Managing the Business Case for Sustainability

The Integration of Social, Environmental and Economic Performance

Edited by Stefan Schaltegger and Marcus Wagner

Managing the Business Case for Sustainability

THE INTEGRATION OF SOCIAL, ENVIRONMENTAL AND ECONOMIC PERFORMANCE

EDITED BY STEFAN SCHALTEGGER AND MARCUS WAGNER

Greenleaf
PUBLISHING

2 0 0 6

Published by Greenleaf Publishing Limited
Aizlewood's Mill
Nursery Street
Sheffield S3 8GG
UK
www.greenleaf-publishing.com

The paper used for this book is a natural, recyclable product made from wood grown
in sustainable forests; the manufacturing processes conform to the environmental
regulations of the country of origin.
Printed in Great Britain by Biddles Ltd, King's Lynn, Norfolk
Cover by LaliAbril.com.

British Library Cataloguing in Publication Data:
  A catalogue record for this book is available from the British Library

  ISBN-10: 1-874719-95-0
  ISBN-13: 978-1-874719-95-3

CONTENTS

PART III
EVIDENCE – STRATEGIES, CASE STUDIES AND
MANAGEMENT SYSTEMS

9 Environmental Management Systems and Competitiveness

FOREWORD

John Elkington
Founder and Chief Entrepreneur, SustainAbility (www.sustainability.com)

This is a critical area—and a key book. With major companies like BP, Shell, Swiss Re and Wal-Mart making a series of major strategic announcements in this area, there is no question that social, environmental and governance issues can have a substantial influence on the economic fortunes of a given company. As a result, the corporate sustainability agenda is finding its way into the pages of publications like the *Harvard Business Review*. While this is welcome, and while there is also growing evidence that some of these issues are surfacing in the boardrooms of major companies, much remains to be done to make this a core element of the corporate governance and top management agenda.

Too often, companies get stuck at the level of visions and strategies, failing to make the necessary next-stage transition to embedding and implantation in day-to-day operations. If—when—the time comes for an executive or manager to decide which of a blizzard of competing priorities proposed by stakeholders should be given priority, there is a growing number of processes and other tools to help; but in the end it is still a matter of judgement. Rather than taking every request for a company's time, money and other resources seriously, today's executives need to know how to cut through the clutter to get to the absolutely key—or 'material'—issues.

There have been many attempts to define and evolve the 'business case' for corporate responsibility and wider sustainability, many of which provide at least some help, in the form of frameworks and guidelines. But surprisingly few bring all of this back to the level of competitiveness in mainstream markets. We need to answer the question, issue by issue, sector by sector, market by market, about how the business success of a company can be improved with outstanding environmental and social performance in conditions where this is still a legal and market option.

These are some of the reasons why I very much welcome this new book, edited by Professor Stefan Schaltegger of the Centre for Sustainability Management (CSM), University of Lüneburg and Dr Marcus Wagner of the Technical University of Munich Business School. They explore how firms currently do—and increasingly should—manage the business case for sustainability. Their book provides probably the most comprehensive collection to date of business case analyses, with contributions from more than 40 experts, investigating business practices, critical success factors, national differences and management approaches that help managers, to use what has now become something of a cliché, 'to do well by doing good'.

FOREWORD

Professor Peter Forstmoser
Chief Executive Officer (CEO), Swiss Re, Zurich

In recent years a broad consensus has been reached among academics and industry leaders that social and environmental issues cannot be separated from economic success. It is now generally accepted that the close connection between social and environmental goals on the one hand and financial goals on the other is a prerequisite for sustainable success. Corporate sustainability has thus become a key management topic, and sustainability strategy and management have found their way from the political arena into the boardroom.

Implementing strategic sustainability goals in business activities is an operational task. When transforming the vision of sustainability into corporate reality, managers will necessarily have to set priorities among the numerous social and environmental topics.

Dealing with business-relevant non-market issues does not mean simply complying with every social and environmental demand made by stakeholders; rather, it entails identifying those social and environmental issues that can, and should, be realised in line with a company's specific business activities. As such, it is a core management task.

The business case of sustainability highlights the interaction between social/environmental performance and business competitiveness. In doing so, it helps answer the question of how business success can be improved by voluntarily delivering outstanding environmental and social performance.

This new book—edited by Professor Stefan Schaltegger of the Centre for Sustainability Management (CSM), University of Lüneburg, and Dr Marcus Wagner of the Business School of the Technische Universität München— examines how corporations should, and do, manage the business case of sustainability. To my knowledge, it provides the most comprehensive collection of analyses currently available in this area: contributions from more than 40 experts—who have investigated business practices, factors in success, national differences and management approaches—can help managers do well by doing good.

I hope the book will serve not only as a reference work on the present state of theory and practice, but also as a guideline for practical implementation.

MANAGING AND MEASURING THE BUSINESS CASE FOR SUSTAINABILITY
Capturing the Relationship between Sustainability Performance, Business Competitiveness and Economic Performance

Stefan Schaltegger[1] and Marcus Wagner[2]

[1]Centre for Sustainability Management, University of Lüneburg, Germany
[2]Dr Theo Schöller Chair in Technology and Innovation Management, Technische Universität München and Centre for Sustainability Management, University of Lüneburg, Germany

Abstract: This introduction provides an overview of the subject of this book, namely how to manage the business case of sustainability. After providing a basic structure of how environmental and social management link to economic success through a number of pathways, various theoretical, empirical and normative approaches to analyse the subject are introduced. Subsequently, the basic link between sustainability performance, competitiveness and economic success is discussed, introducing an inversely U-shaped relationship as a generic case. The chapter then presents the logical corollary of how to measure sustainability performance, business competitiveness and economic success conceptually and empirically, before introducing a framework for the inter-action of factors explaining the relationship of sustainability performance and competitiveness. The chapter ends with an overview of the chapters and con-tributions in this book.

1.   INTRODUCTION

This book deals with the often mentioned—but rarely thoroughly dealt with—'business case of sustainability'. The term 'business case of sustainability' covers the broad area of questions dealing with relevance of voluntary social and environmental activities to the business effects and business success of a company. Or stated differently: how can the competitiveness and business success of a company be improved with voluntarily created outstanding environmental and social performance?

Any attempt to measure and manage sustainability issues in a way such that they have a positive effect on corporate success must take a closer look at the relationship between a company's sustainability performance, its competitiveness and economic performance. Over the last decade, the relationship between environmental and economic performance and, more recently, the interaction between sustainability performance and business competitiveness have received considerable attention—in theory, as well as in management board rooms and on the political stage.

There is no doubt; non-market issues such as environmental and social issues can have a substantial impact on the competitiveness and economic performance of a company. This has been documented in various widely reported cases such as when Shell wanted to sink the Brent Spar oil platform in 1995 or when Nike's sales fell because of NGO pressures accusing the company of purchasing from suppliers involving childwork. There is, furthermore, no dispute that the activities of many companies in actual business practice exceed what can be considered economic in a purely financial sense.

Interestingly enough there is, however, substantial disagreement still about whether management is obliged to focus on business in a more narrow sense relating all activities directly to financial performance or whether management has a social responsibility that requires voluntary social and environmental activities exceeding the compliance with regulations (e.g. Crook 2005; Freeman 1984; Friedman 1997). This dispute is strongly coloured by different ideologies and by perceptions of the social embeddedness and role of a company, ethical perspectives of leadership and the role of stakeholders in a business setting. Apart from different value positions, this dispute is influenced by differing views of how the management of non-market issues and the resulting social and environmental performance of a company relate to business success, i.e. secured existence of the organisation, improved competitiveness and increased economic success. In any case, the two views meet where management can show how voluntary social and environmental management contributes to the competitiveness and economic success of the company.

Managers who are able to systematically analyse how the economic success of a company can be increased through social and environmental activities and who can manage this relationship effectively are still a minority. This is somewhat astonishing because the ability to manage non-market issues can obviously be crucial to the existence and economic success of a company. The economic success and brand value of certain products (e.g. in the sports, textile, food, energy or automotive industries) rely on non-material values communicated and sold to customers. Dealing with business-relevant non-market issues is not the same as replying to each non-market demand of any stakeholder, but a routine managerial task (e.g. Reinhardt

1999, Schaltegger *et al.* 2003) to identify which social and environmental issues influence competitiveness and economic success and how they do so. This is furthermore not a job to be delegated to engineers and scientists in a 'remote' department or shared service unit, but a core strategic management task. If the owners and management do not intend to change it into a non-profit organisation, the integration and management of non-market issues in line with the economic purpose of the company is a constitutional require-ment of the management of any profit-oriented company.

An improved understanding of the link between sustainability perform-ance, competitiveness and business success does not just contribute to a less emotional debate about the social role of a company, but also enables man-agement to realise the 'triple win' potentials that are the basis of any kind of sustainability management of profit-oriented organisations in a market sys-tem. The knowledge of corporate sustainability management can thus be an asset and basis for a competitive advantage of a company. It is, in any case, a prerequisite for the sustainable development of companies and the economy.

The basis of a structured discussion of the link between sustainability performance, competitiveness and economic success is a clear understanding of sustainability performance. The general scientific debate on sustainability, however, is more confusing than enlightening. It mostly circles around the three pillar concept of sustainability that aims at a parallel improvement of social, environmental and economic performance (van Dieren *et al.* 1995). The corporate sustainability and sustainability performance of a company (e.g. Schaltegger and Burritt 2005) would thus be defined by the integrated achievement of social, environmental and economic performance measures (Schaltegger and Wagner 2005). Sustainability performance is, however, often understood as performance in environmental and social terms, thus excluding economic performance. Sustainability performance is thus mostly understood as performance concerning non-market issues and measured in non-economic terms. Hence our suggested structure of the discussion as outlined in Figure 1.

Voluntary environmental and social activities performed with the inten-tion of improving the environmental and social performance of a company constitute corporate social responsibility performance. Environmental and social management applies management methods in a different way to, for example, purely environmental protection or social charity activities. Non-market activities and performance—together with the core business activities and external and other factors—influence company competitiveness. Non-market performance can also have direct influence (e.g. via production costs) on economic success. Competitiveness—describing the relative market position and the ability of the company to meet customer needs better than its competitors—is an important driver of its economic success. Economic

success, especially when positively influenced or created through outstanding social and environmental performance can furthermore be linked to
corporate environmental and social management.

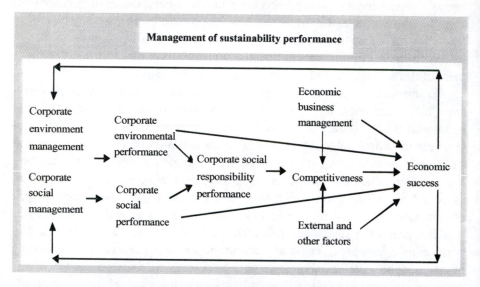

Figure 1. Management of sustainability performance by linking environmental and social
management with competitiveness and economic success

In summary, sustainability performance can be interpreted very broadly as
the overall performance in managing the links and causal relations illustrated
in Figure 1. In a business company, successful management of sustainability
performance is achieved only if the management of environmental and social
issues is in line with increased competitiveness and economic performance.
As a consequence, sustainability management requires an integration of
environmental, social and economic management and thus covers all the
links between non-market and economic issues. It deals with both the
analysis and management of the effects of environmental and social activities on the competitiveness and economic success of a company, as well
as with the analysis and management of the social and environmental effects
of business activities.

Although many studies (mostly correlation-based) have been performed
on the relationship between environmental and economic performance, only
a few take a closer look at the links described in Figure 1. When correlating
selected social or environmental indicators with economic performance
indicators, the management process generally remains a black box. To date,
only some partial aspects of the relationship between sustainability performance, competitiveness and economic performance (e.g. the link between
the environmental and economic performance of companies or the effect of

corporate social responsibility on their financial performance) have been studied from a theoretical as well as an empirical perspective (e.g. Lankoski 2000; Margolis and Walsh 2003; Pearce 2003; Porter 1991; Reinhardt 1999a, 1999b; Schaltegger and Burritt 2005; Schaltegger and Synnestvedt 2002; Wagner and Schaltegger 2003, 2004; Wagner *et al.* 2002, Walsh *et al.* 2003; Ziegler *et al.* 2002). So far, no unique relationship has prevailed in empirical studies. A number of explanations have been put forward for this observation. These include methodological reasons such as the lack or low quality of statistical data or the fact that environmental and sustainability data are often available for short time periods only. Furthermore, some theoretical explanations have been developed (e.g. the influence of different corporate strategies or, on average, a relatively small influence of environmental or sustainability issues in industry) as one factor among many on corporate economic or financial performance. This is the starting point of this book, which aims to compile different insights on various aspects of the link between sustainability performance, business competitiveness and economic success in attempt to provide a comprehensive and structured view of the state-of-the-art in investigating this relationship.

Firstly, the main approaches and questions asked in the context of the link between sustainability performance, competitiveness and economic success are structured. Secondly, we present a basic model for the phenomenological (i.e. observed) relationship between sustainability performance and economic success. Thirdly, the measurement of the link in question is addressed. Fourthly, the phenomenological link is related to a conceptual framework of the interaction of various parameters in bringing about the observed link. Finally, the contributions collected in this book are briefly introduced and related to conceptual considerations.

2.   THEORETICAL, EMPIRICAL AND NORMATIVE APPROACHES

A review of the literature on the link between sustainability performance, competitiveness and economic success shows that the current work can be structured according to:

*   The theoretical questions analysed
*   The empirical research approaches taken
*   The normative conclusions drawn on how the relationship could be managed successfully

Theoretical questions include the analysis of whether, under which circumstances and how environmental and sustainability issues and company activities are related to competitiveness and economic success:

- The proponents asking whether environmental and social issues influence
  competitiveness and economic success at all, however, seem to have
  fallen silent after some obvious cases that attracted mass media interest
  showed that strong links can exist at least in the short term. The accidents
  involving the oil tankers *Exxon Valdez* in Alaska and, more recently, the
  Prestige in Spain, the media spectacle of Brent Spar or the reported
  environmentally driven losses of large re-insurance companies are the
  obvious tips of an iceberg of links between sustainability issues and a
  company's competitiveness and economic performance.
- A frequently analysed question has been to what extent situational factors
  and external conditions have an influence on the relationship between
  environmental and social performance of a company and its economic
  results. Under what circumstances can a strong or weak relationship be
  identified? This question is fairly common among economists and
  political scientists but, despite its close connection, is often not put into
  the context of the 'what and how' question.
- Interestingly enough, the question of how environmental and social
  issues relate to competitiveness has been tackled mostly by investigating
  specific sustainability issues that may be influencing or be influenced by
  a company's competitiveness. Thus, the question is mainly approached
  by asking: what environmental and social issues or company activities
  (such as issuing a sustainability report) relate to competitiveness? The
  cause and effect chain or process linking sustainability with economic
  performance and competitiveness, however, has so far rarely been
  analysed. To avoid confusion, the clear distinction must be made as to
  which direction a causal link is expected: Is the company improving its
  competitiveness through more (or outstanding) sustainability performance? Or: is being very competitive and increasing the company's competitiveness a precondition to improve the sustainability of business
  operations and products?

Empirical research helps to validate or falsify theoretical considerations and
is thus a necessary part of understanding the reality of which environmental
and social issues are related, in which way and under what circumstances to
economic performance:

- Most empirical research in this field is based on more or less sophisticated *regression analyses* searching for correlations (e.g. Ziegler *et al.*
  2002). The findings are very mixed, which is not surprising given that the
  databases are mostly limited in the number of companies and issues

considered as well as in the time period considered. Furthermore, it is rarely clarified what kind of causal link is expected and there is no overarching theoretical framework to structure the analysis provided.

Regression analyses have generally not provided the clear proof or sufficiently significant and generalisable results that the researchers were seeking. For instance, research on the influence of EMAS and ISO 14000 certified environmental management systems has not be able to demonstrate a clear link to the companies' economic performance in terms of their industry average, although many company examples have been analysed and described.

- An increasingly popular empirical approach is to work with case studies (e.g. Holme and Watts 2000). Case studies allow specific causal links and circumstances to be investigated in more depth, but they remain limited in their generalisation for other companies and industries.
- Portfolio studies analyse real or model portfolios of environmentally proactive and environmentally reactive companies, and compare their respective returns (e.g. Edwards 1998). They have however been criticised as only focusing on average performance (Wagner and Wehrmeyer 2002).
- Finally, event studies assess market responses after a positive or negative environmental event and are part of a broader strand of research which assesses the response of capital markets on events related to specific companies or industrial sectors (Blacconiere and Northcut 1996; Jones and Rubin 1999; Hamilton 1995). They also provide mixed results, which have been shown to depend on methodological choices.

To draw normative conclusions is, after all, the reason for analysing the link between sustainability performance, business competitiveness and economic performance. This branch of research will only prove to be valuable if it leads to concepts and methods of how environmental and social management can be better integrated with economic business goals.

Companies do not act 'automatically'—after all, they are neither machines nor do they obey physical laws. Companies are social organisations, characterised by multiple processes based on explicit and implicit decisions of actors. Management and other company actors can only take decisions that improve environmental, social and economic performance simultaneously if they have a clear idea of how these issues are linked and how they can be managed in a mutually beneficial way:

One branch of normative research focuses on how environmental and social issues can be integrated into conventional management methods and tools. This leads to adapted methods such as environmental accounting, environmental audit, eco control and sustainability balanced scorecard (e.g.

Schaltegger and Burritt 2000; Schaltegger and Figge 2000; Strack and Villis 2001) and sometimes feeds back to conventional management research and the improvement of core business management tools.

Other researchers focus on company internal sustainability processes, organisation development and culture (e.g. Martin 2002). Among the main topics are the qualitative analysis and development of environmental learning processes, green organisation development, capacity building for sustainability and green corporate culture development.

Related to the tools-oriented approach as well as to the organisation and culture development approach are the issues of knowledge management and creation, institutional perceptions as a result of organisational or industry culture, and path dependency (e.g. Williander in Chapter 8). The automotive industry, for instance, can be characterised by high entry barriers (high entry costs) creating path-dependent lock-in situations and maintaining an engineering culture that ignores sustainability innovations. This, in turn, influences the mindsets of product developers, marketers and other market actors, making the internal development of sustainable solutions unlikely because of the high entry barriers. As a consequence, managing the link between sustainable product solutions and business success requires the management of new industry and company external knowledge through co-operation and its introduction to the company.

The identification and analysis of causal or other relationships is an important step in most normative approaches. This can be done on the basis of the balanced scorecard (BSC) method (for a general discussion of the BSC, see Kaplan and Norton 1992, 1996) which provides a management method as well as a measurement tool. According to the sustainability balanced scorecard approach (see Figge *et al.* 2002; Schaltegger and Dyllick 2002; Chapter 3 in this book), environmental and social issues can influence five different basic business perspectives that relate to market competitiveness and economic performance:

- Direct financial effects (e.g. fines, penalties, charities, etc.)
- Market effects (effects on the competitiveness of the company in the market such as higher willingness to pay, increased market share, stronger customer binding, etc.)
- Effects on business and production processes (e.g. lower production costs, decreased purchasing costs because of material and resource savings, etc.)
- Effects on learning and organisational development (in this perspective, successful sustainability management creates an organisational culture of sustainability processes, which improve social, environmental and economic performance simultaneously, and is expressed in, for example, more motivated staff, increased innovation rate, less fluctuations, etc.)

- Non-market effects on business performance (e.g. less resistance from neighbours to production sites, strikes, administrative resistance to receive allowances, political resistance, etc.)

Any normative approach of sustainability management will be accepted widely and applied in the majority of companies only if it is based on sound theory and if it proves to be empirically founded. Nevertheless, as with most complex issues in a constantly changing social environment, final proof will not be achieved. This justifies the development and pilot testing of normative approaches of sustainability management and challenges management to obtain an overview of the current state of theory and empirical research.

3. THE BASIC LINK BETWEEN SUSTAINABILITY PERFORMANCE, COMPETITIVENESS AND ECONOMIC SUCCESS

Economic theory provides different perspectives on the relationship between sustainability performance and economic performance from which different predictions about the relationship can be derived. This will be illustrated for the case of environmental performance, but similar lines of argument apply to social performance.

Concerning environmental performance, there is the commonly held 'traditionalist' view of neoclassical environmental economics, which argues that the purpose of environmental regulation is to correct for negative externalities (which diminish social welfare) and that, consequently, environmental regulation (in internalising the costs of the negative externality) corrects a market failure while imposing additional costs on companies. At the level of a specific industry, for example, this is because the share of environmental costs in the total manufacturing costs might be considerably higher than the average (Luken 1997). Furthermore, some industries upstream in the production chain give rise to environmental impacts that are relatively higher than the value added associated with their production activities (Clift and Wright 2000). Based on these considerations, the argument was brought forward that companies in industries with higher environmental impacts face a competitive disadvantage if stringent environmental regulation burdens them with higher environmental compliance costs (relative to total manufacturing or production costs) than other industries. This neoclassical perspective considered market or regulatory failures (in the case that regulation did not take place) as causes of negative (environmental) externalities and developed a set of public policy instruments (e.g. tradable pollution permits, marketable quotas, assigning complete property rights,

environmental taxes, corporate liability standards for companies or command-and-control systems) to address them (for details, see for example,
Endres 1994).

In contrast, the notion (termed the 'revisionist' view) emerged that improved environmental performance is a potential source of competitive
advantage as it can lead to more efficient processes, improvements in
productivity, lower costs of compliance and new market opportunities
(Gabel and Sinclair-Desgagné 1993; Porter 1991, Porter and van der Linde
1995; Schaltegger 1988; Sinclair-Desgagné 1999). In this 'revisionist' view,
environmental regulation is mainly considered to be '... an industrial policy
instrument aimed at increasing the competitiveness of companies, the underlying rationale for this statement being that well-designed environmental
regulation could force companies to seek innovations that would turn out to
be both privately and socially profitable' (Sinclair-Desgagné 1999:2). In the
'revisionist' view (unlike traditional neo-classic economics), companies
facing higher costs for polluting activities have an incentive to research new
technologies and production approaches that can ultimately reduce the costs
of compliance, since innovations can be conceived that also result in lower
production costs (e.g. lower input costs) due to enhanced resource productivity (Porter and van der Linde 1995). In addition, companies can gain 'first
mover advantages' from selling their new solutions and innovations to other
companies (Esty and Porter 1998). According to the 'revisionist' view, at
least in a dynamic, longer-term perspective (but possibly even in the short
term), the ability to innovate and to develop new technologies and production approaches is therefore a greater determinant of competitiveness and
economic success than traditional factors of competitive advantage (Porter
and van der Linde, 1995).

The two views described above can be generalised to the case of
sustainability performance. They are represented in Figure 2, which shows a
monotonously decreasing curve to represent the 'traditionalist' view (of the
relationship between sustainability performance and economic performance)
and an inversely U-shaped curve to represent the 'revisionist' view. The
longer-term dynamics are indicated by the dotted line representing the
efficiency frontier development over time due to technical, regulatory and
market changes.

Given the range of possible relationships, management may want to
know more about the actual link with which the company is confronted. This
requires the measurement of the company-, market-, industry- and country-
specific relationship in question.

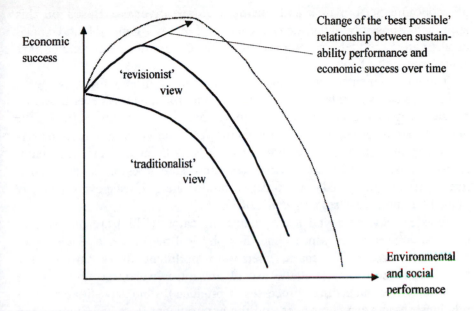

Figure 2. Phenomenological relationship between environmental and social performance and economic success (Source: similar to Schaltegger 1988; Lankoski 2000; Wagner 2000; Schaltegger and Synnestvedt 2002; Wagner 2002; Wagner *et al.* 2002)

4. MEASURING SUSTAINABILITY PERFORMANCE, BUSINESS COMPETITIVENESS AND THE EFFECT ON ECONOMIC SUCCESS

When discussing sustainability performance and business competitiveness measurement, it is necessary to look initially at conceptual aspects. Here, the three pillar view of sustainability perceives the latter to have three dimensions—namely an economic, a social and an ecological/environmental dimension (van Dieren *et al.* 1995). This would suggest defining one measure, which simultaneously assesses all three dimensions. Historically, however, measurement of economic performance and business competitiveness is: (i) much older than the measurement of economic and social performance; and (ii) developed much on its own, leading to a well established body of theory and practice on the measurement. Therefore, while it may seem enticing to develop one measure of sustainable performance spanning all three dimensions, in terms of practicality and also with regard to the feasibility of empirical analysis, it could be more suitable to measure the economic dimension of sustainability separately using established measures of economic performance and business competitiveness. Based on this approach, (possibly integrated) measures for environmental and social performance and their integration with economic performance are considered in this book.

The environmental performance of a company can be defined by means of its physical performance with regard to environmental aspects based on physical environmental performance indicators. An environmental aspect is defined here as an element of an organisation's activities, products or services that interacts with the environment (DIN 1995; next to the term 'environmental aspect', the terms environmental pressure, stressor, environmental intervention, loading and environmental burden are also used synonymously in the literature; see Olsthoorn *et al.* 2001).

Physical environmental performance indicators (EPIs) are one way to describe environmental aspects and thus physical performance. Such physical EPIs can describe mass, energy or pollutant flows through the manufacturing process (e.g. the use of energy or water resources or the emissions of pollutants from processes or products), which constitute a direct relationship between companies and the environment (see e.g. Günther and Kaulich 2004). Physical EPIs can be quantitative (i.e. measured on a continuous, interval or ratio scale) as discussed in the life-cycle assessment literature (e.g. Heijungs *et al.* 1992) or qualitative (i.e. measured on a nominal scale; for example, when assessing whether a company is compliant with regard to specific emissions consent conditions). A fairly popular concept for linking environmental with economic performance is the concept of eco-efficiency measuring value added in relation to environmental impact added or the environmental impact caused per monetary unit earned (Schaltegger and Sturm 1990).

Sustainability performance measures can thus embrace the dimensions of sustainability in a more or less integrative manner. The choice of measure may vary substantially depending on the exact question, industry and company considered and on what factors are part of the respective analysis.

With regard to social performance, the measurement debate is still at a more conceptual level. While there have recently been some activities to operationalise social performance (e.g. GRI 2002 as well as several private sustainability rating companies), this has not yet reached the level of formalisation and coherence found, for example, in environmental life-cycle assessment (see, for example, the various ISO and SETAC standards on this such as SETAC 1991).

With regard to the other core concept, business competitiveness, a first approximation could be to use measures of economic performance such as measures of short-term profitability operationalised in terms of common financial performance ratios. One reason for using economic performance measures instead of indicators of competitiveness might be the difficulty of defining and measuring competitiveness in one dimension. Furthermore, factors that lead to the competitiveness of a company are usually company-internal leading indicators (and hence difficult to observe), which precede the economic outcomes of companies' operations (measured, for example, as financial ratios, profitability/returns, market position or stock market valuation) as lagging indicators (Kaplan and Norton 1992, 1996; Olve *et al.*1999).

While economic performance in the short term can be measured approximately through profitability ratios (e.g. in terms of return on sales [ROS], return on owners' capital employed [ROCE] and return on equity [ROE]—an approach frequently used in empirical studies in the USA and Europe, e.g. Edwards 1998; Hart and Ahuja 1996) to assess the relationship between environmental and economic performance. However, this omits a number of important and more long-term aspects of business competitiveness.

Given the serious difficulties in defining competitiveness, some authors have started to measure sustainable competitiveness as that part of competitiveness that is determined or strongly influenced by the management of environmental and social issues. Lankoski (2000) applies this idea to environmental aspects and points out that economic performance is a multi-causal issue, and that therefore any causal effect on overall economic performance (or overall competitiveness) by a single explanatory factor (such as, for example, environmental performance) is likely to be small. Therefore, an operationalisation of sustainable competitiveness (as a sub-segment of overall business competitiveness) can be based on the self-assessment of companies, an approach successfully used by Sharma (2001) with US and Canadian companies to measure organisational capabilities and competitive benefits, and by Wagner (2003) to assess the influence of strategy choice on the link between environmental performance on environmental competitiveness. Such an approach requires definition of a set of items to approximate a theoretical concept of sustainability competitiveness. Such items can include different drivers that are hypothesised to increase competitiveness, as well as outcomes that are perceived to be results of high competitiveness or environmental competitiveness. The European Business Environment Barometer survey (see, for example, Baumast and Dyllick 2001; Wagner and Schaltegger 2002) uses such a collection of items to allow companies to self-assess the perceived effects of the total of their environmental management activities on a number of drivers and outcomes of competitiveness. An index composed of such items therefore defines a measure of sustainable competitiveness, i.e. the contribution of a company's sustainability management to its overall competitiveness. Sustainable competitiveness is hence defined as that part of competitiveness or economic performance, which can be influenced by corporate sustainability strategies and sustainability management. It needs to be noted that this is still a separate measure of the economic dimension of sustainability; however, it is one that makes reference to the social and environmental dimensions.

5. CONCEPTUAL FRAMEWORK FOR THE INTERACTION OF FACTORS EXPLAINING THE PHENOMENOLOGICAL RELATIONSHIP OF SUSTAINABILITY PERFORMANCE AND COMPETITIVENESS

With regard to empirical analyses, Schaltegger and Synnestvedt (2002) argue that a detailed assessment of the type of social and environmental management a company pursues is particularly important. They consider the frequent lack of theoretical foundations for empirical studies regarding the relationship between environmental and economic performance at least equally important as the statistical and data issues involved, and suggest that a more causal model should be used to explain how the relationship between sustainability performance is brought about through a company's environmental and social management. In general, the original focus of environmental management is the improvement of a company's environmental performance. A company's social and environmental management activities can be understood as being the result of a corporate sustainability strategy (CSS). The relevance of analysing the influence of corporate sustainability strategies (CSS) on the relationship lies in the different views of contingency theory (Lawrence and Lorsch 1967) and strategic choice, and their implications for this influence.

In order to integrate corporate sustainability strategies and other factors into a conceptual framework explaining the 'phenomenological' relationship of sustainability performance and competitiveness, the latter needs to be related to the influence of the former as shown in Figure 3. The 'phenomenological' relationship is represented at the top of Figure 3 and is what is observable. The model also shows the explanatory factors considered most important in causing a certain level of sustainability performance and competitiveness. In the most general form, it should be assumed that each of these factors have a simultaneous influence on both. However, it may well be possible that each factor can be considered to have a predominant influence on either of them, since the key factors influencing sustainability performance most directly and strongly may possibly be relatively distinct to those that influence competitiveness.

Next to the different influences (in terms of directness and strength) the different factors have on sustainability performance and competitiveness, there are two more noteworthy aspects. Firstly, the factors also interact among each other. For example, company size can have an influence on corporate sustainability strategies; it is often argued that small companies are laggards that have a relatively reactive stance towards sustainability management. Country location (via environmental/social regulation) can also have an influence on the technology and processes used in a company (e.g. end-of-pipe or integrated). If the influences and interaction between any two factors are very direct and/or very strong, they need to be taken into account. They can only be neglected if the interaction between them is very weak and indirect compared with the influences each of them has on sustainability performance and/or competitiveness.

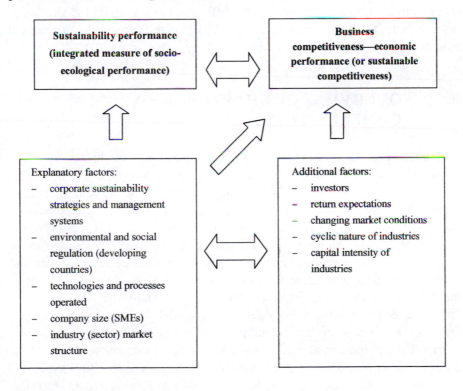

Figure 3. Framework for the interaction of explanatory factors with sustainability performance and competitiveness (based on Wagner and Schaltegger 2003; Wagner 2002)

Secondly, a number of additional explanatory factors need to be considered that have an influence predominantly on business competitiveness/economic performance. Among these are investors and their expectations of return, changing market conditions with regard to demand, supply and prices, the cyclic nature and/or the average capital intensity of the industries under consideration.

As can be seen in the model in Figure 3, the additional factors that mainly have an influence on competitiveness and economic performance can potentially also influence the set of explanatory factors considered to have a major influence on sustainability performance and competitiveness—an interaction that also needs to be accounted for. In order to understand fully the link between sustainability performance, business competitiveness and economic performance, the conceptional framework outlined in Figure 3 can help to categorise work on this link and to point to gaps in the body of knowledge. The contributions chosen for this book reflect and analyse (partly in a comparative perspective) different aspects and themes outlined in this introduction. In this, they often address one or more of the interactions outlined in the above framework. The difficulties experienced by companies when moving towards corporate sustainability raises various theoretical and empirical questions as addressed above.

6.   OVERVIEW OF CHAPTERS AND CONTRIBUTIONS

This book is organised in three parts covering theories, empirical investigations and case studies. Part 1 discusses different conceptual approaches to measure and manage the link between environmental, social and integrative sustainability performance on one hand and competitiveness and economic performance on the other. Chapter 1 deals with the link between the environmental and economic performance of a company; this seems to be the area where most research has been done in the field of sustainability and economic performance. Leena Lankoski from Helsinki University looks at the basic links and treats them step-by-step in an analytical and structured manner in order to bring them together in a model. In her contribution, she defines the concept of environmental profit to describe the incremental impact that environmental performance has on economic performance. Complementary to her investigation, Stefan Schaltegger from the Centre for Sustainability Management at the University of Lüneburg gives an overview of the so called Environmental Shareholder Value concept, which provides a normative approach to how to manage corporate environmental protection in a way that contributes most successfully to shareholder value.

In Chapter 2, social aspects and the link to competitiveness and economic success are addressed. Trevor Goddard from Curtin University considers whether and how social objectives of a company integrate with core corporate objectives and discusses social auditing as the currently prevailing core management tool in this area. A specific part of social aspects that is often in the focus of discussions is what is understood by stakeholder value. Kuno Spirig from Zurich University of Applied Sciences presents a framework linking social performance and competitiveness.

Integrative approaches to measuring and managing sustainability performance with regard to economic success are discussed in Chapter 3. The first two contributions focus on the corporate management level, whereas the second two take a meso- and macro-economic measurement perspective. Marcus Wagner (Dr Theo Schöller Chair in Technology and Innovation Management, Technische Universität München) and Stefan Schaltegger from the Centre for Sustainability Management highlight the development of Sustainability Balanced Scorecards as a strategic management approach for sustainability performance measurement and management whereas Juan Piñeiro Chousa and Noelia Romero Castro from the Department of Finance and Accounting at the University of Santiago de Compostela develop a model of financial analysis at the service of corporate sustainability on basis of different financial indicator methods and strategic management approaches such as the Du Pont return on investment (ROI) scheme, the shareholder value approach and the sustainability balanced scorecard. Frank Figge from the University of Leeds and Tobias Hahn from the Institute for Futures Studies and Technology Assessment Berlin propose an integrated monetary measure of sustainability based on how much the change of social and environmental performance of a company between two periods has contributed to making a national economy more sustainable. This measure is based on an assessment of a company's efficiency relative to that of the total national economy as a benchmark. The chapter ends with a macro-oriented approach of Sonja L. Odom from the Department of Mechanical Engineering at the University of South Carolina, who applies her model of a sustainable systems analysis algorithm to measure the sustainability of industrial operations within the forest products sector in the Edisto River Basin in the USA.

Part 2 covers empirical approaches measuring different links of sustainability performance, competitiveness and company performance from the view of financial markets, at an industry level and for countries. The empirical investigations differ in their methodological approach as well as their industrial and country focus, providing a broad overview of the state of practice and implementation. Chapter 4 provides two theoretical contributions covering Europe and the USA, and two from leading practitioners from the financial market community. Interestingly, the results of the theoretical review for the USA seems to somehow conflict with the empirical analyses for Europe and the experiences of specialised practitioners in sustainable finance operating worldwide.

Klaus Rennings, Michael Schröder and Andreas Ziegler from the Centre for European Economic Research (ZEW) Mannheim investigate econometrically the economic performance of European stock corporations and ask themselves whether sustainability matters. Their main result is that a higher environmental sector performance has a significantly positive influence on the stock performance. In contrast, a higher social sector performance has a negative, but somewhat less significant influence. Dinah A. Koehler from the National Center for Environmental Research reviews US research on capital markets and corporate environmental performance. She states that econometric concerns and model mis-specification consistently undermine the quality of findings and concludes that US capital markets pay attention to environmental news, but that it is a short-term reaction and does not necessarily affect long-term returns or company-level sustainability in the USA. Eckhard Plinke and Andreas Knörzer from Sarasin Sustainability Investments, Bank Sarasin & Co. Ltd., Basel refute the widespread opinion that environmental and social benefits must be bought with financial underperformance of sustainable investments (also known as social responsible investment [SRI]). They conclude that the financial performance of SRI funds is similar to that of 'conventional' funds and that more sustainable companies even tend to outperform the market. While these results apply 'on average', the performance of individual SRI funds varies considerably. They argue that the sustainability approach used and the design of the investment process are important factors in the financial performance of SRI funds.

Niki Rosinski from Generation Investment Management London discusses how the Dow Jones Sustainability Index (DJSI) benchmarks competitiveness and illustrates this for the automotive industry and climate change. He states that, although issues related to sustainable development drive competitive dynamics and the businesses and markets of the future, investors mostly lack a systematic methodology to assess the materiality of issues and to identify likely losers and winners. Using the automotive industry's exposure to climate change, he explores how the DJSI methodology can be used on a disaggregated basis as an issue- and industry-specific framework for benchmarking competitiveness with regard to the risks and opportunities related to sustainable development.

Chapter 5 provides an overview of industry surveys for different industries and countries. Based on a number of surveys, Henning Madsen and John P. Ulhøi from the Aarhus School of Business state that, although positive trends can be observed, a breakthrough in reducing the environmental impact of industrial business activities in Denmark seems to be elusive. They doubt that managers have realised the full potential of the environment as a key strategic factor and conclude that Danish managers seem to focus on short-term results and may have already picked the 'low-hanging fruit', i.e.

implemented all the environmental initiatives with a fast payback potential. David Hitchens, Jens Clausen, Mary Trainor, Michael Keil, Samarthia Thankappan and Wilfried Konrad from the Queen's University Belfast and the Institute for Ecological Economy Research Hanover discuss the relationship between competitiveness, environmental performance and management with a particular focus on small and medium sized manufacturing companies in the furniture industry in the UK, Ireland, Germany and Italy. While no statistically significant relationship between environmental and economic performance could be found in a cross-sectional analysis, environmental initiatives still seem to have an impact on costs and market performance; they stress that external advice on environmental aspects should be available and accessible for small and medium-sized companies. David Hitchens, Frank Farrell, Josefina Lindblom and Ursula Triebswetter from the Queen's University Belfast, the Environment Agency, the Institute for Prospective Technological Studies Seville and the IFO Institute for Economic Research Munich investigate the competitive effects of the EC Integrated Pollution Prevention and Control (IPPC) Directive for the non-ferrous metals sector. IPPC lays down a framework requiring Member States to issue operating permits based on best available techniques (BAT). The economic and environmental performance of plants with varying numbers of BAT are measured and compared in case studies from individual plants. Overall, the study shows that BAT did not stop companies achieving good environmental performance and remaining competitive both nationally and internationally.

Chapter 6 complements the empirical surveys with country perspectives. The first two contributions show developments in environmental management in the Netherlands and Norway, while the other two sections deal with cross-country comparisons of national sustainability performance and the effect on economic stability. Ronald S. Batenburg from the Department of Information Sciences at Utrecht University summarises the results of the European Business Environmental Barometer in the Netherlands. He explains that the Netherlands traditionally takes an upfront position with regard to environmental policy and that corporate environmental policies are progressing in both the technical and managerial sense, and that this has been accompanied with increasing costs for environmental protection since 1993. Bjarne E. Ytterhus from the Norwegian School of Management Sandvika provides an overview of the views of industrial leaders in Norway regarding environmental challenges and the adaptations made by enterprise in relation to the external environment.

In his section, Matthias Bönning from Oekom Research AG Munich develops a country rating approach that enables capital investors to incorporate sustainability criteria into their decisions to invest in government bonds. To examine the link between a country's sustainability performance on the one hand and its credit standing and competitiveness on the other, the results of the country rating are compared with Standard & Poor's Sovereign Credit Rating and two of the World Economic Forum's indices measuring competitiveness. His correlation analysis shows a highly significant positive link between a country's sustainability and underlying economic parameters. He concludes that a country's sustainability performance impacts significantly on its economic performance.

Mathis Wackernagel, Chris Martiniak, Fred Wellington, Chad Monfreda and Steve Goldfinger from Ecological Footprint Network Oakland, the University of San Francisco and the University of Wisconsin-Madison examine how the ecological footprint as an ecological indicator may be able to contribute to the assessment of a country's future economic performance. They contrast national ecological performances measured using the ecological footprint with overall economic performance measures for nations. Starting with the global ecological context and the analysis that humanity's demand on resources exceeds by approximately 20% what the biosphere can regenerate and that this overload is increasing, this section explains how the ecological footprint approach can be used to put economic risks into the context of ecological performance and, in turn, inform assessments of economic stability or competitiveness.

Part 3 deals with empirical surveys and company case studies on the influence of different management systems, strategic management approaches and other factors influencing the business case of sustainability. Ki-Hoon Lee and Robert Ball from POSCO Research Institute (POSRI) Seoul and the Faculty of Management at the University of Stirling Scotland provide a single industry analysis of the influence of perceived strategic importance and management commitment on corporate environmental strategies in the Korean chemical industry. By applying the Miles and Snow typology to study the emergence of corporate environmental strategies and the level of economic performance, this more case-based analysis complements the broader empirical surveys presented in earlier sections. The authors also consider the relevance of environmental strategies as a moderating factor on the relationship between sustainability performance and competitiveness. This is particular underlined by their conclusion that ambitious corporate environmental strategies may well bring about a more positive link between environmental and economic performance.

Holger Petersen from the Umweltbank Nürnberg and the Centre for Sustainability Management at the University of Lüneburg examines the corporate environmental and sustainability strategies used by entrepreneurs to achieve competitive advantages. In the last three decades, an increasing number of entrepreneurs took up environmentalist's ideas and claims against industry to place innovative products on the market. The author discusses strategic opportunities to achieve competitive advantages through an 'ecopreneurship' lens and shows that 'ecopreneurs' base their success on different presumptions to conventional executives. Ulrich Steger from the Institute for Management Development (IMD) Lausanne presents a conceptual and empirical approach of the business case of sustainability, which is well in line with the basic model discussed in this book. The model allows analysis of economically viable sustainability actions by companies , which do not contradict the dominantly economic logic of corporations. The investigation covers nine industries (automotive, aviation, chemical, electric utilities, financial services, food and beverage, pharmaceutical, oil and gas, and technology) and is complemented by a diagnostic tool to help those responsible for sustainability issues in companies to identify the business case specifically for their company. Jodie Thorpe and Kavita Prakash-Mani from the London-based consulting thinktank, SustainAbility Ltd, address the degree to which there is a business case for sustainability in emerging markets. For a large number of companies in various developing countries, the authors assess evidence on whether improved environmental and social performance and management translates into improved economic performance or competitiveness, e.g. in terms of reduced costs or higher sales. Identifying a number of 'sustainability' and 'business success' factors, they show that, to varying degrees, there are reinforcing linkages between sustainability performance and management on the one hand and business success on the other. As the section explains, links depend considerably on company size (e.g. cost savings are often are relevant for SMEs) and the market or industry focus of a company.

Chapter 8 covers a number of instructive company case studies illustrating that the link between sustainability performance, competitiveness and economic business performance can vary substantially from company to company and that its successful management depends largely on good strategy choice and effective implementation. Stefan Seuring and Maria Goldbach from the Supply Chain Management Centre at the Carl von Ossietzky Universität Oldenburg show that leading companies in the textile and apparel industry have, in the meanwhile, found ways to improve the environmental and social performance of their supply chain while remaining competitive in their market. The authors report on two German-based companies (Otto GmbH & Co. KG and Steilmann GmbH & Co. KG) that have introduced measures to improve the sustainability performance of their supply chain, while offering environmentally improved products at competitive prices. Rolf Wüstenhagen from the Institute for Economy and the Environment at the University of St Gallen discusses the impressive success story of one of the world's leading wind generator manufacturer Vestas and presents key milestones in its development from the niche to the mass market. The author analyses success factors in the relationship between the company's sustainability performance and business competitiveness. In a case study analysing Ford and Volvo, Mats Williander from the Fenix Center for Research on Knowledge and Business Creation at Chalmers University of Technology and Business Strategy Manager at Volvo Ltd examines why companies in the automotive sector such as Ford and Volvo do not sell their environmentally best cars in sufficiently high volumes and compares their offers with two alternative and potentially more successful offerings. He concludes that the industry's perceived reluctance towards becoming more environmental friendly may not be rooted in a lack of willingness, ethics or belief in the strategic relevance of environmental issues. Instead, it may be caused by institutionalised perceptions and engineering practices that create a bias in the understanding of consumer expectations. The author indicates that what is perceived as high cost by consumers may be very low and that more innovative solutions addressing not only the monetary issue but also the symbolic, behavioural and organisational attributes of the product may open a major potential for car manufacturers.

Peter A. Stanwick and Sarah D. Stanwick from the School of Accountancy and College of Business at Auburn University show how Honda and Toyota, two companies considered to be in the forefront of addressing environmental issues in the automobile industry, understand how their leadership role is related to sustainability issues with a long term vision of their corporate leaders, as well as the need to be environmentally pro-active in their native country of Japan.

Suzanne Benn and E. Jane Probert from the School of Management at the University of Technology Sydney and the European Business Management School of the University of Wales Swansea compare case studies from two companies based in south Wales, UK, and New South Wales, Australia. The authors argue that the competitiveness of these companies, which have both successfully carried out incremental changes integrating economic aims with environmental improvements and local social sensitivity, is based on the capability of networking with regulators and with the local community as well as the systematic approach to human resource functions.

Chapter 9 as the final chapter of this book focuses on the role of environmental management systems and their impact on competitiveness and corporate economic success—a key issue frequently discussed during the last decade. Thomas Dyllick and Jost Hamschmidt from the Institute for Economy and the Environment at the University of St Gall analyse the effects of the implementation and certification of an environmental management system according to ISO 14001 on the environmental and economic performance of companies in Switzerland. They conclude that mainly positive economic results have been achieved, whereas the environmental goals that were the main drivers when EMAS and ISO 14001 were introduced by the EC and ISO have not been sufficiently achieved.

The contribution of Eric W. Welch, Ashish Rana and Yasuhumi Mori from the University of Illinois at Chicago and the National Institute for Environmental Studies at Ibaraki enlarges the focus with a comparative analysis between the manufacturing industries of Europe, the USA and Japan. The authors report on a comparative, multi-industry study of the adoption of environmental management systems based on ISO 14001 and link this to policy analysis to explain their findings. Like a number of other analyses, they find limited effects of ISO 14001 on companies' environmental performance. These seem to be hindered additionally by institutional and structural barriers to adoption and an adversarial policy regime in the USA. Conversely, a more reciprocal policy regime in Japan is identified as a major factor increasing the success of voluntary initiatives such as environmental management system standards.

The book rounds up with a contribution from Boris Braun from the Department of Geography at the Otto-Friedrich-University Bamberg, who attempts to identify the factors responsible for the successful implementation of standardised corporate environmental management systems. The findings from a multivariate empirical analysis based on a large-scale survey of the implementation of the EMAS system by German manufacturing companies reveal that, irrespective of general characteristics such as size and industry, there is considerable company-specific scope for achieving improvements in environmental protection. The success of environmental management systems correlated positively with profitability. Other important success factors are the environmental commitment of management and employees, but also the integration of companies in information networks and in favourable, innovative regional milieus.

In summary, this book covers a large variety of perspectives and analyses of the multiple links between environmental performance, social performance, competitiveness and the economic success of companies and provides an overview of the current status and an insight on recent new work on the debate and practice. In particular the geographical spread of the research spanning from America to Asia and from northern via western to southern Europe, and including developing and emerging economies, reflects the truly global nature of the issues at the heart of corporate sustainability management. On a conceptual and empirical basis, the research results and experiences in corporate practice show that:

- There is no automatic link—neither a positive nor a negative one—between environmental or social performance and economic performance. Depending on the companies, industries and countries and other issues considered, a more positive or a more negative relationship results in empirical investigations. The focus of investigation has mostly been on linking different levels of sustainability performance. Although crucial for the successful management of the links between environmental, social and economic success, analysis of the kind of environmental and social management activities is limited. First empirical analyses, which put the question 'how' environmental and social issues are managed in the centre of the investigation, confirm the theory of the inversely U-shaped relationship, i.e. it is more important how sustainability is managed than what environmental or social performance level has been achieved.

• A positive link between sustainability performance, competitiveness and economic success is possible and many company examples as well as empirical studies show that it has been realised in practice. However, a differentiated business-oriented approach is necessary to manage social and environmental issues successfully to increase the economic success of business. Sustainability performance, increasing competitiveness and economic success can only go hand-in-hand if they are managed with regard to the specific company and industry situation, and with a clear economic perspective.

So far, companies have been able to manage the link between environmental performance and economic success better than the link between social performance and economic success. A reason for this may be that environmental management has a longer history than explicit social or societal management. In addition, environmental issues can be measured better or more easily than social aspects.

Various approaches and tools exist to support corporate management in analysing the crucial aspects determining the specific link for their own company and to manage successfully the link with a systematic consideration of its specific situation. A general consideration of the basic links and factors of influence as well as a systematic reference to the value drivers of shareholder value provide a structured management support.

Environmental management systems may help to reduce costs, but they do not seem to improve environmental performance. Neither EMAS nor ISO 14001 are able to support an effective management of the link between environmental and economic performance. These standards may, however, help companies with a poor environmental management record to make existing environmental protection activities more efficient through cost reduction. To successfully manage sustainability performance links with competitiveness and economic performance, specific consideration of the basic links and the value drivers of shareholder value is recommended.

REFERENCES

Baumast, A. and Dyllick, T. (2001): *Umweltmanagement-Barometer 2001.* (IWÖ-Diskussionsbeitrag Nr. 93). St Gallen: Institute for Economy and the Environment (IWÖ-HSG), University of St Gallen.

Blacconiere, W.G. and Northcut, W.D. (1997): 'Environmental Information and Market Reactions to Environmental Legislation', *Journal of Accounting, Auditing & Finance* Vol. 12, No. 2, 149-178.

Clift, R. and Wright, L. (2000): 'Relationships between Environmental Impacts and Added Value along the Supply Chain', *Technological Forecasting and Social Change* Vol. 65, 281-295.

Crook, C. (2005): 'The Good Company', *The Economist* 20 January 2005.

DIN (1995): *Umweltmanagementsysteme—Spezifikationen und Leitlinien zur Anwendung.* Berlin: Deutsches Institut für Normung.

Edwards, D. (1998): *The Link between Company Environmental and Financial Performance.* London: Earthscan Publications.

Endres, A. (1994): *Umweltökonomie.* Tübingen: Cansier.

Esty, D. and Porter, M. (1998): 'Industrial Ecology and Competitiveness. Strategic Implications for the Firm', *Journal of Industrial Ecology* Vol. 2, No. 1, 35-43.

Figge, F., Hahn, T., Schaltegger S. and Wagner, M. (2002): 'The Sustainability Balanced Scorecard. Linking Sustainability Management to Business Strategy', *Business Strategy and the Environment* Vol. 11, 269-284.

Freeman, R.E. (1984): *Strategic Management: A Stakeholder Approach.* Marshfield: Pitman.

Friedman, M. (1997): 'The Social Responsibility of Business is to Increase its Profits', in: Beauchamp, T. and Bowie, N. (Eds.): *Ethical Theory and Business.* New Jersey: Prentice Hall, 56-60.

Gabel, L.H. and Sinclair-Desgagné, B. (1993): 'Managerial Incentives and Environmental Compliance', *Journal of Environmental Economics and Management* Vol. 24, 940-955.

GRI (Global Reporting Initiative) (2002): *Sustainability Reporting Guidelines.* Boston, Amsterdam: GRI.

Günther, E. and Kaulich, S. (2004): 'Die ökologische Bewertung in der Software EPM-Kompas', *Umweltwirtschaftsforum* Vol. 12, No. 2, 40-48.

Hamilton, J.T. (1995): 'Pollution as News: Media and Stock Market Reactions to the Toxic Release Inventory Data', *Journal of Environmental Economics and Management* Vol. 28, 98-113.

Hart, S.L. and Ahuja, G. (1996): 'Does it Pay to be Green? An Empirical Examination of the Relationship between Emission Reduction and Firm Performance', *Business Strategy and the Environment* Vol. 5, 30-37.

Heijungs, R., Guinée, J., Huppes, G., Lankreijer, R., Udo de Haes, H. and Sleeswijk, A. (1992): *Environmental Life Cycle Assessment of Products. Guide and Backgrounds.* Leiden: Center of Environmental Science (CML).

Holme, R. and Watts, O. (2000): *Corporate Social Responsibility. Making Good Business Sense.* Geneva: World Business Council for Sustainable Development.

Jones, K. and Rubin, P.H. (1999): *Effects of Harmful Environmental Events on Reputations of Companies.* (Working Paper) Atlanta: Department of Economics, Emory University.

Kaplan, R.S. and Norton, D.P. (1992): 'The Balanced Scorecard—Measures that Drive Performance', *Harvard Business Review* January/February 1992, 71-79.

Kaplan, R.S. and Norton, D.P. (1996): *The Balanced Scorecard.* Boston: Harvard Business School Press.

Lankoski, L. (2000): *Determinants of Environmental Profit*. Helsinki: Helsinki University of Technology.

Lawrence, P. and Lorsch, J. (1967): *Organisations and Environment*. Boston: Harvard Business School Press.

Luken, R. (1997): 'The Effect of Environmental Regulations on Industrial Competitiveness of Selected Industries in Developing Countries', *Greener Management International* Vol. 19, 67-78.

Margolis, J.D. and Walsh, J.P. (2003): 'Misery Loves Companies. Rethinking Social Initiatives by Business', *Administrative Science Quarterly* Vol. 48, 268-305.

Martin, R. (2002): 'The Virtue Matrix. Calculating the Return on Corporate Responsibility', *Harvard Business Review* March, 69-75.

Olsthoorn, X., Tyteca, D., Wehrmeyer, W. and Wagner, M. (2001): 'Using Environmental Indicators for Business? A Literature Review and the Need for Standardisation and Aggregation of Data', *Journal of Cleaner Production* Vol. 9, No. 5, 453-463.

Olve, N.-G., Roy, J. and Wetter, M. (1999): *Performance Drivers*. Chichester: Wiley.

Pearce, B. (2003): *Sustainability and Business Competitiveness. Measuring the Benefit for Business Competitive Advantage from Social Responsibility and Sustainability*. London: Forum for the Future.

Porter, M. (1991): 'America's Green Strategy', *Scientific American* Vol. 264, No. 4, 96.

Porter, M. and Linde, C. van der (1995): 'Green and Competitive: Ending the Stalemate', *Harvard Business Review* September/October 1995, 120-134.

Reinhardt, F. (1999a): 'Bringing the Environment Down to Earth', *Harvard Business Review* July/August 1999, 149-157.

Reinhardt, F. (1999b): 'Market Failure and the Environmental Policies of Companies. Economic Rationales for 'Beyond Compliance' Behavior', *Journal of Industrial Ecology* Vol. 3, No. 1, 9-21.

Schaltegger, S. (1988): *Marktwirtschaftliche Instrumente des Umweltschutzes*. Basel: WWZ.

Schaltegger, S. and Burritt, R. (2000): *Contemporary Environmental Accounting*. Sheffield: Greenleaf Publishing.

Schaltegger, S. and Burritt, R. (2005): 'Corporate Sustainability', in: Folmer, H. and Tietenberg, T. (Eds.): *The International Yearbook of Environmental and Resource Economics 2005/2006. A Survey of Current Issues*. Cheltenham: Edward Elgar, 185-222.

Schaltegger, S., Burritt, R. and Petersen, H. (2003): *An Introduction to Corporate Environmental Management. Striving for Sustainability*. Sheffield: Greenleaf Publishing.

Schaltegger, S. and Dyllick, T. (Eds.) (2002): *Nachhaltig managen mit der Balanced Scorecard. Konzepte und Fallstudien*. Wiesbaden: Gabler.

Schaltegger, S. and Figge, F. (2000): 'Environmental Shareholder Value. Economic Success with Corporate Environmental Management', *Eco-Management and Auditing* Vol. 7, No. 1, 29-42.

Schaltegger, S. and Sturm, A. (1990): 'Ökologische Rationalität', *Die Unternehmung* Vol. 44, No. 4, 273-290.

Schaltegger, S. and Synnestvedt, T. (2002): 'The Link between „Green' and Economic Success. Environmental Management as the Crucial Trigger between Environmental and Economic Performance', *Journal of Environmental Management* Vol. 65, 339-346.

Schaltegger, S. and Wagner, M. (2005): Integrative Management of Sustainability Performance, Measurement and Reporting, *International Journal of Accounting, Auditing and Performance Evaluation (IJAAPE), No. 4*.

SETAC (Society of Environmental Toxicology and Chemistry) (1991): *A Technical Framework for Life-Cycle Assessment*. Washington: SETAC.

Sharma, S. (2001): 'Different Strokes: Regulatory Styles and Environmental Strategy in the North-American Oil and Gas Industry', *Business Strategy and the Environment* Vol. 10, 344-364.

Sinclair-Desgagné, B. (1999): *Remarks on Environmental Regulation, Firm Behaviour and Innovation.* (Scientific Series 99s-20) Montreal: Cirano.

Strack, R. and Villis, U. (2001): 'RAVE. Die nächste Generation im Shareholder Value Management', *Zeitschrift für Betriebswirtschaft* Vol. 71, No. 1, 67-84.

Van Dieren, W. and Köhne, A. (1995): *Mit der Natur rechnen: Der neue Club-of-Rome-Berich—vom Bruttosozialprodukt zum Ökosozialprodukt.* Basel: Birkhäuser.

Wagner, M. (2000): 'A review of studies concerning the empirical relationship between environmental and economic performance of firms: What does theory propose and the evidence tell us?', Paper presented at the Policy Options for Sustainable Technological Innovations (POSTI) Seminar and ESST Annual Conference, BETA, University Louis Pasteur, Strasbourg, 27–28 May (pdf download: http://www.esst.uio.no/posti/workshops/wagner.html), accessed 20 February 2006.

Wagner, M. (2002) *Empirical identification of corporate environmental strategies. Their determinants and effects for companies in the United Kingdom and Germany.* Lüneburg: Centre for Sustainability Management (CSM), University of Lüneburg.

Wagner, M. (2003) *How Does it Pay to Be Green? An Analysis of the Relationship between Environmental and Economic Performance at the Firm Level and the Influence of Corporate Environmental Strategy Choice.* Marburg: Tectum.

Wagner, M. and Schaltegger, S. (2002): *Umweltmanagement in deutschen Unternehmen—der aktuelle Stand der Praxis.* Lüneburg: Centre for Sustainability Management (CSM), University of Lüneburg.

Wagner, M. and Schaltegger, S. (2003): 'How does sustainability performance relate to business competitiveness?', *Greener Management International* (Special edition), Issue 44, 5-16.

Wagner, M. and Schaltegger, S. (2004): 'The Effect of Corporate Environmental Strategy Choice and Environmental Performance on Competitiveness and Economic Performance. An Empirical Analysis in EU Manufacturing', *European Management Journal* Vol. 22, Issue 5, 557-572.

Wagner, M. and Wehrmeyer, W. (2002): 'The Relationship of Environmental and Economic Performance at the Firm Level: A Review of Empirical Studies in Europe and Methodological Comments', *European Environment* Vol. 12, 149-159.

Wagner, M., Schaltegger, S. and Wehrmeyer, W. (2002): 'The Relationship between the Environmental and Economic Performance of Companies: What does Theory Propose and What does Empirical Evidence Tell Us?', *Greener Management International* Vol. 34, 95-108.

Walsh, J., Weber, K. and Margolis, J. (2003): 'Social Issues and Management. Our Lost Cause Found', *Journal of Management* Vol. 29, No. 6, 859-881.

Ziegler, A., Rennings, K. and Schröder, M. (2002): *Der Einfluss ökologischer und sozialer Nachhaltigkeit auf den Shareholder Value europäischer Aktiengesellschaften.* (Discussion Paper No.02-32) Mannheim: Center for European Economic Research.

PART I

THEORY –
CONCEPTUAL APPROACHES

Chapter 1

The Link between Environmental and Economic Performance

ENVIRONMENTAL AND ECONOMIC PERFORMANCE
The Basic Links

Leena Lankoski
Helsinki University, Finland

Abstract: This chapter outlines the basic mechanisms that connect environmental performance with economic performance. It presents possible positive and negative economic outcomes that have been suggested to result from environmental performance improvements and develops an approach that accommodates all the suggested, seemingly contradictory outcomes. It defines the concept of environmental profit to describe the incremental impact that environmental performance has on economic performance, shows that environmental profit is an inverted U-shaped function of environmental performance and draws management implications.

1. INTRODUCTION

Whether there is a link between a company's environmental and economic performance and what is the nature of this link have been extensively debated. While some have argued that there is no reason why the two should be connected, tens of studies have been conducted by a number of researchers since the 1970s to establish whether the relationship is positive or negative.

Drawing from Lankoski (2000), this chapter outlines the basic mechanisms that connect environmental performance with economic performance. Although economic performance may also affect environmental performance by making resources available for environmental improvements, this chapter deals only with the links between environmental and economic performance.

First, possible positive and negative economic outcomes that have been suggested to result from environmental performance improvements are presented. Then, an approach is developed that accommodates and integrates all the suggested, seemingly contradictory outcomes.

Before this, however, two points should be made that are important for understanding and clarifying the environmental–economic performance link. First, environmental performance pertains to the level of harmful environmental impact caused by the activities of a company. The more 'environmentally friendly' a company is, the better its environmental performance. Environmental performance, however, is a multidimensional concept: the activities of a company may cause a multitude of environmental impacts in terms of land use, resource use and pollutant releases to air, water and land. The company may be performing well with regard to one environmental issue and poorly with regard to another. The company's environmental impacts may even be positive with regard to some issues and negative with regard to others. Thus, the dimensions of this concept are not necessarily linked. Moreover, and more importantly for the purposes of this chapter, the dimensions are different when it comes to their link with economic performance. Different environmental issues involve different options for solutions, give raise to different regulatory efforts and provoke different reactions in customers and other stakeholders. Therefore, when assessing the environmental–economic performance link, environmental performance must be considered issue by issue.

Secondly, economic performance is also a multifaceted concept in which different operational measures capture different aspects. For example, some measures of economic performance are indicators of commercial success (growth, market share) while others are indicators of financial success (profitability). Accounting measures portray past performance and stock market measures portray expectations of future performance. In order to grasp conceptually the environmental–economic performance link, it is necessary to move beyond single operational measures of environmental performance and to distinguish between economic values on the one hand and accounting or commercial values on the other (Randall 1987). Thus, in this chapter, all costs and revenues are understood as economic costs and revenues, present and future, including uncertain elements discounted to present time. The concepts are thus significantly broader than the corresponding accounting terms.

2.   THE LINKING MECHANISMS

2.1   Possible Links to Costs

2.1.1   Cost Increases

The core of the argument that improving environmental performance harms
economic performance rests on the premise that environmental performance
improvements result in increased costs. Put simply, the environment is a
factor of production both as a source of raw materials and energy, and as a
sink for pollution and waste. If the company's options are constrained by
limiting the availability of this production factor, production costs will
necessarily rise (see, for example, Palmer *et al.* 1995; Siebert *et al.* 1980).

Installing and operating pollution control or prevention technology is an
obvious source of cost increases. Capital investments such as machinery,
equipment and buildings, as well as operating costs such as energy, labour
and materials are likely to be required. Even if environmental performance
can be improved simply through changing operating practices, costs are still
involved in identifying and analysing possible options (see, for example,
Jaffe *et al.* 1995; Sprenger 1996). Another suggested source of cost increases
is that the implementation of environmental initiatives adversely affects productivity, thus increasing the volume of inputs required to produce a certain
amount of outputs. Productivity may suffer from a change to more environmentally friendly processes and production practices if these are less efficient than the previous ones and if the transitional period involves switching
costs, obsolete capital or production disruptions. Moreover, environmental
investments crowd out other, perhaps more productive investments and inputs aimed at producing environmental quality reduce the amount of
managerial and financial resources the company has available to produce its
saleable output (Jaffe *et al.* 1995).

2.1.2   Cost Savings

To challenge the traditional view, Porter and van der Linde (1995) argued
that instead of cost increases, environmental performance improvements can
often result in net cost savings but that a dynamic perspective is required to
realise these savings. The logic of the argument is that the search for environmental improvements will prompt innovation that results in improved
resource productivity, improved efficiency and avoidance of waste—thus
offsetting the initial environmental costs.

Many other authors have embraced the idea of cost savings from improved environmental performance (for example: Bonifant *et al.* 1995;
Dechant and Altman 1994; Shrivastava 1995). Increased efficiency brings

cost savings in production by reducing the use of purchased inputs, substituting less expensive inputs for hazardous materials, eliminating risky production steps, simplifying designs and recovering valuable materials from waste streams. Regulatory costs are reduced as: less environmental taxes and charges need to be paid and fewer pollution rights purchased; liability costs are reduced; continuous compliance with environmental regulations is ensured, thus avoiding fines and litigation; and anticipating future regulations allows more flexibility and the possibility to influence standard development. Because of lower risks, cost savings are available when obtaining capital and insurance, and savings may also be achieved from good labour and community relations brought by the improved environmental performance. The possibility to obtain cost savings through environmental management is also a core topic in environmental accounting (see, for example, Schaltegger and Müller 1998).

2.2 Possible Links to Revenues

2.2.1 Revenue Losses

The reason why environmental performance improvements could result in revenue losses is that the environmental improvements may have adverse product quality impacts, which reduce sales volume or sales price. Such impacts occur if the environmentally preferable product is—or is perceived to be—less efficient in use, less attractive in appearance, less tasty, of less consistent quality, etc.

2.2.2 Revenue Increases

In addition to cost savings, the other half of the argument by Porter and van der Linde (1995) was that environmental performance improvements may also result in value-improving innovations. These increase the value of the product or service to the customer and, hence, allow increasing revenue through charging a price premium or increasing market share. It is worth noting that the revenue-increasing property of environmental performance improvements may also manifest itself in a less apparent manner—as the ability to maintain the current price or the existing market share in situations where these would otherwise be threatened.

Environmental performance improvements improve the company's general image, which increases customer loyalty and supports sales efforts. Furthermore, they allow the company to attract customers in environmentally conscious market segments, to obtain eco-labels and other means of distinction that affect customer choice favourably, to sell to companies that screen their suppliers using environmental criteria and to tender for contracts to public organisations with an environmental procurement policy. They can also result in better quality, improved safety, lower operating and disposal costs for customers, or higher resale or scrap value—all of which directly increase the value that the customer obtains from the product or service. A separate, growing market in which environmental improvements may open opportunities is that for specific environmental goods and services (see, for example, Gallarotti 1995).

Table 1 summarises the different types of linking mechanisms that have been suggested to exist between a company's environmental and economic performance.

Table 1. Types of suggested links between environmental and economic performance

	Possible links to costs	**Possible links to revenues**
Possible negative links	Environmental performance improvements require managerial time, capital investment and operating expenditure, and thus increase production costs. Environmental performance improvements harm productivity, thus requiring more inputs to produce the desired amount of outputs.	Environmental performance improvements adversely affect product quality, thus reducing sales revenue.
Possible positive links	Environmental performance improvements result in increased efficiency, thus reducing production costs. Environmental performance improvements improve relations with environmental authorities, thus reducing regulatory costs. Environmental performance improvements reduce risk and thus the costs of capital and insurance. Environmental performance improvements improve relations with the employees and the local community, thus reducing related costs.	Environmental performance improvements improve general company image, thus increasing revenue. Environmental performance improvements allow the company to charge a price premium or increase market share in environmentally conscious markets. Environmental performance improvements result in higher product value for customers, thus increasing revenue. Environmental performance improvements open opportunities in the market for environmental goods and services.

3.   A COMBINED PERSPECTIVE

How to make sense of all this? A first consideration is how to combine the suggested positive and negative links. These suggestions may at first sight seem contradictory. However, examined one by one, the suggested cost increases, cost savings, revenue increases and revenue losses are all conceivable. The question is not whether the suggested positive or negative outcomes are correct—both kinds of impacts are possible, even within the context of a single environmental performance improvement. Thus, the positive and negative views need not be incompatible if treated as a pool of possible outcomes out of which a different bundle materialises in each different situation. What is decisive for economic performance is the net impact of the resulting bundle.

A second consideration is how to combine the cost-side and revenue-side links. Taken in isolation, neither cost impacts nor revenue impacts tell the whole story of the relationship between environmental and economic performance. Costs and revenues matter only in comparison to each other. This can be illustrated through iso-profit curves as in Reinhardt (2000). The company's profits are determined by the relationship between its costs and revenues and, along one iso-profit line, the profits remain the same (see Figure 1). An environmental performance improvement may improve a company's economic performance and bring it to a higher iso-profit line if it results in cost savings but has a neutral impact on revenues (case A1), brings both cost savings and revenue increases (A2), or increases revenues while having no net cost impacts (A3). Despite cost savings, an environmental performance improvement will have no impacts on profits if these savings are countered with a corresponding revenue decrease (B1). Similarly, if a revenue increase is accompanied by a corresponding cost increase, the revenue increase will not result in increased profits and the cost increase will not harm economic performance (B2). An environmental performance improvement may harm economic performance and force the company on a lower iso-profit line if it results in a revenue loss with no cost impacts (C1), a simultaneous revenue loss and cost increase (C2), or brings cost increases without any revenue impacts (C3).

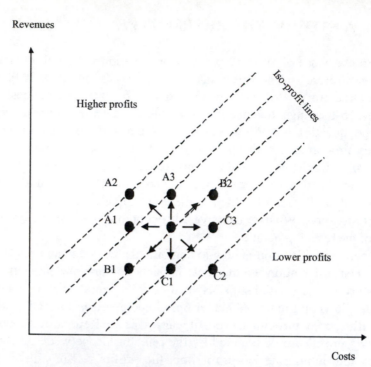

Figure 1. Possible impacts of environmental performance improvements on cost, revenues and profits (Source: modified from Reinhardt 2000)

4.   ENVIRONMENTAL PROFIT: THE CONCEPT

Taking the above considerations into account, it is possible to arrive at a combined perspective on the basic links between environmental and economic performance. For this purpose, it is useful to start by defining a concept to outline exactly what is being looked at—the isolated, incremental economic impact that environmental performance has on economic performance.

Environmental profit refers to the isolated net economic impact of an environmental performance level for a company, i.e. the stream of environment-related costs and revenues over time, discounted to the present. Marginal environmental profit is the corresponding concept relating to a change in environmental performance level. It captures the stream of cost and revenue changes related to an environmental performance change, discounted to the present. Positive marginal environmental profit corresponds to a so-called 'win–win' situation or a shift to a higher iso-profit line. Similarly, negative marginal environmental profit represents a shift to a lower iso-profit line and zero marginal environmental profit represents a move along the original iso-profit line.

To measure environmental profit or marginal environmental profit empirically is very difficult, if not impossible. It would require perfect information on all present and future costs and revenues that relate to a particular environmental performance level or environmental performance change. These are hard to obtain because environmental profit also includes uncertain, intangible and long-term impacts. Thus, only very seldom can environmental profit be expressed as a robust numerical value: it is meant primarily as a vehicle for thinking, not calculating.

Costs and revenues that are unconnected to environmental performance are not counted in environmental profit, but environment-related costs and revenues are counted in conventional economic profit. Hence, environmental profit is a subset of profit. It can be positive, negative or zero regardless of the value of conventional profit. Environmental profit represents the contribution of one particular element, environmental performance, to profit. It should be emphasised that the environmental profit curve incorporates any and all private costs and revenues that relate to environmental performance. Hence, by definition, there can be no trade-offs between environmental profit and 'non-environmental profit'. Put differently, there may initially have been trade-offs between environmental performance and some other attributes that contribute to the company's economic performance, but these are already counted in the costs of and revenues from environmental performance. The isolation of costs and revenues to components that relate to environmental performance from components that do not is important. It guarantees that, when environmental profit is maximised, total profit is also maximised, *ceteris paribus*. Such isolation can, however, be fully made only in the abstract; in practice, many environmental and 'non-environmental' costs are intertwined and difficult to separate. This reinforces the role of environmental profit as a conceptual tool rather than a calculating device.

As defined above, marginal environmental profit equals the net present value of an investment in environmental performance. This analogy reveals how crucial temporal aspects are when thinking about environmental profit. It is typical for investments in environmental performance that, while many costs accrue in the short term, the related revenues are uncertain and may accrue only in the longer term. Due to this temporal asymmetry in the distribution of costs and revenues, the period over which the economic impacts are examined has an important impact on the outcome of the examination. In most cases, the lower the discount rate and, thus, the longer the time period considered the more 'win–win' situations there are. However, certain environmental performance improvements (e.g. a long-term commitment to environmentally friendly forest management practices) may involve an immediate but passing surge of reputational benefits when the decision is announced, while the costs are spread over the longer term. In these cases, a low discount rate diminishes marginal environmental profit. (I am grateful to Professor Markku Ollikainen for pointing out this possibility.)

5.   ENVIRONMENTAL PROFIT: THE CURVE

Much of the literature arguing for a general positive link between environmental and economic performance has tended to simply extrapolate the benefits obtained from improved environmental performance, assuming that further improvements will bring further benefits. However, there is no *a priori* reason why the relationship should be constant across environmental performance levels. Companies that have derived net economic benefits from improving their environmental performance may perhaps not continue to do so up to zero pollution or the socially optimal level of pollution. The cost-reducing opportunities may be limited to a few 'low-hanging fruit' (Walley and Whitehead 1994) and the sales-enhancing potential of environmental performance improvements may also be limited (see, for example, Nehrt 1998).

Hence, the relationship between environmental and economic performance, represented by environmental profit, should be considered a function of environmental performance and may thus be depicted through an environmental profit curve. The curve is developed by extending the traditional neoclassical environmental economics framework to account explicitly for environmental private benefits (cost savings or market revenues). The result is a formal argument that the company-level relationship between environmental performance and economic performance takes the form of an inverted U-shaped function of environmental performance. For other discussions of the relationship between a company's environmental and economic performance in terms of an inverted U-shaped curve, see for example: Schaltegger and Figge 2000 and Schaltegger and Synnestvedt 2002.

5.1   The Standard Model

The costs to a company of environmental performance improvements are usually described in terms of the marginal abatement cost (MAC) curve. This is defined as a measurement of the change in economic costs incurred by a company when improving environmental performance using the least-cost method of abatement at some point in time (Callan and Thomas 1996:112). The shape and position of the MAC curve is source- and issue-specific, but a typical curve increases with improving environmental performance as the curve MAC1 in Figure 2.

The standard treatment involves establishing the MAC function that represents the costs of environmental performance improvements and comparing this with the marginal social benefits obtained from those improvements. However, this treatment assumes no environmental private benefits for companies, only costs. For the location of the social optimum this makes no difference, but it does for the privately optimal level of environmental performance. Without environmental private benefits, companies have no economic incentive to improve their environmental performance voluntarily. Point A in Figure 2 marks the level of environmental performance chosen by a company under this view.

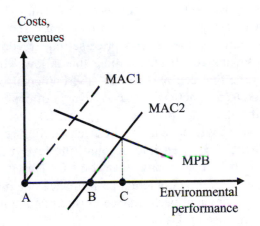

Figure 2. Elements in deriving the marginal environmental profit curve

5.2   Accommodating Cost Savings

As was discussed earlier, environmental performance improvements may result in cost savings. Since the MAC curve is defined through the costs of environmental performance improvements using the least-cost method, it organises pollution abatement alternatives in the order of increasing costs. Accommodating cost savings thus means that the MAC curve shifts down. Sometimes the cost savings serve to reduce the amount of net costs to be paid by the company, but sometimes the savings are so important that the net cost of an environmental performance improvement is, in fact, negative. Hence, the MAC curve may take negative values in the beginning, as shown by the line MAC2 in Figure 2. Taking this into account moves the level of environmental performance chosen by a profit-maximising company to point B in Figure 2.

5.3   Accommodating Differentiation Benefits

Competitiveness is more than cost competitiveness. However, the model does not yet accommodate market benefits from environmental differentiation, even though there is evidence that obtaining such benefits is possible in practice. To examine the impact of the differentiation benefits, it is necessary to integrate an environmental marginal private benefits (MPB) curve in the standard treatment presented above.

The MPB curve accounts for environmental private benefits that accrue in the market through customer preferences and, thus, demand. Traditional microeconomic analysis assumes homogeneous offerings. With differentiation, however, an offering enters a new private market with less intense competition. This increases the seller's price-setting freedom (Mathur and Kenyon 1997). Allowing for differentiation, thus allows for a downward-sloping demand curve that can explain the environmental private benefits. Since differentiation is, in practice, a crucial element of competitive strategy; a downward-sloping marginal private benefit (MPB) curve from environmental performance provision can be inserted in Figure 2. Now when differentiation benefits are taken into account, the level of environmental performance chosen by the company is at point C. This is because, at the profit-maximising level of environmental performance, the marginal revenue from improving environmental performance must equal the marginal cost of environmental performance provision.

5.4   Combining Costs and Revenues

A company's net private benefit from environmental performance is its environmental profit. Some information on the environmental profit function can be obtained indirectly through examining the marginal environmental profit function. Marginal environmental profit is obtained by subtracting marginal abatement costs from environmental marginal private benefits. Since the slope of the MPB curve is negative and that of the MAC curve is positive, the slope of the marginal environmental profit curve is negative. Thus, marginal environmental profit is a decreasing function of environmental performance.

Furthermore, the slope of the marginal environmental profit curve is simultaneously the second derivative of the environmental profit function. It is known that if $f''(x)$ is negative for all x, then the primitive function $f(x)$ must be a concave function (Chiang 1984:243). Correspondingly, the environmental profit function is concave and takes the form of an inverted U-shaped function of environmental performance (the environmental profit curve should not be confused with another inverted U-shaped curve relating environmental and economic variables, i.e. the environmental Kuznets curve that depicts the suggested relationship between per capita income and pollution).

Figure 3 illustrates the environmental profit curve and the marginal environmental profit curve. The environmental performance of a company with regard to an environmental issue determines where on its environmental profit curve or marginal environmental profit curve it is located. To repeat, these curves incorporate the isolated costs and benefits resulting from environmental performance, even though these are in most instances likely to be dwarfed by the non-environmental costs and benefits of business. The curves thus show the direction of the link between environmental performance and economic performance, but not the relative magnitude of environmental profit.

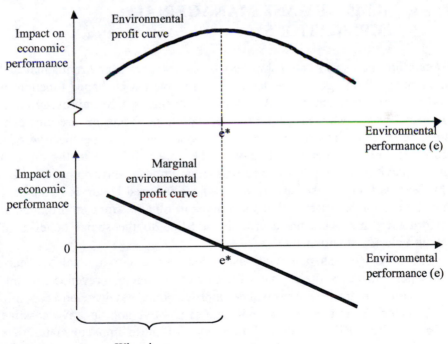

Figure 3. Environmental profit curve and marginal environmental profit curve (Source: Lankoski 2000)

The marginal environmental profit curve is not useful only to derive the environmental profit curve. It is also convenient to examine marginal values. Knowing one point on the environmental profit curve is not sufficient to tell whether the value is high or low, or whether the company has passed its private optimum for environmental performance or not. In contrast, knowing one point on the marginal environmental profit curve suffices to determine whether the company is located in the 'win–win' area or not.

Based on Figure 3, it can be established that improving environmental performance is profitable for a company up to the privately optimal level of environmental performance e^*. At this point, marginal environmental profit equals zero and total environmental profit is maximised. Any further investments in improving environmental performance would decrease profit, but any fewer investments would leave profitable opportunities unused. The area up to the point e^* represents a 'win–win' area where improving environmental performance benefits both the company and the environment, and the drive for profit coincides with sustainable development objectives.

6.   SUMMARY AND MANAGERIAL IMPLICATIONS

To sum up, the basic relationship between a company's environmental and economic performance can be depicted as an inverted U-shaped function of environmental performance. 'Win–win' situations, where improving environmental performance also improves economic performance, are thus possible, but not all situations are 'win–win' ones. From the perspective of a profit-maximising company, it 'pays to be green' only up to the optimal level of environmental performance with regard to each environmental issue. This level is found at the turning point of the inverted U-curve. Remember that the economic benefits that the company obtains from environmental performance improvements accrue in addition to the social benefits of having a cleaner environment.

The inverted U-shaped relationship between environmental and economic performance is the product of both the cost-side and revenue-side impacts that environmental performance improvements may have on economic performance. As was shown, a multitude of positive and negative possible impacts exists on both sides. Which ones of these impacts materialise depends on the specifics of each situation—the characteristics of the company, the environmental issue, the market, etc. Thus, the exact shape and location of the inverted U may vary between cases. Managers, therefore, need to analyse the particular situation of their company in detail to establish the location of the privately optimal level of environmental performance and the size of the 'win–win' area. Moreover, this analysis should be updated continually as the optimal environmental performance level may change with technological solutions or changes in market preferences and the regulatory environment.

Finally, the task of managers is not limited to establishing the profit-maximising point and reacting to it. To an extent, managers may deliberately affect the conditions surrounding the company and thus induce shifts in the environmental profit curve. Further, the theoretical availability of a 'win–win' situation does not mean that the 'win-win' potential will automatically be recognised, pursued and attained. Effective management is required to ensure that the costs of environmental performance improvements are not higher than necessary and that the full potential of market revenues is flowing to the company.

REFERENCES

Bonifant, B.C., Arnold, M.B. and Long, F.J. (1995): 'Gaining Competitive Advantage through Environmental Investments', *Business Horizons* Vol. 38, No. 4, 37-47.

Callan, S. and Thomas, J. (1996): *Environmental Economics and Management: Theory, Policy and Applications*. Chicago: Irwin.

Chiang, A. (1984): *Fundamental Methods of Mathematical Economics*. Singapore: McGraw-Hill.

Dechant, K. and Altman, B. (1994): 'Environmental Leadership: from Compliance to Competitive Advantage', *Academy of Management Executive* Vol. 8, No.3, 7-20.

Gallarotti, G. (1995): 'It Pays to be Green: The Managerial Incentive Structure and Environmentally Sound Strategies', *Columbia Journal of World Business* Vol. 30, No. 4, 38-57.

Jaffe, A.B., Peterson, S.R., Portney, P.R. and Stavins, R.N. (1995): 'Environmental Regulation and the Competitiveness of U.S. Manufacturing: What Does the Evidence Tell Us?', *Journal of Economic Literature* Vol. 33, No. 1, 132-163.

Lankoski, L. (2000): *Determinants of Environmental Profit: an Analysis of the Firm-level Relationship between Environmental Performance and Economic Performance*. Espoo: Helsinki University of Technology, Institute of Strategy and International Business.

Mathur, S.S. and Kenyon, A. (1997): *Creating Value: Shaping Tomorrow's Business*. Oxford: Butterworth-Heinemann.

Nehrt, C. (1998): 'Maintainability of First Mover Advantages When Environmental Regulations Differ Between Countries', *Academy of Management Review* Vol. 23, No. 1, 77-97.

Palmer, K., Oates, W.E. and Portney, P.R. (1995): 'Tightening Environmental Standards: the Benefit-Cost or the No-Cost Paradigm?', *Journal of Economic Perspectives* Vol. 9, No. 4, 119-132.

Porter, M.E. and Linde, C. van der (1995): 'Toward a New Conception of the Environment-Competitiveness Relationship', *Journal of Economic Perspectives* Vol. 9, No. 4, 97-118.

Randall, A. (1987): 'Total Economic Value as a Basis for Policy', *Transactions of the American Fisheries Society* Vol. 116, 325-335.

Reinhardt, F.L. (2000): *Down to Earth: Applying Business Principles to Environmental Management*. Boston: Harvard Business School Press.

Schaltegger, S. and Figge, F. (2000): 'Environmental Shareholder Value: Economic Success with Corporate Environmental Management', *Eco-Management and Auditing* Vol. 7, No. 1, 29-42.

Schaltegger, S. and Müller, K. (1998): 'Calculating the True Profitability of Pollution Prevention', in: Bennett, M. and James, P. (Eds.): *The Green Bottom Line: Environmental Accounting for Management. Current Practice and Future Trends.* Sheffield: Greenleaf Publishing, 86-99.

Schaltegger, S. and Synnestvedt, T. (2002): 'The Link Between 'Green' and Economic Success: Environmental Management as the Crucial Trigger between Environmental and Economic Performance', *Journal of Environmental Management* Vol. 65, 339-346.

Shrivastava, P. (1995): 'Environmental Technologies and Competitive Advantage', *Strategic Management Journal* Vol. 16, 183-200.

Siebert, H., Eichberger, J., Gronych, R. and Pethig, R. (1980): *Trade and Environment: a Theoretical Enquiry.* Amsterdam: Elsevier Scientific Publishing Company.

Sprenger, R.-U. (1996): 'Environmental Policies and Competitiveness', in: Lim, J.-S. (Ed.): *Trade and Environment: International Issues and Policy Options.* Seoul: Korea Environmental Technology Research Institute, 223-266.

Walley, N. and Whitehead B. (1994): 'It's Not Easy Being Green', *Harvard Business Review* Vol. 72, No. 3, 46-52.

HOW CAN ENVIRONMENTAL MANAGEMENT CONTRIBUTE TO SHAREHOLDER VALUE?
The Environmental Shareholder Value Approach

Stefan Schaltegger

Centre for Sustainability Management (CSM), University of Lüneburg, Germany

Abstract: Shareholder value thinking is often considered to clash with environmental management. However, going one step deeper in the analysis shows a more differentiated picture of how voluntary corporate environmental protection influences shareholder value. This contribution centres on the question: what kind of environmental management contributes to increasing shareholder value of a company. The environmental shareholder value approach provides fairly operational conclusions on how the eco-efficiency contribution of alternative environmental management measures can be assessed.

1. INTRODUCTION

It is not just the quantity but primarily the kind of sustainability activities that determines whether they create economic value or not (see Schaltegger and Wagner 2005). The consideration of environmental issues can be of benefit both for the company on one hand and for the environment on the other if—and only if—the respective measures are chosen and managed in the right way. Conventional end-of-pipe technologies will often create high costs without a substantial economic benefit whereas investments in more efficient technologies can often reduce material throughput and related costs in such a way that profitability is increased. Thus, the question arises: what is an economically successful way of environmental management?

As in most complex decision situations, there is no single right way which works for all companies, industries, countries, markets and situations (see, for example, e.g. Reed 1998:4; Schaltegger and Figge 1997:4).

Nevertheless, one general answer makes good sense: if we take a financial market perspective that sustainability management aims to increase the company's value and shareholder value (e.g. Desjardins *et al.* 1999; Feldmann *et al.* 1997; McGuire *et al.* 1981), then corporate environmental and social activities should be linked to, and assessed on, the basis of their effect on shareholder value (Martin 2002; PwC 2004; Schaltegger and Figge 1997:8f., 2000).

With the growing economic relevance of environmental issues, the question arises as to how environmental management influences shareholder value (Desjardins *et al.* 1999; Ellipson 1996; GEMI 2004:2; Reed 1998:2; Repetto and Austin 2000; Schaltegger and Figge 1997, 2000; Wipfli and Hauser 1998; Ziegler *et al.* 2002).

2.   BASIC LINKS BETWEEN ENVIRONMENTAL MANAGEMENT, COMPETITIVENESS AND SHAREHOLDER VALUE

To answer the question as to how corporate environmental and sustainability management is linked with shareholder value requires analysis of causal relationships (Figure 1).

Environmental and sustainability issues can be economically relevant for all the main management decisions in the areas of investments, operations, financing and strategy. Environmental and sustainability management is thus shown as an activity interwoven through these main management decision areas. At a very basic level, management decisions are targeted at the levers of economic success such as sales price, sales, expenses and risk. These economic levers influence competitiveness and the value drivers of shareholder value simultaneously. Furthermore, the level and kind of competitiveness in the customer market (e.g. measured as market share), the labour market (e.g. measured as employment attractiveness), in the financial market (e.g. measured as capital) and the general social and economic environment (e.g. measured as reputation) influences the value drivers and thus shareholder value indirectly. In a more direct way, the economic levers are reflected in the value drivers that determine the value components of the shareholder value. This is where the so-called Environmental Shareholder Value approach (Schaltegger and Figge 1997, 2000; for company cases, see also WBCSD 1997 and, for a survey, Desjardins *et al.* 1999) comes in.

The basic idea of this approach is to assess the economic influence of environmental management from the shareholder perspective by using a conventional concept developed for the calculation of shareholder value. Explanations for the emergence of the shareholder value approach include its focus on future issues and on a cash-based approach to create value, its relative simplicity and its intuitive logic (Schaltegger and Burritt 2000:212f.; Schaltegger and Figge 1997).

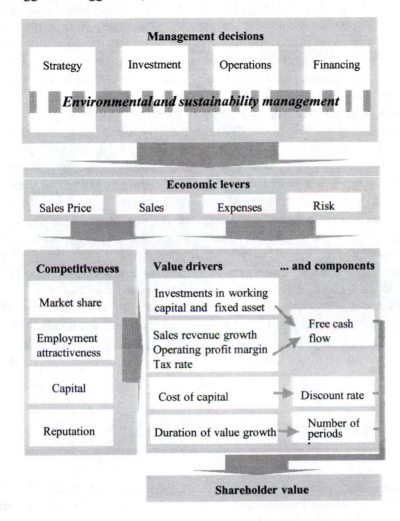

Figure 1. Linking sustainability management and shareholder value

The step between value drivers, value components and shareholder value is described in general by Rappaport (1986). Value drivers are variables with a causal link to the components of the shareholder value formula: investments in fixed assets, investments in current assets, sales revenue growth, net operating margin and rate of tax on income, capital costs and duration of value growth.

Value drivers are affected by environmental interventions to different degrees depending on the nature and size of the company (see Figge 2001; Schaltegger and Burritt 2000:215ff.; Schaltegger and Figge 1997:10ff.; PWC 2004; Wipfli and Hauser 1998). The influence of environmental and sustainability issues on shareholder value depends very much on how their management influences the value drivers. For instance, environment-related investments in effluent treatment plants increase fixed assets and consumables such as chemicals used to neutralise acids lead to higher amounts of current working capital. Sales revenue growth and the net operating margin may be affected, for example, by 'green' or 'fair trade' product lines. The duration of value growth is determined by asking how long a return higher than the market average can be sustained (Rappaport 1986). In contrast to these value drivers, capital costs do not affect the valuation of cash flows but the discount rate. The weighted average cost of capital is calculated on the basis of interest rates on borrowed capital and dividends plus capital gains on equity. Depending on how environmental risk is managed, a higher or lower level of interest rates will influence capital costs.

Following a short review of the fundamentals of shareholder value analysis, the impact of corporate environmental protection measures on shareholder value is discussed below by analysing the links with the so-called value drivers. This allows management to draw conclusions on which environmental protection and green marketing activities are compatible with the shareholder value approach and therefore in line with creating company and shareholder value. Finally, the results of an empirical analysis are discussed.

3.   BASICS OF THE SHAREHOLDER VALUE APPROACH

The shareholder value approach represents a conventional investment calculation used to assess the value of shares on basis of the company's performance. In technical terms, shareholder value (SHV) is the discounted net current value of a company's future free cash flow (Copeland *et al.* 1993:72f.; Rappaport 1986):

$$SHV = \sum_{n=1} \frac{FCF_0}{(1+i)^n} - BC$$

where:
   SHV is shareholder value

FCF$_n$ is the free cash flow in period *n*
BC is the market value of borrowed capital
i is the discount rate

The shareholder value concept is based on expected free cash flows (FCFs). Free cash flows are the cash flows remaining to serve the shareholders after the services of all stakeholders such as customers, employees, etc. have been paid. Thus, the future free cash flows are estimated in a first step. Secondly, corporate value is determined by discounting the expected free cash flows. Third, to arrive at the shareholder value, borrowed capital has to be subtracted from corporate value.

Much has been written on different methods of measuring and managing shareholder value (e.g. Bea 1997; Copeland *et al.* 1993; Hachmeister 1997; Rappaport 1986, 1998).

4. ADVANTAGES AND DISADVANTAGES OF THE GENERAL SHAREHOLDER VALUE APPROACH

Perhaps one of the main reasons for the emergence of the shareholder value method is that cash flow figures reflect basic inflows and outflows of cash and thus cannot be manipulated as easily using accounting practices and standards as accounting figures (Birchler and Spremann 1995; Copeland *et al.* 1993; Schaltegger and Burritt 2000). Unlike most figures used in financial accounting (e.g. net income), shareholder value is a future-oriented long-term indicator (e.g. Volkart 1996:33). Like the basic idea of environmental protection, shareholder value deals with management options to create future benefits.

The key developers and promoters of the shareholder value approach (Rappaport 1986; Copeland *et al.* 1993) did not address environmental issues either in a positive or in a negative way (Schaltegger and Figge 1997, 2000; Wipfli and Hauser 1998). Nevertheless, the approach has been criticised fundamentally as conflicting with environmental and sustainability objectives (e.g. Bosshard 1996; Vontobel 1996:20). Much of this criticism is rather philosophical in character and does not address the methodology.

The shareholder value concept is also confronted with problems from an economic view. The expectations of investors and management are crucial when determining the discount rate and estimating future cash flows. If these expectations do not reflect future company development (e.g. because they neglect future financial impacts of existing environmental contamination), calculations will not show the actual shareholder value. Furthermore, value created in the distant future will often not be considered because, in practice, analysis of future trends is restricted to a period of five to ten years ahead due to the reductionary effects of discounting cash flows. In these circumstances, there is a danger of inappropriate management and investment decisions being made (Figge 2001, 2002). Thus, in terms of the inherent problems related to the shareholder value concept, the quality of the assessment of company value will depend more on the skills and expertise of the assessor than on the choice of assessment method. Nevertheless, the shareholder value approach has gained a lot of support in business practice (see, for example: Krneta 1995; Volkart 1996). This acceptance may be a result of comparatively higher transparency between financial accounting and the shareholder value approach. Complete reliance on accounting figures means that the effects of a large number of standards and practices have to be accepted (Schaltegger and Burritt 2000:204ff.). The shareholder value approach is much more manageable, as only a few variables need to be considered (a forecast of free cash flow, discount rate including risk-free interest rate, and a risk factor). The bottom line effect of accounting standards on the reported profitability is hard or even impossible to analyse for anyone than a few very qualified accountants. In turn, the assumptions on which shareholder value calculations are based are much more transparent for investors and management.

5.   THE ENVIRONMENTAL SHAREHOLDER VALUE APPROACH

The environmental shareholder value concept (Schaltegger and Figge 1997, 2000) describes a straightforward approach to check environmental management options according to their effect on value drivers. Figure 2 shows the basic ideal considerations made by investors (shareholders) when they assess a company. These characteristics of a shareholder's perspective determine the calculation formula of shareholder value and the value drivers.

Investors consider payments as future cash flows that lead to a change of view from a focus on one period to a project view. Project thinking requires the consideration of the length of a project over many periods. Discounting is the method applied to take account of the valuation that future payments are worth less than current payments. This is also influenced by risk. The shareholder value view of profit distinguishes itself from the accounting view of profit. Profitability expectations of investors are that returns must exceed average market profitability for comparable investment options.

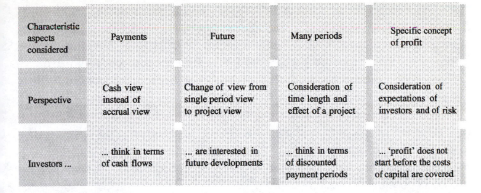

Characteristic aspects considered	Payments	Future	Many periods	Specific concept of profit
Perspective	Cash view instead of accrual view	Change of view from single period view to project view	Consideration of time length and effect of a project	Consideration of expectations of investors and of risk
Investors ...	... think in terms of cash flows	... are interested in future developments	... think in terms of discounted payment periods	... 'profit' does not start before the costs of capital are covered

Figure 2. Characteristics of the investor's shareholder value perspective (similar to Weber and Schäffer 2000:256)

The type of corporate environmental management that is in line with increasing shareholder value is discussed below for the value drivers.

5.1   Investments in Fixed Assets and Working Capital

Investments tie up a lot of capital and have a long-term structural influence on production processes, working procedures and incremental decisions. Traditionally, environmental protection activities were related strongly to large investments in end-of-pipe technologies. Furthermore, conventional investments also have a large structural influence on the extent of the environmental impacts of production.

Investments can increase shareholder value if they generate a return that is higher than the cost of capital. Thus, capital-intensive investments in end-of-pipe technologies, which do not usually generate revenue, reduce shareholder value (see, for example: Ellipson 1996; Schaltegger and Figge 1997) because they require a large amount of capital (e.g. for building a wastewater treatment plant) and because they incur related operating costs (e.g. costs for chemicals used to neutralise acids).

As a consequence, environmental management that changes current environmental protection measures from capital-intensive to capital-extensive (i.e. not capital-intensive) will increase shareholder value. New environmental investments should focus on a minimal increase of fixed assets.

Shareholder value is furthermore influenced by another investment-related value driver—investment in working capital (current assets). Measures that reduce the amount of materials and thus purchasing costs, storage costs and wear and tear of production installations affect shareholder value. This is particularly important for integrated environmental protection technologies such as process optimisation (see, for example, Ellipson 1995). If productivity can be improved through less use of raw materials and semi-manufactured products, smaller inventories and a lower throughput in production processes, economic performance can be increased through environmental management (Schaltegger and Burritt 2000:130ff.; Schaltegger and Müller 1997). Approaches that support this strategy are related to dematerialisation of production (see, for example: Braungart and McDonough 2002; Schmidt-Bleek 1993; von Weizsäcker *et al.* 1997).

Environmental investments and investments with high environmental relevance are in line with a shareholder value orientation if they are capital-extensive (i.e. tie up as little capital as possible in fixed assets) and if they increase the material and energy efficiency of production (i.e. tie up as little capital as possible in working capital).

5.2   Sales Revenue Growth, Profit Margin and Tax Rate

Environmental protection measures involve various operational activities and can influence conventional operational management. Conventional operational management can, in turn, have environmental implications. Investigating operational management in relation to environmental management and its effects on shareholder value takes primarily the first perspective.

Operational influences of environmental management on shareholder value are related to growth in sales revenue, the net operating margin and the rate of income tax.

Sales revenue and profit margins rise through environmental management only if it can increase the perceived benefit of the company's products and services to customers. Sales growth and net operating margin depend on the general economic development of the industry, on how competitive the company is related to other suppliers (e.g. Porter 1989), the industry's image and on the environmental awareness of consumers. In this context, certifications and labels can play a role (e.g. Karl and Orwat 2000). Some consumer goods markets such as in the food retail sector in Switzerland or some niche suppliers in the textile sector in Germany provide good examples of how environmental management can be rewarded with higher sales and competitiveness (e.g. Belz 1999, 2001).

In many developed countries, environmental awareness and consumption patterns are steadily high (for an example from Germany see Kuckartz and Grunenberg 2002) or have increased for the last three decades (e.g. for the U.K.). In some cases, this can also provide new export opportunities for environmental leaders.

A company can increase its shareholder value by improving its competitiveness. Depending on the company's competitive strategy, the kind of environmental management will have to be designed in a different way. Companies following a price leadership strategy will have to focus on environmental measures that result in cost savings; for instance, through a dematerialisation of production processes (e.g. Fischer *et al.* 1997; Schaltegger and Burritt 2000; Schaltegger and Müller 1997), miniaturisation of its products (thus using less materials), etc. (e.g. Braungart and McDonough 2002; Schmidt-Bleek 1993; von Weizsäcker *et al.* 1997). Cost-reducing production process and product innovations may also be driven by taking an environmental perspective (e.g. Fussler and Kolleth 1996).

Companies focussing on product differentiation strategies will have to work out the optimal links between the conventional purchasing criteria of their customers and environmental issues that strengthen their competitive position in terms of these conventional criteria. In this context, the eco-efficiency analysis and matrix is a useful tool with which to compare products (Ilinitch and Schaltegger 1995).

With growing internalisation of external environmental costs, company-internal costs tend to match gradually better with social costs. Thus, cost-reducing environmental measures will tend to become increasingly important in environmental management. Furthermore, when competitors adapt cost-reduction environmental management, competitiveness will be increased mainly through differentiation strategies that widen profit margins or increase sales, or increase the duration of value increase (see Section 4.4).

Furthermore, the company's tax burden may be influenced by how environmental and social issues are managed. Whereas the income tax rate is usually not influenced by sustainability issues, the provision of tax allowances for certain environmental or social activities is an issue in various countries. Integrated clean production technologies often benefit from tax reductions (through shorter write-off periods and subsidies). In addition, more and more environmental impacts are a target of effluent charges, emission taxes or emission trading schemes and thus become economically more relevant.

A modern management accounting system (e.g. Schaltegger and Burritt 2000:87ff.) is necessary to calculate and balance the effect of alternative environmental measures on shareholder value.

5.3　　Cost of Capital

Environmental and social issues, especially when related to reputation, can have a substantial impact on the costs of capital and, thus, a major impact on shareholder value. Many banks and insurance companies tend to underestimate the economic relevance of environmental issues on company specific risk (e.g. Figge 2001). The risks of lending have increased (e.g. Williams and Phillips 1994) with new environmental regulations, and environmental and societal liabilities related to landfills, accidents and products. As a consequence, creditors have started to audit, assess and differentiate companies with low environmental risk from other companies. Examples such as the higher interest rates paid by nuclear power stations to borrow money show that environmental issues do not influence only company-specific availability of capital but also the costs of borrowing capital.

Furthermore, many governments launch subsidy schemes, specific loans and funding programmes to support companies in leadership and innovation for sustainable development. Such government programmes are often targeted on smaller and medium size companies. In some cases, small and medium enterprises (SMEs) can also improve their access to regional capital providers and environmental trust when they can demonstrate a good sustainability performance. The reputational effect of being positively assessed by sustainability rating organisations and by being listed in the portfolio of ethical funds is an important driver for management to engage in sustainability management. However, the direct investment effect of sustainability funds on market capitalisation is still negligible. The so-called 'green bonus' (i.e. to obtain lower interest rates than the market average because of environmental excellence) can be relevant in some distinct cases, but seems irrelevant for larger companies and the majority of industry.

Far more relevant is the impact of environmental risks on the costs of capital (see, for example, Vaughan 1994:39f.). Risks linked to potential environmental problems in the future are now more often considered by banks than in the past and can lead to higher interest rates on borrowed capital. This is especially true for systematic risks that cannot be diversified away through the combination of a large number and broad spread of risks (e.g. Figge 1997, 2001). An example of a systematic environmental risk on a company's shareholder value is the introduction of carbon dioxide (CO_2) emissions trading, which will increase energy costs for all companies if they do not reduce their exposure to this risk. The only way of reducing the financial consequences of this systematic environmental risk is to reduce the company's exposure to the risk by, for instance, improving energy efficiency.

5.4   Duration of Value Growth

In a competitive market, companies can create profits only through innovations that differentiate themselves in their cost structure or in their product-related benefit for customers. Innovations, however, do not provide a competitive advantage for ever. Value growth through innovation is limited in time. In the long run, returns from an investment will decrease until they just cover expenses and the costs of capital. The duration of value growth created through the innovation will vary depending on the duration of patents, how easy the innovation can be copied by competitors, etc.

Another way of increasing shareholder value through sustainability management is thus to increase the time period of a competitive advantage or in the language of finance—the duration of the value gains. This can be achieved in two ways. First, new products that are environmentally or socially problematic may face lower prices, sales or liabilities, which increase costs if this risk is not reduced with good sustainability management. Secondly, environmental or social differentiation may prolong the period for which the higher than average return is achieved. In the second case, shareholder value is increased through a long-lasting price premium as a result of environmental or social innovations.

6. HOW CAN ENVIRONMENTAL MANAGEMENT CONTRIBUTE TO SHAREHOLDER VALUE?

The discussion of what kind of corporate environmental protection can increase shareholder value highlights a large spectrum and variety of possible activities. Measures that combine environmental management with thinking about shareholder value target the improvement of eco-efficiency as the ratio of value added to environmental impact added (or, more generally, as the ratio of economic performance to environmental impact). Eco-efficiency is a ratio and its improvement is the goal. However, eco-efficiency measures can be defined in a more or less narrow way concerning their scope (e.g. as the euro contribution margin of a product unit per kg of CO_2 or as return on equity per total corporate contribution to the greenhouse effect) and time (e.g. for the last period or for many future periods). The environmental shareholder value approach guides the focus of attention to the lasting increase of value through environmental activities. Thus, the management perspective is directed towards future and long-term effects as crucial elements of sustainable development. Furthermore, the environmental shareholder value approach allows management to set clear priorities in environmental management because it does not support every kind of environmental management.

In summary, shareholder value increasing environmental protection is (Schaltegger and Figge 1997:17, 2000):
- Capital-extensive—using 'smarter', smaller and cheaper equipment
- Directed towards dematerialisation, reducing throughput and material consumption in order to reduce purchase, storage and depreciation costs
- Margin widening by reducing the costs of production (through dematerialisation) and by increasing the benefits to customers

- Sales-boosting—increasing customers benefit with more desirable products and services
- Safeguarding the flow of finance and gaining confidence of capital providers by reducing risks and creating a 'green bonus'
- Prolonging the duration of value growth through differentiation, increasing earnings potentials and anticipation of future costs

From a practical perspective, the environmental shareholder value matrix can be a useful tool to structure the assessment of alternative environmental projects and measures (Table 1).

Table 1. The shareholder value matrix (Figge and Hahn 2002)

Value driver / Environmental aspect	Value growth duration	Revenue growth	Operating profit margin		Income tax rate	Investments	Cost of capital
			Price	Costs			
Introduction of a new product	+	++	++	–	0	–	–
...							
...							
...							

++ = significant value creating impact; += value creating impact; 0 = neutral; – = value destroying impact; —— = significant value destroying impact.

The projects are listed and checked for their effect on each value driver. This provides a first overview of conflicting and enforcing effects. The most promising projects can then be examined more in depth and designed in a way that supports the highest possible increase in shareholder value.

7.   LIMITS TO SHAREHOLDER VALUE-ORIENTED ENVIRONMENTAL MANAGEMENT

Corporate environmental management that increases shareholder value conforms with future-oriented long-term financial and market incentives. However, the approach faces important restrictions, which must be kept in mind. From a more technical perspective of finance, financial liquidity is not included explicitly in the calculation of shareholder value and risk is not considered from a management's perspective but only an investor's. Many companies, especially SMEs and very specialised companies, cannot avoid certain unsystematic risks such as accidents through diversification. Unsystematic risks are not considered by investors and hence not reflected in the discount factor. For management, however, avoiding these risks may have a high priority in order to secure the company's existence. This may not only be a technical question of risk but also a societal issue related to stakeholder perceptions and what kind of risks are socially acceptable. The environmental shareholder value approach is obviously limited in its effect by legal, cultural and political circumstances that influence market incentives. Companies are also exposed to the risks of a loss of social acceptance and of legitimacy of their activities and products (e.g. Freeman 1984; Schaltegger and Sturm 1992). Management can only succeed in the marketplace if it does not face problems created by societal stakeholder who have a strong influence on legitimacy and reputation. As a consequence, management may also need to implement measures other than those that have the greatest potential to improve shareholder value. Nevertheless, the environmental shareholder value approach remains a core tool with which to link environmental performance with economic performance.

REFERENCES

Bea, F. (1997): 'Shareholder Value', *Wirtschaftsstudium* No. 10, 541-543 (available only in German).

Belz, F. (1999): 'Integratives Öko-Marketing: Erfolgreiche Vermarktung von ökologischen Produkten im Konsumgüterbereich', in: Bellmann, K. (Ed.): *Betriebliches Umweltmanagement in Deutschland*. Wiesbaden: Gabler, 163-189.

Belz, F. (2001): 'Nachhaltiges Öko-Marketing', *Thexis* Vol. 18, No. 2, 24-29.

Birchler, U. and Spremann, K. (1995): 'Die Eigenmittelrendite als falsche Fährte?', *Neue Zürcher Zeitung* 4 October, 38.

Bosshard, D. (1996): 'Shareholder Capitalism und Stakeholder Capitalism', *GDI Impuls* No. 2, 26-38.

Braungart, M. and McDonough, W. (2002): *Cradle to Grave. Remaking the Way We Make Things.* New York: North Point Press.

Copeland, T., Koller, T. and Murrin, J. (1993): *Valuation: Measuring and Managing the Value of Companies.* New York: Wiley.

Desjardins, J., Tabone, J. and Willis, A. (1999): *Environmental Performance and Shareholder Value Creation. 1999 Survey.* Toronto: The Canadian Institute of Chartered Accountants (CICA).

Ellipson AG (Ed.) (1995): *Ciba's Umweltstrategie* (Ellipson News Winter/Spring 95/96). Basel: Ellipson AG.

Ellipson AG (Ed.) (1996): *The Right Environmental Strategy Increases Shareholder Value* (Ellipson News Autumn/Winter 96/97). Basel: Ellipson AG.

Feldman, S.J., Soyka, P.A. and Ameer, P. (1997): 'Does Improving a Firm's Environmental Management System and Environmental Performance Result in a Higher Stock Price?', *Journal of Investing* Vol. 6, No.4, 87-97.

Figge, F. (2001): *Wertschaffendes Umweltmanagement. Keine Nachhaltigkeit ohne ökonomischen Erfolg. Kein ökonomischer Erfolg ohne Nachhaltigkeit.* Frankfurt: PricewaterhouseCoopers.

Figge, F. (2002): *Stakeholder und Unternehmensrisiko. Eine stakeholderbasierte Herleitung des Unternehmensrisikos.* Lüneburg: Centre for Sustainability Management (CSM).

Figge, F. and Hahn, T. (2002): *Environmental Shareholder Value Matrix. Konzeption, Anwendung und Berechnung.* Lüneburg: Centre for Sustainability Management (CSM).

Fischer, H., Wucherer, C., Wagner, B. and Burschel, C. (1997): *Umweltkostenmanagement: Kosten senken durch praxiserprobtes Umweltcontrolling.* München: Hanser-Verlag.

Freeman, E. (1984): *Strategic Management. A Stakeholder Approach.* Marshfield: Pitman.

Fussler, C. and Kolleth, M. (1996): *Driving Eco Innovation.* London: Pearson.

GEMI (Global Environmental Management Initiative) (Ed.) (2004): *Clear Advantage. Building Shareholder Value. Environment. Value to the Investor.* Washington D.C.: Gemi.

Hachmeister, D. (1997): Shareholder Value, *Die Betriebswirtschaft* Vol. 57, No. 6, 823-839 (available only in German).

Ilinitch, A. and Schaltegger, S. (1995): Developing a Green Business Portfolio, *Long Range Planning* Vol. 28, 2.

Karl, H. and Orwat, C. (2000): 'Economic Aspects of Environmental Labelling', in: Folmer, H. and Tietenberg, T. (Eds.): *The International Yearbook of Environmental and Resource Economics 1999/2000.* Cheltenham: Edward Elgar, 107-170.

Krneta, G. (1995): 'Wem ist der Verwaltungsrat was schuldig?. Plädoyer für ein Spannungs- und gegen ein Schlachtfeld', *Neue Zürcher Zeitung* 11 November, 14.

Kuckartz, U. and Grunenberg, H. (2002): *Umweltbewusstsein in Deutschland 2002. Ergebnisse einer repräsentativen Bevölkerungsumfrage.* Berlin: Bundesumweltministerium.

Martin, R. (2002): Shareholder Value versus Corporate Responsibility?, *Harvard Business Review* Vol. 80, No 3, 5-11.

McGuire, J., Sundgren, A. and Schneeweis, T. (1981): 'Corporate Social Responsibility and Firm Financial Performance', *Academy of Management Journal* Vol. 31, No. 4, 854-872.

Porter, M. (1989): *The Competitive Advantage of Nations.* London: Macmillan.

PwC (PricewaterhouseCoopers) (2004): *Miljø og Shareholder Value. Se Værdien af Miljøarbejde.* Hellerup: PWC.

Rappaport, A. (1986): *Creating Shareholder Value: The New Standards for Business Performance.* New York: Free Press.

Rappaport, A. (1998): *Creating Shareholder Value: A Guide for Managers and Investors* (Revised edition). New York: Simon and Schuster.

Reed, D. (1998): *Green Shareholder Value. Hype or Hit?,* New York: World Resource Institute.

Repetto, R. and Austin, D. (2000): *Pure Profit. Financial Implications of Environmental Performance.* Washington DC: World Resource Institute.

Schaltegger, S. and Burritt R.L. (2000): *Contemporary Environmental Accounting.* Sheffield: Greenleaf Publishing.

Schaltegger, S. and Figge, F. (1997): *Environmental Shareholder Value* (Report 54). Basel: Wirtschaftswissenschaftliches Zentrum/Sarasin.

Schaltegger, S. and Figge, F. (2000): 'Environmental Shareholder Value. Economic Success with Corporate Environmental Management', *Eco-Management and Auditing,* Vol. 7, No 1, 29-42.

Schaltegger, S. and Müller, K. (1997): 'Calculating the True Profitability of Pollution Prevention', *Greener Management International* (Special edition on Environmental Management Accounting) Vol. 17, Spring, 53-68.

Schaltegger, S. and Sturm, A. (1992): *Ökologieorientierte Entscheidungen in Unternehmen.* Bern: Paul Haupt, 2. Ed. 1994.

Schaltegger, S. and Wagner, M. (2006): Integrative Management of Sustainability Performance, Measurement and Reporting, *International Journal of Accounting, Auditing and Performance Evaluation (IJAAPE)*, No. 4, Vol. 4, forthcoming.

Schmidt-Bleek, F. (1993): *Wieviel Umwelt braucht der Mensch? MIPS, das Maß für ökologisches Wirtschaften.* Basel: Birkhäuser.

Vaughan, S. (1994): *Greening Financial Markets.* Geneva: UNEP.

Volkart, R. (1996): 'Langfristige Shareholder-Orientierung. Harmonie mit den Stakeholder-Interessen', *Neue Zürcher Zeitung,* 22 August, 33.

Vontobel, H. (1996): 'Shareholder Value. Ein trüberischer Reiz? Ein Plädoyer wider die Darwinisierung der Sitten', *Neue Zürcher Zeitung* 19 June, 20.

WBCSD (World Business Council for Sustainable Development) (1997): *Environmental Performance and Shareholder Value.* Geneva: WBCSD.

Weber, J. and Schäffer, U. (2000): *Balanced Scorecard und Controlling.* Wiesbaden: Gabler.

Weizsäcker, E. von, Lovins, A. and Lovins, L. (1997): *Factor Four. Doubling Wealth, Halving Resource Use.* London: Earthscan.

Williams, G. and Phillips, T. (1994): 'Cleaning up Our Act. Accounting for Environmental Liabilities. Current Financial Reporting Doesn't Do the Job', *Management Accounting* Vol. 75, 30-33.

Wipfli, C. and Hauser, M. (1998): 'Schaffung von Shareholder Value durch umweltbewusstes Verhalten', *Treuhänder* No. 12, 1389-1394.

Ziegler, A., Rennings, K. and Schröder, M. (2002): 'Der Einfluss ökologischer und sozialer Nachhaltigkeit auf den Shareholder Value europäischer Aktiengesellschaften'. (Discussion Paper No.02-32) Mannheim: Center for European Economic Research.

Chapter 2

Social Performance and Economic Success

DO SOCIAL OBJECTIVES INTEGRATE WITH CORE CORPORATE OBJECTIVES?
The Future of Social Auditing

Trevor Goddard
Curtin University of Technology, Australia

Abstract: This chapter deals with the link between the social objectives and conventional economic objectives of a company. Starting with corporate social responsibility, approaches such as social auditing and reporting area addressed. Subsequently, the business case of a company's voluntary social engagements is discussed for cause-related marketing, ethical relativism, reputation and competitive advantage. Changing the perspective on the company, the social case is afterwards dealt in terms of social justice, stakeholder theory, the deontological argument and the unexpected factor. The chapter ends with a discussion of the role and usefulness of social auditing as an environmental scan.

1. INTRODUCTION

Audits validate corporate performance objectively, verifying actions against standards. This process can report on measures of ethical behaviour and the social impact of a corporation. Social auditing may be a means of assessing and conveying messages to stakeholders about corporate social performance, with tangible advantages for business and the community.

Social audit tools acknowledge the interdependence of business and social issues. The corporate sector requires measures that allow them to use the results as promotional tools with consumers and which link social impact to core business activity. The link between company image, core customer values and social issues builds trust with consumers. This approach focuses corporate attention on concerns raised by the wider community, with stakeholder theory acknowledging the views of wider constituents.

As companies find it harder to 'out-innovate' or 'out-advertise' competitors, strategic activities such as social auditing may build reputation and brand. Corporations may feel that public-spirited initiatives beyond the requirements of law—often involving great expense—make good sense as public confidence is maintained. The use of a social audit tool to verify externally that a company exceeds its required level of corporate social performance can be another tool of competitive advantage. This creates positive correlation between reputation management and commitment to socially responsible activity. This chapter analyses the role of social auditing in bringing the business case and social case for corporate citizenship together.

An increase in social activism has encouraged the corporate sector to acknowledge the need for socially responsible activity in the societal (health, welfare and education) and environmental impacts of core business (Burke and Logson 1996). Social audits measure corporate performance against predetermined criteria (Johnson 2001; Kaptein 1998; Zadek 1994). Subsequently, social audits conducted in a similar manner to financial audits are a mechanism to express corporate social responsibility externally (Johnson 2001; McIntosh *et al.* 1998; Schwartz and Gibb 1999; Svendsen 1998).

Social auditing is part of a wider holistic corporate citizenship movement requiring systemic cultural change in corporations. It must be reflected in a system of behaviour and actions pervading each level of an organisation's mission, policies and practices (Birch 2000b). The effectiveness of a social audit hinges on the value perceived by those requesting the audit. If the standard being audited against cannot be agreed on, or is not valued by wider stakeholders, then the purpose of the audit itself is superfluous (Kaptein 1998; Weiss 1999).

Commentators negating the role of social auditing claim that what needs measuring is not countable and that numerical indicators measuring intrinsic concepts are of limited value (Power 1997). The 'manic nature of global capitalism' gives rise to this new problem of measurement of the way 'citizens of the globe' relate to each other and the impact of cultural diversity (Grieder 1997; Korten 1995; Michelman 1994; Schwartz and Gibb 1999). As Albert Einstein said: 'The things that count cannot be counted' (original source unknown). This chapter explores the influence of social audit tools and their ability to comment on a corporation's social performance and future role by identifying the social and business forces driving their uptake.

2. CORPORATE SOCIAL RESPONSIBILITY

Corporate sector reforms of the 20th century have not restricted the power of capitalism—the first economic system to enjoy relative autonomy from the reigning political system (Michelman 1994). There has been little associated reform dealing with social issues and with moral measurements not prioritised in the power equilibrium between state and free market.

Rapid flux of corporate interactions across multiple boundaries (religion, culture, national and corporate identity) causes ethical dilemmas in environmental management, occupational health and safety, labour law and discriminatory practices (Kegley and Wittkopf 2001). This rate of change often means strategic decisions are 'out of date' before they can be put into operation (Toffler 1990). The capability of the public sector to solve social issues is questioned continually, with societies looking towards the new holders of wealth—the corporate sector—to assist in identifying and rectifying these issues (Birch 2000a; Dignam 2000; Korten 1995; Nolan and Nolan 1995; Quarter 2000). This requires corporate sector engagement with stakeholders that they may not have recognised traditionally.

In 1998, the United Nations estimated that over 53,000 multinational corporations (MNC) and 450,000 global affiliates had assets in excess of US$13 trillion and global sales of more than US$9.5 trillion. Corporations controlling these assets influence access to and the type of employment undertaken by developing communities. With sales of the ten largest corporations exceeding the combined gross national product of the 100 smallest nation states, the rise in MNC power and the paradigm shift of power from nation states to MNC over elements of production is evident (Kegley and Wittkopf 2001).

Corporate performance is a product of the actions, behaviours and intentions of corporations that can be measured, analysed and evaluated in the context of the broader corporate citizenship debate (Zadek 1994). Social audits are part of this process, measuring corporate performance against criteria based on the local standards of a community or industry or the influence of the actions of the corporation on the cultural standing of the community (Freeman 1984; Gray *et al.* 1987, 1997; Greenwood 2001; Griffin 2000).

Corporate social responsibility has descriptive and evaluative components. Social auditing is evaluative, as an 'audit' is a means of reviewing what a corporation has done against predetermined standards (Abt 1977; Brummer 1991; Power 1997). One issue that is debated is the concept of being 'held accountable' for one's actions, both in terms of non-maleficence and beneficence (Spencer *et al.* 2000). Ethically, corporations may be considered to be accountable to not only 'do the right thing', but to actively prevent the wrong thing from being done. This statement of moral implication raises legal implications through negligence and criminal action, issues traditionally linked to individuals (Rawls 1996). Actions taken by a corporate legal entity are greater both in volume and widespread impact than most of the actions a single human being is capable of undertaking (Nozick 1996).

3.   SOCIAL AUDITING AND REPORTING

Audit derives from the Latin 'audire' meaning to listen. The social audit process enables objective measurements of a company's performance against standards and a public statement of trust in the preparation and worthiness of the information provided (Kaptein 1998). This independent examination of record-keeping and business activity expresses an opinion of the reliability and validity of information against predetermined standards. Auditors or group carrying out the audit should be able to demonstrate independence from both the matter and the corporation being audited. In this way, transparency of the process allows for an objective and technical approach that collects forms of evidence through examination of organisational systems and process. The final audit statement should be an expression of a view based on the evidence provided by a corporation and not the intent of the corporation to act, with a defined objective of the audit process (Power 1997).

Social audits define, observe, and report measures of the ethical behaviour and social impact of an organisation in relation to its aims and those of its stakeholders (Leipziger 2001; McIntosh *et al.* 1998). Stakeholders are people who can affect and who are affected by the activities of the corporation (Svendsen 1998; Zadek 1994). Indicators used to create social audit tools are constructs based on observations that are usually quantitative and which tell us something about an aspect of life in which we are interested or about changes that are taking place in it. This information may be objective, in that it claims to show what a position is or how it is changing. It may also be subjective in a sense that it purports to show how changes in position are regarded by the community and constituent groups (Gray *et al.* 1987).

Auditing has developed from the financial industry, while concerns for social issues are steeped in the humanities and social sciences. Each set of disciplines has its own history, philosophies and subsequent means of interpretation and measurement (Capra 1983). Social auditing acknowledges the development of a new paradigm in which social forces and business forces, which while acknowledged individually, have a new relationship in which their interdependence is examined (Korten 1995). For this reason, the business drivers of social auditing and the normative or social drivers should be identified.

Reporting of social impacts on society and the environment has become more strategic and evident of a commitment to transparency and sustainable business (Farmer and Hogue 1985; Hill and Jones 1992; Himmelstein 1997; Kaptein 1998). Most commonly, sections on community relations and philanthropic activity are mentioned in annual reports, but collecting and reporting on comprehensive social and environmental data is still difficult. This has been partly due to a lack of appropriate measurement techniques with which to assess performance (Elkington 1999; Weiss 1999; Wulfson 2001).

The financial costs of social actions can be compiled by an accountant. However, the valuation of these social costs or benefits and the framework used to identify and measure them may prove difficult for executives with limited background in social science and humanities (Abt 1977; Farmer and Hogue 1985; Hill and Jones 1992; Himmelstein 1997; Kaptein 1998). Each industry lives within its own context and community, so there is not likely to be a single form of social auditing standard (Gray *et al.* 1997). This would create a homogenous environment and is not the role of social audit tools (Chatterjee 1998). It is inevitable that no account or representation of an organisation–society interaction can be static through time due to the ever changing issues, concerns and accountabilities that respond to an infinite set of community relations (Abt 1977). These lead to the conclusion among corporate executives that discrete quantitative measures cannot capture social welfare, and that these measures may mislead and distract and may be misused and abused (Gray *et al.* 1987).

4.   THE BUSINESS CASE

4.1   Cause-Related Marketing

Cause-related marketing links a product or company image to a core customer value, deepening relationships and building strong bonds of trust (Wulfson 2001). This focuses corporate attention on concerns raised by the wider community as being important. The wider view of stakeholder theory is employed because a corporation will need to acknowledge the presence of views from a variety of constituents (Jennings 1999).

Research by Business in the Community in the UK shows that, where price and quality are equal, 81% of consumers are more likely to buy a product associated with a cause (Dignam 2000). This is supported by collaborative research (Johnston 2000; Wulfson 2001) demonstrating the influence of individual consumers over interests expressed by corporations. Eighty-six percent of consumers have a more positive image of a company that they see as doing something to make the world a better place to live (Dignam 2000). Supporters of cause-related marketing claim that a long, advertised record of community service also offers corporations greater customer acceptance of price increases and favourable publicity, and wins over sceptical holders of public office who often have control over a company's expansion plans (Meyer 1999; Schwartz and Gibb 1999).

Branding has moved corporations away from individual products and services towards a psychological and anthropological examination of what brands mean to the culture and peoples lives (Klein 2000). Corporations were traditionally subservient to the needs of the people through governance by the sovereign state. However, corporations now have the authority and legitimate power given them by governments to take on the role of a socially influential mechanism. The social audit tool may fill the gap left by governments and may monitor corporate sector influence over issues in which they have limited expertise (Kegley and Wittkopf 2001).

4.2 Ethical Relativism

Global engagement creates ethical discourse through a kaleidoscope of individual and corporate values that do not easily transfer to the international stage (Chatterjee 1998). Social audit tools should reflect the values of the corporation, the community and stakeholders (Wheeler and Sillanpää 1997). Ethical dilemmas arise due to the need to focus on a set of ethical guidelines related to a community, culture or group and the use of boundaries within an ontological mindset (Birsch 1999). Action on the basis of ethical discourse can be initiated on the following levels:

- Cost-benefit approach (consequences, goals and outcomes)—ethnocentric internal method of engagement dealing only with core business activities irrespective of social inputs and cost
- Rule based approach (following codes, rules and law)—operations within the constraints of local guidelines
- Utilitarianism approach (doing the best for most people)—humanistic perspective to meet the needs of the majority of stakeholders
- Categorical Imperative (Kant)—focus on people as 'ends not means', with community sustainability as the reason for MNC being in existence
- Cultural approach (follow local standards)—an epistemological mindset enabling development subservient to the needs of local people (Chatterjee 1998)

4.3 Reputation Management

Reputation management is identified as an important area of future research for corporate social performance (Clark 2000). Studies by McGuire, Fombrun and Shanley (cited by Clark 2000) used Fortune Magazine's Corporate Reputation Index, finding a positive correlation between corporate social performance and financial performance. Social contracts become self-enforcing when corporate gains from maintaining reputation are greater than the loss if the contract was reneged (Crowe 2001; Spencer *et al.* 2000), creating a positive correlation between management of organisational reputation and commitment to socially responsible activity.

4.4   Competitive Advantage

Future-oriented corporations adopt approaches that consider competitiveness and corporate social responsibility as compatible and mutually reinforcing (Khoury *et al.* 1999). The implication for social auditing is that the corporate sector requires tools against which it can measure activity, allowing it to use the results as a means of promotion to consumer markets (Altman 1998).

Corporate social responsibility can be demonstrated through actions beyond legal compliance as a commitment to important social issues as both a means of promotion within the community and preserving customer base, and environmental sustainability—which ultimately sustains a company's core business (Crowe 2001). As companies find it harder to 'out-innovate' or 'out-advertise' competitors, strategic cause programmes that build corporate reputation and brand imaging will become valuable leadership strategies (Meyer 1999). Many companies feel that initiatives beyond legal requirements—often involving great expense—add value because public confidence should be maintained at all costs (Nolan and Nolan 1995). Corporations can create and exploit resources that provide a sustainable and competitive advantage.

5.   THE SOCIAL CASE

5.1   Social Justice

Rawls's theory of justice demonstrates that societal obligation can help to reduce barriers to equality of opportunity, extending to programmes that correct or compensate for disadvantages (Beauchamp and Childress 2001). Corporations are asked to address the triple bottom line, focusing on economic prosperity, environmental quality and the element that corporations have traditionally overlooked—social justice (Elkington 1999). The UN Copenhagen Declaration and Programme of Action recommends that nation states intervene in markets to ensure fair competition and ethical conduct, and to harmonise economic and social development. The UN Human Rights Commission states in Sub-Commission Resolution 1998/12 that: 'unguided globalisation had helped reduce poverty in some of the largest and strongest developing economies but had also produced a widening gap between "winners and losers", and that to create social opportunities requires better management of globalisation internationally' (Third World Network 2001).

5.2   Stakeholder Theory

Stakeholder theory postulates that companies possess explicit and implicit contracts with multiple constituents. Honouring these contracts establishes a reputation that will determine future negotiations and interactions with stakeholders (Elias and Cavana 2001; Etzioni 1998; Svendsen 1998; Wheeler and Sillanpää 1997). Social legitimacy is created through these unwritten contracts, allowing a corporation to continue to operate with the licence of stakeholders as they comply with the implied elements of a contract (Nozick 1996). According to Wulfson (2001), corporate managers should see themselves as stewards or trustees who act in the general public's interests and recognise that business and society are intertwined and interdependent.

A 1992 American Law Institute Report, *Principles of Governance*, actively supports the stakeholder theory espoused by Abt (1977). Birch (2000b) and Korten (1995) also affirm that, by its nature, the modern corporation creates interdependencies with a variety of groups expressing legitimate concerns. These groups include employees, customers, suppliers, and members of the communities in which the corporation operates (Donaldson and Preston 1995). It has been suggested that large corporations should be viewed primarily as social enterprises, as their right to exist and the decisions they make are justified only when measured against the public and social purposes they fulfil (Nozick 1996; Spencer *et al.* 2000; Tam 1998). This is contrasted by the position that corporations fulfil social obligations by being in business and providing employment as a form of societal support (Friedman 1997).

Debate surrounding the need for corporations to adopt socially responsible practices derives from the interpretation of 'constituents'. Friedman's neoclassical economic perspective views corporate executives acting as agents in an official capacity on behalf of stockholders (Michelman 1994). In a holistic sense, these 'constituencies' are not only the stakeholders with a financial interest in the corporation. Several authors (Abt 1977; Korten 1995; Svendsen 1998) have broadly defined 'constituents' and 'stakeholders' to cover employees of the company and their families, shareholders, customers, the local and national community, and the world at large. This has precipitated a debate surrounding the impact that the activities of multinational corporations have on the lives of people around the world (Epstein and Birchard 1999, Griffin 2000).

5.3   Deontological Argument

Theory based in obligation provides a framework with which to view corporate commitment to social responsibility in terms of business not being a means to an end. Kant argued that morality is grounded in reason and not tradition, intuition, conscience, emotion or attitudes such as sympathy. He saw human beings as creatures with rationale powers to resist desire and with the freedom to do so (Beauchamp and Childress 2001). The issue is conflicting obligations. Within a rationalist society where money is the derivative of all action, opportunity cost is a critical measurement within overall cost (Bowie 1997).

5.4 The 'Unexpected Factor'

Corporations learn different operational, management, marketing, recruitment and retention techniques from non-profit organisations, which give their staff access to skill sets outside their normal experiences (Meyer 1999). Through social auditing, the knowledge gained from the social sciences and humanities may be of use to the corporation within a business framework. This reflects the growing recognition that the discipline of management itself is derived from sociology, anthropology and psychology—as all human sciences that bring an emotive side to business counteract the harder mathematical economic and accounting disciplines (Drucker 1999; McMichael 2000; Nozick 1996).

6. ENVIRONMENTAL SCAN

Social auditing represents a paradigm shift from rigorous financial reporting to integrative descriptive and community-based goals (Capra 1983; Dignam 2000; Drucker 1999). This requires a multidisciplinary approach to management even in the absence of externally imposed compliance requirements (Burke and Logson 1996). The tool of environmental scanning derives from the strategic management tool of scenario planning; it discusses the social, technological, economic, environmental and political drivers of change (Schwartz 1996). This model is applied to identify the drivers of change within the sphere of social auditing.

6.1 Social

The shift of values in business from a compliance framework to actively forging closer links between the community and business ensures that corporations are more aware of their affect on and responsibilities towards those in the wider social arena (Zadek 1998). Popular business newsstand publications carry extensive material offering anecdotal evidence of the 'new economy' producing a new 'social contract', where the general public expects the business community to adhere to a higher social standard (Jason

1997; Khoury *et al.* 1999; Korten 1995). This has the effect of becoming a check and balance on keeping current audit tools relevant both by measuring against standards that are deemed important by those who use the results and by ensuring that the corporate sector understands the value of this process (Thurow 1966; Toffler 1990).

There is global uneasiness with the desire to quantify outcomes whose characteristics do not easily lend themselves to objective, large-scale measurement (Giri 2000; Power 1997). The uncontrolled use of mathematics as an end in itself may potentially turn interest groups and the corporate sector against the use of social audit tools as their wide use potentially homogenises the context of each measurement, thus reducing the value of local context in each environment where the audit tool is applied. The development of each tool requires a carefully constructed social acknowledgement of local culture.

Socially responsible investment may be an oxymoron: offering token contributions to a good cause when the investment can grow return on capital input. This allows corporations to get on with the business of profit generation while nurturing foundations and making 'feel-good' public relations gestures (Meyer 1999; Mulgan 2000). It is difficult, however, to criticise these efforts due to the 'good' it brings. In the long-term, ramifications of dependency and control over social directions raise the ethical dilemma of corporate control over welfare and social issues (Rawls 1996).

6.2   Technological

The increasingly interdependent relationship of computing and communications has reinforced the tendency of the corporate sector to move towards functional dispersal of resources in an economic rationalist model (Zadek 1998). As a result, advances in technology have not only become part of the driving force influencing the effectiveness of a social audit, but these changes are part of the impact that a social audit will measure and is required to track.

The dichotomy of technology is that many tools may not sustain the same rate of change that technology itself does in trying to address the affect that it has on the social environment. The absence of an international regulatory authority to determine the criteria of a social audit tool, coupled with the speed of business transactions and information provision, creates uncertainty that corporations may not be prepared to build into their public profile (Svendsen 1998; Toffler 1990).

6.3   Economic

Friedman (1997) argues that the best form of control over the corporate sector—including its ethical and social behaviour—is to allow the consumer to 'voice' opinion through letting the market place determine success or failure. While this may be true, it also allows powerful institutions to dominate those that least threaten their businesses and have the most to lose through exposure to irresponsible social activity (Michelman 1994; Mulgan 2000).

Social auditing can accelerate feedback and learning within an organisation and the wider community. Concurrent measurement against a standard, which is conducted from a social, financial and operational perspective, is one medium in which this feedback can be constructed (Epstein and Birchard 1999). There is potential for future integration of standards through multidisciplinary trained auditors who have the ability to integrate social and financial issues in the context of combined corporation and community issues (Leipziger 2001). Other internationally recognised procedures such as the International Standards Organisation series of quality audit processes have already acknowledged this potential and begun exploring the practicability of this fusion.

How corporations choose to respond to the publication of social audit results may determine the future value and role of social audit tools. While raising issues outside the scope of the actual audit tool, it is directly linked to its use and perceived benefit by both the corporation and the stakeholders interested in the result. There may be some motivation for companies to increase exposure to externally verified audit procedures in the future, based on evidence linking social responsibility with financial performance and long-term economic benefits to be gained by the corporation (Johnston 2000).

6.4   Environmental

Exposure given to action groups (e.g. Greenpeace) and anti-globalisation movements has encouraged the corporate community to take more heed of its responsibility beyond the financial bottom line. This is achieved by addressing ethical practices as part of everyday business rather than superficial offerings that are not represented in practice. Often annual reports or reactive and passive sponsorship of community-based programmes in which they take no long-term or vested interest can be reflective of a lack of connection to the external environment (Nolan and Nolan 1995).

Opportunities for reducing costs and accessing new markets through physical and cultural extensions as a result of globalisation has placed additional pressures on the business unit, which is often asked to look internally without acknowledging the long-term implications of its business practices (Zadek 1998). Environmental issues may suffer to a greater degree than other social issues due to the longevity associated with their impacts as a result of corporate practices. Even if corporate profit and shareholder gain are not enhanced by a corporation's activities, it must abide by the law and take into account ethical considerations as pointed out to it by the community within which it operates (Shore and Wright 2000). Social, ethical and environmental risks are inherent in modern business and should be approached in a similar fashion to conventional financial and physical risks (Crowe 2001).

6.5   Political

Focussing on the outcomes derived from within a community rather than protecting the position of a government is aligned with a stakeholder approach. This is also characteristic of a long-term view—something not often afforded to governments around the world (Mulgan 2000). Rationalist governments appear to encourage rather than regulate MNC involvement in community issues, raising complex problems through the ethics of transnational engagement. Developments in international governance have lagged behind rapid changes in the corporate world, with the growth of business power coinciding with a widespread political trend for governments to withdraw from parts of their traditional role in economic management (Crowe 2001).

Numerical indicators are about management from a distance, increasing the blurred relationship between decision-makers and those whom the decisions affect (Boyle 2002). Political targets established through government indicators are pursued with abandonment of apparent logic as regulatory bodies pursue goals without respect for the means by which they are achieved (Shore and Wright 2000). Communities and corporations may be expected to do what the targets tell them rather than what is actually necessary to maintain sustainable healthy communities (Boyle 2002).

Ethics and responsibility are difficult partners as a corporation deals with social issues that appear distant. Modern capitalism, with the assistance of technology, has made interactions far more emotive, personal, direct and immediate. As a result, the corporate sector cannot escape and politics is ever changing in who it identifies as its constituents and who they can use to achieve their goals (McIntosh *et al.* 1998; Mulgan 2000).

Since formation of the Bretton Woods Institutions (the World Bank and the International Monetary Fund), various forms of global governance have claimed control over aspects of global interactions. These influences have extended to national policies, which governments appear to write with MNC goals and objectives in mind. The 2000 UN World Investment report noted 1,035 changes in laws on foreign investment between 1991 and 1999. Of those changes, 94% increased the freedom of foreign investors and reduced government regulation (Denny 2001). The capacity of governments to manage economies and achieve national objectives in issues ranging from fiscal policy to environmental control appears strained by the activities of MNC in the international environment (Kegley and Wittkopf 2001).

7.   CONCLUSIONS

There are few barriers to the contribution of the accounting profession to the development of this area through professional development and interdisciplinary training to allow for a transition to social issues. This is a cultural change for the accounting profession; a like-minded change could also occur for those with a humanitarian and social background to become trained in the process and scientific rigour of auditing. It would seem that each group of professionals has much to offer the other in the establishment and justification of this new paradigm.

Social auditing attempts to address the ethical issues raised by the exponential growth of MNC transactions. In this dilemma of divergence and convergence of ethical values across nations, the key issue cannot be whose values and morality are adopted but what values and morality should drive the audit tolls established. The challenges to the social auditing movement are mountainous in the need to allow room within standards for a local, national and global context. The current debate over the issue and effects of globalisation and its associated processes will affect the ability of social auditing to become a part of the mainstream accounting and quality control process within corporate structures. This will become increasingly important as the divergence of economies and cultures forms new sets of community characteristics around which the standards of audit tools will be based. A priority for social audit tools will be to remain actively aware of change and to respond in a timely fashion that allows the tools to be adapted effectively to reflect the local environment without compromising international standards.

Ethical values reflect the character of individuals and corporate culture—the character of the business, which is a collection of those individuals. Contemporary literature increasingly shows less differentiation between the individual and the corporation, effectively reducing the distance between a corporation and the effect that its actions have on stakeholders. This results in a strong emotional and physical ease with which the impact of core business decisions on its local and global stakeholders can be identified.

Corporations may need to establish new ideas of what is meant by social equity, environmental justice and business ethics. This requires a higher level of understanding not only of the financial and physical forms of capital, but also of the natural, human and social capital and the effects of its abuse on both the internal dimensions of the organisation and the ability of the external social fabric of society to support corporate sector activities. The social auditing framework lacks definition as social academic disciplines and their practice play second place to pure business and financial models, which have difficulty in acknowledging cost and benefit unless they are measurable in monetary units. The social auditing process exposes corporations to stakeholders through accountable and transparent governance, allowing a public face on consumer/stakeholder input to corporate decisions. These characteristics, while secondary to core business objectives, are important indicators of the link that a social audit will form between a corporation and its identified constituents.

Difficulties identified with using social indicators to establish audit criteria are:

- Emphasis is placed on what is measurable at the expense of what is deemed important. Therefore, what is measured tends to be driven by what is perceived to be most easily measurable.
- The potential for data overload and collation of extraneous data is enormous unless there is a clear philosophical grounding and establishment of the theory behind what is being collected. The development of social auditing cannot grab for issues to measure purely as a means to demonstrate their importance, when that which is being measured may be of no intrinsic value in the first place.
- The complexity of interrelationships between social indicators means there will always be discourse between practitioners, auditors, academics and stakeholders. This needs to be harnessed, driving the issue forward rather than tearing the importance of the process apart through fragmentation of the importance of individual components.

As a result, the challenges for social auditing are:

- Determining what is actually happening (fact versus opinion and view) and choosing an indication that will effectively express this
- Determining what 'should be' by establishing the appropriate and applicable standards for performance
- Determining the boundary of relevance, what is to be included within the scope of the audit and what is not to be included

Social audits may become their own worst enemy through their establishment as a supplement to the traditional financial audit that reviews the single financial line of a corporation. Accountability is important and the auditing culture was, in part, a response to the crude measures of success developed purely from the bottom financial line. The objective of an audit is to enable the auditor to express an opinion whether the report is prepared, in all material respects, in accordance with an identified reporting framework. This framework is the distinguishing feature of auditing over the accounting process. Current social auditing appears, on the surface, to be more consistent with effective stakeholder management and the use of internal structures for promotion of adherence to external requirements. Social auditing has a strong future provided that those who respond to its critics can take the criticism as tools to drive its future change. Of these, the potential to integrate with already substantiated tools, such as the ISO series, may be its strongest chance to develop respect among all stakeholders, including corporations themselves.

REFERENCES

Abt, C. (1977): *The Social Audit for Management*. New York: American Management Association.

Altman, B. (1998): 'Corporate Community Relations in the 1990's: A Study in Transformation', *Business and Society* Vol. 37, No. 2, 221-227.

Beauchamp, T. and Childress, J. (2001): *Principles of Biomedical Ethics* (5th edition). Oxford: Oxford University Press.

Birch, D. (2000a): *Business as a Public Culture: Corporate Governance and Development*. Melbourne: Corporate Citizenship Research Unit, Deakin University.

Birch, D. (2000b): 'The Joined Up Triple Bottom Line and Corporate Citizenship', *The Corporate Citizen* Vol. 1, No. 2, 9-11.

Birsch, D. (1999): *Ethical Insights: A Brief Introduction*. Los Angeles: Mayfield Publishing Company.

Bowie, N. (1997): 'New Directions in Corporate Social Responsibility', in: Beauchamp, T. and Bowie, N. (Eds.): *Ethical Theory in Business* (5th edition). New Jersey: Prentice Hall, 96-107.

Boyle, D. (2002): 'The Storming of the Accountants', *New Statesman* 21 January, 23-24.

Brummer, J.J. (1991): *Corporate Responsibility and Legitimacy: An Interdisciplinary Analysis*. New York: Greenwood Press.

Burke, L. and Logson, J.M. (1996): 'How Corporate Social Responsibility Pays Off', *Long Range Planning* Vol. 29, No. 4, 495-502.

Capra, F. (1983): *The Turning Point: Science, Society and the Rising Culture*. London: Flamingo.

Chatterjee, S. (1998): 'Convergence and Divergence of Ethical Values across Nations: A Framework for Managerial Action', *Journal of Human Values* Vol. 4, No. 1, 5-23.

Clark, C. (2000): 'Differences between Public Relations and Corporate Social Responsibility: An Analysis', *Public Relations Review* Vol. 26, No. 3, 363-380.

Crowe, R. (2001): *Investing in Social Responsibility: Risks and Opportunities*. London: Association of British Insurers.

Denny, M. (2001): 'Back to the Barricades', *The Australian* 27 April, 25.

Dignam, C. (2000): 'Mixing Commerce and Good Causes Benefits Everyone', *Marketing* 24 February.

Donaldson, T. and Preston, L. (1995): 'The Stakeholder Theory of the Corporation: Concepts, Evidence and Implications', *Academy of Management Review* Vol. 20, No. 1, 65-91.

Drucker, P. (1999): 'Creating Community', *Executive Excellence* Vol. 16, No. 10, 5.

Elias, A. and Cavana, R. (2001): *Stakeholder Analysis for Systems Thinking and Modelling* [online] [cited 5 April 2002]. Available from Internet URL: http://www.esc.auckland .ac. nz/Organisations/ORSNZ/conf35/papers/BobCanvana.pdf.

Elkington, J. (1999): *Cannibals with Forks: The Triple Bottom Line of 21st Century Business.* New York: New Society Publishers.

Epstein, M. and Birchard, B. (1999): *Counting What Counts: Turning Corporate Accountability to Competitive Advantage.* Massachusetts: Perseus Books.

Etzioni, A. (1998): 'A Communitarian Note on Stakeholder Theory', *Business Ethics Quarterly* Vol. 8, No. 4, 679-691.

Farmer, R. and Hogue, W. (1985): *Corporate Social Responsibility.* Lexington: D.C Health Company Lexington Books.

Freeman, R. (1984): *Strategic Management: A Stakeholder Approach.* Boston: Pitman.

Friedman, M. (1997): 'The Social Responsibility of Business is to Increase its Profits', in: Beauchamp, T. and Bowie, N. (Eds.): *Ethical Theory and Business* (5th edition). New Jersey: Prentice Hall, 56-60.

Giri, A. (2000): 'Audited Accountability and the Imperative of Responsibility: Beyond the Primacy of the Political', in: Strathern, M. (Ed.): *Audit Cultures.* London: Routledge, 173-195.

Gray, R., Owen, D. and Maunders, K. (1987): *Corporate Social Reporting: Accounting and Accountability.* New Jersey: Prentice Hall.

Gray, R., Dey, C., Dave, O., Evans, R. and Zadek, S. (1997): 'Struggling with the Praxis of Social Accounting, Stakeholders, Accountability, Audits and Procedures', *Auditing & Accountability Journal* Vol. 10, No. 3, 325-345.

Greenwood, M. (2001): 'The Importance of Stakeholders According to Business Leaders', *Business and Society Review* Vol. 106, No. 1, 29-49.

Grieder, W. (1997): *One World Ready or Not: The Manic Logic of Global Capitalism.* London: Penguin Books.

Griffin, J. (2000): 'Corporate Social Performance: Research Directions for the 21st Century', *Business and Society* Vol. 39, No. 4, 479-491.

Hill, C. and Jones, T. (1992): 'Stakeholder-Agency Theory', *Journal of Management Studies* Vol.29, 131-154.

Himmelstein, J. (1997): *Looking Good and Doing Good.* Bloomington: Indiana University Press.

Jason, L.A. (1997): *Community Building: Values for a Sustainable Future.* Westport: Praegen Publishing.

Jennings, M. (1999): *Stakeholder Theory: Letting anyone who's Interested Run the Business—No Investment Required* (Unpublished manuscript). Arizona.

Johnson, H. (2001): 'Corporate Social Audits - This Time Around', *Business Horizons* Vol. 44, No. 3, 29-36.

Johnston, P. (2000): *Business and Community Partnerships.* Sydney: Prime Minister's Business Community Partnerships Initiative.

Kaptein, M. (1998): *Ethics Management: Auditing and Developing the Ethical Content of Organisations.* Dordrecht: Kluwer Academic Publishers.

Kegley, C.W. and Wittkopf, E.R. (2001): *World Politics: Trends and Transformations* (8th edition). Boston: Bedford/St Martins.

Khoury, G., Rostami, J. and Turnbull, P. (1999): *Corporate Social Responsibility: Turning Words Into Action.* Ottawa: The Conference Board of Canada.

Klein, N. (2000): *No Logo.* London: Flamingo.

Korten, D. (1995): *When Corporations Rule the World.* London: Earthscan Publications Ltd.

Leipziger, D. (2001): *SA8000: The Definitive Guide to the New Social Standard.* London: Financial Times Prentice Hall.

McIntosh, M., Leipziger, D., Jones, K. and Coleman, G. (1998): *Corporate Citizenship: Successful Strategies for Responsible Companies.* London: Financial Times Management.

McMichael, P. (2000): *Development and Social Change: A Global Perspective.* Los Angeles: Pine Forge Press.

Meyer, H. (1999): 'When the Cause is Just', *The Journal of Business Strategy* Vol. 20, No. 6, 27-31.

Michelman, I. (1994): *The Moral Limitations of Capitalism.* Brookfield: Aldershot.

Mulgan, G. (2000): 'Ethics, Business and Politics in a Connected World', in: Slaughter, R. (Ed.): *Gone Today Here Tomorrow: Millennium Previews.* St Leonards: Prospect Media Proprietary Limited, 209-220.

Nolan, J. and Nolan, D. (1995): 'The Path to Social Responsibility', in: Stakehouse, M., McCann, D., Roels, S. and Williams, P. (Eds.): *On Moral Business: Classic and Contemporary Resources for Ethics in Economic Life.* Michigan: Williams B. Eerdmans Publishing Company.

Nozick, R. (1996): 'The Entitlement Theory', in: Donaldson, T. and Werhane, P. (Eds.): *Ethical Issues in Business: A Philosophical Approach* (5th edition). New Jersey: Prentice Hall, 262-267.

Power, M. (1997): *The Audit Society: Rituals of Verification.* Oxford: Oxford University Press.

Quarter, J. (2000): *Beyond the Bottom Line: Socially Innovative Business Owners.* Westport: Quorum Books.

Rawls, J. (1996): 'Distributive Justice', in: Donaldson, T. and Werhane, P. (Eds.): *Ethical Issues in Business: A Philosophical Approach* (5th edition). New Jersey: Prentice Hall, 252-261.

Schwartz, P. (1996): *The Art of the Long View.* St Leonards: Australian Business Network.

Schwartz, P. and Gibb, B. (1999): *When Good Companies Do Bad Things: Responsibility and Risk in an Age of Globalisation.* New York: Wiley.

Shore, C. and Wright, S. (2000): 'Coercive Accountability', in: Strathern, M. (Ed.): *Audit Cultures.* London: Routledge, 57-89.

Spencer, E., Mills, A., Routy, M., and Werhane, P. (2000): *Organisational Ethics in Health Care.* Oxford: Oxford University Press.

Svendsen, A. (1998): *The Stakeholder Strategy.* San Francisco: Berrett-Kohler Publishers Incorporated.

Tam, H. (1998): *Communitarianism: A New Agenda for Politics and Citizenship.* London: MacMillan Press.

Third World Network (2001): *The Third World Network* [online] [cited 12 December 2001]. Available from Internet URL: http://www.twnside.org.sg/title/sub12-cn.htm.

Thurow, L. (1966): *The Future of Capitalism: How Today's Economic Forces Shape Tomorrows World.* St Leonards, New South Wales: Allen & Unwin.

Toffler, A. (1990): *Powershift.* New York: Bantam Books.

Weiss, A. (1999): *Cracks in the Foundation of Stakeholder Theory* (Unpublished manuscript).

Wheeler, D. and Sillanpää, M. (1997): *The Stakeholder Corporation: A Blueprint for Maximising Stakeholder Value.* London: Pitman Publishing.

Wulfson, M. (2001): 'The Ethics of Corporate Social Responsibility and Philanthropic Ventures', *Journal of Business Ethics* Vol. 29, 135-145.

Zadek, S. (1994): 'Trading Ethics: Auditing the Market', *Journal of Economic Issues* Vol. 28, No. 2, 631-639.

Zadek, S. (1998): 'Balancing Performance, Ethics and Accountability', *Journal of Business Ethics* Vol. 17, No. 13, 1421-1441.

SOCIAL PERFORMANCE AND COMPETITIVENESS
A Socio-Competitive Framework

Kuno Spirig
Zurich University of Applied Sciences, Winterthur, Switzerland

Abstract: This chapter discusses the relationship between social performance and competitiveness. A socio-competitive model and corresponding analysis show how social performance can influence competitiveness. The analysis differentiates between important stakeholder groups and shows the central role of communication in achieving a competitive advantage through social performance.

1.   CALL FOR ACTION TO INTEGRATE THE SOCIAL DIMENSION IN STRATEGIC DECISIONS

Until now, the social dimension has rarely been considered in strategy development. For the social dimension, as well as for the environmental dimension (Dyllick and Hummel 1996; Hamschmidt and Dyllick 2002), management practices lack strategic management systems to plan, control and advance social performance in order to improve competitiveness. The most important reasons for this are considered to be:

- There is not enough theoretical and empirical knowledge concerning the relationships between social and financial performance and the underlying mechanisms (Wagner and Schaltegger 2003; Schaltegger and Wagner 2006). Therefore, it is essential that future research focuses much more on the areas of social performance and competitiveness.

- There is not only a knowledge gap concerning the question of how social performance influences competitiveness, there is also a methodical gap between the conceptual design of a socially oriented strategic framework with corresponding theoretical explanations and qualitative considerations. The framework should be easily comprehensible and compatible with commercially acceptable costs in general management. A framework for the sustainability balance scorecard (Schaltegger and Dyllick 2002) has been developed and represents a move in the right direction.
- In addition, fact-based knowledge relative to the economic considerations and motivations of managers concerning social performance is lacking. In a market economy, companies compete against each other. Therefore, the management's goal must always be to maintain and improve competitiveness. Only when it has been revealed systematically and traceably how social performance can create competitive advantages will managers start to think how they can integrate the social dimension within their overall company strategy. Because of this lack of systematic and convincing arguments by managers, social actions within companies rather uncoordinated. These so-called social patchwork actions (cf. Table 1) are isolated case studies and critical issue management, forced by external stakeholders such as trade unions or media rather than integrated systematic social management with a competitive orientation. Not only do universal, social and ethical values constitute a rationale to be taken into account for the development of the social dimension of a company, the rationale of keeping and improving competitiveness also has to be considered.
- Unfortunately, most managers do not have enough convincing economic reasons based on sound theory and tools to integrate the social dimension into the overall company strategy. As managers are paid to secure and improve competitiveness, they need to see how social management can increase the competitive advantage of their company. Otherwise, they will not integrate the social dimension into their strategies voluntarily. In comparison with the social dimension, the ecological dimension has already been much better integrated; however, mostly on the operative level (Hamschmidt and Dyllick 2002).

In summary, a number of measures will have to be taken to promote integration of the social dimension into general management:
- Research to develop a theoretical framework and profound empirical knowledge concerning the correlation between social and economic performance
- Development of cost-efficient methods to integrate the social dimension into the general management system using case studies

- Gathering the knowledge and requirements of managers in order to develop market-oriented tools and solutions

Figure 1 illustrates the call for action.

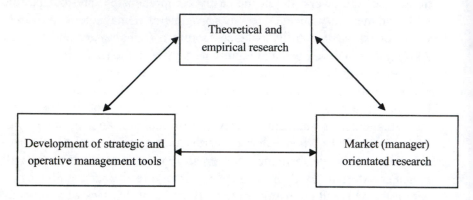

Figure 1. Call for action concerning the socio-competitive dimension

2.   COMPETITIVENESS IS THE LONG-TERM ECONOMIC GOAL OF SOCIAL MANAGEMENT

The question is fundamental: what should the decision criteria be between social and economic performance if there is a conflict of interest? To give an example, should pharmaceutical companies reduce their prices for health-care products so that more people can afford them or should they maximise their profits? The ethical question of how companies should treat social values that reduce competitiveness is the subject of another discussion. This section deals specifically with the reasons for, and the goals of, social management from an economic point of view. We do not pretend that the economic view is the only consideration to be taken into account when determining how to approach the social dimension. However, using a biblical reference as a metaphor, 'The spirit is willing but the flesh is weak,' we can perhaps say that, because market forces dominate, the ethically motivated will for social performance is strong but then weakens. Therefore, we might dare to say that, in the majority of cases, social performance is relevant only if it pays. To promote the deployment and management of corporate social performance inside the economic system, it is highly relevant to identify the intersections of the economic and social dimensions. If the basic interrelations can be revealed, it may be possible to make a good case for management that causes it to no longer view social performance as negligible but rather as a factor of competitiveness. This means a new paradigm: companies begin to see the social dimension as an investment domain in its own right, with its own investment appraisal and its own annual budget. Indeed, social performance measures such as investment in employee measures often act only in the medium term. This should not be a problem because short-term market capitalisation is not relevant to securing and improving the overall competitiveness of a company—given that the psychology-influenced stock market does not always reflect a company's real value.

Box 1. Key definitions of a socio-competitive framework

Most definitions of a socio-competitive framework are currently underdeveloped and difficult to measure (Wagner and Schaltegger 2003). Therefore, this section uses the following definitions:

- **Competitiveness**. A commonly accepted definition is lacking. It would lose explanatory content if reduced to one single factor (e.g. economic performance as returns). We therefore define competitiveness by its result and factors:

  a) *Result of competitiveness* is higher than average customer value that leads to higher profits in the long-term. Only if customers perceive products and services as better than their competitors will a company have long-term higher returns. Results of competitiveness are difficult to measure, i.e. common financial indicators of the accounting system (e.g. profitability ratios as return on sales, return on equity, etc.) are lacking and refer to the past, whereas competitiveness refers to the future.

  b) *Factors of competitiveness*. Porter (1985) sees five forces of competition: supplier power; threat of substitutes; buyer power; barriers to entry; and degree of rivalry. He advises three generic strategies (cost leadership, differentiation and focus) for creating a competitive advantage. Malik (2005) mentions six success factors of competitiveness: market position; innovation; productivity; reputation as good employer; liquidity; and profits. This chapter defines 11 key factors of competitiveness: communication; customer-value; differentiation; employer attractiveness; innovation; market position; productivity; profit needed; reputation; supply chain management; and willingness to pay.

- **Competitive strategies**—long-term plans and actions to secure and improve competitiveness. Such plans are designed to create products and services that customers perceive as more attractive than those of competitors.

- **Social performance**. The Global Reporting Initiative (GRI 2002) sees social performance as part of sustainability performance, which also includes economic and environmental performance. GRI does not define social performance but divides it into five categories: labour practices; decent working conditions); human rights; society; and product responsibility. Freeman's stakeholder theory sees corporations as being responsible to shareholders and other interest groups (Freeman 1984). This chapter defines social performance as the social impact on stakeholders.

- **Social impacts**—outcome of a company's social actions and behaviour.
- **Social perception**. Only the perceived social performance is relevant for competitiveness.
- **Social strategy**—the intentional or unintentional long-term behaviour of a company that affects its social dimension. Social performance is a result of strategy. If a given strategy is not apparent, an analysis of social performance can detect it. In a research project at the Zürich University of Applied Sciences, the author of this chapter is developing frameworks and tools to detect, describe and develop social strategies as part of the overall management system.
- **Social management**—an intentional process to design, control and develop the social dimension (Rüegg-Stürm 2002).
- **Socio-competitive framework**—a theoretical framework, which points out the relationship between corporate social performance and competitiveness.
- **Stakeholders**. This chapter takes into account the stakeholders who, in all probability, have the greatest impact on competitiveness, i.e. customers, employees, the media, suppliers, shareholder, public authorities (state), and non-governmental organisations (NGOs).
- **Sustainability**—based on economic, social and environmental dimensions. It intends to safeguard the balance between all three areas in the long term.

3.   INTERRELATIONS BETWEEN THE TERMS OF A SOCIO-COMPETITIVE FRAMEWORK

3.1   Terms and General Interrelations

Social management has to be based on a common language with applicable and understandable definitions. Only a common terminology enables management to sum up and structure the socio-competitive reality of a company. Common language is a pre-condition for constructive communication relative to the social dimension; thus, the key definitions set out in Box 1. Table 1 shows the relationship and hierarchy of these definitions. At the top of the table is social strategies (A), which reflect the long-term social behaviour of a company. The strategies can be intentional (B1) or unintentional (B2). The strategies can be put into effect by social management (C1), by unstructured measures (patchwork) (C2) or by doing nothing (desert, wilful neglect) (C3).

The handling of the social dimension leads automatically to social performance (D, E1, E2), which in turn creates impacts (F). Even a company with no formal management programme has social performance and social impacts. Thus, analogous to the argument of the constructivist and communications scientist Watzlawick and colleagues (1967), who said it is impossible not to communicate, a company always has a social impact through its social performance. The impacts can be intentional (G1) or unintentional (G2). Social performance influences competitiveness (H)—either through an intentional (J1) or an unintentional (J2) impact. Even if a company is unaware of its social performance, this nevertheless influences its competitiveness. The impact depends on the perception of the stakeholders (K1, K3), as well as the social performance as perceived by the company, its management and its employees (K2, K4). Social performance as an objective fact does not exist in the same way that there are countless definitions for the terms 'social' and 'societal'. From an economic point of view, the perception of the stakeholder is at the centre of socio-competitive management. Therefore, this section shows how social performance—in the perception of different stakeholders—affects diverse key factors of competitiveness.

Table 1. Key definitions of a socio-competitive framework

A	Social strategies (A) (long-term social actions/behaviour)		
B	Intentional social strategies (B1)	Unintentional social strategies (B2)	
C	Social management (C1) (intentional process to design, control and develop the social dimension)	Social patchwork (C2) (little intentional process)	Social desert (C3) (no intentional process)
D	Social performance (D)		
E	Intentional social performance (E1) (result of long-term social actions/behaviour)	Unintentional social performance (E2) (result of long-term social actions/behaviour)	
F	Impacts of social performance on stakeholders (F)		
G	Intentional impacts (G1)	Unintentional impacts (G2)	
H	Impact of social performance to competitiveness (H)		
J	Intentional impact to competitiveness (J1)	Unintentional impact to competitiveness (J2)	
K	Social performance perceived by stakeholder (K1)	Social performance perceived by company (K2)	Social performance perceived by stakeholder (K3)	Social performance perceived by company (K4)

3.2   Requirements of a Socio-Competitive Framework

Social management has to create higher competitiveness through higher than average customer value. This will protect and improve the company's long-term financial performance, as explained in Figure 2. The key question of this section is how a company can influence its competitiveness through social performance. The focus is on theoretical considerations; future research should test its empirical relevance. Valuable models and theories must include sufficient variety to explain the reality (Ashby 1964). The competitive reality is very complex, and the integration of social aspects further increases the complexity of management. This additional complexity constitutes an important counter-argument to the notion of integrating the social dimension into management if it does not improve competitiveness sufficiently. A socio-competitive framework must therefore be:

a) Complex enough so that it can structure and explain reality as a basis for the development of specific socio-competitive strategies
b) Simple enough for a manager to be able to work with
c) Able to show an economic rationale to integrate the social dimension, even if it increases the manager's workload

The additional complexity may also stimulate innovation. A dialogue with stakeholders may stimulate new ideas and may also serve to generate greater flexibility within management.

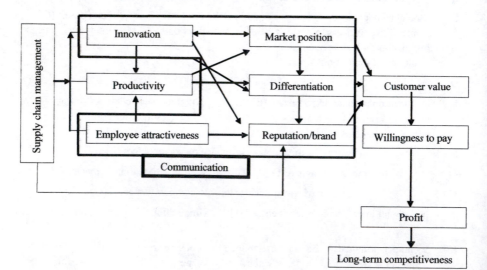

Figure 2. Interaction of the key factors of competitiveness

3.3   Key Factors of Competitiveness and their Interaction

We operationalise competitiveness through 11 key factors (Box 1). If a company performs better than its competitors where these factors are concerned, it should also be more competitive. Arranged in alphabetical order, these factors are:

1. **Communication** poses the question: how are the values and overall performances/differentiation concerning the social dimension communicated to customers and stakeholders?

2. **Customer value** poses the question: how attractive is price, quality, service, image, reputation of products and services?

3. **Differentiation** poses the question: what distinguishes the company and its products from its competitors in the perception of different stakeholder groups (brand/reputation)?

4. **Employee attractiveness** poses the question: how attractive is the company to a competitive workforce regarding corporate culture, salary, social contributions, security of employment, work-life balance, etc?

5. **Innovation** poses the questions: what is the time-frame for any product to reach the market; what is the share of innovative products; what is the share of innovative processes of the company; what is the hit versus miss rate; what is the ratio of new products to sales; what are the new systems and processes, new methods and practices, new structures and technologies?

6. **Market position** poses the question: how good is the market share, the market share of substituting products, the quality of the products, the image of the products and the company?

7. **Productivity** poses the question: how good is a company's overall productivity, capital and knowledge?

8. **Profit** poses the question: how much profit (return on investment, earnings before interest and tax [EBIT]) does the company need to stay in business in the long-term?

9. **Reputation** poses the question: what is the reputation of the company and its products?

10. **Supply chain management** poses the question: how does the integration and management of suppliers operate?

11. **Willingness to pay** poses the questions: how good is the customer's willingness to pay. What are the customer's decision-making factors and underlying motives apart from low price?

Figure 2 shows the assumed interactions of these factors. The suggestions are based on qualitative considerations and are all positive. They are illustrated elsewhere; comments on the most important interactions follow:

- Figure 2 shows that, in the end, all factors of competitiveness influence customer value, i.e. customer satisfaction, customer return rates.
- If customer value is perceived to be higher than that of competitors, the customer will purchase. This results in profit, which is understood as the long-term capacity of a company to preserve and improve competitiveness. Communication (marketing) plays a central role in the perception of customer value.
- An above-average innovation rate influences market position, differentiation and reputation/brand. Employer attractiveness promotes productivity and innovation.
- Communication plays a central role for many factors of competitiveness: employer attractiveness; reputation/brand; innovation; market-position; and differentiation. In order to simplify Figure 2, the factors in question are connected by a frame rather than by arrows. Communication of social performance must be credible and understandable to the internal and external stakeholders—but especially to the customer. Brand and credibility are part of the performance for which the customer is willing to pay. It is a challenge and a task at the same time to integrate social performance in the overall performance of products and services in a bid to improve competitiveness.

3.4   Social Performance has Become More Important as a Competitive Factor

The key question of a socio-competitive framework is: does social performance lead to competitive advantage, parity or disadvantage? The answer depends on the current and future competition situation of a company. It is impossible to fix a business case in advance and with a guarantee. Therefore, one should work with probabilities, estimations and scenarios to evaluate the impact of social performance.

However, it does seem that social performance has become increasingly important for competition; in most cases, not as a core performance attribute of a product or service, but as a pre-condition for market success. Some fair-trade products are the exception, i.e. fair-trade bananas or products from social institutions; in such cases, social performance is the key selling proposition in competition with ordinary products.

In the area of liberalisation, stakeholders expect more and more social performance from companies. As a consequence, moral values are becoming increasingly important to competition and investments in social performance become necessary to secure and improve competitiveness. The socio-competitive framework of this section provides the basis for analysis and the development of socio-competitive strategy.

4. IMPORTANCE OF STAKEHOLDER PERCEPTION AND COMPANY REPUTATION FOR COMPETITIVENESS

Reputation strongly influences purchasing decisions and willingness to pay. Therefore, the way in which different stakeholders perceive the company is crucial for achieving competitiveness.

Branding is an important instrument with which to influence stakeholder perception. Branding differs between competitors and increases willingness to pay. Social performance is beginning to play an increasingly important role as part of the brand image of a company. Violation of social performance expectations (i.e. laws) may not lead only to imprisonment, fines and other penalties, but also to a temporary loss of credibility since stakeholders such as NGOs can influence the reputation and the brand of a company (e.g. the Shell or Nike examples). Reputation and brand are important customer values especially when products are materially identical, i.e. T-shirts or coffee. If the quality is identical, the product with the better brand and reputation elicits higher customer value and an increased willingness to pay. So, a T-shirt with a higher social performance can—if the higher social performance is apparent to the customer—gain a competitive advantage and higher profits through better sales.

4.1 Social Performance must be Communicated to Create Competitive Advantage

It is essential to build up brand and reputation in the customers' perception. Companies ought to communicate social performance to customers and other stakeholders both intensively and in the long-term; otherwise, social performance may be forgotten. Communication is an important way of improving reputation/brand in order to create a competitive advantage. The media is therefore a powerful instrument as an independent, critical reporter and intermediary. For economic reasons, companies are often suspected of being less than truthful about their social performance. NGOs, on the other hand, tend to enjoy huge public confidence. NGOs with their independent assessment of social performance thus play an important role in integrating social performance into the reputation and brand of a company. Companies should try to enter into an active dialogue or collaborate with NGOs, as this can result in a positive image transfer of NGO credibility to the reputation and brand of the company.

4.2   Social Performance must be Stakeholder Oriented

The internal preferences of a company may influence social performance and its communication. However, social performance must also provide an answer to the expectations of the stakeholders. Stakeholders must appreciate the social performance of a company. Only then will social performance improve competitiveness. Communicating involves building up a demand-oriented relationship with the customer. The social issues of greatest concern to customers are: human rights; mass redundancies; wages; wage spread; discrimination; support for families; safety; and pricing. Furthermore, social performance deficiencies should be communicated in an appropriate manner as this promotes credibility and helps to disprove allegations of 'social' manipulation.

5.   HOW SOCIAL PERFORMANCE INFLUENCES THE KEY FACTORS OF COMPETITIVENESS

The following considerations are not definite predictions but working hypotheses. The relationships between social performance and competitiveness are described at a very general level. Discussion of specific influences such as stakeholder expectations, company size, market development, economic sector, country location, regulation and macro-culture is outside the scope of this chapter.

Stakeholders have different expectations. If specific stakeholder expectations are fulfilled better and/or differently by one company in relation to another, then this also influences competitiveness. For each stakeholder, Tables 3–9 show possible links between social and competitive dimensions and their directions. Table 3 outlines the possible social performance measures that could influence competitiveness. The columns indicate the key factors of competitiveness. Each symbol explains the relation between social performance and factors of competitiveness. The factor 'productivity'—defined as the ratio between input and output—is subdivided into output and input (costs of social performance, i.e. wages, risk exposition, etc.). Symbols in the intercepts between rows and columns describe the possible relationship between perceived social performance measure and a specific competitiveness factor. Table 2 explains the symbols representing the socio-competitive links.

Table 2. Symbols indicating the relationship between social performance and competitiveness

Symbol	Explanation
+	presumed positive impact on a specific factor of competitiveness
–	presumed negative impact on a specific factor of competitiveness
n	presumed no impact on a specific factor of competitiveness
–/+	presumed negative or positive impact on a specific factor of competitiveness
n/+	presumed neutral or positive impact on a specific factor of competitiveness
–/n	presumed negative or neutral impact on a specific factor of competitiveness

Table 3 shows the socio-competitive links between customer-orientated social performance and its impacts on the key factors of competitiveness.

Table 3. Influence of customer-oriented social performance on competitiveness

	Supply chain management	Innovation	Productivity (output)	Productivity (input)	Differentiation	Reputation	Employer attractiveness	Market position	Communication	Customer value	Willingness to pay	Profit
Measures												
Gathering and consideration of customer-oriented social values and expectation	+	+	–/+	n	n	n	n/+	n	n	n	n	+
Credible and recipient oriented information about social strategies and measures	n	n	n	n	+	+	+	+	+	+	+	+
Credible measures	–/n	+	–/+	–	+	+	n/+	+	+	+	+	–/+

6. CUSTOMER EXPECTATIONS

Customer values and perceptions are central to competitiveness. Purchasing decisions decide the economic destiny of a company—to secure and improve competitiveness means to influence and to fulfil its customer expectations better than its competitors. The perceived customer value (including brand image) is central to this.

This section cannot separate the specific social expectations of different customer groups. Each company must do this for itself. To be relevant, social performance must create higher than average customer value, i.e. lower or higher prices, better product features, better customer services or better ethical value (reputation, brand, good conscience).

6.1   Customer Communication

Each product and service has social impacts during its life-cycle. For most customers, however, social performance is an invisible element and thus an irrelevant aspect of products and services. To make it relevant for customers, and therefore for competitiveness, a company must make its social performance visible. Companies must convince customers that social performance improves their customer value and should, therefore, be considered when making purchasing decisions. Finally, the company has to be perceived by customers as having products and services of a higher than average social performance value.

To make social performance relevant to purchasing decisions, companies must communicate actively to gain competitive advantage. Possible instruments for achieving this include: building up brand names such as Max Havelaar or gaining a corporate image as a socially responsible company such as The Body Shop. Further measures include: public relations (media); advertising; product information; point-of-sale-information; events; customer dialogue (face-to-face or internet); and competitions. Externally controlled social labels and the integration of independent NGOs in communication measures are helpful for making communication credible.

6.2   The Influence of Employee-Oriented Social Performance on Competitiveness

Table 4 shows the socio-competitive links between employee-oriented social performance and its impact on the key factors of competitiveness.

Table 4. Influence of employee-oriented social performance on competitiveness

	Supply chain management	Innovation	Productivity (output)	Productivity (input)	Differentiation	Reputation	Employer attractiveness	Market position	Communication	Customer value	Willingness to pay	Profit
Possible measures Company is better than average competitor in terms of social contribution, security of employment, training and education, diversity and opportunity, professional training, health and security, diversity, human rights, non-discrimination, freedom of association and expression, collective bargaining, child labour, disciplinary practices, indigenous rights, forced and compulsory labour	n/+	+	+	–	+	n/+	+	n/+	n/+	n/+	n/+	–/+
Result Employee recruitment: better quality of human resources (improved attractiveness for highly skilled professionals)	+	+	+	+	+	n/+	+	n/+	n/+	n/+	n/+	+
Result Less employee turnover (improved retention, less brain drain and knowledge-loss, greater loyalty)	+	+	+	+	+	n/+	+	+	n/+	n/+	n/+	+
Result Fewer costs due to accidents and diseases (i.e. improved insurance conditions)	+	+	+	+	+	n/+	n	+	n/+	+	n/+	+
Result Improved corporate culture (more integrity)	+	+	+	+	+	n/+	+	+	+	I	n/+	+
Result Higher co-operation (improved knowledge sharing)	+	+	+	+	+	n/+	+	+	n/+	+	n/+	+
Result Cost savings through higher flexibility of employees and more goodwill, i.e. flexible working hours	+	+	+	+	+	n/+	+	+	+	+	n/+	+
Result Internal and external reputation as a good employer	+			+	+	n/+	+	+	n/+	+	+	+

Table 4 shows that employee-oriented social performance may, in many cases, support competitiveness. The impact on the key competitive factors—reputation, communication and customer value—depends on the specific social performance communication strategy employed by a company. There are three important arguments why employee-oriented social performance is vital for competitiveness:

1. **The impact on knowledge-management**: economy is more and more knowledge-based. A particularly strong rate of growth is evident in the service industries sector (Pfarr and Linne 2001). Knowledge is doubtless the most important production factor in the industrialised nations, being central to stimulate innovation. Employees carry and advance knowledge; they always remain the owner of their knowledge and they have the competence to generate it and apply it to teamwork. Companies depend on employee motivation to both produce and share knowledge. Therefore, employees have to be motivated in order for them to co-operate and share their knowledge, which in turn obliges companies to design extrinsic incentives. Employee-oriented social performance appears a powerful instrument for stimulating knowledge-production and diffusion. Therefore, employee-oriented social performance is always knowledge management and, as such, influences competitiveness.

2. **The impact on quality of service**. Services are intangible. A customer cannot display and inspect them before purchasing. Therefore, the reputations of the different competitors govern purchasing decisions strongly. Above average quality of service confirms reputation, while below average performance destroys it. It is essential to motivate employees to produce a competitive quality of service, which is perceived as excellent by the customer and better than those of competitors. However, unless the service is below the threshold of formalised quality criteria, a company cannot measure its quality and customers may therefore be systematically disappointed by the attitude of company employees. To address this situation, it is vital that employee-oriented social performance is an important component of service-management, reputation management and, as a consequence, competitiveness.

3. **The impact on corporate culture**. Corporate culture influences the behaviour of employees as an informal governance mechanism. Corporate culture does not specify in detail the actions of employees. Instead it provides a general framework of duties and rights. Employee-oriented social performance can support the creation of corporate culture with high ethical and communication values focused on customer needs. This may promote loyalty and integrity towards a company and customers alike and also go a long way towards reducing the risks of bribery, bullying and other negative elements. A positive corporate culture de-

creases the costs of monitoring and increases customer-oriented quality of service, know-how building and innovation.

6.3 Impact of State-Oriented Social Performance on Competitiveness

Table 5 shows the socio-competitive links between state-oriented social performance and its impact on the key factors of competitiveness.

Table 5. Influence of state-oriented social performance on competitiveness

	Supply chain management	Innovation	Productivity (output)	Productivity (input)	Differentiation	Reputation	Employer attractively	Market–position	Communication	Costumer value	Willingness to pay	Profit
Possible measures:												
A) Illegal social performance: violation of socially oriented laws, regulations, additional requirements (i.e. employment law, minimum pay legislation, occupational health and safety regulations, tax regulations)	–/+	–	–/+	+	n	–	–	–/+	n	–	–	–/+
B) Fulfilment of state-oriented social performance: compliance to socially oriented laws, regulations, additional requirements (i.e. employment law, minimum pay legislation, occupational health and safety regulations, tax regulations)	–/n or n/+	–	n	–	+	+	+	n	n/+	n/+	n	–/n+
B) Social performance higher than state demands: i.e. social benefits wages, occupational health and safety measures, taxes)	–/n	n/+	n/+	–	n/+	+	+	n/+	n/+	n/+	+	n/+

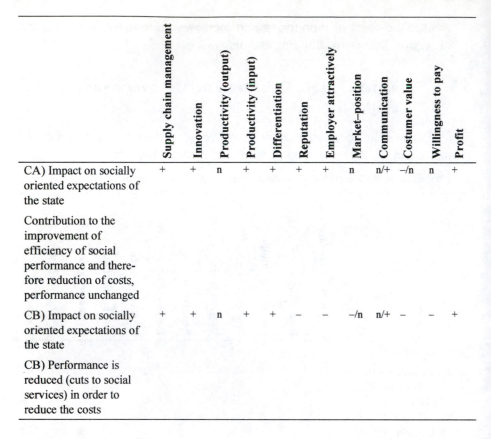

	Supply chain management	Innovation	Productivity (output)	Productivity (input)	Differentiation	Reputation	Employer attractively	Market–position	Communication	Costumer value	Willingness to pay	Profit
CA) Impact on socially oriented expectations of the state	+	+	n	+	+	+	+	n	n/+	–/n	n	+
Contribution to the improvement of efficiency of social performance and therefore reduction of costs, performance unchanged												
CB) Impact on socially oriented expectations of the state	+	+	n	+	+	–	–	–/n	n/+	–	–	+
CB) Performance is reduced (cuts to social services) in order to reduce the costs												

State-oriented social performance expectations are transmitted by different representatives of the state: authorities; ministries; representatives of the people in Parliament; administrations; professional associations; police and courts. Does the realisation of their expectations influences competitiveness? And, if it does, how? The following considers different ways of producing state-oriented, social performance and its impact on competitiveness:

- **Violation**. Most expectations of the state refer to employees (cf. Table 4). Today, national regulators and supranational organisations such as the International Labour Office (ILO) are more vigilant and demanding with regard to social performance. The violation of regulations may lead to sanctions and the loss of company credibility, reputation and legitimacy, especially when a fraud is publicised in the media or interest groups organise product boycotts and public protests. It is, therefore, an increasingly difficult and costly strategy for companies to improve their competitiveness by lowering production costs through unlawful measures. A violation strategy could be successful in markets where high rivalry and price are the only competition factors, e.g. in commodities.

- **Complying**. This means compliance with social performance regulations. Can a competitive advantage be gained when almost every company is compliant? It may be possible by offensive communication measures designed to convince customers that the social performance of a specific company is better than that of its competitors—even if, in reality, there is no difference. In this case, communication is the key to competitive advantage, not social performance. Companies should also know if their customers expect them to be responsible for the legal compliance of their suppliers as is the case in Southern countries.

- **Cost reduction by reducing inefficiencies**. A legal way of reducing costs is by eliminating administrative inefficiencies caused by the state without reducing social performance. This can improve the competitiveness of a specific company. It is also possible for an entire national economic sector to reduce administrative inefficiencies and create a comparative advantage on the global market.

- **Reduction of expectations**. A large, globally active company or a whole economic sector such as the machine construction industry could lobby to reduce the state's social demands and, thus, also its costs. This would improve competitiveness in the global market. Reduction of the state-oriented social performance level is always a difficult and controversial issue. If social performance/reputation is an important purchasing argument, negative media coverage can have a strong negative influence on a single company or, indeed, on a whole economic sector.

- **Improvement of expectations**. Here a company makes a commitment to new state regulations such as those concerning bribery and corruption, political contributions of companies, competition regulations, social justice and social security. Stronger regulations can improve the competitive position of a company wanting to avoid corruption costs or no longer wanting higher costs than those of its competitors with a lower social performance. Companies that make an honest commitment to increasing social justice and security can hope to improve their reputation and receive positive media coverage.

6.4   Impact of Media-Oriented Social Performance on the Key Factors of Competitiveness

Table 6 shows the socio-competitive links between media-oriented social performance and its impact on the key factors of competitiveness.

Table 6. Influence of media-oriented, social performance on competitiveness

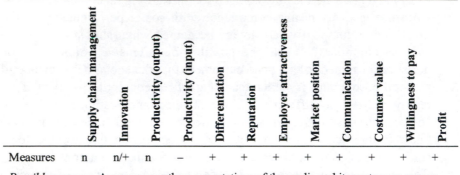

	Supply chain management	Innovation	Productivity (output)	Productivity (input)	Differentiation	Reputation	Employer attractiveness	Market position	Communication	Costumer value	Willingness to pay	Profit
Measures	n	n/+	n	–	+	+	+	+	+	+	+	+

Possible measure. A company gathers expectations of the media and its customers concerning social performance. It provides media actively with credible and recipient-oriented information about social strategies and measures.

- **Relevance of media.** For customers, media reports are cues for brand, for company reputation and for the quality of products and services. Every day, the media communicate the most important social values and ethical expectations of the macro-culture in which a company sits. The media has a strong influence on customer perception of a company's social performance. The media can support or destroy reputation and are therefore an influence on, and a driving force behind, competitiveness.
- **Interest of media.** The media are like all economic entities in a competitive environment, with the main areas of competition being news value, interesting personalities, sensations and conflicts. The social performance expectations placed on companies depend on the political position of the media. Media tend to prefer critical reports because they sell better. A better social performance than its competitor can help a company to reduce the risk of negative reports.
- **Media-oriented social performance communication.** The media are very important in setting the agenda of critical societal issues. Thus in order to keep and improve their competitiveness, companies should try to achieve better media reports than their competitors. Some measures for this goal are:
  - *Reduce the probability of negative reports.* Identify critical social performance issues as perceived by the company and the stakeholder (to include wages, human rights, job security, etc.). Prepare answers. Prepare reliable, consistent, professional, social reporting compliant with established standards. Prepare a professional report about problems. Establish a constructive dialogue with stakeholders.
  - *Improve the probability of positive reports.* Build up professional public relations activities on social performance. Organise regular contacts with the media. Offer success stories involving interesting

personalities. Accept and discuss apparent problems openly and sincerely (balanced coverage of issues). Communicate more intensely and better with the media.

6.5 Impact of Supplier-Oriented Social Performance on the Key Factors of Competitiveness

Table 7 shows the socio-competitive links between supplier-oriented social performance and its impact on the key factors of competitiveness.

Table 7. Impact of supplier-oriented social performance on the key factors of competitiveness

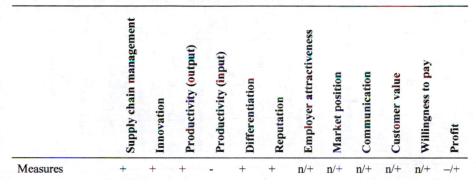

	Supply chain management	Innovation	Productivity (output)	Productivity (input)	Differentiation	Reputation	Employer attractiveness	Market position	Communication	Customer value	Willingness to pay	Profit
Measures	+	+	+	-	+	+	n/+	n/+	n/+	n/+	n/+	–/+

Possible measures. A company provides for its suppliers to have a better than average social performance regarding: social contribution; security in employment; training and education; diversity and opportunity; health and security; diversity; human rights; non-discrimination; freedom of association and collective bargaining; use of child labour; disciplinary practices; security practices; indigenous rights; forced and compulsory labour; living wages; wages spread; and external control of standards.

The impact of supplier-oriented social performance is probably the same as with the employee-oriented social performance. Social expectations for suppliers probably originate from three sides of a company buying products and services from a supplier:
- From the suppliers themselves
- From the employees of the supplier and the trade unions
- From NGOs, the media and customers (who may be based outside the supplier countries)

Particularly sensitive social issues are wages (much lower than in the customers' countries), child labour, the black market economy and lack of social assurances. The reputation of a company depends on the realisation of the social values of its customers and not those of the suppliers' countries. Most customers, media and NGOs believe companies to be responsible for the social situation of their supplier companies. In many cases, it is not only the employees' social situation that is affected, but also that of their family and community (e.g. those supplying cotton).

6.6 Impact of NGO-Oriented Social Performance on the Key Factors of Competitiveness

Table 8 shows the socio-competitive links between NGO-oriented social performance and its impact on the key factors of competitiveness.

Table 8. Impact of non-governmental organisation-oriented social performance on the key factors of competitiveness

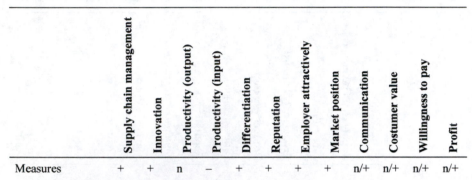

	Supply chain management	Innovation	Productivity (output)	Productivity (input)	Differentiation	Reputation	Employer attractively	Market position	Communication	Costumer value	Willingness to pay	Profit
Measures	+	+	n	–	+	+	+	+	n/+	n/+	n/+	n/+

Possible measure. A company gathers values and expectations of NGOs concerning social performance. It actively provides credible and recipient-oriented information about social strategies and measures.

- **NGOs influence competitiveness**. NGOs increasingly observe and criticise the social performance of companies. NGOs do not shy away from making public their values and expectations regarding social performance. As important representatives of public opinion with a broad presence in the media, NGOs influence both the brand and reputation of a company (e.g. media campaigns, purchasing boycotts, strikes and protests). In the area of social issues, the most important NGOs are trade unions, works councils, development organisations and consumer organisations. To gain a competitive advantage, a company has to introduce measures to convince NGOs that its social performance conforms to their values better than the social performance of its competitors.
- **Dialogue supports competitiveness.** First, constructive dialogue can create mutual understanding, collaboration and innovation with many positive effects:
  (a) It detects emerging conflicts early in the day
  (b) It stimulates innovation to resolve existing or future conflicts such as job security versus production flexibility

(c) The dialogue improves efficiency (costs) and the level of social performance as perceived by the NGOs

Secondly, the dialogue brings trust and thus improves reputation and brand. In the end, all these elements will improve competitiveness, if the dialogue and its results are better than those of the competition.

- **Success factors for a competitive oriented interaction with NGOs**. A successful dialogue needs professional preparation. Identify critical issues (e.g. wages, human rights and job security) in the perception of the NGOs. Prepare answers to difficult questions. Prepare reliable and consistent social disclosure such as using established standards. Know the NGO critics in detail. Prepare enough resources for a good dialogue in terms of time and personnel.

6.7 Impact of Shareholder-Oriented Social Performance on the Key Factors of Competitiveness

Table 9 shows the socio-competitive links between customer-oriented social performance and its impact on the key factors of competitiveness.

Table 9. Influence of shareholder-oriented social performance on competitiveness

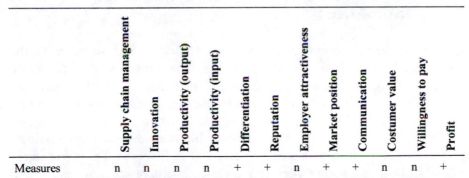

	Supply chain management	Innovation	Productivity (output)	Productivity (input)	Differentiation	Reputation	Employer attractiveness	Market position	Communication	Costumer value	Willingness to pay	Profit
Measures	n	n	n	n	+	+	n	+	+	n	n	+

Possible measure. A company gathers values and expectations of shareholders concerning social performance. It actively provides shareholders with credible and recipient-oriented information about social strategies and measures.

- **Social performance is relevant to investment decisions**. Companies compete for capital providers in three dimensions, i.e. liquidity, security and profit. More and more investors see a positive link between social performance and intangible value drivers such as human capital, brand image and reputation. Social performance becomes part of their decision-making. Managers of socially oriented funds and socially oriented indices are particularly interested in social performance information. Subsequently, a better than average social performance and a professional level of communication, adapted to investor needs, can lead to a competitive advantage.

- **Social performance can lower the cost of capital and insurance**. Higher social performance creates a competitive advantage if investors perceive the social performance of a specific company as higher than that of its competitors. As a rule, a company must also prove that its higher social performance improves its shareholder value compared with that of its competitors. This creates a higher than average investor value such that investors will prefer investments in this company. The costs of its own and foreign capital will consequently fall. Banks and insurance companies grant cheaper loans and better insurance conditions if a company can show that its higher than average social performance reduces credit and liability risks.

- **Communication measures**. Companies have to integrate social performance in their investor relations to prove to them that social performance influences company policy and creates a competitive advantage. Communication has to be in a suitable language and give convincing socio-economic reasons that are understood by the financial markets.

7.   SUMMARY

Until now, social performance has been limited mainly to securing the legitimacy of a company. This chapter has shown that social performance also has important impacts on competitiveness and can both secure and improve it. Important stakeholder groups are connected with key factors of competitiveness. The tables in this chapter illustrate, in a pragmatic and easily understandable way, the relations between different stakeholder-oriented social performance measures and competitiveness. These considerations can help managers to develop socio-competitive scenarios and could provide a basis for integrating the social dimension in order to increase competitiveness.

Social performance is not usually a visible attribute of products and services. It needs professional stakeholder-oriented communication. To develop the power of social performance for competitiveness, it is necessary to integrate the social dimension into corporate and marketing communication, so as to build up brand and reputation. Social performance thus becomes visible—it enters into customer perception, influences purchasing decisions and leads to a competitive advantage.

The complex reality does not allow the creation of simple receipt strategy formulae to use social performance as a tool for competitiveness. The socio-competitive framework, presented in this chapter, helps managers to:

- Understand the relationship between social performance and competitiveness
- Gather initial ideas in order to use their potential to create economic value
- Develop in-house, socio-competitive strategies with the help of a theoretical framework and appropriate definitions

Each company must find a specific way to use the economic potential of social-performance (cost leadership, innovation, branding, differentiation, developing human resources). The development and realisation of socio-competitive strategies is perhaps the most powerful instrument to advance corporate social responsibility. This is because market success promotes social performance.

In conclusion, social performance is much more than charitable donations and secure legitimacy. It is a part of, and a tool, for improved competitiveness.

REFERENCES

Ashby, R.W. (1964): *An Introduction to Cybernetics.* Boston: Routledge & Kegan Paul.

Dyllick, T. and Hummel, J (1996): *Integriertes Umweltmanagement: Ein Ansatz im Rahmen des St. Gallen Management-Konzepts.* St. Gallen: Institut für Wirtschaft und Ökologie an der Hochschule St. Gallen.

Freeman, E.R. (1984): *Strategic Management. A Stakeholder Approach.* Boston: Pitman.

GRI (Global Reporting Initiative) (2002): *Global Reporting Guidelines.* Boston: GRI.

Hamschmidt, J. and Dyllick, T. (2002): 'ISO 14001: Profitable? Yes! But is it Eco-effective?', *Greener Management International* Vol. 34, 43-54.

Malik, F (2005): 'Die sechs Schlüsselgrößen des Unternehmenserfolges', *Manager Magazin* 13 January [online]. Available from Internet URL: http://www.manager-magazin.de/koepfe/artikel/0,2828,336518,00.html.

Pfarr, H. and Linne, G. (2001): *Pathways to a Sustainable Future.* Düsseldorf: Hans Böckler Stiftung.

Porter, M.E (1985): *Competitive Advantage. Creating and Sustaining Superior Performance.* New York: Free Press.

Rüegg-Stürm, J (2002): *Das neue St.Gallen-Management-Modell.* Berne: Haupt.

Schaltegger, S. and Dyllick, T. (Eds.) (2002): *Nachhaltig managen mit der Balanced Scorecard.* Wiesbaden: Gabler.

Schaltegger, S. and Wagner, M. (2006): 'Integrative Management of Sustainability Performance, Measurement and Reporting', *International Journal of Accounting, Auditing and Performance Evaluation (IJAAPE)*, Vol. 3, No. 1.

Schaltegger, S., Herzig, C., Kleiber, O. and Müller, J. (2003): 'Werkzeuge des unternehmerischen Nachhaltigkeitsmanagements', *UmweltWirtschaftsForum* Vol. 11, No. 4, 60-65.

Wagner, M. and Schaltegger, S. (2003): 'How Does Sustainability Performance Relate to Business Competitiveness?', *Greener Management International* Issue 44, 5-16.

Watzlawick, P., Beavin, J. and Jackson, D. (1967): *Pragmatics of Human Communication.*
New York: W.W. Norton and Co.

Chapter 3

Integrative Approaches

MAPPING THE LINKS OF CORPORATE SUSTAINABILITY

Sustainability Balanced Scorecards as a Tool for Sustainability Performance Measurement and Management

Marcus Wagner[1] and Stefan Schaltegger[2]

[1]*Dr Theo Schöller Chair in Technology and Innovation Management, Technische Universität München and Centre for Sustainability Management, University of Lüneburg, Germany;*
[2]*Centre for Sustainability Management, University of Lüneburg, Germany*

Abstract: Sustainability performance management is a newly emerging term and area in the debate about business and corporate social responsibility. It aims to addressing the social, environmental and economic (performance) aspects of corporate management in general and corporate sustainability management in particular. The management of sustainability performance in all its perspectives and facets requires a sound management framework which, on the one hand, links environmental and social management with competitive strategy and business management and, on the other, integrates environmental and social information with economic business information. This chapter discusses how Sustainability Balanced Scorecards as a strategic information and management approach play a role in this and what empirical evidence there is for this approach being successful in practice. In addition, links to sustainability accounting as a supporting measurement approach and sustainability reporting as a communication and reporting instrument are established.

1. INTRODUCING SUSTAINABILITY PERFORMANCE MEASUREMENT AND MANAGEMENT

Sustainability performance measurement and management addresses the social, environmental and economic (performance) aspects of corporate management in general and corporate sustainability management in particular (Schaltegger *et al.* 2003; Schaltegger and Wagner 2005). Management of sustainability performance in all its perspectives and facets requires a sound management framework which, on one hand, links environmental and social management with the business and competitive strategy and management and, on the other, integrates environmental and social information with economic business information. Sustainability performance measurement (and management) needs to be distinguished conceptionally from sustainable performance—a term that also features frequently in the scientific and practitioners' debate. To us, sustainable performance refers conceptually to a normative evaluation of the conventional performance of a company. Depending on the perspective of the person using the term, the attribute 'sustainable' may apply only to economic performance or to overall performance in a number of dimensions. Taking a broader sustainability-related view (at least at an aggregate level), three dimensions, namely the environmental, economic and social dimensions should be covered, thus approaching the term and coverage of sustainability performance. Sustainable performance understood in this latter way would mean overall levels of performance under which the long-term existence of the company is ensured (sustainable organisation development). This state would necessarily be a Pareto optimal situation with regard to the whole of the company's environmental, social and economic performance, since any other situation would imply that the company could improve in one of the three sustainability dimensions without lowering its performance in at least one of the remaining two. However, organisational Pareto optimality does not necessarily ensure that all performance dimensions are at levels sufficient for the longer-term existence of the company (unless, for example, safe minimum standards for each dimension are defined along the reasoning of proponents of strong sustainability). This is because Pareto optima do not specify a particular distribution of improvements to different performance and time dimensions.

Other than the term 'sustainable performance', the term 'sustainability performance measurement' (and management) does not only refer to a normative evaluation of a given organisational performance, but also to the performance of the organisation in terms of the sustainable development of the economy and society as a whole. Sustainability performance thus includes sustainable organisational development and performance, and also covers the effects of the organisation on its stakeholders and the broader environment. Sustainable performance is thus a multidimensional topic covering various different links between social, environmental and/or economic factors within the company, as well as between the company and its constituencies, the economy and society at large. Sustainability performance measurement and management is more generic in the sense that it also includes the analysis of states of unsustainable performance—partly with the aim of transforming them into states of sustainable organisational performance. To speak of sustainable performance measurement and management here would be misleading since sustainability is the subject and goal, and not an attribute of performance measurement and management. Of course, performance measurement or management that results in performance for sustainable development could, in principle, be referred to as sustainable performance. But, if the outcome is the focus of attention, sustainability performance may be the preferred term for such a performance achievement. Furthermore, it seems necessary to acknowledge the multidimensional character of sustainability due to substantial differences in what type of sustainability issues are relevant for a given company, industry, market, point of time or country. Considering sustainability performance measurement and management as a multidimensional approach that aims to identify which issues are relevant to a company, corporate sustainability and sustainable development leads to a differentiation of approaches and tools for sustainability management. This is necessary to link social and environmental management successfully with competitiveness and economic success because what creates success is people, processes, systems, incentives and structures—all factors varying substantially between companies and their specific situation.

Early empirical research into environmental and social management and reporting during the 1980s focussed first on the societal (i.e. environmental and social) performance of corporations (partly as a result of dissatisfaction with the early empirical work on social performance) and, secondly, on a more theoretical discussion of how to define and measure environmental and social performance (or exchangeable corporate social responsibility performance), corporate social responsibility or corporate citizenship—all of which are constitutional elements of the concept of what is nowadays called sustainability management. Two examples that illustrate the first approaches to measuring environmental and/or social performance are the development of life-cycle assessment (LCA) approaches (see, for example: Heijungs *et al.* 1992; Hofstetter and Heijungs 1996; ICI 1997; Wright *et al.* 1997) or social indicator developments (e.g. Epstein and Roy 2003; GRI 2002; Hoffmann *et al.* 1997; Holme and Watts 2000; Keeble *et al.* 2002). An example of the latter approach is that corporate social responsibility (CSR) is considered to be the subset of corporate responsibilities that addresses a company's voluntary or discretionary relationships with its societal and community stakeholders. This means that, in most cases, CSR is typically undertaken with some intention of improving an important aspect of society or relationships with communities or non-governmental or non-profit organisations (Caroll 1979). CSR defined in this way is frequently operationalised in terms of community relations, philanthropic activities, multi-sector collaborations or volunteer activities, which cover only very limited aspects of the broader definition.

Resulting from this first phase of sustainability performance measurement is a whole range of tools and measurement systems used in socially responsible investment contexts. These have significantly increased requirements on qualitative as well as quantitative data and on physical as well as monetary data. This, in turn, makes benchmarking and analysis more difficult. For example, comparison of the performance of a company with the average of all those in one (narrowly defined) industrial sector is increasingly more difficult than a comparison with a national average. Such an industry comparison is commonly encountered as the 'best-in-class' approach pursued by many companies active in socially responsible investment.

However different the approaches may be, a common feature is that they do not integrate business issues particularly with social and environmental activities and they do not consider the general economic relevance of corporate societal engagement. CSR activities often result in the establishment of a parallel organisation in the company (e.g. environmental departments and delegates or employee relations) dealing with non-economic issues and measuring non-economic aspects of performance.

We see primarily three problems with such an approach. First, parallel or supplementary developments contrast with the basic vision of sustainability to integrate social, environmental and economic issues. Secondly, sustainable development and corporate sustainability require participation and stakeholder involvement—not just with societal stakeholders but also with conventional business managers. Business strategy and sustainability communications and reporting should therefore be linked with sustainability performance management. Thirdly, the building up parallel organisational structures with satellite management and measurement methods always faces the danger of being cut back in times of less good economic performance by the company. Parallel developments tend to be managed as a discretionary activity. Furthermore, such a satellite approach to the measurement, management and reporting of social and environmental issues conflicts, in most organisations, with business reality.

This is why sustainability performance measurement and management requires a framework approach that links business strategy with sustainability performance measurement and management and also integrates reporting and communication in this context. This chapter therefore focuses on the use of Sustainability Balanced Scorecards in the context of sustainability performance measurement and management.

2.   A FRAMEWORK FOR SUSTAINABILITY PERFORMANCE MEASUREMENT AND MANAGEMENT

2.1   Need for a Framework

Sustainability performance measurement and management can be defined (Bennett and James 1997) as the measurement and management of the interaction between business, society and the environment. Issues and perspectives of sustainability performance measurement and management can be analysed at three levels: the level of individual sustainability performance indicators; the level of the overall performance measurement system; and the level of the relationship of this overall system with the external environment (Neely 1993). The first level has been analysed extensively (see, for example, Schaltegger and Burritt 2000 or Olsthoorn *et al.* 2001)—at least for the aspect of environmental performance. The focus of the remainder of this section is on the second level, the overall performance measurement system. The third level, i.e. the system's relationship to the external business environment, is examined in the last section.

The development of sustainability performance measurement is driven by The interests of various stakeholders (James and Wehrmeyer 1996). These aim primarily to support regulatory data requirements (Freedman and Jaggi 1988), pressure group demands for detailed information and data (Seidel 1988), internal environment-related decision-making and the requirements of financial institutions (banks, insurers and funds) (Lascelles 1993). Customer interests in environmental and social performance (Wells *et al.* 1992) and the requirements of environmental and social management standards (Gilbert 1994) are also important drivers. Another set of driving forces stems from the ultimate objectives of sustainability performance measurement and management. These issues include whether sustainability performance measurement and management should be business-linked or solely oriented towards environmental and social improvements and whether they should be more long-term or short-term orientated (James and Wehrmeyer 1996). This, in turn, leads to the question of whether sustainability performance measurement and management should take a life-cycle approach or a more site-orientated one (Schaltegger 1997).

Clearly all these forces are interrelated and depend on stakeholder interests. In other words, what is understood by sustainability performance is influenced by the stakeholder environment of a company. As a consequence, sustainability performance measurement requires management to define the goals and criteria of what is understood by corporate sustainability performance in a communicative interaction with stakeholders and to establish an information, measurement and reporting systems that support the management and communication of those indicators and issues considered vital to stakeholders and the key to business success.

2.2 Sustainability Performance Measurement and Management using a Sustainability Balanced Scorecard

The Sustainability Balanced Scorecard (Hahn and Wagner 2002; Schäfer and Langer 2005; Schaltegger and Dyllick 2002; Schaltegger 2004; van der Woerd and van den Brink 2003) is one of the most promising instruments for better integration of the environmental, social and economic aspects of corporate sustainability measurement and management. The Balanced Scorecard is very popular and has experienced rapid diffusion as a management tool. Because of this and its multidimensional conception, it is well placed to address the major challenges of corporate sustainability management efficiently. The Sustainability Balanced Scorecard, which in addition to issues addressed by the conventional Balanced Scorecard addresses non-market issues of major business relevance, combines performance measurement simultaneously with performance management in all dimensions of sustainability (Hahn and Wagner 2002; Hahn *et al.* 2002; Schaltegger and Dyllick 2002).

In reality, environmental and social performance indicators rarely stand alone and separate from each other (see, for example, Schaltegger and Burritt 2000). Thus, the issues are:

- How to combine them into an overall performance measurement system covering all significant environmental and social performance aspects of a company's operations
- How to determine what indicators are needed in an overall performance measurement system to measure and report the achievement of predefined goals

An overall performance measurement system can, for example, be defined mainly by the industry sector, resulting in a set or subset of sector-specific indicators. Other determinants could be the level of public concern, the strictness of national legislation and the size of the organisation (James and Wehrmeyer 1996). Yet another set of determinants could result from the relative importance of stakeholders to the company (Figge and Schaltegger 2000). Much of the discussion is about identifying a suitable 'balanced scorecard' of monetary and non-monetary (i.e. physical) indicators (Bennett and James 1997). This is why the Sustainability Balanced Scorecard (SBSC) approach seems suitable for linking performance measurement with reporting and management.

The starting point of the Balanced Scorecard (BSC) is the business strategy operationalised through four to five management perspectives based on cause and effect chains. The conventional Balanced Scorecard approach (Kaplan and Norton 1997, 2001, 2004) emerges in its original form from weaknesses of conventional management accounting (Johnson and Kaplan 1987) and distinguishes a financial perspective, a customer perspective, a business process perspective and a learning and development perspective (Kaplan and Norton 1997, 2002; Olve *et al.* 1999). The Sustainability Balanced Scorecard also integrates non-market issues with a possible fifth perspective (Figge *et al.* 2002; Hahn and Wagner 2002; Schaltegger and Dyllick 2002). The perspectives are linked with cause and effect chains. Beyond being a performance measurement system, the BSC also embeds this into an overall management concept (see, for example, Kaplan and Norton 2001).

A number of essential steps need to be completed to develop a SBSC (see Hahn and Wagner 2002 and Hahn *et al.* 2002 for detailed descriptions and examples): identification and analysis of the environmental and social exposure of the business; development of cause and effect chains; and the definition of key performance indicators.

In order to link sustainability reporting with performance measurement and management, the following steps should be adopted:
1. Identifying the environmental and social exposure of the business
2. Analysing the strategic relevance of environmental and social aspects
3. Developing causal chains and the strategy map
4. Defining key performance indicators and developing the measurement methods necessary to create the respective performance information
5. Considering identified key sustainability performance indicators within the company's internal and external communication and reporting activities
6. BSC implementation and revision, and reporting on sustainability indicators

The first step aims to identify those environmental and social aspects relevant to a specific company. Since these may differ depending on the company and the business field (e.g. depending on products, production processes, site location), it is necessary to identify them specifically, based on criteria matrices (see Hahn *et al.* 2002:71 for a detailed explanation of how this is achieved). The second step in the SBSC process is the identification of strategically relevant environmental and social aspects, i.e. the subset of environmental and social aspects that could have a material impact on the company's business success. Identification is carried out in an order consistent to the logic of the conventional BSC, i.e. starting from the financial perspective and then progressing through the customer perspective and process perspective to the learning and development perspective. An important addition here (specific to the SBSC) is an analysis of non-market aspects of corporate activity captured through a dedicated non-market perspective (see Schaltegger 2004:511f. for a discussion of the interaction of market and non-market aspects of corporate activity). The development of causal chains as a third step is important to reflect linkages between strategically relevant social and environmental aspects and the company's business goals and corporate activities in order to assess the potential influence of environmental and social aspects on business success. Strategy maps are an important instrument used here; these are also becoming increasingly relevant for conventional BSC development (Kaplan and Norton 2004). A strategy map focuses on the essential linkages within a company and aims to describe concisely the business model (Gaiser and Wunder 2004). Target levels, performance indicators and activities can then be formulated and implemented. The sustainability performance indicators defined in this process reflect the first level of sustainability performance measurement and management and provide an important link to sustainability reporting.

The last step of the SBSC process is the implementation and review of the resulting SBSC. Here it is important to ensure that the SBSC is reviewed continuously in terms of the underlying strategy, indicators and activities. As well as being a performance measurement tool, this step brings out more fully the strength of the BSC method as a management system.

Once this process of SBSC development is complete, the result is a hierarchical causal chain network that enables successful strategy enactment (see Kaplan and Norton 1997:28 for more details on this crucial aspect). Based on this, the relevant sustainability performance indicators are defined. Figure 1 provides an example of such a strategy map based on the Sustainability Balanced Scorecard.

Once the Sustainability Balanced Scorecard (including the strategy map and the performance indictors for the measurement of the key performance indicators) is developed for the company, the management challenge is to integrate this sustainability performance measurement system with internal company business information and reporting systems. An important comment should be made here about the distinction between value- and values-oriented SBSC approaches. While a number of generic elements can be easily identified, which are common to all Sustainability Balanced Scorecard approaches, the various approaches often have different philosophies.

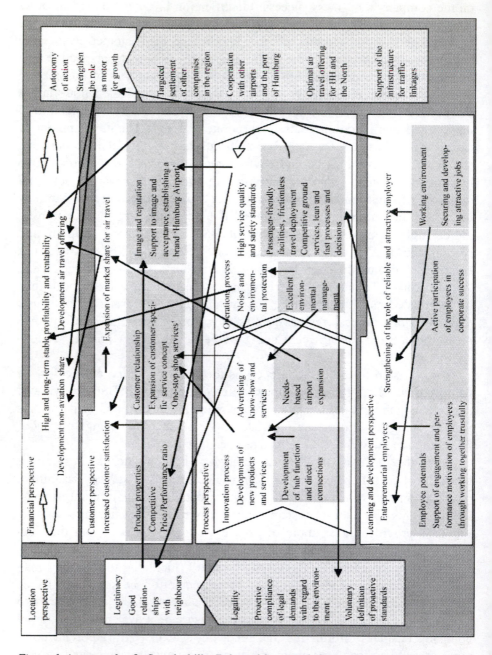

Figure 1. An example of a Sustainability Balanced Scorecard (Source: based on Diaz Guerrero *et al.* 2002)

One important demarcation can be made between approaches that maintain the predominance of the financial perspective of the conventional BSC as the target perspective (e.g. Hahn *et al.* 2002) and those that argue for the equal or higher relevance of other perspectives (e.g. Gminder *et al.* 2002). Against what has been said above with regard to trading-off (weak sustainability) or not (strong sustainability) performance dimensions, such differences seem to be well justified. A Sustainability Balanced Scorecard is a tool for implementing strategies—whatever their contents.

2.3 Empirical Potential of a Sustainability Balanced Scorecard

In order to evaluate to what degree the SBSC idea formulated in the last section has practical viability beyond single case studies, the main characteristics of the conventional BSC (objectives, indicators, target values and measures) are analysed with regard to their usage being dependent on the linkage between corporate strategy and sustainability aspects as proposed for the SBSC. The focus here is on the linkage of environmental aspects with the assumption that a similar situation could be expected for social aspects. The data used was collected in during European Business Environment Barometer (EBEB), a biennial survey carried out in several European countries on the state of environmental management in practice (Baumast and Dyllick 2001; Kestemont and Ytterhus 2001). Data used in this chapter refer to the last survey round in 2001 and to Germany only. The questionnaire used for gather data during this survey can be found at: http://www.agf.org.uk/pubs/pdfs/UK.pdf. A total of 332 companies in the manufacturing industry provided responses. The most important instruments used in this chapter are a set of management activities that link directly to the BSC method (e.g. usage of quantitative performance indicators and target levels for these, as well as the existence of programmes to achieve these targets) and a specific question on whether companies link their environmental activities to management activities targeted to achieve economic success (e.g. increased competitiveness or financial performance). The hypothesis based on the SBSC concept and method formulated in the last section would be that the extension of the BSC concept towards a SBSC and the implementation of the latter should have good chances for realisation in practice provided the use of specific management activities or features that are central for a BSC are found with higher likelihood in companies that link their environmental activities with general management activities or corporate strategy considerations aimed at economic success. In short, we propose that, if companies that integrate their environmental and corporate strategy considerations are those that are also more likely to use core elements of the BSC methods, then the SBSC stands a better chance of succeeding than if this was not the case.

Table 1. Cross-tabulation of written environmental policy and environmental activities linked to management activities targeted towards economic success

| | | **Environmental activities linked to management activities targeted towards economic success** | | | | | |
		Not at all	**Some-what**	**Partly**	**Very much**	**Fully integrated**	**Total**
Written environmental policy	Yes	5.0%	6.0%	23.8%	12.1%	6.7%	53.5%
	No	14.5%	9.2%	12.1%	4.3%	0.7%	40.8%
	N/A	2.5%	0.7%	2.5%	-	-	5.7%
Total		22.0%	16.0%	38.3%	16.3%	7.4%	100.0%

N/A means that the activity was not applicable to this company.

Table 1 shows that the hypothesised relationship exists for the use of a written policy. This can be a starting point for deriving sustainability objectives for the company.

Table 2. Cross-tabulation of the usage of quantitative environmental performance indicators and linkage of environmental aspects to activities aimed at economic success

| | | **Environmental activities linked to management activities targeted towards economic success** | | | | | |
		Not at all	**Some-what**	**Partly**	**Very much**	**Fully integrated**	**Total**
Usage of quantitative indicators to measure environmental performance	Yes	4.7%	4.0%	17.3%	8.7%	5.8%	40.4%
	No	15.2%	10.8%	17.7%	6.9%	1.4%	52.0%
	N/A	2.2%	1.4%	2.9%	1.1%	-	7.6%
Total		22.0%	16.2%	37.9%	16.6%	7.2%	100.0%

N/A means that the activity was not applicable to this company.

With regard to the usage of quantitative environmental performance indicators, it is also found that companies that link environmental and competitiveness considerations are more likely to have adopted the former (Table 2), which provides better fit with the BSC method. Differences with those companies without linkage of environmental and economic aspects are, however, less pronounced than in the case of a written environmental policy.

Table 3. Cross-tabulation of quantitative environmental targets and environmental activities linked to management activities targeted towards economic success

| | | Environmental activities linked to management activities targeted towards economic success | | | | | |
		Not at all	Some-what	Partly	Very much	Fully integrated	Total
Quantitative environmental targets	Yes	4.6%	6.4%	22.7%	12.1%	6.0%	51.8%
	No	14.9%	8.5%	13.5%	3.5%	1.1%	41.5%
	N/A	2.5%	1.1%	2.1%	0.7%	0.4%	6.7%
Total		22.0%	16.0%	38.3%	16.3%	7.4%	100.0%

N/A means that the activity was not applicable to this company.

As can be seen from Table 3, which also features quantitative environmental targets (i.e. existence of target values for the indicators used), the usage probability is higher for companies that link environmental to corporate strategy/performance considerations. This linkage has a similar strength to the one for a written environmental policy, possibly because such targets are often associated closely with a policy. This is actually confirmed by Table 4, which shows that existence of a written environmental policy is closely associated with quantitative environmental targets.

Table 4. Cross-tabulation of environmental policy and environmental targets

| | | Written environmental policy | | | |
		Yes	No	N/A	Total
Quantitative environmental targets	Yes	145	22	0	167
	No	25	106	4	135
	N/A	4	4	14	22
Total		174	132	18	324

N/A means that the activity was not applicable to this company.

Finally, Table 5 looks at whether the existence of a programme to achieve environmental targets is linked to the degree with which a company integrates its environmental activities with management considerations targeting economic success. It shows that there is a similar link for the existence of implementation programmes and measures aimed at achieving pre-defined targets as for the previously analysed three core elements of the conventional BSC.

This association has a similar range of strength to that for a written environmental policy and environmental targets. Again, the mechanism behind this is that companies are only likely to have an implementation programme when they have environmental targets and, as was shown above, the existence of targets is closely associated with the availability of a written policy as targets are usually derived from policies.

Table 5. Cross-tabulation of the existence of a programme to achieve environmental targets and linkage of environmental activities to management activities aimed at economic success

| | | Environmental activities linked to management activities targeted towards economic success | | | | | |
		Not at all	Some-what	Partly	Very much	Fully integrated	Total
Programme to achieve environmental targets	Yes	3.5%	5.3%	22.7%	11.3%	5.7%	48.6%
	No	16.3%	9.6%	13.1%	4.3%	1.4%	44.7%
	N/A	2.1%	1.1%	2.5%	0.7%	0.4%	6.7%
Total		22.0%	16.0%	38.3%	16.3%	7.4%	100.0%

N/A means that the activity was not applicable to this company.

Overall, the empirical analysis confirms the suitability of the approach of integrating sustainability aspects in the conventional BSC according to the approaches described in the previous section. Therefore, an SBSC has a good basis in business reality for being implemented successfully. The feasibility deriving it conceptually is illustrated in the case study shown in Figure 1.

However, the somewhat weaker linkage of quantitative indicators to integration of environmental, economic and, possibly, also social aspects towards an integrated sustainability management also points to a potential weakness. This because the effect is largely due to companies stating they have a written policy, targets and a programme to implement them but, in some cases, not appearing to use quantitative indicators. As this is a core element of performance measurement based on the BSC method, it limits somewhat the potential of companies that otherwise express conditions conducive for the implementation of a SBSC.

Following this detailed look at SBSC tools and their practical feasibility, the next section takes a broader look by discussing how the increasing incidence of sustainability reporting should be integrated into sustainability performance measurement and the role a SBSC can play in this.

2.4   Integration of Sustainability Reporting and Sustainability Performance Measurement

Several papers and recent initiatives on environmental, social and sustainability reporting stress:

- The need for greater standardisation of accounting and reporting procedures (Bennett and James 1998; Marsanich 1998; Skillius and Wennberg

1998; MEPI 2000; James and Bennett 1996; Ditz and Ranganathan 1997; CERES 1998)

- The need for systematic measurement of sustainability (Wehrmeyer and Tyteca 1998) and eco-efficiency (WBCSD 1998; ISO 1999)
- The consideration of life-cycle thinking (Bennett and James 1998)
- A narrower but deeper analysis of core areas of environmental and social performance (Bennett and James 1998).

Some initiatives point to the need to use sector-specific performance indicators within an overall performance measurement system to mirror sector-specific social and environmental impacts (CERES 1998). The implications of these considerations of performance measurement, management and reporting are illustrated in the remainder of this section through a focus on environmental performance. Similar arguments can be formulated for social performance and thus for sustainability performance as a whole.

A trend that emerges from these initiatives in terms of environmental performance is that relative indicators aimed at measuring efficiency, rather than effectiveness, are proposed increasingly for performance measurement (NRTEE 1997). Linked to this, another trend is the proposal of key resource flows/areas around which to cluster measurement and indicators of environmental performance (Ditz and Ranganathan 1997; Gee and Moll 1998). Areas proposed are quantities and types of materials used, quantities and types of energy consumption or generation, non-product output (i.e. waste generated before recycling) and pollutant release to air, water and land.

There are clear consequences for performance management and reporting from the major trends, issues and developments of overall performance measurement systems. The objective of achieving comparable, transparent and complete (environmental) performance indicators implies the need to adopt a standard set of universally reported indicators. It thus requires the development of accounting and reporting standards ensuring high information quality (Schaltegger 1997; Wagner 2004, 2005). It also has probable affects on reporting requirements since it provides incentives for tracking environmental performance in a standardised way (Ditz and Ranganathan 1997). These developments could therefore form the basis for consistent standards of accountability for environmental performance. Such standardisation is likely to result from the combined efforts of governments, international standards and ratings organisations and intercompany co-operation, possibly facilitated by industry associations.

Sustainability performance measurement, management and reporting as practical means for internally measuring and externally communicating social and environmental performance improvements face the challenge of serving diverse audiences with different information needs. One model could be a type of 'generic' performance measurement and reporting that concentrates on key information that is relevant to all major target audiences (Azzone *et al.* 1997). The guidelines produced by the Global Reporting Initiative (GRI) follow this direction. But to become effective within a company, the sustainability indicators relevant for its success have to be selected from the general framework. The trend for standardisation of reporting indicators and the strive for a core set of broadly applicable metrics makes it necessary for corporate managers to identify, select and focus on those indicators that best relate and reflect core areas of performance. This requires a systematic approach such as the SBSC to determine which indicators are strategically relevant. The strategically relevant indicators, in turn, define both the data collection needs and the focus of the sustainability accounting approach. Furthermore, the respective accounting information provides the main information content for sustainability reporting if reporting needs to address those sustainability issues important to stakeholders which are also of core strategic relevance to the company.

3.   CONCLUSIONS AND OUTLOOK

Although the type of sustainability reporting described as the endpoint of the above process would be a very structured and focused way of communicating on the basis of a strategically determined integrated measurement of sustainability performance, the practical and historical evolution of sustainability reporting (for overviews, see Elkington *et al.* 1998; KPMG 1996; UBA 1999) is currently much more strongly influenced by a number of contingent factors external to the company. These are the publication of guidance documents or quasi-standards for environmental and sustainability reporting such as, for example, European Communities (1993), Müller and de Frutos (1994) or IRRC (1995), which may imply a system lock-in (see, for example, Clausen and Klaffke 2000 and IMUG *et al.* 2000 for a discussion of such aspects). The guideline developments are driven by general societal and political factors discussed in various groups or based on a multi-stakeholder consultation process. In addition, specific reporting competitions (e.g. future e.V and IÖW 1998) and rankings may provide incentives for some 'tuning' of reports towards specific formal aspects of these competitions rather than basing them on a fully consistent performance measurement and management system. From a reputation, signalling and marketing perspective, these developments would no doubt have to be considered by corporate management. But for efficient achievement of the best sustainability performance with those social and environmental activities that contribute most to the company's business success and shareholder value, other priorities may have to drive sustainability performance measurement and management.

REFERENCES

Azzone, G., Brophy, M., Noci, G., Welford, R. and Young, W. (1997): 'A Stakeholders' View of Environmental Reporting', *Long Range Planning* Vol. 30, No. 5, 699-709.

Baumast, A. and Dyllick, T. (2001): *Umweltmanagement-Barometer 2001* (Discussion Paper No. 93). St. Gallen: Institute for Economy and the Environment IWÖ-HSG.

Bennett, M. and James, P. (1997): *Environment-Related Performance Measurement: Current Practice and Trends.* Ashridge: Ashridge Management College.

Bennett, M. and James, P. (1998): *Environment under the Spotlight - Current Practice and Future Trends in Environment-Related Performance Measurement for Business.* London: Association of Chartered Certified Accountants (ACCA).

Caroll, A.B. (1979): 'A Three-dimensional Conceptual Model of Corporate Performance', *Academy of Management Review* No. 4, 497-505.

CERES (Coalition for Environmentally Responsible Economies) (1998): *Global Reporting Initiative* (GRI) [online] [cited 21 September 1998]. Available from Internet URL: http://www.ceres.org/reporting/globalreporting.html.

Clausen, J. and Klaffke, K. (2000): 'Kommunizieren oder Erbsen zählen', *Ökologisches Wirtschaften* No. 5, 4.

Diaz Guerrero, A., Möller, D. and Wagner, M. (2002): 'Sustainability Balanced Scorecard in der Flughafen Hamburg GmbH', in: Schaltegger, S. and Dyllick, T. (Eds.): *Nachhaltig managen mit der Balanced Scorecard.* Wiesbaden: Gabler, 229-258.

Ditz, D. and Ranganathan, J. (1997): *Measuring Up. Towards a Common Framework for Tracking Corporate Environmental Performance.* Washington D.C.: World Resources Institute (WRI).

Elkington, J., Kreander, N. and Stibbard, H. (1998): 'The Third International Survey on Company Environmental Reporting: The 1997 Benchmark Survey', *Greener Management International* Vol. 21, 99-111.

Epstein, M.J. and Roy, M.-J. (2003): 'Improving Sustainability Performance: Specifying, Implementing and Measuring Key Principles', *Journal of General Management* Vol. 29, No. 1, 15-31.

European Communities (1993): *EU Regulation (EEC) No. 1836/93 of 29 June 1993 Allowing Voluntary Participation by Companies in the Industrial Sector in a Community Eco-Management and Audit Scheme.* Brussels: European Communities.

Figge, F. and Schaltegger, S. (2000): *What is Stakeholder Value? Developing a Catchphrase into a Benchmarking Tool.* Lüneburg/Geneva/Paris: University of Lüneburg/Pictet in association with United Nations Environment Programme (UNEP).

Figge, F., Hahn, T., Schaltegger, S. and Wagner, M. (2002): 'The Sustainability Balanced Scorecard. Linking Sustainability Management to Business Strategy', *Business Strategy and the Environment* Vol. 11, No. 5, 269-284.

Freedman, M. and Jaggi, B. (1988): 'An analysis of the association between pollution disclosure and economic performance', *Accounting, Auditing and Accountability Journal* Vol. 1, No.2, 43-58.

future e.V. and IÖW (Eds.) (1998): *Umweltberichte und Umwelterklärungen: Ranking 1998. Zusammenfassung der Ergebnisse und Trends.* Munich: future e.V.

Gaiser, B. and Wunder, T. (2004): Strategy Maps und Strategieprozess', *Controlling* No. 8/9, 457-463.

Gee, D. and Moll, D (1998): *Information for Sustainability: Eco-Efficiency Indicators.* Copenhagen: European Environment Agency (EEA).

Gilbert, M. (1994): 'BS7750 and the Eco-Management and Audit Regulation', *Eco-Management and Auditing* Vol. 1, No. 2, 6-10.

Gminder, C., Bieker, T., Dyllick, T. and Hockerts, K. (2002): 'Nachhaltigkeitsstrategien umsetzen mit einer Sustainability Balanced Scorecard', in: Schaltegger, S. and Dyllick, T. (Eds.): *Nachhaltig managen mit der Balanced Scorecard.* Wiesbaden: Gabler, 95-147.

GRI (Global Reporting Initiative) (2002): *Sustainability Reporting Guidelines.* Boston: GRI.

Hahn, T. and Wagner, M. (2002): 'Sustainability Balanced Scorecard', in: Lutz, U., Döttinger, K. and Roth, K. (Eds.): *Betriebliches Umweltmanagement: Grundlagen; Methoden; Praxisbeispiele.* Düsseldorf: Symposium Publishing, Section 02.10.

Hahn, T., Wagner, M., Figge, F. and Schaltegger, S. (2002): 'Wertorientiertes Nachhaltigkeitsmanagement mit einer Sustainability Balanced Scorecard', in: Schaltegger, S. and Dyllick, T. (Eds.): *Nachhaltig managen mit der Balanced Scorecard.* Wiesbaden: Gabler, 43-94.

Heijungs, R., Guinée, J., Huppes, G., Lankreijer, R., Udo de Haes, H. and Sleeswijk, A. (1992): *Environmental Life Cycle Assessment of Products: Guide and Backgrounds.* Leiden: CML.

Hoffmann, J., Ott, K. and Scherhorn, G. (Eds.) (1997): *Ethische Kriterien für die Bewertung von Unternehmen. Frankfurt-Hohenheimer Leitfaden.* Frankfurt a.M.: IKO.

Hofstetter, P. and Heijungs, R. (1996): 'Definitions of Terms and Symbols', in: Udo de Haes, H. (Ed.): *Towards a Methodology for Life Cycle Impact Assessment.* Brussels: SETAC Europe, 31-39.

Holme, R. and Watts, P. (2000): *Corporate Social Responsibility. Making Good Business Sense.* Geneva: WBCSD.

ICI (1997): *Environmental Burden: The ICI Approach.* London: ICI.

IMUG, IÖW, IFEU and Öko-Institut (2000): *German Environmental Institutes' Common Statement of Position on the GRI Sustainability Reporting Guidelines.* Hannover: IMUG.

IRRC (Investor Responsibility Research Centre) (1995): *Environmental Reporting and Third Party Statements.* Washington DC: IRRC/Global Environmental Management Institute.

ISO (International Standards Organisation) (1999): *Environmental Management—Environmental Performance Evaluation—Guidelines (ISO 14031:1999).* Brussels: ISO.

James, P. and Bennett, M. (1996): *Environment-Related Performance Measurement in Business - From Emissions to Profit and Sustainability?* Ashridge: Ashridge Management Research Group.

James, P. and Wehrmeyer, W. (1996): 'Environmental Performance Measurement', in: Groenewegen, P., Fischer, K., Jenkins, E. and Schot, J. (Eds.): *The Greening of Industry Resource Guide and Bibliography.* Washington DC: Island Press, 111-136.

Johnson, H. and Kaplan, R. (1987): *Relevance Lost: The Rise and Fall of Management Accounting.* Boston: Harvard Business School Publishing.

Kaplan, R. and Norton, D. (1997): *Balanced Scorecard: Strategien erfolgreich umsetzen.* Stuttgart: Schäffer-Poeschel.

Kaplan, R. and Norton, D. (2001): *The Strategy-Focused Organisation.* Boston: Harvard Business School Press.

Kaplan, R. and Norton, D. (2004): *Strategy Maps.* Boston: Harvard Business School Press.

Keeble, J., Topiol, S. and Berkeley, S. (2002): 'Using Indicators to Measure Sustainability Performance at a Corporate and Project Level', *Journal of Business Ethics* Vol. 44, No. 2, 149-158.

Kestemont, M.P. and Ytterhus, B. (2001): *International Business Environment Barometer 1997 - Final Report to the EC*. Louvaine-la-Neuve: UCL [online] [cited 9 Oktober 2001]. Available from Internet URL: www.iag.ucl.ac.be/recherches/cese/research/int_bus_env_ baro.htm

KPMG (1996): *The KPMG UK Environmental Reporting Survey 1996*. London: KPMG.

Lascelles, D. (1993): *Rating Environmental Risk*. London: Centre for the Study of Financial Innovation.

Marsanich, A. (1998): *Environmental Indicators in EMAS Environmental Statements*. Milano: Fondazione Eni Enrico Mattei (FEEM).

MEPI (2000): *Website of the 'Measuring Environmental Performance of Industry (MEPI)' project* [online] [cited 3 December 2000]. Available from Internet URL: http://www. environmental-performance.org

Müller, K. and Frutos, J. de (1994): *Environmental Reporting and Disclosures. The Financial Analysts View*. London: Workings Group of Environmental Issues of the Accounting Commission of the European Federation of Financial Analysts Society (EFFAS).

Neely, A. (1993): *Performance Measurement System Design. A Process-Based Approach*. Cambridge: University of Cambridge/Manufacturing Engineering Group.

NRTEE (National Roundtable on the Environment and the Economy) (1997): *Backgrounder: Measuring Eco-Efficiency in Business*. Ottawa: NRTEE.

Olsthoorn, X., Tyteca, D., Wehrmeyer, W. and Wagner, M. (2001): 'Using Environmental Indicators for Business. A Literature Review and the Need for Standardisation and Aggregation of Data', *Journal of Cleaner Production* Vol. 9, No. 5, 453-463.

Olve, N., Roy, J. and Wetter, M. (1999): *Performance Drivers*. Chichester: Wiley.

Schäfer, H. and Langer, G. (2005): 'Sustainability Balanced Scorecard. Managementsystem im Kontext des Nachhaltigkeits-Ansatzes', *Controlling* Vol. 17, No. 1, 17-21.

Schaltegger, S. (1997): 'Economics of Life Cycle Assessment: Inefficiency of the Present Approach', *Business Strategy and the Environment* No. 6, 1-8.

Schaltegger, S. (2004): 'Unternehmerische Steuerung von Nachhaltigkeitsaspekten mit der Sustainability Balanced Scorecard', *Controlling* Vol. 16, No. 8/9, 511-516.

Schaltegger, S. and Burritt, R. (2000): *Contemporary Environmental Accounting*. Sheffield: Greenleaf Publishing.

Schaltegger, S. and Dyllick, T. (Eds.) (2002): *Nachhaltig managen mit der Balanced Scorecard. Konzepte und Fallstudien*. Wiesbaden: Gabler.

Schaltegger, S. and Figge, F. (2000): 'Environmental Shareholder Value. Economic Success with Corporate Environmental Management', *Eco-Management and Auditing* Vol. 7, No. 1, 29-42.

Schaltegger, S. and Sturm, A. (1990): 'Ökologische Rationalität', *Die Unternehmung* No. 4, 273-290.

Schaltegger, S. and Sturm, A. (1998): *Eco-Efficiency by Eco-Controlling. Theory and Cases* (2nd edition). Zürich: vdf.

Schaltegger, S. and Sturm, A. (2000): *Ökologieorientierte Entscheidungen in Unternehmen. Ökologisches Rechnungswesen statt Ökobilanzierung: Notwendigkeit, Kriterien, Konzepte* (3rd edition). Bern: Paul Haupt.

Schaltegger, S. and Wagner, M. (2005): Integrative Management of Sustainability Performance, Measurement and Reporting, *International Journal of Accounting, Auditing and Performance Evaluation (IJAAPE)*, No. 4.

Schaltegger, S., Burritt, R. and Petersen, H. (2003): *An Introduction to Corporate Environmental Management*. Sheffield: Greenleaf Publishing.

Seidel, E. (1988): 'Ökologisches Controlling', in: Wunderer, R. (Ed.): *Betriebswirtschaftslehre als Management- und Führungslehre* (2nd edition). Stuttgart: Schäffer-Poeschel, 301-322.

Seidel, E. (1992): 'Entwicklung eines betrieblich-ökologischen Rechnungswesens. Schlüssel zu einer tatsächlichen Ökologisierung des Wirtschaftens', in: Seidel, E. (Ed.): *Betrieblicher Umweltschutz. Landschaftsökologie und Betriebswirtschaftslehre.* Wiesbaden: Gabler, 229-246.

Skillius, A. and Wennberg; U. (1998): *Continuity, Credibility and Comparability: Key Challenges for Corporate Environmental Performance Measurement and Communication.* Lund: IIIEE, Lund University.

UBA (1999): *EG-Umweltaudit in Deutschland–Erfahrungsbericht 1995 bis 1998.* Berlin: Umweltbundesamt.

Wagner, M. (2004): 'Sustainable Reporting? The Link of Environmental Reports and Environmental Performance', *Corporate Environmental Strategy. International Journal for Sustainable Business* No. 11, 21-28.

Wagner, M. (2005): 'Environmental Performance and the Quality of Corporate Environmental Reports: The Role of Environmental Management Accounting', in: Rikhardsson, P., Bennett, M., Schaltegger, S. and Bouma, J.J. (Eds.): *Implementing Environmental Management Accounting: Status and Challenges.* Dordrecht: Kluwer Academic Publishers: 105-122.

WBCSD (World Business Council for Sustainable Development) (1998): *Eco-efficiency Metrics and Reporting* (Eco-efficiency Brief No. 1). Geneva: WBCSD.

Wehrmeyer, W. and Tyteca, D. (1998): 'Measuring Environmental Performance for Industry: From Legitimacy to Sustainability?' *The International Journal of Sustainable Development and World Ecology* No. 5, 111-124.

Wells, R., Hockman, M., Hochman, S. and O'Connell, P. (1992): 'Measuring Environmental Success', *Total Environmental Quality Management* Summer, 315-327.

Woerd, F. van der and Brink, T. van den (2003): *Implementation of a Business Sustainability Scorecard. Pilot Study in a Sector of Industry* (Paper presented at the 11th International Conference of the Greening of Industry Network, 12-15 October). San Francisco: The Greening of Industry Network.

Wright, M., Allen, D., Clift, R. and Sas, H. (1997): 'Measuring Corporate Environmental Performance: The ICI Environmental Burden System', *Journal of Industrial Ecology* Vol. 1, No. 4, 117-127.

A MODEL OF FINANCIAL ANALYSIS AT THE SERVICE OF SUSTAINABILITY

Juan Piñeiro Chousa and Noelia Romero Castro
Department of Finance and Accounting, University of Santiago de Compostela, Spain

Abstract: The maximisation of shareholder value can no longer be considered an iso-lated objective. Managerial theory has started to integrate sustainability issues into different areas (accounting, finance, marketing, etc.) and to develop new tools and instruments or adapt existing ones to allow the strategic management of sustainability by companies and capital markets. Financial analysis—con-sidered traditionally as an appropriate tool to assess a company's financial and economic situation and to guide the decision-making processes of companies and financial markets—should embrace sustainability issues into its logic under some kind of scheme or framework that allows the evaluation of a company's sustainable management system and the impact of sustainability issues on financial performance. An integrated model is needed that takes account of the social, environmental and economic/financial performances of a company and their expression under both quantitative and qualitative, accounting and non-accounting, physical and monetary data. In this chapter, we propose a conceptual model for the financial analysis of company value creation oriented to sustainability.

1. INTRODUCTION

In traditional corporate finance, decision-making aims to maximise the value of the company, the shareholder value (Rappaport 1986; Copeland *et al.* 1993) or the share price when the company is traded publicly and the markets are considered to be efficient. There is a close relationship between financial decisions and company valuation, which is subject to internal and external constraints affecting those decisions. The former refer to the structure and concentration intensity of ownership, the management's share in that ownership structure, the mechanisms used to solve conflicts of interest, the established compensation system, etc. External restrictions are imposed by the status of the company's economic and financial environment, the degree of development of financial markets, the power of financial institutions within the economic system, the regulatory framework and society's general demands.

Damodaran (2001) argues that, in order to recognise share price maximisation as the only objective in decision-making, it is necessary to assume that: (1) managers are responsive to the company's owners, with or without compensation systems or other mechanisms to promote such behaviour; (2) shareholder value is not being increased at the expense of bondholders; (3) markets are efficient as long as reliable and updated information is revealed to them; and (4) there are no significant social costs and these can be easily traced and charged to the company.

Every company creates some kind of social and/or environmental impact (cost or benefit), such that the maximisation of shareholder value cannot result in the maximisation of the society's wealth. Thus, problems in meeting social objectives arise when achieving the financial objective mentioned above. In many cases, managers ought to perform in a socially responsible manner, not only because they must comply with regulation, but also because it is the only way to maximise shareholder value. However, in many other situations, conflicts can arise between the owners' demands and those of other stakeholders or society as a whole.

Managers are, thus, confronted with the need to give an answer to the requirements of an increasingly wide range of stakeholders that conforms with the company's environment. In the field of sustainable development, the increasing pressure from society—and especially from governments—has transformed the management of environmental, social and economic issues into a key element in guaranteeing the company's survival in the medium/long term and in contributing to its ability to generate shareholder value. Once CEOs and boards of directors have started to realise the urgent and unavoidable character of the integration of social responsibility criteria into their companies' management systems, the hard task of aligning the classic objective of shareholder value creation with objectives of sustainable development has begun.

A consequence of acknowledging the existence of externalities derived from business activities is that the traditional divergence between the company's behaviour and the neoclassical assumption of value maximisation behaviour is recognised. Faced with complex problems and in the absence of full information, it is evident that the behaviour of economic agents is at present intended to be rational, although in a limited way (Simon 1982). In addition, companies do not operate exclusively in the commercial–economic sphere but interact with other spheres such as the socio-cultural or legal spheres (Figge *et al.* 2002; Schaltegger 1999; Schaltegger and Sturm 1990, 1994) that conform to a model of socio-economic rationality (Hill 1985).

In this way, the new perceptions about society and the environment are complemented by the verification that economic agents behave rationally, but they are subject to restrictions derived from the uncertainty generated by a lack of information that results in incomplete contracts and the delegation of responsibility that originates from the principal/agent problem. The lack of information and the existence of asymmetric information are, therefore, the first pitfalls in the process of integrating the management of sustainability into the decisions of companies and financial markets. Thus, it is in this field that the major efforts have been developed to promote that process and to contribute to the binding of environmental, social and financial objectives. Examples include the Global Reporting Initiative (GRI), the Eco-Management and Audit Scheme (EMAS) and ISO 14001. One of the main obstacles to this route has been the absence of an adequate approach that links both financial and sustainability objectives in terms of profitability and risk—the terms best understood by companies and financial markets as they are part of their own language.

2.   LINKING FINANCIAL MANAGEMENT AND SUSTAINABILITY: WHY IS A NEW APPROACH NEEDED?

It is essential to analyse in depth the particular features and elements defining the relationship between the environmental and social performance of a company and its financial performance to provide managers and the members of financial markets with the theoretic foundations on which they can base their decision-making processes and develop analysis and management tools that allow them to carry out actions that are financially, socially and environmentally sustainable. Once the market has incorporated sustainability into its strategies, a 'sustainability circle' will have closed inside which the market requires an environmentally and socially responsible behaviour from companies that limits their risk and ensures a sustainable value creation., On the other hand, companies will need market support to face the financial requirements derived from their commitment to sustainable development. Such support takes the form of a lower cost of capital for those companies willing to assume the sustainability challenge.

In recent years, an increasing number of studies have tackled the analysis of the linkage between the financial performance of a company and its environmental and social performance, attempting to find a correlation or a conceptual link between them (see, for example, Griffin and Mahon 1997; Pava and Krausz 1996; Schaltegger and Figge 1997, 2000; Schaltegger and Synnestvedt 2002; Wagner 2001, 2003). But, as Zadek (2000) argues, some

studies linking sustainable development with improved financial performance are not sufficiently conclusive. In addition, one question remains
unanswered: what comes first, corporate social performance or financial performance?

But is this the correct or more appropriate approach of the research? As
Reed (1998) suggests with regard to the environmental perspective of
sustainability: 'The appropriate question for main-stream investors is not: do
investors care about critical environmental events? Clearly they do. Nor is it:
do investors have to sacrifice returns in order to limit the universe of possible companies in which to invest to those with decent environmental
records? They do not. Nor is it: is there a statistical relationship between environmental and financial performance? There appears to be a positive one,
but the vast majority of equity money is managed using investment styles
that are not built primarily around statistical relationships. The meaningful
question today is: does an understanding of a company's environmental and
social strategies and positioning add a useful insight to what investors
already know about selecting stocks?'

In this sense, Feldman *et al.* (1996) take an existing model of valuation
and add environmental variables in order to see if they increase the
explanatory power of the model. They ask what we believe is the most appropriate question: what does environmental performance tell us that we do
not know about financial performance yet? The study concludes that both the
variables for environmental performance and the quality of the environmental management system add value to a model of risk for stocks.

Our contribution is thus based on the belief that it is necessary to adapt
existing tools and models of financial analysis in order to incorporate the
impact of sustainability issues on the economic and financial performance of
the company.

Some important advances have been already made in integrating sustainability considerations into the strategic and financial management of companies (for a review of concepts and instruments, see German Federal
Ministry for the Environment and Federation of German Industries 2002).
This integration has focused mainly on the environmental perspective, as this
was the first sustainable development dimension to attract the attention of
governments and business. Advances in the field of environmental and
ecological accounting (Bartolomeo *et al.* 2000; Bennett and James 1998,
1999; Burritt 1997; Burritt *et al.* 2002; EPA 1995; Gray *et al.* 1993;
Schaltegger 1996; Schaltegger and Burritt 2000; Schaltegger *et al.* 2000),
and the design of various instruments and tools of environmental and/or
sustainability management have only partially applied the language, knowledge and tools of corporate financial theory to the orientation of the

decision-making processes of the different economic agents when incorporating sustainability objectives.

In this sense, the absence of fundamental approaches to the incorporation of sustainable development considerations into the traditional financial analysis of the company is especially significant. This is not only a tool to assess a company's past financial performance but also its strengths and weaknesses for the future. The information that such analysis provides is critical for all the company's stakeholders when developing their decision-making processes.

Our aim is to provide companies with a methodology that allows them to focus on the environmental and social activities that generate significant financial and/or non-financial benefits and to integrate financial considerations into every major sustainable development decision, as well as to provide the financial community with appropriate decision-making tools and rules to be able to assess a company's sustainable management system and support its sustainability as well as its financial objectives.

2.1 Financial Analysis and Ratio Analysis

The financial analysis is the assessment of the company's past, present and future financial conditions in order to identify its financial strengths and weaknesses. Although it has been argued that it is focused on the past and its reliance on accounting measures has been criticised (Cohem 1994; Mattessich 1995), we believe that financial analysis provides the context of a company's current performance by showing where it is now and that it has an influence on its expectations by showing developments that will change future performance.

The aim of the financial analysis varies as a function of the strategic objective pursued:

- When the objective is to bring about a change in the company in order to develop a project, the financial analysis aims to identify the strategies and the internal development possibilities (i.e. value creation).
- When the objective is to solve the company's problems, the primary objective of the diagnostic will be to clarify the causes of the value destruction symptoms.

The financial analysis plays an important role in the achievement of either of these two objectives since the global character of the financial function allows it to deal with the main economic aspects of the company (commercial, productive, environmental, etc.) that affect, to a certain extent, the achievement of the main objective of maximising shareholder value.

Ratios (i.e. the mathematical relation between two quantities) are of major importance in financial analysis because they: inject a qualitative measurement; demonstrate in a precise manner the adequacy of a key item on a financial statement regarding another item; and provide comparisons between companies in the same industry as well as year-to-year comparisons within a single company. In this sense, it is generally assumed that financial ratio analysis can be developed under two perspectives (Marion 1999):

- **Diachronic perspective**—where it is necessary to collect information on the evolution in time of the essential variables of the diagnostic
- **Synchronic perspective**—where the value of the company's ratios is compared with the same figures for its sector in order to draw conclusions on each individual ratio and to determine whether the company's situation is good, standard or bad. Pyle and White (1974) argue that sector membership is the best base for comparisons.

Unfortunately, earlier attempts to relate important elements of financial statements through key financial ratios suffered from a lack of systematic application due to a lack of awareness of the main principle of cause and effect. Most analysts have essentially given equal weight and equal value to all ratios, simply creating a 'laundry list' of calculations with no indication of which ratios might be the most important. Ratios are not equal in importance. Some ratios lead and others follow, while some represent cause and some effect. Certain key factors are primary, causing changes in other important measures of a company's operating performance and basic financial structure.

Cause–effect ratio analysis derives from the following assumptions:

- The different ratios do not have the same importance for the analysis. Disregarding the sector membership factor, some key ratios are primary, driving changes in the rest of the relevant measures on the economic performance and financial structure of the company. Identifying the former as causes and the latter as effects is the best way of reflecting the different relative weight of each ratio.
- The analysis acts in an inductive manner: the immediately visible situation is the effect; the cause or causes must be searched.
- Understanding the meaning and significance of each individual ratio is not enough to ensure appropriate use of the ratio analysis. It is also not enough to simply develop it through diachronic and synchronic comparisons. The ratio analysis potential and its strategic value for financial analysis are based on two fundamental methodological principles: the breakdown of each ratio in its main components; and the definition of relationships between the different ratios.

2.2   Breaking Down Ratios: the DuPont Ratios Pyramid

The DuPont system (Figure 1) is used to dissect a company's financial statements and to assess its financial condition. It merges the income statement and the balance sheet into two summary measures of profitability, ROA (Return on Assets) and ROE (Return on Equity), which are broken down into other ratio figures as follows:

$$ROE = \frac{\text{Net Income}}{\text{Total Assets}} \times \frac{\text{Total Assets}}{\text{Common Equity}}$$

$$ROA = \frac{\text{Net Income}}{\text{Sales}} \times \frac{\text{Sales}}{\text{Total Assets}}$$

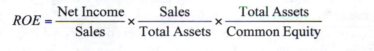

$$ROE = \frac{\text{Net Income}}{\text{Sales}} \times \frac{\text{Sales}}{\text{Total Assets}} \times \frac{\text{Total Assets}}{\text{Common Equity}}$$

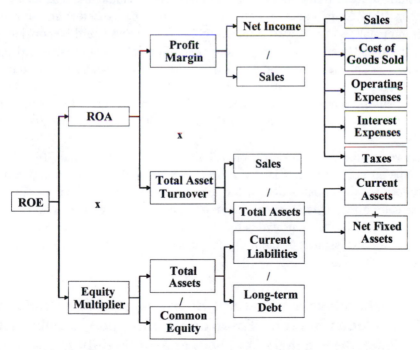

Figure 1. DuPont ratios pyramid

The main contributions of this approach to the financial analysis are that it helps to:
* Identify sources of strength and weakness in current performance
* Focus attention on value drivers

2.3   Defining Cause–Effect Relations: Balanced Scorecard/Sustainability Balanced Scorecard

The Balanced Scorecard (Kaplan and Norton 1992, 1996, 2001) is based on the establishment of cause–effect relationships between key strategic indicators through four perspectives of a company's management (financial, customer, learning and growth, and internal business processes) with the financial perspective as the endpoint. It aims to make the contribution and transformation of soft factors and intangible assets into long-term financial success explicit and thus controllable.

As long as sustainability issues fall frequently into this category of soft factors and intangible assets (Senn [1986] cited in Figge *et al.* 2002), several authors have suggested the application of the Balanced Scorecard approach to sustainability (Elkington 1997; Figge *et al.* 2002; Hahn and Wagner 2001; Johnson 1998; Schaltegger and Dyllick 2002) in order to select and develop environmental and social performance indicators, which could be considered in the balanced scorecard through their integration into the four standard perspectives or through the creation of an additional perspective (non-market perspective; Figge *et al.* 2002). A third possibility would be to formulate a specific environmental and/or social scorecard, but this should only be done after the development of one (or both) of the former variants (Figge *et al.* 2002).

However, the definition of a hierarchical chain of cause and effect relationships proposed in the balanced scorecard methodology lacks a systematic procedure for the construction of the leading and lagging indicators defined across categories. This is where financial analysis through cause and effect ratios, as defined above, provides the most valuable contribution to the management and assessment of the impact of sustainability issues on shareholder value.

2.4   Shareholder Value and Environmental Shareholder Value Concepts: Towards a Conceptual Framework for the Financial Analysis of Sustainability

The concept of shareholder value, coined by Rappaport (1986), was applied for the first time to the environmental field by Schaltegger and Figge (1997), who considered which forms of corporate environmental management can help to improve shareholder value or can destroy it. Subsequently, these authors proposed a complementary concept, the 'stakeholder value' (Figge and Schaltegger 2000), which focuses on who creates added value, how it is distributed, and to whom. Although the concept of stakeholder value is not a valuation method, the authors proposed a methodology to measure it in an effort to incorporate a perspective other than the shareholder perspective in the value-oriented management of a company according to the principles of sustainability.

Without rejecting the addition of a new perspective focused on other stakeholders, our model is based on the incorporation of sustainability issues into the traditional shareholder perspective. SustainAbility (2001) identified six financial drivers of the sustainable value creation: customer attraction; brand value and reputation; licence to operate; human and intellectual capital; innovation and risk profile. We have integrated these six value drivers into Rappaport's model of shareholder's added value to make the link between a company's environmental management and its capacity to create value more evident (Figure 2). This allows us to define the framework under which to develop our model of financial analysis of sustainability through cause and effect ratios.

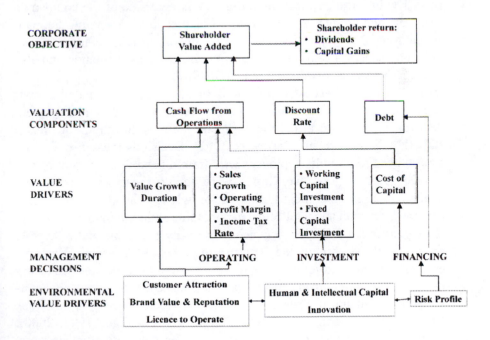

Figure 2. Conceptual model of financial analysis of sustainability

The six financial value drivers of sustainability can be seen as catalysts of the sustainability decision-making process of a company's management aimed at creating a sustainable shareholder value. These six indicators should drive those operating, investment and financing decisions that, ultimately, will result in a specific value of all the measures (ratios in our model) that explain the company's financial, environmental and social performance; the final result being some measure of the value created (shareholder value, share price, etc.). The six drivers (the definitions are taken from SustainAbility's *The Business Case* programme) do not only influence decisions individually but also as a consequence of their interrelations. Their influence on sustainability decision-making can be depicted as follows:

- **Customer attraction** is defined as the company's ability to attract and retain customers through interesting products, attractive brands, a strong reputation, customer service and/or particular corporate activities. Its influence on management decisions from a sustainability perspective will require the evaluation of issues such as product features and composition (operating decisions) and will also require being aware of its impact over the company's capacity to sustain its growth (Boiral and Joly 1992; Ottman 1998).

- **Brand value and reputation** is defined as the value of the company's corporate and product brands. From a sustainability viewpoint, the management needs to recognise that every decision made (operating, investment or financing) could inflict lasting damage on its reputation and also endanger its value growth duration (ABI 2001).

- **Human and intellectual capital** is defined as the accumulated knowledge and skill set of a company's employees. Again, every management decision made could affect the company's ability to attract and retain staff (Hardjono and van Marrewijk 2001). Decisions must also account for the need to provide employees with training and development opportunities and a good working environment; these are investment decisions. It is also important to acknowledge the importance of a company's human and intellectual capital in its ability to innovate.

- **Risk profile** is the degree to which a company's tangible and intangible assets are at risk through the exposure to potential 'disasters' or gradual erosion due to long-term decline. It will directly affect the financing decisions of the company to the extent that the financial system internalising sustainability risks by affecting the credit concession decisions (ABI 2001; Feldman *et al.* 1996; Schaltegger and Figge 1997, 2000). Decisions on operating and investment issues must pre-empt negative events and minimise the damage if such events occur by focusing on the expected or pursued performance of the other five drivers.

- **Innovation** is defined as a company's ability to maintain competitive advantage by regularly designing and delivering new and improved products, services and business models. There is a relationship between the regulatory enforcement of environmental and social corporate responsibility and companies innovation activities (Bhatnagar and Cohen 1998; Gabel and Sinclair-Desgagné 2001; Porter 1991; Porter and van der Linde 1995; Sinclair-Desgagné 1999). Investment decisions will be depend directly on the company's innovation policy and innovation can provide companies with better approaches to sustainability (economically, socially and environmentally speaking).
- The **licence to operate** is the level of acceptance of the company by its stakeholders. The company must ensure that its operating, investment and financial decisions do not endanger its licence to operate, as well as shaping this licence through those decisions (Arnold and Day 1998). The company's licence to operate has an obvious link with its value growth duration.

This conceptual framework links management decision-making with the simultaneous achievement of financial and sustainability objectives through six financial value drivers of sustainability. Using this framework, we have developed a model of financial analysis based on the definition of cause–effect relations between ratios that reflect the company's financial, environmental and social performance.

2.5 Model of Financial Analysis of Sustainability

Our model, called Model of Financial Analysis of Sustainability, suggests a number of conceptual relationships between some significant ratios reflecting the financial as well as the environmental and social performances of a company, linked by means of mathematical expressions (multiplying or dividing ratios). The relations defined are therefore far from subjective. In Figure 3, we focus on the analysis of those financial and environmental performances that are the most easily quantifiable. The inclusion of qualitative measures proves difficult in our model as defined (it is based on mathematical relations between ratios), but we recognise that these qualitative factors should be considered as many of them exert a significant influence over those mathematical relations. Nevertheless, the final aim of the model is to translate all those factors into quantitative measures. For example, the company's value growth duration, which has some subjective and qualitative character, is transformed into a quantitative measure by making it dependent on the sector rate of growth, the company's market share goals and its growth capacity (measured as the profit that has not been distributed in dividends to shareholders).

Following the claims that signalled the importance of using both monetary and physical information (Burritt *et al.* 2002), embraced under the concept of eco-efficiency (Schaltegger and Sturm 1990, 1994, 1996; Schaltegger and Burritt 2000), some ratios are formed on the base of the data that could be taken from sources such as eco-balances, environmental profit/loss accounts and internal/cost/environmental accounting systems.

Obviously, the list of ratios that could be created is almost infinite. It is therefore necessary to identify, in each particular case, which are the most relevant, which will depend on variables such as sector/subsector membership, company size, etc.

The result of identifying the relevant ratios and defining the relationships between them can be modelled in the form of a pyramid similar to that of the DuPont methodology. In this model (Figure 3), the main causes that deliver the results (shown at the top) can be found at the base, being the final effect ratio, the price per share, which is directly dependent on the ROE, the cost of equity capital and the rate of future growth. Figure 3 merely shows part of the model.

As an example of how this methodology can improve the financial analysis by considering environmental issues, we will look at the implications of the analysis on a particular ratio, the sales/fixed assets ratio. From a traditional perspective, when the value of this ratio is high, it is believed to reflect the efficient use of the capital invested in the company's site and the likely reduction of the financial leverage of the company's capital structure (owing to the improved ROA, which would lead to a higher profit that would allow the reduction of total liabilities). This line of thought would imply following the path drawn in Figure 4 on our model.

But if we assume that the company's management is delaying the adoption of a new cleaner technology and that this is why the value of the sales/fixed assets ratio is so high, we can conclude that this is not good from an environmental perspective. Although the financial result is good, it is not accompanied by good environmental performance. But how can we detect this situation if we only follow the path we have just described? It is necessary to broaden the analysis, taking into account other areas of the company's management and analysing in depth the cause–effect chain to identify other signals of the real environmental (and financial?) situation of the company.

From a theoretical point of view: what could be the expected result of not updating or removing the dirty technology? More emissions (both in kg and euros)? More waste? More fines?

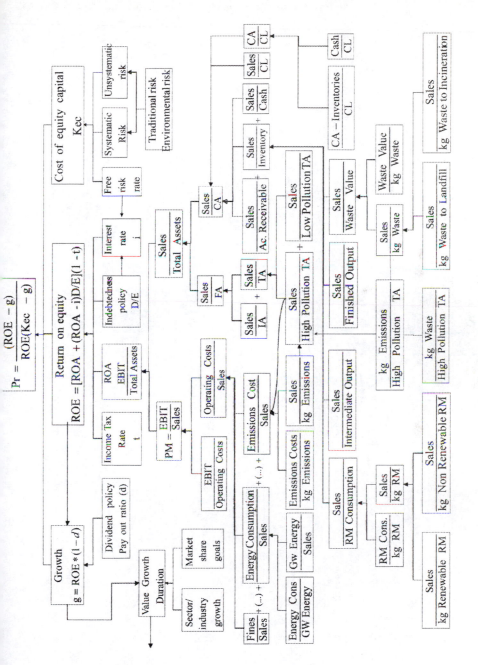

Figure 3. Model of financial analysis of sustainability

CA = Current Assets; CL = Current Liabilities; D = Debt; d = Payout Ratio; E = Equity; EBIT = Earnings before Interest and Tax; FA = Fixed Assets; g = Growth; i = Interest Rate (cost of debt); IA = Intangible Assets; Kec = Cost of Equity Capital; PM = Profit Margin; RM = Raw Materials; ROA = Return on Assets; ROE = Return on Equity; t = Income Tax Rate; TA = Tangible Assets

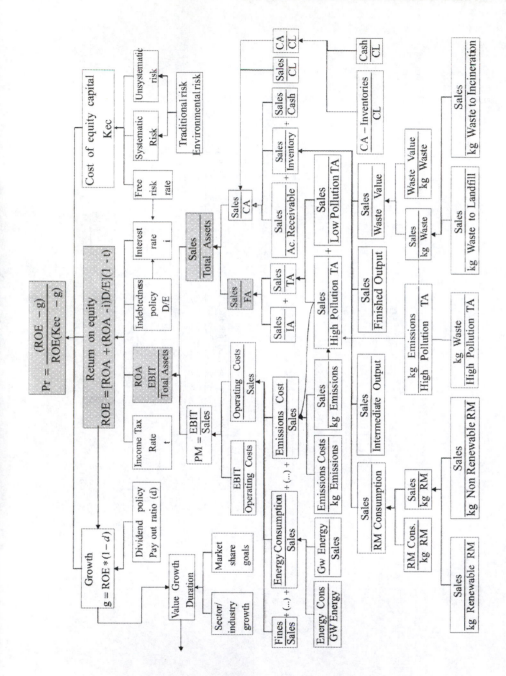

Figure 4. Top-focused financial analysis of sustainability

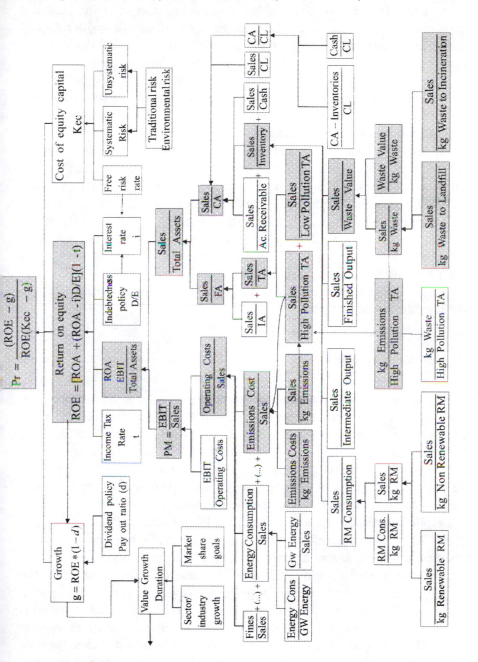

Figure 5. Extended financial analysis of sustainability

The analysis of ratios such as sales/waste value, cost of emissions/sales, environmental fines/sales, etc. can add valuable information to the financial ratio analysis. Although a high sales/fixed assets ratio may be signalling an improved ROA and ROE, other ratios may be signalling the opposite. A high cost of emissions/sales ratio and/or a high environmental fines/sales ratio will limit profit generation and a low sales/waste value ratio will reduce the sales/current assets ratio, thus compensating for the high value initially found for the sales/fixed assets ratio.

The company's manager could have to explain to its shareholders that the increment in the sales/fixed assets ratio has been compensated by the reduction of the sales/current assets ratio in such a way that the ratio sales/total assets remains unchanged and does not affect the ROA, while the profit margin has fallen such that the final impact is a reduction of the ROA. Furthermore, the possible damage to the company's image would reduce its sales, cause the loss of market share and limit its potential for growth, all with a final impact on the share price (Pr).

In this way, we have expanded the analysis to look for causes at the bottom of the pyramid (Figure 5).

3.   SUMMARY

Once it became evident that the financial objective of maximising share-holder value cannot be considered alone and that companies and financial markets need to embrace sustainability principles in order to achieve that objective, managerial theory started to integrate sustainability issues into its different areas (accounting, finance, marketing, etc.) and to develop tools and instruments and adapt existing ones to allow the strategic management of sustainability by companies and the capital markets.

Despite the frequent criticisms regarding the reliance of financial analysis on past and accounting information, it has traditionally been considered an appropriate tool to assess a company's financial and economic situation. Thus it could also provide valuable information when analysing the company's environmental and social performance and their relationship with financial performance. The use of ratio analysis and cause–effect rationale is a valid alternative for the development of the financial analysis of sustainability. They allow the identification of sustainability activities that generate significant financial and/or non-financial benefits and provide the financial community with an appropriate decision-making tool to evaluate a company's sustainable management system and the impact of sustainability issues on its financial performance.

As long as environmental reporting becomes the norm and not the exception and the availability of information is no longer an obstacle for the strategic management of sustainability and its integration into the decision-making processes of companies and financial markets, the model of financial analysis of sustainability presented in this chapter will help to uncover a company's true financial, environmental and social situation. This will result in better decisions and contribute to the simultaneous achievement of financial and sustainability objectives.

REFERENCES

ABI (Association of British Insurers) (2001): *Investing in Social Responsibility. Risk and Opportunities*. London: Association of British Insurers.

Arnold, M.B. and Day, R.M. (1998): *The Next Bottom Line. Making Sustainable Development Tangible*. Washington D.C.: WRI Reports.

Bartolomeo, M., Bennett, M., Bouma, J.J., Heydkamp, P., James, P. and Wolters, T. (2000): 'Environmental Management in Europe: Current Practice and Further Potential', *The European Accounting Review* Vol. 9, No. 1, 31-52.

Bennett, M. and James, P. (1998): 'The Green Bottom Line', in: Bennett, M. and James, P. (Eds.): *The Green Bottom Line: Environmental Accounting for Management, Current Practice and Future Trends*. Sheffield: Greenleaf Publishing, 30-60.

Bennett, M. and James, P. (1999): 'Key Themes in Environmental, Social and Sustainability Performance Evaluation and Reporting', in: Bennett, M. and James, P. (Eds.): *Sustainable Measures: Evaluation and Reporting of Environmental and Social Performance*. Sheffield: Greenleaf Publishing, 29-74.

Bhatnagar, S. and Cohen, M.A. (1998): *The Impact of Environmental Regulation on Innovation: A Panel Data Study*. Nashville: Vanderbilt Center of Environmental Management Studies.

Boiral, O. and Jolly, D. (1992): 'Stratégie, Compétitivité et Ecologie', *Revue Française de Gestion* June/July, 80-95.

Burritt, R.L. (1997): 'Corporate Environmental Performance Indicators: Cost Allocation—Boon or Bane?', *Greener Management International* Vol. 17, Spring, 89-100.

Burritt, R.L., Hahn, T. and Schaltegger, S. (2002): 'Towards a Comprehensive Framework for Environmental Management Accounting—Links Between Business Actors and Environmental Management Accounting Tools', *Australian Accounting Review* Vol. 12, No. 2, 39-50.

Cohem, E. (1994): *Analyse Financière*. Paris: Collection Gestion.

Copeland, T., Koller, T. and Murrin, J. (1993): *Valuation. Measuring and Managing the Value of Companies*. New York: Wiley.

Damodaran, A. (2001): *Corporate Finance: Theory and Practice* (2nd edition). New York: Wiley.

Elkington, J. (1997): *Cannibals with Forks: The Triple Bottom Line of 21st Century Business*. Oxford: Capstone Publishing.

EPA (US Environmental Protection Agency) (1995): *Introduction to Environmental Accounting*. Washington DC: EPA.

Feldman, S.J., Soyka, P.A. and Ameer, P. (1996): *Does Improving a Firm's Environmental Management System and Environmental Performance Result in a Higher Stock Price?* (Working Paper). Fairfax: ICF Kaiser International.

Figge, F., Hahn, T., Schaltegger, S. and Wagner, M. (2002): 'The Sustainability Balanced Scorecard—Linking Sustainability Management to Business Strategy', *Business Strategy and the Environment* No. 11, 269-284.

Figge, F. and Schaltegger, S. (2000): *What is 'Stakeholder Value'?. Developing a Catch-phrase into a Benchmarking Tool.* Lüneburg: University of Lüneburg/Bank Pictet in association with UNEP.

Gabel, L.H. and Sinclair-Desgagné, B. (2001): 'The Firm, its Procedures and Win-Win Environmental Regulations', in: Folmer, H., Gabel, L.H., Gerkin, S. and Rose, A. (Eds.): *Frontiers of Environmental Economics.* Cheltenham: Edward Elgar, 148-175.

German Federal Ministry for the Environment and Federation of German Industries (Eds.) (2002): *Sustainability Management in Business Enterprises. Concepts and Instruments for Sustainable Development.* Lüneburg: Centre for Sustainability Management.

Gray, R.H., Bebbington, J. and Walters, D. (1993): *Accounting for the Environment.* London: Chapman Publishing.

Griffin, J. and Mahon, J. (1997): 'The Corporate Social Performance and Corporate Financial Performance Debate: Twenty Five Years of Incomparable Research', *Business and Society* Vol. 36, No. 1, 5-31.

Hahn, T. and Wagner, M. (2001): *Sustainability Balanced Scorecard. Von der Theorie zur Umsetzung.* Lüneburg: Centre for Sustainability Management.

Hardjono, T.W. and Marrewijk, M. van (2001): 'The Social Dimensions of Business Excellence', *Corporate Environmental Strategy* Vol. 8, No. 3, 223-233.

Hill, W. (1985): 'Betriebswirtschaftslehre als Managementlehre', in: Wunderer, R. (Ed.): *Betriebswirtschaftslehre als Management- und Führungslehre.* Stuttgart: Schäffer-Poeschel, 111-146.

Johnson, S.D. (1998): 'Identification and Selection of Environmental Performance Indicators. Application of the Balanced Scorecard Approach', *Corporate Environmental Strategy* Vol. 5, No. 4, 34-41.

Kaplan, R. and Norton, D. (1992): 'The Balanced Scorecard- Measures that Drive Performance', *Harvard Business Review* January/February, 71-79.

Kaplan, R. and Norton, D. (1996): *The Balanced Scorecard: Translating Strategies into Action.* Boston: Harvard Business School Press.

Kaplan, R. and Norton, D. (2001): *The Strategy-Focused Organisation: How Balanced Scorecard Companies Thrive in the New Business Environment.* Boston: Harvard Boston School Press.

Marion, A. (1999): *Le Diagnostic d'Entreprise, Méthode et Processus.* Paris: Economica.

Mattessich, R. (1995): *Critique of Accounting; Examination of the Foundation and Normative Structure of an Applied Discipline.* London: Quorum Books.

Ottman, J.A. (1998): 'Five Strategies for Business Reinvention: The Development of Sustainable Products', *Corporate Environmental Strategy* Vol. 5, No. 5, 81-89.

Pava, M. and Krausz, J. (1996): 'The Association between Corporate Social- Responsibility and Financial Performance: the Paradox of Social Cost', *Journal of Business Ethics* Vol. 15, 321-357.

Porter, M. (1991): 'America's Green Strategy', *Scientific American* Vol. 264, No. 4, 96.

Porter, M. and Linde, C. van der (1995): 'Green and Competitive: Ending the Stalemate', *Harvard Business Review* Vol. 73, No. 5, 120-33.

Pyle, W.W. and White, J.A. (1974): *Fundamental Accounting Principles* (6th edition). Homewood: Irwin.

Rappaport, A. (1986): *Creating Shareholder Value. The New Standard for Business Performance.* New York: The Free Press.

Rappaport, A. (1998): *Creating Shareholder Value: A Guide For Managers and Investors.* New York: The Free Press.

Reed, D.J. (1998): *Green Shareholder Value, Hype or Hit?* Washington DC: World Resources Institute.

Schaltegger, S. (1996): *Corporate Environmental Accounting.* London: Wiley.

Schaltegger, S. (1999): 'Öko-Effizienz als Element des sozio-ökonomisch vernünftigen Umweltmanagements. Ein Kriterium unter vielen', *Ökologisch Wirtschaften* No. 3, 12-14.

Schaltegger, S. and Burritt, R.L. (2000): *Contemporary Environmental Accounting.* Sheffield: Greenleaf Publishing.

Schaltegger, S. and Dyllick, T. (Eds.) (2002): *Nachhaltig managen mit der Balanced Scorecard.* Wiesbaden: Gabler.

Schaltegger, S. and Figge, F. (1997): *Environmental Shareholder Value* (WWZ/Sarasin Basic Research Study No. 54). Basel: WWZ.

Schaltegger, S. and Figge, F. (2000): 'Environmental Shareholder Value: Economic Success with Corporate Environmental Management', *Eco-Management and Auditing* Vol. 7, No. 1, 29-42.

Schaltegger, S., Hahn, T. and Burritt, R.L. (2000): *Environmental Management Accounting. Overview and Main Approaches.* Lüneburg: Centre for Sustainability Management.

Schaltegger, S. and Sturm, A. (1990): 'Ökologische Rationalität', *Die Unternehmung* No. 4, 272-290.

Schaltegger, S. and Sturm, A. (1994): *Ökologieorientierte Entscheidungen in Unternehmen* (2nd edition). Bern/Stuttgart: Haupt Verlag.

Schaltegger, S. and Sturm, A. (1996): *Eco-Efficiency through Eco-Controlling. For the Implementation of EMAS and ISO 14001* (2nd edition). Zurich: vdf.

Schaltegger, S. and Synnestvedt, T. (2002): 'The Link between 'Green' and Economic Success. Environmental Management as the Crucial Trigger between Environmental and Economic Performance', *Journal of Environmental Management* Vol. 65, No. 4, 339-346.

Senn, J.F. (1986): *Ökologieorientierte Unternehmensführung: theoretische Grundlagen, empirische Fallanalysen und mögliche Basisstrategien.* Frankfurt a. M.: Lang.

Simon, H.A. (1982): *Models of Bounded Rationality.* Cambridge: MIT Press.

Sinclair-Desgagné, B. (1999): *Remarks on Environmental Regulation, Firm Behaviour and Innovation* (Scientific Series 99s-20, May). Montreal: Cirano.

SustainAbility (2001): *Buried Treasure. Uncovering the Business Case for Corporate Sustainability.* London: SustainAbility Ltd.

Wagner, M. (2001): *A Review of Empirical Studies Concerning the Relationship between Environmental and Economic Performance.* Lüneburg: Centre for Sustainability Management.

Wagner, M. (2003): *An Analysis of the Relationship between Environmental and Economic Performance at the Firm Level and the Influence of Corporate Environmental Strategy Choice* (PhD Thesis). Lüneburg: University of Lüneburg.

Zadek, S. (2000): *Doing Good and Doing Well: Making the Business Case for Corporate Citizenship.* New York: Conference Board.

SUSTAINABLE VALUE ADDED
A New Approach to Measuring Corporate Sustainable Performance

Frank Figge[1] and Tobias Hahn[2]
[1]School of the Environment, University of Leeds, UK,
[2]Institute for Futures Studies and Technology Assessment, IZT, Germany

Abstract: Only companies that contribute positively to all three pillars of sustainability
at the same time contribute to sustainability. Companies will, however, only
exceptionally contribute simultaneously to all three dimensions. There is usually some kind of trade-off and contributions to sustainability are thus quite
difficult to assess in practice. There is a quasi-unlimited number of environmental and social impacts. In practice, companies will always have a better
performance with respect to some impacts and a worse performance with
respect to others. Drawing on the technique developed by Modigliani and
Modigliani (1997) for the financial markets, this chapter shows how different
environmental and social impacts and economic performance can be aggregated. Unlike existing assessments, it does not fall back on external costs that
are impossible to determine in practice. It determines, in a similar way to the
pricing of risk in the financial markets, the cost of environmental and social
impacts via opportunity costs. Sustainable Value Added takes into account
both eco- and social- efficiency and effectiveness, and expresses in monetary
terms by how much a company contributed to more sustainability. Sustainable
Value Added thus provides a shift in focus from a cost-based to a value-based
assessment of corporate contributions to sustainability.

1.   INTRODUCTION

The assessment of the sustainable performance of companies has experienced increasing attention in academic literature and practice in recent years. Based on different perceptions of the concept of sustainability (weak vs. strong sustainability) at the macro level (e.g. Harte 1995; Norton and Toman 1997; Pearce *et al.* 1989; Stern 1997), corporate contributions to sustainability focus on the micro level of economic activity. On the one hand, the assessment of corporate sustainable performance by taking into account the external effects of private economic activities has been proposed in the literature (Atkinson 2000; Huizing and Dekker 1992). These authors argue, that to assess the sustainable performance of companies, value added figures have to be corrected by the external costs induced by a company. While being theoretically sound, however, such absolute measures suffer from the problems that accompany the monetarisation of external environmental and social effects (see, for example: Rees and Wackernagel 1999; Steer and Lutz 1994). On the other hand, relative measures to assess corporate sustainable performance have been proposed (e.g. Schaltegger and Burritt 2000; Schaltegger and Sturm 1990). Such relative measures of eco-efficiency relate the value added of a company (in monetary terms) to the environmental damage caused by these activities (in physical terms). From a viewpoint of sustainability, however, the major shortcoming of eco- and social efficiency considerations is that they do not take eco- and social effectiveness, i.e. absolute changes of the environmental and social burden, into account (for eco-effectiveness, see, for example, Ullmann 2001).

In this chapter, we propose Sustainable Value Added as a new approach for the assessment of corporate sustainable performance, which overcomes the shortcomings of existing measures. Taking an opportunity cost perspective makes it possible to elude the problems associated with monetarisation of external effects. Unlike existing measures, eco- and social effectiveness is considered. In addition, Sustainable Value Added represents an integrated measure, which allows the expression of corporate sustainable performance in a single unit.

The remainder of this chapter is organised as follows. Section 2 introduces the concept of Environmental Value Added, on which Sustainable Value Added is built. In Sections 3 and 4, Sustainable Value Added is introduced and developed for the single and multiple impacts case, respectively. In Section 5, we discuss the main findings and further implications of the new concept before drawing conclusions in Section 6.

2. THE CONCEPT OF ENVIRONMENTAL VALUE ADDED

Eco-efficiency indicators are very popular today for the measurement of corporate environmental performance. However, one problem with eco-efficiency indicators is that they are expressed in synthetic units such as € per carbon dioxide (CO_2). Therefore, this chapter introduces the concept of Environmental Value Added (Figge 2001)—a concept that expresses the eco-efficiency of a company in comparison with a benchmark in absolute monetary terms.

The notion of efficiency is not new in economics. Efficiency considerations are used whenever desired and undesired aspects need to be balanced. A good example is risk–return considerations in financial management. It is usually assumed that investors like return and dislike risk. When they decide where to invest, investors therefore take two aspects into account—risk and return. There are a number of ratios that are used to describe the relation of risk to return. The best known ratios are those proposed by Sharpe (1966), Jensen (1968) and Treynor (1965).

There are a number of difficulties associated with the use of risk return ratios. In response to these difficulties, Modigliani and Modigliani (1997) proposed a new risk–return measure. This new measure expresses the relation between risk and return in a monetary unit and thus facilitates its interpretation. As shown by Figge (2001), eco-efficiency can be measured in a similar way.

Environmental Value Added corresponds to the economic value that is created by a level of eco-efficiency above the benchmark level. Environmental Value Added measures are therefore analogous to Economic Value Added (Stewart 1991)—the economic value of an eco-sur-efficiency.

The Environmental Value Added concept is easy to depict graphically (Figure 1). The slopes of the two lines through points A and B reflect the eco-efficiency of the company (line through point A) and the benchmark (point B). The steeper the slope the more value is created per environmental impact added. Therefore, a steeper slope reflects a higher level of eco-efficiency. In the example depicted in Figure 1, the company has a higher eco-efficiency than the benchmark (Clift and Wright [2000] compare the eco-efficiency of economic activities to a benchmark in order to arrive at a dimensionless indicator that expresses whether the economic activities are more or less eco-efficient than the benchmark chosen). At the eco-efficiency of the benchmark, 5 € can be produced with 10 units of environmental impacts. In contrast, the company generates 10 € with the same amount of environmental impacts. It generates therefore an Environmental Value Added of 5 € (line AC).

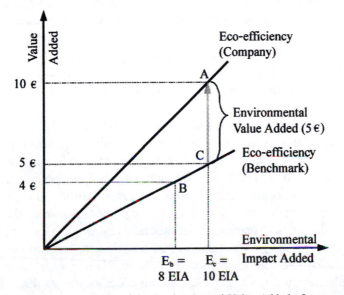

Figure 1. Graphical representation of the Environmental Value Added of a example company (Source: Figge 2001).

More technically, Environmental Value Added (EnVA) can be expressed as the product of the value spread and the level of resource use (Figge 2001). This gives the following:

EnVA = (Eco-efficiency~company~ − Eco-efficiency~benchmark~) × Environmental
impact added~company~.

More formally, this translates to:

$$EnVA = \left(\frac{VA_c}{EIA_c} - \frac{VA_b}{EIA_b} \right) \cdot EIA_c \qquad (1)$$

where VA_c and VA_b are the value added and EIA_c and EIA_b the environmental impact added of the company and the benchmark, respectively.

To analyse the social dimension of corporate contributions to sustainability, we propose to define social performance, in analogy to environmental performance, via social 'bads'. Thus, social efficiency is used here in a similar way to the concept of eco-efficiency (Callens and Tyteca 1999). Consequently, we define social performance via social impacts. Less social impacts are preferred to more social impacts, i.e. the less social impacts the higher social performance. Social Value Added (SoVA) can then be calculated analogously to Environmental Value Added.

Economic activity leads to a wide range of environmental and social impacts. Environmental or Social Value Added can be calculated for every single environmental or social impact, respectively. As a result, a range of EnVAs and SoVAs is obtained, reflecting every relevant environmental and social impact of a company (e.g. a greenhouse potential EnVA, an ozone-depleting potential EnVA, as well as a work accidents SoVA or an unpaid overtime SoVA).

The Environmental Value Added concept provides the basis for Sustainable Value Added (SusVA). It serves to introduce a relative perspective because it assesses the eco-efficiency of a company compared with a benchmark. By doing so, it introduces an opportunity cost perspective to the assessment of corporate contributions to sustainability. The EnVA (or SoVA) indicates the extra value that is gained or lost due to the use of a given amount of environmental (or social) resources in a company in comparison to its use in a benchmark. In addition, it helps to convert eco-efficiency ratios into meaningful monetary terms. However, as shown above, it is not sufficient to look at eco- and social efficiency to evaluate corporate contributions to sustainability. Instead, effectiveness aspects have to be taken into account. This will be done in the following sections by introducing Sustainable Value Added.

3.   THE SINGLE IMPACT CASE

Based on the discussion of Environmental Value Added, we now introduce Sustainable Value Added as a new approach to measure corporate contributions to sustainability that includes both efficiency and effectiveness considerations. In this section, we develop the derivation of Sustainable Value Added for a single impact case, i.e. in order to keep the argument understandable, we consider only eco-efficiency, economic and environmental effectiveness for the time being, and reduce eco-effectiveness to one environmental impact. In Section 4, this will be extended to the more realistic situation of multiple environmental and social impacts.

3.1   Changes in Efficiency and Effectiveness

As noted above, an increase in eco-efficiency can lead to decreasing eco-effectiveness. A company that is more eco-efficient might, for example, increase its competitiveness, which in turn might result in a higher demand and eventually in an increased consumption of resources. In other words, the improvements in eco-efficiency might be over-compensated by a growth effect (e.g. Dyllick and Hockerts 2002). This effect is illustrated in Figure 2, where we compare the company's change in eco-efficiency between the two periods t_0 and t_1. In addition, the absolute changes in economic and environmental performance (effectiveness) are taken into consideration.

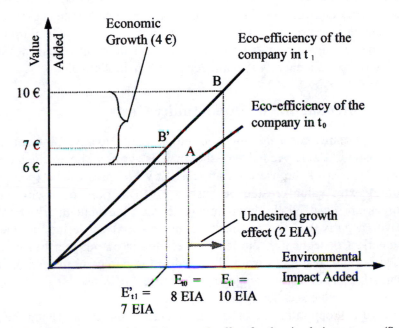

Figure 2. Graphical representation of the growth effect for the simple impact case (Source: Figge and Hahn 2002)

The company in Figure 2 used 8 EIA in t_0 to create 6 € Value Added (point A in Figure 2). Thus, the eco-efficiency of the company in t_0 is 0.75 €/EIA. In t_1, the economic output of the company increased to 10 € Value Added using 10 EIA (point B in Figure 2). This translates into an eco-efficiency of 1 €/EIA. in t_1. To find out if the company contributed to more sustainability during the period under observation, it is necessary to compare the performance of t_1 to the performance of t_0. The eco-efficiency of the company improved between t_0 and t_1. With the improved eco-efficiency, the company created a Value Added of 10 € in t_1, which translates in a change in economic output (economic growth) of +4 € (see Figure 2). However, the absolute level of environmental impacts added also rose between t_0 and t_1. Despite the increase of eco-efficiency, the company used 2 EIA more (undesired growth effect) than in the period before (line $E_{t0}E_{t1}$ in Figure 2). Economic growth has therefore overcompensated for the increase in eco-efficiency. Eco-effectiveness has decreased, which can be interpreted as an undesired (environmental) growth effect.

This assessment procedure can be generalised. To assess corporate contributions to sustainability during a period, changes in eco-efficiency and changes in economic and eco-effectiveness must be considered. If economic, environmental and social performances attain at least the level of the preceding period, strong contributions to sustainability are achieved. In Figure 2, environmental performance deteriorates because the eco-efficiency improvement is overcompensated for by economic growth. Thus, up to this point, one would be tempted to conclude that there has been no strong contribution to sustainability (Schaltegger and Burritt 2000:53).

3.2   Introduction of Opportunity Costs

So far, opportunity costs are not taken into account. However, the concept of Environmental Value Added has shown it is worthwhile to consider the opportunity cost of the use of resources. EnVA expresses the (positive or negative) extra value created because a given amount of environmental resources are used by the company instead of the benchmark. EnVA is positive (negative) if the company is more (less) eco-efficient than the benchmark. Consequently, the level of economic output that has not been realised because resources were allocated to the company instead of to the benchmark represents the foregone value of resource use by the company. This foregone value is called opportunity cost.

In Figure 3, opportunity costs are introduced to the graph. Using the same example as before, opportunity cost is added as the eco-efficiency of the benchmark, which is given by the line EE$_b$. In the example, the eco-efficiency of the benchmark is 0.5 €/EIA. The choice of benchmark depends on the desired significance of EnVA. In the context of corporate contributions to sustainability, the most obvious question to answer is whether a company has contributed to the sustainability of the national economy during the period of time under observation. Therefore, we propose to choose the national economy as a benchmark. Consequently, EE$_b$ indicates the eco-efficiency of the national economy, which is given by the ratio between the gross domestic product (GDP) and the environmental impacts created by all entities of that economy.

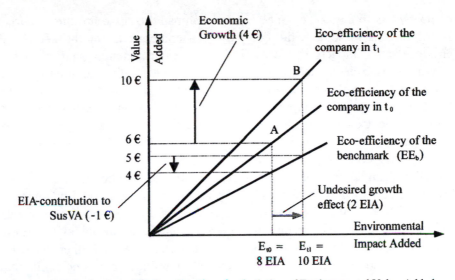

Figure 3. Introduction of the benchmark and calculation of Environmental Value Added

3.3 Calculation of Sustainable Value Added for the Single Impact Case

As shown in Section 3.1, improvements in eco-efficiency may not be sufficient for strong corporate contributions to sustainability. Eco- (and social) effectiveness must also be considered. In the example above, the improvement of corporate eco-efficiency has been over-compensated by economic growth, causing an undesired deterioration of the company's environmental performance. However, taking the opportunity cost perspective into account allows the question to be answered of whether it was more sustainable that the company used the additional resources instead of someone else, or not. This is expressed by Sustainable Value Added. We now show in detail how Sustainable Value Added can be explained and calculated for the single impact case.

The eco-efficiency of the benchmark indicates how efficiently the national economy uses an environmental resource. To become more sustainable at a national level, resources should be allocated to those companies that are more eco-efficient. This can hold true even if eco-efficiency and, thus the eco-effectiveness of the company, deteriorate during the period under observation.

If we assume that companies use environmental (and social) resources to create value, other less efficient companies will agree to sell a resource if selling the resource creates more value than using it. Since eco-efficiency shows how much value is created per EIA, it also corresponds to the price a company has to pay to convince another company to 'give up' the resource. Based on this reasoning, the company can compensate for the additional environmental impacts it causes by buying environmental (and/or social) resources from benchmark companies. The price for this compensation is given by the eco- (or social-) efficiency of the benchmark, which we have previously identified as opportunity cost. (We will assume that the eco- (and social-) efficiency of the benchmark does not change during the period under observation. This assumption is realistic if we consider a short period of time and if many companies make up the benchmark. The concept could also consider changing eco- and social efficiency by the benchmark. This would, however, complicate the reasoning without providing additional insights). It is crucial to note that, in this context, compensation does not mean paying victims of external effects to make them accept these impacts as it does in approaches that rely on monetarisation of external effects. Rather, it means paying the companies of the benchmark to reduce their environmental (and/or social) impacts to the extent to which the company has caused a deterioration of its environmental (and/or social) performance. In other words, compensation here means paying the companies of the benchmark for giving up some of the resources they would otherwise use. As a result, the total level of impacts is unchanged.

To find out if the company can pay for the compensation of any additional environmental impact it has caused, it is necessary to compare the additional funds at its disposal (= economic growth) to the cost (=price × quantity) of the additional environmental impacts. The price per EIA, as explained above, corresponds to the eco-efficiency of the benchmark. The quantity equates to the additional environmental impacts caused. The company can afford to pay the compensation of a deteriorated environmental performance as long as economic growth at least equals the cost of compensation. More formally, this condition is expressed as follows:

$$VA_{t1} - VA_{t0} \geq EE_b \cdot (EIA_{t1} - EIA_{t0}) \qquad (2)$$

It follows that, for the single impact case, Sustainable Value Added is created if additional value has been created after negative changes in eco-effectiveness have been compensated for. Sustainable Value Added for the single impact case therefore equals economic growth minus the cost of compensation. This is expressed by the following formula:

$$\text{SusVA}_{si} = EG - EE_b \cdot (EIA_{t1} - EIA_{t0}) \qquad (3)$$

where SusVA_{si} is the Sustainable Value Added for the single impact case, EE_b is the eco-efficiency of the benchmark, $EG = VA_{t1} - VA_{t0}$ representing economic growth, and $EIA_{t1} - EIA_{t0}$ the additional environmental impacts that need to be compensated for. For the example depicted in Figures 2 and 3, $SusVA_{si}$ results in 4 € – 0.5 €/EIA (10 EIA – 8 EIA) = 3 €. This result is also shown graphically (Figure 3). Economic growth results in two additional EIA ($EIA_{t1} - EIA_{t0}$), which have to be compensated for. The cost of compensation depends on the value created by the benchmark per EIA, i.e. on the eco-efficiency of the benchmark. The segment between the two cross sections of E_{t0} and E_{t1} with line EE_b reflects the cost of compensation. This segment corresponds to 1 € in our example. In general, the cost of compensation for additional EIA can be seen as the EIA-contribution to Sustainable Value Added. It is negative (–1 €) in our example.

So far, we have considered the case where an improvement in corporate eco-efficiency from t_0 to t_1 was overcompensated for by economic growth and environmental effectiveness thus deteriorated. In this context, Sustainable Value Added indicates whether economic growth has created enough scope to compensate the undesired growth effect in eco-effectiveness through buying environmental impacts added from benchmark companies. In this example, part of the economic growth must therefore be given up. In order to generalise the argument further, it is necessary to look at the case where there are both improved eco-efficiency and economic growth, but where economic growth has not led to an undesired growth effect in terms of additional environmental impacts. For this purpose, consider point 'B' in Figure 2. With the same performance level in t_0 and the same improvement of the eco-efficiency as previously in t_1, the company now grows only from 6 € in t_0 to 7 € Value Added in t_1. As a result, environmental impacts reduce from 8 EIA in t_0 to 7 EIA in t_1. Thus, economic effectiveness still improves (+1 €, though to a lesser degree) and environmental effectiveness now also improves (–1 EIA). Corporate effectiveness improves in all dimensions. Therefore, no compensation is necessary to achieve a strong contribution to sustainability. In other words, there is no need to buy any environmental impact added from benchmark companies to ensure that the overall level of resource consumption is maintained. But since we want to find out how economic effectiveness changes when eco-effectiveness remains unchanged, the 1 EIA saved are now valued at their opportunity cost. This corresponds to the revenue the company would obtain if it decided to 'sell' to benchmark companies the EIA it no longer needs. The term that constituted a cost above now becomes a revenue. In this case, therefore, the Sustainable Value Added single impact ($SusVA_{si}$) of the company exceeds its economic growth by the value the benchmark companies create with the environmental resources saved by the company under investigation. The company now has a second source of revenue. Equation (3) still holds true for this case. $SusVA_{si}$ here is 1€ –0.5 €/EIA (7 EIA – 8 EIA) = 1.5 €. Note that, in this calculation, the term for 'cost of compensation' shows up as negative and thus constitutes a revenue; hence, SusVAsi > economic growth. In this case the EIA-contribution to Sustainable Value Added is a revenue and thus positive (+0.5 €).

We can now generalise the reasoning developed so far. Sustainable Value Added (here for the single impact case) examines whether changes in the economic, environmental and/or social performance of a company during a given period have contributed to sustainability relative to a benchmark (e.g. relative to the national economy). It expresses in monetary terms by how much the performance of a company in a period t_0 to t_1 has contributed to make the national economy more sustainable. For this purpose, an opportunity cost perspective is introduced. Following the requirement that the overall effectiveness has to be maintained, the SusVA examines a situation of an overall constant level of resource consumption. It calculates and expresses in monetary terms the extra value a company creates under the condition of a maintained overall level of resource consumption.

4.   THE MULTIPLE IMPACTS CASE

The multiple impacts case allows us to consider an unlimited amount of environmental and social impacts.

A positive Sustainable Value Added for the multiple impacts case occurs as long as economic growth exceeds the average of all costs and revenues from compensation of any changes in eco- and/or social effectiveness. In the multiple impacts case, n environmental and m social impacts represent the complete bundle of environmental and social resources used by a company to create a given level of economic output. These resources contribute complimentarily to value creation. In order to value these resources at their opportunity costs, it is necessary to take into account the weight at which these resources contribute to value creation at the benchmark level. The weight of a resource depends on how much output is created when one resource unit is added. To arrive at the relative weight of one resource relative to another resource, these weights are compared with each other. Put differently, the weight of a resource relative to another resource depends on how much more value it creates when one unit is added relative to when one unit of another resource is added. This is also given by the relation of the respective eco- and social efficiencies of the benchmark level. As the additional use of each environmental and social resource is valued with the eco- or social efficiency of the benchmark in order to ascertain the costs and revenues from the compensation of any changes in eco- and/or social effectiveness, it follows that the average of these costs and revenues represents the opportunity cost of the additional bundle of environmental and social resources used up by a company. In other words, the cost of compensation for every additional environmental (EIA_i) and/or social impact (SIA_j) is averaged and this opportunity cost is compared to economic growth. More formally, this condition is expressed by:

$$VA_{t1} - VA_{t0} \geq \frac{1}{n+m}\left(\sum_{i=1}^{n} EE_{i,b} \cdot \left(EIA_{i,t1} - EIA_{i,t0}\right) + \sum_{j=1}^{m} SE_{j,b} \cdot \left(SIA_{j,t1} - SIA_{j,t0}\right) \right)$$

(4)

where VA_{t1} and VA_{t0} are the Value Added of the company in t_1 and t_0, n and m the number of relevant environmental and social impacts, $EIA_{i,t0}$ and $EIA_{i,t1}$ represent the eco-effectiveness for environmental impact i in t_0 and t_1, and $SIA_{j,t0}$ and $SIA_{j,t1}$ the social effectiveness for social impact j in t_0 and t_1, and with $EE_{i,b}$ and $SE_{j,b}$ as the eco- or social efficiency of the benchmark for environmental resource i and social resource j, respectively. In general terms, the two sum functions on the right side of expression (4) stand for the average of all costs and revenues from changes in any corporate eco- or social effectiveness, respectively. Thus, the formula for Sustainable Value Added for the multiple impacts case is as follows:

$$SusVA = EG - \frac{1}{n+m}\left(\sum_{i=1}^{n} EE_{i,b} \cdot \left(EIA_{i,t1} - EIA_{i,t0}\right) + \sum_{j=1}^{m} SE_{j,b} \cdot \left(SIA_{j,t1} - SIA_{j,t0}\right) \right)$$

(5)

where $EG = (VA_{t1} - VA_{t0})$ represents economic growth. It is now clear that the formula developed above for the single impact case (see Equation 3) represents just a special case of the general formula for Sustainable Value Added shown in Equation (5). It follows that Sustainable Value Added in general is calculated by deducting the total opportunity cost that results from changes in corporate eco- or social effectiveness from the economic growth of the company. (We assume that SIA and EIA can be traded on a market [the benchmark] and that the seller of the SIA or EIA will ask for a price that corresponds to the value that EIA or SIA can create if used in the seller's company. This ratio [value created per environmental or social impact added used] corresponds to eco- and social efficiency of the benchmark. Moreover, we assume that environmental and social impacts can be bought separately at that price. This last assumption should be quite realistic whenever there is a large number of companies with different eco- and social-efficiencies). A positive SusVA indicates that a company has succeeded to create an extra value compared with a benchmark while keeping overall resource consumption at the level of the preceding period for all the resources it uses. Instead of remunerating victims for accepting externalities, environmental and social resources are (partly) reallocated between different users. This does not imply any substitution of different forms of environmental, social or economic capital as assumed by the concept of weak sustainability. Money transfers serve only to make the affected users accept the reallocation. Thus, the sum of costs and revenues for which economic growth is adjusted in Equation (5) reflects the net amount of money that results after settling all changes in corporate eco- and social effectiveness with benchmark companies. Establishing a micro–macro link, this equates to the net contribution of the company to the economic growth of the benchmark (e.g. as measured by GDP in the case of an entire economy). The sum of all SusVAs of the companies of the benchmark describes the net economic growth of the benchmark, i.e. the economic growth for an unchanged level of environmental and social impacts.

5.   MAIN FINDINGS AND FURTHER IMPLICATIONS

Sustainable Value Added, the measure presented in this chapter, takes a very prudent stance. It assumes, on one hand, that we do not know if or to which degree resources can be substituted. A combination of a higher economic and a lower environmental and/or social performance might be acceptable for some decision-makers, but it will not meet general approval. From this point of view, only a company that enhances economic, eco- and social effectiveness simultaneously contributes to sustainability. On the other hand, it presupposes that social and environmental resources are used by companies to create economic value and that companies will therefore agree to refrain from using a resource if they are compensated for the foregone value.

Sustainable Value Added integrates these two basic aspects. It only allows corporate eco- or social effectiveness to decline if these negative effects are settled by reallocating resources from other users to the company and paying them for refraining from producing environmental or social damage. This is achieved by taking an opportunity cost perspective into account. As a consequence, the total amount of environmental and social impact added remains constant at the benchmark level and there is no substitution of any forms of environmental, social or economic capital. Taking up the company perspective, Sustainable Value Added expresses in monetary terms whether the company has been able to create a positive extra Value Added after it has taken into account any changes in eco- and social effectiveness for every single relevant environmental or social impact. A positive Sustainable Value Added occurs only if there is a positive remainder in economic output after all changes in eco- and social effectiveness have been settled. Thus a strong contribution to sustainability has been achieved. Moreover, as Sustainable Value Added is expressed in monetary units, it does not only allow us to assess whether a company has exhibited a strong contribution to sustainability. It also serves to express to what extent the company has contributed positively or negatively to sustainability. By taking into account changes in corporate eco- and social efficiency as well as changes in corporate economic, eco- and social effectiveness, the concept of Sustainable Value Added gives a comprehensive picture of corporate contributions to sustainability.

Sustainable Value Added measures the surplus value adjusted for changes in eco- and social effectiveness, and is thus expressed in monetary terms such as the Euro. This reflects the change in economic output when environmental and social effectiveness are unchanged. However, stakeholders who pursue environmental goals such as environmental pressure groups might be more interested to learn if, and by how much, the environmental impact is reduced when economic output and social burdens are kept constant. In order to meet such claims, Sustainable Value Added can also be expressed in terms of a specific environmental or social impact, i.e. in physical units. For this purpose, the monetary Sustainable Value Added has to be divided by the relevant eco- and social efficiency of the benchmark, respectively. If it is, for example, divided by the eco-efficiency of an impact of the benchmark (e.g. CO_2), it shows how many environmental impacts can be reduced while keeping the effectiveness of the economic, social and the remaining environmental dimensions constant. In other words, converting Sustainable Value Added into physical units shows by how much a specific environmental burden caused by a company (e.g. CO_2) can be reduced by using the sustainable surplus (measured by monetary Sustainable Value Added) for paying other polluters of the benchmark for refraining from their polluting activities.

Sustainable development posits that capital stocks must be kept constant in order to ensure intragenerational and intergenerational prosperity (constant capital rule). Following this logic, the existing approaches to measuring sustainability have focused mainly on resource stocks. As it looks at corporate performance during a period, Sustainable Value Added deals with resource flows. The underlying assumption during the development of our concept is that a constant consumption of environmental and social resources over time equals a unchanged level of sustainability. Obviously, there are cases where maintaining the present level of resource consumption may not lead to sustainable outcomes. In such cases, resource flows have to be steadily reduced in order to achieve constant stocks of critical capital. This is achieved by introducing flow reduction targets. Such targets can easily be incorporated into the calculation of Sustainable Value Added. For this purpose, Equation (5) for calculating Sustainable Value Added for the multiple impacts case is modified slightly. By introducing resource specific reduction factors α_i and β_j for environmental and social resource flows, respectively, the formula is extended to integrate resource flow reduction targets as shown in Equation (6).

$$SusVA = EG - \frac{1}{n+m}\left(\sum_{i=1}^{n} EE_{i,b} \cdot \left(EIA_{i,t1} - \alpha_i EIA_{i,t0}\right) + \sum_{j=1}^{m} SE_{j,b} \cdot \left(SIA_{j,t1} - \beta_j SIA_{j,t0}\right)\right) \quad (6)$$

Consider a case where CO_2 emissions are to be reduced by 10% each year. For integrating this target when calculating Sustainable Value Added, α_{CO2} would be 0.9. As a consequence, the cost of compensation for a change in CO_2 emission would only be zero or positive and thus not lower Sustainable Value Added if the absolute level of CO_2 emission was reduced by 10% each period. Such an introduction of reduction targets brings the more flow-oriented approach of Sustainable Value Added in line with the stock-based concept of sustainable development.

A positive Sustainable Value Added is not a guarantee that undesired changes in corporate eco- and social effectiveness will be settled really. Instead it shows that there are enough funds created to pay for the reduction of the additional environmental or social damage by compensating less efficient users for giving up their impact-causing activities. There are three conditions for the reduction of environmental and social impacts. First, there have to be enough funds available to pay others to reduce their impacts. Secondly, the company has to be willing to actually spend these funds. Thirdly, there has to be some kind of market or trading scheme for environmental and social impacts. Sustainable Value Added does not give any information on the willingness to spend these funds or if there is a market or trading scheme.

Including external costs in the standard graphical representation (for the sake of simplicity we fall back on the simple impact case) reveals an interesting phenomenon (see Figure 4). In our example, the eco-efficiency of the company exceeds opportunity costs (C > B) and a positive Environmental Value Added is therefore observed. Opportunity cost, however, exceeds external costs (B > A). It would therefore be 'cheaper' to remunerate the victims of the externality than to pay another company for the reduction of the environmental impacts. As explained earlier, Sustainable Value Added as presented in this chapter is based on the assumption of strong sustainability. Paying victims for accepting externalities is, however, based on weak sustainability and indemnifying victims would therefore result in a loss of eco- and/or social effectiveness. The difference between opportunity costs and external costs (line AB) thus reflects the 'price' of strong over weak sustainability.

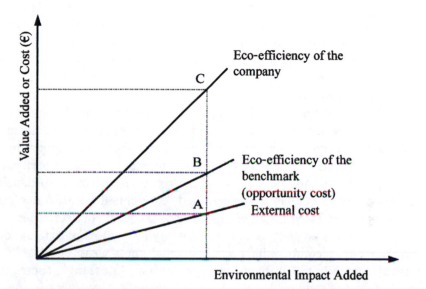

Figure 4. Environmental Value Added and external cost (Source: Figge and Hahn 2002)

Opportunity costs are not necessarily higher than external costs. Thus, there can also be a price of weak over strong sustainability, and it would be cheaper for companies to pay for the reduction of environmental impacts than for their acceptance. This example shows that strong sustainability is not necessarily more restrictive or more costly for business than weak sustainability.

Two important conclusions can be drawn from this analysis. First, if we presuppose weak sustainability, taking only opportunity costs into account might result in a sub-optimal use of resources. This is the case whenever external costs are below opportunity costs and it would thus be cheaper to pay the victim for the acceptance than other companies for the avoidance of an externality. In this case, a least-cost analysis should provide useful insights. Secondly, if a resource cannot be substituted, indemnifying victims for externalities is not a viable option. Companies can then only try to identify others that use the resource less efficiently in order to buy from them reductions of environmental and/or social impacts. The price of these reductions is reflected by opportunity costs. External costs are in that case unimportant.

6.   CONCLUSION

Sustainable Value Added as presented in this chapter constitutes an unprecedented way to measure corporate contributions to sustainability. The concept can be used in practice as it is based exclusively on information that is available in the market today. It requires information on the eco- and social efficiency of the company and a benchmark, as well as information on the company's economic performance. Environmental and social impacts do not have to be monetarised.

Sustainable Value Added is measured in monetary terms but it is not only a monetary measure. Rather it considers the efficiency and effectiveness of all three dimensions of sustainability. Because it shows the amount of value created while ensuring a constant environmental and social performance, Sustainable Value Added is based on the paradigm of strong sustainability. Put differently, Sustainable Value Added represents the extra value created by a company adjusted for all changes in eco- and social effectiveness. Compensation, in this context, does not mean paying victims of external effects to make them accept these impacts; this would imply weak sustainability and thus substitutability of different forms of capital. In contrast, compensation for calculating Sustainable Value Added means paying other less eco- or social-efficient users of resources to reduce the environmental and/or social impacts in question by that exact amount. This results in a constant overall level of eco- and social effectiveness. As only identical environmental or social impacts are considered in that kind of compensation, substitutability between different forms of capital does not matter. From the perspective of the former users of the resources, selling the avoidance of environmental and social impacts will be more profitable than their previous activity.

Sustainable Value Added as presented in this chapter is limited because it does not indicate whether a company is sustainable. It shows, however, how much a company has contributed to more sustainability. This contribution can be expressed in economic, environmental or social terms. When expressed in economic terms, Sustainable Value Added expresses in monetary terms the sustainable performance of the company relative to a benchmark. Sustainable Value Added thus allows us to determine whether a company has in fact contributed to sustainability or if it just enhanced its eco- and/or social efficiency. A sustainable measure to be adopted in practice has to be easy to understand and to communicate, and be meaningful at the same time. Because Sustainable Value Added is based on data available today and it translates corporate contribution to sustainability into one monetary, environmental or social unit, Sustainable Value Added is a step in this direction.

REFERENCES

Atkinson, G. (2000): 'Measuring Corporate Sustainability', *Journal of Environmental Planning and Management* Vol. 43, No. 2, 235-252.

Callens, I. and Tyteca, D. (1999): 'Towards Indicators of Sustainable Development for Firms: A Productive Efficiency Perspective', *Ecological Economics* Vol. 28, No. 1, 41-53.

Clift, R. and Wright, L. (2000): 'Relationships between Environmental Impacts and Added Value along the Supply Chain', *Technology Forecasting and Social Change* Vol. 65, No. 3, 281-295.

Dyllick, T. and Hockerts, K. (2002): 'Beyond the Business Case for Corporate Sustainability', *Business Strategy and the Environment* Vol. 11, No. 2, 130-141.

Figge, F. (2001): 'Environmental Value Added: ein neuer Ansatz zur Messung der Öko-Effizienz', *Zeitschrift für angewandte Umweltforschung* Vol. 14, No. 1-4, 184-197.

Figge, F. and Hahn, T. (2002): *Sustainable Value Added—Measuring Corporate Sustainable Performance beyond Eco-Efficiency* (2nd edition). Lüneburg: Centre for Sustainability Management.

Harte, M. J. (1995): 'Ecology, Sustainability, and Environment as Capital', *Ecological Economics* Vol. 15, No. 2, 157-164.

Huizing, A. and Dekker, H.C. (1992): 'Helping to Pull our Planet out of the Red: An Environmental Report of BSO/Origin', *Accounting, Organisations and Society* Vol. 17, No. 5, 449-458.

Jensen, M.C. (1968): 'The Performance of Mutual Funds in the Period 1945-1964', *Journal of Finance* Vol. 23, No. 2, 389-416.

Modigliani, F. and Modigliani, L. (1997): 'Risk-Adjusted Performance', *Journal of Portfolio Management* Vol. 23, No. 2, 45-54.

Norton, B. and Toman, M. (1997): 'Sustainability: Ecological and Economic Perspectives', *Land Economics* Vol. 73, No. 4, 553-568.

Pearce, D., Markandya, A. and Barbier, E.B. (1989): *Blueprint for a Green Economy.* London: Earthscan.

Rees, W. and Wackernagel, M. (1999): 'Monetary Analysis: Turning a Blind Eye on Sustainability', *Ecological Economics* Vol. 29, No. 1, 47-52.

Schaltegger, S. and Burritt, R. (2000): *Contemporary Environmental Accounting: Issues, Concepts and Practice.* Sheffield: Greenleaf Publishing.

Schaltegger, S. and Sturm, A. (1990): 'Ökologische Rationalität', *Die Unternehmung* Vol. 44, No. 4, 273-290.

Sharpe, W.F. (1966): 'Mutual Fund Performance', *Journal of Business* Vol. 39, No.1, 119-138.

Steer, A. and Lutz, E. (1994): 'Measuring Environmentally Sustainable Development', in: Serageldin, I. and Steer, A. (Eds.): *Making Development Sustainable. From Concepts to Action.* Washington D.C.: The International Bank for Reconstruction and Development/ The World Bank, 17-20.

Stern, D. (1997): 'The Capital Theory Approach to Sustainability: A Critical Appraisal', *Journal of Economic Issues* Vol. 31, No. 1, 145-173.

Stewart, G.B. (1991): *The Quest for Value. The EVA Management Guide.* New York: Harper Business.

Treynor, J.L. (1965): 'How to Rate Management of Investment Funds', *Harvard Business Review* Vol. 43, No. 1, 63-75.

Ullmann, A. (2001): 'From Eco-Efficiency to Eco-Effectiveness: Prolegomena to a Gaian Theory of Strategic Management', *Academy of Management Interactive Paper Upload*

System Paper 31761 [online] [cited 4 February 2002]. Available from Internet URL: http://aomdb.pace.edu/InteractivePapers/pdf/31761.pdf.

ACKNOWLEDGEMENTS

Both authors were working at the Centre for Sustainability Management (CSM) when the chapter was written.

SUSTAINABLE ANALYSIS OF INDUSTRIAL OPERATIONS
A Proof of Concept Demonstration Study

Sonja Lynn Odom
Laboratory for Sustainable Solutions, Department of Mechanical Engineering, University of South Carolina, USA

Abstract: The Sustainable Systems Analysis Algorithm (SSAA), a heuristic decision-support and evaluation methodology, was applied as a static proof of concept demonstration to the sustainability of industrial operations within the forests products industry sector in the Edisto River Basin. This research, dubbed the Sustainable Industrial Development Simulator (SIDS), followed the steps outlined in the SSAA methodology beginning with stakeholder identification; selection, weighting and measurement of Sustainability Performance Indicators (SPIs); followed by a descriptive analysis of the resulting Sustainability Directives (*SDs*). The results showed that the Indicator Measuring Units (IMUs) were not contributing toward industrial sustainability under existing operating conditions. An internal modifications scenario was introduced and the SPIs were re-measured. The results derived from the scenario showed that, as each company/IMU theoretically manipulated attainable modifications within their respective subsystem operations; improvements were seen in each IMU's scenario derived (*SD*).

1.   INTRODUCTION

Improved environmental performance has largely been a result of compliance with government statutes. Yet, restrictive environmental regulations—along with their associated cost of implementation—have also been a driving factor for the relocation of polluting industries to a more economically competitive area hosting regulations that are weak or non-existent. The command and control nature of the US regulatory structure has impeded and often discouraged greater (more valuable) manufacturing efficiency and has been perceived as a cost for doing business (Matson and Goreham 1997).

Weiss (1993) argues that the short-term 'search for competitiveness can lead to later environmental damage that will in turn undermine competitiveness.' The environment as a business strategy can provide competitive advantage to companies in the areas of improved process and manufacturing efficiency, increased access to market, regulatory leverage and improved stockholder value (NAE 1999). In discussing manufacturing strategy in the context of green manufacturing state, Dangayach and Deshmukh (2001) stated: 'today companies are under pressure from stakeholders to be eco-efficient. Those companies that can manage their resources efficiently are likely to gain competitive advantage. Eco-efficiency means to run manufacturing operations more innovatively, responsively and ultimately on a sustainable competitive basis.' Spencer-Cooke (1998) maintained that '[t]he first step toward managing sustainability is to recognise that it is more than environmental performance.' And Sillanpää (1998) asserts: 'ultimately there must be an integration of economic, ecological and social accounting methodologies if our aim is to establish a holistic methodology for assessing progress or contributions toward sustainable development.'

Within the realm of approaching a sustainable future, it is important to know where we want to go. Determining where that is will require collaborative stakeholder involvement and assessment tools that serve to guide their decisions. It is essential to determine a frame of reference from which to identify if change has taken place and, while it is not necessary to know an exact endpoint, it is imperative to establish a desirable direction for change (IISD 1997). The Sustainable Systems Analysis Algorithm (SSAA) methodology was designed to provide such a framework based on systems thinking while incorporating the ambiguous concept of sustainability. It is generally accepted that sustainability is an 'ethical guiding principle' for anthropogenic behaviour with dimensions in both time and space, and that systems thinking offers an objective foundation for evaluating, integrating and understanding quantitative and qualitative information over time.

The SSAA is a universal decision-support and evaluation approach expected to provide a much-needed impetus for sustainable performance evaluation once a system and the desired scope of analysis are defined. The framework thus far developed has the ability to compare products, processes, facilities and communities within a region, and regions with states and counties.

The Sustainable Industrial Development Simulator (SIDS)/SSAA demonstration research was initiated with the formation of a 39-member multistakeholder group, which collectively engaged in the selection and weighting of a set of Sustainable Performance Indicators (SPIs). The final lists consisted of five economic, four social and five environmental indicators. A separate group of companies known as the Indicator Measuring Units

(IMUs) measured the SPIs with respect to their industrial facilities under existing operating conditions. Each IMU SPI measurement was then transformed into a correlating contribution factor—a value representative of each measurement's contribution towards system sustainability. The SPI importance weight factor and correlating contribution factor values were utilised to derive a sustainability directive (*SD*)—a line segment of magnitude and direction determined by its three mutually perpendicular reference points representing the economic, social and environmental dimensions within the circumscribed sustainability space. A *SD* was derived for each IMU subsystem and collectively over the participating IMUs. The results showed that the IMUs were not contributing toward sustainability under existing operating conditions according to the SPIs selected as important to the at-large stakeholder group. A scenario involving internal modifications influenced by the introduction of Sustainability and Industrial Ecology (IE) concepts was presented and the SPIs were re-measured. The scenario-derived results showed that, as each company theoretically manipulated attainable modifications within their respective subsystems, improvements were seen in each IMU's scenario derived *SD*. This demonstration has provided the proof of concept needed for continued research that improves this decision-support and performance evaluation methodology and ventures to include the assessment of *SD* derivation over time.

2.   UNDERLYING CONCEPTS OF THE SSAA METHODOLOGY

Sustainability is a complex idiomatic term—an *a priori* concept that has proven impractical to define, yet is approached in an *a posteriori* manner. Among those embracing the concept, there are deep divisions on a precise meaning and discussions of whether one should be given. Shearman (1990) recognised that anthropocentrism and non-anthropocentrism are the dividing ethics of sustainability, with anthropocentrism taking centre stage in the sustainability debate. The two foremost conflicting anthropocentric views among the champions of sustainability are the concepts of 'critical limits' and 'competing objectives' (Farrell and Hart 1998). These differ in theme and scope, but are mutually concerned for both intra- and intergenerational equity. The SSAA methodology is theoretically grounded in the 'competing objectives' view of sustainability because it characterises a sustainable system as one that through continual improvement endeavours to balance, in a positive direction, its three inextricably linked dimensions—economic, social and environmental. Yet, it abets the integration of the 'critical limits' view via the dimensional indicators chosen for measurement and evaluation.

Figure 1 depicts the SSAA systems theory framework for incorporating and transforming sustainability aspect indicators into decisions and actions that will serve to guide policy in a sustainable direction.

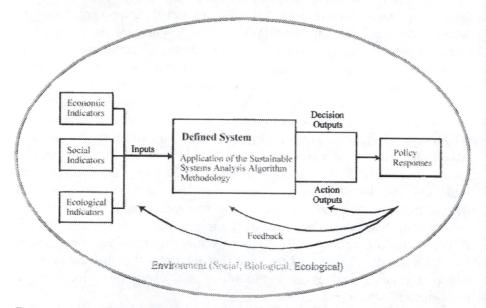

Figure 1. A sustainable systems theory framework (Source: adapted from figures and discussion in Easton 1957: Figure 1; Easton 1965: Diagram 3)

This framework conforms to the major steps in performing systems analysis as outlined in *SCOPE 34* (SCOPE 1988:35). The SSAA System Modelling and Performance Evaluation component (see Figure 2) takes place within the 'defined system' of Figure 1, resulting in the decision and action outputs that are then evaluated and improved upon. The feedback loop ensures that continuous improvement is sought at all stages of the assessment process as advocated by Deming (1986) via the Shewhart cycle. As time and space dimensions are considered, the 'defined system' within this framework becomes multiple-system and static modelling becomes dynamic.

3.   AN OVERVIEW OF THE SSAA FRAMEWORK VIA THE SIDS DEMONSTRATION

The development of the SIDS demonstration model after defining the system and scope of analysis followed the SSAA steps outlined in Figure 2. These are:
• Identification of appropriate stakeholders

- Selection and importance weighting of SPIs
- Determination of appropriate indicator measurement methods and correlating contribution factor transformations
- Measurement of SPIs
- Calculation and analysis of *SDs*
- Introduction of design scenarios (optional)

In Figure 2, solid lines represent consecutive activities, while dashed lines represent concurrent and dotted lines represent optional activities. All of these steps and a description of the *SD* are discussed in subsequent sections.

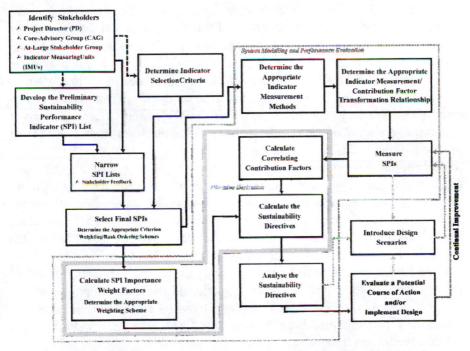

Figure 2. The general steps of the sustainable systems analysis algorithm

The smaller dashed 'box' in Figure 2 isolates those components of the algorithm that are direct inputs to the calculation of the sustainability directive. The larger dashed 'box' isolates those components that correspond to the 'generation of solutions' and 'modelling' steps of systems analysis, as outlined in *SCOPE 34* (SCOPE 1988:35), which occur within the 'defined system' of Figure 1. The dashed arrows designate concurrent activities.

4.   SSAA PRELIMINARIES: DEFINITION OF
SYSTEMS AND SCOPE OF ANALYSIS

As advocated in Gustavson *et al.* (1999), the SIDS demonstration utilised a
systems approach with an overall boundary defined by ecology, the Edisto
River Basin (ERB), a two-million acre rural watershed covering portions of
12 counties and over 325 miles of navigable rivers in South Carolina's
coastal plain. The ERB represents approximately one-tenth of the total area
of the state and the Edisto River is one of the longest free-flowing
blackwater rivers in the USA. In November 1993, a 39-member Edisto River
Basin Task Force (ERBTF) was formed. This multi-year, citizen-based effort
concluded its extensive resource assessment and planning process in January
1996. This recognised the significance of the river basin and the importance
of sustaining the area's resources for the benefit of the community and local
economy. A comprehensive final report, *Managing Resources for a Sustainable Future: the Edisto River Basin Project*, was published in October 1996.

Land use data from 1989 show that 56% of the basin land cover is for-
ested (S.C. Water Resources Commission 1993). South Carolina derives
approximately 20% of its total annual cash receipts from timber and forest
products in the ERB. Among its many recommendations, the ERBTF identified economic development as a crucial element in its regional sustainable
development strategy. It was the aspiration of this task force that future
industrial development should address and minimise environmental impact
to the basin yet enhance the quality of life for the local residents. In addition,
ERBTF recommendations directly addressed the development of 'manufacturing facilities that utilise wood products' (S.C. Department of Natural Resources 1996). Therefore, the scope of analysis of this demonstration effort
was focused on the potential for sustainable industrial development within
the lumber and wood products (L&WP) industrial sector. The internal operations of participating L&WP company IMUs, the 'hetrarchical' subsystems became an integral part of the SIDS analysis.

4.1   Stakeholder Identification

During the initial exploration of the opportunity to apply the SSAA as per
the system and scope of analysis defined, it was determined that the follow-
ing groups should be represented as stakeholders:
• Wood products companies
• Local, state and federal government
• Local economic development agencies
• Local advocacy groups/non-governmental organisations (NGOs)
• Academia/research

Within the context of the SIDS demonstration, stakeholder identification began with the establishment of a ten-member core advisory group (CAG). Six were from academia/research, two from state government, one from local government and one from industry. The tasks of the CAG included weighting the SPI selection criteria and ranking the narrowed intermediate list of indicators to form the final list to be sent out to the at-large group for importance weighting. Members of the CAG were also called upon to provide assistance and feedback in determining selection criteria, appropriate indicator measurement methods and contribution factor transformations.

The CAG expanded into an at-large stakeholder group representative of the diverse membership of those with a vested interest in the defined systems and scope of analysis. Forty-five individuals were initially contacted for participation as a stakeholder in the SIDS demonstration. Of these, 39 (87%) responded to form the at-large stakeholder group: four L&WP companies; 15 federal, state and local government; four ERB economic development agencies; nine local advocacy/NGO groups; and seven academia/research. Of those representing government, two were at the federal level, nine at the state level and four at the local level. The academia/research sub-division included researchers in economics, environmental resource management, sociology, industrial ecology/eco-industrial development and sustainability. This group participated actively in the initial selection and importance weighting of final SPIs.

The stakeholder group was then broadened to include the IMUs—those research participants who actually measured the selected SPIs. Of the 34 L&WP companies (including logging operations) in the ERB, 12 were targeted to participate as IMUs in the development of the SIDS demonstration model. Seven agreed to a presentation of the research. Of these, four participated in the indicator measurement and *SD* analysis phases. To avoid disclosure, the identity of each company is not revealed and they are referred to in subsequent sections as IMUi.

4.2 The Indicator Selection Process

Concurrent to identifying stakeholders, a preliminary list of SPIs was generated and the selection criteria for final SPI selection were determined. The potential SPIs were grouped according to sustainability dimension (i.e. economic, social and environmental) using a 'topic-based' framework as described by Hart (1998). The initial SPI lists of 25+ indicators in each dimension was expanded to more than 60 before evolving into narrowed lists following open feedback from stakeholders and ranking according to 'appropriateness of use' given the scope of the demonstration and each

IMU's ability to measure. The narrowed list evolved into the final SPI list via weighting of criteria and scoring the indicators.

A selection limit of at least three and at most five SPIs in each dimension was an initial constraint. The final list consists of five economic, four social and five environmental SPIs. These are provided in Tables 1, 2 and 3, respectively; they are rank ordered according to their indicator selection score and shown with their stakeholder assigned importance weight factor.

Table 1. Final list of SIDS demonstration Economic Indicators, rank ordered according to indicator selection score and shown with their respective importance weight factor.

Rank	Economic Indicators	Importance Weight Factor
1	Energy consumption per $ value of product shipments.	0.205
2	Materials consumption ratio: product output per unit of raw material input.	0.166
3	Waste disposal cost per $ value of product shipments.	0.149
4	Total cost savings due to conservation of energy within the industrial process or facility.	0.247
5	Percent investment in R&D for product, process or facility operation improvement influenced by IE and sustainability concepts (e.g. dematerialisation, minimal energy consumption and minimal generation of residue during manufacture, use of recycled materials, use of renewable energy resources, development of sustainable strategies, etc.).	0.233

Table 2. Final list of SIDS demonstration Social Indicators, rank ordered according to indicator selection score and shown with their respective importance weight factor

Rank	Social Indicators	Importance Weight Factor*
1	Percentage of employees participating in collaborative training programmes (i.e. job skills, potential operational perturbations, new technology, environmental awareness and stewardship, sustainability).	0.198
2	Percentage of employees able to earn a living wage including a benefits package (health care insurance and vacation/sick time).	0.347
3	Identification and support of champions for implementing industrial ecology (e.g. employee involvement programme in place, number of employee suggestions received that result in a cost savings reward).	0.140
4	Percentage of employees that take advantage of company policies that encourage pursuit of higher education (i.e. flex-time, reduced hours, tuition reimbursement).	0.316

* Values may not add up due to rounding.

Table 3. Final list of SIDS demonstration Environmental/Ecological Indicators, rank ordered according to indicator selection score and shown with their respective importance weight factor

Rank	Environmental Indicators	Importance Weight Factor*
#1	Routine water quality/chemistry measurements at the facility for water either accumulating onsite or leaving the site boundary, in compliance with National Pollutant Discharge Elimination System (NPDES) permit limits and Safe Drinking Water Act (SDWA) maximum contaminant levels (MCLs.)	0.282
#2	Reduction in the purchase, storage and use of toxic chemicals in production.	0.195
#3	Reduction in the amount of unusable solid, liquid or gaseous residues (including hazardous/non-hazardous and/or toxic/non-toxic) released or transferred as a result of the production process.	0.154
#4	Ratio of the amount of process output material being discarded of as unusable waste compared with the amount of process output material being recycled or re-used.	0.199
#5	Ratio of renewable energy consumed to fossil fuel consumed in production.	0.169

*Values may not add up due to rounding.

4.3 Determining the Importance Weight Factor

There are numerous multi-criteria decision-making (MCDM) weighting schemes in use for determining the importance of individual metrics based on relevance to overall project goals and incorporating the preferences of individual stakeholders. The problem seems to lie in determining the most apt method to use—in that, if the weights derived are inappropriate, then the results of the evaluation will be erroneous. As quoted in Rogers and Bruen (1998), it is understood that the 'lack of consistency between different approaches [makes] the process of ... weighting the weak link within the decision-aid process.' They outline a simple, straightforward importance weighting technique using Hinkle's (1965) 'resistance to change grid', which is based on the Personal Construct Theory—a theory from psychology devised by Kelly (1963). This 'resistance to change grid' technique was incorporated to establish SPI importance weight factors during the SIDS demonstration and involved a series of pair-wise comparisons of bipolar indicator-constructs. Stakeholders were asked to indicate on which indicator-construct they would remain the same if they were forced to change on one. The number of times any one indicator-construct 'resisted change' designated its relative importance with respect to the other constructs presented. This process produced a set of raw scores, which were then averaged to obtain SPI importance weight factors. The importance weights for each SPI that resulted of this process are provided in Tables 1, 2 and 3 for the economic, social and environmental dimensions, respectively.

4.4 Indicator Measurement and Contribution Factor Transformation

Once the SPIs are selected, an appropriate method of measurement and transformation into a correlating contribution factor (i.e. normalisation within sustainable ranges) must be determined. Simple linear or binary relationships were incorporated to perform this task for the SIDS demonstration. These relationships were derived from industry-specific data and/or advice from members of the CAG. The 14 SIDS SPI measurement methods and correlating contribution factor transformations are discussed in detail in Chapter 8 of Odom (2001). An abbreviated example is provided in Box 1.

Box 1. An abbreviated example of the indicator measurement/contribution factor transformation development, specifically for the first economic indicator of the SIDS demonstration—the Energy Intensity ratio

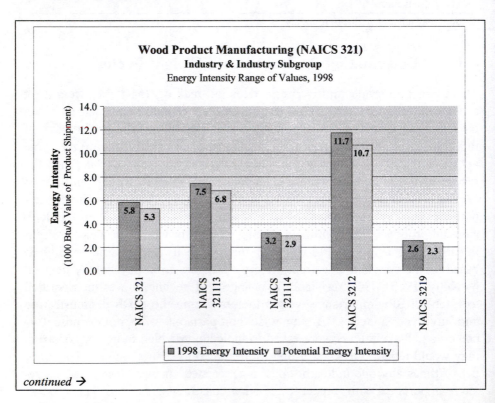

continued →

Figure. Range of actual and potential energy intensity values across the wood products manufacturing subgroups for 1998 (Source: actual values are calculated from 1998 energy consumption data in US Department of Energy [2001] and dollar value of product shipments data in US Department of Commerce [2001]. Potential values are based on a Motor Challenge Program report recommendation published by US Department of Energy, Office of Energy Efficiency and Renewable Energy [1998: 67])

As shown in the figure above, US energy intensity estimates from statistical data within the wood products manufacturing (WPM) group range from 2,600 BTUs/US$ for wood preservation to 11,700 BTUs/US$ for veneer, plywood and engineered WPM. The range of values that will correlate the transformation of the Energy Intensity indicator measurement ($\vartheta_{m_{il}}$) into its associated contribution factor (μ_{il}) is ascertained in consideration of the historical and current macro and micro energy intensity estimates available for the L&WP industry group.

Knowing that the south census region estimates have been historically higher than US estimates, it is assumed that the slightly higher values than those presented in the figure above will be more representative of this local region. The defining bounds sought for the indicator measurement/contribution factor transformation will therefore extend from 2,000 to <12,000 BTUs/US$ value of product shipments.

The Energy Intensity indicator, el, will be measured for each IMU as:

$$\vartheta_{m_{il}} = \frac{E_{C_i}}{V_{PS_i}} \tag{T-1}$$

where Ec_i is equal to the amount of total first use of energy consumed for all purposes in BTUs and V_{PS_i} is equal to the US$ value of product shipments for IMUi. The contribution factor for this indicator, μ_{il}, is correlated to equal -1 when $\vartheta_{m_{il}}$ ≥ 12.0 and to equal 1 when $\vartheta_{m_{il}} \leq 2.0$. Otherwise, as $\vartheta_{m_{il}}$ ranges from a value <12.0 to a value ≥ 2.0, the contribution factor correlation becomes a bounded linear function.

The SIDS IMUs were given a baseline indicator measurement survey for the purpose of gathering data specific to the SPI measurement calculations. Via the defined correlation functions, these SPI measurements were transformed into their respective SPI contribution factors. The calculation of indicator specific weighted utility functions involved multiplying the SPI importance weight factor by its correlating contribution factor. The results of the SSAA modelling effort were used to create a three-dimensional framework for observing the relationship between the economic, social and environmental/ ecological aspects of the industrial system in the form of a sustainability directive. These results are discussed in a subsequent section.

4.5   The Sustainability Directive: a Directional Bearing

The sustainability directive is a line segment extending from the origin (0, 0, 0) to a point located in sustainability space, circumscribed by a cube of dimension ±1 (see Figure 3). Three mutually perpendicular reference points representing the three dominant dimensions of sustainability determine the magnitude and direction of *SD*. The overall System Sustainability Directive is defined as follows:

$$\overrightarrow{SD} \equiv M\vec{i} + \Theta\vec{j} + E\vec{k} \tag{1}$$

where *M*, Θ, and *E* represent the total characteristic economic, social and environmental contributions of all subsystems analysed within the system and are the orthogonal projections of *SD*, and $\vec{i}$, $\vec{j}$, and $\vec{k}$ are the unit directives in these directions, respectively.

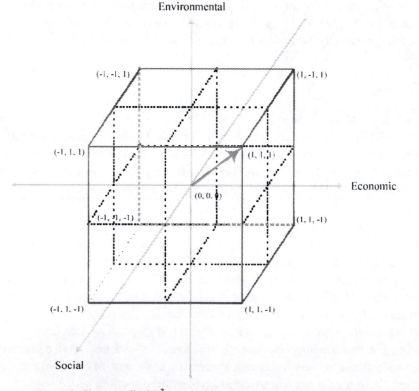

Figure 3. Circumscribed R^3 sustainability space with centre at the origin

Depicted is the Ideal Sustainability Directive:

$$\overrightarrow{SD}_{Ideal} = \langle 1, \; 1, \; 1 \rangle$$

The total economic (M), social (Θ) and environmental (E) contributions toward system sustainability made by participating IMUs included in the systems analysis is inferred to be the summation of the individual contributions divided by the total number of participating IMUs.

By adding the subscript i, an expression representing the individual IMU 'hetrarchical' systems within the overall system, SD_i is obtained:

$$\overrightarrow{SD_i} \equiv M_i \vec{i} + \Theta_i \vec{j} + E_i \vec{k} \tag{2}$$

The distinct contribution of a single IMU is characterised as a linear summation of the SPI contribution factor multiplied by its corresponding importance-weighting factor (i.e. the weighted utility functions) derived for each attribute indicator selected for analysis. The economic contribution toward system sustainability for IMU$_1$ is expressed as:

$$M_1 = \mu_1 \cdot \omega_\mu = \sum_{j=1}^{n_\mu} \mu_{1j} \omega_{\mu j} = \mu_{11} \omega_{\mu 1} + \mu_{12} \omega_{\mu 2} + \cdots + \mu_{1n_\mu} \omega_{\mu n_\mu} \tag{3}$$

where μ_{1j} is the contribution factor transformation value correlated with the measurement of economic indicator, j, and $\omega_{\mu j}$ is the 'state of sustainability' importance weight factor derived for this economic indicator. Similar equations express the same relationships for individual IMUs with regard to the social and environmental dimensions.

The Ideal Sustainability Directive, $SD_{Ideal} = (1,1,1)$, is the maximisation of the individual utility functions (e.g. the independent $\mu_{ij} \cdot \omega_{\mu j}$ terms of Equation 3) inferring that, in order to achieve sustainability, the three competing dimensions are equally balanced (see Figure 3). The contributing components of a directive that cause it to situate outside the solitary positive octant are considered unsustainable. Therein lies the stimulus to further investigate those indicants that have contributed to the unsustainable activities of the system. But this does not dictate that all directives that lie within the solitary positive octant are ultimately sustainable and analysis ends. Moving towards sustainability is a dynamically evolving process of planning, doing, evaluating and acting. The SSAA methodology is viewed as a synergist for the introduction of system modifications that strive for continual improvement of project parameters toward the ideal direction.

5.   INTRODUCTION OF DESIGN SCENARIOS

For the ERB SIDS demonstration, a design scenario involving internal modifications to existing operations and policies based on sustainability and industrial ecology related concepts was introduced. These concepts include dematerialisation, minimal energy consumption and minimal generation of residue during manufacture, use of recycled materials, use of renewable energy resources, development of sustainable strategies, etc.

In the design scenario survey, each IMU was asked to consider the effects of the potential modifications when responding to the survey questions, thereby re-measuring the baseline indicators with respect to any changes that may or may not occur as a result of implementing such concepts. A sample of potential modifications presented to the SIDS IMUs is provided in Box 2.

Box 2. Selected design scenario considerations presented to SIDS demonstration IMUs for consideration when exploring potential internal modifications to existing operations

---

SIDS IMUs were asked to consider internal modifications to their existing operations based on sustainability and IE concepts as a design scenario for continued SSAA analysis. The following modifications were offered for consideration.

1) Energy saving opportunities that contribute to lower energy consumption and cost saving due to energy conservation such as:
    • Reducing or controlling pump or fan speeds
    • Matching pump size to load
    • Installing microprocessor controls on compressor systems
    • Insulating steam lines
    • Sizing motors to fit the load
    • Energy efficient lighting
2) Reducing or replacing hazardous or toxic maintenance cleansers
3) Researching potential uses for current waste streams
4) Designing a bark collection system
5) Reducing the amount of toxic chemicals purchased for use, stored and/or used on site
6) Setting up a non-existent educational assistance policy
7) Making an effort to increase the number of employees pursuing higher education
8) Setting up a non-existent employee-championing program
9) Allocating management support, time and money to an existing employee-championing program
10) Increase participation in collaborative training programs
11) Encouraging employees that are pursuing higher education to conduct research or independently engage in R&D on topics such as:

> • Potential uses of treated lumber waste
> • Finding substitutes for toxic chemicals used in production
> • Potential solar kiln design

5.1   The 'State of Sustainability' Results and Analysis

The results of this demonstration included the SD_i calculations prepared for each participating IMU and a composite (overall) SD calculation for both the baseline study and the internal modifications scenario. Visual representations and descriptive analysis of the SDs derived as part of this proof of concept demonstration follow the numerically calculated results. Analysis includes the simple determination of in which octant of the circumscribed sustainability space each sustainability directive resides and straightforward inferences based on the survey results. From the calculations made, it was shown which IMUs were providing a positive measure toward sustainable industrial development in the ERB and which were negative contributors, according to the SPIs selected and measured. Comparisons between the baseline study and the internal modifications scenario revealed which indicators were improved upon by which IMU via an indicator assessment grid.

6.   BASELINE STUDY

The baseline survey, distributed to obtain SPI measurement data, requested that each IMU respond with data derived from fiscal year 2000. The M$_{Baseline}$, $\Theta_{Baseline}$ and E$_{Baseline}$ column vectors were calculated as:

$$\begin{bmatrix} M_1 \\ M_2 \\ M_3 \\ M_4 \end{bmatrix} = \begin{bmatrix} -0.083 \\ -0.292 \\ -0.145 \\ 0.038 \end{bmatrix} ; \begin{bmatrix} \Theta_1 \\ \Theta_2 \\ \Theta_3 \\ \Theta_4 \end{bmatrix} = \begin{bmatrix} -0.531 \\ -0.113 \\ -0.560 \\ -0.039 \end{bmatrix} ; \text{ and } \begin{bmatrix} E_1 \\ E_2 \\ E_3 \\ E_4 \end{bmatrix} = \begin{bmatrix} 0.459 \\ -0.601 \\ -0.434 \\ -0.382 \end{bmatrix} .$$

These individual $SD_{Baseline_i}$ results represent the linear summation of the dimensional SPI weighted utility function calculations for the four participating IMUs. The resulting $SD_{Baseline}$ equation and a visual representation of each IMU baseline study directive in sustainability space (shown as an inset offering an enlarged view) are provided in Figures 4–7. Note the axis direction and rotation carefully, as it changes to provide a clearer view of each SD_i in its respective octant.

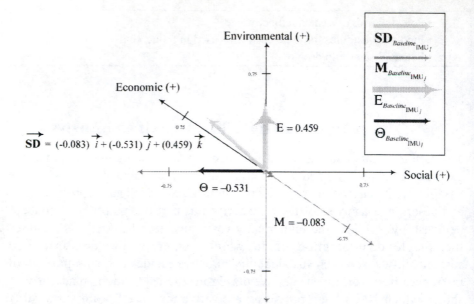

Figure 4. Visual interpretation of the sustainability directive for IMU₁ resulting from the Baseline Study

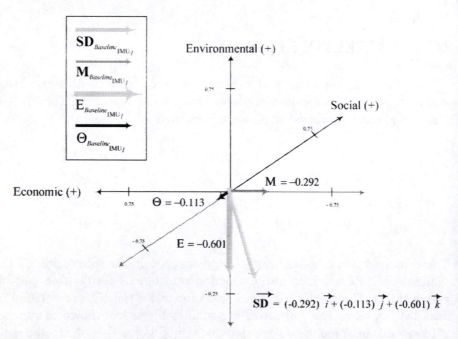

Figure 5. Visual interpretation of the sustainability directive for IMU₂ resulting from the Baseline Study

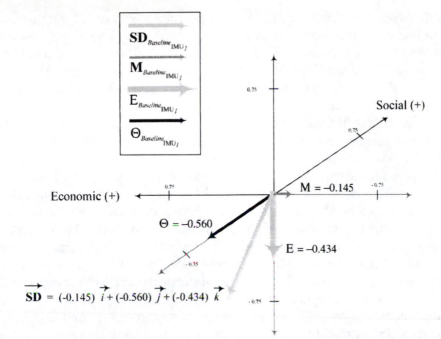

Figure 6. Visual interpretation of the sustainability directive for IMU₃ resulting from the Baseline Study

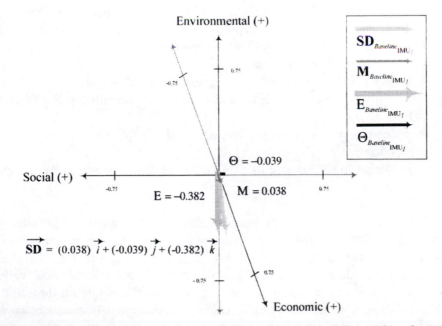

Figure 7. Visual interpretation of the sustainability directive for IMU₄ resulting from the Baseline Study

In the economic dimension, only IMU$_4$ provides a very small but positive contribution to the composite group, while only IMU$_1$ provides a positive contribution in the environmental dimension. All IMUs performed poorly in the social dimension. This places IMU$_1$ in the (-1, -1, 1) octant, IMU$_2$ and IMU$_3$ in the (-1, -1, -1) octant and IMU$_4$ in the (1, -1, -1) octant as depicted in Figures 4–7.

With respect to the economic dimension, all IMUs performed well with respect to energy consumption. This may have been the result of incomplete data that provide a full accounting of energy consumption at each respective facility, as the values provided in the surveys were noticeably below industry averages. This may be an area that could benefit from further research into the accurate accounting of resources. With respect to the second economic indicator ($m2$; the 'materials efficiency' indicator), two of the IMUs reported performing within the ranges of the contribution factor transformation and two were below the minimum threshold value of having an input/output efficiency of 80%. All IMUs were within contribution factor ranges with respect to waste disposal cost, yet all performed poorly with respect to energy conservation activities, having no activity to report. And finally, of the three IMUs reporting performance of R&D, only one was above the threshold values established as 'sustainable'.

Within the social dimension, all four IMUs reported having no collaborative training or employee-championing programmes. Although these SPIs received the lowest importance weighting of the four in this dimension, they contributed heavily toward a non-sustainable path. All four IMUs reported having a percentage of employees earning a 'living wage', which contributed positively toward sustainability. IMU$_2$ reported the largest percentage of employees pursuing higher education.

With respect to the environmental dimension, only IMU$_1$ had:

- Water quality measurements within NPDES permitting limits and SDWA MCLs
- A reduction in the purchase, storage and use of toxic chemicals in production
- A reduction in the amount of residue released or transferred from their facility

Two IMUs did not measure for water quality, which contributed negatively toward this SPI overall. The consumption of energy from renewable resources was zero at all IMU facilities. Although it was expected that this SPI would provide a positive contribution, it in fact contributed negatively. IMU$_2$ and IMU$_4$ had 'discard/recycle' ratios below the minimum threshold, while IMU$_3$ was within the positive range of indicator 'e4' measurements, which translated into a positive contribution factor. IMU$_1$ was slightly over the transition value; thus, their weighted utility function value was slightly below zero.

Assuming each IMU affects systems sustainability equally, an average of the dimensional calculations resulted in the composite $SD_{Baseline}$. The directive equation takes the form of:

$$\overrightarrow{SD}_{Baseline} = (-0.121)\vec{i} + (-0.311)\vec{j} + (-0.240)\vec{k} \qquad (4)$$

This is visually represented in the (-1, -1, -1) octant of the circumscribed sustainability space as depicted in Figure 8.

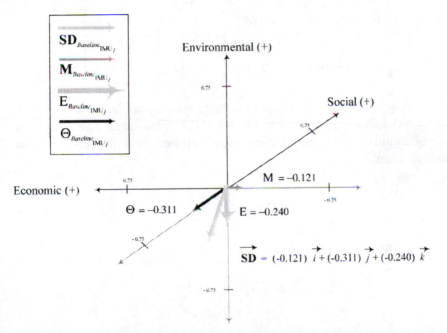

Figure 8. Visual interpretation of the *composite sustainability directive* resulting from the Baseline Study

While the $\overrightarrow{SD}_{Baseline}$ is comparatively less negative in the economic dimension, it is clearly not 'pointing' in the sustainable direction as defined by the constraints of the weighted indicator measurements and the contribution factor transformation utility functions.

7. INTERNAL MODIFICATIONS SCENARIO

It was hypothesised that if IE and sustainability concepts were implemented, such implementation would have a positive effect on the SPI measurements. Therefore, their influence was expected to cause a shift of the resulting *SDs* to a more positive endpoint. Starting with the fiscal year 2000 data provided in the baseline survey, the indicators were re-measured taking these theoretical modifications into account and the resulting M*Scenario*, Θ*Scenario* and E*Scenario* column vectors were calculated as:

$$
\begin{bmatrix} M_1 \\ M_2 \\ M_3 \\ M_4 \end{bmatrix} = \begin{bmatrix} -0.062 \\ 0.054 \\ 0.166 \\ 0.532 \end{bmatrix} ; \begin{bmatrix} \Theta_1 \\ \Theta_2 \\ \Theta_3 \\ \Theta_4 \end{bmatrix} = \begin{bmatrix} -0.135 \\ 0.055 \\ -0.037 \\ 0.609 \end{bmatrix} ; \text{and} \begin{bmatrix} E_1 \\ E_2 \\ E_3 \\ E_4 \end{bmatrix} = \begin{bmatrix} 0.532 \\ -0.293 \\ -0.129 \\ 0.377 \end{bmatrix}.
$$

The resulting individual *SDScenario* equations and visual representations in sustainability space are provided in Figures 9–12. Note the axis direction and rotation carefully, as it changes to provide a clearer view of each *SDi* in its respective octant.

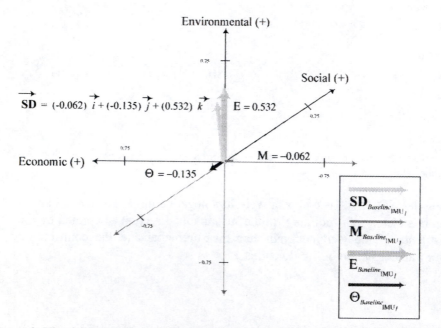

Figure 9. Visual interpretation of the sustainability directive for IMU₁ resulting from the introduction of the Internal Modifications Scenario

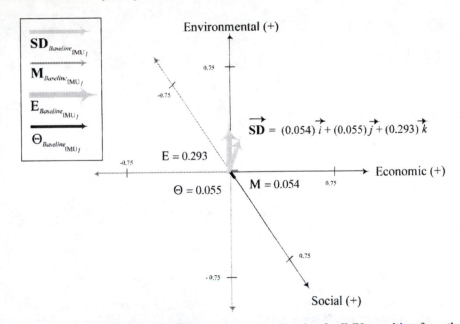

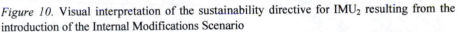

Figure 10. Visual interpretation of the sustainability directive for IMU₂ resulting from the introduction of the Internal Modifications Scenario

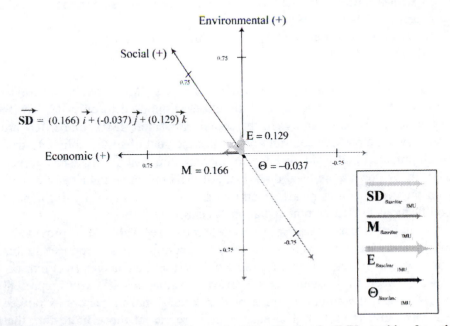

Figure 11. Visual interpretation of the sustainability directive for IMU₃ resulting from the introduction of the Internal Modifications Scenario

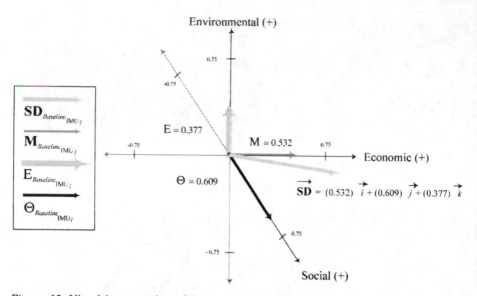

Figure 12. Visual interpretation of the sustainability directive for IMU₄ resulting from the introduction of the Internal Modifications Scenario

It is obvious from the individual IMU directives depicted that:

- IMU*₁* still resides in the (-1, -1, 1) octant
- IMU*₂* has shifted from the (-1, -1, -1) octant to now reside in the (1, 1, -1) octant
- IMU*₃* has shifted from the (-1, -1, -1) to the (1, -1, -1) octant
- IMU*₄* has shifted from the (1, -1, -1) to the (1, 1, 1) octant

In the economic dimension, three of the four IMUs (IMU*₂*, IMU*₃*, and IMU*₄*) are now 'pointing' in the positive direction as opposed to only IMU*₄* with respect to the baseline study. In the social dimension, IMU*₂* and IMU*₄* are now showing a positive contribution toward the goal of sustainable industrial development. Finally, in the environmental dimension IMU*₄* has joined IMU*₁* to take on a more ideal direction. All IMU indicator contributions have been augmented as a result of applying the IE/sustainability influenced modifications to their current operations as expected.

An indicator-assessment grid was generated (see Table 4) to provide an insight into which SPIs were affected by the modifications introduced in this scenario. The grid is a difference table comparing the changes (Δx) that occurred between the 'baseline' and 'scenario' evaluations. The rows represent the IMUs and the columns represent the dimensional indicators as ranked and listed in Tables 1–3. The shaded cells represent those indicators that were augmented by the IMU modifications introduced. The addition of a '+' to the cell is a gauge signifying how much change took place. As can be seen, no SPI measurements/transformation values in this scenario caused movement in a negative direction; only one indicator was augmented by a change >0.50; and eight were augmented <0.10 over their 'baseline' values. This grid purposely does not specify whether an SPI measurements/transformation value changed from being negative to being positive; it is intended to show only that movement (of the scenario derived directive endpoints) in the positive direction has taken place.

Although the modifications introduced had the intended 'positive' effect sought, the IMUs did not apply the opportunity offered by this scenario to its fullest potential. As can be seen in Table 4, only 22 out of the possible 56 opportunities to effect a change were pursued, This provides insight into which of the SPIs each IMU felt were theoretically achievable and reveals that the transition toward sustainability will, in fact, be an evolutionary *a posteriori* process.

Table 4. Indicator-assessment grid for comparison between the baseline study and internal modifications scenario

IMU_i	Economic Indicator, m_j					Social Indicator, s_j				Environmental Indicator, e_j				
	$j=1$	$j=2$	$j=3$	$j=4$	$j=5$	$j=1$	$j=2$	$j=3$	$j=4$	$j=1$	$j=2$	$j=3$	$j=4$	$j=5$
I=1						++								
i=2				++			+					++		
i=3			+				+	++			+	+		
i=4			++		++			++		+++	+			

A shaded cell indicates that this SPI increased for this IMU between the baseline study and the design scenario.

$0 < \Delta x < 0.1$	+	$0.1 < \Delta x < 0.25$	++	$0.25 < \Delta x < 0.5$	+++	$\Delta x > 0.5$

$0 > \Delta x$

The resulting composite directive, depicted in Figure 13, takes the form of:

$$\overrightarrow{SD_{Scenario}} = (0.173)\vec{i} + (0.123)\vec{j} + (0.122)\vec{k} \qquad (5)$$

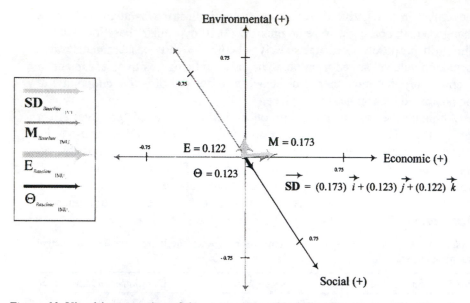

Figure 13. Visual interpretation of the composite sustainability directive resulting from the introduction of the Internal Modifications Scenario

The composite internal modifications scenario directive has shifted into the (1, 1, 1) octant of the circumscribed sustainability space. While this directive is at less than 20% of its potential in all three dimensions, it is assumed that continued implementation of IE concepts under the conditions of well understood indicator measurements will continue to augment the results over time. This is, of course, assuming that IE concepts will result only in augmented indicator measurements.

The interlinkages that exist between the selected SPIs are complex and further analysis, at this point, would have limited value. Continued (dynamic) analysis beyond the scope of this demonstration and using the SSAA methodology will involve actual implementation of the design scenarios.

8.   CONCLUSION

Research focused on the development of sustainability performance and evaluation methodologies has placed emphasis on the relationships between economy and ecology bound by the confines of existing economic theory. The research presented contributes an evaluation technique that attempts to collectively observe the three inextricably linked dimensions of sustainability. The optimistic objectives of such a framework are to provide the ability to compare systems (e.g. products, processes, facilities, and communities within a region, and regions with states and counties) in a 'panarchical' fashion. Although the SSAA methodology, as demonstrated in the SIDS application, is an approach that dissects the problem into small parts and applies linear relationships between the economic, social and environmental dimensions, it is viewed as a heuristic (self-educating) process that can continuously reinterpret the situation, and assess the decision and action outcomes via subsequent evaluation of policy responses.

This proof of concept demonstration revealed that the wood products company participants—the 'hetrarchical' systems in this research—are not contributing toward industrial sustainability under current operating conditions within the ecologically bounded system known as the Edisto River Basin. This application of the SSAA has illustrated visually that, based on the indicators selected and weighted as important by a diverse at-large stakeholder group, the ERB IMUs are currently in the (-1, -1, -1) octant. It was further demonstrated that, with the introduction of IE and sustainability concepts via internal modifications to industrial operations and policy, the baseline measurements could be enhanced.

The stakeholders who participated in this research responded favourably when asked about their experience. Future research applications suggested upon the completion of this research included:

- Determining if forest-related certification criteria provide for sustainable products
- Investigating the marketing insight provided by comparing directives derived from individual stakeholder group weightings.

Sustainability is seen as an evolutionary goal where the 'state of sustainability' changes with time as discussed by Iyer-Raniga and Treloar (2000). This emphasises the dynamic nature of evaluating sustainability—in this case, sustainable industrial development and the need for continuous improvement in this procedurally rational process. This research strives to be more than just an academic manuscript; it is an invitation to respond. If humanity is to move forward with an attempt to understand our complex earth systems and our role in it, as 'sustainability' has called upon us to, we must (as George A. Kelly championed), overcome barriers built by more than two thousand years of 'constructive' thought.

REFERENCES

Dangayach, G.S. and Deshmukh, S.G. (2001): 'Manufacturing Strategy: Literature Review and Some Issues', *International Journal of Operations and Production Management* Vol. 21, No. 7, 884-932.

Deming, W.E. (1986): *Out of the Crisis*. Cambridge: MIT Center for Advanced Engineering Study.

Easton, D. (1957): 'An Approach to the Analysis of Political Systems', *World Politics* Vol. 9, No. 3.

Easton, D. (1965): *A Framework for Political Analysis.* Englewood Cliffs: Prentice-Hall.

Farrell, A. and Hart, M. (1998): 'What does Sustainability Really Mean? The Search for Useful Indicators', *Environment* Vol. 40, No. 9, 4-9.

Gustavson, K.R., Lonergan, S.C. and Ruitenbeek, H.J. (1999): 'Selection and Modeling of Sustainable Development Indicators: A Case Study of the Fraser River Basin, British Columbia', *Ecological Economics* Vol. 28, No. 1, 117-132.

Hart, M. (1998): *Indicators of Sustainability: Everything you want to know about Indicators.* North Andover: Hart Environmental Data [online] [cited 15 September 1999]. Available from Internet URL: http://www.subjectmatters.com/indicators/Indicators/index.html.

Hinkle, D. (1965): *The Change in Personal Constructs from the Viewpoint of a Theory of Construct Implications* (Ph.D. Dissertation). Ohio: The Ohio State University.

IISD (International Institute for Sustainable Development) (1997): *Assessing Sustainable Development: Principles in Practice.* Winnipeg: IISD.

Iyer-Raniga, U. and Treloar, G. (2000): 'A Context for Participation in Sustainable Development', *Environmental Management* Vol. 26, No. 4, 349-361.

Kelly, G.A. (1963): *The Theory of Personality: The Psychology of Personal Constructs.* New York: W.W. Norton & Co. Inc.

Matson, J.V. and Goreham, E.A. (1997): *Zero Emissions Discharge, the Ultimate Solution to Sustainable Industrial Development* (Presented at the DeLange-Woolands Conference, 3rd March 1997). Houston: Rice University.

NAE (National Academy of Engineering) (1999): *Industrial Environmental Performance Metrics: Challenges and Opportunities.* Washington D.C.: National Academy Press.

Odom, S.L. (2001): *The Sustainable Systems Analysis Algorithm (SSAA): A Decision-Support and Evaluation Methodology Applied to Promote Sustainable Industrial Development* (Ph.D. Dissertation). Columbia: University of South Carolina.

Rogers, M. and Bruen, M. (1998): 'A New System for Weighting Environmental Criteria for Use within ELECTRE III', *European Journal of Operational Research* Vol. 107, No. 3, 552-563.

S.C. Department of Natural Resources, Water Resources Division (1996): *Managing Resources for a Sustainable Future: The Edisto River Basin Project Report.* Columbia: S.C. Department of Natural Resources, Water Resources Division

S.C. Water Resources Commission (1993) *Assessing Change in the Edisto River Basin: An Ecological Characterisation.* Columbia: S.C. Water Resources Commission.

SCOPE (Scientific Committee on Problems of the Environment) (1988): *SCOPE 34 - Practitioner's Handbook on Modelling of Dynamic Change in Ecosystems.* New York: Wiley.

Shearman, R. (1990): 'The Meaning and Ethics of Sustainability', *Environmental Management* Vol. 14, No. 1, 1-8.

Sillanpää, M. (1998): 'A New Deal for Sustainable Development in Business: Taking the Social Dimension Seriously', *Greener Management International* Vol. 23, Autumn, 93-115.

Spencer-Cooke, A. (1998): 'A Dinosaur's Survival Kit—Tools and Strategies for Sustainability' in: Roome, N.J. (Ed.): *Sustainable Strategies for Industry: The Future of Corporate Practice.* Washington DC: Island Press, 99-114.

US Department of Commerce, Bureau of Census (2001): *1999 Annual Survey of Manufactures: Value of Product Shipments* (M99(AS)-2). Washington D.C.: US Government Printing Office.

US Department of Energy, Energy Information Administration (2001): *Manufacturing Energy Consumption Survey: Manufacturing Consumption of Energy 1998* (DOE/EIA-0512(98)). Washington D.C.: US Government Printing Office.

US Department of Energy, Office of Energy Efficiency and Renewable Energy, Office of Industrial Technologies (1998): *United States Industrial Motor Systems Market Opportunities Assessment.* Burlington: Xenergy Inc.

Weiss, E B. (1993): 'Environmentally Sustainable Competitiveness—A Comment', *Yale Law Journal* Vol. 102, No. 8, 2123-2142.

ACKNOWLEDGEMENTS

This research was supported in part by two National Science Foundation Graduate Research Traineeship Grants, No. GER-9553409 and No. 9554556; a United States Department of Agriculture/South Carolina Forestry Commission Grant, No. 01-DG-11083145-060; and a grant from the Center for Manufacturing and Technology at the University of South Carolina.

PART II

EMPIRICAL SURVEYS – FINANCIAL MARKETS; INDUSTRY AND COUNTRY SURVEYS

Chapter 4

Views from the Financial Markets

THE ECONOMIC PERFORMANCE OF EUROPEAN STOCK CORPORATIONS
Does Sustainability Matter?

Klaus Rennings, Michael Schröder and Andreas Ziegler
Centre for European Economic Research (ZEW), Germany

Abstract: Concerning the relationship between sustainability and economic performance, this chapter examines the effect of environmental and social performance on the stock performance of European stock corporations. Stock performance is measured as the average monthly stock return for the period 1996–2001. The sustainability performance is measured both by an evaluation of the environmental or social risks of the industry to which a company belongs and by an evaluation of the environmental or social activities of a company relative to the industrial average. We apply two-stage econometric approaches, which include recent insights from empirical finance. The most important result is that a higher environmental sector performance has a significantly positive influence on the stock performance. In contrast, a higher social sector performance has a negative influence. This effect is somewhat less significant. The variables of corporate environmental and/or social activities relative to the industry average have no significant effect.

Companies can have very different motives for improving their environmental or social performance. One important goal of environmentally friendly behaviour, for example, is the intrinsic motivation to protect living conditions on Earth. This behaviour does not necessarily need an economic justification. However, for investors, shareholders or managers, it is important to know the relationship between environmental or social activities of companies and the economic performance. Beyond the general relationship between sustainability and economic performance, it is further necessary to identify specific success factors of firms with a positive relationship. In other words, firm managers are interested in the question: which management system or strategy is able to decrease costs and to increase sales (see Schaltegger and Synnestvedt 2002)?

The relationship between sustainability and economic performance is also a relevant issue for policy decisions. An example is the disclosure regulations for socially responsible investment (SRI). While SRI regulation can increase the transparency of SRI, it can be expected that the acceptance and diffusion of SRI (and thus the acceptance and diffusion of SRI regulation) in the future will crucially depend on economic success. In the SRI discussion, an integrated perspective of environmental and social performance is understood as sustainability performance. In this chapter, based on econometric estimations, we analyse the effect of different variables measuring sustainability performance on the economic performance of European corporations quoted on the stock exchange. As a measure of economic or financial performance, we consider the stock performance, since this concept is widely used. The concrete measure is the average monthly stock return.

The sustainability performance is measured independently both by an evaluation of the environmental or social risks of the industry to which a company belongs and by an evaluation of the environmental or social activities of a company relative to the industry average. Concerning the first measure, it should be noted that companies can hardly influence the environmental or social risks of their respective sector. However, particularly large companies are able to restructure their investments towards industries with a higher sustainability performance. The second measure of sustainability performance refers to corporate activities to reduce the sector-specific environmental or social risks. Such behaviour can be motivated, for example, by compliance with environmental regulation. Especially environmentally friendly behaviour can also be motivated by the attainment of cost reductions due to lower energy or material use and less waste production, or higher market shares due to product integrated environmental innovations. These activities may lead to a higher stock performance due to an improved management of natural resources. As Schaltegger and Synnestvedt (2002) have pointed out, important success factors are: consumers' willingness to pay, inefficiencies of existing natural resources management, financial importance of environmental issues to reach a critical mass and management quality. For example, a recent large-scale survey on effects of the European Eco-Management and Audit Scheme (EMAS) showed that EMAS firms are more innovative and competitive if the R&D department is closely involved in the EMAS development (see Rennings *et al.* 2003).

For the econometric analysis of the effect of sustainability performance on economic performance, we include recent insights from empirical finance, which have not been considered in previous studies. The finance literature agrees that the estimated (so-called) beta parameters of the capital asset pricing model (CAPM) are not sufficient to explain the cross-sectional variation in average stock returns. An increased explanatory power has been identified when the market capitalisation and the book-to-market value ratio are used as explanatory variables (see Fama and French 1992). A lower market capitalisation and a higher book-to-market value ratio tend to lead to higher average stock returns. Against this background, Fama and French (1993) have developed a multifactor model which uses the market capitalisation and the book-to-market value ratio for the construction of two additional factors to explain the expected stock returns. If econometric studies about the effect of sustainability performance on stock returns are exclusively based on the CAPM (such as Muoghalu *et al.* 1990, Hamilton 1995, Konar and Cohen 1997, Khanna *et al.* 1998, Yamashita *et al.* 1999 or Butz and Plattner 1999), parameter estimations may be biased because of omitted variables. In this chapter, we examine two different two-stage econometric approaches in order to avoid these potential biases.

The next section compares the methodology used to examine the relationship between sustainability and economic performance with those used in previous studies. We then describe our theoretical approach and the data for the econometric analysis, followed by a specification of the applied econometric approaches and a summary of the most important results. The last section draws some conclusions.

1.   LITERATURE REVIEW

The three approaches that are predominant in the literature are: portfolio analysis, event studies and panel or cross-sectional studies.

1.1   Portfolio Analysis

Portfolio analysis is used to investigate whether SRI funds (or indices) exhibit a different performance from funds (or indices) with a more general investment universe. Such studies compare the economic (or financial) performance of portfolios consisting of companies with a higher sustainability performance with portfolios that consist of companies with a lower sustainability performance. If, for example, there is no difference between the two types of funds or indices, then it follows that an investment in SRI funds will not result in a worse performance than conventional investments. Portfolio studies consider either existing funds (see White 1995; Statman 2000; Kreander *et al.* 2000; Schröder 2003) or virtual funds constructed by the researcher (see Cohen *et al.* 1997; Yamashita *et al.* 1999).

It should be noted that the financial success of existing funds depends heavily on the ability of the fund management. Portfolio studies cannot separate these management effects from sustainability performance effects.

But the main weakness of analyses of fund performance in general is that only the average economic performance of all corporations in the portfolio is considered (see also Wagner 2001). Consequently, the specific form of the influence of sustainability performance variables on the economic (or financial) performance can hardly be separated from other influences (particularly from the ability of the fund management, but also, for example, from the market capitalisation or from regional peculiarities) within this methodology. The identification of isolated effects needs econometric methods that include all relevant variables to explain the economic performance besides the variables of interest (here, the sustainability performance variables).

1.2   Event Studies

Event studies investigate the effect of news on the performance of single stocks (see e.g. Muoghalu *et al.* 1990; Hamilton 1995; Klassen and McLaughlin 1996; Konar and Cohen 1997; Blacconiere and Northcut 1997; Khanna *et al.* 1998; but a combination of event studies and analyses of fund performance can be found in Yamashita *et al.* 1999). These events typically have the character of negative news, such as information about hazardous accidents or the emission data according to the Toxics Release Inventory (TRI). Only a few studies consider the effects of positive news, such as information about companies winning environmental awards (see e.g. Klassen and McLaughlin 1996; Yamashita *et al.* 1999). Indeed, it can be argued that the sustainability performance of companies cannot be measured by special events. But the main weakness of event studies is their short-term character. Thus, short-term over-reactions of stock markets are possible, which may be compensated over time. Consequently, the investigation of the general effect of sustainability performance on economic performance needs long-term consideration.

1.3   Panel and Cross-sectional Studies

Panel and cross-sectional studies analyse the characteristics of companies concerning their environmental and social behaviour. These studies investigate the relationships between certain characteristics of companies and their economic performance. In our case, we used standard models of asset pricing, the CAPM and the multifactor model, to try to find out whether sustainability performance can improve the pricing of the stocks. In contrast to event studies, the analysis concentrates on characteristics of companies and not on specific news about the companies. In contrast to portfolio analysis, we do not analyse a portfolio of stocks but single stocks.

Therefore, we consider a longer time-horizon in the econometric analysis of this chapter. This methodology has received increasing attention in recent years owing to the restrictions of analyses of fund performance and event studies on sustainability performance (see Hart and Ahuja 1996; Butz and Plattner 1999; Yamashita et al. 1999; Konar and Cohen 2001; King and Lenox 2001; Thomas 2001; Wagner et al. 2002). It should be noted that other econometric analyses with longer observation periods that examine the influence of sustainability performance on the economic performance of corporations differ in the inclusion of the explanatory variables. Owing to these differences in the included explanatory variables and in the selected observation periods and regions, the results of the studies cannot be compared. But the previous studies particularly differ in the measures of the sustainability and economic performance. These differences also exist in event studies and in analyses of fund performance.

In this chapter, we use the stock performance as a measure of the economic performance of companies. In corporations quoted on the stock exchange, the stock performance can be calculated as the total return of stocks including both changes of stock prices and cash flows to the investor. The concrete measure of the stock performance is the average monthly stock return for the period 1996 to 2001. The approach based on stock return differs from other studies using accounting data and, thus, measures such as Tobin's Q, return on assets, return on sales, return on equity or return on capital employed as a measure of economic performance (see Hart and Ahuja 1996; King and Lenox 2001; Konar and Cohen 2001; Wagner et al. 2002). In contrast to other stock return-based econometric analyses with longer observation periods (see Butz and Plattner 1999; Thomas 2001) or event studies (see Muoghalu et al. 1990; Hamilton 1995; Klassen and McLaughlin 1996; Konar and Cohen 1997; Khanna et al. 1998), more advanced approaches, especially the multifactor model of Fama and French (1993), are applied in this study.

Furthermore, we use two different and independent measures for sustainability performance. The first measure evaluates the environmental and/or social risks of the industry to which a company belongs (compared with other industries). The second measure evaluates the environmental and/or social activities of a corporation relative to the industry average. In contrast, most previous studies only use one-dimensional and narrower measures of environmental performance. For example, these approaches refer to temporary environmentally friendly behaviour that has been published in newspaper articles (see Klassen and McLaughlin 1996; Yamashita et al. 1999) or to temporary behaviour that is harmful to the environment leading to lawsuits or penalties due to non-compliance with environmental regulation (see Muoghalu et al. 1990).

Such negative consequences are often considered in addition to the emission data according to the TRI (see Cohen *et al*. 1997; Konar and Cohen 2001). Several other studies use only the TRI data (or other emission data, see e.g. Wagner *et al*. 2002) to measure the environmental performance of companies (see Hamilton 1995; Hart and Ahuja 1996; Konar and Cohen 1997; Khanna *et al*. 1998; King and Lenox 2001). However, the TRI data seem to be a weak indicator for environmental performance as a whole since they do not give any information about pollution from non-toxic substances such as carbon dioxide emissions or through energy and material use. Other aspects, such as the existence of an environmental management system, are not included either. Consequently, general conclusions about the environmental performance cannot be drawn. Furthermore, a selectivity problem arises because studies based on the TRI data include only those companies (in the USA) that have actually emitted certain harmful substances.

Moreover, the measure of environmental performance (e.g. with emission data) often mixes two independent constituents: the comparison of corporate environmental activities with those of other corporations in the sector and sector-specific influences. Both components should be evaluated separately. But only a few studies analyse these constituents. Cohen *et al*. (1997), for example, examine the corporate environmental activities compared with other corporations of the industry in their analysis of fund performance. Most notably, King and Lenox (2001) even investigate both constituents separately in their econometric analysis with longer observation periods. Finally, most studies examine only the environmental performance and neglect the social dimension of sustainability performance. The social part of sustainability performance has been considered only in the investigation of ethical funds so far (see Statman 2000; Kreander *et al*. 2000; Schröder 2003). In contrast, the social dimension is generally missing in econometric studies, with the exception of the examination of Butz and Plattner (1999).

2. THEORETICAL APPROACH AND DATA

One theoretical basis of our analysis is the multifactor model of Fama and French (1993), which measures the link between three risk factors (market risk, market capitalisation, book-to-market value ratio) and the expected return of stocks. Thus, Fama and French propose the expansion of the traditional CAPM (including only market risk) by two additional variables to explain the expected stock returns. The arising multifactor model usually has a stronger explanatory power than the CAPM (see Fama and French 1996; Davis *et al*. 2000; Berkowitz and Qiu 2001). Owing to the success of this model, it is now a standard model for empirical asset pricing. Thus, we also use this model to find out whether the sustainability performance can explain part of the expected returns of European stocks in addition to the aforementioned three risk factors.

The sustainability performance could be particularly relevant to correct the book-to-market factor. The book-to-market factor has a positive coefficient in the stock return regressions. Thus, a higher book-to-market value should coincide with a higher average stock return. The sustainability performance is a correction of the book-to-market factors, as those parts of the firm value that characterise 'sustainability performance' are not properly accounted for in the book value. In general, the degree of sustainability of a company is at least partly characterised by organisational structures, which cannot therefore be part of the usual book value as they are not valued in the balance sheet. Another example is that firms can in many cases write off environmentally relevant investments more quickly than other investments. As a consequence, companies with a high degree of sustainability performance have a book-to-market value that is too low compared with companies with a low degree of sustainability performance. A positive coefficient for the additional factor 'sustainability performance' could thus correct for this underestimate of the book-to-market value. In other words, a positive coefficient of the sustainability performance could explain above-average stock returns of those companies with a relatively high degree of sustainability performance.

In our econometric analysis, we use data about the sustainability performance of companies that stem from the Swiss bank Sarasin & Cie in Basle. This bank has evaluated approximately 300 European corporations quoted on the stock exchange (date: September 2001) using environmental and social criteria. The stock corporations under consideration cover about 80% of the stock index of Morgan Stanley Capital International (MSCI) Ltd for Europe. On the one hand, many of the evaluated companies are large. These companies are important for their sector and serve as a reference for the sustainability performance evaluation. On the other hand, corporations with lower market capitalisation that are relevant because of their sustainability profile are also evaluated. Overall, large corporations are over-represented in the sample compared with their ratio in the population of all European corporations quoted on the stock exchange. However, this aspect is less relevant for the econometric estimations, since the market capitalisation is included as a control variable to explain the average monthly stock return.

Concerning the sustainability criteria, these approximately 300 companies have been evaluated by a technique developed by Sarasin & Cie. Although the evaluation criteria were developed by Sarasin & Cie, there are large overlaps with evaluation criteria from other rating agencies and with evolving international standards of sustainability reporting, such as the guidelines developed by the Global Reporting Initiative (2000). On the one hand, the measure of sustainability performance refers to the industry of the company: that is, the extent of environmental and/or social risks an industry might have. Environmental criteria are the use of resources, emissions and the degree of centralisation. Besides the degree of centralisation, social criteria for the evaluation of sectors are the pressures on social stability and the damage of individual values or rights. On the other hand, the evaluation of sustainability performance refers to the activities of a corporation to reduce the sector-specific environmental and/or social risks relative to the sector average. Environmental criteria are drawn from the life-cycle approach of a product: that is, corporate activities aiming at a reduction of environmental impacts are evaluated along the entire value chain (pre-production, production, use of products and services). Social criteria are drawn from the stakeholder approach. This means that corporate activities are evaluated considering the relationships with different stakeholders (general public, suppliers, investors, employees, clients, competitors). All these different types of sustainability performance are evaluated on a five-stage scale (but in the econometric analysis, dummy variables derived from the corresponding ordinal variables are also used).

It should be noted that not all of the approximately 300 originally evaluated European stock corporations are included in the econometric analysis. First of all, only those corporations are examined that have been quoted on the stock exchange during the complete period from January 1996 to August 2001. Furthermore, corporations are not considered if they have merged or been taken over during this observation period. In addition, we only include companies when all relevant financial data is provided in the database we used, Thomson Financial Datastream. All total return stock indices (which contain both changes of stock prices and cash flows to the investor) to compute the stock returns, in addition to data on the market capitalisation and on the book value, must exist for the companies during the complete observation period. Altogether, 214 out of the approximately 300 originally evaluated European corporations quoted on the stock exchange were suitable for consideration.

The period January 1996 to August 2001 was chosen in order to get a sufficiently large number of companies with all relevant data. We could have increased the number of stock corporations by using a shorter period, but the time-series used for the estimation of the CAPM and the multifactor model should not be too short. Therefore, the applied time interval of 5–6 years seems to be a reasonable compromise between the needs of a relatively large number of observations and a long observation period. This observation period covers both the strong worldwide increase in stock prices that occurred up to the beginning of 2000 and the following decrease, particularly in the technology sector. The final date (August 2001) of the period was chosen to avoid the influence of the stock market disturbances that appeared after the terrorist attack of 11 September in New York on the estimation results.

In the econometric analysis, we (partially) use the market capitalisation and the book-to-market value ratio of each company at the beginning of the observation period (i.e. in January 1996) as control variables to explain the average monthly stock returns. These two variables are denominated in Swiss Francs (SFR) according to the Thomson Financial Datastream database. Note that some corporations split their equity capital into different types of stocks: for example, common and preferred stocks. In these cases, the market capitalisation and the book-to-market value ratio and especially the stock returns are calculated using that type of equity capital with the highest number of stocks in 2001. In order to check for a possible distortion of the estimation results due to the neglect of a relevant type of equity capital, the econometric analysis was also performed using those companies with only one essential type of equity capital. But the consideration of these 175 (out of 214) companies does not yield qualitatively different results.

Besides the financial variables, country dummies are always used and industry dummies are partly used as additional control variables to explain the average monthly stock returns. These dummy variables cover potential influences on the stock performance that are country and sector-specific. The 214 European companies included in the econometric analysis stem from the United Kingdom, Switzerland, Germany, the Netherlands, France, Sweden, Italy, Austria, Spain, Denmark, Finland, Norway and Belgium. The industry dummies refer to the technology, banking, insurance and construction sectors. For the econometric analysis, we calculate the stock returns using total return stock indices from the Thomson Financial Datastream database, denominated in SFR. Furthermore, the estimation of the CAPM and the multifactor model requires the inclusion of the return on a market portfolio of stocks and the risk-free interest rate. In this respect, the return on a market portfolio of stocks is calculated using the Financial Times Stock Exchange (FTSE) Eurotop 300 index (this index covers the 300 European companies with the highest market capitalisation). The risk-free interest rate is represented by the return of a Swiss government bond with a constant duration of one month.

3.   ECONOMETRIC ANALYSIS

We used two econometric approaches in order to get robust results. Both approaches include two steps. Our first approach was based on the CAPM model. In a second step, the CAPM is extended by using all three risk factors mentioned above as control variables. Thus, the second approach is fully based on the multifactor model according to Fama and French (1993).

In the first stage of the first econometric approach, the CAPM is estimated for each of the 214 European companies under consideration using the ordinary least squares (OLS) method. Thus, the excess return of the stocks is explained only by the excess return on the market portfolio of stocks. As a result, one receives the corresponding estimated beta parameter for each of the companies. These parameter estimates are then used as control variables to explain the average monthly stock returns between 1996 and 2001 in the second-stage regression model. In the second-stage regression model, we also consider the two variables, market capitalisation and book-to-market value ratio, proposed by Fama and French (1992) as explained above. Note that these two variables were constructed at the beginning of the observation period to avoid problems with the use of the endogenous variables. Furthermore, country and sector dummies are considered as additional control variables. In particular, the currently interesting sustainability performance variables discussed above are included as explanatory variables in the second-stage regression model.

A multifactor model is estimated for each of the 214 European companies under consideration in the first stage of the second econometric approach (for details, see Ziegler *et al.* 2002). The results are the corresponding three (OLS) estimated parameters for each of the companies. Similar to the first approach, we use these (now three for each company) parameter estimates as control variables to explain the average monthly stock returns. Furthermore, country and sector dummies are included again. Since the market capitalisation and the book-to-market value ratio are considered in the derivation of the multifactor model, these variables are not considered as control variables. But the most important explanatory variables in the second-stage regression model are again the sustainability performance variables.

The econometric analysis with both approaches (see in detail Ziegler *et al.* 2002) shows that a higher environmental sector performance (i.e. a lower degree of environmental risks) has a significantly positive effect on the average monthly stock return between 1996 and 2001. According to this result, the stock market rewards investments in stock corporations of clean sectors (with otherwise similar economic characteristics, e.g. concerning financial variables) with a premium. This influence is particularly strong for companies with the two highest evaluations of environmental sector performance compared with companies with lower evaluations. In contrast, a higher social sector performance has a negative effect on the average monthly stock return. Consequently, the stock market penalises investments in stock corporations of sectors with a high social performance (and other-wise similar economic characteristics) with a negative premium. But the latter effect is statistically less robust than the former effect.

Some sectors with a very high evaluation of environmental performance are often considered as sectors with a lower overall sustainability perfor-mance. This is particularly true for the banking and the insurance sectors. Both industries have the second lowest evaluation of social performance. In further examinations, variables of an overall sustainability performance (i.e. environmental and social performance) of the sector are included to explain the average monthly stock return between 1996 and 2001. These variables have no significant influence in most cases because of the obvious rivalry between the positive effect of a high environmental sector performance and the negative effect of a high social sector performance. But some of these variables actually have a significantly positive effect. Thus, investments in stock corporations of sectors with a high overall sustainability performance seem to be at least as good as investments in other stock corporations (with otherwise similar economic characteristics). Accordingly, this restriction of the investment universe should not reduce the average stock return of the investor.

Finally, a significant effect on the average monthly stock return between 1996 and 2001 was not found for any variable of the corporate environ-mental and/or social activities relative to the sector average. Consequently, neither a strong environmental behaviour nor a strong social behaviour of the management of a company can improve the stock performance. But, obvi-ously, this sustainable behaviour does not have a negative influence, either. Thus, when it comes to the average monthly stock return, such corporate environmental or social activities can be increased without economic losses. Concerning the investor view, investments in stock corporations with higher environmental and/or social activities compared with the other corporations of the sector do not result in lower average monthly stock returns than investments in other stock corporations (with otherwise similar economic characteristics).

4.   CONCLUSIONS

Summing up the results of this econometric analysis, the question posed in this chapter concerning the economic performance of companies can be answered with: yes, single components of sustainability do matter. A higher environmental sector performance has a significantly positive effect on the stock performance, whereas a higher social sector performance has a (statis-tically less robust) negative effect. In contrast, variables of an overall sustainability performance of the sector rarely have, and variables of the corporate environmental and/or social activities relative to the sector average never have, a significant influence on the average monthly stock return. Concerning the latter result, more corporate environmental or social activities obviously do not lead to a better economic performance compared with corporations in the same sector that do not enforce such activities. Thus, it can be expected that, because of a lack of incentives, companies do not install or improve environmental or social management systems voluntarily, although this would be desirable from a social perspective. As a consequence for environmental policy, it can be stated that voluntary measures will hardly substitute for environmental regulation.

Furthermore, the results are relevant with regard to the international trend of SRI disclosure regulation for pension funds. In 2000, the United Kingdom introduced an obligatory statement of investment principles (SIP) for pension funds. In this statement, the funds must declare their environmental, social and ethical investment criteria. A similar regulation has been introduced in Germany by the so-called Riester-pension reform: that is, voluntary additional private savings for retirement. The certificate for the Riester-pension requires that the investor declare his investment policy, including environmental, social and ethical criteria. Moreover, nearly all governments and international organisations (including multinational firms and/or business associations) have signed commitments to the principles of sustainable development in the meantime. Regarding the results of this study, these governments and organisations (including all their dependencies) should consider an extended SIP in the sense that funds with a higher sustainability performance are preferred in general.

Concerning the econometric analysis of this chapter, it should be noted that the results are based on the examination of the average monthly stock returns of European corporations quoted on the stock exchange during the period 1996 to 2001. The region under consideration and the observation period could strongly influence the estimation results about the effect of sustainability performance on economic performance. To our knowledge, there are no comparable studies for European companies using this observation period especially using these measures of sustainability and economic performance as well as applying these econometric approaches. Therefore, the results of this chapter cannot be directly compared with the results of other econometric analyses with longer observation periods that mostly concentrate on the USA. The time horizon used in this study is also relatively short. The period 1996 to 2001 is, among other things, characterised by a strong general increase in stock prices up to the beginning of 2000 and then by a collapse particularly in the technology sector. Although possible sector effects are controlled for by including additional dummy variables, there might be an influence on the estimation results that stems from the specific observation period.

Methodically, another difficulty is the fundamental assumption of the econometric models used in this chapter. The models imply that the variables of the (average) sustainability performance (between 1996 and 2001) influence the average monthly stock return (between 1996 and 2001). But it might also be possible that a relatively successful company (or sector) can afford to increase the environmental or social performance. If such a reverse effect existed, the estimations of the parameters would be biased. With regard to the causality of the relationship between environmental and economic performance, lagged explanatory variables are often used in other studies. That is, the effect of environmental performance on the economic performance one or more years later is examined (see Hart and Ahuja 1996; King and Lenox 2001; Konar and Cohen 2001). But all these studies are based on the TRI data. Despite the problem of subjectiveness, it seems that the evaluations applied in this chapter are a better indicator for the entire environmental performance than measures based on the TRI data. In the future, we should also use lagged explanatory variables within the econometric models. But the necessary time-series of sustainability performance evaluations are not yet available.

If we were able to apply such time-series of sustainability performance evaluations, we could connect these lagged explanatory variables with panel models (one example for the application of panel models is King and Lenox 2001). In the framework of such models, possible intertemporal effects on the endogenous variable such as the stock return could be considered. If intertemporal effects existed and if they were not modelled, the estimation of the parameters would be biased. But, as already mentioned, the conditions for the application of panel models are time-series of evaluations of the environmental and/or social performance, which are not yet available. Finally, it should be noted that the causality problem of the relationship between sustainability and economic performance can be analysed by simultaneous equation models. One example for the application of such models is Wagner *et al.* 2002, but this study also uses only emissions data to operationalise environmental performance. Thus, the consideration of simultaneous equation models with sustainability performance evaluations would be another field of research in future investigations.

REFERENCES

Berkowitz, M.K. and Qiu, J. (2001) *Common Risk Factors in Explaining Canadian Equity Returns*. Discussion paper; University of Toronto.

Blacconiere, W.G. and Northcut, W.D. (1997) 'Environmental Information and Market Reactions to Environmental Legislation', *Journal of Accounting, Auditing and Finance* Vol. 12 No. 2: 149-178.

Butz, C. and Plattner, A. (1999) *Nachhaltige Aktienanlagen: Eine Analyse der Rendite in Abhängigkeit von Umwelt- und Sozialkriterien*. Basel: Sarasin Studie.

Cohen, M.A., Fenn, S.A. and Konar, S. (1997) *Environmental and Financial Performance: Are They Related?* Discussion paper; Nashville: Vanderbilt University.

Davis, J.L., Fama, E.F. and French, K.R. (2000) 'Characteristics, Covariances, and Average Returns: 1929 to 1997', *Journal of Finance* Vol. 55 No. 1: 389-406.

Fama, E.F. and French, K.R. (1992) 'The Cross-Section of Expected Stock Returns', *Journal of Finance* Vol. 47 No. 2: 427-465.

Fama, E.F. and French, K.R. (1993) 'Common Risk Factors in the Returns on Stocks and Bonds', *Journal of Financial Economics* No. 33: 3-56.

Fama, E.F. and French, K.R. (1996) 'Multifactor Explanations of Asset Pricing Anomalies', *Journal of Finance* Vol. 51 No. 1: 55-84.

Global Reporting Initiative (2000) *Sustainability Reporting Guidelines on Economic, Environmental, and Social Performance*. Boston: Global Reporting Initiative.

Hamilton, J.T. (1995) 'Pollution as News: Media and Stock Market Reactions to the Toxics Release Inventory Data', *Journal of Environmental Economics and Management* No. 28: 98-113.

Hart, S.L. and Ahuja, G. (1996) 'Does It Pay To Be Green? An Empirical Examination of the Relationship between Emission Reduction and Firm Performance', *Business Strategy and the Environment* No. 5: 30-37.

Khanna, M., Rose, W., Quimio, H. and Bojilova, D. (1998) 'Toxics Release Information: A Policy Tool for Environmental Protection', *Journal of Environmental Economics and Management* No. 36: 243-266.

King, A. and Lenox, M. (2001) 'Does It Really Pay To Be Green?', *Journal of Industrial Ecology* Vol. 5 No. 1: 105-116.

Klassen, R.D. and McLaughlin, C.P. (1996) 'The Impact of Environmental Management on Firm Performance', *Management Science* Vol. 42 No. 8: 1,199-1,214.

Konar, S. and Cohen, M.A. (1997) 'Information as Regulation: The Effect of Community Right to Know Laws on Toxic Emissions', *Journal of Environmental Economics and Management* No. 32: 109-124.

Konar, S. and Cohen, M.A. (2001) 'Does the Market Value Environmental Performance?', *Review of Economics and Statistics* Vol. 83 No. 2: 281-289.

Kreander, N., Gray, R.H., Power, D.M. and Sinclair, C.D. (2000) *Evaluating the Performance of Ethical and Non-Ethical Funds: A Matched Pair Analysis*. Discussion paper; University of Dundee.

Muoghalu, M.I., Robison, H.D. and Glascock, J.L. (1990) 'Hazardous Waste Lawsuits, Stockholder Returns, and Deterrence', *Southern Economic Journal* Vol. 7 No. 2: 357-370.

Rennings, K., Ziegler, A., Ankele, K., Hoffmann, E. and Nill, J. (2003) *The Influence of the EU Environmental Management and Auditing Scheme on Environmental Innovations and Competitiveness in Germany: An Analysis on the Basis of Case Studies and a Large-Scale Survey*. Discussion paper no. 03-14; Mannheim: Zentrum für Europäische Wirtschaftsforschung (ZEW).

Schaltegger, S. and Synnestvedt, T. (2002) 'The Link between "Green" and Economic Success: Environmental Management as the Crucial Trigger between Environmental and Economic Performance', *Journal of Environmental Management* No. 65: 339-346.

Schröder, M. (2003) *Socially Responsible Investments in Germany, Switzerland and the United States: An Analysis of Investment Funds and Indices*. Discussion paper no. 03-10; Mannheim: Zentrum für Europäische Wirtschaftsforschung (ZEW).

Statman, M. (2000) 'Socially Responsible Mutual Funds', *Financial Analysts' Journal* Vol. 56 No. 3: 30-39.

Thomas, A. (2001) 'Corporate Environmental Policy and Abnormal Stock Price Returns: An Empirical Investigation', *Business Strategy and the Environment* No. 10: 125-134.

Wagner, M. (2001) *A Review of Empirical Studies Concerning the Relationship between Environmental and Economic Performance*. Lüneburg: Centre for Sustainability Management, University of Lüneburg.

Wagner, M., Van Phu, N., Azomahou, T. and Wehrmeyer, W. (2002) 'The Relationship between the Environmental and Economic Performance of Firms: An Empirical Analysis of the European Paper Industry', *Corporate Social Responsibility and Environmental Management* No. 9: 133-146.

White, M.A. (1995) 'The Performance of Environmental Mutual Funds in the United States and Germany: Is There Economic Hope For Green Investors?', *Research in Corporate Social Performance and Policy* No. 1 (suppl.): 323-344.

Yamashita, M., S. Sen and M.C. Roberts (1999) 'The Rewards for Environmental Conscientiousness in the US Capital Markets', *Journal of Financial and Strategic Decisions* Vol. 12 No. 1: 73-82.

Ziegler, A., Rennings, K. and Schröder, M. (2002) *Der Einfluss ökologischer und sozialer Nachhaltigkeit auf den Shareholder Value europäischer Aktiengesellschaften*. Discussion paper no. 02-32; Mannheim: Zentrum für Europäische Wirtschaftsforschung (ZEW).

ACKNOWLEDGEMENTS

This study is part of the research project 'Improving the Environmental and Sustainability Transparency of Financial Markets', funded by the German Ministry of Education and Research (BMBF). We are grateful to Andreas Knörzer, Eckhard Plinke, Christoph Butz, Paschen von Flotow, Rolf Häßler, Elke Eberts and two anonymous referees for useful comments on earlier versions of the chapter. On top of that, special thanks are dedicated to Ilja Karabanow and Thomas Rohrmann for their untiring commitment during data analysis.

CAPITAL MARKETS AND CORPORATE ENVIRONMENTAL PERFORMANCE
Research in the United States

Dinah A. Koehler
Economics and Decision Sciences Research, National Center for Environmental Research,
US Environmental Protection Agency, USA

Abstract: A series of empirical analyses in the USA reviewed in this chapter provide insight into whether there is a systematic relationship between environmental and financial performance and whether it is strong enough to inform both regulatory and corporate environmental strategy. The findings seem to imply that capital markets react long-term to environmental performance. However, a closer look at the research indicates that US capital markets pay attention to environmental news, but that it is a short-term reaction and will not necessarily affect long-term returns or company-level sustainability. Econometric concerns and model misspecification consistently undermine the quality of findings.

1.   INTRODUCTION

The 1990s saw a proliferation of empirical research in the United States on the relationship between capital markets and corporate environmental performance. The focus thus far is on measures of environmental performance, and the long-term implications for sustainability can only be conjectured. After perusing this literature, the curious reader is left questioning how to interpret the finding of a statistically significant contemporaneous correlation between measures of environmental performance and financial performance from time t to $t+n$. A viable interpretation depends on whether we believe **and** can demonstrate that environmental expenditures improve company profitability in a structural way. A first plausible mechanism is that environmental performance (A) leads to changes in financial performance (B) (Hart and Ahuja 1996; King and Lenox 2001, 2002). Secondly, it may be a matter of reverse causality, where profitable companies can afford to invest in environmental performance, B to A (Konar and Cohen 1997b). In addition to these two possibilities, researchers consider a third; there may be another factor C that is affecting both A and B, and this omitted variables bias may be responsible for the statistical relationship (Holthausen 1994). These omitted variables could include various environmental management strategies applied in the company-specific setting that affects both environmental and economic performance (Schaltegger and Synnestvedt 2002) or R&D (McWilliams and Siegel 2000). Additional omitted variables are plausible. Guided by multiple discussions with finance professors, management scholars and environmental professionals, this chapter reflects my possible explanations for the statistical relationship found in this literature by delving more deeply into finance economics research.

The reader will note that my reflections are motivated by a concern with model uncertainty, where the debate centres on which form of model to employ. Another potential concern in this research is parameter uncertainty, which focuses on random and systematic (i.e. biased) measurement error and lack of data for key inputs to a specific model. Uncertainty, however, is not to be confused with variability, which refers to the variability inherent to particular parameters of an analysis such as the great variability in market capitalisation of companies that can change dramatically over time. Statistical methods can be employed to reduce the effects of parameter uncertainty and variability in statistical modelling. Experienced analysts expend more energy debating model structure, which has a greater impact on results by leading to either over- or under-estimation of a relationship. By definition, a model is a simplification of reality and thus all models are definitively false—though some models are better at predicting outcomes than others (Morgan and Henrion 1990). This makes the matter of model choice central to any analysis, particularly when a meta-analysis of a wide variety of studies combined would be difficult and time-consuming. The literature reviewed here is no exception, with largely incomparable models and results that paint a mixed picture of the relationship between corporate environmental performance and the reactions of capital markets.

Providing further support for a concern with model choice, Wagner *et al.* (2002) note that the results of research to date are highly variable and inconclusive with respect to whether a change in financial performance in association with a change in environmental performance is positive, negative or dynamic over time. Theoretical schools support each outcome. Traditionally, economists posit that investment in environmental technology comes at a net cost to the company. Thus, Palmer *et al.* (1995) argue that compliance with environmental regulations will always be costly, forcing companies to face a trade-off between social benefits and private costs. Alternatively, companies can gain competitive advantage through innovation offsets that outweigh the costs of compliance (i.e. net financial gain) in a dynamic view of the world (Porter 1991; Porter and van der Linde 1995a, 1995b) or increased productivity due to efficiency gains, which should be reflected in changes in company cash flows (King and Lenox 2001; Reinhardt 1999a; Schaltegger and Synnestvedt 2002). Porter and van der Linde theorise that the perceived trade-off between minimising private costs and maximising public gain that underlies most environmental regulation has been over-stated. This appears likely, not because companies benefit from innovation offsets, but because empirical evidence indicates that regulations do not have an adverse effect on competitiveness due to the low costs of compliance (Jaffe *et al.* 1995). Other mechanisms are based on various stakeholder pressures such as changes in consumer, customer or investor preference that ought to guide a company's engagement in voluntary measures beyond compliance and bespeaks a basic business objective (HBR 1994; Reinhardt 1999a, 1999b). In an effort at synthesis, Wagner *et al.* (2002) and Schaltegger and Synnestvedt (2002) propose that a company can initially gain competitive advantage from investment in environmental improvement up to an optimum, after which point further investment comes at a net cost as low-hanging fruit have already been harvested (Walley and Whitehead 1994).

This chapter does not review all research in detail; it has been summarised and classified elsewhere (Margolis and Walsh 2001; Wagner *et al.* 2002). It focuses on a number of key papers that are exemplary of the research paths taken and discuss the significance of model choice on results. The remainder of this chapter is organised as follows. Section 2 introduces the mechanism underlying changes in stock prices and how these can affect corporate behaviour. Section 3 introduces the research, followed by a discussion with reference to theoretical models and financial empirical results in Section 4 and proposals for future research in Section 5. Finally, the chapter concludes that regulation will play a critical role in strengthening the impact of capital markets on corporate environmental behaviour.

2. HOW CAPITAL MARKETS AFFECT CORPORATE BEHAVIOUR

While much of the literature focuses on company environmental strategy formulation with respect to economic motivation and financial consequences, too little attention has been given to the conditions under which capital markets can be of influence. The potential reaction of capital markets to new information on company pollution can be explained with two basic scenarios. In the first scenario shown in Figure 1, information on expected environmental liabilities or clean-up costs enters the market at time t causing the stock price to drop because investors expect decreased earnings and dividend payments. Any change in stock price corresponding to a negative or positive company-specific event equals the change in the company's present value—to the extent that the marginal financial benefit of acting on the information does not exceed the marginal cost for market participants (Jensen 1978). The return (i.e. the market's discount rate) is unchanged if the fundamentals of the company do not change. This is the cash flow news effect.

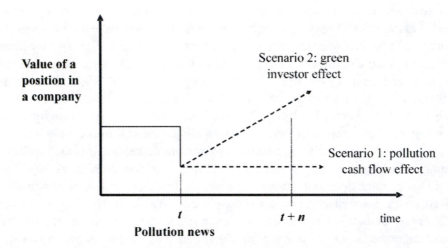

Figure 1. Capital market reaction to environmental news

If the drop is on the day of the news release, we can say with a high degree of confidence that the environmental news caused the drop in stock price for that company. If the price drop is gradual over several days $(t+n)$, then we can no longer be as certain because other news may have interfered. This scenario is best tested using the event study methodology described in the next section.

A short-term negative price movement does not, however, offer a compelling reason to argue that there is a long-term business case for environmental or sustainable investments. Short-term price movements do not provide enough substance to formulate buy/sell strategies unless we believe sustainability to be a matter for day traders arbitraging on momentum. We thus turn to the second basic scenario, the green investor effect, also shown in Figure 1. Imagine that 'green' investors worried about sustainability become aware of pollution news and decide to sell 'dirty' stocks, which reduces their price. Based on finance research (Chopra *et al.* 1992; DeBondt and Thaler 1985; LaPorta 1996), we can expect neutral investors who do not care about environmental performance to buy cheaper 'dirty' stocks anticipating a higher return. This is the expected returns news scenario and returns here are no longer constant. The effect on price can be a temporary panic and share price bounces back quickly. Alternatively, when investor's 'green' preferences are more long-lived, the price effect is more long-term requiring multi-period analyses. Whether the green investor effect is short-lived or long-lived, the dividend is not necessarily affected if there is no change in cash flows. In this scenario, green investor preferences consistently drive stock price changes for 'dirty' companies, whether or not such a company faces an immediate environmental expenditure.

Finally, to explain how changes in stock price can affect corporate behaviour, consider that as the stock price of 'dirty' companies falls, investors will demand compensation with a higher return. Therefore the cost of capital for such companies will increase. If the difference in price between 'dirty' and 'clean' stocks increases and begins to exceed the investment necessary to augment a dirty technology, then 'dirty' companies will invest expecting an increase in stock price. As a result, 'clean' companies may eventually achieve a lower expected return and hence a lower cost of capital (Heinkel *et al.* 2001). If an environmental effect is found, it should be greater for small companies than for large companies, which exhibit greater risk due to the cash flow effects of investment projects and thus have a higher correlation between returns and cash flow news (Vuolteenaho 2000)—unless the deep pockets of large companies are specifically targeted in environmental liability proceedings.

3.   EVIDENCE AND EVOLUTION OF LITERATURE

A cursory glance through the literature shows a great variety of methodological approaches. The vast majority of empirical analyses use a company's market value as the measure of financial performance, which places this research more under the rubric of finance economics. Other academic disciplines are organisational behaviour and accounting. Given the preponderance of research into whether capital markets value company environmental performance, the following section is organised to provide insight into whether the response of capital markets to environmental news is temporary or permanent. In modelling work on short- and long-term effects of environmental performance on financial performance, a key assumption has been constant returns; this follows from the random walk theory of stock prices. In other words, returns are not predictable in efficient markets and, every day, 'the stock market return is like the result of flipping the same coin, over and over again' (Cochrane 1999). Under the assumption of constant returns, i.e. a constant market discount rate, researchers model the relationship between environmental and financial performance without accounting for risk. I return to this important issue in Section 4.

3.1   Short-Term Event Studies

The classic framework for understanding the financial value of environmental information is the market efficiency hypothesis. Here the assumption is that all known determinants of stock returns are incorporated into stock prices and prices are updated continuously to reflect new information. If prices do not move when new information is revealed, then the market is already efficient with respect to that information. Campbell (1991) points out that, because stock returns are unpredictable under the strict random walk theory, unexpected movements in stock prices are due only to news about future dividends (i.e. cash flow news). Since the first study of this phenomenon by Fama *et al.* (1969), event studies have been widely used to test market efficiency with respect to new information.

Event studies offer the strongest econometric results of causality when they are limited to one or at most five trading days after the event to ensure that confounding news does not obscure the effect of interest. Most environmental event studies to date find a significant negative impact of pollution news on stock prices. Thus, for example, in the five trading days following the 1986 explosion at Union Carbide's plant at Bhopal in India, which left approximately 4,000 people dead and another 200,000 injured, the market value of Union Carbide's common stock price fell approximately $1 billion or 27.9% (from $3,443 million to $2,483 million) (Blacconiere and Patten 1994). Furthermore, the stock price of Union Carbide suffered a sustained drop in returns for over one month and pulled down the stocks of 47 chemical companies for at least 10 days after the accident. Similarly, following the *Exxon Valdez* oil spill, the stock of Exxon suffered a sustained drop over six months (Jones *et al.* 1994; White 1996), with a value loss ranging from $4.7 billion to $11.3 billion depending on the length of the event window. Hamilton (1995) found that, when Toxic Release Inventory (TRI) data were first released to the public in 1989, the stock value of TRI-reporting companies dropped by an average of $4.1 million. Similarly, Konar and Cohen (1997a) found that for 40 out of 130 companies that suffered the greatest drop in stock price after the 1989 TRI release, 32 significantly reduced their reported TRI releases per dollar of revenue by 1992. Khanna *et al.* (1998) evaluated investor reactions to repeat annual release of TRI data in 1989–1994 for 91 chemical companies and found significant negative abnormal returns on the day following the release of TRI data in four out of their six sample years (1991–1994). They concluded that capital markets reward and punish different levels of environmental performance measured by changes in TRI emissions.

It should be no surprise that capital markets react negatively to major events such as the Bhopal incident or *Exxon Valdez* oil spill. It is more surprising that capital markets react negatively to routine events such as annual TRI releases, which are not emitted illegally. TRI event studies merit a closer look. Re-analysing Hamilton's (1995) results for the 1989 TRI release, Cram and Koehler (2000) utilised Zellner's (1962) seemingly unrelated regressions (SUR) and found that previous researchers had overestimated the significance of the TRI effect because they failed to account for contemporaneous correlation across companies. Contemporaneous correlation arises when all sample companies experience the same event (e.g. TRI release to the public) on the same day—'clustering.' When event clustering is not adjusted for, researchers are more likely to eject the null hypothesis of no significant change in returns. In contrast to Hamilton, Cram and Koehler found that, with SUR, the aggregate average TRI impact on stock prices is no longer significant. However, they did find a statistically significant stock market reaction to the news for each individual company on the event day and that approximately half of the total 368 companies had an abnormal drop in stock price on the event date. This ambiguous result could equally be assigned to chance and puts into question the finding of a TRI effect isolated in event studies.

According to these analyses, environmental events are cash flow news, as evidenced by a short-lived negative market reaction. In fact, we should not expect the market response to be sustained unless markets are slow to incorporate environmental cash flow news into stock price, as has been documented in the post-earnings drift literature. However, US capital market players react to news about a significant accident or fine regardless of whether it involves damage to the environment and public health or not. This does not prove irrevocably that environmental investments or sustainability will eventually result in an increase in stock price. It simply means that capital markets are efficient with respect to information related to future environmental expenditures, and that this news leads to a short-term decrease in stock price. The drop in stock price does not necessarily tell us whether capital markets have incorporated the indirect social costs or reputation costs of pollution. In fact, in their event study Karpoff *et al.* (1998) found that the drop in stock price is comparable in dollar value to the fines and penalties issued by the government. A drop in stock price is more likely to indicate what capital markets believe to be the direct expected expenditures in cleaner technology or cleaning up—in other words, the costs of being eco-efficient. It is notable that these are perceived as short-term costs and not short-term benefits, indicating that the U-shaped relationship theorised by Schaltegger and Synnestvedt (2002) is not achieved in the USA.

Several concerns complicate the analysis of Scenario 1, which are primarily parametric in nature. In the USA, the average costs of compliance are low or not reported, and thus will have a limited negative impact on share prices. The other main problem is that some types of environmental information (e.g. minor accidents, spills or mandated release of TRI emissions) are not indicative of a cash flow impact. In general, environmental events are a difficult area to evaluate with event study methodology since they are difficult to define clearly and tend to be regulation driven and hence more readily anticipated (Blacconiere and Northcut 1997; Bosch 1996; Dasgupta 2001). The market will tend to price in their effect gradually, which may not lead to a statistically significant signal or a specific 'event' date at any point in time (Campbell *et al.* 1997; Campbell 2000a; Schipper and Thompson 1983). McWilliams and Siegel (1997) and McWilliams *et al.* (1999) note various intractable methodological concerns with event studies in the corporate social responsibility literature (including environmental events) that undermine the many contradictory findings. Most importantly, findings of short-term price changes do not offer compelling proof of a systematic or sustained effect of environmental performance on company financial performance.

The results of empirical analysis depend on:

- The economic model of normal returns chosen (i.e. how many and which variables)
- The assumption of rational expectations given investors' information (investor biases)

In other words, can investors be expected to act rationally in their stock buying/selling strategy given certain information? Finance researchers warn that, in reality, market efficiency can be easily rejected because an incorrect equilibrium model was used in the analysis or the market may not be acting efficiently (Campbell *et al.* 1997).

3.2   Long-Term Market Value Studies

Long-term models evaluating the relationship between company performance and stock performance draw from various schools of thought such as accounting, asset pricing and organisational behaviour, yet most suffer from model misspecification. Thus, for example, Holthausen (1994) re-analyses the balance sheet model used by Barth and McNichols (1994; Campbell *et al.* 1996) to evaluate the effect of estimated Superfund liability on market value of equity (MVE). Rather than assume as did Barth and McNichols that capital markets can rationally estimate environmental liabilities from sources other than a company's financial statements, Holthausen assumed that the market's assessment of environmental liability was exactly equal to what companies accrue in their financial statements. Despite assuming the market is fully informed of Superfund liabilities, his simulations show that changes in companies' market value are still greater than expected. As an explanation, Holthausen points out that Barth and McNichols assumed that measurement errors associated with assets, liabilities and their proxy for environmental liabilities are uncorrelated with each other and with the net asset value of all omitted variables. This is likely to be false, since book values of assets and liabilities are predominantly historical cost measures likely to induce correlation in the measurement errors of both variables. In conclusion, it is not clear from Barth and McNichols' work whether there is a Superfund effect, even though they found that the market recognises Superfund liability in excess of amounts (on average to 28.6% of MVE) accrued by 477 companies named as the Principal Responsible Party (PRP) between 1982 and 1991.

King and Lenox (2001) used Tobin's q to isolate the incremental effect of TRI emissions on company market value and re-visit Hart and Ahuja's (1996) analysis. After controlling for several determinants of company value (e.g. company size and capital intensity), they found a negative association between TRI emissions and Tobin's q for 652 companies between 1987 and 1996, but cannot offer any insight into the mechanism underlying the association. Using the same model, Dowell *et al.* (2000) found that, for a biased sample of 89 manufacturing and mining companies between 1994 and 1997, the adoption of international environmental standards can improve a company's financial value compared with companies adopting a US standard abroad. However, a more likely explanation is that a third factor affects both Tobin's q and the measure of environmental performance. To test this concern, King and Lenox controlled for company fixed effects in their model and found that the TRI effect remains significant, though they point out that this model can also obscure evidence of other potentially significant company specific attributes of importance to TRI emissions levels. These may or may not be directly related to a company's environmental strategy. Other researchers have started to address this concern, noting that gains in company financial performance associated with environmental performance may be coincidental (interact) with the adoption of the latest technology (Dowell *et al.* 2000), R&D expenditures (McWilliams and Siegel 2000), environmental management approach (Schaltegger and Synnestvedt 2002) or variables that could increase company productivity or company growth (measured in % annual change in sales) (Russo and Fouts 1997). This endogeneity concern can undermine these approaches.

Garber and Hammitt (1998) use the capital asset pricing model (CAPM) (Lintner 1965; Markowitz 1952; Sharpe 1964) to analyse the effect of Superfund liability on the cost of equity capital for a biased sample of 73 chemical companies from 1976 to 1992. Theorising that Superfund liability should depress current stock price in a 'wealth effect' (i.e. cash flow effect) and increase company risk (the CAPM *beta*) for these chemical companies, Garber and Hammitt augmented the traditional CAPM model of expected returns with a measure of Superfund liability (e.g. number of Superfund sites). They found no significant incremental effect of Superfund liability on *beta* for the full sample after controlling for industry-wide effects. Yet after dividing the sample into large and small companies, 23 large companies with market capitalisation above $1 billion experienced an increase in *beta*, which was not extended to 54 small sample companies with market capitalisation under $500 million. Garber and Hammitt postulated that investors have more information on Superfund liability for large chemical companies leading to a higher discount rate relative to small companies. Therefore for larger chemical companies (by market capitalisation) that pollute, this is associated with a higher *beta*. Since the use of CAPM does not specifically permit estimation of a Superfund cash flow affect on returns and the event study method is difficult to apply as Superfund events are hard to isolate, Garber and Hammitt provided their own estimate. They concluded that any potential cash flow effect is minimal relative to the market value of equity and debt, and hence cannot diminish the increase in cost of capital for large chemical companies.

Use of the traditional CAPM will overstate the Superfund liability effect on expected returns. Since 1992, finance economists note that the CAPM *beta* does not predict returns due to an omitted variables problem and should not be used for cost of capital estimation. CAPM has been under attack since 1981 when Banz (1981) found that, between 1926 and 1975, the shares of companies with large market values had smaller risk adjusted returns on average than similar small companies. The 'size effect' continued to puzzle researchers until Fama and French (1992) presented evidence that when stocks were sorted by size (market capitalisation) and *beta*, high-*beta* stocks have no higher returns than low-*beta* stocks of the same size. Furthermore, small stocks have a low market value relative to book value. To account for these anomalies, Fama and French (1993) combined all three (*beta*, size and book equity to market equity) in a three-factor model and found that size and book-to-market (B/M) have the strongest relation to returns. In addition to the 'size effect', others argue that ratios of market value to accounting measures, return on human capital, gross domestic product (GDP) forecasts and momentum undermine CAPM. The debate rages on, with some finance economists asserting that findings of CAPM anomalies are entirely spurious or that CAPM is actually untestable (Roll 1977). Without accounting for at least *beta*, size and book equity to market equity, the results generated by

Garber and Hammitt (1998) cannot be conclusive. A seemingly positive relationship between Superfund and *beta* can become negative or be cancelled out completely by the inclusion of omitted variables. Therefore, cost of equity capital estimation using the traditional CAPM *beta* is hopelessly imprecise (Fama and French 1997; Botosan 1997).

More recently, Stone *et al.* (2001) compared the returns of several KLD social screens with the S&P500 index from 1984–2001. Using the F-F results, they controlled carefully for size (market capitalisation), B/M (growth), dividend yield and *beta* by matching 20 fractile portfolios on these variables. They found no significant cost or benefit of social screening on portfolio returns. In fact, they suggested that in a market adverse to risk bearing, growth, size and/or high price-earning ratios, socially responsible portfolios could do worse because of their factor exposures. While portfolio comparisons may yield different results from a F-F model regression analysis (Fama 1998), Stone *et al.* (2001) used an empirically convincing equilibrium model of asset returns as the starting point of their analysis. Similarly, after adjusting the performance of various US, UK and German ethical funds for style tilts using the Cahart (1997; Jegadeesh *et al.* 1993) four-factor model (*beta*, size, B/M, momentum) and controlling for survivorship-bias, Bauer *et al.* (2002) found no significant difference in risk-adjusted returns between ethical and conventional funds from 1990 to 2001.

4.   DISCUSSION

This brief overview of the research in the USA shows that model uncertainty tends to consistently undermine the quality of findings. We can trace an evolution from simple analysis of the relationship between company performance and stock price changes using few control variables, matching on one variable, few data years and industry-specific runs to more complex models more closely aligned with finance economics research. As yet, the research does not illuminate a monotonic relationship between environmental and financial performance. Researchers have yet to demonstrate that environmental expenditures improve company profitability in a structural way and that it is not a matter of reverse causality where profitable companies can afford to invest in environmental performance. A more likely explanation for the findings to date is that various omitted variables affecting both environmental and financial performance are responsible for the apparent statistical relationship.

Market returns are driven primarily by revisions in capital market expectations of the profitability of future transactions. This makes it more difficult to justify using contemporaneous accounting values and organisational characteristics to evaluate market returns, when it is changes in company fundamental information that drive the market's valuation of a company's future earnings. Finance economist John Campbell notes that the type of cross-sectional models employed in this research (even an improved CAPM), which regress stock returns on contemporaneous innovations to variables of plausible significance, make it hard to distinguish between cash flow (Scenario 1) and expected return news (Scenario 2) (Campbell 1991). Finding a correlation between environmental and financial performance at any time between the release of pollution news to the markets at t to $t+n$ does not tell us why or how capital markets interpreted the news. Are real costs involved or are investors simply nervous about pollution? Without knowing whether cash flow changes underlie changes in emission levels and/or whether capital markets consider this important cash flow news, it is hard to conclude that capital markets encourage companies to spend money for environmental quality improvements.

Recent developments in accounting and finance research help understand the challenge of adopting an analytical model. Campbell and Shiller (1988) argued that accounting studies assessing whether securities respond to earnings announcements or other news do not necessarily ask whether the response is 'consistent with a particular fundamental valuation model for the security price' that correctly predicts stock price behaviour (Fama 1976). According to Lee (1999), accounting research in the second half of the 1990s was marked by a gradual shift away from studies that focus exclusively on the contemporaneous association between accounting information and returns (i.e. stock prices) toward a research objective focused on using accounting information in a predictive role. He notes that the residual income model, which expresses company value as the sum of its invested capital and the discounted present value of the residual income from future activities, is a promising baseline model, variations of which have been used to evaluate the value-relevance of environmental information (Li *et al.* 1999; Feltham *et al.* 1995). By emphasising the need to improve the forecasting of key valuation parameters, accounting research is converging with the search for a fundamental valuation model by finance economists. This same shift needs to be made by researchers of environmental and financial performance.

According to professor of finance, Eugene Fama, anomalies can only be studied relative to an equilibrium model representative of economic theory of factors affecting stock valuation (Fama 1998). Equilibrium models proposed by finance economists include state variables such as interest rates, investor psychology and business cycles (Hirschleifer 1970) that influence the market's discount factor (i.e. market risk as a function of investor preferences), which behaves stochastically (Cochrane 2001). Shiller (1981) and LeRoy and Porter (1981) demonstrated that simplified asset-pricing models of constant returns and changing expectations of dividend cash flows do not fully describe the volatility of post World War II stock prices. In a variance decomposition of stock returns, Campbell (1991) determined that variance about news of future cash flows accounts for a third to a half of the variance in unexpected stock returns (defined as the excess of dividend growth over the commercial paper rate). The remainder is due to news about future expected returns. In the 1980s, researchers also noted that this excess volatility is closely related to the predictability of multi-period returns, which increases over intervals of several years (DeBondt and Thaler 1985; Campbell and Viceira 1999; Fama and French 1988). In fact, as the number of years used to compute returns increases (1, 3, 10 years), the constant-expected return model is rejected even more strongly. Two common econometric methods are to use risk-adjusted returns and a multi-factor model that accounts for various sources of market risk. Without adopting current finance economics approaches to evaluate the impact of environmental performance on market value of equity, some of these anomalies attributed to a lack of market efficiency might instead be the result of a mis-specified pricing model (Ball 1978).

An equilibrium model of market returns reflecting the market conditions under which environmental performance might affect stock returns in fact yields very different results. In a compellingly simple manner, Heinkel *et al.* (2001) demonstrated that the number of green investors is key to affecting stock prices as in the second scenario outlined in Section 2. They design an equilibrium model of capital markets assumed to be efficient with two types of risk-averse investors—neutral investors who are insensitive to environmental concerns and green investors who have preferences on company environmental performance. These investors are faced with opportunities to invest in three types of companies:

- Acceptable companies with clean technology
- Reformed companies that invest to make their technologies acceptable
- Unacceptable companies that do not invest in cleaner technology

After conducting sensitivity analysis on various parameters, Heinkel *et al.* (2001) noted that a key determinant of whether a polluting company will reform is the fraction of funds controlled by green investors. They concluded that it is necessary to have at least 25% green investors to change corporate environmental investment strategy. A generous estimate suggests that, in 2001, 11.75% of all US investing managed by professionals involved a social screen. Green investors are not likely to affect stock prices. In fact, when Heinkel *et al.* (2001) calibrated their model at 10% green investors, no polluting company would invest to become acceptable to green investors, unless the expenditures were 1% of expected cash flow. In this latter case, approximately 10% of polluting companies would opt to invest in cleaner technology.

When green investors are still price takers, as is the case in US capital markets, we cannot expect a green investor effect as described in Scenario 2 (see Figure 1). This should raise our scepticism of the long-term effects on stock returns found in this research. A more conservative view of the research to date indicates that the response of US capital markets to environmental performance can best be described by Scenario 1: information on expected environmental liabilities or clean-up costs hits the market at time *t* causing an immediate stock price drop without necessarily affecting returns. Environmental news is more likely to be received as cash flow news and capital markets will promptly incorporate these costs in share price. This implies that capital markets do not exhibit a long-term response to environmental performance (Campbell 2000b).

5.   FUTURE RESEARCH

Future research paths should focus on probing the short-term mechanism of Scenario 1. A central challenge of explaining a cash flow news effect is how to estimate company-level environmental expenditures and whether they are properly reported to the investing public, i.e. parameter uncertainty. Furthermore, if expenditures are involved, are they an immediate cost or a future cost? Do they reflect the social costs of pollution?

Researchers struggle to estimate environmental expenditures mostly because these data are hard to find and under-reporting continues to be a widespread problem. Around 1990, rising concern about corporate under-reporting of Superfund liability forced the Securities and Exchange Commission (SEC) to refocus on environment, and the SEC and Environment Protection Agency (EPA) drafted a Memorandum of Understanding for information provision. From 1990 to 1995, the EPA Office of Enforcement and Compliance Assurance (OECA) provided quarterly data to the SEC Division of Corporate Finance. The information highway was interrupted due to OECA reorganisation and has not been taken up again by the SEC. A 1998 OECA study on the disclosure of environmental legal proceedings in registrants' 10-K statements in 1996 and 1997 found a 74% non-reporting rate. The growing corporate environmental reporting movement may become a credible plug for this gap. However, availability of financial data related to environmental management is limited by the capability of company managers to collect and disseminate voluntarily such information, which is scattered throughout the company and facility, in particular, and often of minimal financial import (Ditz *et al.* 1995; Koehler 2001). Researchers therefore must undertake their own cost estimates or very rarely use the US Census Bureau's Pollution Abatement Cost and Expenditure survey (PACE).

Various methods to evaluate the financial implications of environmental expenditures at the company level are explored. Most companies claim that the costs of Superfund clean-up are hard to estimate and thus do not recognise the liability in their financial statements early on in the long clean-up (sometimes up to 30 years). Therefore, Barth *et al.* (1997) had to use EPA's Record of Decision cost estimates and EPA Haz-site reports instead of company reported information to estimate liability. They noted that it is difficult to estimate site remediation costs using publicly available data. Unfortunately, they found that the numbers of Superfund sites per company and not their cost estimate is the strongest predictor of the Superfund liability effect on MVE. Similarly unable to isolate a significant cash flow affect of Superfund liability on stock prices, Garber and Hammitt (1998) assumed average costs of $41.1 million in addition to 20% transactions costs discounted at 5% based upon previous research. Other methods include scenario analysis of the impact of new regulations on different industries (Austin and Sauer 2002; Repetto and Austin 2000) and real options to evaluate off-balance sheet items (Cortazar *et al.* 1998). Business scholars and economists still struggle with how to translate environmental risk into financial risk, particularly when regulation does not provide adequate guidance. For example, levels of many TRI chemical emissions that are not associated with a clear legal liability are not indicative of future expenditures and do not obviously pose a financial risk.

At the 3rd EPA workshop on capital markets and corporate environmental performance in October 2002, researchers noted the need to evaluate the social impacts of pollution to permit comparison of the public and private cost/benefit of 'internalising' externalities. The methods of cost benefit analysis employed by the EPA when new regulations are under consideration would be helpful in determining the social impacts and costs associated with pollution. Researchers discussed various additional outstanding questions such as whether shareholder dialogue or SRI screens can affect corporate behaviour and/or stock price changes. What are the conflicting interests preventing more investment in pollution reduction? Is there a difference between how small and large companies allocate resources to environmental compliance? Do earnings shocks affect pollution levels? Are markets informed of environmental externalities and what is the role of regulation in promoting transparency? Under what circumstances can capital markets supplement, complement or substitute for regulation? Finally, it worth mentioning that the literature focuses exclusively on environmental damage from production technologies and remediation, which in fact misses a major source of environmental damage—product use. From the perspective of sustainability, corporate environmental performance measures should cover production processes, product use and disposal as in the life-cycle assessment (LCA) framework.

6.   CONCLUSIONS

This debate has been sparked in part by the perception that the expected future constraints imposed by sustainability need to be addressed, either by regulation or by markets. Where government action is often slow in coming and potentially unfair, scholars and commentators put unrealistic faith in the potential of markets to incorporate environmental externalities first. In fact, the fervent desire to demonstrate that capital markets reward corporations for their environmental expenditures has often coloured the research and how it is interpreted (Dixon 2002). Capital markets are consumers of information and when the information on the cost of pollution is not obviously in the public domain, we should not naively expect an impact on share prices. Researchers should focus on defining and estimating the social costs that are to be recouped via markets or regulation. To date, most cost estimates cover private sector expenditures in clean technology or remediation, but do not incorporate social cost estimates. Finally and most importantly, the minority in most capital markets, 'green' investors are still price takers, implying that shareholder pressures will not change corporate behaviour on average unless there is more systematic change in the form of regulation. That regulation can have a supply side slant where companies are forced to internalise social costs in their pricing structure, or a demand side focus where capital market players are required to account for the social impacts of their investments. The UK government has spearheaded the latter route. Only with additional regulation forcing internalisation of environmental externalities will capital markets systematically become more responsive to information on the total impacts of pollution and begin to exert the long-term pressures necessary to promote corporate sustainability.

REFERENCES

Austin, D. and Sauer, A. (2002): *Changing Oil: Emerging Environmental Risks and Share-holder Value in the Oil and Gas Industry*. Washington D.C.: WRI.

Ball, R. (1978): 'Anomalies in Relationships between Securities. Yields and Yield Surrogates', *Journal of Financial Economics* No. 6, 103-126.

Banz, R.W. (1981): 'The Relationship between Return and Market Value of Common Stocks', *Journal of Financial Economics* Vol. 9, No. 1, 3-18.

Barth, M.E. and McNichols, M.F. (1994): 'Estimation and Market Valuation of Environmental Liabilities Relating to Superfund Sites', *Journal of Accounting Research* Vol. 32, Supplement 1994, 177-209.

Barth, M.E., McNichols, M.F. and Wilson, G.P. (1997): 'Factors Influencing Companies. Disclosures about Environmental Liabilities', *Review of Accounting Studies* No. 2, 35-64.

Bauer, R., Koedijk, K. and Otten, R. (2002): *International Evidence on Ethical Mutual Fund Performance and Investment Style.* Maastricht: Limburg Institute of Financial Economics, Maastricht University.

Blacconiere, W.G. and Patten, D.M. (1994): 'Environmental Disclosures, Regulatory Costs, and Changes in Firm Value', *Journal of Accounting and Economics* Vol. 18, 357-377.

Blacconiere, W.G. and Northcutt, W.D. (1997): 'Environmental Information and Market Reactions to Environmental Legislation', *Journal of Accounting, Auditing & Finance* Vol. 12, No. 2, 149-178.

Bosch, J.C., Eckard, E.W. and Lee, I. (1996): *Environmental Regulations and Stockholders' Wealth: An Empirical Examination.* Denver: College of Business, University of Colorado at Denver.

Botosan, C. (1997): 'The Effect of Disclosure Level on Cost of Equity', *The Accounting Review* Vol. 72, 323-350.

Cahart, M. (1997): 'On persistence in mutual fund performance', *Journal of Finance*, Vol. 52, No. 1, 57-82.

Campbell, J.Y. (1991): 'A Variance Decomposition of Stock Returns', *The Economic Journal* Vol. 101, March, 157-179.

Campbell, J.Y. (2000a): 'Asset Pricing at the Millennium', *Journal of Finance* Vol. 55, No. 4, 1515-1567.

Campbell, J.Y. (2000b): 'Strategic Asset al. location: Portfolio Choice for Long-Term Investors', *NBER Reporter* Fall, 8-12.

Campbell, J.Y. and Shiller, R. (1988): 'Stock Prices, Earnings, and Expected Dividends', *Journal of Finance* Vol. 43, 661-676.

Campbell, J.Y. and L.M. Viceira (1999): 'Consumption and Portfolio Decisions When Expected Returns are Time Varying', *Quarterly Journal of Economics* Vol. 114, 433-495.

Campbell, K., Sefcik, S.E. and Soderstrom, N.S. (1996): 'Site Uncertainty, Allocation Uncertainty and Superfund Liability Valuation', *Journal of Accounting and Public Policy* Vol. 17, No. 4/5, 331-366.

Campbell, J.Y., Lo, A. and Craig MacKinlay, A. (1997): *The Econometrics of Financial Markets.* Princeton: Princeton University Press.

Chopra, N., Lakonishok, J. and Ritter, J.R. (1992): 'Measuring Abnormal Performance: Do Stocks Overreact?', *Journal of Financial Economics* Vol. 31, No. 2, 235-268.

Cochrane, J. (1999): 'New Facts in Finance', *Economic Perspectives* Vol. 23, No. 3, 36-58.

Cochrane, J. (2000): 'Asset Pricing', *NBER Reporter* Fall, 1-7.

Cochrane, J. (2001): *Asset Pricing.* Princeton: Princeton University Press.

Cortazar, G., Schwartz, E.S. and Salinas, M (1998): 'Evaluating Environmental Investments: A Real Options Approach', *Management Science* Vol. 44, No. 8, 1059-1070.

Cram, D.P. and Koehler, D.A. (2000): *Pollution As News: Controlling for Contemporaneous Correlation of Returns in Event Studies of Toxic Release Inventory Reporting.* Cambridge: MIT Sloan School of Management, Harvard School of Public Health.

Dasgupta, S. and Laplante, B. (2001): 'Pollution and Capital Markets in Developing Countries', *Journal of Environmental Economics and Management* Vol. 42, No. 3, 310-335.

DeBondt, W.F. and Thaler, R.H. (1985): 'Does the Stock Market Overreact?', *Journal of Finance* Vol. 40, No. 3, 557-581.

Ditz, D., Ranganathan, J. and Banks, R.D. (1995): *Green Ledgers: Case Studies in Corporate Environmental Accounting.* Baltimore: World Resources Institute.

Dixon, F. (2002): 'Financial Markets and Corporate Environmental Results', in: Esty, D. and Cornelius, P.K. (Eds.): *Environmental Performance Measurement, The Global Report 2001-2002.* New York: Oxford University Press, 54-65.

Dowell, G., Hart, S. and Yeung, B. (2000): 'Do Corporate Global Environmental Standards Create or Destroy Market Value?', *Management Science.* Vol. 46, No. 8, 1059-1074.

Fama, E.F. (1976): *The Foundations of Finance.* New York: Basic Books.

Fama, E.F. (1998): 'Market Efficiency, Long-Term Returns and Behavioral Finance', *Journal of Finance Economics* Vol. 49, No. 3, 283-306.

Fama, E.F. and French, K.R. (1988): 'Permanent and Temporary Components of Stock Prices', *Journal of Political Economy* Vol. 96, No. 2, 246-273.

Fama, E.F. and French, K.R. (1992): 'The Cross-Section of Expected Stock Returns', *Journal of Finance* Vol. 47, No. 2, 427-465.

Fama, E.F. and French, K.R. (1993): 'Common Risk Factors in the Returns on Stocks and Bonds', *Journal of Financial Economics* Vol. 33, No. 1, 3-56.

Fama, E.F. and French, K.R. (1997): 'Industry Costs of Equity', *Journal of Financial Economics* Vol. 43, No. 2, 153-193.

Fama, E.F., Fisher, L., Jensen, M.C. and Roll, R. (1969) 'The Adjustment of Stock Prices to New Information', *International Economic Review* Vol. 10, No. 1, 1-21.

Feltham, G.A. and Ohlson, J.A. (1995): 'Valuation and Clean Surplus Accounting for Operating and Financial Activities', *Contemporary Accounting Research* Vol. 11, No. 2, 689-731.

Garber, S. and Hammitt, J.K. (1998): 'Risk Premiums for Environmental Liability: Does Superfund Increase the Cost of Capital?', *Journal of Environmental Economics and Management* Vol. 36, No. 3, 267-294.

Hamilton, J.T. (1995): 'Pollution as News: Media and Stock Market Reactions to the Toxics Release Inventory Data', *Journal of Environmental Economics and Management* Vol. 28, 98-113.

Hart, S.L. and Ahuja, G. (1996): 'Does it Pay to be Green? An Empirical Examination of the Relationship between Emission Reduction and Firm Performance', *Business Strategy and the Environment* Vol. 5, 30-37.

HBR (1994): 'The Challenge of Going Green', *Harvard Business Review* July/August, 37-50.

Heinkel, R., Kraus, A. and Zechner, J. (2001): 'The Effect of Green Investment on Corporate Behavior', *Journal of Finance and Quantitative Analysis* Vol. 36, No. 4, 431-449.

Hirschleifer, J. (1970): *Investment, Interest and Capital.* Englewood Cliffs: Prentice-Hall.

Holthausen, R.W. (1994): 'Discussion of Estimation of Market Valuation of Environmental Liabilities Relating to Superfund Sites', *Journal of Accounting Research* Vol. 32, Supplement 1994, 211-219.

Jaffe, A.B., Peterson, S.R., Portney, P. and Stavins, R. (1995): 'Environmental Regulation and the Competitiveness of U.S. Manufacturing: What Does the Evidence Tell Us?', *Journal of Economic Literature* Vol. 33, No. 1, 132-163.

Jegadeesh, R. and Tietman, S. (1993): 'Returns to Buying Winners and Selling Losers: Implications for Stock Market Efficiency', *Journal of Finance* Vol. 48, No. 1, 65-91.

Jensen, M. (1978): Some Anomalous Evidence Regarding Market Efficiency', *Journal of Finance Economics* Vol. 6, 95-101.

Jones, J.D., Jones, C.L. and Phillips-Patrick, F. (1994): 'Estimating the Costs of the Exxon Valdez Oil Spill', *Research in Law and Economics* Vol. 16, 109-149.

Karpoff, J.M., Lott, J.R. and Rankine, G. (1998): *Environmental Violations, Legal Penalties, and Reputation Costs* (John M. Olin Law & Economics Working Paper No. 71). University of Chicago Law School.

Khanna, M., Quimio, W.R.H. and Bojilova, D. (1998): 'Toxics Release Information: A Policy Tool for Environmental Protection', *Journal of Environmental Economics and Management* Vol. 36, No. 3, 243-266.

King, A. and Lenox, M. (2001): 'Does it Really Pay to be Green? Accounting for Strategy Selection in the Relationship between Environmental and Financial Performance', *Journal of Industrial Ecology* Vol. 4, No. 4, 105-116.

King, A. and Lenox, M. (2002): 'Exploring the Locus of Profitable Pollution Reduction', *Management Science* Vol. 48, No. 2, 289-299.

Klassen, R.D. and McLaughlin, C.P. (1996): 'The Impact of Environmental Management on Firm Performance', *Management Science* Vol. 42, No. 8, 1199-1214.

Koehler, D.A. (2001): 'Developments in Health and Safety Accounting at Baxter International', *Eco-Management and Auditing* Vol. 8, No. 4, 229-239.

Konar, S. and Cohen, M.A. (1997a): 'Information as Regulation: The Effect of Community Right to Know Laws on Toxic Emissions', *Journal of Environmental Economics and Management* Vol. 32, 109-124.

Konar, S. and Cohen, M.A (1997b): *Why do Companies Pollute (and Reduce) Toxic Emissions?* Nashville: Owen Graduate School of Business, Vanderbilt University.

LaPorta, R. (1996): 'Expectations and the Cross Section of Stock Returns', *Journal of Finance* Vol. 51, No. 5, 1715-1742.

Lee, C.M. (1999): 'Accounting-Based Valuation: Impact on Business Practices and Research', *Accounting Horizons* Vol. 13, No. 4, 413-425.

LeRoy, S.F. and Porter, R.D. (1981): 'Stock Price Volatility: Tests Based on Implied Variance Bounds', *Econometrica* Vol. 49, 97-113.

Li, Y. and McConomy, B.J. (1999): 'An Empirical Examination of Factors Affecting the Timing of Environmental Accounting Standard Adoption and the Impact on Corporate Valuation', *Journal of Accounting, Auditing & Finance* Vol. 14, No. 3, 279-319.

Lintner, J. (1965): 'The Valuation of Risk Assets and the Selection of Risky Investments in Stock Portfolios and Capital Budgets', *Review of Economics and Statistics* Vol. 47, No. 1, 13-37.

Margolis, J.D. and Walsh, J.P. (2001): *People and Profits? The Search for a Link between a Company's Social and Financial Performance*. Mahwah: Lawrence Erlbaum Associates Publishers.

Markowitz, H. (1952): 'Portfolio Selection', *Journal of Finance* Vol. 6, 77-91.

McWilliams, A. and Siegel, D. (1997): 'Event Studies in Management Research: Theoretical and Empirical Issues', *Academy of Management* Vol. 40, No. 3, 626-657.

McWilliams, A. and Siegel, D. (2000): 'Corporate Social Responsibility and Financial Performance: Correlation or Misspecification?', *Strategic Management Journal* Vol. 21, No. 5, 603-609.

McWilliams, A., Siegel, D. and Teoh, S.H. (1999): 'Issues in the Use of the Event Study Methodology: A Critical Analysis of Corporate Social Responsibility Studies', *Organisational Research Methods* Vol. 2, No. 4, 340-365.

Morgan, M.G. and Henrion, M. (1990): *Uncertainty: A Guide to Dealing with Uncertainty in Quantitative Risk and Policy Analysis*. Cambridge: Cambridge University Press.

Palmer, K., Oates, W.E. and Portney, P.R. (1995): 'Tightening Environmental Standards: The Benefit-Cost or the No-Cost Paradigm?', *Journal of Economic Perspectives* Vol. 9, No. 4, 119-132.

Porter, M. (1991): 'America's Green Strategy', *Scientific American* Vol. 264, 168.

Porter, M. and Linde, C. van der (1995a): 'Towards a New Conception of Environment-Competitiveness Relationship', *Journal of Economic Perspectives* Vol. 9, No. 4, 97-118.

Porter, M. and Linde, C. van der (1995b): 'Green and Competitive', *Harvard Business Review* September-October, 120-134.

Poterba, J. and Summers, L. (1988): 'Mean Reversion in Stock Returns: Evidence and Implications', *Journal of Financial Economics* Vol. 22, 27-60.

Reinhardt, F.L. (1999a): 'Bringing the Environment Down to Earth', *Harvard Business Review* Vol. 77, No. 4, 149-157.

Reinhardt, F.L. (1999b): 'Market Failure and the Environmental Policies of Companies', *Journal of Industrial Ecology* Vol. 3, No. 1, 9-21.

Repetto, R. and Austin, D. (2000): *Pure Profit. The Financial Implications of Environmental Performance*. Washington D.C.: World Resources Institute.

Roll, R. (1977): 'A Critique of the Asset Pricing Theory's Tests: Part I', *Journal of Financial Economics* Vol. 4, No. 2, 129-176.

Russo, M.V. and Fouts, P.A. (1997): 'A Resource-Based Perspective on Corporate Environmental Performance and Profitability', *Academy of Management Journal* Vol. 40. No. 3, 534-559.

Schaltegger, S. and Synnestvedt, T. (2002): 'The Link between 'Green' and Economic Success: Environmental Management as the Crucial Trigger between Environmental and Economic Performance', *Journal of Environmental Management* Vol. 65, No. 4, 339-346.

Schipper, K. and Thompson, R. (1983): 'The Impact of Merger-Related Regulations on the Shareholders of Acquiring Companies', *Journal of Accounting Research* Vol. 21, No 1, 184-221.

Sharpe, W. (1964): 'Capital Asset Prices: A Theory of Market Equilibrium under Conditions of Risk', *Journal of Finance* Vol. 19, 425-442.

Shiller, R. (1981): 'Do Stock Prices Move too Much to be Justified by Subsequent Changes in Dividends', *American Economic Review* Vol. 71, No. 3, 421-436.

Stone, B.K., Guerard, J.B., Gultekin, M.N. and Greg, A. (2001): *Socially Responsible Investment Screening: Strong Empirical Evidence of No Significant Cost for Actively Managed Value-Focused Portfolios*. Provo: Brigham Young University, Dept. of Finance.

Vuolteenaho, T. (2000): *What Drives Firm-Level Stock Returns?* (Working Paper) Cambridge: Harvard University.

Wagner, M., Schaltegger, S. and Wehrmeyer, W. (2002) 'The Relation between the Environmental and Economic Performance of Companies: What Does Theory Propose and What Does Empirical Evidence Tell Us?', *Greener Management International* Vol. 34, Summer, 95-108.

Walley, N. and Whitehead, B. (1994): 'It's Not Easy being Green', *Harvard Business Review*, May/June, 46-52.

White, M.A. (1996) *Investor Response to the Exxon Valdez Oil Spill*. Charlottesville: McIntire School of Commerce, University of Virginia.

Zellner, A. (1962): 'An Efficient Method of Estimating Seemingly Unrelated Regressions and Test for Aggregation Bias', *Journal of the American Statistics Association* Vol. 57, 348-368.

ACKKNOWLEDGEMENTS

The author wishes to thank Donald Cram for providing invaluable insight in the formative stages of this review, Bill Blackburn, John Campbell, Mark

Cohen, Randy Cohen, Dan Esty, Jim Hammitt, Kai Hockerts, Patrick Hofstetter, Barry Korb, Mike Lenox, Greg Norris, Ludo Phalippou, Forest Reinhardt and John Spengler for their helpful discussions of earlier drafts of this paper, in addition to seminar participants at Harvard School of Public Health, the 2nd and 3rd EPA Workshop on Environmental and Financial Performance, EPA's National Center for Environmental Economics and INSEAD. The Yamaguchi Endowment and the Robert and Patricia Switzer Foundation have supported this research. This work was completed at Harvard School of Public Health and the Wharton School at University of Pennsylvania. It does not necessarily affect EPA policy.

SUSTAINABLE INVESTMENT AND FINANCIAL PERFORMANCE

Does Sustainability Compromise the Financial Performance of Companies and Investment Funds?

Eckhard Plinke and Andreas Knörzer
Sarasin Sustainability Investments, Bank Sarasin & Co. Ltd, Basel, Switzerland

Abstract: Sustainable investment (also known as socially responsible investment [SRI]) combines goals of appropriate financial returns, contribution to environmental protection and contribution to socially responsible economic development. It is a widespread opinion, however, that the environmental and social benefits must be bought with financial underperformance. A review of recent statistical research concludes that, on average, good environmental and social performance does not compromise financial performance. The financial performance of SRI funds is similar to that of 'conventional' funds and more sustainable companies even tend to outperform the market. While these results apply 'on average', the performance of individual SRI funds varies considerably. The chapter argues that the sustainability approach used and the design of the investment process are important factors in the financial performance of SRI funds.

1.   DOES SUSTAINABILITY UNDERMINE PERFORMANCE?

'Sustainable development' has become the major global model for balancing economic development with the protection of the natural environment (e.g. reduction of greenhouse gas emissions) and the reduction of social imbalances (e.g. the growing gap in standards of living between industrialised and developing countries). A contribution of the financial sector to sustainable development is 'sustainable investment'—also known as 'socially responsible investment' (SRI). SRI funds invest in equities (or bonds) of companies, which are not only financially attractive but which also act responsibly towards environment and society. Bank Sarasin is one of the leading providers of sustainable asset management in Europe.

Sustainable investment has grown rapidly over the last several years internationally. Nevertheless, many investors are still uncertain about the financial performance of SRI funds:

- For a given risk level, the returns of SRI funds were worse than those of 'conventional' funds because the number of equities 'fit for investment' is reduced ('non-sustainable' equities are sorted out). From a portfolio theory point of view, this conclusion is evident as portfolio diversification opportunities are reduced. Practical evidence from the management of SRI funds shows, however, that enough sustainable equities can be found to allow for adequate portfolio diversification. The theoretical argument is true, but of small practical relevance only.

- 'Good environmental and social performance is not for free': Additional costs (e.g. for investment in pollution control equipment or above-average salaries) may reduce the profitability of companies. However, on the other hand, companies that care for the environment and their stakeholder relations can avoid risks such as product liability claims or reputational risks, which imply even higher costs (e.g. problems with child labour in the case of Nike and Adidas).

As a conclusion, factual arguments indicate a positive or at least neutral impact of sustainability on financial performance. The question of statistical evidence remains.

When analysing the financial performance of SRI funds, two levels must be distinguished:

1. **Company level (Section 2).** SRI equity funds tend to systematically outperform (underperform) if sustainable companies perform better (worse) financially than the market. The company level can be regarded as the systematic component of outperformance or underperformance of SRI funds, independent from the investment process and quality of the portfolio management.

2. **Investment process level (Section 3).** The 'investment process' comprises such performance-determining factors as the quality of the portfolio management (not specific to sustainability), potential restrictions to portfolio diversification due to the screening out of non-sustainable companies, and integration of sustainability-related information with financial relevance into investment decisions.

A complete statistical analysis of the performance pattern of SRI funds must take into account both levels. For example, if the statistical analysis gives clear evidence for a financial outperformance of sustainable companies, this does not necessarily mean that SRI funds outperform as well; for example, because the number of equities fit for investment is reduced so much that portfolio diversification is compromised. On the other hand, a statistical financial underperformance of more sustainable companies does not necessarily lead to underperformance of SRI funds; for example, because the sustainability analysis provides an information advantage for portfolio managers, which allows better 'stock picking' in the investment process.

2.   DOES MORE SUSTAINABILITY COMPROMISE THE STOCK PERFORMANCE OF COMPANIES?

Most of the numerous studies which have been carried out in recent years concluded that the statistical impact of environmental and social perform-ance on financial performance of companies is positive (Figure 1), i.e. sus-tainability 'pays off' rather than costs. However, the investigative framework of most studies is limited (for example, they cover limited periods, are limited to the analysis of individual events or are limited to environmental aspects), which makes it hard to draw general conclusions.

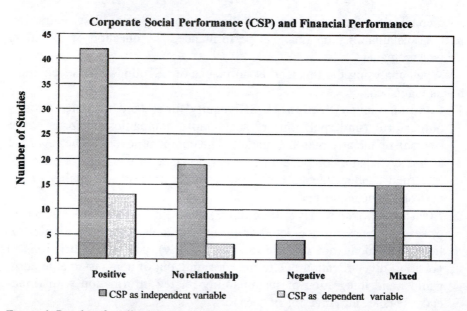

Figure 1. Results of studies investigating the relationship between corporate social perform-ance (CSP) and financial performance (Source: Margolis and Walsh 2001)

In 2002, the research institute ZEW (Mannheim) in co-operation with Bank Sarasin carried out a more comprehensive study on the issue (Plinke 2002;

Ziegler *et al.* 2002), analysing the financial performance (average stock price returns) of 200 European companies over the period January 1996 to August 2001.

The study is an econometric study. That is to say, working within the framework of 'linear regression models' derived from related financial theories, the average share performance is explained by various influencing factors:

$$\text{Financial performance} = f \text{ (financial variables + environmental/social variables)}$$

In other words, the financial performance of a company is explained by different variables derived from financial models, as well as variables that measure the company's environmental and social performance.

The environmental and social performance was measured by the companies' Sarasin Sustainability Rating, which consists of two dimensions (see Figure 2):
- The sustainability of the company within its industrial sector resulting from the comparison with the other companies of the sector (Company Rating)
- The sustainability of the industrial sector itself (Sector Rating)

The rating methodology for both dimensions is based upon a risk philosophy. The exposure to major environmental and social risks (e.g. contribution to climate change or reliance on suppliers or production sites in countries with low social and environmental standards) determines the Sector Rating. The activities of a specific company to control these sector-specific risks (e.g. energy conservation programmes, control and improvement of working conditions of suppliers) are the basis of the Company Rating.

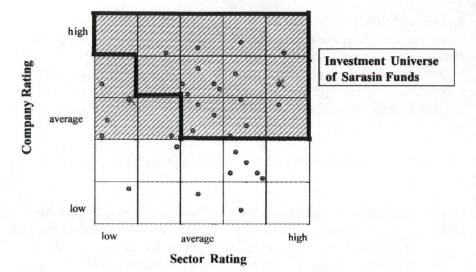

Figure 2. Environmental and social rating of companies with the Sarasin Sustainability Matrix®

Each company is positioned within the Sarasin Sustainability Matrix® according to its industry and company ratings. The shaded area in Figure 2 indicates the kind of rating a company must have in order to qualify for inclusion in a sustainable equity portfolio. In low-sustainability sectors (i.e. sectors with a 'low' rating such as the petroleum industry or 'below-average' such as energy utilities), only companies with a much higher than average company rating will qualify. In more sustainable industries (e.g. renewable energies with a 'high' sector rating), even average companies will qualify.

The study used two alternative financial models:

1. **Capital Asset Pricing Model (CAPM).** According to this model, there is a linear correlation between the performance of a share and the market performance. This correlation is described by the market risk.

2. **Multifactor model (MFM).** This model (named after Fama and French) is an extension of the CAPM and, in many studies, has proved to be more revealing. As well as market performance, it also takes into account the performance advantages of low versus high market capitalisation and a high versus low ratio of net asset value to market value.

The study produced the following conclusions:

• A good environmental and social performance has no significant adverse impact on a company's average stock price performance, i.e. sustainability does not compromise financial returns. On the other hand, opting for high sustainability does not have any significant positive impact on average share performance either.

- There is a positive relation between the environmental Sector Rating and the financial performance, i.e. environmentally beneficial sectors such as water utilities, software, telecommunications, etc. tend to outperform financially. Although the social evaluation of the industry tends to have a negative effect, the influence of the sustainability of the sector is positive overall—though the findings were significant in only one of the two models (Figure 3, right).

- Finally, a negative correlation between sustainability rating and market risk was found. Compared with other companies in the same sector, equities of more environmentally aware and socially responsible companies have a lower risk of price fluctuations relative to the market as a whole.

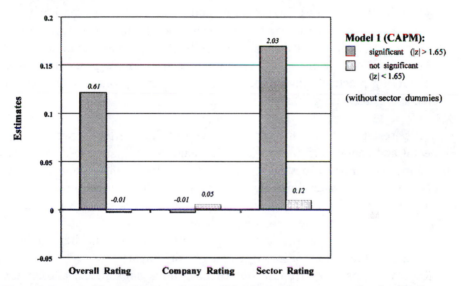

Figure 3. Impact of the environmental and social rating on the average stock price (the figure on top of the bars show the parameter values of the z-statistics)

Due to limitations in the underlying data, the study tended to estimate too negatively the influence of environmental and social performance on share performance. Moreover, bearing in mind that most investigations carried out on this topic in recent years found a positive correlation between environmental/social performance and share performance, the conclusion seems justified that a company's environmental and social performance tend to have a positive impact on its financial performance.

Furthermore, it seems that partial aspects of the sustainability of a company have positive impacts as well:

- A recent study by the Institute of Business Ethics (UK) analysed statistically the relationship between the ethical behaviour and financial performance of companies in the FTSE 250 index between 1997 and 2001

(Webley and More 2003). It was found that, for three out of four measures of financial performance (economic value added [EVA], market value added [MVA] and stability of the price/earnings ratios), companies with codes of ethics or codes of conduct in place ranked better than companies without codes.

- Another recent study analysed statistically the impact of corporate governance on the financial performance of companies in the EU (Bauer and Guenster 2003). It found that the return of a portfolio of well-governed companies (companies with a good corporate governance rating, using a quite comprehensive rating methodology) was significantly better than a portfolio of 'bad governance' companies in the period 2001–2002. It was also found that better corporate governance ratings resulted in a higher valuation of companies. However, an additional analysis of the impact of corporate governance on operating performance (net profit margin and return on equity) revealed negative results. As a potential explanation, it was argued that well-governed companies were more prudent in their accounting practices, thus understating short-term profits. In the longer run, such 'accounting effects' level off.

The latter result points to an important aspect of the relation between environmental and social performance and financial performance, i.e. long-term and short-term impacts may be different. In the long run, a good environmental and social performance tends to have a positive impact on financial performance, as it helps to reduce risks. These risks, which are associated with environmental and social factors, include:

- Reputation risks, e.g. consumer boycott of companies in the headlines for use of child labour or improper use of test animals
- Regulatory risks, e.g. phase-out of hazardous substances, carbon tax affecting consumers with high energy consumption
- Liability risks, e.g. asbestos claims (such claims have resulted in a number of bankruptcies)

These risks are 'latent' in nature, i.e. it is not possible to predict if and when they will become material (different from accidents and other stochastic risks for which probabilities can be given), and the damage can be devastating (e.g. bankruptcy). Their appearance depends largely on the prevailing macro-economic, political and regulatory environment. For example, it is unlikely that an effective international climate protection agreement will be negotiated in the near future. Under these conditions, a company that 'sits and waits' may be better off in the short-term than a company that actively reduces energy consumption and increases the use of renewable energies, requiring costly investments. In an environment with an effective and restrictive climate protection policy, the situation is reversed.

Thus, the explanatory power of the statistical analyses carried out so far may be limited as the time periods and the number of companies considered may be too limited to account properly for the specific nature of environmental and social risks and to reveal results of universal applicability—this may apply even for the most comprehensive studies. As a consequence, the positive long-term effect of a good environmental and social performance on financial performance may be underestimated by the different studies.

3. DO SUSTAINABLE EQUITY PORTFOLIOS HAVE A DIFFERENT FINANCIAL PERFORMANCE THAN 'CONVENTIONAL' ONES?

Rather than the return of individual stocks, the investor is interested in the performance of entire SRI portfolios or funds. This is the combined result of the company level, which tend to be positive (Section 2), and the investment process level.

A glance at the actual results of SRI funds suggests that, on average, differences in the financial performance between SRI funds and 'conventional' funds are small—if they exist at all. A recent comprehensive statistical analysis of more than 40 German, Swiss and US SRI funds carried out by ZEW (Mannheim) confirms this impression: '...it is relatively reliable that the performance of SRI funds is comparable to that of conventional funds' (Schröder 2003:23). The analysis used Jensen's alpha (extra-return which is not explained by the risk exposure of the fund) to measure out- or under-performance.

Another similar analysis of nearly 100 German, UK and US SRI funds (Bauer *et al.* 2002) also did not find a statistically significant deviation of the performance of SRI funds and conventional funds. However, variations in time and countries were found; German and US SRI funds underperformed in the beginning of 1990s, but they matched conventional fund performance during the period 1998–2001. This is explained by a 'learning effect'. One aspect is certainly that the investment philosophy of many of the first SRI funds was very much focussed on certain environmentally beneficial sectors (e.g. pollution control technologies). Later, the 'best in class' philosophy emerged which, by searching for the most sustainable companies in each industry sector, opened the investment universe to virtually all economic sectors and made much more diversified portfolios possible.

The result of a non-significant difference in the performance between SRI funds and conventional funds apply 'on average', while non-negligible differences between the individual SRI funds were observed. The ZEW study showed that the equity funds managed by Sarasin (ValueSar, Oekovision) were among the top performers, with a positive (though not statistically significant) extra return. The studies did not delve deeper into the reasons for these differences, but practical experiences suggest that the design of the investment process matters for good financial performance in addition to the sustainability concept used:

- The Sarasin sustainability approach emphasises environmental and social risks (e.g. related to climate change or product safety problems) rather than ethical goals, thus establishing a direct link between sustainability rating and business performance of companies.
- The investment process of most Sarasin SRI funds is based on 'active' stock selection. The results of the ZEW study suggest that the passively managed SRI funds or SRI indices tended to perform worse than the more actively managed SRI funds (although this not statistically significant in most cases). For some SRI indices, even a significant underperformance was observed. An explanation could be that the positive effect of the individual investments—as more sustainable companies tend to perform better financially (company level, Section 2)—is partially balanced by negative portfolio diversification effects due to the reduction of the number of stocks fit for investment. The actively managed funds are less oriented toward conventional stock indices and rely more on 'stock picking', i.e. the identification of promising individual stocks. In this process, the information from the sustainability analysis of the related companies can have a financial value added to the 'usual' financial information. This allows fund managers to identify the most successful investments (e.g. conflicts with employees impairing motivation, use of potentially hazardous substances that may be affected by legal restrictions).

4.   CONCLUSIONS

Recent research studies conclude that, on average, a good environmental and social performance does not compromise the financial performance of SRI funds. This may be the result of the combination of a positive performance contribution of the individual investments (more sustainable companies tend to perform better financially) and a slightly negative contribution of the portfolio diversification restriction (due to the reduced number of companies fit for investment in SRI funds). However, the different statistical studies may still underestimate the positive long-term effect of a good environmental and social performance on a company's financial performance, as the number of companies and the length of the time intervals analysed may still be too limited to account adequately for the 'latent' character of environmental and social risks.

Though the result of a similar performance of SRI funds and conventional funds applies 'on average', some SRI funds have outperformed. It can be assumed that this is, at least partially, attributable to the investment process design and the sustainability concept used. Sarasin SRI funds are managed with a more active approach integrating environmental, social and financial information for stock selection. According to the results of the studies, the more actively managed funds tended to outperform the passively managed funds and SRI indices.

REFERENCES

Bauer, R. and Guenster, N. (2003): *Good Corporate Governance Pays Off! Well-Governed Companies Perform Better on the Stock Market* (Working Paper). Maastricht: University of Maastricht.

Bauer, R., Koedijk, K. and Otten, R. (2002): *International Evidence on Ethical Mutual Fund Performance and Investment Style* (Working Paper). Maastricht: University of Maastricht.

Margolis, J.D. and Walsh, J.P. (2001): *Misery Loves Companies: Wither Social Initiatives by Business?* (Discussion Paper) Boston: Harvard University.

Plinke, E. (2002): *Aktienperformance und Nachhaltigkeit. Hat die Umwelt- und Sozialperformance einen Einfluss auf die Aktienperformance?* (Sarasin Study, Nov. 2002) Basel: Sarasin & Cie.

Schröder, M. (2003): *Socially Responsible Investments in Germany, Switzerland and the United States—An Analysis of Investment Funds and Indices* (ZEW Discussion Paper No. 03-10). Mannheim: Zentrum für Europäische Wirtschaftsforschung (ZEW).

Webley, S. and More, E. (2003): *Does Business Ethics Pay?* London: Institute of Business Ethics IBE.

Ziegler, A., Rennings, K. and Schröder, M. (2002): *Der Einfluss ökologischer und sozialer Nachhaltigkeit auf den Shareholder Value europäischer Aktiengesellschaften* (ZEW Discussion Paper No. 02-32). Mannheim: Zentrum für Europäische Wirtschaftsforschung (ZEW).

BENCHMARKING COMPETITIVENESS AND MANAGEMENT QUALITY WITH THE DOW JONES SUSTAINABILITY INDEX
The Case of the Automotive Industry and Climate Change

Niki Rosinski
Sustainable Asset Management (SAM), Zurich, Switzerland

Abstract: While realising that issues related to sustainable development drive competitive dynamics and shape businesses and markets of the future (Hilton and Ruth 2003), investors lack a systematic methodology allowing for the assessment of the materiality of issues and the identification of likely losers and winners. The matter is further complicated by the fact that the impact on competitive dynamics is both issue- and industry-specific. Using the automotive industry's exposure to climate change, this chapter explores how the Dow Jones Sustainability Index (DJSI)—besides being a proven approach to construct indexes tracking the performance of companies embracing sustainability—could fill this gap. The chapter concludes that the DJSI methodology can be used on a disaggregated basis as an issue- and industry-specific framework for benchmarking competitiveness regarding risks and opportunities related to sustainable development.

1. THE DJSI METHODOLOGY: A PROVEN METHODOLOGY FOR INDEX CONSTRUCTION

As traditional investment metrics and historic corporate information increasingly concede importance to future-oriented, forward-looking and intangible indicators of the health of a company and its attractiveness to an investor, indexing the performance of companies addressing sustainability attempts to provide investors with the insights they seek. Thus, as an investment insight, equity research in relation to sustainability must be (Flatz 2002; Internet URL: http://www.sustainability-indexes.com):

- Forward-looking
- Based on industry-specific value drivers

- Transparent
- Capable of adding value to existing valuation methods

Assessing corporate sustainability aims to incorporate the characteristics mentioned above and offers insight across most equity asset classes and investment styles. Recent studies (Garz and Volk 2002) demonstrate that stock portfolios incorporating sustainability display stronger performance attributes across all investment styles compared with conventional portfolios. Accordingly, the Dow Jones Sustainability Index (DJSI) is based on the hypothesis that a portfolio of stocks that incorporates sustainability will be expected to outperform comparable portfolios, at least in the long run. Under this hypothesis, companies embracing global sustainability trends are likely to achieve a higher return on equity (ROE) and/or a lower required rate of return (RRR) than companies that ignore these trends. Higher ROE may result from a better understanding of investment opportunities or from lower non-operating costs because of a better understanding of risks.

Since its launch in 1999, the DJSI has tracked the performance of companies leading in terms of integrating sustainability in their business strategy. The Dow Jones Global Index of the 2,500 largest companies in market capitalisation, of the total universe of more than 5,000 companies, is used as a basis for the DJSI World investable universe. The selection of the DJSI components pursues a mixed approach incorporating both numeric and market capitalisation-weighted elements. The DJSI reflects the selection of the 10% best companies in terms of corporate sustainability in each of the 50 industry sectors as defined by Dow Jones Indexes, while ensuring that the DJSI represents at least 20% of the market capitalisation in each industry. This approach ensures that the DJSI meets the requirements of traditional indexes and investors (Flatz 2002).

As the primary selection rule for the DJSI, the objective of the DJSI methodology is to aggregate the performance of a company in terms of specific criteria into an overall sustainability performance score (Flatz 2002). The DJSI methodology is based on the hypothesis that continually reinvention by companies in line with market, societal and environmental realities and changes (Doering *et al.* 2002) to ensure their own sustainability is a key to longevity and profitability of businesses (De Geus and Senge 1997). These market, ecological and social changes are trends that need to be considered and managed effectively—by maximising the opportunities and minimising the risks they present—if a company is to contribute to a sustainable future for itself and the parts of the systems in which the business is embedded. As a result, global trends can affect the dynamic balance of underlying competitive forces across industries.

Consequently, the DJSI methodology starts with a systematic analysis of issues on an industry-basis (Porter 1982). This analysis helps to identify issues and trends that hold the largest potential to affect competitiveness and value creation in an industry. The analysis translates into a structure similar to a business case matrix (SustainAbility and UNEP 2001). This matrix forms the basis for selection of criteria geared to differentiate between leaders and laggards for the DJSI. While some issues hold potential for value creation and destruction across all industries, some are specific to just one or a small set of industries. Therefore, the DJSI methodology is based, to a large extent, on business cases that are both issue-specific and industry-specific. The following examples illustrate the materiality of a set of global issues:

- **Corruption**. The global trend of social imbalances and inequalities in developing and emerging countries is compounded by corrupt practices. From a business point of view, corruption creates unstable and high-cost operating environments. Companies in the extractive sector, such as oil and gas, appear to be most exposed as a result of their continuous expansion in developing countries with large oil and gas fields. Companies see additional pressure on their licence to operate by coalitions such as Publish What You Pay (Internet URL: http://www.publishwhatyoupay.org) and the Extractive Industries Transparency Initiative (EITI) (Internet URL: http://www.transparency.org) that call for transparency on payments made to the host governments in resource-rich countries.

- **Biodiversity**. The continuous loss of biodiversity and ecosystems threatens valuable ecological goods and services. Hence, biodiversity is a strategic business issue. The business case for biodiversity ranges from reducing environmental liabilities to access to the growing market for biotechnology. While the pharmaceutical sector seems to be most exposed, biodiversity also holds a strong potential for value creation in other sectors. The UN Conference on Trade and Development and the World Trade Organisation (WTO) estimate that the eco-tourism market is worth around US$ 260 billion/year and that the annual sales of organic food and drinks in the USA, Japan and the EU are likely to approach US$ 60 billion in 2005, up from US$ 20 billion in 2000 (Cooper 2003).

- **Climate change**. There is increasing concern that human activities are leading to increased accumulations of greenhouse gases (GHGs) in the atmosphere, which are altering the Earth's climate patterns. The Intergovernmental Panel on Climate Change (IPCC; Internet URL: http://www.ipcc.ch) reports that global average temperatures rose by around 0.6°C over the last century, with 1998 being the hottest year since records started in 1861. A recent empirical study (Garz and Volk 2003) revealed that global financial markets bear a combined market value at risk (MVaR) of around US\$ 210–915 billion. The study concluded that climate change is not yet incorporated in stock prices. Therefore, companies in highly exposed sectors such as oil and gas and transport risk incurring significant discounts on their market valuation.

Following the identification of material issues across industries, a further challenge is to select relevant and quantifiable criteria to underscore issues affecting value creation in an industry. These criteria are compiled in an industry-specific matrix and aggregated in a sustainability score—an important selection factor for the DJSI. By virtue of the relative exposure to material issues, the number of criteria varies across industries. The aggregated sustainability score can be based on up to 30 criteria for companies that operate in sectors exposed to a wide range of issues.

To be able to apply the DJSI methodology as a benchmarking tool for issue-specific competitiveness of companies in a specific sector, criteria can be disaggregated: criteria relevant for a specific issue can be isolated and then structured accordingly. To illustrate this, the issue of climate change in the automotive industry is used as an example below.

2. TAKING THE DJSI METHODOLOGY BEYOND INDEX CONSTRUCTION

2.1 Management Quality of Car Makers in Dealing with Climate Change Challenges

Following the broader look at how an issue corresponds to competitive forces on an industry level, identification of relevant criteria requires the assessment of an issue's potential for value creation and value destruction on the shareholder value concept proposed by Rappaport (1986) by identifying potentially affected value drivers.

A key metric for measuring value creation in the automotive industry is Return on Capital Employed (ROCE). ROCE is defined by volume and price. Volume and price in turn are influenced by a number of value drivers, including gross domestic product (GDP) per capita, consumer behaviour, new models, brand strength, capacity utilisation and costs (Deutsche Bank 2002).

Climate change impacts the core business model of the auto industry. Value drivers affected include:

- **New models**. New models may translate into sales growth. Climate risk therefore impacts the core product of the auto industry as climate policy and climate-conscious consumer behaviour are increasingly shaping framework conditions and thus the product line-up of car makers. More rigorous emissions regulations put pressure on product policy and force redesigns of existing models or diversification into new product segments (e.g. smaller cars). As a result, car makers that combine high margins with relative better fuel economy of their product line-up could carve out a competitive advantage.

- **Brand strength**. Brand strength can translate into higher margins. In the main car markets, superior fuel economy is increasingly perceived as an attribute of product quality (Ganguli *et al.* 2003), a key driver for brand value. Technology leadership regarding climate change can help to differentiate a car maker's brand in the highly competitive auto industry. As a result, investments in lower carbon strategies can strengthen a car maker's brand and competitiveness.

- **Costs**. Changes in government policy and technological innovations increase costs throughout the life-cycle of the industry's core product. Moreover, capital expenditure on lower carbon technologies is expected to increase as car makers aim to demonstrate technology leadership in advanced propulsion systems such as hybrid electric vehicles or fuel cell vehicles. Car makers that are able to both increase operational efficiency and set de facto standards for lower carbon technologies have the potential for a sustainable competitive advantage.

This overview highlights the materiality of climate risks for competitiveness and value creation in the auto industry. Moreover, it indicates that there is a competitive premium on lower carbon strategies that aim to reduce the carbon intensity of the product line-up and profits.

Taken a step further, the DJSI methodology can be used to assess relative competitiveness in addressing risks and opportunities derived from climate change. More generally, companies derive competitiveness from a combination of:

- A business strategy that is well aligned with the challenges of the business environment
- Capabilities or competences that allow a company to capitalise on this strategy

In the auto industry, climate change risks have resulted in lower carbon strategies that aim to (Rosinski 2002):

- Enhance the overall fuel economy of the core product
- Prepare for commercialisation of advanced propulsion systems that allow for carbon-neutral mobility
- Mitigate climate-related risks through, for example, reducing emissions from operations

To assess relative issue-specific and industry-specific competitiveness of a company and thus a company's ability to capitalise on a challenge, the DJSI methodology tests the competence of companies in addressing industry-specific challenges. Competences are assessed via indicative proxies or assessment criteria. These assessment criteria are designed to describe and quantify a company's potential to gain a future competitive premium and thus sustained future value generation.

To illustrate how the DJSI methodology can help to assess the competence of a car maker in managing climate risks, relevant climate-related criteria of the DJSI assessment methodology for the automotive industry are highlighted below. In summary, they are designed to provide a robust indication of a car maker's management quality in dealing with climate change challenges. This allows benchmarking of a car maker's competitiveness against its peers:

1. **Carbon intensity of product line-up**—helps to assess relative exposure to climate risk and provides an indication of how much value could be at stake relative to industry peers. Underlying indicators include a review of fuel economy on both a segment and a market basis.
2. **Quality of lower carbon strategy**—indicates the relative ability of a car maker to reduce the carbon intensity of its product line-up in future through the introduction of lower carbon technologies. Indicators include relative well-to-wheel GHG emissions of engine/fuel choices.
3. **Greenhouse gas strategy**—indicates the scope and sophistication of organisational capabilities to mitigate climate risks. Among others, indicators test emissions trading capabilities.

The above criteria tests differ in their focus. While the two first criteria concentrate on the product competence, the latter focuses on the process competence of car makers to address climate change. This reflects the fact that, across the life-cycle of a car, an estimated 80–90% of GHG emissions occur during its useful life in the hands of customers. Consequently, the emphasis is on fuel economy. The three criteria and their respective assessment for the DJSI are explored in more detail below:

- Carbon intensity of product line-up
- Quality of lower carbon strategy
- Greenhouse gas strategy

2.2   Carbon Intensity of Product Line-Up

This criterion draws fundamentally on two key indicators:
1. Average corporate fuel economy across different product segments (e.g. passenger cars, light trucks)
2. Average corporate fuel economy of product line-up in key automotive markets (North America, Europe, Japan)

2.2.1   Average Corporate Fuel Economy across different Product Segments

Fuel economy has proved to be a quantifiable and relevant indicator to understand both the relative global warming impact of car makers, as well as their exposure to stricter legislation or changing consumer behaviour (UCS 2002). Therefore, average corporate fuel economy is used as a key indicator to differentiate companies for the DJSI in the automotive industry. Fuel economy is largely determined by the product mix. Car makers with a bias in key segments such as large sport utility vehicles (SUVs) and pick-up trucks tend to display a lower fuel economy compared with peers with a bias in segments such as small and compact cars. Recognising these structural differences, the DJSI methodology adopts a differentiated approach, benchmarking car makers segment by segment. Consequently, car makers that display above average fuel economy across all relevant segments rank highest on this criterion.

2.2.2   Average Corporate Fuel Economy of Product Line-Up in Key Automotive Markets (North America, Europe, Japan)

In the USA, efforts to address the risks posed by oil dependence led to the design of Corporate Average Fuel Economy (CAFE) standards in 1975. CAFE standards distinguish between passenger cars and light trucks. The fuel economy standard for cars is currently 27.5 mpg (approx. 200 g carbon dioxide/km [CO_2/km]) and 20.7 mpg (approx. 268 g CO_2/km) for light trucks. The distinction between cars and light trucks emerged as a loophole for car makers as it allows the building of vehicles with low fuel economy as soon as they are classified as light trucks. Another de facto loophole exists through the Alternative Motor Fuel Act, which allows car makers to gain CAFE credits by selling cars and light trucks that can run on gasoline and/or on ethanol fuel—so-called flexible fuel vehicles (UCS 2002). In reality, however, flexible fuel vehicles run mostly on gasoline and no reduction of climate intensity is gained. Following proposals from the National Highway Traffic Safety Administration (NHTSA) and an initiative by Democrats

McCain/Lieberman, momentum has risen for stricter and harmonised CAFE standards for cars and light trucks.

As a result, the DJSI methodology draws on CAFE as a differentiator for car makers in the context of the US market. The indicator explicitly excludes credits gained through sales in flexible fuel vehicles to allow for a more accurate reflection of real performance. Car makers that exceed current fuel economy requirements without credits for both cars and light trucks rank highest.

In Europe, the Association of European Car Makers (ACEA) is voluntarily committed to achieving an industry-wide CO_2 emissions average of 140 g/km (approx. 39.5 mpg) by 2008—a 35% reduction in emissions from today's levels. During 2003, ACEA reviewed whether it can meet the further reduction targets of 120 g/km by 2012 proposed by the European Commission. Japanese and Korean car makers have also signed up to this agreement. Due to their specific product mix, progress toward the 2008 target differs among car makers. As a result, the DJSI methodology ranks car makers based on their performance against the latest corporate average fuel economy of their European fleet. Consequently, car makers beating the European average are ranked highest.

In order to meet Kyoto Protocol targets, the Japanese transport sector has been mandated to reduce its CO_2 emissions by 16% by 2010. To meet this sectoral target, the Japanese government has introduced regulations to improve the fuel economy of cars by 23% of 1995 levels by 2010. The specific fuel economy targets are determined by vehicle weight. In addition, the government has set a longer-term goal of averaging 2 litres of gasoline per 100 km by 2025. For the context of the Japanese market, the DJSI methodology ranks car makers based on their performance against their overall fuel economy across all weight classes (ranging from less than 702 kg to more than 2,266 kg). Car makers that show above average fuel economy in most weight classes are ranked highest.

2.3   Quality of Lower Carbon Strategy

This criterion includes the following indicators:
- Business case for advanced vehicle technology—distribution of sales across engine technologies including internal combustion engine, hybrid electric, fuel cell
- Relative well-to-wheel CO_2 emissions of technology/fuel options

2.3.1   Business Case for Advanced Vehicle Technology

To accommodate increasingly strict emissions regulation in their key markets, car makers can draw on a range of technology options, ranging from more efficient diesel and gasoline engines to hybrids and fuel cells. For some markets, the technology pathway seems to be set. In Japan, hybrid technology is strongly backed by both government and car makers. Europe, in contrast, appears to be geared for diesel (SSMB 2002).

However, there are signals that hybrids could play an increasingly important role across all markets and might have a long lead time on longer-term technologies such as fuel cells. While the European 140 g/km target should be feasible through improved fuel efficiency of gasoline and diesel-powered internal combustion engines alone, accommodating the stricter 120 g/km target is likely to require the introduction of hybrid options into the market. As a result, car makers that build up robust options in key engine technologies such as advanced diesel and gasoline engines (e.g. hybrids and fuel cells) are likely to benefit from a growing market for lower carbon technologies.

The DJSI methodology focuses on three key technology options that are expected to hold strong market potential:
- Advanced internal combustion engine
- Hybrid technology
- Fuel cell technology

Sales distribution across these technology options is used as an indicator for market readiness and competitiveness of car makers with respect to advanced vehicle technologies such as hybrid. Consequently, car makers that display above average share of sales in advanced vehicle technology rank highest because they have stronger potential to capitalise on their first-mover advantage by setting de facto standards.

2.3.2   Well-to-Wheel CO2 Emissions of Technology/Fuel Options

The shift from gasoline to alternative fuels is generally seen as a promising way to reduce CO_2 emissions. However, the potential to reduce carbon emissions depends on the primary energy source used to produce the fuel. Therefore, the relative GHG emissions of fuel options are increasingly evaluated over the entire fuel cycle, ranging from fuel extraction at the well through useful energy at the wheels (Greene and Schafer 2003). For example, carbon-free hydrogen fuel can be produced through electrolysis, using electricity from renewable energy such as solar energy. This would result in a carbon-free well-to-wheel fuel cycle. However, more than 50% of hydrogen worldwide is currently produced from natural gas, which contains methane—a greenhouse gas. Following this pathway, substituting gasoline through hydrogen would not yield a significant total reduction in GHGs (Greene and Schafer 2003). Due to cost barriers, it is not expected that hydrogen could be produced from renewable primary energy sources in the short term. This example illustrates the importance of considering the whole fuel cycle when evaluating the viability of fuel/technology options. As a result, the DJSI's indicator is based on capital expenditure for technology/ fuel combinations pursued by car makers. This allows testing of the efficiency of resource allocation, i.e. whether the technology/fuel options are likely to yield significant reductions in carbon emissions compared with today's gasoline combustion engine (Weiss *et al.* 2003). Consequently, car makers rank highest whose resource allocation yields the strongest reduction of GHG emissions across the fuel cycle.

2.4   Greenhouse Gas Strategy

This criterion draws partly on the World Resources Institute/World Business Council for Sustainable Development (WRI/WBCSD) GHG Reporting Protocol (http://www.ghgprotocol.org) and includes the following indicators:
• Scope and verification of GHG inventory
• Robustness of management of climate change issues

2.4.1   Scope and Verification of GHG Inventory

Pressure to set up GHG inventories comes from two main factors:
• Introduction of flexible mechanisms under the Kyoto Protocol, e.g. emissions trading
• Investor demand for transparency on exposure to climate risks

In 1997, the Kyoto Protocol established an institutional framework for the international effort to mitigate the consequences of climate change. The Protocol aims to reduce future GHG emissions in 37 developed countries to 5.2% below their 1990 levels by 2008–2012. So far, countries representing 43.9% of the volume of GHG emitted in the baseline year have ratified the Protocol. With the ratification of the Russian Federation, this number stands at 61.3%, well above the 55% required for full enforcement of the Kyoto protocol (Garz *et al.* 2003). The Kyoto protocol has been enforced and national systems have been implemented to meet the international targets. Emission trading schemes have been introduced, starting with the European Union in 2005. While the USA has pulled out of the Kyoto Protocol, voluntary initiatives backed by leading US companies are emerging, e.g. the

Chicago Climate Exchange (Internet URL: http://www.chicagoclimatex. com).

Emissions trading will result in a price for carbon. Therefore, GHG emission data will become key financial information. The WRI/WBCSD GHG Reporting Protocol was developed to assure accuracy and reliability. Ultimately, GHG emission data will have to be as accurate and reliable as other financial metrics. External verification of the data provides for additional assurance of quality.

Recently, the Carbon Disclosure Project (Internet URL: http://www. cdproject.net)—backed by a group of large institutional investors—asked the 500 largest companies in the world, as measured by market capitalisation, to identify the business implications of their exposure to climate-related risks, including reporting of corporate GHG emissions (Innovest 2003).

Similarly, the DJSI methodology draws on indicators that are based on the extent to which companies are prepared for a Kyoto world. Consequently, the companies that rank highest are those that are prepared to provide comprehensive and accurate information on their GHG baseline.

2.4.2   Robustness of Management of Climate Change Issues

As pre-requisite, accurate and reliable GHG baseline data should be complemented by a robust GHG mitigation strategy. Besides the flexible mechanisms negotiated for the Kyoto Protocol (emissions trading, joint implementation and clean development mechanisms), there are a number of additional measures to reduce GHG emissions. The options may differ across different markets. As a result, the DJSI methodology is based on the hypothesis that companies that have gained experience in a broad range of GHG reduction options will be in a strong competitive position in a Kyoto world. Consequently, companies rank highest that have gained experience in a wide range of options—implying a strong hedge against difference in the implementation of the Kyoto mechanisms across markets.

3.   CONCLUSION

In summary, the set of criteria outlined above provides a robust framework to assess both exposure and quality of strategy among car makers. In illustration, Figure 1 shows hypothetical results from a company in the automotive industry benchmarked against its peers. In this case, the car maker shows superior competence in dealing with the issue and has the potential to translate the climate challenge into a competitive advantage.

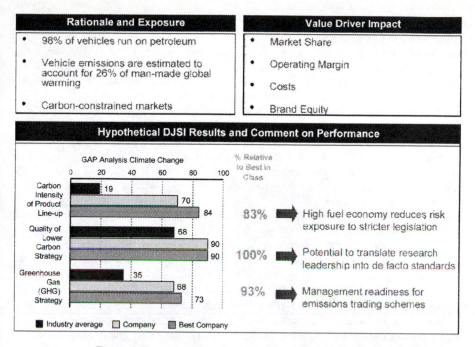

Figure 1. Example of benchmarking (hypothetical example)

The case of the automotive industry demonstrates that the DJSI methodology can be used as a robust tool to assess competitiveness with respect to industry-specific challenges at a company level. In combination with the analysis of affected industry-specific value drivers outlined above, investors can then translate this insight into the key ratios used in standard financial models such as margins and sales.

REFERENCES

Cooper, G. (2003): 'A business case for biodiversity?' *Environmental Finance*, April, 26-28.

De Geus, A. and Senge, P. (1997): *The Living Company*. Boston: Harvard Business School Press.

Deutsche Bank (2002): 'The Drivers', *Global Equity Research*.

Doering, D.S., Cassara, A., Layke, C., Ranganathan, J., Revenga, C., Tunstall, D. and Vanasselt, W. (2002): *Tomorrow's Markets: Global Trends and Their Implications for Business* (A collaboration of World Resources Institute, United Nations Environment Programme, World Business Council for Sustainable Development). Washington D.C.: WRI.

Flatz, A. (2002): 'Corporate Sustainability and Financial Indexes', in: Esty, D. and Cornelius, P.K. (Eds): *Environmental Performance Measurement: The Global Report 2001-2002*. New York: Oxford University Press, 66-81.

Ganguli, N., Kumaresh, T.V. and Satpathy, A. (2003): 'Detroit's New Quality Gap', *The McKinsey Quarterly* No. 1, 148.

Garz, H. and Volk, C. (2002): *More Gain Then Pain.* London/Düsseldorf/New York: WestLB Panmure Pan European Equity.

Garz, H. and Volk, C. (2003): *Von Economics zu Carbonomics: Value at Risk durch Klimawandel.* London/Düsseldorf/New York: WestLB Panmure Pan European Equity.

Greene, D.L. and Schafer, A. (2003): *Reducing Greenhouse Gas Emissions from U.S. Transportation.* Arlington: Pew Center on Global Climate Change.

Hilton, H. and Ruth, S. (2003): 'Financial Markets and Environment —What Counts?', *CERA Decision Brief* April.

Innovest (Ed.) (2003): *Carbon Finance and the Global Equity Markets* (Carbon Disclosure Project February 2003). London: Carbon Disclosure Project.

Porter, M.E. (1982): *Competitive Strategy.* New York: Free Press.

Rappaport, A. (1986): *Creating Shareholder Value: The New Standard for Business Performance.* New York: Free Press.

Rosinski, N. (2002): 'Climate Looms Large on Car Makers' Road Map', *Environmental Finance* September, 24-25.

Schaltegger, S. and Figge, F. (2000): 'Environmental Shareholder Value. Economic Success with Corporate Environmental Management', *Eco-Management and Auditing* Vol. 7, No. 1, 29-42.

SSMB (Salomon Smith Barney) (2002): 'Diesel Market Update', *Equity Research: Europe.*

SustainAbility and UNEP (United Nations Environment Program) (2001): *Buried Treasure: Uncovering the Business Case for Corporate Sustainability.* London: SustainAbility.

UCS (Union of Concerned Scientists) (2002): *Automaker Rankings: The Environmental Performance of Car Companies.* Cambridge: UCS.

Weiss, M.A., Heywood, J.B., Schafer, A. and Natarajan, V.K. (2003): *Comparative Assessment of Fuel Cell Cars.* Cambridge: MIT Press.

Chapter 5

Industry Surveys

HAVE TRENDS IN CORPORATE ENVIRONMENTAL MANAGEMENT INFLUENCED COMPANIES' COMPETITIVENESS?

Henning Madsen and John P. Ulhøi
The Aarhus School of Business, Denmark

Abstract: Over the past two to three decades, corporate environmental management has gradually developed into a more mature discipline. Many companies have incorporated environmental considerations into their activities in order to eliminate or reduce the impact of these activities on the natural environment. The question is, however, whether managers perceive corporate environmental initiatives as a challenge leading to new strategic options and, eventually, increased competitiveness, or whether they regard it as yet another burden. Based on a number of surveys, this chapter discusses contemporary trends in the implementation of environmental management systems in Danish industry up to the beginning of the new millennium in an attempt to identify any related effects on competitiveness.

The last decade or so has seen an increase in concern about environmental issues, especially in the West, where the many unpleasant side-effects of industrial production have captured the headlines more and more often. This, in turn, has led to an increasing public and political focus on the negative consequences of present production and ways of life, which could threaten conditions for future generations. This has resulted in a spate of environmental legislation and agreements at international, regional, national and local levels, as well as voluntary initiatives.

Business organisations tend to regard this either as yet another burden or as a new challenge. It is now almost a decade since mainstream industrial economists, such as Porter and van der Linde (1995a, 1995b), strongly opposed the reactive view that environmental regulations were just another burden that could erode competitiveness. Rather, they argued, by constantly looking for innovative solutions to increasing environmental regulation, companies would be able to tackle the challenge proactively, which could make them more, not less, competitive.

The concept of corporate environmental management was introduced more than a decade ago to help managers handle this new situation. The application of this concept has been described in terms of strategic advantages (see, for example, Welford and Gouldson 1993; Welford 1995; Ulhøi 1993), which may lead to increased competitiveness.

However, interest in implementing the principles behind corporate greening seems to have slowed of late, in part because of the perceived decreasing influence of various stakeholders, including customers (Madsen and Ulhøi 2001). In other words, the market mechanism does not seem to motivate companies to take environmental initiatives beyond those strictly required by legislation. Put another way, they seem to be less motivated to adopt attitudes and positions that may give them a competitive advantage.

The question is, therefore, whether there have been any substantial changes in the adoption of corporate environmental management in recent years that can reverse this negative impression. That is, have companies discovered the strategic advantage of being ahead of environmental regulations or avoiding environmental regulation costs by adopting an innovative attitude? This chapter addresses the question of strategic importance based on evidence from a number of surveys of Danish industrial companies carried out during the last decade. The chapter is organised as follows. The next section outlines the background and theoretical context of the study, followed by an introduction to the methodological approach used. The research findings are then discussed and discussions and implications of the findings are presented. The last section offers a conclusion to the chapter.

1. BACKGROUND AND THEORETICAL CONTEXT

Contemporary corporate environmental and resource management theory is inspired by the concept of environmental sustainability, which is basically concerned with how the quality and quantity of raw materials can be indefinitely maintained without degrading the soil, disrupting natural habitats, polluting watercourses, deteriorating the absorptive capacity of the environment and so on. As the Brundtland Report puts it: 'How can we meet the needs of the present generation without compromising the ability of future generations to meet their own needs?' (WCED 1987). However, as pointed out by Welford (1995), strategies are needed to translate this conceptual idea into practical reality.

Corporate environmental management can be considered as an attempt to translate the concept of environmental sustainability into an operational tool for company managers, since it is concerned with how companies analyse, handle and solve their environmental problems (see, for example, Ulhøi 1993). But, as Welford (1995) points out, it is only a first step towards more universal sustainable attitudes and behaviour. Nonetheless, it is an important step, since it enables companies to go from reactive pollution prevention (end-of-pipe solutions) to a more proactive platform, where environmental issues are more or less integrated in all functional areas (clean-at-source solutions).

Adopting the principles of corporate environmental management includes the formulation of an environmental strategy, which has clear relations to other strategic issues, such as corporate goals and product positioning. In other words, it must be considered as an element that can influence a company's competitive position. Reactive pollution prevention normally implies extra production costs: that is, a negative influence on competitiveness. On the other hand, a proactive attitude normally indicates an innovative climate. The result could be cost savings or improvements in a product's value, which in turn will make the company more competitive (Porter and van der Linde 1995a). However, it is important to note that the temporary adoption of a proactive environmental approach will not necessarily give a competitive advantage (Aragón-Correra and Sharma 2003). A proactive environmental attitude requires continuous and dynamic development centred on organisational learning processes for new innovations to defend or improve the competitive position (Ulhøi 1997).

Another way of looking at the environment–competitiveness relationship is to compare a company's environmental performance with its economic performance. This has been discussed frequently in recent years, and many valuable contributions have been presented (see, for example, the overview and discussion in Wagner and Wehrmeyer 2002 and Schaltegger and Synnestvedt 2002). However, an applicable formulation of such a relationship still has hurdles to overcome.

There are several unresolved challenges. First, factors other than environmental performance may contribute to economic performance, and with it competitiveness. A proactive environmental strategy may not always be linked to a positive competitive advantage, but depends on other factors in the general business environment (Aragón-Correra and Sharma 2003). This means that the effect of environmental performance must be isolated from other factors influencing economic performance (Schaltegger and Synnestvedt 2002). Second, while it may be relatively easy to develop an expression for economic performance, it is less straightforward to measure the interaction between business activities and the environment, that is, a company's environmental performance. One way is to construct standardised indicators to facilitate comparison (see, for example, the overview and discussion in Olsthoorn *et al*. 2001). However, there are many diverging approaches to environmental indicators at company level, measuring different aspects of the business environmental interaction. In addition to different ways of measuring the environmental consequences of business activities, it is not at all certain that we can isolate these consequences from the natural variation in the environment (Ulhøi *et al*. 1996a). Furthermore, as indicated by Olsthoorn *et al*. (2001), the time dimension must also be considered, since some environmental impacts cannot be observed immediately. Finally, in light of the societal dimension involved, it is debatable whether we can rely solely on company information when evaluating environmental performance. Shifting the focus to sustainable performance does not diminish the importance of this question.

However, companies do not carry on their business activities in a vacuum. As described by Freeman (1984), they are embedded in a web of stakeholders representing different and often conflicting interests. It has even been hypothesised that adopting stakeholder principles and practices results in a better economic performance (Donaldson and Preston 1995). Therefore, relationships with stakeholders ought to be included in a general evaluation of corporate environmental performance (see, for example, Lober 1996). And companies' impact on the environment has become increasingly important to most of the key stakeholders: for example, consumers, regulators, politicians and NGOs (Madsen and Ulhøi 2001). Companies themselves are aware of this, although some observers argue that much of their environmental rhetoric represents ill-concealed attempts to control the direction, if not the content, of the debate/dialogue on environment and sustainability with their stakeholders (Welford 1997).

Despite suspicions of the degree of altruism underlying corporate environmental actions and pronouncements, the fact remains that businesses, particularly in industry, have been the target of vast amounts of environmental regulation, with which they have generally been forced to comply. But the general impression of the greening of industry leaves much to be desired. Many companies seem to be at pains to go beyond compliance (see, for example, Madsen and Ulhøi 1995), claiming that they are deeply conscious of the environmental problems facing society, and gladly adopt and champion the use of concepts such as sustainability and sustainable development, but often without previous analysis of the wider implications involved, including the competitive advantages.

Any evaluation of the rate of adoption of corporate environmental management, including its potential impact on competitiveness, must be based on the elements involved in the adoption process. Of primary interest here are the drivers that force management to take the environmental challenge seriously and introduce corporate environmental management into their company. One example is the influence of various stakeholders on initiatives related to environmental issues in order to improve the company's environmental performance. However, it is important to stress that, when information is collected from companies directly, it is the influence as perceived by managers that is important. Column 1 in Table 1 shows the various relevant stakeholders who can potentially influence a company's decisions regarding environment-related initiatives. As suggested by Madsen and Ulhøi (2001), the influence of these stakeholders can be categorised into three groups: namely, stakeholders with a direct influence on companies' decision processes, stakeholders with whom companies have a market-based relationship and stakeholders with only a very indirect and limited influence.

A second element is the stage at which the decision to adopt and implement corporate environmental management has been taken. In order to determine where initiatives should be taken, a company audit is normally carried out in order to identify the company's own impact on the environment. This is important for raising awareness of why initiatives are needed, and is also normally a first step towards implementing one of the known certification schemes, such as ISO 14000 or EMAS. Column 2 in Table 1 shows a list of potential sources of the impact of a company's business activities on the natural environment.

Table 1. Details of the elements considered in relation to the four main topics (basis for the measurement scales)

1. Stakeholders	2. Impact areas	3. Areas for initiatives and improvements
• Employer and industrial associations (1999 only)	• Extraction of raw materials	• Reduction of waste
• Distributors	• Suppliers' production processes	• Soil protection
• Owners/shareholders	• The company's own production process	• Reduction of discharges
• Business networks (1999 only)	• The company's total logistics	• Reduction of water consumption
• Unions (1999 only)	• Use of the company's products	• Reduction of airborne emissions
• Financial institutions	• Discharge of the company's products	• Noise reduction
• Consumer organisations	• Recycling of the company's products	• Reduction of energy consumption
• R&D institutions		• Reduction or substitution of raw materials
• International regulations		• Improvements in the working environment (the internal environment)
• Competitors		
• Customers		
• Suppliers		
• Local regulations		
• Employees (1999 only)		
• Employees/unions (1995 only)		
• Environmental organisations		

1. Stakeholders	2. Impact areas	3. Areas for initiatives and improvements
• National regulations • Press and media		

Two final elements concern the actual actions (initiatives) taken and the results (improvements) achieved, and as such these are the factual cores of corporate environmental management. Details of environmental initiatives are generally industry-specific. However, it is possible to list a number of potential areas that should be valid across industries. These are shown in column 3 of Table 1.

Thus, an evaluation of the adoption of corporate environmental management must include four main topics:
- Influence from various stakeholders to take environmental initiatives, as perceived by managers
- Impact of the company's business activities, as perceived by managers
- Initiatives related to environmental issues
- Improvements resulting from actual initiatives

This approach is what Olsthoorn *et al.* (2001) characterise as management indicators. Though not an ideal way to analyse the environmental performance of companies in more exact terms, it provides an opportunity to evaluate the situation as perceived by management in order to identify the awareness of competitive advantages. Thus, by analysing the adoption of corporate environmental management in Danish industry, we can evaluate the extent to which the competitive advantages advocated by Porter and van der Linde (1995a, 1995b) have been recognised.

2. METHODOLOGY

Information on the adoption of corporate environmental management in Danish industry has been collected in regular surveys over the last decade. The survey instrument used is a structured questionnaire primarily based on the four topics mentioned above. In addition to a pilot survey in early 1994, two full-scale surveys have also been carried out, one in late 1995 and another in late 1999. In all surveys, samples of industrial companies with more than ten employees were drawn randomly from an electronic database. For the purpose of this chapter, only data from the two full-scale surveys are compared.

The initial sample consisted of 517 companies in 1999 and 562 in 1995, approximately 10% of the companies in the population. The sampled companies were initially contacted by telephone for the purpose of identifying the person responsible for environmental matters and obtaining his or her consent to participate in the survey. Some respondents did not wish to participate in the survey, so 440 questionnaires were sent to the remaining companies in 1999 and 498 in 1995.

In 1999, a total of 308 completed questionnaires were returned, equivalent to a response rate of 70.0% compared with the number sent and 59.6% compared with the original sample. The figures in 1995 were 54.7% and 48.4%, respectively. This can be considered to be a quite satisfactory result regarding the validity of the analyses.

For each of the four basic topics in the questionnaire a measurement scale was constructed based on the items included in each topic (see Table 1). The responses were given on a five-point Likert scale, so that questions could be answered by expressing either the degree of agreement/disagreement or the level of perceived impact or influence.

Various statistical techniques have been used to analyse the data. For the purpose of this chapter, the primary technique used is the so-called profile analysis, which is a special version of a multivariate analysis of variance (see, for example, Johnson and Wichern 1992). By means of this technique, it is possible to identify differences in responses to the same topic in two surveys. The three basic hypotheses in this model (parallel profiles, coincident profiles and level profiles) will all be tested at a 5% level of significance. Any differences identified will be further evaluated by means of simultaneous confidence intervals based on the Bonferroni principle, at an identical level of significance. In this way, the individual items causing the differences can be identified and described.

3.   RESULTS

3.1   General Trends

In order to compare the general development in adoption of corporate environmental management in Danish industry from 1995 to 1999, the responses to the individual items within each topic have been compressed into an index from 0 to 10. This enables the overall development to be visualised even if the measurement scales for the individual topics include an unequal number of items. The results are presented in Figure 1.

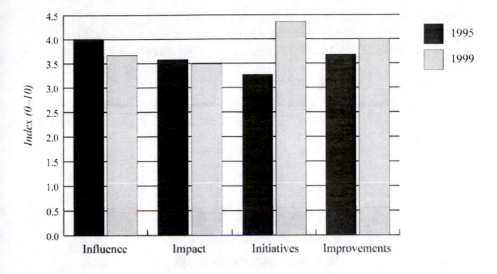

Figure 1. General tendency in the development of perceived stakeholder influence, perceived own impact, reported initiatives and reported improvements

As can be seen from Figure 1, in 1995, perceived stakeholder influence was higher than perceived own impact, which in turn was higher than the level of initiatives. On the other hand, the level of achieved improvements was approximately the same as perceived own impact. In 1999, the perceived influence from stakeholders was still higher than perceived own impact. But in 1999, the level of initiatives was remarkably higher than in 1995, and the level of achieved improvements also increased. The level of initiatives was even higher than the achieved improvements in 1999. However, it should be noted that the overall level in both 1995 and 1999 fluctuates around 3.5, which indicates a relatively low level.

The dual tendency of the observed fluctuations is confirmed by a profile analysis, since the profiles are not parallel. This is because the development in perceived influence from stakeholders and initiatives taken were both significant, but in opposite directions. The former decreased significantly from 4.13 to 3.66, whereas the latter increased significantly from 3.19 to 4.36. Perceived own impact and achieved improvements do not differ significantly, even where changes in the absolute values can be observed. However, the increase in achieved improvements is almost significant.

3.2 Stakeholder Influence

As noted above, the perceived influence from stakeholders regarding environmental initiatives decreased significantly from 1995 to 1999. Details of this development are presented in Figure 2. Obviously, stakeholders can be split into two groups according to the perception of their influence. The first group consists of stakeholders such as owners/shareholders, employees, customers and various kinds of regulation. The perceived influence from stakeholders in this group fluctuates around a level equal to 3. The other group consists of the remaining stakeholders, and the perceived influence fluctuates around a level equal to 2. But perceived influence in general decreased from 1995 to 1999. The two exceptions are local regulations and competitors.

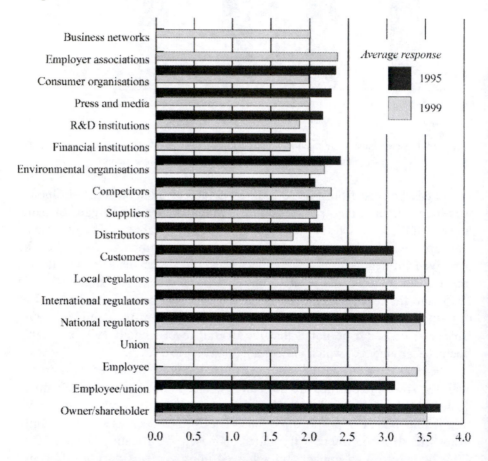

Figure 2. Development in perceived influence of a range of stakeholders on environment-related initiatives (average responses, originally measured on a 5-point likert scale, ranging from 1 = no influence to 5 = very high influence)

As can be seen in Figure 2, the 1999 survey included two new stake-holders: employer/industrial associations and business networks. Further-more, in the 1995 survey, employees and unions were treated as a single stakeholder, whereas they were split into two separate stakeholders in 1999. When comparing the combined perceived influence in 1995 with individual perceived influence in 1999, it is worth noting the differences in perception of influence between employees and unions.

A profile analysis of the perceived stakeholder influence makes it possible to conclude that the profiles in 1995 and 1999 are not parallel. This is basically due to a significant decrease in the perceived influence from four stakeholders: distributors (from 2.16 to 1.79), consumer organisations (from 2.35 to 1.99), press and media (from 2.31 to 2.00), and research and development institutions (from 2.17 to 1.88). Furthermore, the decrease in perceived influence from international regulations is almost significant (from 3.11 to 2.81). However, as mentioned above, there are two exceptions to the general decreasing tendency. For local regulations, there is a significant increasing tendency (from 2.69 to 3.53), whereas the increasing tendency for competitors is almost significant (from 2.05 to 2.28). The change in perceived influence from the remaining stakeholders confirms the decreasing tendency, although none of them is significant.

3.3 Own Impact

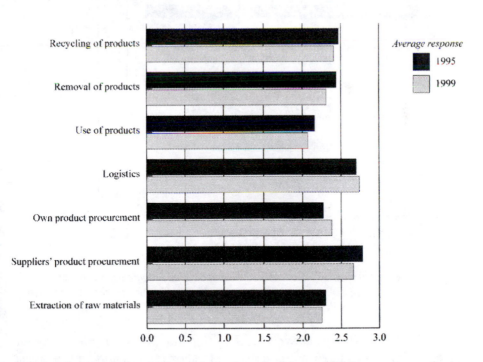

Figure 3. Respondents' perception of the environmental impact of their own company due to its business activities (average responses, originally measured on a 5-point likert scale, ranging from 1 = no impact to 5 = very high impact)

As can be seen in Figure 3, the general perception is that the companies do not have a major environmental impact. The level ranges from an average of 2 to 3 for the individual items included in the measurement scale, equivalent to the response options 'very little' and 'little' impact, respectively.

Even if differences can be observed between the perception of environmental impact in 1995 and 1999, these differences are not significant when the development is evaluated using a profile analysis. In other words, the profiles are not only parallel but they are also coincident. But the profiles do not level. The significant differences between the levels of the individual scale items are obvious from Figure 3.

3.4   Reported Initiatives

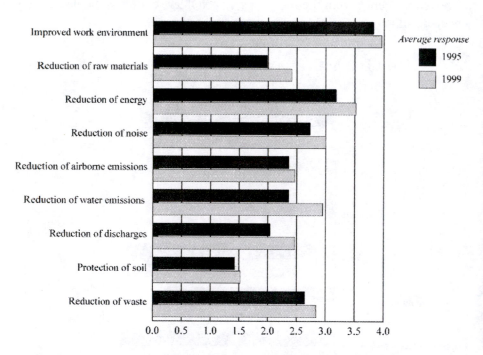

Figure 4. Reported level of initiatives on environmental issues within a number of areas (average responses, originally measured on a 5-point likert scale, ranging from 1 = no impact to 5 = very high impact)

In the general overview above (see Fig. 1), initiatives on environmental issues in the companies was the only topic showing a significant increase from 1995 to 1999. The details of this development are presented in Figure 4. As can be seen in the figure, an increasing tendency can be observed within all areas included in the measurement scale. In general, initiatives related to the working environment show the highest level, followed by reductions in energy consumption. Reductions in water consumption, noise and waste come next. There are only a few initiatives directly related to soil protection.

The profile analysis reveals that the situation in 1999 is identical to that in 1995, but at a significantly higher level, i.e. the two profiles are parallel but not coincident. This result supports the visual impression of Figure 4. However, it turns out that the result is due to a significant increase in the number of initiatives in only four out of the nine areas. These four areas are: reduction in water consumption (from 2.33 to 2.96); reduction in discharges (from 2.00 to 2.47); reduction in consumption of raw materials (from 1.96 to 2.41); and reduction in energy consumption (from 3.14 to 3.53). The change in initiatives concerning noise reduction is almost significant (from 2.68 to 3.00). In other words, the changes in initiatives concerning the working environment and reduction of solid waste are positive but not significant.

3.5   Reported Improvements

The level of improvements achieved does not fully match the level of initiatives taken, as a comparison of Figures 4 and 5 shows. The situation in Figure 5 looks very much the same as in Figure 4, only at a lower level.

The general insignificant tendency between 1995 and 1999 is partly confirmed by a profile analysis based on the individual areas included in the measurement scale. Parallel profiles can be accepted, but at a level of significance less than 0.05 (0.027). If the hypothesis of parallel profiles is accepted, it is possible to accept that the profiles are coincident too. But they do not level. A detailed interpretation of this result shows that there is a significant increase in improvements in the reduction of water consumption (from 2.35 to 2.81) and the reduction in raw materials consumption (from 1.99 to 2.35). Furthermore, almost significant increases can be found in improvements in the reduction of discharges (from 2.08 to 2.37) and the working environment (from 3.49 to 3.75).

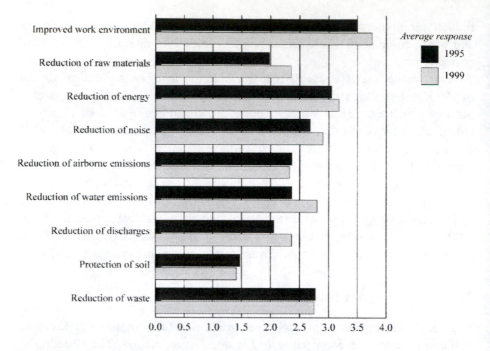

Figure 5. Reported level of improvements achieved within a number of areas (average responses, originally measured on a 5-point likert scale, ranging from 1 = no impact to 5 = very high impact)

4.   DISCUSSION AND IMPLICATIONS

Individuals often tend to overestimate their own performance. In order to deal with such a potential bias, it would be necessary to check each participating company to see whether the respondent's statement matched actual performance. This would not only be very time-consuming and expensive, but probably also generate resistance to participating in the study in the first place. Given that the present study is entirely based on the self-perception of the respondent, therefore, it cannot be said to be free from bias; that is, the results reported in the previous section may give too optimistic an impression.

The general tendency observed in the adoption of corporate environmental management in Danish industry over the last decade indicates a positive development, due to the increase in initiatives taken and improvements achieved (cf. Fig. 1). However, it is possible that this development has just removed a burden from managers so they do not feel the same influence from stakeholders any more, and that improvements actually have reduced the company's own impact. Furthermore, as noted in relation to Figure 3, no significant difference between 1995 and 1999 can be observed concerning the perception of the companies' own impact. There are two possible interpretations of this result. Either the increase in initiatives has not yet produced a reduction in the environmental impact of the companies, or the initiatives do not have a significant effect.

As could be observed from Figure 5, the major change in achieved improvements is related to cost reduction. This seems to indicate that many initiatives focus on 'picking the low-hanging fruit': for example, as an immediate reaction to the increase in taxes on water and energy consumption and charges on waste deposits introduced by the government and local authorities. However, as mentioned by Porter and van der Linde (1995a), this has an impact both on competitive position and environmental performance. On the other hand, it could indicate that companies avoid taking more serious and costly initiatives, which only pay in the longer term, as also mentioned above.

With regard to stakeholder influence, it is interesting to note the development between 1995 and 1999, since it is in contrast to expectations expressed in 1995. When asked about the expected future influence of the stakeholders included in Figure 2, the general response in 1995 was that it could be expected to increase (Madsen and Ulhøi 1996b). But the perception in 1999 does not seem to confirm this. However, in 1999, the majority of respondents generally expected an increase in stakeholder influence in the future. One possible explanation for this is that managers always think they are under the influence of various stakeholders.

The fact that legislation still seems to be one of the major drivers of environment-related initiatives is a negative development as regards competitiveness. This has been reported in several surveys over the years (e.g. Fineman and Clarke 1996; Ulhøi *et al.* 1996b; Madsen and Ulhøi 1996a). But two positive aspects can also be identified. First, the perceived influence from competitors seems to have increased. This could indicate an increasing market-based influence, even if the influence from customers has not changed. Second, there is an increase in the perceived influence from local regulations. This may be a particularly Danish phenomenon, since environmental control functions are normally handled by local authorities in Denmark (city or county). Recently, these authorities have taken a more proactive approach, rejecting the traditional control function and adopting a more dialogue-based contact with companies.

This new approach is in line with the rationale of stakeholder management (see Madsen and Ulhøi 2001) and the call for more flexibility in regulations (Porter and van der Linde 1995a). Moreover, the presence of a statutory health and safety scheme, which is compulsory for many industrial companies, may also influence perceptions. Even though this scheme focuses on the working environment, there are clear derived effects on the natural environment. Furthermore, it underlines the observation by Donaldson and Preston (1995) that employees are considered important stakeholders in many European countries. However, as it is compulsory, compliance with the statutory health and safety scheme may not, in itself, result in a competitive advantage.

Though there are differences in the sampling procedure used, it is possible to compare trends in environmental initiatives with a similar survey from Switzerland (Baumast and Dyllick 2001). In contrast to the increasing tendency in environmental initiatives in Danish industry (cf. Fig. 4), the Swiss result indicates a decline from 1997 to 2001. This could indicate different stages in the adoption of corporate environmental management in the two countries, but it might also be due to differences in industrial structure or managerial attitudes, for example. However, there is insufficient information for a more detailed evaluation of this difference.

There are several implications from the results of this survey. First, it seems obvious that political initiatives—for example, regulations—are still needed, since market forces do not seem to play an influential role. However, regulation is typically an all 'stick' approach to changing behaviour, which leaves the competitive situation unchanged. The challenge for politicians, therefore, is to introduce initiatives with a strong 'carrot' element, which can really change the attitude and behaviour of customers and consumers as well as managers. What is needed, therefore, is more flexibility in regulations, as called for by Porter and van der Linde (1995a) and by Aragón-Correra and Sharma (2003). More flexible regulations might provide the basis for continuous improvements that will influence the competitive situation, unlike rigid compliance with strict regulations.

Business managers increasingly need to recognise the potentialities for competitiveness of introducing corporate environmental management. When they are forced—one way or another—to focus on short-term results, they lack the motivation to introduce more costly initiatives leading to more long-term and lasting effects, but which do not pay back immediately. This echoes the remark by Donaldson and Preston (1995) that response to social and ethical considerations is often consistent with long-run increases in profit and value. Clearly, both market mechanisms and political initiatives play an important role in changing this situation.

5.   CONCLUSION

Corporate environmental management has been available to managers for a number of years. But, as the results of the survey presented in this chapter demonstrate, the rate of adoption does not seem to be convincing. Positive trends can be observed, but a breakthrough in reducing the environmental impact of industrial business activities still seems to be elusive. Could it be that we just haven't seen the full effect of the increase in initiatives observed between 1995 and 1999? Or could it be that managers do not acknowledge the competitive advantage of corporate environmental management?

One plausible explanation for the recent decrease in corporate greening is that managers generally have to focus on core/bottom-line issues. In other words, besides environmental issues, the general business climate also has to be taken into account. Another reason may be that, in the first wave of corporate greening, companies experienced a fast return on their investment. This means that many companies have already 'picked the low-hanging fruits': that is, implemented all the environmental initiatives with a fast payback potential. The next level of corporate greening activities is likely to require a longer payback time, since it will involve the implementation of more advanced or expensive cleaner technologies and be increasingly difficult and expensive to improve waste sorting and treatment. Finally, the managerial mind-set is proving to be a major brake on the speed of corporate greening. The question is whether managers have realised the full potential of the environment as a key strategic factor, which, in order to achieve a dynamic and innovative organisation, and with it a competitive advantage, needs to be implemented from the design phase of product development through each link in the overall business process.

Managers seem to have to constantly focus on short-term results. This is not conducive to the long-term perspective needed for more serious environmental initiatives. The important question is, therefore, are we able to change our behaviour and attitudes in daily life in order to promote and motivate a change in managerial behaviour? Do we have to rely on politicians alone, or do we also have a responsibility ourselves, one which we do not take seriously? In other words, who is to blame for the slow progress—or are we overreacting?

REFERENCES

Aragón-Correra, J.A. and Sharma, S. (2003) 'A Contingency Resource-Based View of Proactive Corporate Environmental Strategy', *Academy of Management Review* Vol. 28 No. 1 (January 2003): 71-88.

Baumast, A. and Dyllick, T. (2001) 'Umweltmanagement-Barometer Schweiz: Erste Ergebnisse zur Befragungsrunde 2001', in: Baumast, A. and Dyllick, T. (Eds.): *Umweltmanagement-Barometer 2001*. IWÖ-Diskussionsbeitrag nr. 93; St Gallen: Institut für Wirtschaft und Ökologie, Universität St Gallen, 35-44.

Donaldson, T. and Preston, L.E. (1995) 'The Stakeholder Theory of the Corporation: Concepts, Evidence, and Implications', *Academy of Management Review* Vol. 20 No. 1 (January 1995): 65-91.

Fineman, S. and Clarke, K. (1996) 'Green Stakeholders: Industry Interpretations and Response', *Journal of Management Studies* Vol. 33 No. 6: 715-730.

Freeman, R.E. (1984) *Strategic Management: A Stakeholder Approach*. Boston: Pitman.

Johnson, R.A. and Wichern, D.W. (1992) *Applied Multivariate Statistical Analysis*. Englewood Cliffs: Prentice Hall, 3rd edn.

Lober, D.J. (1996) 'Evaluating the Environmental Performance of Corporations', *Journal of Managerial Issues* Vol. 8 No. 2 (Summer 1996): 184-205.

Madsen, H. and Ulhøi, J.P. (1995) 'The Greening Situation of Danish Companies', in: Wolff, R. and Ytterhus, B. (Eds.): *Environmental Management: Where do we Stand?* Oslo: Cappelen Akademisk Forlag.

Madsen, H. and Ulhøi, J.P. (1996a) 'Environmental Management in Danish Manufacturing Companies: Attitudes and Actions', *Business Strategy and the Environment* Vol. 5 No. 1: 22-29.

Madsen, H. and Ulhøi, J.P. (1996b) 'Environmental and Resource Management: Managerial Implications and Empirical Evidence', in: Ulhøi, J.P. and Madsen, H. (Eds.): *Industry and the Environment: Practical Applications of Environmental Management Approaches in Business*, Proceedings of the 3rd Conference of the Nordic Business Environmental Management Network. Aarhus: The Aarhus School of Business.

Madsen, H. and Ulhøi, J.P. (2001) 'Integrating Environmental and Stakeholder Management', *Business Strategy and the Environment* Vol. 10 No. 2: 77-88.

Olsthoorn, X., Tyteca, D., Wehrmeyer, W. and Wagner, M. (2001) 'Environmental Indicators for Business: A Review of the Literature and Standardisation Methods', *Journal of Cleaner Production* No. 9: 453-463.

Porter, M.E. and van der Linde, C. (1995a) 'Green and Competitive: Ending the Stalemate', *Harvard Business Review* Vol. 73 No. 5 (September/October 1995): 120-133.

Porter, M.E. and van der Linde, C. (1995b) 'Toward a New Conception of the Environment–Competitiveness Relationship', *Journal of Economic Perspectives* Vol. 9 No. 4 (Autumn 1995): 97-118.

Schaltegger, S. and Synnestvedt, T. (2002) 'The Link between "Green" and Economic Success: Environmental Management as the Crucial Trigger between Environmental and Economic Performance', *Journal of Environmental Management* No. 65: 339-346.

Ulhøi, J.P. (1993) 'Corporate Environmental and Resource Management: What, Why and How?', *International Journal of Management* No. 10: 440-451.

Ulhøi, J.P. (1997) 'A Stakeholder Approach to Green Innovation', in *Proceedings of the 4th International Meeting of the Decision Sciences Institute*, Sydney, Australia, 20–23 July 1997.

Ulhøi, J.P., Madsen, H. and Hildebrandt, S. (1996a) 'Green New World: A Corporate Environmental Business Perspective', *Scandinavian Journal of Management* Vol. 12 No. 3: 243-254.

Ulhøi, J.P., Madsen, H. and Rikhardsson, P.M. (1996b) *Training in Environmental Management: Industry and Sustainability (Part 1): Corporate Environmental and Resource Management and Educational Requirements*. Luxembourg: Office for Official Publications of the European Communities.

Wagner, M. and Wehrmeyer, W. (2002) 'The Relationship of Environmental and Economic Performance at Firm Level: A Review of Empirical Studies in Europe and Methodological Comments', *European Environment* No. 12: 149-159.

WCED (World Commission on Environment and Development) (1987) *Our Common Future* ('The Brundtland Report'). Oxford: Oxford University Press.

Welford, R.J. (1995) *Environmental Strategy and Sustainable Development: The Corporate Challenge for the 21st Century*. London: Routledge.

Welford, R.J. (1997) *Hijacking Environmentalism: Corporate Responses to Sustainable Development*. London: Earthscan Publications.

Welford, R.J. and Gouldson, A. (1993) *Environmental Management and Business Strategy*. London: Pitman.

COMPETITIVENESS, ENVIRONMENTAL PERFORMANCE AND MANAGEMENT OF SMEs

David Hitchens[1], Jens Clausen[2], Mary Trainor[1], Michael Keil[3] and Samarthia Thankappan[4]

[1] *Queen's University Belfast, UK;* [2] *Borderstep Institut für Innovation und Nachhaltigkeit, Germany;* [3] *IÖW, Germany;* [4] *Cardiff University, UK*

Abstract: This chapter presents some of the results of a four-year study which sought to measure the relationship between firm competitiveness, management environmental culture, the importance of external advice on the use of cleaner production and the firm's environmental performance among small and medium-sized European manufacturing firms (SMEs) in the United Kingdom, Republic of Ireland, Germany and Italy for three industrial sectors. Using the example of the furniture sector, this chapter concentrates on the relationship between the firm's use of environmental initiatives and its competitive performance. Cost and market drivers appear to be almost as important as regulation, and the environmental initiatives adopted by firms in the industry did have an impact on both cost and market performance. Nevertheless, a statistically significant relationship between overall environmental and economic performance could not be shown. Moreover, regarding the other two hypotheses, there was no evidence of a relationship between environmental performance and management's environmental attitudes, while the relevance of external advice is that, although it is important, SMEs fail to take up available advice, which is often of good quality. The policy implications of the research are that environmental policy towards SMEs should not in these cases be constrained by concerns over competitiveness implications; firms' attitudes to the environment are not irrespective of their current environmental performance. External advice is important but is not valued by the firms.

The major aim of the EU-funded project, 'The relationship between competitiveness, environmental performance and management of small and medium-sized European manufacturing firms' (1998–2002), was to identify and weigh the importance of factors that promote and constrain the adoption of environmental initiatives by small and medium-sized enterprises (SMEs). The objective is to inform how policy can overcome obstacles to the adoption of cleaner technology. Central to the research is the testing of a set of hypotheses, which, *inter alia*, relate the adoption of cleaner technologies to competitiveness, management culture and the importance of the provision of information. The manufacturing sectors considered are those dominated by SMEs where product and process environmental response by the firm is important. Of these, furniture, textile finishing and fruit and vegetable processing were chosen. More specifically the focus is on European SMEs (in this study taken as employing fewer than 500 persons). Variations within the EU with respect to environmental regulation are exemplified by a study of firms (and plants) across four member states: Germany, north-east Italy, Republic of Ireland and the United Kingdom. This article outlines the scientific background, the research objectives and presents the main findings on the competitiveness implications for the adoption of environmental initiatives by the furniture sector. The conclusions summarise some of the main findings of the whole study.

1.   SCIENTIFIC BACKGROUND AND OBJECTIVES

The adoption of clean technologies has been slow and uneven and action has mainly involved good housekeeping; major changes involving large capital spending, or material substitution, process redesign or reformulation have been relatively rare (OECD 1985, 1995; Ashford 1993). The problem is particularly acute among SMEs because they are additionally handicapped by lack of information and resources to invest in cleaner technologies (OECD 1990). While the dominant influence on a company's investment in environmental initiatives is the need to comply with regulations (Irwin and Hooper 1992; CIA 1993; Whitaker 1993; Department of the Environment 1994; Green *et al.* 1994), survey data indicates that many businesses are not fully aware of their legal environmental responsibilities while some managers go beyond the 'compliance only' approach and see benefits to be derived from an effective environmental programme (Winter and Ledgerwood 1994).

This study focuses on the characteristics and experience of those above-average environmental performers, in comparison with the average performers in the industry, and more specifically it seeks to test the following hypotheses to explain an above-average take-up of environmental initiatives:

1. The relationship between investment in environmental initiatives and firm competitiveness is likely to involve positive feedback in both directions.
2. The role of management and the culture of the business organisation are important to the take-up of environmental initiatives.

3. The dissemination of information about environmental initiatives is likely to be a critical determinant of diffusion.

This chapter concentrates on the findings following an investigation of the first hypothesis for the furniture sector. This hypothesis acknowledges two-way causality, as follows.

The competitive performance of firms may be defined from the input or output side (Jacobson and Andréosso-O'Callaghan 1996). Where competitiveness is defined from the input side (i.e. representative of the likely explanations of competitiveness) the measure is based on strengths in physical and human capital endowment, R&D spending, etc. These are also factors that are known to influence the adoption of cleaner production technologies. Moreover, much consideration has been given to those circumstances under which environmental regulation increases or reduces innovation and hence the potential for competitive impacts (OECD 1985, 1987, 1995; Geiser 1991; Green *et al.* 1994; ECMT/OECD 1994; Wallace 1995; Porter and van der Linde 1995; Lanjouw and Mody 1996; Jaffe and Palmer 1997; Jenkins 1997; Environmental Law Institute 1999; Jaffe *et al.* 2000; Schaltegger and Synnestvedt 2002). Furthermore, above-average competitive performance implies that the firm has a management capability to respond to environmental pressures with best-practice solutions (Gabel and Sinclair-Desgagné 1998; Sinclair-Desgagné 1999).

Output-side indicators of competitive performance, such as profitability, market share, productivity, patents and firm growth, not only measure (in principle) the consequences of the adoption of clean technologies (OECD 1987, 1995; Porter 1990; ENDS 1994; CBI 1994) but also provide the resources and opportunities for the adoption of cleaner production methods and products. Moreover, where investment in environmental initiatives arises through environmental regulation, there is no convincing evidence that this has a systematic negative impact on competitiveness (Cropper and Oates 1992; Roberts 1992; OECD 1993; Jaffe *et al.* 1995; Glass 1996; Adams 1997; Jenkins 1998; Day 1998; Ekins and Speck 1998; Jaffe 1999; Wagner 2001; Vasilopoulos 2001).

2.   RESEARCH METHOD

The countries considered in the study are the United Kingdom (UK), the Republic of Ireland (ROI), Germany and Italy. The justification for this set of sample countries is provided by the extent to which they vary with respect to both environmental performance and competitiveness. There was broad coverage in all countries except Italy, where the investigation was concentrated in the north-east. The UK (including Northern Ireland) and ROI data were aggregated since there was insufficient variation in economic and environmental requirements to justify treating them as separate jurisdictions.

The research method adopted involved three strands and was the same for each of the industries selected: furniture, textile finishing and fruit and vegetable processing.

1. A short questionnaire was distributed by post[1] to firms in the sector and consisted of a series of questions on the economic characteristics and performance of the firm, the environmental strategy and the environmental initiatives adopted. For the latter, firms were asked to record the drivers, economic effects, obstacles and facilitators to adoption. The target response for each country was 100.

2. Face-to-face interviews were held with the managers of manufacturing firms using a semi-structured questionnaire. In each country and for each sector 33 firms were targeted. The questionnaire sought information on the economic characteristics and performance of the firm and on the adoption of environmental initiatives. This aspect was covered in some detail and included questions on environmental management, the use of environmental management systems and the take-up of a range of environmental initiatives including investment and running costs required, environmental impacts, effect on labour, skills and so forth. Constraints on the take-up of initiatives and the importance of different sources of advice as well as cultural attitudes were also addressed.

3. Interviews were held with providers of advice including consultants, suppliers, customers and public institutions. Advisors interviewed were either specialists in the particular industry or generalists serving a range of industrial sectors. Advisors were asked to consider a typical advisory input and the impact on the client firm of this input, how well the firm collaborated, the drivers for use of the service, barriers to the adoption of advice and so on.

Standard sources of information such as trade and telephone directories, business information publications and the Internet were used to identify the samples in each sector for the distribution of the short questionnaire. The selection of firms for the face-to-face interviews was made by careful consideration of the type of product manufactured, the number of employees and the extent to which, on the basis of information available, the firm could be categorised as compliance only or beyond compliance in terms of its environmental performance. Firms were then matched between compliance only, compliance plus and excellence. Products in the furniture sector, which

---

[1]   In Italy a slightly different approach was taken in administering the short questionnaire because of an extremely poor response to the initial mailing. The researchers opted for telephone interviews, starting with the larger firms, to achieve the target of 100 responses.

is the sector used for illustration in this article, included household furniture (chairs, tables, sofas, beds, kitchen cupboards), office furniture (desks and chairs) and flat-pack products as well as complete items.

The measurement of environmental performance was central to the project and a mix of methods was used to develop a comprehensive indicator. Taking into account the facts that controlling procedures in SMEs are rarely sophisticated and environmental performance indicators such as those proposed by ISO 14031 (environmental performance evaluation) cannot be expected to be readily available in the average SME, a set of questions was identified, which provoked meaningful, comprehensive and comparable responses in most interviews. The general idea of environmental performance measurement was:

- To evaluate the effort behind environmental management systems
- To evaluate the number and quality of process-oriented environmental protection activities and to take into account to what degree the firm is aware of its success
- To evaluate the range and quality of product-oriented environmental protection activities and the related activity concerning marketing and market communication

The individual activities taken into account varied from sector to sector. For example, solvent reduction was an important activity in furniture production but was of no importance in fruit and vegetable processing. In that sector, it was subsequently replaced by water protection, which in turn is unimportant in furniture manufacturing.

The responses to the environmental initiative questions were used to allocate scores (eco-points) by counting and weighting of initiatives undertaken by individual SMEs with slight differences between sectors; eco-points were obtained for environmental management activities (9–10 eco-points), environmental process control (12–15 eco-points) and activities concerning environmental raw material and products (6–8 eco-points). On the basis of the sum of eco-points, three environmental performance groups were established: 'compliance only', 'compliance plus' and 'excellent'. Table 1 shows the details of the scoring system used in the furniture sector for the responses to the face-to-face interviews.

Table 1. Environmental measurement system for the furniture industry

Variables	Points for rating				
	0	1/3	2/3	1	2
1. Environmental management					
Is there someone whose job involves addressing the environmental aspects?	No			Yes	
Do you have an environmental policy?	No	Discussion only	Draft version	Official version	
Do you have an environmental improvement programme?	No	Targets, not documented	Draft version	Official version	
Does an environmental team exist?	No	One meeting in past 12 months	Two meetings in past 12 months	Three+ meetings in past 12 months	
Do you evaluate environmental performance of suppliers?	No	Yes, there were tests	Yes, for many suppliers	Protocols for every supplier	
Is a management system according to EMAS or ISO 14001 implemented or planned in the next three years?	No			Yes	
Was the EMS certified externally?	No			Yes	
Which instruments of environmental communication do you use?	None			One	Two or more
2. Environmental process control					
Are activities in solvent reduction in place?	None			One	Two or more
What environmental effect was achieved?	Not known			Known	
Which waste-streams do you separate?	Up to two separated waste-streams			Three to five separated waste-streams	Six or more separated waste-streams

Variables	Points for rating				
	0	1/3	2/3	1	2
What environmental effect was achieved?	Unknown			Known	
Are energy-saving activities in place?	None			One	Two or more
What environmental effect was achieved?	Unknown			Known	
Are environmentally friendly packaging activities in place?	None			One	Two or more
What environmental effect was achieved?	Unknown			Known	
3. Ecological raw material and products					
Do you have products with a defined ecological marketing strategy?	No			Yes	
Do you avoid certain substances within raw materials?	None			One substance avoided	Two+ sub-stances avoided
Do you use natural/ecological materials?	No			One material	Two or more materials
Is there a declared eco-design scheme?	No			Yes	
Have you ever had an award for good design?	No			Yes	

Based on the face-to-face interviews, competitiveness was measured using both output and input indicators. The output measures of performance used were productivity, labour growth and the destination of sales, particularly exports, while the input measures included the level of R&D, qualifications of workers and the age of machinery. There is no simple theoretical or empirical relationship between the variables that would allow the construction of a competitiveness index. Therefore these variables and their relationship with environmental performance were analysed separately.

3. ENVIRONMENTAL PERFORMANCE AND COMPETITIVENESS

In general, the furniture industry in the UK/ROI has gradually expanded during the 1990s whereas in Germany the industry has experienced difficulties with competition from Eastern Europe. This position was reflected in the responses to the questions concerning current profitability and expectations of growth over the next three years. In the UK/ROI respondents were extremely optimistic: just over 90% of the responses stated that they operated in profit and almost 80% forecasted growth in sales. In contrast, in Germany, the expectations were more reserved, with about half of the companies operating in profit and forecasting growth. In Italy, despite its strong export market, the situation was similar.

In terms of environmental initiatives, Table 2 shows that Germany, as expected, undertook substantially more initiatives (as measured using eco-points) than either of the other countries. On the basis of analysis of variance tests, there was a statistically significant difference (at $\alpha = 0.01$) in the average number of eco-points between Germany and the other countries but not between the UK/ROI and Italy. Similar results were obtained for the

Table 2. Sample size, eco-points and environmental performance groups, face-to-face interviews

	United Kingdom/ Republic of Ireland	Germany	Italy
Sample size	32	32	33
Total number of eco-points	201	508	193
Average number of eco-points	6.28	15.89	5.86

Environmental performance groups

	Number of firms	Average number of eco-points	Number of firms	Average number of eco-points	Number of firms	Average number of eco-points
Compliance only	17	4.68	9	9.84	32	5.63
Compliance plus	15	8.08	12	14.48	1	13.33
Excellence	–	–	11	22.37	–	–

compliance only and compliance plus performance groups with Germany outperforming the other countries.[2]

On the whole there was little evidence that firms that were more active in environmental protection were more competitive than other firms (Table 3). For the British/ Irish sample a significant correlation was observed between environmental performance and productivity. The age of machinery was also significant although based on a reduced sample size. In Germany the only measure to show a significant relationship with environmental performance was exports. Hence, few competitive variables correlated with environmental performance and where they did this was not the case across all samples.

a The percentage of sales exported and the size of the firm were significantly correlated ($r = 0.71$ at $a = 0.01$, $n = 30$); thus this statistic has been calculated using partial correlation while controlling for the effect of size.

Table 3. Correlation between economic and environmental performance of furniture firms

	Expected sign	Correlation coefficient	Level of significance	Number of observations
United Kingdom/Republic of Ireland				
Exports (%)	+	−0.058	ns	32
Age of machinery	−	−0.497	0.05	16
Productivity (turnover per capita)	+	0.558	0.01	27
R&D (% of total employ)	+	0.011	ns	30
Growth (employment, 1993–98)	+	0.112	ns	26
Qualifications (% of total employ)	+	−0.277	ns	17
Germany				
Exports (%)	+	0.511[a]	0.01	30
Age of machinery	−	−0.228	ns	24
Productivity (turnover per capita)	+	0.058	ns	32
R&D (% of total employ)	+	−0.106	ns	25
Growth (employment, 1993–98)	+	−0.034	ns	32

[2] Since there was just one compliance plus firm in Italy there was no comparison made between Italy and the other countries in this category.

	Expected sign	Correlation coefficient	Level of significance	Number of observations
Qualifications (% of total employ)	+	0.197	ns	30
Italy				
Exports (%)	+	−0.182	ns	33
Age of machinery	−	0.206	ns	32
Productivity (turnover per capita)	+	Not available		
R&D (% of total employ)	+	Not available		
Growth (employment, 1993–98)	+	0.205	ns	31
Qualifications (% of total employ)	+	-0.128	ns	32

ns = not significant

Data source: 98 face-to-face interviews with furniture firm representatives: UK/ROI, 32; Germany, 33; Italy, 33.

Table 4 shows the average value of the competitiveness measures for the UK/ROI for environmental performance groups. Although there was significant positive correlation between the size of the firm and environmental performance ($r = 0.459$, at $\alpha = 0.01$) for the sample as a whole, as expected there was no significant difference in average employment between the compliance only and compliance plus groups because these data were matched. Hence, the effect of size has been controlled for. For the UK/ROI data, employment growth was the only competitiveness variable to show a significant difference on the basis of a Mann–Whitney test.[3]

Table 4. UK/Republic of Ireland average competitiveness by environmental performance group

	Compliance	Compliance plus	P-value	Number of observations
Average turnover (£ million)	7.36	17.01	0.114	28
Average productivity (output per head, £)	68,337	89,584	0.554	27
Average level of exports (%)	21	14	0.285	32
Average employment per firm	100	115	0.762	32

[3]   It was not possible to undertake a similar analysis for Germany since this data had not been matched by plant size and the latter was correlated with the number of eco-points ($r = 0.53$ at a = 0.01).

	Compliance	Compliance plus	P-value	Number of obser- vations
Average employment growth (%)	6.5	96.5	0.024	26
Average development staff per firm	2.04	4.75	0.378	31
Average qualified staff as a percentage of all staff	65.6	30.7	0.095	17
Average wages (£ per hour)	6.63	6.27	0.584	26
Average age of machinery (years)	7.83	7.12	0.449	16
Sample size	17	15		32
Average number of eco-points	4.68	8.08	0.018	32

Data source: 32 face-to-face interviews with furniture firm representatives

In summary, there was limited evidence to support the hypothesis that the more competitive the firm the more environmental initiatives it will undertake. It is also worth noting the reverse, that there were no results that pointed in the often-supposed direction that a high level of environmental activity is a burden on the economic performance of the companies. Companies that showed a high number of environmental initiatives were no less competitive than the average. They did not suffer from any obvious disadvantage, but they made use of the better image and cost reduction possibilities that may compensate for the additional efforts.

The take-up of environmental initiatives across the countries is shown in Table 5. In all countries, there was almost universal adoption of initiatives aimed at reducing waste. Initiatives to reduce packaging and energy use also had a high level of take-up while the use of non-toxic and/or natural materials was not as prevalent in the UK/ROI as in Germany and Italy. Initiatives associated with solvent reduction or environmental management systems were less common and tended to be associated with the better-performing firms, while eco-design was the least common initiative, usually found only in the top-performing firms.

Table 5. Environmental initiatives adopted, percentage of firms, face-to-face interviews

Initiative	UK/ROI	Germany	Italy
Waste reduction	96.8	100.0	100.0
Energy efficiency	68.7	81.3	69.7
Re-usable packaging	71.8	75.0	100.0
Solvent reduction	65.6	53.1	42.4
Materials change	53.1	96.9	94.0
Environmental management	62.5	40.6	30.3

Initiative	UK/ROI	Germany	Italy
Environmental communication[a]	–	53.1	–
Eco-design	18.7	46.9	0.0

[a] No data collected for the UK/ROI and Italy.

In general, most environmental initiatives were quite well integrated into the investment strategy of the firm and the need to comply with regulation was not seen as the sole reason for undertaking such initiatives. Table 6 shows that the fundamental housekeeping type of initiatives associated with efficiency gains were mainly driven by cost and to a lesser extent regulation. As the initiatives become more technically demanding, regulation (environmental and health and safety) and the market become the key drivers. Finally, for initiatives that were related to design, environmentally friendly inputs and management systems, the market was the dominant driver.

Table 6. Dominant drivers (cited by >20% of firms), face-to-face interviews

Initiative	UK/ROI	Germany	Italy
Waste reduction	Cost: 65% Regulation: 33%	Regulation: 50% Cost: 28%	Regulation: 85%
Energy efficiency	Cost: 82%	Cost: 73%	Cost: 87%
Re-usable packaging	Cost: 74%	Cost: 43% Market: 23%	Regulation: 24% Cost: 12%
Solvent reduction	Regulation: 62% H&S: 19%	Market: 33% H&S: 22%	Regulation: 57% H&S: 29%
Materials change	Market: 54%	Market: 74%	–
Environmental management	Market: 55% Regulation: 20%	Market: 69%	H&S: 83%
Environmental communication	–	Market: 65%	–
Eco-design	Market: 100%	Market: 85%	–

Respondents were asked to assess the implications of undertaking individual initiatives in terms of positive, negative or neutral effects on labour, sales, costs, productivity, profits, price, market position and image. At the aggregate level, there were 144 of these effects arising from 140 initiatives in the UK/ROI, 240 from 172 initiatives in Germany and 88 from 146 initiatives in Italy. These gave a ratio of effects to initiatives of 1.03, 1.40 and 0.60, respectively. For a few of the initiatives there was a certain degree of uniformity in terms of effects: for example, energy initiatives invariably resulted in reduced costs in all the countries. However, there was also evidence of variability in effect across country for the same initiative: for example, waste reduction in Germany showed a zero cost effect whereas in the UK/ROI there was a net reduction in costs. In Italy the impact of re-usable packaging was falling productivity while in the UK/ROI and Germany this activity was associated with increased productivity.

In general, the net effect of implementing environmental initiatives was to increase sales and reduce costs, which led to increased productivity. Cost-driven initiatives such as waste reduction, energy efficiency and re-usable packaging had the greatest economic impact on the firm, particularly in the UK/ROI. Market-driven initiatives such as eco-design and choice of environmentally conscious raw materials did lead to increased sales and productivity. There was little increase in labour associated with the initiatives. In Germany net labour increase was associated with most of the initiatives while in the UK/ROI it was the management initiatives that exhibited the greatest net gains in labour. The German dataset contained some additional information on environmental communication and showed that this activity led to a definite improvement in market position and company image.

In terms of constraints to the adoption of environmental initiatives there was general agreement between the countries and the firms, irrespective of economic or environmental performance, that the most important constraints were: (i) the difficulties faced in raising capital for a new investment; and (ii) that the regulations were too uncertain to allow managers the scope to plan for putting new technologies into practice. The British/Irish managers reinforced the latter by commenting on the shortage of good-quality advice. In addition, in the UK/ROI, a lack of management time was considered to be an important constraint.

4.   CONCLUSION

There is clearly no convincing evidence that firms with a better economic performance adopt more environmental initiatives.

Despite competitive advantages, which may variously take the form of above-average profitability, growth and associated R&D, skills and modernity (these are sub-hypotheses considered above), there was only scattered evidence to suggest that any of these was important. The policy implication follows that strong environmental performance is not constrained by the initial competitive status of the firm. This finding was further underlined by evidence from the research that firm constraints on the adoption of environmental initiatives did not differ according to the firm's current environmental performance (compliance, compliance plus, excellence). Capital or skills were a constraint irrespective of the level of environmental performance already achieved. However, there was evidence that environmental performance can be a function of the size of the firm, and that was demonstrated for a number of environmental initiatives, notably environmental management, but also some technical initiatives. There was also evidence that improvements in environmental performance were associated with increasing technical complexity of the additional initiatives adopted and the take-up of environmental management initiatives.

The economic effects of individual initiatives were in general positive (although this differed by sector with more firms in the textiles and fruit and vegetable industries reporting positive effects). There was some evidence that for two sectors payoffs were smaller for very small firms. Moreover, the ratio of positive economic benefits arising from any particular initiative rose as the firm moved up the environmental performance ladder. This supports the finding that improved environmental performance is not associated with a worsening of economic performance. In fact, at the firm level competitiveness was found to be generally unrelated to environmental performance. Strong environmental performance was not associated with a weakening of competitive performance.

Reports on the economic effects of individual initiatives indicated variation across countries, across sectors and within sectors between positive and negative economic experiences. While, as stated above, on average the experience was positive, for any single firm there is a probability that the experience could be negative. It does not therefore follow that all firms can improve their environmental performance with, on average, positive economic outcomes.

The obstacles to the adoption of environmental initiatives reported by firms were capital constraints, poor payback, low priority, lack of management time and an absence of the correct skills and/or advice. The obstacles noted by firm advisors were broadly similar: lack of resources (both time and capital), scepticism about the benefits to be derived from the environmental initiatives, and, rather differently, resistance to change, and the view that environmental performance is a necessary constraint on the activities of the firm and an interruption to production-related activities.

The advisors also highlighted the lack of demand for their services (as indicated by the low take-up of even free services). They emphasised the need for external expertise, especially where the technicalities of the environmental initiative are outside the scope of the business of the SME. Like the SMEs themselves they would emphasise the need for correct skills but a lack of take-up of those skills.

A widely quoted barrier to the take-up of clean technologies was the firm's culture. This was emphasised in many of the interviews with advisors and is one of the three important hypotheses considered in this study. The survey indicated, however, that positive environmental attitudes were quite common, and were positively held irrespective of the firm's environmental performance.

Policy should not be constrained by the expected impact on competitiveness of pressure to improve the environmental performance of firms. However, it must be recognised that the same pressure can lead to different economic impacts on what look like similar firms. Firms need more expert help than they seek or realise they need, to adopt environmental initiatives. Poor environmental performance is not the outcome of a negative attitude to the environment.

REFERENCES

Adams, R. (1997) 'Linking Financial and Environmental Performance', *Environmental Accounting and Auditing Reporter* Vol. 2: 4-7.

Ashford, N.A. (1993) 'Understanding Technological Responses of Industrial Firms to Environmental Problems: Implications for Government Policy', in: Fischer, K. and Schot, J. (Eds.): *Environmental Strategies for Industry.* Washington, DC: Island Press, 277-301.

CBI (Confederation of British Industry) (1994) *Environment Costs.* London: CBI.

CIA (Chemical Industries Association) (1993) *Survey of Investment Intentions.* London: CIA.

Cropper, M.L. and Oates, W.E. (1992) 'Environmental Economics: A Survey', *Journal of Economic Literature* Vol. 30: 675-740.

Day, R.M. (1998) *Beyond Eco-efficiency: Sustainability as a Driver for Innovation.* Washington, DC: World Resources Institute Sustainable Enterprises Initiative.

Department of the Environment (1994) *Top Management's Attitudes to Energy and the Environment.* London: HMSO.

ECMT (European Conference of Ministers of Transport)/OECD (Organisation for Economic Co-operation and Development) (1994) *Internalising the Social Costs of Transport.* Paris: ECMT/OECD.

Ekins, P. and Speck, S. (1998) 'The Impacts of Environmental Policy on Competitiveness: Theory and Evidence', in: Barker, T. and Köhler, K. (Eds.): *International Competitiveness and Environmental Policies.* Cheltenham: Edward Elgar, 33-70.

ENDS (1994) *Integrated Pollution Control: The First Three Years.* London: Environmental Data Services Ltd.

Environmental Law Institute (1999) 'Introduction', proceedings of the *Conference on Cost, Innovation and Environmental Regulation: A Research and Policy Update*, Washington, DC, 30 April 1999. Washington, DC: Environmental Law Institute.

Gabel, H.L. and Sinclair-Desgagné, B. (1998) 'The Firm, Its Routines and the Environment', in: Tietenburg, T. and Folmer, H. (Eds.): *International Yearbook of Environmental and Resource Economics.* Cheltenham: Edward Elgar.

Geiser, K. (1991) 'The Greening of Industry', *Technology Review* Vol. 94: 64-73.

Glass, N. (1996) 'Competitiveness and the Environment', paper presented at the *Conference on Environmental Economic Policies: Competitiveness and Employment*, Dublin, Ireland, October 1996.

Green, K., McMeekin. A. and Irwin, A. (1994) 'Technological Trajectories and R&D for Environmental Innovation in UK Firms', *Futures* Issue 26: 1,047-1,059.

Irwin, A. and Hooper, P. (1992) 'Clean Technology, Successful Innovation and the Greening of Industry', *Business Strategy and the Environment* No. 1: 13-24.

Jacobson, D. and Andréosso-O'Callaghan, B. (1996) *Industrial Economics and Organisation*. Maidenhead: McGraw-Hill.

Jaffe, A.B. (1999) 'Environmental Regulation and Competitiveness: An Interpretative Update', *Environmental Law Institute–Carnegie Mellon University Symposium on Environmental Regulation and Innovation*, Washington, DC, 30 April 1999.

Jaffe, A.B. and Palmer, K. (1997) 'Environmental Regulation and Innovation: A Panel Data Study', *Review of Economics and Statistics* No. 79: 610-619.

Jaffe, A.B., Peterson, S.R., Portney, P.R. and Stavins, R.N. (1995) 'Environmental Regulation and the Competitiveness of US Manufacturing: What Does the Evidence Tell Us?', *Journal of Economic Literature* No. 33: 132-163.

Jaffe, A.B., Newell, R.G. and Stavins, R.N. (2000) 'Environmental Policy and Technological Change', *Environmental Resource Economics* No. 22: 41-69.

Jenkins, R. (1997) 'Environmental Regulation and International Competitiveness', *Workshop on Environmental Regulation, Globalisation of Production and Technological Change*, UNU/INTECH, Maastricht, Netherlands, 14–15 March 1997.

Jenkins, R. (1998) *Environmental Regulation and International Competitiveness: A Review of Literature and Some European Evidence*. Discussion paper no. 9801; Maastricht: United Nations University, Institute for New Technologies.

Landjouw, J.O. and Mody, A. (1996) 'Innovation and the Diffusion of Environmentally Responsive Technology', *Research Policy* No. 25: 549-571.

OECD (Organisation for Economic Co-operation and Development) (1985) *Environment Policy and Technological Change*. Paris: OECD.

OECD (1987) *The Promotion and Diffusion of Clean Technologies*. Paris: OECD.

OECD (1990) *Promoting the Development and Dissemination of Environmentally-friendly Technologies*. Paris: OECD.

OECD (1993) *Pollution Abatement Expenditures in OECD*. Environmental Monographs no. 75; Paris: OECD.

OECD (1995) *Technologies for Cleaner Production and Products*. Paris: OECD.

Porter, M. (1990) *The Competitive Advantage of Nations*. New York: The Free Press.

Porter, M. and van der Linde, C. (1995) 'Towards a New Conception of the Environment–Competitiveness Relationship', *Journal of Economic Perspectives* No. 9: 97-118.

Roberts, P. (1992) 'Business and the Environment: An Initial Review of the Recent Literature', *Business Strategy and the Environment* No. 1: 41-50.

Schaltegger, S. and Synnestvedt, T. (2002) 'The Link between "Green" and Economic Success: Environmental Management as the Crucial Trigger between Environmental and Economic Performance', *Journal of Environmental Management* No. 65: 339-346.

Sinclair-Desgagné, B. (1999) *Remarks on Environmental Regulation, Firm Behaviour and Innovation*. Scientific Series no. 20; Montreal: CIRANO.

Vasilopoulos, M. (2001) *Clean Technology Adoption by Firms*. Seville: Institute for Prospective Technological Studies, JRC, European Commission.

Wagner, M. (2001) *A Review of Empirical Studies Concerning the Relationship between Environmental and Economic Performance*. Lüneburg: Centre for Sustainability Management.

Wallace, D. (1995) *Environmental Policy and Industrial Innovation*. London: Earthscan Publications/Royal Institute of International Affairs.

Whitaker, B. (1993) *The Business Case for the Environment and the Roles of Legislation and Economic Instruments in Enhancing the Environmental Performance of British Business*.

Environmental Management Working Group Papers; London: Advisory Committee on Business and the Environment.

Winter, L. and Ledgerwood, G. (1994) 'Motivation and Compliance in Environmental Performance for Small and Medium-Sized Companies: A Model Based on Empirical Evidence from a Pilot Investigation of Small Businesses in the English West Midlands', *Greener Management International* Issue 7: 62-72.

ACKNOWLEDGEMENTS

The authors would like to thank Wilfried Konrad for his contribution to the project.

IPPC AND THE IMPACT OF BEST AVAILABLE TECHNIQUES (BAT) ON THE COMPETITIVENESS OF EUROPEAN INDUSTRY

Survey of the European Non-Ferrous Metals Industry

David Hitchens[1], Frank Farrell[2], Josefina Lindblom[3] and Ursula Triebswetter[4]

[1]*School of Management and Economics, Queen's University Belfast, Northern Ireland;* [2]*Environment Agency, Bristol, UK;* [3]*Institute for Prospective Technological Studies (IPTS), Seville, Spain;* [4]*IFO Institute for Ecological Research, Munich, Germany*

Abstract: Integrated Pollution Prevention and Control (IPPC) Directive 96/61/EC lays down a framework requiring Member States to issue operating permits that contain conditions based on best available techniques (BAT). This chapter reports the likely impact of the implementation of IPPC on the competitiveness of existing plants in the non-ferrous metals sector. The approach is based on individual plant case studies where the economic and environmental performance of plants with varying numbers of BAT are measured and compared. The BAT requirements for the non-ferrous metals industry are summarised into ten requirements. Companies at risk of closure from IPPC have fallen behind in the development of their processes and face higher than average differential compliance costs. Overall, there was no evidence from the study that BAT hindered companies from achieving good environmental performance and remaining competitive—both nationally and internationally. What is important is that plants are given time to adapt to the Directive's requirements.

1.   INTRODUCTION

Integrated Pollution Prevention and Control (IPPC) Directive 96/61/EC lays down a framework requiring Member States to issue operating permits that contain conditions based on best available techniques (BAT). It requires the European Commission to organise an exchange of information between Member States and the industries concerned with best available techniques. The European IPPC Bureau (EIPPCB), which is located at the Institute for Prospective Technological Studies (IPTS) at Seville in Spain, organises this exchange of information and produces BAT reference documents (BREFs), which cite techniques that Member States are required to take into account by 2007 when issuing permits (Sevilla Process 2000).

Permits must contain conditions based on BAT as defined by the Directive. That these techniques are 'available' requires that they should be 'developed on a scale which allows implementation in the relevant industrial sector, under economically and technically viable conditions, taking into consideration the costs and advantages, whether or not the techniques are used or produced inside the Member State in question, as long as they are reasonably accessible to the operator' (Article 2, para 11).

This chapter reports on the impact of the implementation of IPPC on the competitiveness of existing plants in the non-ferrous metals sector based on the Non-Ferrous Metals BREF (IPPC 2001a). This is one of three industries studied by Hitchens *et al.* (2001). The other two were cement (Cement and Lime BREF; IPPC 2001b) and pulp and paper (Pulp and Paper BREF; IPPC 2001c). The principal methodology adopted is a case study approach contrasting the economic performance of plants that have adopted all or most of the elements of BAT with the performance of other plants in the various industries. The following questions arise:

- Whether companies or plants are able to maintain competitiveness in the long run after the adoption of BAT
- To what extent the industry as a whole can maintain the level of sectoral output as before.

2.   WHAT ARE THE EXPECTED IMPACTS?

The principal concern is whether the requirement to meet emission standards associated with BAT renders companies uncompetitive in the face of international competition from companies and plants in less stringently regulated countries. In general, the outcome depends on whether the policy requires that the company redirects resources from other profitable opportunities as this can lead to a rise in costs and prices and the loss of markets. There is an alternative view, however, (Porter 1990; Porter and van der Linde 1995) that regulation creates external pressure to overcome organisational inertia to reduce or eliminate the cost of compliance (Gabel and Sinclair-Desgagné 1998; Sinclair-Desgagné and Gabel 1997). In addition, it improves competitiveness by eliminating waste and the inefficient use of resources. In developing this hypothesis, Porter built on early work on the co-optimisation of economic growth through technological innovation (Ashford *et al.* 1985).

2.1   Factors Influencing the Relationship

A number of factors are likely to be important influences on the impact of regulation on competitiveness. The greater is the differential cost penalty relative to foreign competitors, the greater the negative impact on the output and employment of companies in an industry following compliance. The most significant factors are environmental costs in total costs, the greater the degree of price competition between companies and the greater the sensitivity of demand to price increases. On the other hand, industries that are characterised by higher rates of investment may be more able to take advantage of cost-reducing clean technologies. Consumer preferences may shift in favour of green products and cleaner production (OECD 1993a)

In addition, the characteristics of an industry (e.g. plant size, technology, R&D expenditure) may impact on its ability to absorb compliance costs or diffuse clean technologies (Hitchens 1999; Jenkins 1998; Klassen and McLaughlin 1996; OECD 1987; Vasilopoulos 2001a), while institutional variables such as regulation and science policy may impact the industry's previous adoption and diffusion of clean technology (Burton and Hansen 1993; Hultberg *et al.* 1999; Rogers 1995).

2.2   Measures of Competitiveness

At the company level, definitions of competitiveness revolve around quality, price and profitability relative to domestic and foreign producers. This suggests measures should consider costs, prices, profitability, non-price factors, quality etc. (Buckley *et al.* 1988). But since measures of profitability may be affected by market power, some measure of productivity may be used given the positive association between productivity and competitive performance (Jenkins 1998).

At the industry level, performance is usually related to performance in international trade. The questions addressed are whether highly regulated industries suffer in terms of exports, whether production moves abroad and whether there is increasing investment by companies overseas. Rather less attention has been paid to those companies that actually trade, although stringent regulations can prohibit the trade of non-complying imports.

At the national level, most commentators emphasise the need to judge the competitiveness impact of environmental regulation by measuring the effect on productivity (though there is much debate; see, for example, Krugman 1996). For example, the OECD (1992) defines a nation's competitiveness as 'the degree to which it can, under free and fair market conditions, produce goods and services which meet the test of international markets, while simultaneously maintaining and expanding the incomes of its people over the longer term'.

This chapter is concerned primarily with the impact of the introduction of BAT on plants and companies. A range of indicators are used to proxy competitiveness including profitability, productivity and impact on costs.

3.   FINDINGS OF PREVIOUS STUDIES

What do previous studies in the area tell us about the relationship between regulation and competitiveness? The outcome of surveys conducted by Roberts (1992), Cropper and Oates (1992), OECD (1993b), Jaffe *et al.* (1995), Glass (1996), Adams (1997), Jenkins (1998), Day (1998) Ekins and Speck (1998), Jaffe (1999), Wagner (2001) and Vasilopoulos (2001b) suggest that there is no strong universal relationship between environmental pressures and competitive performance. In particular, there is no empirical evidence that environmental standards have a systematic negative impact on competitiveness at the macro-economic or micro-economic level

Evidence supporting the Porter hypothesis has tended to be anecdotal, and hence suffers from a possible selection bias. More recent discussions have concentrated on the circumstances under which environmental regulation increases or reduces innovation, and hence the potential for competitive impacts (Environmental Law Institute 1999, Geiser 1991, Jenkins 1997, Schaltegger and Synnestvedt 2002). Porter emphasised a number of favourable conditions. These would exclude BAT-type standards because they are backward-looking, conservative, restrictive and provide little or no incentive for further progress (Jaffe *et al.* 2002). However, IPPC does not prescribe BAT. BREFs (Litten 2000) provide a dynamic list of best available techniques; hence, it still provides a stimulus to equipment-producing companies and engineers to improve their technologies and methods. Moreover, while regulators must enforce legislation, they must be flexible in how they do this. It is a weak stimulus to innovation not a disincentive to environmental innovations (Gislev 2000).

4. RESEARCH METHOD

The main approach adopted for the three sectors was based on individual plant case studies where the economic and environmental performance of plants with varying numbers of BAT was measured and compared (Hitchens *et al.* 1998, 2000). The application of this general methodology differed slightly between the industries studied. In this chapter, we concentrate on the method adopted to investigate the relationship in the non-ferrous metal industry (Farrell and Hitchens 2001) and draw together conclusions for the whole study.

5. THE NON-FERROUS METALS STUDY

At least 42 non-ferrous metals plus ferro alloys, carbon and graphite are produced in the EU. They are used in a variety of applications in the metallurgical, chemical, construction, transport and electricity generation/transmission industries.

Non-ferrous metals are produced from a variety of primary and secondary raw materials. Primary raw materials are derived from ores that are mined and treated further before they are metallurgically processed to produce crude metal. The treatment of ores is normally carried out close to the mines. Secondary raw materials consist of indigenous scrap and residues, and may also undergo some pre-treatment to remove coating materials.

In Europe, ore deposits containing metals in viable concentrations have been progressively depleted and few indigenous sources remain. Most concentrates are therefore imported from a variety of sources worldwide.

Recycling constitutes an important component of the raw material supplies of a number of metals. Copper, aluminium, lead, zinc, precious metals and refractory metals (among others) can be recovered from their products or residues and can be returned to the production process without loss of quality in recycling. Overall, secondary raw materials account for a high proportion of the production, thus reducing the consumption of raw materials and energy.

The product of the industry is either refined metal or what is known as 'semis' or semi-manufactured material, i.e. metal and metal alloy cast ingots or wrought shapes, extruded shapes, foil, sheet, strip, rod, etc.

The structure of the industry varies metal by metal. No companies produce all non-ferrous metals, though there are a few pan-European companies producing several metals, e.g. copper, lead, zinc and cadmium.

5.1   Sectors Studied

The study focused on five products and the impact of BAT on plants producing those products:

- Production of copper cathodes from primary raw materials. There are four primary smelters in the EU and all were studied. This sector competes directly with smelters that operate on a worldwide basis.
- Production of copper from secondary raw materials. Four of the six secondary smelters in the EU were studied. This sector again operates against strong international competition.
- Production of aluminium ingots from secondary raw materials. There are 80 secondary smelters in the EU and 13 were studied. This sector also operates against strong international competition.
- Production of lead ingots from secondary raw materials. Six of the 30 secondary smelters in the EU were studied. The market for lead is now closely linked to lead–acid battery demand.
- The recovery of salt slag and the production of Waelz oxide. Eleven of the 17 plants in the EU were studied. Waelz oxide is a crude form of zinc oxide produced by the treatment of electric arc furnace dust from the steel industry. It is an important route for the recycling of secondary zinc and represents the largest source. Other sources of secondary zinc are normally recycled by galvanizers or in small plants designed for the treatment of zinc residues. These sectors have developed as a waste treatment facility for parts of the non-ferrous metals industry.

5.2   IPPC Requirements

The BAT requirements for the non-ferrous metals industry can be summarised by a number of common requirements governing:

- Storage and handling of all materials
- Pre-treatment of materials
- Process control
- Management and supervision of all of the stages
- The production process used
- The collection of fumes and gases (prevention of fugitive emissions)
- Air pollution abatement plant used
- Water and effluent
- Residues and waste
- Energy efficiency/recovery.

These ten BAT factors, which apply to the industry in general, are summarised in Table 1. The BAT factors are frequently interdependent.

Table 1. BAT factors, investment cost and impact

BAT factor	Example	Investment cost	Economic characteristic	Impact cost (–ve)/ benefit (+ve)
1 Storage and handling	Enclosure	100,000 to 200,000 €	Prevents up to 5% loss of raw material	Negative to neutral
2 Pre-treatment	Swarf centrifugation	120,000 €	10% increase in throughput	Positive
3 Process control	Interactive system	100,000 €	10% increase in productivity	Positive
4 Management and supervision	Environmental system	50,000 €	Productivity increase	Positive
5 Metallurgical process	Metal pumping system	300,000 €	10% increase in yield	Positive
6 Fume collection, enclosure, hooding, molten transfers	Increased fan capacity	50,000 €	Ongoing operating cost	Negative
	Furnace enclosure	200,000 €	Dust recovered	Negative
	Intelligent dampers	50,000 €	Dust recovered	Neutral
	Launder system	100,000 €	Dust recovered	Neutral
7 New or upgrade of abatement **Dust**	Change from electrostatic precipitator (EP) to fabric filter	1,000,000 €	Ongoing operating cost	Negative
Sulphur dioxide (SO$_2$)	Modern bags	100,000 €	6 month payback	Positive
Volatile organic compounds (VOCs)	Scrubber	1000000 €	Ongoing operating cost	Negative
	Afterburner	500,000 €	Ongoing operating cost	Negative
8 Wastewater treatment	Change of reagent to sodium hydrosulphide (NaHS)	50,000 €	Equal operating cost	Neutral
9 Process residues	Greater mixing in furnace	20,000 €	Residue reduced to 30%	Positive
10 Energy efficiency/ recovery **Oxygen (O$_2$)**	Oxy-fuel burners	50,000 €	Reduction in gas volume and 30% increase in capacity	Positive

5.3 Focus on Fugitive Emissions

The relatively good standard of existing air and water pollution abatement systems means that extensive investment in new or replacement abatement plant is not a priority for most plants in the industry. More importantly, there are significant variations in the effectiveness of fume capture and the extent of fugitive emissions in the sector. Fugitive emissions often represent the major environmental impact as well as a health and safety issue. Implementation of IPPC and the adoption of BAT are therefore likely to focus on controlling the process well and making incremental changes in gas extraction systems. Improvements in fume capture might need higher capacity fans or better control of the gas volumes caused by process surges.

The main effect of IPPC in this sector will be to reduce air emissions from non-captured or fugitive sources.

Several of the BAT factors focus on the 'front end' of the process. The techniques aim to improve material storage and handling and to increase efficiency by reducing process variations and therefore the potential for fugitive emissions. Such techniques can also improve productivity.

6. IMPACT OF BAT ON EXISTING PROCESSES AND COMPETITIVENESS

6.1 Method for Measuring BAT

An experienced regulator, who also has industrial process experience, conducted interviews and made the assessment and judgements of the impact of BAT on the competitiveness of sample plants using an environmental assessment methodology and a questionnaire.

The environmental assessment procedure is based on the Operator Performance and Risk Assessment (OPRA) methodology (EP OPRA 2002) developed by the Environment Agency in the UK, which has been used for more than five years. The scheme marks environmental standards against a number of headings, which include the BAT factors. The factors are scored out of 5 depending on the standard achieved. The use of BAT achieves a score of 4; see Table 2. Other important criteria that can influence the environmental and economic performance of a plant are also measured using this methodology and are reported as factors either influencing the take-up of BAT or acting as an obstacle.

6.2   Factors Influencing Environmental and Economic Performance

The environmental performance of a plant is the sum of the scores on each of the BAT factors measured using OPRA methodology. This has been compared with the economic performance of the plant quantified as productivity performance and metal yield, across all plants with some data available on compliance costs and profitability across sample plants. A number of factors, which may influence the BAT 'score' e.g. national regulation, were also measured and compared. In addition the importance to the eco-eco performance relationship of in house skills, technical age, ownership, plant size and technology were also considered.

Table 2. Scoring method for environmental assessment

BAT Factor	Criteria for Measuring the Strength of the BAT Factor				
	Score of 1	Score of 2	Score of 3	Score of 4	Score of 5
Generic description	None of the techniques are used	Some of the techniques are used Development considered	Most of the techniques are used Some development	All of the techniques are used Some development	All of the techniques are used or exceeded Constant development
1 Storage and handling	Open storage of dust-forming material VOC emissions from tanks	Shielded storage of dust-forming material	Shielded storage of dust-forming material Oily material in bunded areas, tanks back-vented	Covered, shielded storage of dust-forming material Oily material in bunded areas' tanks back-vented	Enclosed storage of dust-forming material Oily material in bunded areas; tanks back vented
2 Pre-treatment	No pre-treatment	Some pre-treatment to optimise the size	Some pre-treatment to remove organic material or optimise the size	Pre-treatment to remove organic material or optimise the size	Effective pre-treatment. e.g. to remove organic material and blend the furnace charge to provide a constant feed

BAT Factor	Criteria for Measuring the Strength of the BAT Factor				
	Score of 1	Score of 2	Score of 3	Score of 4	Score of 5
3 Process control	Manual control of process and abatement No procedures/in structions No monitoring of parameters Frequent process deviations	Manual control Poorly written procedures/in structions Poor monitoring of parameters Frequent process deviations	Operating procedures available and implemented Control of some process operations, e.g. combustion conditions Limited process deviations	Effective operating procedures available and implemented Control of some process operations, e.g. combustion conditions Limited process deviations	Fully automatic control based on key process parameters Comprehensive procedures/ instructions being followed Rare process deviations
4 Management and supervision	Ineffectively managed, poorly defined reporting structure and no clearly identified responsible person No identifiable supervision Breakdown maintenance only	Poor management control but skills present Poor supervision but skills present Some planned maintenance	Fair management control with skills present Improvements being made Controlled by responsible person Maintenance is planned	Plant effectively maintained and managed with well-trained, competent personnel aware of all consequences Fully trained, responsible operators reacting to process variations	Commitment to planned maintenance Environmental performance demonstrated within management policy Fully trained foremen or supervisors reacting to process variations
5 The process	Basic process not included in the BREF conclusions on BAT	Some processes included in the BAT conclusions	Majority of process included in the BAT conclusions	Process included in the BAT conclusions including the control and monitoring aspects	Process included in the BAT conclusions, combined with effective, continuous development
6 Fume collection	Open or semi-sealed furnaces with inadequate extraction systems	Open or semi-sealed furnaces with fair extraction systems	Semi-open furnaces with good extraction of gases	Semi-sealed furnaces with good extraction of gases	Sealed or fully enclosed furnaces with good, high volume extraction

| BAT Factor | Criteria for Measuring the Strength of the BAT Factor | | | | |
	Score of 1	Score of 2	Score of 3	Score of 4	Score of 5
7 Abatement or upgrade of abatement	Basic process not included in the BAT conclusions. Replacement or total upgrade needed	Some of the process included in the BAT conclusions Some upgrade needed, e.g. improved filter bags	Majority of the process included in the BAT conclusions Upgrade needed in near future, e.g. continuous monitoring	All of the process included in the BAT conclusions including the control and monitoring aspects No upgrade needed Regular maintenance carried out	Process included in the BAT conclusions combined with good monitoring and control systems No upgrade needed Regular maintenance and improvement
8 Wastewater treatment	Basic process not included in the BAT conclusions	Some of the process included in the BAT conclusions	Majority of the process included in the BAT conclusions	Process included in the BAT conclusions	Process included in the BAT conclusions with effective, continuous development.
9 Process residues	No attempts to minimise or re-use process residues	Some attempts to minimise or re-use process residues	Effective attempts to minimise or re-use process residues	Good minimisation practices	Good minimisation practices with continual reviews
10 Energy efficiency/ recovery	No energy recovery Possibilities not investigated	No energy recovery Possibilities investigated	Limited energy recovery Some investigation of other opportunities	Energy recovery practised where plant design showed possible areas	Energy recovery Continuous investigation of other opportunities

6.3   Plants Sampled

The sample included primary and secondary copper plants, secondary aluminium plants, secondary lead plants and the associated processes for the recovery of salt slag and production of Waelz oxide. The range of sizes of sample plants was representative of the non-ferrous metals industry as a whole in the EU and, importantly, included SMEs (see Table 3).

Table 3. Site visits for the sectors studied

Metal Produced	No. of plants in EU	No. of plants visited
Primary copper	4	4
Secondary copper	6	5
Secondary aluminium	50	17
Secondary lead	30	11
Salt slag	10	7
Waelz oxide	7	4

6.4 Findings on Environmental and Economic Performance Relationship

Companies that have developed their environmental standards, already exploited cleaner technology and adopted effective methods for controlling the process also have a competitive advantage. The observations on-site confirmed that these companies not only have high environmental standards, but also have higher productivity and lower energy usage. These companies were profitable and reported that they foresaw no problems in implementing IPPC. Figures 1 and 2 show examples of this positive relationship. This result is not surprising as the underlying principles of IPPC are to reduce the consumption of energy and raw materials. Increases in yield will produce more metal for a given operating cost, improve profitability and prevent emissions of waste products to all environmental media.

6.5 Additional Costs Arising from Implementation of IPPC

The site visits suggested that many companies in the sector were using elements of BAT and that most companies were already using satisfactory process and abatement plant. The absent BAT factors were those relating to the collection of process gases and controlling the process (e.g. management and operator skills). Differential compliance costs for IPPC would have generally been low because the missing factors can be corrected with minimal capital expenditure.

Table 4 lists differential costs for the uptake of IPPC that have been quoted by the companies or calculated from the costs available. The estimates are based on the environmental assessment methodology and anticipate the adoption of all the BAT factors.

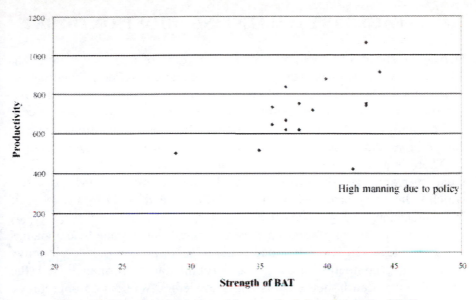

Figure 1. Secondary aluminium—labour productivity and strength of BAT

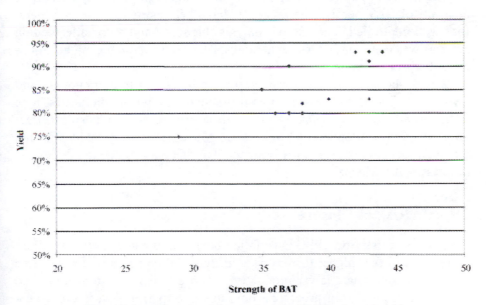

Figure 2. Secondary aluminium—strength of BAT and metal yield

7.   FACTORS FACILITATING ADOPTION OF BAT

During the site visits, it was apparent that a group of front end factors that relate to how a process is managed, developed and controlled is important in differentiating between good and poor performers at both an economic and environmental level. These factors include the technical age of the process and a number of skill factors that include training, innovation, operator competence, management and supervision, and the elements of maintenance.

There is a strong influence of technical age on economic and environmental performance. The successful development of furnaces and processes, which reduce technical age, are in turn influenced strongly by the level of innovation employed by a company.

A large number of process improvements have been made by companies using high levels of innovation and skills to solve problems. They improve productivity, competitiveness and environmental performance. All the projects have used in-house skills and knowledge. Without an appropriate focus, the presence of these skills and knowledge alone does not necessarily improve a company's competitiveness and environmental performance.

The site visits showed that companies with higher productivity have more elements of BAT because the processes have been optimised and are therefore well controlled. The use of analysis, blending and automatic feeding systems was common in these companies. The use of these techniques minimises fugitive emissions.

Size of the company and ownership were found not to be important and SMEs were equally successful in environmental and economic issues. Size of the installation (throughput of metal), however, did have a positive effect on productivity. Adoption of EMAS (Eco-Management and Audit Scheme) did not affect environmental performance, but this may be due to the relative newness of the scheme.

7.1   Risk of Closure

Companies at risk from IPPC have fallen behind in the development of their processes and face higher than average differential compliance costs. These companies have much lower productivity and efficiency than average and have not optimised their processes. For such poor performers, improvement to the 'front end' of a process is very important, followed by development of the process itself. Skills and the way that they are implemented and directed can be used to improve both these elements. For example, in cases where under-designed gas collection is the main issue, process improvements can reduce gas volumes to a level that is acceptable—though some plants need to up-rate fan sizes and possibly the size of abatement plant.

Table 4. Likely impact of IPPC on a selection of sample plants

Differential impact due to IPPC	Motivation driver and obstacles	Work needed	Effect on emissions	Likely project cost €	Effect on productivity	Economic effect		Capital and running cost
						Margin	Yield	
Improved fan capacity	Some fugitive emissions	Increase fan capacity by 25,000 m³/h	Reduction of fugitive emissions	120,000 € = 1.2 €/t over 5 years	No change	- 2 €/t*	No effect	1 €/t* 50 kWh
Optimisation of extraction	Small fugitive emissions	Survey and adjustment of extraction	Reduction of fugitive emissions	Minor	No change	No change	No change	Minor effect
Optimisation of extraction	Some fugitive emissions	Survey and adjustment of extraction	Reduction of fugitive emissions	Minor	No change	No change	No change	Minor effect
No anticipated costs	Use of all BAT factors	None	No reduction needed	Nil	No change	No change	No change	No change 8 companies in the sample
Improved fan capacity	High level of fugitive emissions	Increase fan capacity by 50,000 m³/h	Reduction of fugitive emissions	240,000 € = 0.6 €/t over 5 years	No change	- 2 €/t*	No effect	1 €/t* 100 kWh
Reduced gas volume	High level of fugitive emissions	Use of oxygen if feasible	Reduction of fugitive emissions	Minor	Increase possible	+ 2 €/t	No effect	< 1 €/t

No likely effects on Employment and Skills. * Based on increased electricity usage

The improvement of skills is an area where many companies have had success by adapting established systems. Many of these improvements relate to management issues. Table 4 summarises the competitive advantages and disadvantages reported by companies.

8.   ENVIRONMENTAL COSTS AND COMPANY COMPETITIVE ADVANTAGES AND DISADVANTAGES

The main advantages reported during the study of implementing IPPC requirements were:
*   Labour quality, efficiency, process control, knowledge of process and reject rate
*   Price, quality of products and marketing
*   Transport charges and markets
*   Scale and raw material price
*   Flexibility (raw materials, products and general)
*   Environmental cost and image

The disadvantages reported were:
*   Transport
*   Environmental cost
*   Raw material type and price
*   Products and scale
*   Location
*   Inability to use difficult raw materials

The environmental cost disadvantage reported in six cases referred to that arising from existing legislation. Significantly, those companies that thought that environmental costs were a disadvantage were not using all or most of the BAT factors and were less efficient performers. Companies that reported environmental costs as an advantage had all the BAT factors.

9.   CONCLUSIONS

There was no evidence from the study of any of the three sectors (pulp and paper, cement and non-ferrous metals) that BAT hindered those companies already using BAT and achieving good environmental standards from remaining competitive both nationally and internationally.

It did not follow, however, that an early implementation of BAT by other companies or plants in the industries studied would similarly have little or no impact on their competitive performance. The study lists the characteristics of the BAT plants visited that helped those companies reach BAT standards and remain competitive.

Advantageous factors included the stringency of the national regulations of the country within which the plant was located and the plant's history of adopting BAT and other clean technology. Other factors that helped the relationship included plant size and growth, the technical age of plant and machinery, and the extent of in-house R&D and skills.

The study concluded that there are other plants that would have technical, financial and other difficulties in a speedy implementation of all BATs. In cement, there are special problems for small, old and independent kilns in adjusting to BAT investment requirements and simultaneously remaining competitive in the short-term. Sufficient time for planning investments is important in the cement industry.

In the paper and pulp study, the possible speed of upgrading differs between sites. For example, it may be possible to combine environmental investments with other investments (for capacity increase or quality improvement). These opportunities play a major role in determining whether or not a company should invest in a single jump or choose a stepwise approach.

For each industry, individual industry reports emphasised the importance of prioritising environmental initiatives and the need to take care over the timing of these initiatives and the time taken to undertake them.

While similar findings may apply to other industries subject to IPPC, it is important to check economic impacts when BREFs are being considered. The recently published Economic and Cross-Media Effects BREF (IPPC 2005) includes a methodology to check the competitiveness implications of BAT at the BREF development stage.

REFERENCES

Adams, R. (1997): 'Linking Financial and Environmental Performance', *Environmental Accounting and Auditing Reporter* Vol. 2, No. 10, 4-7.

Ashford, N., Ayers, C. and Stone, R. (1985): 'Using Regulation to Change the Market for Innovation', *Harvard Environmental Law Review* Vol. 9, No. 2, 419.

Buckley, P.J., Pass, C.L. and Prescott, K. (1988): 'Measures of International Competitiveness: A Critical Survey', *Journal of Marketing Management* Vol. 4, No. 2, 175-200.

Burton, D.F. and Hansen, K.M. (1993): 'German Technology Policy: Incentive for Industrial Innovation', *Challenge* Vol. 36, No. 1, 37-48.

Cropper, M.L. and Oates, W.E. (1992): 'Environmental Economics: A Survey', *Journal of Economic Literature* Vol. 30, No. 2, 1675-1740.

Day, R.M. (1998): *Beyond Eco-efficiency: Sustainability as a Driver for Innovation.* Washington D.C.: World Resources Institute Sustainable Enterprises Initiative.

Ekins, P. and Speck, S. (1998): 'The impacts of Environmental Policy on Competitiveness: Theory and Evidence', in: Barker, T. and Köhler, J. (Eds.): *International Competitiveness and Environmental Policies.* Cheltenham: Edward Elgar, 33-70.

Environmental Law Institute (1999): *Introduction* (Proceedings of the Conference on Cost, Innovation and Environmental Regulation: A Research and Policy Update). Washington D.C.: Environmental Law Institute.

EP OPRA (Environmental Protection Operator and Pollution Risk Appraisal) (2002): *Risk Screening Methodology for the Environmental Agency's Regulation under the Pollution Prevention and Control Regulations* (Version 1 November 2002).

Farrell, F. and Hitchens, D. (2001): *The Impact of Best Available Techniques (BAT) on the Competitiveness of European Non-Ferrous Metals Industry.* Seville: Institute for Prospective Technological Studies, JRC, European Commission.

Gabel, H.L. and Sinclair-Desgagné, B. (1998): 'The Firm, its Routines and the Environment', in: Tietenberg, T. and Folmer, H. (Eds.): *International Yearbook of Environmental and Resource Economics 1998/99.* Cheltenham/Northampton: Edward Elgar, 89-118.

Geiser, K. (1991): 'The Greening of Industry', *Technology Review* Vol. 94, No. 6, 64-73.

Gislev, M. (2000): *European Innovation and Exchange of Information about BAT* (Paper presented at the European Conference on the Sevilla process: A Driver for Environmental Performance in Industry, Stuttgart, 6-7 April 2000).

Glass, N. (1996): *Competitiveness and the Environment* (Paper presented at the Conference on Environmental Economic Policies: Competitiveness and Employment, Dublin, October 1996).

Hitchens, D. (1999):'The Implications for Competitiveness of Environmental Regulations for Peripheral Regions in the EU', *Omega - International Journal of Management Science* Vol. 27, No. 1, 101-114.

Hitchens, D., Birnie, J.E., McGowan, A., Triebswetter, U. and Cottica, A. (1998): *The Firm, Competitiveness and Environmental Regulation.* Cheltenham: Edward Elgar.

Hitchens, D., Triebswetter, U., Birnie, J.E., Thompson, W., Bertossi, P. and Messori, L. (2000): *Environmental Regulation and Competitive Advantage, A Study of Packaging Waste in the European Supply Chain.* Cheltenham: Edward Elgar.

Hitchens, D., Farrell, F., Lindblom, J. and Triebswetter, U. (2001): *The Impact of Best Available Techniques (BAT) on the Competitiveness of European Industry.* Seville: Institute for Prospective Technological Studies, JRC, European Commission.

Hultberg, P.T., Nadiri, M.I. and Sickles, R.C. (1999): 'An International Comparison of Technology Adoption and Efficiency: A Dynamic Panel Model', *Annales d'Economie-et-de-Statistique* No. 55/56, 449-474.

IPPC (Integrated Pollution Prevention and Control) (2001a): *Reference Document on Best Available Techniques in the Non Ferrous Metals Industry.* Seville: IPTS.

IPPC (Integrated Pollution Prevention and Control) (2001b): *Reference Document on Best Available Techniques in the Cement and Lime Manufacturing Industry.* Seville: IPTS.

IPPC (Integrated Pollution Prevention and Control) (2001c): *Reference Document on Best Available Techniques in the Pulp and Paper Industry.* Seville: IPTS.

IPPC (Integrated Pollution Prevention and Control) (2005): *Reference Document on Economics and Cross-Media Effects.* Seville: IPTS.

Jaffe, A.B. (1999): *Environmental Regulation and Competitiveness: An Interpretative Update* (Symposium on Environmental Regulation and Innovation). Mellon: Environmental Law Institute-Carnegie Mellon University.

Jaffe, A.B., Peterson, S.R., Portney, P.R. and Stavins, R.N. (1995): 'Environmental Regulation and the Competitiveness of US Manufacturing: What Does the Evidence Tell Us?', *Journal of Economic Literature* Vol. 33, No. 1, 132-163.

Jaffe, A.B., Newell, R.G. and Stavins, R.N. (2002): 'Environmental Policy and Technological Change', *Environmental and Resource Economics* Vol. 22, No. 1/2, 41-69.

Jenkins, R. (1997): *Environmental Regulation and International Competitiveness* (Workshop on Environmental Regulation, Globalisation of Production and Technological Change, UNU/INTECH, Maastricht, 14-15 March).

Jenkins, R. (1998): *Environmental Regulation and International Competitiveness: A Review of Literature and some European Evidence* (Discussion Paper # 9801). Maastricht: The United Nations University, Institute for New Technologies.

Klassen, R.D. and McLaughlin, C.P. (1996): 'The Impact of Environmental Management on Firm Performance', *Management Science* Vol. 42, No. 8, 1199-1213.

Krugman, P.R. (1996): 'Making Sense of the Competitiveness Debate', *Oxford Review of Economic Policy* Vol. 12, No. 3, 17-25.

Litten, D. (2000): *BAT Reference Documents: What are They and What are They Not* (Paper presented at the European Conference on The Sevilla process: A Driver for Environmental Performance in Industry, Stuttgart, 6-7 April 2000).

OECD (Organisation for Economic Cooperation and Development) (1987): *The Promotion and Diffusion of Clean Technologies*. Paris: OECD.

OECD (Organisation for Economic Cooperation and Development) (1992): *Technology and the Economy: The Key Relationships*. Paris: OECD.

OECD (Organisation for Economic Cooperation and Development) (1993a): *Environmental Policies and Industrial Competitiveness*. Paris: OECD.

OECD (Organisation for Economic Cooperation and Development) (1993b): *Pollution Abatement Expenditures in OECD* (Environmental Monographs No. 75). OECD: Paris.

Porter, M. (1990): 'The Competitive Advantage of Nations', *Harvard Business Review,* November/December, 73-93.

Porter, M. and Linde, C. van der (1995): 'Towards a New Conception of the Environment-Competitiveness Relationship', *Journal of Economic Perspectives* Vol. 9, No. 4, 97-118.

Roberts, P. (1992): 'Business and the Environment: An Initial Review of the Recent Literature', *Business Strategy and the Environment* Vol. 1, Part 2.

Rogers, E.M. (1995): *Diffusion of Innovations* (4th edition). London: The Free Press.

Schaltegger, S. and Synnestvedt, T. (2002): 'The Link between 'Green' and Economic Success: Environmental Management as the Crucial Trigger between Environmental and Economic Performance', *Journal of Environmental Management* Vol. 65, No. 4, 339-346.

Sevilla Process (2000): *Proceedings of the European Conference on The Sevilla process: A Driver for Environmental Performance in Industry* (Stuttgart, 6-7 April 2000).

Sinclair-Desgagné, B. and Gabel, H.L. (1997): 'Environmental Auditing in Management Systems and Public Policy', *Journal of Environmental Economics and Management* Vol. 33, No. 3, 331-346.

Vassilopoulos, M. (2001a): *Industrial Competitiveness and Environmental Regulation*. Seville: Institute for Prospective Technological Studies, JRC, European Commission.

Vassilopoulos, M. (2001b): *Clean Technology Adoption by Firms*. Seville: Institute for Prospective Technological Studies, JRC, European Commission.

Wagner, M. (2001): *A Review of Empirical Studies Concerning the Relationship between Environmental and Economic Performance*. Lüneburg: Centre for Sustainability Management.

Chapter 6

Country Surveys

THE MUTUAL RELATIONSHIP BETWEEN THE ENVIRONMENTAL CONTEXT AND MANAGEMENT IN THE NETHERLANDS

Ronald S. Batenburg

Department of Information Sciences, Utrecht University, the Netherlands

Abstract: In this chapter, the Structure Conduct Performance (SCP) model is used to describe how Dutch manufacturing companies judge their influence on a number of environmental problems during 2001. With regard to the 'Structure' element, it appears that, in particular, companies in the textile and energy industries indicate that their activities negatively influence the use of energy, water and non-renewable resources. In contrast to their expectation, however, their 'Conduct' (an array of potential environmental actions) is not above average in all cases. Instead, companies from other industries such as the manufacture of electrical optical equipment take significant measurements on toxic inputs and waste water. But in terms of 'Performance', the expectation that active companies are more positive about the estimated effects of their environmental actions is supported empirically.

1.   INTRODUCTION

Around the turn of the 21st century, the Dutch economy can be characterised as a service, transportation and knowledge economy. About 70% of registered companies operate in the service sector, 13% in agriculture and 17% in construction and manufacturing. The profit and non-profit service sectors contribute most to gross domestic product (GDP). A large part of the Dutch economic growth originates from transportation, retailing and re-exportation. Lately, the IT service industry has contributed significantly to the proliferation of the Dutch economy. A high average level of education, jobs and professions typically characterises the Dutch labour force. In 2001, about half of the labour force was occupied in the service sector (Statistics Netherlands 2002).

The traditional manufacturing industries in the Netherlands lost their economic position during the 1960s and 1970s as many activities lost the worldwide competition for products such as steel, automotives, ships, textiles and food. In particular, the production of high turnover consumer products disappeared from Dutch sites and moved to countries with cheap labour. However, some large multinational companies in the traditional industries still have their base in the Netherlands (e.g. Philips, Shell, Unilever and Akzo Nobel). Most of their core production and assembly has, however, have been outsourced through complex networks of holdings, groups, plants, units and divisions.

Given this characterisation of the economy, the Netherlands traditionally takes an upfront position with regard to environmental policy. Although the number of Dutch manufacturing companies is relatively limited, this sector has been subject to significant environmental policy measures since the early 1970s. Framework laws, regulations and legislation to control environmental damage from industrial activities have been extensively developed, debated and researched. A typical example is the Covenant on Packaging Waste, which was agreed between the Environment Ministry and industry in 1991. This Covenant was developed through a consultative approach—an example of the Dutch 'Polder' tradition of multi-party collaboration and negotiation. Environmental policy in the Netherlands is implemented and executed at the provincial and municipal level. At these levels, licences are granted under the Environmental Management Act and contain conditions with regard to water management. In addition, the Netherlands aims to play a significant role in international debates in provoking collective environmental measurements in numerous fields.

Environmental management and sustainable development are not only major issues in Dutch policy, but also in commercial and academic Dutch communities. Numerous initiatives in this field are undertaken at various levels and from different perspectives. At the business level, environmental policy is progressed in both a technical and a managerial sense. Life-cycle analysis, environmental annual reports and supply chain management have become important tools. Dutch enterprises invested 450 million euros in environmental protection in 2002, almost 50 million euros more than in 2001. Most of these investments were spent on anti air pollution measures. In addition, environmental costs for Dutch companies increased to almost 2.1 billion euros in 2002. Costs for environmental protection have been increasing every year since 1993 (Statistics Netherlands 2003). However, there has been a decreasing interest in green issues by the public in recent years as indicated, among other things, by opinion polls and the diminishing number of students opting for environmental studies.

2.   EUROPEAN BUSINESS ENVIRONMENTAL BAROMETER (EBEB)

2.1   The EBEB Approach

The Netherlands joined the European Business Environmental Barometer (EBEB) project in 1997. This international joint survey effort provided the first quantitative insight in the environmental policies of 550 Dutch companies during the period 1995–1997. This chapter reports on the next wave of EBEB with Dutch participation—the 2001 survey—and outlines the Dutch situation at the beginning of the 21st century. In 2001, 347 companies contributed to the EBEB survey. Out of 2,000 questionnaires sent, the response was almost 17%. In 1997, the response was 25%. This decline demonstrates the decreasing interest of Dutch companies (managers) in participating in survey research, particularly in the main target group of environmental research, i.e. medium and large industrial companies.

The lower the response, the more important is the matter of bias or pre-selection in sampling. In this research, the variation in industry type and employees size is especially important. These two basic characteristics determine many factors and conditions relevant to the environmental behaviour of the Dutch companies. Table 1 shows the division of response by industry and size; note that the relevant variation is present within the sample. Companies that produce energy (coke, oil and fuel), textiles and clothing, and transport products are present in small numbers, but this is accordance to their proportional representation in Dutch national statistics as most manufacturing companies in the Netherlands are active in food products, tobacco and metal products. For instance, in terms of production value, the Netherlands accounts for one quarter of tobacco products in the European Union (Statistics Netherlands 2001). In addition, comparison with the Dutch national statistics shows that survey response is also non-selective with regard to company size. Most respondents are in the mid-size category with up to 250 employees. For these reasons, this chapter is based on unweighted results from the 2001 EBEB survey.

Table 1. Response on the EBEB-2001 survey by size and industry

| Industry | Number of employees | | | | |
	50–99	100–249	250–499	500+	Total
Food products, tobacco	14	24	8	7	53
Textile products, clothing	1	3	1	1	6
Wood products	7	1		2	10
Pulp paper products		11	2		13
Publishing, printing	4	5	3	5	17
Energy (coke, oil, fuel)		1		2	3
Chemical products, fibres	3	7	2	4	16
Rubber and plastic	8	15	4		27
Non-ferrous mineral products	6	5	1		12
Metal products	23	37	18	13	91
Machines equipment	11	9	4	5	29
Electrical, optical equipment	3	2	3	3	11
Transport products	1	3	1	1	6
Other	11	19	5	18	53
Total	**92**	**142**	**52**	**61**	**347**

2.2   Background of Analysis

There are many ways in which to present the results of a survey as large as the EBEB 2001. Within the context of the Netherlands, this chapter focuses on the interrelation and interaction between manufacturing companies and their environments. As outlined above, manufacturing companies in the Netherlands are confronted with significant forces from policy, international competition and restructuring of the national economy and labour market. A general question in this respect refers to the (subjective) interpretation of the macro context by managers of these companies. In particular, the first question to examine is how companies judge the potential negative effects of their activities on a number of environmental areas. Following this step from the macro context to the micro level of the company itself, the next step focuses on the environmental actions of companies, which are expected to vary according to the interpretation of the environmental problem area; however, this assumption will also be influenced by other factors. Finally, the question can be directed to the effects of the environmental actions as interpreted by the respondents, i.e. the environmental managers of the participating companies. This step brings us back at the macro level of the environmental problem areas themselves and their relevance to the manufacturing industry in the Netherlands in 2001, the date of the survey.

The plan of presentation in this chapter is inspired by the so-called structure–conduct–performance approach. This theoretical concept has become well known for its explicit alignment of external conditions with organisational action and performances in general. The model originates from the perspective that stresses the importance of the external context in understanding organisational strategy, structure and behaviour. It marked the beginning of classic strategic management as an academic field of interest, with Ansoff, Bain and Porter as the main academic representatives. Although the approach has been criticised for its dominant focus on external analysis (Barney 1991), the approach suits the modelling of the chain- and cross-boundary behaviour of organisations as examined it in this context. Within the context of environmental management, this approach promised to be a fruitful inspiration. Obviously, the natural environment drives environmental management and practices directly. In addition, stakeholders form part of the structural context of companies. Environmental managers react or anticipate by constructing policies and take actions. As a result, companies make achievements in environmental position and outcomes. As will be shown in the following sections, the questionnaire used by the EBEB 2001 project is well suited to operationalise this conceptual framework.

3.   MAIN RESULTS

3.1   'Structure': Environment Problem Areas

Companies differ in their involvement with environmental issues by the nature of their activities. Data from Statistics Netherlands show that enterprises in the mining, manufacturing, energy and water supply industries spent about 105 million euros on improving water quality. Some 45 million euros were invested in the abatement of soil pollution. Another 40 million euros were invested in the reduction of waste pollution and 20 million euros in reducing noise. The EBEB 2001 survey data allow a closer and better look at the environmental behaviour of manufacturing companies, especially with regard to the variation in the environmental problem areas with which companies are coping.

The top five environmental problem areas that Dutch respondents judged as most negatively influenced by their industrial activities were selected for an initial examination (Table 2). In total, 13 different problem areas were presented to the respondents. In Table 2, the top five problem areas plus one other area—landscape damage—are broken down by industry. This enables types of environmental problem to be mapped with types of industry, i.e. industrial processes and activities. The mean values in Table 2 indicate the extent to which respondents believe their activities contribute to the environmental problem area: the higher the mean score, the higher the negative impact of the company to the problem area according to the respondent.

Table 2. Negative impact of company activities on six environmental problem areas, by industry (mean judgments of respondents on a five-point scale)

			Environmental problem areas			
Industry	**Use of water**	**Use of energy**	**Non-renewable resources**	**Use of toxic inputs**	**Waste water**	**Land-scape damage**
Food products, tobacco	2.94	2.98	2.08	1.61	2.77	1.63
Textile products, clothing	3.00	4.00	3.60	2.20	3.00	1.50
Wood products	1.00	2.75	2.00	2.00	1.40	1.33
Pulp paper products	2.15	3.23	1.82	2.00	2.25	1.50
Publishing, printing	2.21	2.94	2.21	2.31	2.13	1.20
Energy (coke, oil, fuel)	2.33	3.33	3.00	2.50	2.67	2.00
Chemical products, fibres	2.25	2.94	2.81	2.69	2.53	1.64
Rubber and plastic	2.08	3.30	2.72	1.86	1.65	1.47
Non-ferrous mineral products	2.10	2.91	2.45	2.00	1.82	1.56
Metal products	2.00	3.03	2.08	2.07	2.18	1.38
Machines equipment	1.81	2.84	2.40	2.13	2.00	1.33
Electrical, optical equipment	1.67	3.17	1.80	2.20	1.73	1.50
Transport products	2.25	2.50	1.80	2.00	2.00	1.25
Other	2.26	2.66	2.47	1.98	2.30	1.29
Total	**2.22**	**2.97**	**2.29**	**2.05**	**2.24**	**1.45**

As in many other countries and in previous survey years, the use of energy is at the top of the list as most negatively influenced by industrial activities. The other problem areas show total averages close to that of energy use. Remarkably, two of the top five problem areas as judged by Dutch industries are problems concerning water, i.e. the use and its waste variant.

In Table 2, landscape problems are judged as relatively unimportant the responding companies in terms of an environmental problem area related directly to their activities.

Broken down by industry, the negative impact on water use and waste water is prominent in the textile, food products and energy industries. These industries also report high negative impacts on energy use and non-renewable resources. The energy, rubber and plastic industries have similar impacts in these problem areas. Companies that produce energy and chemical products, in particular, have high negative impact on toxic inputs. As can be expected, the energy industry is of major concern with regard to landscape impacts, but also with toxic inputs.

From Table 2, it appears that environmental problems indeed vary by industry. The variation is understandable by type of core activity but, from the overall picture, it also becomes clear that the high negative impacts are concentrated within a few sectors of Dutch industry. Companies in the textile and energy industries are most prominent in judging their activities as very influential in four out of five of the environmental problem areas.

With regard to this analysis, however, it has to be noted that these types of self-assessment questions in questionnaires have important limitations. Clearly, incentives to provided social desirable answers may stop respondents from judging the own environmental impacts of their industrial activities objectively. Although the confidentiality of the survey is stressed, companies (respondents) still have strong incentives to protect their reputation by underestimating the negative impact of their activities. This aspect will be returned to in the next steps of the analysis.

3.2   'Conduct': Environmental Actions

The list of top five environmental problem areas in Table 2 provides the input to the next step of the analysis. What significant actions did Dutch companies undertake during the three years up to 2001 to cope with their negative impact on these different environmental areas? This question was presented to respondents with three simple answer categories:

- No (no significant actions undertaken)
- Yes (significant actions undertaken)
- Not relevant (used to pre-select only relevant cases)

In practice, companies have a large spectrum of potential green organisational routines consisting of many different technical and organisational activities (Hass 1996). For the sake of simplicity, the analysis in this chapter is limited to the distinction between 'actions' in general and no significant environmental actions at all.

Naturally, one would expect strong correlations between problem areas and actions. The Dutch industries judged to have high negative impacts on water use and waste water, for instance, will probably adopt strong environmental actions in this field. However, this expectation is based on several assumptions, which will be discussed later. First, Table 3 presents the proportion of companies that took action in relation to the environmental problem areas broken by industry.

Table 3. Actions undertaken by companies by environmental problem areas and industry (% that ticked 'yes' on taking significant actions with regard to the problem area)

| Industry | Environmental problem area | | | | | |
	Use of water	Use of energy	Non-renewable resources	Use of toxic inputs	Waste water	Land-scape damage
Food products, tobacco	75.47	82.35	53.85	40.00	82.35	14.29
Textile products, clothing	40.00	50.00	60.00	75.00	60.00	0.00
Wood products	16.67	85.71	42.86	71.43	40.00	33.33
Pulp paper products	76.92	71.43	45.45	80.00	92.31	0.00
Publishing, printing	50.00	76.47	50.00	82.35	53.33	0.00
Energy (coke, oil, fuel)	66.67	100.00	0.00	0.00	100.00	0.00
Chemical products, fibres	66.67	93.75	21.43	73.33	86.67	25.00
Rubber and plastic	52.00	85.19	61.90	78.95	28.57	7.69
Non-ferrous mineral products	72.73	63.64	63.64	25.00	60.00	50.00
Metal products	60.94	79.55	40.00	70.97	57.75	11.76
Machines equipment	34.78	55.56	18.18	60.87	38.10	8.33
Electrical, optical equipment	45.45	91.67	33.33	80.00	88.89	0.00
Transport products	20.00	33.33	33.33	50.00	25.00	33.33
Other	63.64	76.92	55.26	81.08	61.90	5.88
Total	**59.52**	**77.22**	**44.05**	**68.88**	**63.80**	**11.19**

The variation in actions undertaken by environmental area is more or less comparable with the overall variation found in the previous analysis. The use of energy is mentioned by over three-quarters of the companies as an area where they take significant action. This is in accordance with the high negative impacts that companies judged themselves to have in this area (see Table 2). The other environmental areas receive less attention in terms of significant actions. Less than half of respondents indicated that they take significant actions on the use of water—a level below that which could be expected. Landscape damage, an environmental area previously judged as a problem outside the scope of most companies, is accordingly subject to little environmental action; only 11.2% ticked this area.

From an examination of on the different industries, it appears that companies in the textile and energy industries did not take as many actions with regard to the environmental problem areas as they previously judged themselves to have highly negative impacts on. Here, the expected relation between problem recognition and actions seems to be absent. On the other hand, companies in the food and tobacco industries indicate that they are highly active in the same environmental problem areas as they mentioned earlier (use of water and waste water). The same is true for the chemical products industry, which takes significant actions with regard to the use of energy—as would be expected. Manufacturers of electrical and optical equipment take above average actions on toxic inputs and waste water. This was not expected from their negative impact on these areas as reported in Table 2.

As a first conclusion, it can be stated that the general rank order of environmental problem areas by problem recognition (Table 2) resembles that by actions (Table 3). However, the picture is less clear if we take a closer look at the different industries. Industries that judged themselves to have serious negative impacts on a certain environmental area do not systematically show above average action in response to the problem. Vice versa, some industries appear to be frontrunners in taking environmental actions in one field while having considerable negative impacts in quite different problem areas. The expected relation between problem recognition and consequential actions is therefore analysed more specifically in (Figures 1–6), which show scattergram plots of the industry scores on both variables for each of the six environmental areas studied in more detail in EBEB survey 2001.

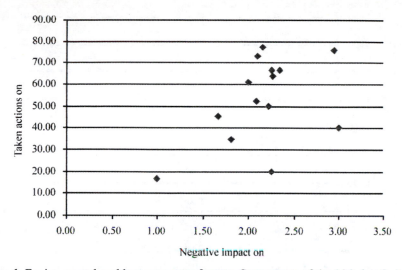

Figure 1. Environmental problem area: use of water. Scattergram of the 14 industries' score on negative impact versus actions undertaken.

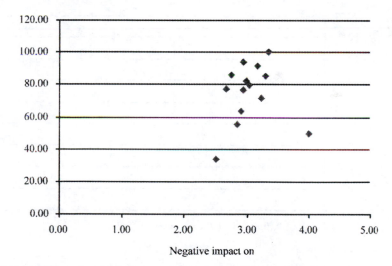

Figure 2. Environmental problem area: use of energy. Scattergram of the 14 industries' score on negative impact versus actions undertaken.

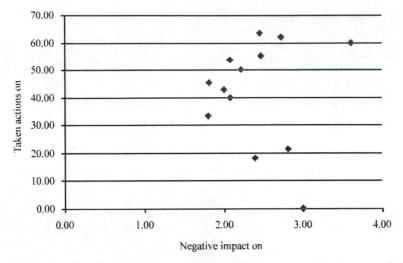

Figure 3. Environmental problem area: non-renewable resources. Scattergram of the 14 industries' score on negative impact versus actions undertaken.

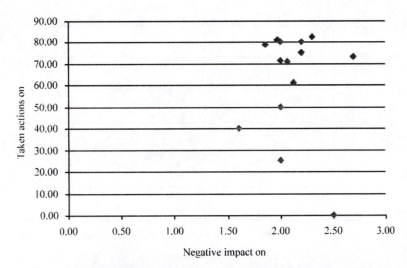

Figure 4. Environmental problem area: use of toxic inputs. Scattergram of the 14 industries' score on negative impact versus actions undertaken.

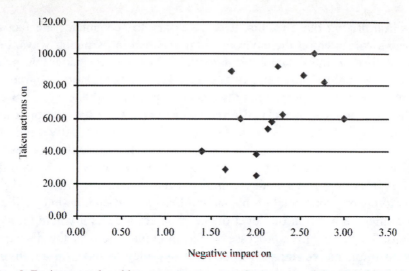

Figure 5. Environmental problem area: waste water. Scattergram of the 14 industries' score on negative impact versus actions undertaken.

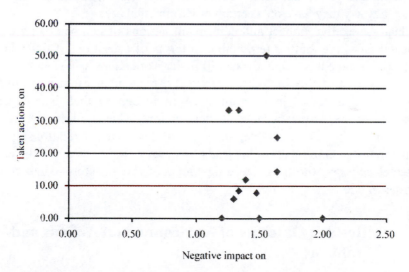

Figure 6. Environmental problem area: landscape damage. Scattergram of the 14 industries' score on negative impact versus actions undertaken.

Figures 1–6 demonstrate that, at an industry level, the positive relationship between negative impact and actions taken upon the environmental areas is recognisable. The upward line can be most clearly drawn through the scatter plot in the case of use of water, use of energy and waste water. The other environmental problem areas show a somewhat broader pattern. It is clear that some industries can diverge strongly from the expected straight correlation between the two variables.

In interpreting these results, it is necessary to account for the fact that managers will interpret the environmental problem in particular ways. From many studies on individual environmental behaviour, we know that people consider the natural environment as a collective 'good' or resource. For different reasons, people are not always convinced that the level of environmental problems can be related directly to their own behaviour or responsibility. Respondents might think, for example, that their negative impact on water use is relatively strong, but take little action because they believe the problem is determined much more by other industries or factors beyond their control. In addition, respondents might argue that they contribute significantly to the environmental problems, but believe that their actions will have only a minor impact on the level of the problem area as a whole (see next section). These cognitive processes offer an explanation for the divergence between the negative impact respondents say they to have on an environmental problem area and the actions they devote to these problems. Another argument would be that companies take actions merely as a reaction to the pressure from stakeholders such as local government. This could explain why companies undertake more actions than can expected from the negative impact they say they have on a certain environmental area.

Finally, negative impact and significant actions of companies on environmental areas are multi-interpretable in terms of causality. At first glance, one might assume that respondents will undertake actions as a reaction to the negative impact of their activities. However, respondents that indicate that many actions are taken in a certain area might believe that their negative impact to the area is low because of these actions. This is, of course, hard to capture from the data available, since it implies a causal relationship that cannot be tested empirically. This leads to a focus on the results of the environmental actions—the third building block of the structure–conduct–performance model.

3.3   'Result': Outcome of Environmental Actions and Problems

This examines how respondents judged the effects of their environmental actions over the last three years. In some sense, this judgment is affected by the same measurement problems as noted in previous sections. However, it is based on the same list of environmental areas and can be specified with regard to the same classification of industries, thus making it a relevant extension of the previous analysis.

Respondents were asked to indicate the effect of their actions on five point scales. Cases were omitted if no action was undertaken on a certain area. The respondents are equally positive about the effects of their environmental activities with regard to the use of water, energy, toxic inputs and waste water. The energy use problem is less prominent in this part of the analysis.

It is important to note that the five-point scale in this case varies from 1 (no effect) to 5 (very much effect). An average score of 2.6 on the use of toxic inputs, for example, thus indicates that respondents believe that their actions had between 'little' and 'some' effect.

With regard to the industries, the overall score of the paper pulp industry is striking to a certain extent. The food and tobacco industries indicate that they had relatively success with their actions in the fields of water and energy use and waste water. Other highlights are the scores of the electrical and optical equipment industry on the use of toxic inputs, which is comparable with result from Table 3. The respondents from the transport products industry indicate that their actions to reduce the water use and toxic inputs were relatively successful. This cannot be related to the combination in previous tables.

Table 4. Positive effect of company actions towards six environmental problem areas, by industry (mean judgments of respondents on a five-point scale)

Industry	Environmental problem area					
	Use of water	Use of energy	Non-renewable resources	Use of toxic inputs	Waste water	Land-scape damage
Food products, tobacco	2.79	2.73	1.96	2.00	3.02	1.41
Textile products, clothing	1.83	2.33	2.00	1.75	2.40	1.33
Wood products	1.33	1.80	1.67	2.50	1.50	1.00
Pulp paper products	2.75	2.27	3.00	2.71	2.90	1.25
Publishing, printing	2.46	2.57	2.42	3.40	2.58	1.80
Energy (coke, oil, fuel)	2.33	3.00	1.00	1.00	3.33	1.50
Chemical products, fibres	2.21	2.53	2.22	2.69	3.00	1.60
Rubber and plastic	2.57	3.23	2.30	2.67	1.84	1.17
Non-ferrous mineral products	2.44	2.30	2.63	2.33	2.75	1.75
Metal products	2.63	2.59	1.83	2.59	2.67	1.38
Machines equipment	2.26	2.26	2.00	2.70	2.44	1.33
Electrical, optical equipment	2.25	2.55	2.13	3.13	2.33	1.00
Transport products	3.00	2.40	1.50	3.25	2.00	0.00
Other	2.76	2.65	1.86	2.49	2.72	1.40
Total	**2.56**	**2.61**	**2.03**	**2.60**	**2.67**	**1.38**

4. CONCLUSION: STRUCTURE–CONDUCT–PERFORMANCE?

The trilogy of analysis presented in this chapter is concluded by relating the three EBEB 2001 survey questions (variables) to the level of the individual companies (respondents). Performing correlation analyses tests the main expectation that the three components will have a certain relationship with each other. In the previous section, this expectation was tested by comparing overall and industry averages. This has advantages in terms of direct interpretations of the Dutch industrial sectors, but disadvantages with regard to the number of observations for statistical analysis. Table 5 presents the results of the correlation analysis.

It is remarkable that the correlation between 'actions' and 'effects' are positive and strong for all problem areas. The effects between the 'impact' and 'actions' are only significant for the three areas highlighted in the previous section, i.e. the use of water, use of energy and waste water. In addition, there is also a direct correlation between 'impact' and 'effects' for these areas.

Table 5. Correlation between the negative impact companies say they have ('impact'), significant companies have undertaken ('actions') and the perceived effect of company actions ('actions) on six environmental problem areas (correlation coefficients)

| | Environmental problem area | | | | | |
	Use of water	Use of energy	Non-renewable resources	Use of toxic inputs	Waste water	Land-scape damage
Correlation between:						
Impact ⇔ actions	0.25**	0.15*0.15	0.01	0.00	0.27**	0.02
Actions ⇔ effects	0.55**	0.43**	0.34**	0.38**	0.60**	0.39**
Impact ⇔ effects	0.26**	0.19**	0.07	0.00	0.28**	0.17

This final analysis shows that the mutual relationship between environmental context and the behaviour of companies is partly supported by the Dutch dataset from the EBEB 2001 survey project. The extent to which respondents believe that their company has a negative impact on the environment is followed by significant actions in the field of water and energy use and waste water, but not with regard to the use of non-renewable resources, toxic input and landscape damage. To a lesser extent, the same holds true for the respondents' judgment of the positive effect of their company's environmental actions. In the case of water and energy use and waste water, significant actions are highly correlated with positive effects on these environmental problem areas. The answers of the respondents to the other three environmental areas also support such a relationship but to a lesser degree.

These results might be due to the fact that water and energy are generally prominent environmental areas within the Dutch manufacturing industries. As elaborated above, food products, tobacco and metal products dominate the Dutch industrial structure. Operations in these industries depend on the use of energy and water as part of their inputs and have severe consequences for waste water as part of the emission process. Other environmental problems such as landscape damage and the use of toxic inputs are limited in their application to the total sample of industries in this survey. This might explain why the relationship is absent between recognition of these problems and significant actions, but present for the subjective relation between actions and their effects.

REFERENCES

Barney, J. (1991): 'Firm Resources and Sustained Competitive Advantage', *Journal of Management* Vol. 17, No. 1, 99-120.

Hass, J. (1996): 'Environmental ('Green') Management Typologies: An Evaluation, Operationalisation and Empirical Development', *Business Strategy and the Environment* No. 5, 59-68

Statistics Netherlands (2001): *Industry Monitor 2001/01.* Voorburg/Heerlen: Statistics Netherlands.

Statistics Netherlands (2002): *The Year in Figures, 2002.* Voorburg/Heerlen: Statistics Netherlands.

Statistics Netherlands (2003): *Press Release PB03-124.* Voorburg/Heerlen: Statistics Netherlands.

Wagner, M. and Schaltegger, S. (2002): *Umweltmanagement in deutschen Unternehmen. Der aktuelle Stand der Praxis.* Lüneburg: Centre for Sustainability Management.

THE NORWEGIAN ENVIRONMENTAL BUSINESS BAROMETER

Bjarne E. Ytterhus
Norwegian School of Management (BI), Sandvika, Norway

Abstract: The Norwegian Environmental Business Barometer is a survey of the views of industry leaders regarding environmental challenges and the adaptations made by the enterprise in relation to the external environment. The method used is a questionnaire. The survey has been conduced several times over the last decade. This chapter presents some core results from the Norwegian survey. In the last Norwegian Environmental Business Barometer carried out in 2001, the sample consisted of 679 industrial enterprises, each with more than 50 employees. The response rate was 23% or 153 enterprises.

1.   OVERALL DESCRIPTIVE RESULTS

This section gives details of the 2001 survey and presents a descriptive overview of the results. The results are given in more detail in subsequent sections.

1.1   Objectives

The objective of the Norwegian Business Environmental Barometer is to map how the chief executive officers in Norwegian manufacturing companies perceive:
*   The driving forces behind companies' environmental strategies and actions
*   The implementation by companies of environmental strategies and actions
*   Economic and environmental performance

To achieve these objectives, a questionnaire based upon the international survey called European Business Environmental Barometer was used. The questionnaire is structured in a similar way to the OECD Pressure–State–Report model. The hypotheses are:

- Environmental stakeholders have an influence on companies' environmental policy and actions
- Environmental activities are implemented by introducing environmental management systems and environmental actions along the value chain
- Environmental actions affect both economic and environmental performance

1.2 Project Description

The survey was carried out by post in spring 2001. The Norwegian sample consisted of 679 manufacturing companies with more than 50 employees; the response rate was 22%. The respondents were chief executive officers and heads of environmental, health and safety departments within companies. The most represented sectors are listed in Table 1.

Table 1. The most represented sectors: number of respondents and response rates by sector

	Number of respondents	Response rates
Basic metals and fabricated metal	35	22%
Food products and beverage	28	25%
Pulp, paper product and publishing	21	27%
Rubber and plastic products	15	28%
Chemicals and chemical products	10	22%
Wood, cork and straw	10	16%
Others	32	
Total	**151**	**22%**

Since the questionnaire was sent to most Norwegian manufacturers with 50 employees or more, the results are representative of the industry structure in Norway. A response rate of 22% is quite good for this kind of survey.

Previous reports have shown that large companies have implemented more environmental activities than smaller companies (Ytterhus and Skjaker 1999) Thus, we might expect a relatively higher answer rate by large companies since environmentally active companies may answer questionnaires more often than others. The number of employees was used to characterise company size. The number of respondents by company size is shown in Table 2.

Table 2. Number of responses by size of the company

Company size (number of employees)	Number of responses	Percentage (%)
50–99	66	44
100–250	46	30
251–500	21	14
More than 500	18	12
Total	**151**	**100**

Some over-representation by large companies is observed in the total distribution of companies in terms of the number of respondents due to company size. This weakness should be borne in mind when interpreting the results given in the rest of the chapter. On the other hand, however, there is a large sample with a quite good response rate compared with a similar survey executed in 1997. In addition, the 2001 results are consistent with previous findings. Some general trends on environmental drivers, obstacles and activities in Norwegian manufacturing companies are thus be presented below with some confidence.

1.3 Environmental Stakeholders

Senior managers, employees and environmental authorities, together with owners and corporate customers, are considered by the survey respondents the most important stakeholders. A comparison of the results between the studies of 1998 and 2001 shows a high degree of agreement.

Stakeholders in general—such as environmental and consumer organisations as well as the press and other media—exert very limited environmental pressure on enterprises and environmental pressure from banks barely registers.

Business leaders also feel little environmental pressure from consumers. They do not believe, to any large extent, that consumers are prepared to pay more for environmentally friendly products and perceive 'low demand for environmentally friendly products' to be an important obstacle to the implementation of further environmental activities.

1.4 Obstacles to Environmental Activities

Leading companies in Norway believe that the most important obstacles to the implementation of environmental activities are that:
• They are too costly

- They do not give any competitive advantage
- There is little demand for environmentally friendly products

1.5   Strategic Environmental Activities

Nine out of ten enterprises that responded to the 2001 survey had completed a status review—a mapping of the procedures in relation to statutory environmental requirements—and had included environmental information in their annual report. Seven out of ten enterprises had a written environmental strategy in 2001, whereas in 1998 this applied to only five out of ten enterprises. As many as 45% of the enterprises had training schemes relating to environmental issues during 2001 compared with only 17% in 1998. The reason for this increased training may be that the most important obstacle to carrying out environmental activities in 1998 was 'a lack of qualified staff'.

1.6   Operational Environmental Activities in Relation to the Value Chain of the Enterprise

According to reports from the enterprises in the 2001 survey, the most frequently implemented environmental activities consisted of reducing the discharge of effluents to water and measures related to waste management. These improvements (the percentage share who answered affirmatively is given in brackets) were as follows:

- Activities to reduce the amount of waste (80%)
- Activities to reduce discharge of effluents to water (71%)
- Activities to recycle packaging (67%)

Thus, the most frequently reported environmental activities took place in the last part of the value chain. However, more enterprises than previously emphasised environmental factors in connection with purchasing; in 2001, 52% answered in the affirmative compared with 38% in 1998.

The respondents implemented fewer environmental activities directed towards their products compared with environmental activities with respect to waste and recycling related to production processes.

1.7   Conclusions Regarding Environmental Activities

During the period 1998–2001, environmental activities directed towards strategic adaptations showed a positive development. More companies carried out environmental reporting, environmental audits and training schemes related to environmental issues. Almost half of respondents had a written environmental strategy in 1998, but this share had increase to seven out of ten in 2001.

Operational environmental activities are still implemented to a larger degree in production processes and in the fields of waste management and recycling than elsewhere. Product-related environmental activities such as environmentally friendly design and environmental labelling are still relatively limited.

1.8   Environmental Activities and Results

To a certain extent, the companies supported the concept of eco-efficiency in the environmental area. Environmental activities are considered to have a positive effect on 'soft' values such as satisfaction among employees, management and owners, as well as on the profile of the enterprise. Furthermore, environmental activities are expected to lead to cost reductions.

A classification into 'green enterprises' and 'environmental laggards' based on the number of environmental activities implemented by the respondents gives the following results:
- 'Green enterprises' have more employees and larger turnover per employee than 'environmental laggards'
- 'Green enterprises' are more profitable per employee than 'environmental laggards' (in terms of operating result per employee)

These results are consistent with the study carried out in 1998.

2.   ENVIRONMENTAL STAKEHOLDERS AND OBSTACLES TO THE IMPLEMENTATION OF ENVIRONMENTAL ACTIVITIES

2.1   Environmental Stakeholders

Authorities, customers, employees and competitors are examples of stakeholders in an environmental context. Since enterprises are players in social systems, they have to take into account the demand made by their stakeholders in order to survive in the long-term. The stakeholders that make demands on enterprises in an environmental context can be classified in three groups:
- Political (environmental) authorities, etc.
- General stakeholders (environmental organisations, etc.
- Parties that have financial interests relating to environmental issues (customers, financial institutions, etc.).

Enterprises adapt to the demands from the stakeholders in various ways:
- Minimum solutions where the enterprise, for instance, observes statutory environmental requirements. This means that they pursue a neutral strategy.
- A proactive strategy where the enterprise implements activities beyond the statutory requirements. Examples of such activities include the introduction of environmental control systems and certification, and the environmental labelling of products. These are non-statutory environmental activities. However, cost reductions through, for example, the reduced use of energy and less waste will make it profitable for enterprises to implement an environmental management system. Moreover, environmental labelling may give enterprises a competitive advantage.

Figure 1 summarises the relations between the demands made by stakeholders and the adaptations made by the enterprises.

Figure 1. Demands made by stakeholders and adaptation by enterprises

In relation to the stakeholder model, the survey asked the following question: 'To what extent have the implementation of environmental activities in your enterprise been influenced by the following players.' At this point were listed various political, general interest groups and financial players that could be considered stakeholders in relation to an enterprise's environmental activities. Five alternative responses (not at all, a little, partly, much and very much) were permitted; the results are shown in Figure 2.

In 2001, industrial leaders considered the following interest groups as the most important stakeholders for the implementation of environmental activities:
- Senior management
- Employees
- Environmental authorities
- Owners
- Corporate customers

Players from whom the enterprises felt little pressure included consumers, consumer, environmental organisations and the press/media. Banks were reported to exert hardly any 'environmental pressure' at all.

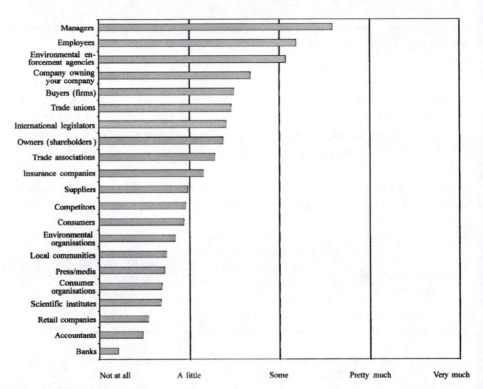

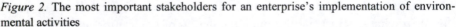

Figure 2. The most important stakeholders for an enterprise's implementation of environmental activities

2.2   Environmental Trends: Stakeholders Associated with Environmental Activities in Industry

Since the first Environmental Business Barometer was completed in 1993/94, the most important stakeholders relating to environmental activities in industry have been national authorities, owners, employees and customers. Political and, to some extent, financial stakeholders have also exerted 'environmental pressure'. The pressure from general interest groups has been low. Similarly, the financial institutions and particularly the banks are perceived by the leading companies themselves as applying little pressure.

Table 3 compares the results from the surveys in 1998 and 2001 in terms of stakeholder pressure. In the 1998 survey, no distinction was made between corporate customers and (end) consumers.

Table 3. A comparison of stakeholders that try to influence industry to implement environmental activities, 1998 and 2001

Ranking		Results	
		1998	**2001**
	1	Management	Management
	2	Environmental enforcement agencies	Employees
Best	3	Owners	Environmental enforcement agencies
	4	Employees	Owners
	5	Buyers	Buyers (companies)
	1	Consumer organisations	Consumer organisations
	2	Competitors	Scientific institutes
Worst	3	Suppliers	Retail companies
	4	Retail companies	Accountants
	5	Banks	Banks

The comparison shows that the leading companies have retained their perception from the previous survey that.

- Senior managers, employees and the environmental authorities, together with owners and corporate clients, are the most important stakeholders from an environmental perspective
- General interest groups such as environmental and consumer organisations, as well as the press/media represent a very limited stakeholder interest
- Among financial institutions, insurance companies exert a slight 'pressure' whereas banks are perceived as 'environmentally passive'

2.3   Obstacles

What obstacles may have made it difficult to implement environmental activities? Among others, this question is relevant for environmental authorities when deciding how to stimulate environmental adaptation in business and industry.

In the survey the following question was asked: 'To what extent may the following obstacles have made difficult the implementation of environmental activities in your enterprise?' A similar question formed part of the 1988 survey. It was therefore possible to compare the opinions of the business leaders as to what the biggest obstacles were in 1998 and 2001 (Table 4).

Table 4. The biggest obstacles to the implementation of environmental activities: comparison of the results from the 1998 and 2001 surveys

Ranking	Largest obstacles	
	1998	2001
1	Lack of skilled human resources	Too costly
2	Too costly	No competitive advantage
3	No market demand for green product	No market demand for green product
4	No competitive advantage	No legal requirements
5	No technical solutions available	Lack of skilled human resources

There is agreement between the 1998 and 2001 surveys as to most important obstacles as perceived by the business leaders. In 2001, 'too costly' is classified as the most important obstacle. Both in the Norwegian survey and even more clearly in the European study from 1998, financial circumstances were seen as an important obstacle. Both in 2001 and 1998, 'low demand for environmentally friendly products' was perceived as an important obstacle.

The comparison, however, shows one important difference: In 1998, the 'lack of competent personnel' was considered to be the most important obstacle, in the 2001 survey, this seems to be a less important obstacle to the implementation of environmental activities.

3.   ENVIRONMENTAL ACTIVITIES

Previous sections have described the attitudes, stakeholders and obstacles to the implementation of environmental activities as perceived by leading Norwegian companies. This section presents the results of the mapping of activities that have actually been carried out. Environmental activities are carried out within enterprises both at the strategic and the operational level:
*   Strategic activities are developed through internal processes and are implemented through adjustments of the enterprise's management systems
*   Operational environmental activities can be associated with the individual functions in the enterprise such as purchasing, production, logistics and marketing

3.1   Strategic Environmental Activities

Procedures for the initiation, implementation and follow-up of environmental actions over time are established through environmental management systems. An environmental management system (EMS) enables the enterprise to co-ordinate and carry out environmental actions. EMAS and ISO

14001 are examples of systems that qualify for certification. Enterprises may also introduce an EMS without seeking certification. Through different questions related to environmental management systems allowed the mapping of the extent to which Norwegian industrial enterprises have focused on the different elements that standardise such systems.

First, the status for implemented strategic environmental activities is presented followed by an examination of the changes that have taken place during the period 1998–2001. Figure 3 shows the proportion of enterprises confirming that they have implemented strategic environmental activities.

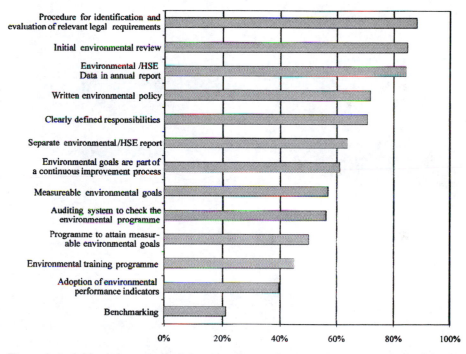

Figure 3. Activities in respect of environmental control systems (percentage share of the enterprises that responded affirmatively).

Almost nine out of ten enterprises reported that they had carried out an analysis of the situation, clarified routines in relation to statutory requirements and included environmental information in their annual report. Furthermore, seven out of ten enterprises had prepared a written environmental policy, whereas 45% had set up training programmes in the environmental area.

3.2   Implementation of Strategic Environmental Activities

Four indicators were selected to demonstrate the development of the implementation of environmental activities during the period 1998–2001. These were:

- Environmental reporting
- A written environmental strategy
- Environmental auditing
- Training related to the environmental issues

The results are shown in Figure 4.

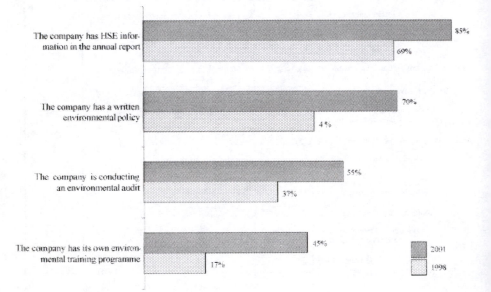

Figure 4. Strategic environmental actions in 1998 and 2001: share of enterprises that confirmed that the activity had been carried out

The degree of implementation of strategic environmental activities shows a positive development for all four indicators.

- The greatest progress is seen with respect to training. The reason for this may be that, in 1998, 'lack of competent personnel' was reported to be the most important obstacle to the implementation of environmental activities.
- Both environmental reporting and environmental auditing were carried out in an increasing number of enterprises in 2001.
- Whereas in 1998, five out of ten enterprises had a written environmental strategy, this share had increased to seven out of ten enterprises in 2001.

3.3   **Operational Environmental Activities**

Operational environmental activities can be associated with functions such as purchasing, production and marketing. Table 5 shows operational environmental activities along the value chain and provides a picture of whether the bulk of the activities are implemented early or late in the value chain. Previous studies showed that activities directed towards production and waste management had a high score (Ytterhus and Skjaker 1999). Table 5 shows, in brackets, the proportion of the respondents that had implemented operational environmental activities in the various parts of the value chain.

Table 5. Share of companies that have implemented operational environmental activities in the value chain

Inputs	Procure-ment	Produc-tion	Logistics	Waste and recycling
Using less material per unit of production (61%)	Demanding that suppliers take environmental actions (43%)	Reducing emissions to surface water (71%)	Reducing negative environmental effects of packaging (48%)	Reduced solid waste (80%)
Reduced energy use (55%)	Taking environmental performance into account in selection of supplier (52%)	Reducing noise (55%)	Reduced energy use in transport (25%)	Packaging recycling (67%)
Reduced water use (53%)		Implementation of cleaner technology (51%)		Material re-cycling within the company (55%)
Substitution of hazardous inputs (52%)		Reducing emissions to air (47%)		Product recycling (52%)
Substitution of non-renewable materials (23%)				

Relatively speaking, the majority of environmental activities are implemented in the last parts of the value chain, cf. the three most frequently reported environmental activities:
- Reduced amount of waste (80%)
- Reduced discharge of effluents to water (71%)
- Recycling of packaging (67%)

Activities directed towards the input factors increased after the 1998 study:
- Reduced use of water (53% in 2001 as against about 40% in 1998)
- Reduced use of materials for each produced unit (61% in 2001 as against 50% in 1998)
- More enterprises take environmental factors into account in connection with purchasing (51% in 2001 as against 38% in 1998)
- Activities to replace 'hazardous' input factors show little change from 1998 to 2001

3.4   Environmental Activities Directed Towards Products

Traditionally, environmental activities within the scope of 'cleaner production' have been directed towards processes and operational changes rather than towards reducing the effects of the products on the environment. Gradually, however, product-oriented environmental policies have become more significant. A study of the changes in the effects of environmental activities directed towards products can be made by looking at Table 6, which presents a comparison of the results from the 1998 and 2001 surveys.

Table 6. Environmental actions towards products: percentage of companies accomplishing actions in 1998 and 2001

Activity	Degree of accomplishment (%)	
	1998	2001
'Green' design of a new product	30	42
Information given to consumers about environmental effects of products	40	48
Eco-labelling	20	24

In 2001, four out of ten enterprises made use of environmentally friendly design compared with three out of ten enterprises in 1998.

An increased number of enterprises reported giving information to customers about the environmental effects of their products (48% in 2001 compared with 40% in 1998).

However, the number of enterprises that provide environmental labels on their products shows little change from 1998 to 2001.

Fewer enterprises carry out product-related environmental activities compared with operational activities directed towards production, waste and recycling.

4.   ECONOMIC AND ENVIRONMENTAL PERFORMANCE

Traditionally, the prevailing view on the relationship between environmental activities and the enterprise's goals has been that environmental activities increase costs and thus reduce profitability. During the 1990s, however, concepts such as eco-efficiency and 'win–win' strategies have generally been more accepted by business and industry. The essence of eco-efficiency is 'to produce more by using less'. In real terms, this means adding more value without a corresponding increase in the effects on the environment. If an enterprise can reduce the use of energy or other input factors, this will be beneficial to the environment and the enterprise may save money. Environmental activities may also result in a more positive profile for the enterprise. Overall, cost reductions and an improved image in the markets due to environmental activities may led to 'win–win' situations with benefits for both the enterprise and the environment.

In order to map the opinion of leading Norwegian companies regarding eco-efficiency, the following question was posed: 'What effect do you think the environmental activities have had on the goals of the enterprise?' Figure 5 lists 16 alternative sub-goals and summarises the response to this question.

The leaders believe that environmental activities have had a positive effect on the large majority of the sub-goals and that they have most affected 'soft' factors such as the following:
• Satisfaction among employees, management and owners
• The profile of the enterprise

The leaders further believe that environmental activities may have a positive effect on long-term profits and cost reductions. Environmental activities may lead to better insurance terms, but have no effects on the terms under which the banks provide loans.

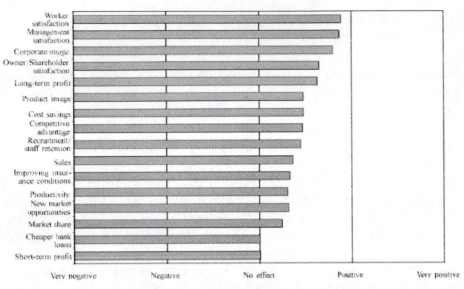

Figure 5. Effect of environmental actions on company objectives

From the results, it can be concluded that the leading companies conditionally support hypotheses on eco-efficiency and win–win strategies in an environmental context. The results from 2001 are in agreement with those from 1998.

4.1   Results for 'green enterprises' and 'environmental laggards'

In order to indicate what characterises the environmentally most active enterprises compared with 'environmental laggards', the enterprises were classified according to what extent they had implemented an EMS. 'Green enterprises' were defined as the 20% best, whereas 'environmental laggards' were those that had made the least progress in this respect.

Table 7 presents characteristics of 'green enterprises' and 'environmental laggards' by turnover per employee and number of employees.

Table 7. Characteristics of green enterprises and environmentally lagged, measured by turnover per employee and number of employees

	Turnover per employee (1,000 NOK)	No. of employees
'Green enterprises'	2,696	301
'Environmental laggards'	1,614	109

NOK = Norwegian krone

Table 7 shows that 'green enterprises' differ from 'environmental laggards' with respect to size; in general, 'green enterprises' are larger than 'environmental laggards. This result is in agreement with previous studies (Ytterhus and Skjaker 1999).

4.2 Environmental Activities and Profitability

Comparing profitability for 'green enterprises' and 'environmental laggards' gives an indication as to whether it pays to be 'green' (Table 8). Two indicators are used for profitability—operating profit per employee and an economic indicator determined by a question in the questionnaire.

Table 8. Comparison of profitability in 'green enterprises' and 'environmental laggards'

	Operating profit per employee (1,000 NOK)	Economic indicator*
'Green enterprises'	138	4.0
'Environmental laggards'	46	3.5

*An economic indicator of '3' means 'sufficient to create a balance', whereas '4' means 'sufficient to create a small profit'.

A value of 138 in Table 7 indicates that 'green enterprises' are more profitable than 'environmental laggards'. However, it is not possible to draw the direct conclusion that 'green enterprises' are more profitable because they have implemented more strategic environmental actions than 'environmental laggards' (see Figure 6). Innovative enterprises will often be the first to adapt their strategy to new challenges.

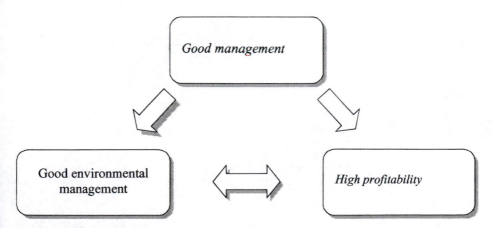

Figure 6. Relations between 'good' management, environmental activities and profitability

The hypothesis, therefore, is that enterprises with good management will also implement environmental management systems to improve both their competitiveness and their profitability. Consequently, good management is characterised by both good environmental management and high profitability simultaneously.

REFERENCES

Betz, F. and Strannegård, L. (1997): *International Business Environmental Barometer.* Oslo: Cappelen Akademisk Forlag.

Kestemont, M.P. and Ytterhus, B.E. (2000): *European Business Environmental Barometer* [online]. Available from Internet URL: http://www.bi.no/users/fag86010.

Wagner, M. and Schaltegger, S. (2002): *Umweltmanagement in deutschen Unternehmen. Der aktuelle Stand der Praxis.* Lüneburg: Centre for Sustainability Management (CSM).

Wolff, R. (1995): *The Nordic Business Environmental Barometer.* Oslo: Bedriftsøkonomenes Forlag.

Ytterhus, B.E. and Aasebø, S. (1995): *Buskerud Miljøbarometer.* Oslo: Handelshøyskolen BI.

Ytterhus, B.E. and Refsum, S. (1996): *Norsk Miljøbarometer 1996.* Oslo: Handelshøyskolen BI.

Ytterhus, B.E. and Skjaker, O.C. (1999): *Norsk Miljøbarometer 1998.* Oslo: Handelshøyskolen, BI.

SUSTAINABILITY PERFORMANCE OF COUNTRIES

Based on the Example of Oekom Research AG's Country Rating

Matthias Bönning
Oekom Research, Munich, Germany

Abstract: While socially responsible investment (SRI) has long had a permanent place in the investment culture of Anglo-Saxon countries, the market has only recently been able to establish itself in continental Europe. It is, above all, the good financial performance of investments and increased demand from institutional investors that have led to the significantly higher-than-average growth of this segment of the market. Whereas the market has focused traditionally principally on shares in listed companies, recent years have seen a significant expansion in the demand for fixed-interest-bearing forms of investment. In the course of this development, Oekom Research AG developed a Country Rating in 2001, which enables capital investors to incorporate sustainability criteria into their decisions on investing in government bonds. To examine the link between a country's sustainability performance on the one hand and its credit standing and competitiveness on the other, a study was carried out comparing the results of Oekom Research's Country Rating with Standard & Poor's Sovereign Credit Rating as well as with two of the World Economic Forum's indices measuring competitiveness. Correlation analyses showed that a highly significant association exists between the sustainability-related results of the Country Rating and the underlying economic parameters. Consequently, the hypothesis can be advanced that a country's sustainability performance impacts significantly on its economic performance.

1.   THE SUSTAINABILITY INVESTMENT MARKET

In the evaluation of companies and countries, the sustainability rating has established itself in recent years as a tool to complement the conventional financial rating. It serves primarily as a basis for investment decisions in the field of sustainability investment. While this investment sector was formerly only of niche interest, today it concerns a rapidly growing number of private and institutional investors. The reasons for this are diverse:
Investments in ethical and environmental funds are registering significantly higher volume growth rates than conventional investments
*   The yields achieved are on average at least on a par
*   The concept of sustainability investment is meanwhile also being promoted on the political level, e.g. by national governments or the European Commission.

The growing importance of the market has also led to a higher level of professionalism and institutionalisation among the relevant players, e.g. the founding of international umbrella organisations and the development of transparency guidelines and quality standards for fund providers and rating agencies.

The basic idea behind sustainability investment is the conscious inclusion of environmental, social and cultural criteria to supplement classical financial research—be it through the inclusion of appropriate 'soft factors' in order to obtain a fuller picture of the indicators relevant to the success of corporate and of social and government actions, i.e. risk- and opportunity-related indicators, or in order to integrate the ethical views of a particular investor into the capital investment process. Sustainability ratings can help to identify those companies and countries worldwide which, as issuers of securities, are more progressive and innovative than average with regard to sustainable development.

In the USA and the UK—the countries with the longest tradition in the field of 'socially responsible investment' (SRI)—sustainability investments now form a permanent feature of the overall investment market, with double-digit growth rates being recorded annually (e.g. Eurosif 2003). According to a study by the Social Investment Forum, more than 10% of all funds in the USA currently operate using ethical, environmental or social criteria (Social Investment Forum 2001). The enormous volumes in the USA are attributable not least to the activities of institutional investors (e.g. church investors and pension funds), which began decades ago to orient their capital investments according to ethical criteria and are consequently seen as the initiators of the SRI scene as a whole.

In continental Europe, this development began only a few years ago. Starting from a previously comparatively small market share, the volumes of investment concerned have multiplied several times in the space of a few years. For example, while the overall volume of all public funds in German-speaking countries grew by just 30% between 1998 and 2002, the sustainable funds segment managed to grow by 600% over the same period, from 300 million euros to 2.1 billion euros, and thus showed significantly higher growth than the market as a whole (Bank Sarasin 2003). The reasons for this growth lie first in the rising importance of the market for institutional investors such as church investors and foundations that would like to bring their capital investments more closely into line with environmental and social criteria. Secondly, the field of sustainability investment is increasingly being seen by banks and fund management companies as an interesting and lucrative area. Both developments can be traced back to the proven competitive yields of the investments concerned, as a result of which earlier prejudices based on there being an intrinsically lower yield on sustainable investments have largely been dispelled (e.g. Garz *et al.* 2002; Oekom Research 2003; Plinke 2002). Accordingly, the number of public funds licensed for marketing in the German-speaking countries saw a significant rise in 2002 to over 100, representing more than an eight-fold increase compared with 1998 (Institut für Ökologie und Unternehmensführung an der European Business School e.V. 2003). Experts are proceeding on the assumption that this is just the start of a long-term upward trend. Thus, the Deutsche Aktieninstitut [German Share Institute], for example, envisages the future development of the market as being very positive, with annual growth rates of 30-40%. It is believed that a share of 5–10% of the overall investment fund market is viewed as being achievable over the next ten years—a marked increase compared with the current market share, which still lies at below 1% (Leven 2003).

2. OEKOM RESEARCH AG'S COUNTRY RATING

2.1 Introduction

Oekom Research AG is among the pioneers in German-speaking countries of ratings based on environmental and social criteria. Its experience in the area of corporate ratings extends back to 1994, when the first environmental ratings were performed and published. In 1999, the rating approach was extended to include the social and cultural dimensions and, in 2001, a Country Rating was established alongside the Corporate Rating. The Country Rating can be used to evaluate the world's most common government bonds according to relevant criteria.

Oekom Research AG's sustainability research has, for many years, been employed as a factor in the asset management of more than 17 different fund management companies. Consequently, it currently influences capital investments totalling about 800 million euros.

Over many years, the sustainable investment market has been restricted predominantly to shares and has thus ignored other major investment options. Above all, this has restricted the opportunities for, and consequently the demand from, risk-averse investors. In order to extend the range of investments to include government bonds, Oekom Research developed the Country Rating and successfully launched it onto the market in 2001. It now forms the decision-making basis for around ten bond portfolios, which invest according to sustainable development principles and administer a volume of funds totalling over 300 million euros.

2.2   Rating Structure

The Country Rating was developed in collaboration with experts from science and research and uses 150 sustainability indicators to evaluate a country's general institutional framework and its actual performance in the environmental and social spheres. Financial indicators are built into the evaluation only to the extent that they impact directly on social and environmental areas (e.g. per capita income, expenditure on education and health). In order to take adequate account of previous research results and rating methodologies, the design of the rating's structure was based on existing and recognised models. The structure of the environmental section of the rating therefore to a large extent follows the Pressure–State–Response concept developed by the Organisation for Economic Co-operation and Development (OECD), which is the presentation of:

*   Environmental pressures (Country Rating: 'Environmental Stresses')
*   The state of the environment (Country Rating: 'Environmental Systems')
*   The political and social response (Country Rating: 'Institutional Capacity and Politics').

For the social section of the Country Rating, a structure in line with that of the environmental section was chosen, based on the fundamental concept of the 'Seven Freedoms' of the United Nations Development Programme with the added inclusion of further important criteria. Actual social conditions and the infrastructure of the country are examined, taking general political and social conditions as a starting point. The structure of the Country Rating is illustrated in Table 1.

Table 1. Structure of the Country Rating

Social Rating	Environmental Rating
1 Institutional Capacity and Politics	*1 Institutional Capacity and Politics*
– Political system and basic rights	– Institutional capacity
– Participation in international treaties	– Political programme
– Public spending	– Participation in international treaties
– Non-governmental institutions	
– Political stability	
– Corruption and money laundering	
2 Human and Social Conditions	*2 Environmental Systems*
– Equal rights	– Soil and land use
– Health	– Water
– Education	– Biodiversity
– Employment and income	
– Personal safety	
– Population change	
3 Infrastructure	*3 Environmental Stresses*
– Basic infrastructure	– Soil constraints
– Medical facilities	– Water constraints
– Educational facilities	– Biodiversity
– Access to information flows	– Air emissions
	– Energy
	– Waste

2.3　Rating Indicators

Using this rating structure, over 150 separate indicators have been selected. With the aid of these indicators, the complex circumstances of the respective areas under investigation can be modelled adequately. Quantitative indicators are used principally, with the addition of individual qualitative criteria (e.g. for evaluating the granting and observance of basic rights). When the selection was made, special emphasis was placed on the functional context, relevance, data availability and data quality. In order to make the rating applicable to all countries worldwide, value was also attached to the universal relevance of criteria, irrespective of geographical location, development status, etc. Moreover, the set of indicators is updated regularly so as to adapt it to social trends and new scientific findings.

The following example of a qualitative indicator illustrates the classification hierarchy and the qualitative description of the concrete facts and circumstances. The example given in Table 2 is the indicator 'Prohibition of forced or compulsory labour' for Australia.

Table 2. Example of a qualitative indicator

Example 1: qualitative indicator

Classification hierarchy
Social Rating
1. Institutional Capacity and Politics
1.1. Political system and basic rights
1.1.10. Prohibition of child and forced labour
1.1.10.1 Prohibition of forced or compulsory labour

Evaluation of item 1.1.10.1 for Australia

'Although there are no laws prohibiting it, forced labour, including forced and bonded labour by children, generally is not practised; while there were instances of such practices in the past, there were no reports of this activity during 2002. Trafficking in persons, particularly in women (but also children) for the sex trade, is a limited but growing problem.'

Table 3 gives an example of a quantitative indicator illustrates the classification hierarchy and quantitative data analysis based on the example of 'Share of energy by coal' for Germany.

Table 3. Example of a quantitative indicator

Example 2: quantitative indicator

Classification hierarchy
Environmental Rating
3. Environmental Stresses
3.5. Energy
3.5.3 Energy supply by primary source
3.5.3.1 Share of energy by coal

Evaluation of item 3.5.3.1 for Germany

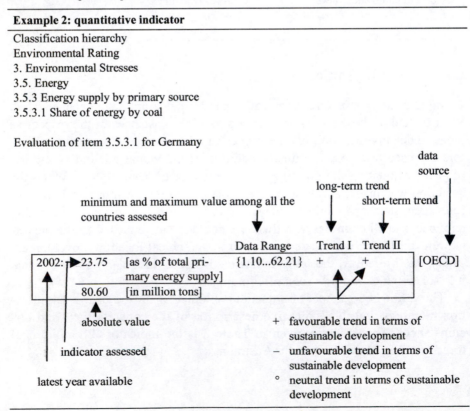

2.4   Evaluation

As part of the rating, each individual indicator is evaluated separately for each country. For the evaluation of qualitative indicators, an evaluation handbook was developed for each criterion, which lists all the realistic forms that the indicator takes and gives these corresponding grades. Included here are both forms that are typical for OECD countries and those that are encountered in newly industrialised and developing countries. This approach is designed to ensure that the rating can be applied equally to all countries worldwide.

Where a quantitative criterion is involved, then in addition to the absolute level of the indicator in the cross-national survey, the evaluation also takes into account the trend over time for the country concerned. For the example in Table 3, this means that first the level of the absolute share of coal in the total energy volume of Germany compared with the corresponding values for other countries is evaluated. Since power generation from coal has to be rated rather negatively from the sustainability viewpoint (e.g. because of the comparatively high emissions of carbon dioxide [CO_2]), the lower the proportion turns out to be for a country, the more positively it is evaluated. In the example chosen, this proportion fluctuates among the countries surveyed between 1.10% and 62.21% (see 'data range' in Table 3). Secondly, the development over time of this proportion within a country is evaluated using a short-term and a long-term trend indicator. The plus signs in the example show that the proportion of coal in Germany has developed positively from the sustainability viewpoint, i.e. has steadily decreased.

This differentiated approach enables, over and above a description of conditions at a particular point in time (i.e. the country survey with regard to the level of the indicator in a particular year), the inclusion in the evaluation of social and environmental developments within a country.

Whereas with qualitative indicators, the facts and circumstances specific to each particular country are evaluated absolutely, quantitative data are, for comparability purposes, generally related to a benchmark figure. In the social section, the data here are primarily expressed in terms, for example, of the domestic population (or relevant subsets), the proportion of the population connected to public sewage works, the proportion of the able-bodied population who are unemployed or the proportion of women in parliament. Monetary budget variables such as expenditure on education, health or development aid are generally expressed in relation to the gross national product (GNP). The indicators selected in the environmental section are mainly efficiency indicators, i.e. they compare the environmental performance of a country in relation to its economic performance. An example of this is the level of domestic water or energy consumption relative to the gross domestic product (GDP). It is thus the level of efficiency of the management of natural resources that goes into the evaluation rather than absolute environmental consumption levels.

The overall rating score is determined for the individual hierarchical levels of the rating on the basis of the grading of each individual criterion and the weighting in each case. The grading scale extends here from A+ (the best grade) to D–. Using these grades, a ranking list is drawn up for all the countries examined, which serves as the basis for the decisions of investors. Investors can stipulate individually whether, for example, they wish to invest in the best 10 or 20% of countries or more generally in countries that have been evaluated as above average.

Alongside this best-in-class method, i.e. the comparative evaluation of general conditions and of the performance of different countries, Oekom Research also offers its customers a facility for excluding, by means of a large number of exclusion criteria, investment where defined social conditions or political decisions apply. These include, for example:

- Authoritarian regimes
- Use of the death penalty
- Major corruption or money laundering
- Grave human rights violations
- Production of nuclear power
- Rejection of climate protection obligations

2.5   Data Sources

In gathering data for its Country Rating, Oekom Research first uses statistical datasets produced by supranational organisations that collect relevant data at regular intervals and make the results available in publications and databases. In addition, Oekom Research examines information from numerous other renowned institutions and non-governmental organisations (NGOs), which are generally specialists in individual subject areas such as human rights, conflict research or corruption. As far as possible, plausibility checks and cross-checks of the given data are conducted in order to ensure a high degree of accuracy.

Compared with purely domestic data collection systems and sources, the organisations described offer the advantage of guaranteeing a high degree of comparability of data between individual countries. Countries' domestic data, by contrast, differ significantly in many cases in terms of underlying definitions, system boundaries, etc. and are therefore not usually suitable for cross-national comparisons. The sources used include, for example:

- Amnesty International
- BBC
- Food and Agriculture Organisation (FAO)
- Financial Action Task Force on Money Laundering (FATF)
- International Confederation of Free Trade Unions
- National Defence Council Foundation
- OECD
- Stockholm International Peace Research Institute (SIPRI)
- Transparency International
- UN Development Programme
- US Department of State
- World Health Organisation (WHO)
- World Bank
- World Resources Institute (WRI)

In line with past demand from investors, it is above all the OECD countries that have previously been subjected to ratings. In principle, however, the structure of the rating has been designed so that it can also be used to analyse newly industrialised countries or developing countries. In many cases, however, the status of a country's development also affects the availability and quality of data and information needed for the rating. For example, certain data that is relevant for the rating is, in many developing countries, not yet being collected or else only to a limited extent. Given the current status of information, distortions of the situation in less developed countries can not be ruled out.

3.   SUSTAINABILITY AND MACROECONOMIC COMPETITIVENESS

Due to the complexity and the generally long-term nature of the relevant processes affecting sustainability, their micro- and macro-economic effects cannot always be defined clearly. As far as companies are concerned, there have recently been numerous studies that have failed to identify any systematic underperformance in companies that are above average in terms of sustainability. Many cases even recorded a higher level of competitiveness, which was expressed in an above average share price performance. This link is frequently underpinned by potential savings in raw materials, lower entrepreneurial risk, higher rates of innovation, etc. The three most common approaches to explaining this are as follows:

1. **High sustainability performance leads to high financial performance.** Integration of sustainability criteria into a company's strategy achieves value gains, e.g. cost reductions as a result of greater energy and raw material efficiency.
2. **High financial performance leads to high sustainability performance.** More profitable companies can afford greater environmental protection and higher standards of social provision.
3. **Good management leads to high financial and sustainability performance.** Companies with a higher sustainability performance are distinguished by better and more innovative management overall, which also leads to improved financial performance.

Corresponding scientific research on a macro-economic level (i.e. the analysis of the impact of a country's sustainability performance on its economic performance) is still rare. The following study has been designed to contribute to this analysis:

In the area of government bonds, the most decisive factors for investors may be, above all, the credit standing of the debtor country and the minimisation of the financial risk associated with it. There is obviously a positive correlation between a country's credit standing and its competitiveness. Accordingly, an investigation should be made of a possible link between a country's high sustainability performance on the one hand and its high credit standing and competitiveness on the other. To this end, the results of Oekom Research's Country Rating are compared below with Standard & Poor's (S&P) Sovereign Credit Rating and two of the World Economic Forum's competitiveness indicators.

As part of a correlation analysis, the country-specific rating results from Oekom Research's Country Rating were first compared with Standard & Poor's corresponding Long Term Foreign Currency Sovereign Credit Ratings (Standard & Poor's 2003). The results are shown in Figure 1. With a coefficient (according to Pearson) of more than 0.8, a significant positive correlation (significance level of 1%) is revealed between these two parameters; this means that countries with a high sustainability performance also have, on average, a high financial credit standing. In particular, it is noted that the Scandinavian and Central European countries that top the sustainability rating generally have a credit rating of at least AA+, while the countries doing badly in the Country Rating such as Mexico, Turkey and Russia fail to score higher than a BBB. Only the USA, which in the sustainability rating of 31 countries was ranked in only 25th place, achieves a high credit rating of AAA—unusual for a country in this position.

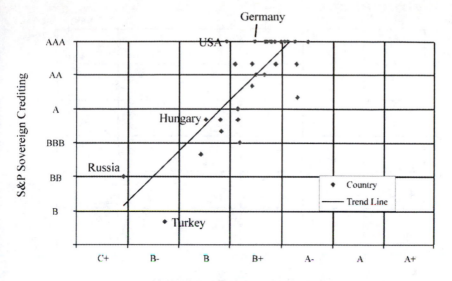

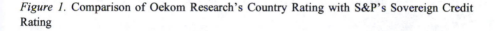

Oekom Research Country Rating

Figure 1. Comparison of Oekom Research's Country Rating with S&P's Sovereign Credit Rating

The results of Oekom Research's Country Rating were additionally compared as part of a correlation analysis with two indices published by the World Economic Forum that focus explicitly on the competitiveness of a country (World Economic Forum 2003). The Growth Competitiveness Index (GCI) is based on three economic variables that are supposed to be fundamental to medium-term and long-term economic growth: technology; public institutions, e.g. the legal framework; and the macro-economic environment

Thus, while the GCI analyses the fundamental growth determinants, the Micro-economic Competitiveness Index (MICI), in contrast, examines the factors influencing the productivity of a country, i.e. the quality of domestic companies and the micro-economic business environment.

Because the results of the CGI and MICI are shown as a league table, Oekom Research's Country Rating has also been presented as a ranking list in the comparison below. In contrast to the comparison above, the parent population here comprises just 30 rather than 31 countries, since Luxembourg has not been included in the World Economic Forum's indices. The results are shown in Figures 2 and 3. Here too, a clearly significant though slightly weaker correlation is revealed, with coefficients (according to Spearman) of 0.69 and 0.61 respectively (significance level of 1%). Again, it is principally the USA which, despite a very low sustainability rating, has to date exhibited a high competitiveness rating.

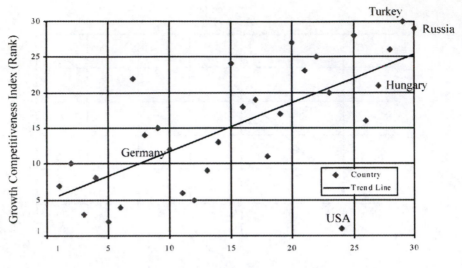

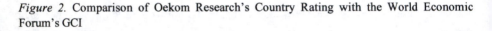

Figure 2. Comparison of Oekom Research's Country Rating with the World Economic Forum's GCI

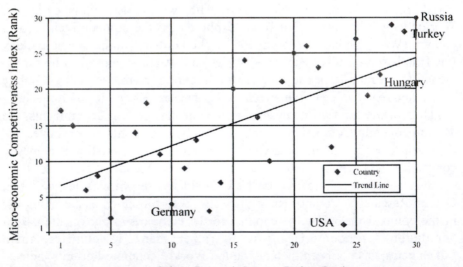

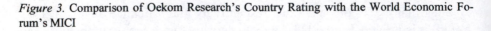

Figure 3. Comparison of Oekom Research's Country Rating with the World Economic Forum's MICI

A comparison of a country's economic competitiveness on the one hand and of (non-economic) social and environmental facts and circumstances on the other shows a significant positive correlation between the two dimensions. However, because the study did not explicitly analyse how sustainability performance influences economic performance, no clear conclusions can be drawn regarding the causality.

In recent years, other authors have developed specific theoretical models and conducted research on this influence, mainly with regard to environmental parameters. For example, the environmental Kuznets curve suggests an inverted U-shape of pollution compared with per capita GDP growth in developed countries. Based on this model, some authors assume that environmental damage has a negative impact on the growth process, i.e. that it inhibits economic growth (Stern *et al.* 1996). Sturm *et al.* (1996) found that the level of eco-efficiency contributes to national competitiveness (Sturm *et al.* 1999).

Other plausible examples of this assumed impact of social and environmental indicators on a country's economic competitiveness are the quality of the education and healthcare systems, the protection of fundamental civil rights, political stability, corruption and money laundering. According to Transparency International (TI), the most prominent NGO worldwide in the battle against corruption, the consequences of bribery and nepotism in the economic sector are frequently underestimated: 'Corruption makes countries poor', says Peter Eigen, head of TI (Läsker 2003).

In principle, therefore, the hypothesis can be advanced that a country's sustainability performance has a significant impact on its economic performance. In order to prove this causality for a broad spectrum of sustainability-related parameters, additional research seems to be necessary. The sustainability-based Country Rating could then provide an important contribution to the overall assessment of countries' competitiveness and thereby also become an integral part of conventional financial ratings.

REFERENCES

Bank Sarasin (2003): *Bank Sarasin erweitert Angebot nachhaltiger Rentenfonds in Deutschland und Österreich* [online] [cited 17 May 2003]. Available from Internet URL: www.ecoreporter.de.

Eurosif (2003): *Socially Responsible Investment among European Institutional Investors—2003 Report.* Paris: Eurosif.

Garz, H., Volk, C. and Gilles, M. (2002): *More Gain than Pain—SRI: Sustainability Pays Off.* London/Düsseldorf/New York: WestLB Panmure Pan European Equity.

Institut für Ökologie und Unternehmensführung an der European Business School e.V. (2003): *Einhundert Fondsprofile online* [online] [cited 1 August 2003]. Available from Internet URL: www.nachhaltiges-investment.org.

Läsker, K. (2003): ' "Korruption macht Länder arm"– Peter Eigen, Chef von Transparency International', *Süddeutsche Zeitung* No. 160, 18.

Leven, F.-J. (2003): *Marktentwicklung für nachhaltige Finanzprodukte* (Workshop Kommunikation und Vertrieb von nachhaltigen Finanzprodukten, 14 November 2003) Hannover: imug.

Oekom Research (2003): *Sustainability as a Style of Investment Offering Double Dividends—A Collaborative Project between Oekom Research and Morgan Stanley Private Wealth Management.* Munich: Oekom Research.

Plinke, E. (2002): *Aktienperformance und Nachhaltigkeit.* Basel: Bank Sarasin/ZEW/ebs.

Social Investment Forum (2001): *2001 Report on Socially Responsible Investing Trends in the United States.* Washington D.C.: Social Investment Forum.

Standard & Poor's (2003): *Sovereign Ratings History since 1975.* London: Standard & Poor's.

Stern, D.I., Common, M.S. and Barbier, E.B. (1996): 'Economic Growth and Environmental Degradation: The Environmental Kuznets Curve and Sustainability', *World Development* Vol. 24, No. 7, 1151-1160.

Sturm, A., Wackernagel, M. and Müller, K. (2000): *The Winners and Losers in Global Competition. Why Eco-Efficiency Reinforces Competitiveness. A Study of 44 Nations.* Chur/Zürich: Rüegger.

World Economic Forum (2003): *The Global Competitiveness Report 2002—2003.* Oxford: Oxford University Press.

Zürcher Kantonalbank (2002): *Nachhaltigkeitsrating für Staaten: OECD-Staaten im Vergleich.* Zürich: Zürcher Kantonalbank.

DOES A NATION'S ECOLOGICAL PERFORMANCE AFFECT ITS ECONOMIC STABILITY?

The Potential for Enhancing Sovereign Credit Risk Assessments with Ecological Resource Accounts

Mathis Wackernagel[1], Chris Martiniak[1,2], Fred Wellington[3], Chad Monfreda[4], Steve Goldfinger[1], Justin Kitzes[1] and Deborah Cheng[1]

[1]*Global Footprint Network, Oakland, CA, USA;* [2] *University of Michigan Business School, USA;* [3]*World Resources Institute, Sustainable Enterprise Program, and formerly Environmental Management Program, University of San Francisco, USA;* [4]*Sustainability and Global Environment Program, University of Wisconsin, Madison, USA*

Abstract: This chapter examines how ecological indicators may be able to contribute to assessments of a country's future economic performance. We use Ecological Footprint accounts to track a country's ecological performance and contrast results from this analysis with overall economic performance measures for nations such as sovereign credit ratings published by leading sovereign rating agencies. Our starting point is the global ecological context: humanity's demand on resources exceeds by approximately 20% what the biosphere can regenerate and this overshoot is increasing. This reality is neither reflected in current prices for resources or waste emissions, nor does future scarcity inform today's prevailing assessments of a country's future economic performance. With increasing global scarcity, it is likely that a country's resource situation will become an increasingly significant factor in its economic performance as prices for ecological goods and services are adjusted either through international agreements for protecting the biosphere's regenerative capacity or, in absence of such agreements, by the more brutal reality of actual physical limits being encountered. This chapter explains how the Ecological Footprint, a comprehensive measure of human demand on the biosphere, can be used to put economic risks into the context of ecological performance and, in turn, inform assessments of economic stability or competitiveness.

1.   INTRODUCTION: SOVEREIGN CREDIT RISK ASSESSMENTS AND THEIR BLIND SPOTS

Financial analysts assess investment risk. Risk assessments are essential to investors since higher financial risks are only acceptable if the investment opportunity also generates a higher return. Hence, investors depend on reliable tools to guide their investment decisions.

One large investment universe is the bond (or debt) market. With a nominal value of over 37 trillion dollars in 2001, it exceeds the value of the globe's annual economic output (International Monetary Fund 2002:Table 4.1). Over a quarter of these bonds are internationally traded. Out of these 37 trillion dollars, over 18 trillion dollars are government issued debts—some by nations (sovereigns), some by their regions or cities (Bank for International Settlements 2003:86).

This chapter focuses on national debts and the corresponding sovereign credit risk assessments. But it has implications for other kinds of investments too. With increased levels of international capital flows, perceived risks associated with sovereign credit affect other investments significantly as well. This is because capital markets are influenced by the financial industry's most respected risk assessments, i.e. of sovereigns.

Hence, sovereign risk assessments shape the performance of national economies that issue debts in two ways. First, nations with higher credit risk pay higher interest rates as investors demand a premium for bearing higher levels of risk. Secondly, the credit risk of local governments and businesses operating within that country are considered to be equal to or higher than the country's risk. Thus, poor sovereign credit rating becomes an additional cost factor for businesses in these countries. This makes reliable risk assessments the interest of both investors as well as debtors.

The risk of bonds is a function of the debtor's ability to repay the credit. The biggest risk is default of the debtor, which, prior to the wave of sovereign debt defaults in the 1990s, investors believed to be a remote risk in the modern era of global currency markets. While this principally occurred in dollar-denominated debt, the long held dictum that countries would 'honour their own coin' was proved wrong when Russia defaulted in 1998 on its rouble-denominated debt.

But risks go beyond default. A country's sluggish or erratic economic performance—potentially impacting its ability to pay on time—can also amount to an investment risk. Hence, many indices attempt to provide foresight about a country's economic condition beyond the likelihood of a default.

The most influential risk measures for sovereign debt are sovereign credit ratings provided by rating services such as Standard and Poor's (S&P) and

Moody's Investors Services. In spite of their sophistication, these rankings are not always reliable predictors of economic performance, as exemplified in the 1997/8 South-East Asian currency crisis. Thus, analysts and the investment community understand that these tools may have blind spots.

This chapter addresses an increasingly critical area of risk omitted by these assessments, i.e. ecological risks. It extends the arguments put forward in an earlier study that addressed the links between economic competitiveness and both eco-efficiency and ecological demands (Sturm *et al.* 2000). This chapter builds on the premise that ecological risks are bound to become more significant as humanity increases its demand on natural resources. The chapter suggests that ecological risk analysis can help to link countries' resource constraints to economic effects—aspects not readily apparent utilising traditional financial risk measurement methodologies. It then shows how national accounts based on the Ecological Footprint, a measure of human demand on nature, can be used to evaluate this ecological risk and its potential impact on national economies.

2. THE ORIGIN OF THE ECOLOGICAL BLIND SPOT IN ASSESSMENTS OF FINANCIAL RISK

Neoclassical economics has viewed the natural world as an unlimited source of raw materials for production. Even environmental economics, one of its sub-disciplines, sees ecological constraints merely as a market failure and not a fundamental material limitation (Norgaard 2002; Rees and Wackernagel 1999). Trusting that social preferences represent ecological necessities in timely and accurate ways, most economists ignore or reject ecological limits as an underlying material constraint on the human economy.

This often silent assumption is apparent in most neoclassical economic theories. Economic inputs, throughputs and outputs, however, all have an effect on the global ecosystem of which we are a part, and income and wealth are tightly linked with resource consumption. Hence, some economists, in dialogues with ecologists and biologists, now argue that economics needs to recognise that:

- Natural resources are not infinitely abundant
- Exceeding ecological limits is not always self-evident to market players
- Ecological constraints must become part of economic models

This emerging field of 'ecological economics' (as distinct from environmental economics) stresses that the human system is dependent on the natural system in which it is embedded, and that this relationship is becoming increasingly significant for the human economy as its scale is approaching that of the natural systems on which it depends (Daly and Farley 2003).

While ecological economics may seem like a fundamental shift in world view, its ideas evolve from traditional economic theories. Essentially, ecological economics extends the concept of capital to all assets, some of which are sometimes ignored. In addition to financial and manufactured capital (machines and infrastructure), it also considers:

- Human capital (formerly labour capital), which includes both physical and intellectual capital
- Social (cultural) capital, which includes the complex web of interpersonal connections, arrangements, rules and norms that allow human society to exist
- Natural capital (formerly considered as simply land capital), which includes ecological systems, mineral deposits, flora and fauna, and other benefits of the natural world

Stated differently, ecological economic theory takes into account the fact that the global socio-economic system has transformed from one where the limits to economic growth were a function of 'human-generated' capital to one where natural capital is increasingly becoming a limiting factor. It also recognises that these forms of capital are not infinitely substitutable among each other. Some economists have called this an evolution from 'empty-world economics' to 'full-world economics' (Costanza *et al.* 1997; Daly 2005).

Economic theory suggests that maximising production depends on increasing the supply or productivity of the scarcest (or limiting) factor. Therefore, in the face of natural capital constraints, future economic productivity would rely on maintaining natural capital assets. Since current growth in human and manufacturing capital is a function of the supply and utilisation of natural capital and since natural capital and human-made capital are largely complementary and not substitutable, expanding economies increase the pressure on natural capital stocks and ecosystems, and threaten the liquidation of these natural assets. Thus, countries have a vested interest not merely in recognising their dependence on natural capital, but also in encouraging the maintenance of the natural capital stocks upon which they depend.

These insights about natural capital and the economy are not fully incorporated in current economic practice, which continues to create mathematical models for calculating and describing societal welfare that leave out natural capital. Obvious examples are the Systems of National Accounts in which gross domestic products (GDPs) include income from depletion of natural capital (timber sales, fishing harvest, etc.), but exclude any corresponding cost beyond extraction efforts (El Serafi and Luke 1989).

This systematic distortion can lead to dangerous blind spots in economic analyses. It is curious that economists have been resistant to including a broader array of assets into their analyses. But with economic theory influencing the measures of economic value and risk used by economic and financial institutions, this omission of natural capital distorts the accuracy of these institutions' risk assessments.

For example, credit rating agencies such as Moody's Investor Services and Standard & Poor's assess governmental securities primarily by analysing aggregates of economic statistics—statistics that are influenced by ecological pressures. These statistics include:

- Economic structure and performance (GDP, population, gross national product [GNP], inflation, unemployment, imports and exports, exports as percentage of GDP)
- Fiscal indicators (Government revenues and expenditures as percentage of GDP, government debt, etc.)
- External payments and debt (exchange rate, account balance, foreign currency debt, debt service ratio, etc.)
- Monetary and liquidity reserves (interest rates, domestic credit, foreign exchange reserves, liquidity ratios, etc.)

The basic function of risk assessment is to identify relative investment risk in order to facilitate optimal allocation of economic resources. An ecological blind spot may lead to a misallocation of these resources, with very real consequences.

Sovereign risk assessments analyse how easily governments can finance their debts. Governments can take on debt through private institutions such as investment banks or other lending institutions (e.g. International Finance Corporation or the World Bank). Governments can also issue debt securities through domestic or international public markets. Systematic blind spots in underlying financial risk assessments, caused by an overly narrow view of the economic theories informing these assessments, are therefore not only 'sub-optimal', but can negatively impact both the creditors and the debtors.

The Ecological Footprint method can reduce this blind spot by evaluating ecological risks and putting them into an economic context. This analytical tool can be utilised to augment and complement existing financial and economic methods for assessing sovereign credit risk. The next section explains how this tool works.

3.   **ASSESSING THE ECOLOGICAL**
        PERFORMANCE OF A COUNTRY WITH THE
        ECOLOGICAL FOOTPRINT

Ecological Footprint Accounts provide a way of documenting the resource situation of a country by measuring the extent to which national economies stay within or exceed the regenerative capacity of their land and sea territory. Such biophysical resource accounting is possible because resources and waste flows can be tracked. The Ecological Footprint measures how much biologically productive land and sea area a population (an individual, a city, a country or all of humanity) requires for the resources it consumes and for the absorption of its waste, given prevailing technology. Measured in 'global hectares' (gha) (i.e. bio-productive hectares with world average capacity to produce useful biomass), Ecological Footprints are calculated based on official government data and reflect annual changes in resource efficiency and technology.

This tool addresses one critical research question: how much of the biosphere's regenerative capacity is available to, and used within, a given country. In focusing on this primary question, it does not cover all issues concerning ecological health. For instance, it does not measure the level of degradation of local ecosystems or the intensity by which these ecosystems may be used. But it does show the extent to which the size of human economies are approaching or exceeding the size of the ecosystems that support them.

Figure 1 shows how human demand compares with the regenerative capacity of the biosphere. Over the last 40 years, humanity's draw on nature has grown from using 70% of the biosphere's capacity to using 120%—or the equivalent of 1.2 Earths (Wackernagel *et al.* 2002:9269; WWF 2004; EEA/GFN 2005). With a population of over 6 billion people and an average Ecological Footprint of 2.2 global hectares per person, the world is currently operating with an ecological debt of 0.4 global hectares per person (EEA/GFN 2005). This overuse is possible because resources can be harvested more rapidly than ecosystems can regenerate them—by liquidating natural capital rather than living off its interest. Examples include overfishing, over-harvesting timber or depleting water tables. Overshoot is similar to the overdraft concept in the finance world: the act of drawing on a bank accounts for more than the account balance allows.

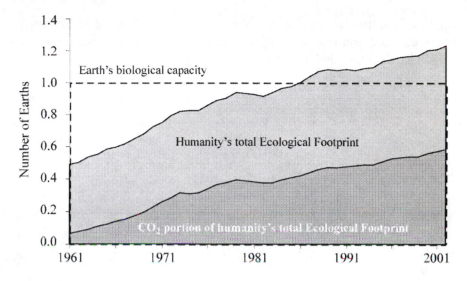

Figure 1. Human demand compared with the Earth's regenerative capacity. This graph compares human demand on nature with the regenerative capacity of the Earth for each year from 1961–2002) (Source: Wackernagel *et al.* 2002:9269; latest updates EEA/GFN 2005)

This overshoot is the globe's ecological deficit. It represents the amount by which the Ecological Footprint of humanity exceeds the biological capacity of the space available to humanity. Individual nations can also run ecological deficits if their Ecological Footprint exceeds the biological capacity of the country. To compensate for a deficit, nations can either import resources or deplete their natural capital stock. But for the planet as a whole, the only option is depletion since there is no inter-planetary resource trade.

Table 1 presents the Ecological Footprint, the biological capacity and the resulting ecological deficit or reserve for 22 selected countries (EEA/GFN 2005) Note that countries with biological capacity exceeding their footprint show an ecological reserve (positive value) and countries with biological capacity smaller than their footprint show an ecological deficit (negative value).

As Table 1 indicates, many countries consume resources at rates that they cannot sustain with their own environmental systems. In fact, these 22 countries alone, representing two-thirds of the world's population, have a combined ecological deficit of 0.6 global hectares per person (2.4 billion gha).

Frequently, wealthy nations protect their own local ecosystems by importing goods and services from ecosystems in other countries. This technique is effective as long as resources remain available in other countries for purchase and importing countries have sufficient financial capital. As the

supply of available resources shrinks and resource demand increases, resource conflicts continue to arise. Irregular supply therefore will affect certain industries earlier and, to a greater extent, than others.

Table 1. Country comparison

	Population (millions)	Ecological Footprint (global ha/cap)	Biological Capacity (global ha/cap)	Ecological Deficit (-) or Reserve (+) (global ha/cap)
WORLD	**6225.0**	**2.2**	**1.8**	**- 0.4**
Argentina	38.0	2.2	6.7	4.5
Australia	19.5	7.0	11.3	4.4
Brazil	176.3	2.1	10.1	8.0
Canada	31.3	7.8	14.3	6.5
China	1302.3	1.6	0.8	- 0.8
Egypt	70.5	1.4	0.5	- 0.9
France	59.9	5.6	3.2	- 2.4
Germany	82.4	4.4	1.8	- 2.6
India	1049.5	0.8	0.4	- 0.4
Indonesia	217.1	1.2	1.0	-0.2
Italy	57.5	3.9	1.1	- 2.8
Japan	127.5	4.4	0.8	- 3.6
Korea, Rep.	47.4	4.4	0.6	- 3.8
Mexico	102,0	2.4	1.7	- 0.7
Netherlands	16.1	4.5	0.8	- 3.7
Pakistan	149.9	0.6	0.4	- 0.3
Philippines	78.6	1.1	0.6	- 0.6
Russia	144.1	4.4	7.0	2.6
Sweden	8.9	6.6	9.8	3.2
Thailand	62.2	1.5	1.0	- 0.4
United Kingdom	59.3	5.6	1.6	- 4.0
USA	291.0	9.8	4.7	- 5.0
Combined	*4191.3*	*2.5*	*1.9*	*-0.6*

In the last column, negative numbers indicate an ecological deficit,
positive numbers an ecological reserve. Note that numbers may not sum due
to rounding. Data for year 2002 (Source: EEA/GFN 2005)

The pressure behind the global trend of a growing overall Footprint (as
shown in Figure 1) is likely to persist. Higher incomes correlate with larger

footprints, and the world economy continues to expand. World population also continues to grow. But there is no immutable law that says this global trend of increased demand on nature has to persist. For instance, if efficiency gains exceed increases in demand, the overall pressure on ecosystems would decrease. Unfortunately, over the past few decades efficiency gains have not kept up with the overall increase in resource demand, making it likely that the overall global trend of a growing Footprint will persist for some time.

Recognising these trends makes it clear that the remaining natural capital is an increasingly crucial asset. As a result, countries may begin to reconsider the importance of their biological wealth. The ecological deficit/reserve is one way to measure this wealth (see Figure 2).

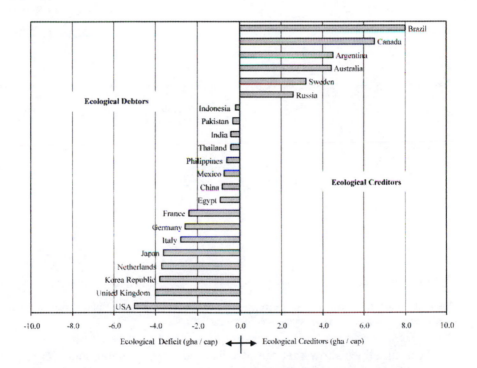

Figure 2. Comparison of national ecological reserves or deficits (per capita)

The size of the ecological deficit (or reserve, if positive) summarises a country's consumption of nature relative to its biological capacity. It shows, in aggregate terms, to what extent a country's consumption of resources matches or exceeds the regenerative capacity of the ecosystems within its territory. Data for year 2002 (EEA/GFN 2005).

In addition to the aggregate results that Ecological Footprint accounts generate, they also provide information on different components. For instance, specific aspects of demand can be singled out and their performance plotted over time. Figure 3 shows an example for Mexico (EEA/GFN 2005). National trends in the biocapacity and in the import, export and production footprints of agriculture and forestry products are compared. Biocapacity (dashed line) represents the per capita sum of available cropland, pasture and forest. Production (solid line) represents the aggregate demand on local ecosystems for running the Mexican economy (excluding carbon dioxide [CO_2] since Mexico sets aside no significant CO_2 sequestration areas). Some of this production footprint (or resource demand of the Mexican economy) is exported, while some resources are imported. This is depicted in the two lines in the lower part of the figure.

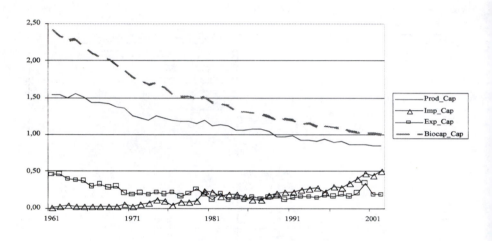

Figure 3. Mexico agriculture and forestry products

This time series tracks the Mexican economy's demand on its own biological capacity and identifies the biological capacity embodied in the trade flows.

These timelines show that the Mexican economy's compound demands for cropland, pasture and forest have created a production footprint that approached national biological capacity over time. Figure 3 also shows that net exports in renewable terrestrial resources have decreased steadily over time. By the mid-1980s, Mexico had become a net footprint importer for forest and agricultural products.

Another significant trend becomes evident for Mexico: the ecological assets per person are declining rapidly. As its population grew from 38 million in 1961 to over 100 million in 2002, its per capita ecological assets fell by more than 50% in spite of technology-induced productivity gains in agriculture.

Such biophysical analysis of a country's situation can assist financial analysts in identifying regional and local ecological resource limits, dependencies on net imports of ecological services (a cost factor that can become an increasing economic liability), as well as specific areas of overuse. Moreover, these accounts can identify net dependence on ecological services from elsewhere.

Note that some of the ecological services that countries import are not paid for. Examples include fishing in international waters, the use of waste sinks in other countries and emissions of CO_2 into the global commons. Economists call the use of these 'free' ecological services costs that are externalised onto the global commons. Footprint accounts allow analysts to track such demands on the global commons, which may be free today but may become an economic liability in the future.

4.   HOW THE ECOLOGICAL FOOTPRINT CAN HELP ANALYSE A COUNTRY'S ECONOMIC STABILITY

To explain how the Ecological Footprint tool can support financial analysts in their risk assessments, standard financial ratings are compared below to ecological deficits, as calculated with the Ecological Footprint accounts (see Figure 4).

Figure 4 compares sovereign credit rankings to the nations' net dependency on importing ecological services. While the dots representing each country are quite scattered, the overall trend suggests that the bigger the ecological deficit, the more financial analysts consider these countries to be creditworthy. This could give rise to three possible interpretations:

a) This weak, but visible negative trend connecting lower credit risk and higher ecological deficit could mean that having ecological assets makes it more difficult for countries to compete economically.

b) The scattered distribution could suggest that ecological performance is a negligible factor that does not significantly affect the risk.

c) The counter-intuitive correlation between higher creditworthiness and higher ecological deficits could mean that sovereign credit risk may be assessed inadequately. In other words, it may be that large discrepancies in the relative ecological situations of countries are not adequately represented in current credit risk analyses.

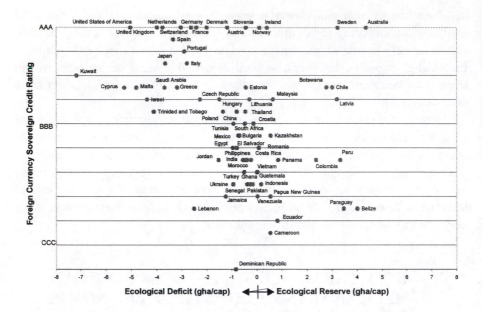

Figure 4. Sovereign Credit Risk Rating in comparison with a country's ecological reserve or deficit

This graph compares financial rating to the Ecological Deficit for 80 countries for whom both sovereign ratings and footprint assessments are available (EEA/GFN 2005 for ecological deficit, S&P 2005 for credit rating). An Ecological Deficit of 8 global hectares per person means that the average person's Ecological Footprint in that country exceeds that country's per capita Biological Capacity by 8 global hectares (an 8 global hectare per person reserve would mean that the capacity exceeds the footprint by that amount). AAA rating stands for highest creditworthiness, CCC for the lowest; the most recent available data are used for both the Ecological Deficit as well as for the risk assessments of long-term foreign currency sovereign credit. The graph reveals that some countries ranked high in creditworthiness operate within the bounds of their ecological capacity, while others ranked of equal creditworthiness are operating well beyond the bounds of long-term ecological productivity.

The first interpretation is difficult to reconcile with biophysical reality. It essentially suggests that (ecological) assets are a liability. In other words, it would mean that having resources available would be a curse for the economic performance of the country. Taken to an extreme, this logic could suggest that humanity would be better off without a planet. Another possible way of reading this interpretation would be the following: in the current economic context, running an ecological deficit provides economic benefits in excess of the costs associated with the ecological deficits. If this is the case, this would prompt financial risks and volatility since it would encourage all countries to accelerate their ecological deficit spending and liquidate their natural capital—not a comforting trend given that the world is ecologically finite.

The second interpretation may be valid in the current economic context. Today, importing ecological services and imposing environmental externalities on the global commons is still cheap. Hence, economic performance may not yet be determined by environmental factors. However, this is likely to change in the future. It may be possible to obscure a country's ecological reality in the short-run through strong currencies, new access to less exploited resources and cheaper exploitation methods. But in the longer-run, ecological scarcity will significantly affect the cost of resource consumption and waste emission. While waste can currently be emitted at almost zero cost, this will become increasingly expensive due to international treaties such as the Kyoto Protocol (on carbon dioxide), the Montreal Protocol (on ozone destroying gases) and the Basel Convention (on the export of hazardous industrial wastes).

The third interpretation, which stems from the fact that countries with the same credit rating can have quite distinctly different ecological situations, suggests that current financial risk rankings suffer from ecological blind spots. There is some intuitive logic to this interpretation, since resource-rich countries such as New Zealand, Australia, Canada, Finland, Brazil and Sweden seem to have more resource choice—or a higher 'ecological degree of freedom'. These countries have a head start since their ecological assets provide opportunities for economic activities that resource poor countries do not have. But the overall trend in Figure 4 seems to suggest the opposite, which could mean that the ratings are inadequate.

Current analysis cannot determine which of these three interpretations is correct, but all of them point to issues of significant importance for financial risk analysis. The Ecological Footprint provides a tool to explore these interpretations—a research tool to statistically test hypotheses about the relationship of ecological assets, resource use and economic performance. But even without further research, the Ecological Footprint can stress test conventional economic risk assessments. By this we mean that Footprint results can help challenge financial risk assessments and pick out the cases where some effect from the ecological assets or liabilities of the particular country would be expected.

For instance, comparing two or more countries might generate questions about how ecological performance impacts economic performance. As shown in Figure 4, Canada and Australia have more ecological opportunities than Switzerland and the UK—factors that the sovereign credit rankings currently ignore. Hence, analysts can use the Ecological Footprint to identify countries with similar ratings but disparate ecological contexts and reconsider their relative risk assessments. Financial analysts may still come to the same conclusion regarding credit risk but, by testing their results against the ecological situation of the country, they can make their risk assessment more informed and hence more robust.

5.   CONCLUSIONS

Ecological analysis suggests that the global overshoot of the biosphere's regenerative capacity is becoming a growing threat to the steady provision of resources and ecological services upon which economies depend. Anticipating these risks is wise not only for countries, but especially for investment analysts trying to predict sovereign competitiveness and continuing economic health. The Ecological Footprint may be valuable in assessing this risk since it is an effective tool for monitoring countries' ecological performance and resource dependencies.

While the Ecological Footprint can support at present sovereign credit risk analysis through stress testing, it can also support sovereign credit analysis through empirical analysis of international trade, economic sectors, resource production, resource consumption, resource efficiency, energy composition and time trends. For instance, Ecological Footprints can track a nation's demand on ecological resources such as timber, food and energy, and measure this demand in a way that makes it directly comparable to the ecological capacity available within the country. By linking economic and environmental databases, these analyses can help identify and quantify hidden economic strengths and weaknesses.

- **Trade balances**. How reliant is a country on importing or exporting natural resources? Can a country's domestic ecological capacity support continued resource export earnings or are those earnings temporary?
- **Ecological efficiency**. Does a country generate maximum revenue per unit of resource consumption? Or do inefficient technologies and practices leave room for improvement?
- **Sectoral analysis**. What does the prevailing composition of energy sources mean for future climate treaties such as the Kyoto Protocol? Is there extra capacity to expand resource use or are key industries facing ecological risk?
- **National security**. If globalisation becomes more expensive due to terrorism and security costs, how will that affect countries' resource supplies and competitive advantages? What effect would war have on the ability of countries to secure resources for consumption and production?
- **Resource dependency**. As resources become scarce, how able are different countries to absorb higher resource costs, implement efficient tech-

nologies and production methods, or make the transition to new products for export?

In addition, Ecological Footprint accounts add an ecological perspective to existing economic indicators:

- **GDP.** Ecological constraints identified by the Footprint could hamper the ability for certain industries to expand, thus affecting the rate of industrial and agricultural production.
- **Imports/exports**. Footprinting can document trends of natural resource trade flows and the strength of sectors such as tourism, agriculture and fishing.
- **Domestic credit**. Footprinting can analyse whether loans to resource-dependent industries are backed by sufficient ecological capacity;
- **Foreign exchange reserves.** Footprinting can identify potential pressure on foreign exchange revenues from deficiencies of natural capital.

The investment community is constantly searching for ways to make their assessments of risk more reliable and predictive. With the increasing importance of ecological limits in an ever more crowded world, ecological measures like the Ecological Footprint offer additional intelligence. Incorporating measures of ecological risk can help assess sovereign credit worthiness by analysing risks that may not be readily apparent in traditional financial risk assessment methodologies.

REFERENCES

Bank for International Settlements (2003): 'BIS', *Quarterly Review* December [online] [cited 10 December 2003]. Available from Internet URL: http://www.bis.org/publ/qtrpdf/r_qa0312.pdf#page=86.

Costanza, R., Cumberland, J., Daly, H., Goodland, R. and Norgaard, R.B. (1997): *An Introduction to Ecological Economics.* Boca Raton: St Lucie Press.

Daly, H. (2005): 'Economics in a Full World', *Scientific American*, September 2005, 100-107.

Daly, H. and Farley, J. (2003): *Ecological Economics: Principles and Applications.* Washington D.C: Island Press.

EEA/GFN (European Environment Agency and Global Footprint Network) (2005): *The 2005 Edition of the Ecological Footprint Accounts (with Results up to 2002)*. Copenhagen: EEA [online] [after October 2005] available from Internet URL: http://www.eea.eu.int/main.

El Serafi, S. and Lutz, E. (1989): 'Environmental and Resource Accounting: An Overview', in: Ahmad, J., El Serafi, S. and Lutz, E. (Eds.): *Accounting for Sustainable Development.* Washington D.C.: The World Bank.

IMF (International Monetary Fund) (2002): *Global Financial Stability Report: Market Developments and Issues* [online] [cited 10 December 2003]. Available from Internet URL: http://www.imf.org/External/Pubs/FT/GFSR/2002/03/.

Norgaard, R. (2002): 'Optimists, Pessimists, and Science', *BioScience* Vol. 52, No. 3, 287-292.

Rees, W.E. and Wackernagel, M. (1999): 'Monetary Analysis: Turning a Blind Eye on Sustainability', *Ecological Economics* Vol. 29, No. 1, 47-52.

Standard and Poor's (2003): *Standard and Poor's Sovereign Ratings History since 1975* [online] [cited 20 September 2005]. Available from Internet URL: http://www2.standardandpoors.com/servlet/Satellite?pagename=sp/sp_article/ArticleTemplate&c=sp_ar ticle&cid=1099333608002&b=10&r=1&1=EN#ID645.

Sturm, A., Wackernagel, M. and Müller, K. (2000): *The Winners and Losers in Global Competition: Why Eco-Efficiency Reinforces Competitiveness: A Study of 44 Nations.* Chur/Zürich: Rüegger.

Wackernagel, M., Monfreda, C., Erb, K., Haberl, H. and Schulz, N. (2004): 'Ecological Footprint Time Series of Austria, the Philippines, and South Korea for 1961-1999: Comparing the Conventional Approach to an 'Actual Land Demand' Approach' *Land Use Policy* (forthcoming).

Wackernagel, M., Schulz, N., Deumling, D., Callejas Linares, A., Jenkins, M., Kapos, V., Monfreda, C., Loh, J., Myers, N., Norgaard, R. and Randers, J. (2002): 'Tracking the Ecological Overshoot of the Human Economy' *Proceedings of the National Academy of Sciences* Vol. 99, No. 14, 9266-9271.

WWF (2004): Living Planet Report 2004. Gland: WWF International, Global Footprint Network and UNEP WCMC.

PART III

EVIDENCE –
STRATEGIES, CASE STUDIES
AND MANAGEMENT SYSTEMS

Chapter 7

Strategies and the Business Case for Sustainability

ACHIEVING SUSTAINABLE CORPORATE COMPETITIVENESS
The Strategic Link between Top Management's (Green) Commitment and Corporate Environmental Strategy

Ki-Hoon Lee[1] and Robert Ball[2]
[1] KwangWoon University, Korea; [2] University of Stirling, UK

Abstract: Current prescriptions for organisational eco-change, which are often driven by a desire to show companies the 'right way forward', are often dominated by rhetoric and are reliant on the assumption that organisations will voluntarily become greener. There is little evidence to support any of these assumptions. Assuming that the primary motivating force for business corporations is the pursuit of organisational sustainability through the attainment of competitive advantage, corporate contributions to sustainability must stem from self-interest and survival instincts. This study seeks to develop a corporate understanding of emerging environmental concerns and their impacts on organisational survival and profitability. By focusing on the strategic assessment of change drivers—top management's commitment and strategic importance of green issues—this chapter studies 15 companies in the Korean chemical industry and develops four strategic response models ranging from lagging to proactive catalyst. This study finds that top management's commitment has a direct and indirect impact on corporate environmental responses and strategy.

Business activities cannot avoid exerting an influence on conditions in the natural environment in some way. During the past few decades, however, the environmental disaster in Bhopal and the *Exxon Valdez* oil spill in Alaska have contributed to an increasing awareness of the effect of business activities on the natural environment.

There has been considerable discussion about the relationship between businesses and the natural environment (Schmidheiny 1992; Hawken 1993; Hawken *et al.* 1999). Even though there are some pessimistic ideas concerning the potential for establishing environmentally friendly business activities (Walley and Whitehead 1994), a common theme is that businesses cause environmental problems but can also contribute to their solutions.

Corporate environmental management has been recently developed in order to assist companies in reducing, evaluating, monitoring and controlling their environmental impact. Implementation of this in business, however, presents a challenge to management, since it implies fundamental changes in some of the ways of operating a company (Hawken 1993).

Many academic researchers have explored the relationship between environmental and financial performance (Ingram and Frazier 1980; Jaffe *et al.* 1995; Edwards 1998; Stanwick and Stanwick 1998; Toms 2000; Wagner 2001; Edwards *et al.* 2002). Little attention, however, has been paid to other factors, such as top management or CEO's commitment, which influence corporate environmental and economic performance. Top managers' (green) commitment and understanding of corporate environmental management will influence the extent to which companies may take innovative and risk-taking strategies or defensive and risk-avoidance strategies.

This study applies Miles and Snow's 1978 typology to corporate environmental management in the Korean chemical industry. In particular, the study explores how top management's (green) commitment influences the formulation of different types of corporate environmental strategy and different environmental and financial performance.

1. THE MILES AND SNOW 1978 TYPOLOGY IN BUSINESS STRATEGY

Business strategy has been a highly significant aspect of business research in the last two decades, and several typologies of business strategy have been developed, such as those of Miles and Snow (1978) and Porter (1980). Typologies are classification schemes which provide 'a means for ordering and comparing organisations and clustering them into categorical types' (Rich 1992: 758). One of the reasons why researchers commonly use typologies is 'to provide a parsimonious framework for describing complex organisational forms and for explaining outcomes' (Doty and Glick 1994: 230).

Miles and Snow (1978) propose that organisations develop distinctive and relatively enduring patterns of strategic behaviour to co-align the organisation with its environment. According to Miles and Snow, an organisation can be classified as a defender, prospector, analyser or reactor depending on the pattern of interaction between the organisation and its environment. Prospectors perceive a dynamic, uncertain environment and maintain flexibility to combat environmental change. The prospector seeks to identify and exploit new products and market opportunities. Prospectors' characteristics include a diverse product line; multiple technologies; a product or geographically divisionalised structure; skills in product research and development, market research and development engineering. In contrast, defenders perceive the environment to be stable and certain, and thus seek stability and control in their operations to achieve maximum efficiency. The defender is characterised by a narrow and relatively stable product-market domain, single capital-intensive technology; a functional structure; and skills in production efficiency, process engineering and cost control.

Analysers stress both stability and flexibility and attempt to capitalise on the best of both of the preceding strategic types. According to Miles and Snow, the analyser operates in two differing types of product-market domain, one relatively stable, the other changing. Given different market demands, analysers enact a diversity of behaviours. Thus they are characterised by a limited product line; search for a small number of related product and market opportunities; cost-efficient technology for stable products and project technologies for new products; skills in production efficiency, process engineering and marketing. In reactor organisations, managers perceive change and uncertainty but are unable to respond effectively. Reactors, therefore, lack a consistent strategy and act only when the environment forces them to do so, thus performing poorly. Table 1 summarises these four strategic patterns.

Table 1. Miles and Snow's 1978 typology of business strategy

Strategic variable	Archetypes	Features
Strategic pattern	Prospector	Turbulent domain, always seeking new product and market opportunities, uncertain environment, flexible structure
Strategic pattern	Defender	Stable domain, limited product range, competes through low cost or high quality, efficiency paramount, centralised structure
Strategic pattern	Analyser	Hybrid, core of traditional products, enters new markets after viability established, matrix structure
Strategy lacking	Reactor	Lacks coherent strategy, structure inappropriate to purpose, misses opportunities, unsuccessful

Source: adapted from Lee 2001

The strategic choice perspective of Miles and Snow (1978) suggests that a firm's competitive advantage can be sought through proactive strategies (prospector), conservative strategies (defender) or a hybrid alternative (analyser). A prospector strategy has innovative, future-oriented, risk-taking and proactive characteristics (Miller and Friesen 1983). Firms using this strategy concentrate on identifying and capitalising on emerging market opportunities. These firms maintain strategic flexibility and strive to gain competitive advantage with speed, surprise and sound execution (Tan 1996). Conversely, a defender strategy corresponds to a non-adaptive, defensive and risk-averse orientation (Banerjee 2001). Firms adopting this strategy tend to be rigid and conservative organisations that deliberately reduce costs and risks by selecting a stable, narrowly defined product or market domain (Wright *et al.* 1995). As a hybrid strategy between prospector and defender, an analyser strategy may be an appropriate choice for those firms seeking both risk-adjusted efficiency and emerging market opportunities (Miles and Snow 1978; Hambrick 1983). These firms defend existing product markets through efficiency-oriented strategies while cautiously penetrating new markets with intensified product/ market innovations (Venkatraman and Prescott 1990).

Miles and Snow's (1978) typology has implications for proactive–reactive type corporate organisational responses regarding green issues. Proactive organisations (prospectors) would seek green market opportunities and develop green products even though their environment is uncertain and turbulent. In contrast, reactive organisations (reactors) would ignore green opportunities or new markets because of lack of strategy and commitment. As Miles and Snow point out, managerial interpretations of the environment, particularly at board level, significantly influence whether organisations become proactive or reactive.

2.   CORPORATE RESPONSES TO GREEN ISSUES: CORPORATE GREENING MODELS APPROACH

As mentioned above, considerable attention has recently been paid to corporate environmental management. Corporate environmental management has focused in particular on the development of typologies of environmental management approaches (Arthur D. Little 1989; Hunt and Auster 1990; Roome 1992; Post and Altman 1992, 1994; Sadgrove 1992; Scallon and Sten 1996). Table 2 shows these eight different corporate greening models as mentioned above.

Most of these typologies suggest that companies' strategic responsiveness to environmental issues describes a continuum, which ranges from reactive compliance with legislation at the lower end to proactive practices at the upper end. To illustrate this we can elaborate on one of the best-known models. Roome (1992) categorises four different levels of corporate response. The lowest level, non-compliance, reflects a firm that fails to address the requirements of environmental regulation and other external pressures.

Table 2. Corporate greening response models

ADL 1989	Hunt and Auster 1990	Roome 1992	Post and Altman 1992, 1994	Sadgrove 1992	Scallon and Sten 1996	Brockhoff et al. 1999	Winn and Angell 2000
Problem-solving	Beginner	Non-compliance	Adjustment	Laggard	Compliance	Defender	Deliberate reactive
Compliance	Fire fighter	Compliance	Adaptation/ anticipation	Punished	Alignment	Escapist	Unrealised
Assurance	Pragmatist	Compliance plus	Innovation	Conformer	Expansion	Dormant	Emergent active
	Proactivist	Leading edge/ excellence		Leader	Integration	Activist	Deliberate proactive

Firms at this level are identified as having little strategic vision and a limited understanding of the environmental issues within their business activity. The second level, compliance, reflects a firm that has a more aware attitude. However, firms in this level are still reactive, pursuing a minimum level of environmental commitment to avoid legal action or loss of market share. The third level, compliance plus, reflects a firm that takes a more proactive stance. Firms at this level are becoming aware of the potential competitive advantage to be gained from environmental commitment and leadership. In addition, such firms often take actions beyond existing environmental legislation and requirements. The fourth level, leading edge/excellence, is that of the environmental champion. Roome (1992) sees firms at this final level achieving commercial and environmental excellence through innovative solutions to environmental problems.

3. ENVIRONMENTAL (GREEN) COMMITMENT

It is very often claimed that top managers strongly influence the implementation of corporate environmental management (Ghobadian *et al*. 1998; Lee 2001). It would be useful to identify levels of commitment of decision-makers (and particularly top management on green issues).

Ghobadian *et al*. (1998) categorise environmental commitment as:

- Restrained commitment
- Speculative commitment
- Conditional commitment

Restrained commitment refers to companies that may want to make an environmental statement, but do not perceive any real need to follow up this statement with action. Thus, the category of restrained commitment can involve 'greenwashing', which, according to Hoffman (1997), reflects 'the symbolic activities taken by some companies to demonstrate their environmental commitment, while their underlying practices and values remain unchanged' (1997: 157). Ghobadian *et al*.'s second type, speculative commitment, reflects companies that become leaders in the environmental field because they identify business opportunities such as increased market share, increased profitability, or reduced cost structure leading to competitive advantage. Thus, speculative commitment can be categorised as 'opportunity seeking'. Conditional commitment is shown by companies that take different actions in different circumstances or countries. That is, companies' environmental commitment depends on the prevailing business conditions—in particular, operational factors. They may seek more proactive stances where their interests are best served by, for example, investing relatively heavily in environmental technology and pollution reduction systems. In contrast, they will take more reactive actions where their interests are best served by such actions. This commitment can be categorised as 'it all depends'.

4.   ENVIRONMENTAL AND FINANCIAL PERFORMANCE

Corporate greening can impact on a company's environmental and financial performance. The relationship between environmental and financial performance remains unclear, although evidence is beginning to emerge that there can be a positive relationship between proactive greening behaviour and the firm's financial situation. Stead and Stead (1995) have found that enhanced greening activity results in reasonable financial returns and investment payback periods. Some scholars argue for the existence of an early-mover advantage in strategic management (Porter and van der Linde 1995a, 1995b; Shrivastava 1995). According to Porter and van der Linde (1995a, 1995b), stringent environmental regulation can improve firms' competitiveness and, as a result, will lead to a positive relationship between environmental and financial performance for the firm. This proposition is called the Porter hypothesis.

Klassen and McLaughlin (1996) report a positive relationship between the receipt of environmental awards and financial performance, with a corresponding negative relationship between environmental crises and financial performance. However, Jaffe *et al.* (1995) suggest that there is little evidence that environmental regulations impact on financial performance at all. Walley and Whitehead (1993) support the view of Jaffe *et al.* (1995). They argue that environmental investments are too costly to gain an adequate return on investment within the short term, say within five to ten years. Unclear outcomes of environmental investments in future financial periods bring great uncertainty for decision-makers at board level. They also found that there are more executives who have a wait-and-see attitude instead of taking early steps towards environmental sustainability. More recently, Edwards (1998) carried out a European portfolio analysis on the relationship between environmental and financial performance. He found limited support for the Porter hypothesis. In 69% of the comparisons between portfolios of environmentally high-performing firms and other firms, the former demonstrate better performance. Thomas and Tonks (1999) examined the correlation between excess stock market returns and environmental activities and features of firms based on UK data. They found that the adoption of an environmental policy by firms with sound pollution records improves their stock market returns.

5. THE KOREAN CHEMICAL INDUSTRY: GENERAL BACKGROUND

The chemical industry has one of the longest industrial histories in Korea. In 2001, total production in the chemical products industry, total sales and total profitability increased by 10%, 11.5% and 1.4%, respectively. In the same year, total exports amounted to US$115.2 billion and imports amounted to US$25.2 billion (Bank of Korea 2001). In addition to strengthened international competitiveness, the Korean chemical industry has rapidly increased its overseas direct investments since the 1990s. Overseas investments contributed to Korean firms' expanding share in the world market and acquisition of advanced technology in capital-intensive industries.

Since March 1998, however, excess capacity and international competitiveness have brought pressure from the government to restructure the industry. As a result of the government-initiated industrial restructuring drive, mainly aimed at eliminating overlapping businesses, the three national industrial complexes at Daesan in South Chungchong Province, Yeochon in South Cholla Province, and Ulsan in South Kyongsang Province were criticised for restructuring under a series of mergers and asset swaps among the top five *chaebols*. In addition, the government has a mandate to set environmental standards and to investigate environmental pollution. For example, environmental impact assessment (EIA) is a compulsory part of environmental management in the industry.

The industry has begun to be aware that pressure over green issues arises not only internationally but also domestically. Thus, investment in environmental technology and pollution reduction facilities has increased. However, the traditional strategy for environmental investment involves complying with minimum regulation standards. Historically, the major source of international competitiveness of the Korean chemical industry has been relatively cheap labour. Increasing environmental investment to meet stricter environmental regulation can be an obstacle to gaining competitiveness in international markets. However, executives of the industry seem to have reconsidered the importance of corporate environmental management. How environmental management can bring benefits to the industry was discussed at the annual meeting of the chemical industry association in 1998. The main outcome of the meeting was to promote high environmental standards and to take proactive steps in corporate environmental management.

6.   RESEARCH METHODOLOGY

As discussed above, management plays a critically important role in handling green issues. Therefore, we decided to address the research question: 'How do executives perceive green issues and how and why do executives integrate given issues in strategic management?'

A case study approach was adopted in that it allowed for in-depth studies of individual companies and for comparisons between them to take place. Fifteen companies were used as case studies. Case study information consisted of written documents, responses to a written questionnaire and interviews with around five senior executives of each company. Each of the 15 companies represented a single case study. The main issues tackled in each case study are top-level commitment to strategic issues and business responses to environmental issues.

In top-level commitment, the following issues are included:
• Top-level responsibility
• Environmental policy
• Strategic planning
• Stakeholder involvement

In business responses to environmental issues, the following are included:
• Environmental performance
• Environmental report
• Environmental management system (EMS)
• Environmental standards
• Records of fines and penalties
• Environmental liability
• Eco-products

In order to evaluate companies' performance on these issues, an environmental sustainability evaluation sheet was developed. This consisted of indicators of performance in 19 sub-areas. These were consolidated into 11 main areas. Appendix 1 shows the performance of each of the 15 companies against each indicator.

The results obtained from this analysis were assessed by doing a conceptually clustered matrix analysis (Miles and Huberman 1994). According to Miles and Huberman, a conceptually clustered matrix is developed by bringing together items that 'belong together' (1994: 127).

Before carrying out the cluster analysis it was considered desirable to consolidate the evaluative indicators. This grouping process reduces the number of indicators and helps to identify common themes.

The authors found it possible to identify the following themes: top-management commitment, strategic importance of green issues and operational performance on green issues. Top-management commitment includes top-level responsibility and environmental policy. The rating score for top-management commitment can be calculated by adding the score for top-level responsibility and environmental policy. Strategic importance of green issues includes strategic planning and stakeholder involvement. The rating score for strategic importance of green issues can thus be calculated by adding the score for stakeholder involvement and strategic planning. Operational performance on green issues includes environmental performance, environmental report, environmental management system, environmental standards, record of fines and penalties, environmental liability and eco-products. The rating score of operational performance of green issues can be calculated by adding the scores on these issues (see Appendix 2 for more details).

7.   RESULTS OF THE STUDY

Corporate greening is considered to be a complex and multi-dimensional process. Identifying the key elements in the study is not easy but from the case studies, three themes have been identified. As mentioned above, the cluster analysis method is used for identifying groups of strategic behaviour. The results for the cluster analysis of the 15 companies across the three dimensions of corporate greening are shown in Table 3 (see Appendices 1 and 2 for more details).

Table 3. The output of cluster analysis: corporate greening pattern

| | | Dimensions of corporate greening | | |
| | | Corporate greening themes | | |
Cluster	Company	Top management's commitment	Strategic importance of green issues	Operational performance of green issues
1	3	M	VL	VL
2	9, 12, 13	M	H	H
3	4, 14, 15	H	H	H
4	1, 2, 5, 6, 7, 8, 10, 11	M	M	M

H = high, M = moderate, L = low, VL = very low

The results of the cluster analysis identify four patterns of corporate greening behaviour. Similarities and differences between the clusters are particularly important so that general patterns of greening behaviour can be identified and a more coherent descriptive profile of the clusters can be developed.

7.1   Cluster 1

Company 3 has very low scores on strategic importance and operational performance on green issues. The dimension related to top management's commitment on green issues has a medium rating. Such low scores would indicate that the company is facing some difficult challenges both from within the organisation and from the outside. In addition, detailed case study data shows environmental performance was poorer in 2000 and 2001, the final two years of the study. Because of this, the company has had to pay a number of fines for exceeding their effluent consent levels. There were also demonstrations by local residents protesting against the air pollution and noise that result from the manufacturing process. In addition, environmental groups found suspicious pipelines from the company facilities on the banks of the local river. Environmental groups reported their findings to a local court, and investigators were sent to examine the issues.

Although the company has had to make substantial investments to comply with environmental legislation, there is a definite focus on regulation compliance only. The management is trying to implement some changes but the strategic consideration and operational performance are very weak and there is not much more than the expectation of compliance. Not surprisingly, there was no positive relationship between environmental performance and financial performance in the period 1997–2001.[1]

Cluster 1 characteristics can be summarised as follows:

- A reactive approach to environmental management with lack of top-management commitment and strategic consideration
- Lack of staff who hold responsibility for legal compliance and environmental issues
- Weak commitment on international environmental standards for new and existing operations
- Absence of linkage between financial performance and environmental performance

---

[1]   The indicators for environmental performance include air emissions (kg/day), water consumption and waste (kg/day). The indicators for financial performance include turnover, total investment and environmental investment.

7.2   Cluster 2

Companies 9, 12 and 13 have high scores in strategic importance of, and operational performance on, green issues with a medium score on top-management commitment. All three companies have no major waste problems and they are not dealing with products or processes that have high environmental risks. The major feature that these three companies have in common is that they are all voluntarily implementing changes in their companies that reduce their impact on the natural environment.

This group of companies maintains a good environmental performance record by reducing emissions from their facilities by investing in advanced process technology and strategically focusing their product range. At the same time, end-of-pipe environmental protection for the treatment of exhaust air and waste-water as well as waste disposal is becoming less necessary.

These companies have discovered that the investment in new technology can reduce environmentally hazardous emissions as well as reduce cost through adoption of increasingly efficient production methods. There are significant positive relationships between environmental performance and financial performance. For example, environmental investment has increased while turnover also increased. At the same time, environmental performance with respect to air has improved. Overall, environmental effectiveness and cost efficiency correlate well together. Thus, it is possible to conclude that there is a positive relationship between environmental and financial performance in this group.

The drivers for improved environmental consciousness were primarily external in nature arising from governmental regulations and market opportunities to tap the growing demand for environmentally compatible products.

Characteristics of this cluster are:

- Desirability of making early financial investment in environmental protection and technology development
- Top-management commitment to environmental issues is critical for success
- Effective decentralisation of environmental specialists in the different business units
- Environmental considerations should be viewed as an inseparable part of business performance. It is useful to set quantitative targets for different environmental performance measures.

7.3   Cluster 3

Companies 4, 14 and 15 in Cluster 3 show high scores in the three different areas of top-management commitment, strategic importance and operational performance of green issues. These companies have very sound environmental performance records in the last five years. This group of companies has achieved superior environmental performance compared with companies in clusters 1 and 2. These companies consider their reputation and corporate image very seriously. The CEO at Company 4 said:

> A weak or poor reputation can threaten goodwill, co-operation and ulti-mately the company's licence to operate. Such a threat now faces our company. Its reputation is mixed, with some areas of important strength. But it also has negative associations which, if left unchecked, are likely to undermine the company's ability to operate smoothly and efficiently—in other words, its ability to serve its stakeholders and, in particular, its shareholders.

All these companies are aware of green issues and regard them as business opportunities rather than threats. Thus, with top management's support, these companies have a proactive strategy in environmental invest-ment and technology development. The CEO at company 14 said, 'There is growing awareness that addressing green concerns does not depend on a tremendous investment but more on a proactive approach, managerial ability and commitment tied to smart investment.'

The initial cost of incorporating green concerns is indeed an investment rather than an expense. It is an investment that has significant impact on the overall business. Those companies with the skills to manage these issues do so at a fraction of the cost, and far more effectively than those without an integrating approach. The companies manage to keep a certain level of environmental investment each year while showing very good environmental performance.

There are a number of important drivers leading to an emphasis on environmental issues. These are governmental regulations, increasing public awareness of environmental issues, corporate image and reputation, demands from customers and the media. The effect has been for both environmental and financial performance to show a positive increase.

The following are the characteristics of Cluster 3 companies:

- A proactive approach to environmental management; setting specific targets for future environmental performance for outcomes, inputs and processes is critical for success
- Benchmarking of their competitor companies in international and domes-tic markets
- Top-management understanding of green issues and support for these bring much more attention to operational performance
- Adopting their own environmental quality standards in cases where existing laws and regulations are not adequate

- Communicating their commitment to environmental quality to their employees, shareholders, suppliers, customers and the local communities in which they operate
- Recognising and responding to the community's questions about their operations
- Actively participating with government agencies and other appropriate groups to ensure that the development and implementation of environmental policies, laws, regulations and practices serve the public interest and are based on sound scientific judgement

7.4   Cluster 4

Companies 1, 2, 5, 6, 7, 8, 10 and 11 show a medium-level rating on top management's commitment, strategic importance and operational performance on green issues. All eight companies have been focusing on reducing their operating costs and have not focused on environmental issues more than is required by the regulations. Most investments made were primarily to reduce cost with environmental improvement a secondary consideration. More detailed case study data shows no clear sign of significant reduction in pollution levels or waste.

For example, company 8 is primarily focused on complying with regulations with regard to its operations, but is taking a much more aggressive approach with regard to its products. The company stays very well informed about the types of chemical included in its products and is attempting to reformulate any product that contains chemicals that require special permits. For example, when chlorofluorocarbons (CFCs) were banned, the company had to find replacements for the propellants in its aerosol spray paints. This strategy helps the company to keep its compliance costs down since the company avoids using certain chemicals, thus avoiding the costs of obtaining permits and disposing of hazardous wastes. The company has not faced any major environmental problems related to its business activities.

Cluster 4 companies have been identified as lacking the following characteristics:

- Providing ongoing education and training for employees to effectively deal with day-to-day environmental responsibilities as well as environmental emergencies
- Complying with and exceeding requirements of all applicable environment-related laws and regulations
- Adopting their own environmental quality standards in cases where existing laws and regulations are not adequate

- Communicating their commitment to environmental quality to their employees, shareholders, suppliers, customers and local communities in which they operate
- Recognising and responding to the community's questions about their operations
- Actively participating with government agencies and other appropriate groups to ensure that the development and implementation of environmental policies, laws, regulations and practices serve the public interest and are based on sound scientific judgement
- Regularly assessing and reporting to management and board of directors on the status of their compliance with this policy and with environmental laws and regulations

Based on the analysis of the four different clusters, the corporate greening response pattern shown in Table 4 is produced. Cluster analysis identified four different groups of companies. These are labelled as lagging, defensive compliance, environmentally sensitive and proactive catalyst. Lagging indicates a minimum level of corporate greening while proactive catalyst refers to a maximum level of corporate greening in given cases. Only one company is labelled as lagging while the majority of companies are positioned as defensive compliance. Some companies are situated in environmentally sensitive and proactive catalyst.

Table 4. Four patterns of corporate greening response and its characteristics

Cluster	Label	Characteristics
1	Lagging	• Fines and penalty records are the company's experience with environmental issues. • Main focus is on compliance of regulations. • Lack of top-management commitment • Environmental issues are a regulatory burden rather than strategic issues. • There is no potential benefit, only cost for environmental investment.
4	Defensive compliance	• To comply with requirements of all applicable environment-related laws and regulations • The company does not view green issues as strategically important. • Environmental investment is for cost-effectiveness.
2	Environmentally sensitive	• The company views environmental issues as strategically important. • All plant sites meet regulatory compliance. The company views early investment in

Cluster	Label	Characteristics
		environmental protection or improvement as cost-saving or even profit-making opportunities in the near future.
		• Full usage of environmental risk assessment for environmental investment
3	Proactive catalyst	• Green issues are viewed as strategically important.
		• There is high top-management commitment and support.
		• There is a belief that early investment saves costs and makes profits.
		• There is a direct link between green issues and corporate image and reputation.
		• Continuous investment in environmental protection and technology

8.   CONCLUSION

This chapter began with a criticism of mainstream management theory, which largely ignores environmental and ecological issues. In order to understand corporate environmental management, we studied top management's commitment and its impact on corporate environmental responses and strategies. Based on the findings from the study, the following conclusions can be drawn.

First, few companies are positioned in the 'lagging' type of corporate environmental management. The common characteristic of lagging companies is that top executives view 'green' issues as a serious regulatory burden or threat. Thus, companies in the 'lagging' category try to meet the minimum level of regulatory legislation.

Second, the majority of Korean chemical companies are situated in 'defensive compliance'. Since the characteristic of this category is complying with legislation while avoiding extra cost, many companies do still pay attention to regulations rather than identify new business or market opportunities. In this case, top executives do not consider green issues as new opportunities. Rather, they think of these issues as extra costs.

Third, some leading companies are positioned as 'environmentally sensitive' or 'proactive catalyst'. The main characteristic of these companies is looking for new business opportunities through corporate environmental management. In other words, achieving leadership and competitive edge in corporate greening will bring better environmental and financial performance. In addition, continuous commitment and improvement is another main characteristic in these two groups. The main difference between the two groups is dependent on explicit environmental goals as a main business goal. The 'environmentally sensitive' group has rather business-oriented goals while the 'proactive catalyst' group has more balanced environmental and financial goals.

REFERENCES

Arthur D. Little (1989) 'A Survey of Executives and Environmental Managers', in: Arthur D. Little (Ed.): *Hitting the Green Wall*. London: Arthur D. Little.

Banerjee, S.B. (2001) 'Corporate Environmental Strategies and Actions', *Management Decision* Vol. 39 No. 1: 36-44.

Bank of Korea (2001) *Industrial Statistics*. Seoul: Bank of Korea.

Brockhoff, K., Chakrabarti, A. and Kirchgeorg, M. (1999) 'Corporate Strategies in Environmental Management', *Research Technology Management* July/August 1999: 26-30.

Doty, D. and Glick, H. (1994) 'Typologies as a Unique Form of Theory Building: Toward Improved Understanding and Modeling', *Academy of Management Review* Vol. 19 No. 2: 230-251.

Edwards, D. (1998) *The Link between Company Environmental and Financial Performance*. London: Earthscan Publications.

Edwards, P., Birkin, F. and Woodward, D. (2002) 'Financial Comparability and Environmental Diversity: An International Context', *Business Strategy and the Environment* Vol. 11 No. 6: 343-359.

Ghobadian, A., Viney, H., Liu, J. and James, P. (1998) 'Extending Linear Approaches to Mapping Corporate Environmental Behaviour', *Business Strategy and the Environment* Vol. 7 No. 1: 13-23.

Hambrick, C. (1983) 'Some Tests of the Effectiveness and Functional Attributes of Miles and Snow's Strategic Type', *Academy of Management Journal* No. 26: 5-26.

Hawken, P. (1993) *The Ecology of Commerce*. New York: HarperCollins.

Hawken, P., Lovins, A. and Lovins, L.H. (1999) *Natural Capitalism: The Next Industrial Revolution*. London: Earthscan Publications.

Hoffman, A. (1997) *From Hersey to Dogma: An Institutional History of Corporate Environmentalism*. San Francisco: New Lexington.

Hunt, C. and Auster, E. (1990) 'Proactive Environmental Management: Avoiding the Toxic Trap', *Sloan Management Review* Vol. 31 No. 2: 7-18.

Ingram, R. and Frazier, K. (1980) 'Environmental Performance and Corporate Disclosure', *Journal of Accounting Research* No. 187: 614-622.

Jaffe, B., Peterson, R., Portney, R. and Stavins, R. (1995) 'Environmental Regulation and the Competitiveness of US Manufacturing: What Does the Evidence Tell Us?', *Journal of Economic Literature* No. 33: 132-163.

Klassen, D. and McLaughlin, P. (1996) 'The Impact of Environmental Management on Firm Performance', *Management Science* Vol. 42 No. 8: 1,199-1,214.

Lee, K.-H. (2001) *Towards Sustainable Development: A Business Management Perspective on 'Greening' in the Korean Chemical Industry*. PhD thesis; Stirling, UK: Stirling Business School, University of Stirling.

Miles, E. and Snow, C. (1978) *Organizational Strategy, Structure and Process*. New York: McGraw-Hill.

Miles, M. and Huberman, A. (1994) *Qualitative Data Analysis*. London: Sage.

Miller, D. and Friesen, H. (1983) 'Strategy-making and Environment: The Third Link', *Strategic Management Journal* No. 4: 221-235.

Porter, M.E. (1980) *The Competitive Advantage of Nations*. New York: The Free Press.

Porter, M.E. and van der Linde, C. (1995a) 'Green and Competitive: Ending the Stalemate', *Harvard Business Review* Vol. 73 No. 5: 120-134.

Porter, M.E. and van der Linde, C. (1995b) 'Toward a New Conception of the Environment–Competitiveness Relationship', *Journal of Economic Perspectives* Vol. 9 No. 4: 97-118.

Post, J. and Altman, B. (1992) 'Models of Corporate Greening: How Corporate Social Policy and Organizational Learning Inform Leading-edge Environmental Management', *Research in Corporate Social Performance and Policy* No. 13: 3-29.

Post, J. and Altman, B. (1994) 'Managing the Environmental Change Process: Barriers and Opportunities', *Journal of Organizational Change Management* Vol. 7 No. 4: 64-81.

Rich, P. (1992) 'The Organizational Taxonomy: Definition and Design', *Academy of Management Review* No. 17: 758-81.

Roome, N. (1992) 'Developing Environmental Management Strategies', *Business Strategy and the Environment* Vol. 1 No. 1: 11-24.

Sadgrove, K. (1992) *The Green Guide to Profitable Management*. London: Gower.

Scallon, M. and Sten, M.J. (1996) 'Environmental Positioning for the Future: A Review of 36 Leading Companies in the Pacific Northwest Region of the United States of America', *Greener Management International* Issue 13 (January 1996): 49-65.

Schmidheiny, S. (1992) *Changing Course: A Global Business Perspective on Development and the Environment*. Cambridge, MA: The MIT Press.

Shrivastava, P. (1995) 'Ecocentric Management for a Risk Society', *Academy of Management Review* Vol. 20 No. 1: 118-137.

Stanwick, P. and S. Stanwick (1998) 'The Relationship between Corporate Social Performance, and Organizational Size, Financial Performance, and Environmental Performance: An Empirical Examination', *Journal of Business Ethics* Vol. 17 No. 2: 195-204.

Stead, W. and Stead, J. (1995) *Management for a Small Planet*. London: Sage.

Tan, J. (1996) 'Regulatory Environment and Strategic Orientations: A Study of Chinese Private Entrepreneurs', *Entrepreneurship: Theory and Practice* No. 1: 31-44.

Thomas, A. and Tonks, I. (1999) 'Corporate Environmental Policy and Abnormal Stock Price Returns: An Empirical Investigation'. Proceedings of the *1999 Eco-Management and Auditing Conference*, University of Leeds, UK, 1–2 July 1999. Leeds: ERP Environment, 335-344.

Toms, S. (2000) *Environmental Management, Environmental Accounting and Financial Performance*. London: CIMA.

Venkatraman, N. and Prescott, E. (1990) 'Environment–Strategy Coalignment: An Empirical Test of its Performance Implications', *Strategic Management Journal* No. 11: 1-23.

Wagner, M. (2001) *A Review of Empirical Studies Concerning the Relationship between Environmental and Economic Performance: What Does the Evidence Tell Us?*. Lüneburg: Centre for Sustainability Management.

Walley, N. and Whitehead, B. (1994) 'It's Not Easy Being Green', *Harvard Business Review* Vol. 72 No. 3: 36-44.

Winn, M. and Angell, A. (2000) 'Towards a Process Model of Corporate Greening', *Organization Studies* Vol. 21 No. 6: 1,119-1,147.

Wright, P., Kroll, M., Pray, B. and Lado, A. (1995) 'Strategic Orientations, Competitive Advantage and Business Performance', *Journal of Business Research* No. 33: 143-151.

Appendix 1. Evaluation indicators and company ratings

Evaluation indicator	Companies														
	1	2	3	4	5	6	7	8	9	10	11	12	13	14	15
1. Top-level responsibility	2	2	1.5	2	1.5	2	2	2	1.5	2	2	2	2	2	2
2. Environmental policy	0.5	1	0.5	1	0.5	0.5	0.5	0.5	0.5	0.5	0.5	0.5	0.5	1	1
3. Stakeholder involvement	1	1	0.4	1.2	1	1.2	0.5	0.6	1.3	1.3	1.2	1.2	1.3	1.4	1.5
4. Strategic planning	0.25	0.5	0.25	0.25	0.25	0.25	0.25	0.25	0.25	0.25	0.25	0.25	0.25	0.25	0.5
5. Environmental performance	0.35	0.35	0	0.35	0.1	0.35	0.1	0.35	0.35	0.35	0.35	0.35	0.35	0.35	0.35
6. Environmental report	0.2	0.2	0	0.2	0	0.2	0	0.2	0.2	0.2	0.2	0.2	0.2	0.2	0.2
7. Environmental management system	1.7	1.3	0.2	1.3	1.1	1.3	1.3	1.1	1.3	1.3	1.1	1.1	1.3	1.3	1.1
8. Environmental standard	1.1	1.3	0	1.3	1.1	1.3	1.1	1.1	1.1	1.1	1.1	1.1	1.1	1.1	1.1
9. Record of fine and penalty	1	1	0.25	1	1	1	1	1	1	1	1	1	1	1	1
10. Environmental liability	0	0	0	0	0	0	0	0	0	0	0	0	0	0	0
11. Eco-product	0.5	0.5	0	2	0.5	1	0.5	0	2	0.5	0	2	2	2	2
Total	8.6	9.15	3.1	10.6	7.05	9.1	7.25	7.1	9.5	8.5	7.7	9.7	10	10.6	10.75

Appendix 2. Dimensions of corporate greening

Company	Dimensions of corporate greening Corporate greening themes		
	Top management's commitment	Strategic importance of green issues	Operational performance of green issues
1	2.5	1.25	4.85
2	3	1.5	4.65
3	2	0.65	0.45
4	3	1.45	6.15
5	2	1.25	3.8
6	2.5	1.45	5.15
7	2.5	0.75	4.0
8	2.5	0.85	3.75
9	2.5	1.55	5.95
10	2.5	1.55	4.45
11	2.5	1.45	3.75
12	2.5	1.45	5.75
13	2.5	1.55	5.95
14	3	1.65	5.95
15	3	2.0	5.75

ECOPRENEURSHIP AND COMPETITIVE STRATEGIES

Striving for Market Leadership by Promoting Sustainability

Holger Petersen
Umweltbank Nürnberg and Centre for Sustainability Management (CSM), University of Lüneburg, Germany

Abstract: Ecopreneurship combines entrepreneurship with ecological goals. It is about gaining competitive advantage with an entrepreneurial spirit and approach. The question is: what kind of competitive strategies do successful green entrepreneurs use and how are they able to combine environmental values with economic success? This chapter gives a conceptual and empirical overview of competitive strategies of ecopreneurs.

1. COMPETITIVE ADVANTAGES OF ECOPRENEURS: CREATING VALUE OUT OF GREEN IDEAS

Companies use a variety of general strategies to achieve competitive advantages. On the one hand, these strategies are shaped by the unique characters, ideas, experiences and personal aims of individual decision-makers. On the other hand, competitive strategies have to participate in general developments that continuously generate new consumer needs and business opportunities. Consequently, companies are challenged to realise general opportunities in a unique way of creating value (Porter 1997).

A key development at present is the drive for sustainability. In the last three decades in particular, an increasing number of entrepreneurs have adopted environmentalists' ideas and claims against industry to place innovations in the market. These ecopreneurs base their success partly on assumptions that differ from those of conventional executives (Isaak 1999; Larson 2000; Schaltegger and Petersen 2002; Schaper 2003; Schick *et al.*

2003). This chapter discusses strategic opportunities to achieve competitive advantages through an ecopreneurship lens.

An explorative survey of 64 German, Austrian and Swiss companies produced empirical results explaining essential competitive advantages that ecopreneurs can attain on their way to market leadership. Representatives of these companies satisfied two conditions. First, they have made solutions for ecological problems their core business and, secondly, they are market leaders in specialised sectors for ecological food, clothes, body-care, mobility, regenerative energy, packing, building materials or other products. Such companies are referred to as 'sustainable champions'. Sustainable champions are predominantly, small- and medium-sized enterprises (SMEs) founded within the last three decades and managed by successful ecopreneurs. Most of them occupy small but increasingly international market niches (Petersen 2003). Typical examples are Enercon (wind turbines), Auro Naturfarben (natural paints), Dennree (logistics for ecological food) or Remei (textiles).

The next section outlines the parameters of a business definition, showing differences between a 'green' and a conventional business. An explorative study is then introduced, including its methods and key findings. The subsequent section classifies the leading ecological ideas that inspired ecopreneurs to found their business and explains the importance of a number of competitive advantages on the route to market leadership. In accordance with the three parameters of a business definition, the final section follows up the development of competitive advantages from the outset.

2. STARTING WITH A BUSINESS DEFINITION

A strategy to achieve competitive advantages starts with a business definition outlining a business field. Abell (1980) suggested considering three dimensions of a business definition:

- Functions—what are the benefits of a product or service for the customers?
- Technology—which methods, skills and instruments are used to realise the benefit?
- Customer groups—who is willing to pay an attractive price for the benefit?

Each dimension enables a company to develop competitive advantages. It may be through the eminent ability to create products including a new set of benefits, or a leading technological position, or excellent access and nearness to attractive customer groups (Treacy and Wiersema 1993). Advantages such as these are useful anchors on which to gradually define, develop and widen a business. Those planning for the future should proceed from the dimension that is dominant for their business success (Abell 1980). Possible paths are shown in Figure 1.

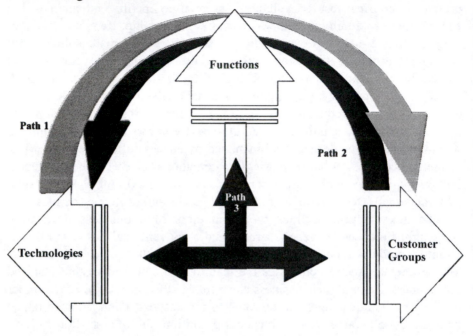

Figure 1. Paths to outline a business field (Source: Petersen 2003:238)

If an enterprise controls an innovative technology, it is reasonable to follow Path 1 in Figure 1. A technology is generally able to fulfil different functions; for example, a fuel cell is useful for mobility or to provide electricity for appliances. After fixing the main function of their technology, entrepreneurs look for customer groups that their products will appeal to (Prahalad and Hamel 1990).

Path 2 starts, in the opposite way, from a customer group. If customers generally prefer a specialist supplier or a trademark, an entrepreneur can take advantage of this to widen the assortment of products available on the market. A key question, especially for a chain of shops or a mail order business, may be (Hanan 1974): what other needs of the customers are worth thinking about? Having explored some additional needs, a company should be able to realise the benefits through the use of suitable techniques and skills.

Paths 1 and 2 are favourable approaches for enterprises that are already established in the market. In both cases, a company connects technological opportunities with the lifestyle of a customer group (Hamel and Prahalad 1994). The aim on its path will be the generation of higher benefits by crossing the functional dimension (shown in the middle of Figure 1). However, people developing a start-up company do not normally have superior resources or competitive advantages such as a leading technology or a cultivated access to customers at their disposal. They have to follow Path 3, starting from an individual's perspective onto the functional dimension. The only advantages that start-ups are normally equipped with are based on the skills of their founders (Schick *et al.* 2003); first, the possession of an original but practical idea about how to combine attractive benefits and, secondly, the ability to make it work.

What does all this mean for an ecopreneur's way of business and how does it differ from conventional companies? Like every entrepreneur, an ecopreneur is striving for innovation and for increased sales with higher benefits from a customer group willing to pay for convincing solutions (Timmons 1986). Starting with functions, conventional entrepreneurs want to make profits by creating individual benefits for their customers. Ecopreneurs also want to create public benefits. They care about ecological sustainability—a public 'good'. Their special task is to extract private benefits from a public 'good' by promoting sustainability. Such benefits can be associated with healthcare, wellness, status, ethical sense, cost savings, etc. In this way, solutions for customers' problems are combined with solutions for the 'free rider' problem. Attractive additional benefits have to be attainable for people who are willing to pay for them.

What does it mean for the technology dimension? Ecopreneurs use agricultural, chemical, biological or physical knowledge ranging from a low-tech to a high-tech level. There are thousands of possibilities but one demand—production is part of the product. To sell ecological goods means also having production methods that are either non-polluting or less-polluting. For example, organic crops are desirable because of their organic cultivation. The special challenge is not only to realise and to control eco-efficient methods but also to bring transparency to them for the customer. Thus, ecopreneurs also need methods to ensure and to demonstrate the ecological advantage of the technologies used to produce their products.

The third dimension refers to customers. At the beginning, ecopreneurs are pioneers, ahead of the mass market. Without a hard core of 'pioneer' customers, they will walk alone for a short while until they run out of cash. Like ecopreneurs, 'pioneer' customers are not only curious and conscious of the environment, but also convinced of their self-effectiveness, safe in the knowledge that general progress is a result of many small individual steps. As an active part of the environmental movement, many ecopreneurs begin with a personal network of equally minded people and with an affinity to their customers. Out of these roots, they develop a friendly relationship with their customers, who share their visions and ethical values (Ripsas 1999).

This community of pioneer customers has four functions. The first is to pay the bill. Secondly, they give advice on how to improve products and services. Their third function is to spread news of an innovation by word of mouth to other customers and, ultimately if possible, to the mass market. In the best scenario, these pioneer customers constitute a 'happy elite', who cultivate a lifestyle to which many people aspire. The task for ecopreneurs may be to make the happiness of this 'elite' available and attainable for everyone. The fourth and final function of pioneer customers is to remain loyal even if the boom seems to be over and business with more opportunistic customers is poor for a while.

3.   EXPLORATIVE STUDY

This section outlines the measurement, analysis and results of the explorative survey of 64 German, Austrian and Swiss companies mentioned in Section 1. It focuses on the following questions:
*   What business ideas have incited ecopreneurs?
*   What competitive advantages are essential for a successful turnover?

3.1   Measurement and Analysis

A total of 126 companies from Germany, Austria and Switzerland were asked to outline their market position and competitive advantages. These selected companies appeared to fulfil the following criteria:
*   The company produces or sells innovative products and services that contribute to solving or reducing environmental problems.
*   These products and services are core business.
*   The company is a leader in its sector.

Companies matching these criteria were designated 'sustainable champions'. Of the 126 companies contacted, 74 agreed to complete a short questionnaire. Of the 74 respondents, 64 confirmed that their company saw themselves as having an ecological core business and that they had reached the highest turnover in their market sector—absolutely or together with one or two similar-sized competitors. Only data from these selected 64 'sustainable champions' was used in the subsequent analysis.

The questionnaire gathered information about the:
*   Number of employees
*   Market position
*   Business definition
*   Competitive advantages

Twelve possible advantages were given (see Table 1 in Section 3.4). This selection corresponds to similar questionnaires (e.g. Schmitt 1997:212) and to lists published in management literature relevant to the subject (e.g. Thürbach 1991:110). Companies were asked to answer the question using a scale with six levels (see Section 3.4). In most cases, it was answered by senior managers. Complementary to the questionnaire, the websites of the chosen companies provided information about their innovations and history.

In order to examine the received data, the companies were classified. In the first instance, this classification was intended to demonstrate the general characteristics of the chosen sample such as size, age or internationalisation (see Section 3.2). In addition, the companies where divided into groups of leading ecological ideas (see Section 3.3). The next step involved the investigation of competitive advantages. For this purpose, the average importance of each given advantage was determined. A varimax rotated factor analysis was then run to reduce the answers to the essential competitive advantages of ecopreneurship. The results are shown in Section 3.4.

3.2   General Findings

The sustainable champions in Germany, Austria and Switzerland that responded to the survey were engaged in a wide variety of industries. Most of them operated in industries such as nutrition (N = 12), followed by mechanical engineering (N = 11) and retail (N = 7). Two-thirds were from the manufacturing sector and about a third from the service sector. Most of the companies had been operating for less than 20 years; half were founded in 1985 or later. They were predominantly small or medium in size. Size as reflected by the number of employees ranged from two to 15,000 with a median of 60.

The size of a company is connected with its level of internationalisation. A majority (N=36) of the sustainable champions were selling goods internationally and 11 claimed a leading position in the world market. A quarter (N=15) of them were leaders in the European market. More than half of the participating companies (N=34) saw themselves in a leading position at a national level, though many were also selling goods to other countries. Regional market leaders (N=4) where only accepted as 'sustainable champions' in a small number of business fields with fragmented structures such as car sharing, tool hire service or organic bakery.

3.3   Business Ideas

The four main patterns revealed by the survey are summarised in Figure 2. Depending on their technical skills and their position in the value chain, ecopreneurs can normally be distinguished according to how they follow the ideas of 'nature', 'regeneration', 'thrift' or 'conservation'.

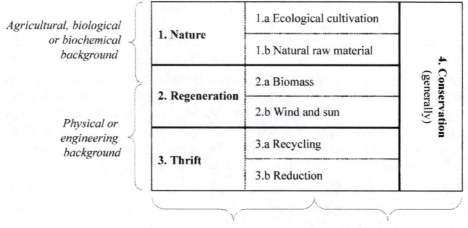

Figure 2. Leading ideas of ecopreneurs (Source: Petersen 2003:121)

The most frequent issue adopted by the questioned sustainable champions (39%) was the idea of 'nature'. This assumes the avoidance of synthetic materials, especially synthetic fertilisers and pesticides. Ecopreneurs are challenged to replace these synthetic materials with natural ones—starting off in agriculture and afterwards in the manufacturing of food, clothes, soaps, cosmetics, furniture, paints, building materials, etc. Companies such as Auro Naturfarben or Hess Natur introduce their main idea in their name. Toxicity to humans is an essential argument for customers to buy only natural articles; in particular, those suffering from allergies often prefer natural products. But there are other less tangible benefits as shaping a lifestyle including a better taste, aesthetic preference and emotional attachment to nature.

The second idea refers to the regeneration of transformed energy and materials. Some promoters of 'regeneration' use chemical and engineering knowledge to explore the feasibility of using biomass (2.a) as a raw material for packaging, as a source of heat and electricity, or as a substitute for diesel fuel. The use of biomass helps to solve waste problems by putting materials back into circulation. Another possibility is the transformation of wind and sun energy (2.b) into useful energy through the invention and use of new engineering methods. In each case, there is an ecological benefit by using renewable sources and by reducing greenhouse gas emissions to atmosphere.

There are some private benefits too. For example, putting a solar cell on the roof installs a status symbol of science, wealth and personal independence. Packing made out of starch is suitable for composting. Technical standards, learning effects and economies of scale, however, are actually not sufficient to generate competitive advantages compared with conventional products in many cases. In such cases, ecopreneurs and customers have to look for financial incentives offered by governments, e.g. lower taxes for regenerative fuel or subsidies for buying solar cells. Sometimes, regenerative energies and products can only be spread effectively by ecopreneurs and government working together (their strategies have to mesh with each other).

The third leading idea, 'thrift', is based on opportunities to save primary raw materials. Companies that represent this idea sell either products made out of recycled materials and remanufactured scrap (3.a) or products and services that lead to a significant reduction in material and energy use (3.b), e.g. energy efficient domestic appliances or car-sharing. Most of the private benefits are economic incentives—which not only environmentalists are interested in. Additionally some enterprises that are engaged in trading or a service business have adopted the idea of 'conservation' in a more general way. For example, mail order houses, banks and consultancies that have been founded to promote ways of doing business leading to sustainability.

3.4 Competitive Advantages

A critical matter for strategic planning is the question: which advantages are decisive for increasing sales? To determine the relevance of 12 possible advantages, respondents were asked to estimate the importance for their market success on a scale from 1 (not important) to 6 (really important). The average values in Table 1 illustrate the importance of each one.

This analysis suggests that 'credibility' and 'repute of the company' are most important for sustainable champions, followed by 'uniqueness of supply'. The analysis also indicates that 'ecological performance of supplies', 'ability to set trends', 'cultivated relationships to customers', 'competent after-sales services' and the 'ability to realise new product ideas' are also relevant. 'Well-known brand names', 'comfortable access to supply' and 'technological superiority' have reached a lower level of persuasive power. But, as expected, the importance of these items depends on the general characteristics of the companies. Brand names, for example, are more important for bigger companies and the relevance of technological superiority is a matter for industrial sectors. 'Low prices' are not relevant for most of the sustainable champions in the survey.

Table 1. Relative importance of given competitive advantages

Competitive advantage	Importance for market success 1 = not important; 6 = really important	
	Mean	Standard deviation
Credibility	5.2	1.1
Reputation of the company	5.0	1.1
Uniqueness of supply	4.8	1.3
Best ecological performance	4.6	1.4
Ability to set trends	4.6	1.4
Good customer relationships	4.6	1.2
Competent after-sales services	4.5	1.4
Ability to realise new product ideas	4.5	1.3
Well-known brand names	4.2	**1.6**
Comfortable access to supply	4.0	1.4
Technological superiority	3.9	**1.7**
Low prices	2,8	**1,6**

In order to reduce the number of items, the data were subjected to a factor analysis (Table 2). Items with a loading >0.5 belong to the according factor.

Table 2. Factor analysis of competitive advantages

	Loading				
	Factor 1 *Reputation*	**Factor 2** *Creativity*	**Factor 3** *Exclusivity*	**Factor 4** *Nearness to company*	**Factor 5** *Competence*
Reputation of the company	**0.903**	0.184	0.069	0.093	0.150
Credibility	**0.820**	-0.099	0.355	0.207	0.089
Well-known brand names	**0.697**	0.418	0.006	-0.283	-0.005
Ability to set trends	0.183	**0.898**	-0.016	0.061	0.176
Ability to realise product ideas	0.047	**0.857**	0.227	0.156	0.105
Low prices	-0.169	0.020	**-0.833**	0.230	-0.005
Uniqueness of supply	0.070	0.245	**0.782**	0.149	0.078

	Loading				
	Factor 1 *Reputation*	**Factor 2** *Creativity*	**Factor 3** *Exclusivity*	**Factor 4** *Nearness to company*	**Factor 5** *Competence*
Comfortable access to supply	-0.073	0.002	-0.170	**0.865**	0.041
Good relationships to customers	0.456	0.242	0.241	**0.608**	-0.119
Technological superiority	0.027	0.180	0.100	-0.083	**0.899**
Competent after-sales services	0.398	0.190	-0.016	0.478	**0.609**
Best ecological performance	0.340	0.477	0.423	-0.165	0.218

Loadings with a factor >0.5 are shown in bold.

Five factors collectively account for 78% of the variance in the data. Based on the according items, these were interpreted as 'reputation', 'creativity', 'exclusivity', 'nearness to customers' and 'technical competence'. 'Best ecological performance' is the only item that failed to load onto any factor (i.e. no value exceeded 0.5). In addition, only one high loading is negative; together with uniqueness, exclusive goods do not to have low prices.

The final stage of the analysis is to look at the correlation between the importance of competitive advantages and the leading ideas of green business (Table 3). Given the topic of this book, the importance of 'best ecological performance' is a special point of interest.

Table 3. Importance of 'best ecological performance' for market success

Leading ideas	Best Ecological Performance		
	Mean	**N**	**Standard deviation**
Nature	5.2	25	1.1
Regeneration	4.4	16	1.5
Thrift	3.8	16	1.4
Conservation	5.3	7	0.8
Altogether	4.6	64	1.4

The survey results show that ecopreneurs following the ideas of 'conservation and 'nature' are mostly entitled to the claim high ecological quality for their business performance. The idea of 'regeneration' seems to contain a lower and 'thrift' the lowest demand on ecological performance.

Possible reasons for this have already been mentioned in Section 3.3. The ideas of 'conservation' and 'nature' take the integrated view of ecological aims for granted. Arguments for customers to buy such products are based on reduced toxicity and on lifestyle principles. It is not therefore not surprising that the importance of 'uniqueness' is above average for those companies. The idea of 'thrift' is driven by cost savings—a feature that attracts not only environmentalists.

Although these findings are instructive, they represent just a snapshot. The next section deals with the development of competitive advantages—a key challenge for ecopreneurs (see Porter 1991).

4. PATHS TO COMPETITIVENESS

This section outlines strategies on how to occupy and manage new business fields, starting from the foundation of a 'green' enterprise up to an established market position.

The only advantages with which 'green' start-ups are normally equipped with depend on having original but practical ideas on how to combine attractive benefits with a solution to environmental problems and the ability to make it work. Both the unique idea and its realisation depend on the characteristics of ecopreneurs, who can obtain their inspiration not only from their profession but also from their private lives. Promising ideas often result from a mental connection between professional and private experiences. After finding a gap in the market, ecopreneurs are challenged to turn it into a profitable niche by creating an innovation. In particular, this will include an additional benefit for customers who are interested in environmental conservation.

Sooner or later, every good business idea meets with resistance. On the one hand, ecopreneurs have to solve technical and organisational problems—first during the development of new products to market maturity and, afterwards, when production begins. They also have to ensure that their products and production methods have a real ecological advantage. On the other hand, ecopreneurs have to open the markets—capital markets as well as markets for goods. They face the challenge of convincing investors such as 'business angels' (venture capitalists) and 'launching customers' (first customers) of their performance and opportunities. As mentioned before, it is helpful at that point to start with a personal network and with affinity to the favoured customers. Such relationships often result from earlier participation in conversation projects or actions.

After the first steps are taken, a start-up seeks shelter in its occupied niche from possible competitors. This niche may be very special. As long as a couple of loyal pioneer customers agree to pay prices above the production and transaction cost, there is a basis of subsistence. And, as long as the niche is small and insignificant for large-scale enterprises, there is little danger of being ousted from the market by imitators. For the present, creativity of action and exclusivity of unique supplies offer sufficient reasons to stay in the niche.

Afterwards, when business is going well, there is time to widen it gradually by adding further products supplies and modifications (Simon 1996:66). But the more an enterprise turns to expansion, the more it attracts competitors—and the more it has to develop additional competitive advantages. The Dutch company Yarrah, for example, has grown into a considerable international supplier of organic pet food within only a few years. Masterfoods Limited, the producer of Whiskas® and a European market leader for conventional pet food, could not ignore this threat any longer and is now developing its own organic product range to reclaim its lost share of the market.

How to protect the market position in comparable situations of competition? Many health food shops listed Yarrah's organic pet food are soon as it was ready for the market; they did not sell Whiskas because such shops tend to avoid brand names that are readily available in conventional supermarkets. Many customers have got used to buying Yarrah food for their pet. As customers' trust in Yarrah organic pet food increased, the brand name has become more and more well-known. Thus, Yarrah has built up two additional advantages— reputation and a protected access to customers.

This company has probably improved its core competence for producing and commercialising pet food, but that should not be a real advantage over well- skilled suppliers such as Masterfoods. In contrast, enterprises in other industries such as Enercon or Auro Natufarben have reached technical superiority because multinational companies such as FKI or BASF ignored the emerging industries of wind and natural chemistry, respectively, for too long. Their only chance to make up ground in a short time is to take possession of these pioneers. This is probably the reason why FKI acquired DeWind, another German supplier of wind turbines.

5. CONCLUSION

In addition to creativity and exclusivity of unique supplies, ecopreneurs strive for three general advantages:
- Reputation

- Protected access or nearness to customers
- Technical superiority.

This consideration corresponds to the investigation of sustainable champions in the survey reported in this chapter. These advantages increase the margin allowing higher prices. It is also possible to gain advantages through low prices, but this is not typical of sustainable champions.

However, the most important advantage of sustainable champions seems to be reputation. This is based on:
- Credibility
- Confidence in a company
- The ecological quality of its supply
- Brand names
- The personal reputation of a well-known ecopreneur (often but not always)

Reputation is an essential advantage to underline technological superiority as well as nearness to customers. Conventional entrepreneurs probably also value the good reputation of their products too. However, reputation is much more essential if customers cannot inspect the ecological quality of a product by taking a close look at it (Bech-Larsen and Grunert 2001). This is especially true if ecopreneurs follow the leading ideas of 'nature' or 'conservation', as these are mostly linked to the ecological quality of their business performance. Although the ecological performance of ecopreneurs following the ideas of 'regeneration or 'thrift' are lower, every business idea includes essential potentials for sustainability.

REFERENCES

Abell, D.F. (1980): *Defining the Business: The Starting Point of Strategic Planning*. Englewood Cliffs, New Jersey: Prentice-Hall.

Bech-Larsen, T. and Grunert, K.G. (2001): 'Konsumentscheidung bei Vertrauenseigenschaften: Eine Untersuchung am Beispiel des Kaufes von ökologischen Lebensmitteln in Deutschland und Dänemark', *Marketing ZFP* Vol. 3, 188-197.

Hamel, G. and Prahalad, C.K. (1994): *Competing for the Future*. Harvard: Harvard Business School Press.

Hanan, M. (1974): 'Reorganise Your Company around its Markets', *Harvard Business Review* November/December, 63-74.

Isaak, R. (1999): *Green Logic: Ecopreneurship, Theory and Ethics*. West Hartford: Kumarian Press.

Larson, A.L. (2000): 'Sustainable Innovation through an Entrepreneurship Lense', *Business Strategy and the Environment* Vol. 9, 304-317.

Petersen, H. (2003): *Ecopreneurship und Wettbewerbsstrategie: Verbreitung ökologischer Innovationen auf Grundlage von Wettbewerbsvorteilen*. Marburg: Metropolis.

Porter, M.E. (1991): 'Towards a Dynamic Theory of Strategy', *Strategic Management Journal* Vol. 12, 95-117.

Porter, M.E. (1997): 'Nur Strategie sichert auf Dauer hohe Erträge', *Harvard Business Manager* Vol. 3, 42-58 (Translation of: 'What is Strategy?', *Harvard Business Review*, November/December 1996).

Prahalad, C.K. and Hamel, G. (1990): 'The Core Competence of the Corporation', *Harvard Business Review* May/June, 79-91.

Ripsas, S. (1999): *Unternehmensgründung im Umweltschutz* (Discussion Paper No. Po1-501). Berlin: Wissenschaftszentrums Berlin (WZB).

Schaltegger, S. and Petersen, H. (2001): *Ecopreneurship: Konzept und Typologie* (Reihe: Analysen zum Rio Management Forum 2000). Luzern: RIO Impuls.

Schaper, M. (2003): 'The Essence of Ecopreneurship', *Greener Management International* Theme Issue: Environmental Entrepreneurship, 26-30.

Schick, H., Marxen, S. and Freimann, J. (2003): 'Sustainability Issues for Start-up Entrepreneurs', *Greener Management International* Theme Issue: Environmental Entrepreneurship, 59-70.

Schmitt, E. (1997): *Strategien mittelständischer Welt- und Europamarktführer*. Wiesbaden: Gabler.

Simon, H. (1996): *Die heimlichen Gewinner: Die Erfolgsstrategien unbekannter Weltmarktführer*. Frankfurt am Main: Campus.

Thürbach, R.-P. (1991): 'Mittelständisches Überlegenheitspotential sichern und ausbauen', in: Jahn, E. (Ed.): *Auf der Suche nach Erfolgspotentialen*. Stuttgart: Schäffer-Poeschel, 95-111.

Timmons, J. (1986): 'Growing Up Big', in: Sexton, D. and Smilor, R. (Ed.) *The Art and Science of Entrepreneurship*. Cambridge: Ballinger, 153-167.

Treacy, M. and Wiersema, F. (1993): 'Drei Wege zur Marktführerschaft', *Harvard Business Manager* Vol. 3, 123-131 (Translation of: 'Customer Intimacy and other Value Disciplines', *Harvard Business Review* January/ February 1993).

BUILDING A BUSINESS CASE FOR CORPORATE SUSTAINABILITY

Ulrich Steger
Institute for Management Development (IMD), Lausanne, Switzerland

Abstract: This chapter looks at evidence to support the business case for sustainability. Based on a sustainable business model, the real drivers for corporations becoming more sustainable are searched for. The same 'chicken and egg' question comes back again and again: are companies more successful because they are run in a sustainable manner or is it that already successful companies are those that apply sustainability successfully too? Is there a new breed of CEOs who are less driven by short-term and who look to the longer-term, seeking to build a solid reputation on the basis of a sustainable approach? What are the tools that currently exist to measure the direct and indirect effects of sustainability on the bottom line?

1. RESEARCH NEEDS AND OBJECTIVES

The evidence of the impact of corporate actions for sustainable development on the financial bottom line is highly inconclusive (Griffin and Mahon 1997; Pava and Krausz 1996; Wagner *et al.* 2002; Wagner and Schaltegger 2003). Basically, three streams can be identified:

- The first, which is more political and normative, claims a 'win–win–win' (Elkington 1994) reality by referring to best practice companies. However, as the role models run into financial difficulties—as was experienced with examples such as The Body Shop, Levis and Interface—the arguments become less compelling.
- The second stream, predominantly a US-driven approach, tries to establish empirical evidence based on correlations (e.g. Aupperle *et al.* 1985;

Davidson III *et al.* 1990; McGuire *et al.* 1988; Moore 2001). Results differ widely depending on measures, time frames and assumptions.

- The third group assumes, pragmatically, that there is or could be a positive correlation and focus on the development of toolsets to manage corporate sustainability action and recommend an appropriate organisational setting (Epstein and Wisner 2001; Sharma *et al.* 1999; Zadek 1999). This stream of research follows, implicitly, the tendency of managers to jump on the 'how' because the 'why' and 'what' are assumed to be 'givens'.

However, it is far from clear why and what companies should do to contribute to sustainable development. Even leaving aside the fuzziness of sustainability concepts and the many variants of the definition itself, a majority of companies do not—or only sporadically and on an ad hoc basis—engage in such actions (and, in other cases, the sustainability claim is rejected by important stakeholders, e.g. in the nuclear industry). Companies are, after all, predominantly economic entities and their fundamental licence to operate in a market economy is based on satisfying demand and making a profit (as a measure of value added) along the way.

The first research requirement was therefore to establish a framework to define economically viable sustainability actions by companies that do not contradict the dominantly economic logic of corporations. Secondly, there was a need to cover the whole spectrum of questions from 'why' to 'how' in order to understand what companies are doing and how this fits into the economic logic of a business case. A disadvantage of many previous studies was that they tried to be too general. Circumstances and issues differ widely from industry to industry, and even from company to company or country to country (Lankoski 2000:96). Therefore, our research at the Institute of Management Development (IMD) (see Acknowledgements) focused on the following nine industries:

- Automotive
- Aviation
- Chemical
- Electric utilities
- Financial services
- Food and beverage
- Pharmaceutical
- Oil and gas
- Technology

In all these industries, the same approach was applied and answers were sought to the following questions:

- What are the sustainability issues and why are they relevant for the companies?
- What are the value drivers in companies that are, or could be, positively or negatively impacted?
- How are these issues currently managed—from awareness, strategy and organisational design to the tools used?

Based on the resulting empirical evidence, a diagnostic tool was developed to help 'sustainability officers'—or whoever is responsible for these aspects in companies—to identify the business case for their company.

The research is based on more than 400 interviews with global companies and stakeholders from 16 countries in Europe, North America and Japan, and 850 questionnaires returned by general managers and sustainability officers in addition to an extensive review of publicly available information. The industry reports are nearing completion and can be downloaded from IMD's website at Internet URL: http://www.imd.ch/research/projects/bcs), and a number of companies are currently testing the diagnostic tools. An interactive example is available for use from the same website.

1.1   The Research Concept of Externalities and the 'Smart Zone'

Through their operations, companies (and others such as consumers) create external effects in addition to their market-valued activities. These can be positive (e.g. 'spill over' from research, income multiplier effects in local communities) or negative (pollution is a classical example). It is expected that governments (or entities external to the market process) will 'internalise' these externalities into market-relevant costs—particularly if the impact of the externalities is not acceptable to important stakeholders who are affected by them, e.g. the investment and operating costs of pollution control equipment to protect people living near an industrial plant.

However, not all externalities are internalised; if this were the case, one would end up in a static (but not Pareto-optimal) equilibrium. The externalities created by innovation are a telling example; so far, nobody has claimed compensation for the fossil fuel industry for potential job losses and stranded assets resulting from the growth of renewable energy sources (even if these sources were in a position to compete).

Sustainability issues emerge when important stakeholders press for internalisation, often to reduce the negative impact of corporate operations. In the past, the demand was directed primarily at governments because they were expected to do this job. Companies did not voluntarily do so because they perceived that it harmed their economic activity by increasing costs.

The tables have now turned and there are two reasons why companies are now the target of such stakeholder claims:

- First because, as a result of globalisation, national states have lost the power to be effective 'internalisers'(Steger 2002).
- Secondly, although in many cases internalisation is economically disadvantageous, companies basically have three levers to internalise externalities themselves without harming their economic goals:
  - Technological innovation is often, though not always, more advantageous in all three dimensions of sustainability
  - Management concepts can be applied to reduce (negative) externalities or to generate more positive externalities
  - Influencing customers to shift their demand to more 'sustainable' goods and services

An example of the first lever is the array of clean technologies that have emerged in recent decades, often way above legal standards and, at the same time, more cost-effective. With regard to the second lever, an example can be found in the supply chain management and outsourcing strategy of some multinationals, which substitute capital-intensive production 'at home' with labour-intensive processes in developing countries. Finally, an example of the third lever is the introduction of 'eco-labels' by retailers to attract more buyers for their (relatively) environmentally friendly products.

A corporate business case for sustainability is therefore dependant on three pre-conditions:

- An insufficiently internalised externality becoming a sustainability issue through the demand of an important stakeholder
- A relevance of this sustainability issue for the company because the issue affects value drivers (Rappaport 1986), e.g. turnover or brand reputation
- The possibility of using one of the above-mentioned levers to manage/ tackle sustainability issues with, at the very least, no negative economic consequences

But if a business case exists (our central hypothesis in the research), the way that companies are exhausting this potential is very variable across sectors and countries. Secondly, there are potentially many barriers and promoting factors. The former include the mindset of managers (Rojsek 2001), corporate culture (Corbett and van Wassenhove 1993), knowledge gaps, regulatory barriers, investor behaviour, etc. The latter include public or market pressures, new business opportunities, top management leadership and nurturing corporate culture. In terms of a research methodology, all this was formulated in detail as hypotheses and translated into an interview guideline and questionnaire.

The diagnostic tools, which should help sustainability officers to develop company-specific business cases, are based on the results of the empirical investigation. The key paradigm of the diagnostic tool can be visualised in the 'Smart Zone', which covers the area of the business case as the zone where the company creates additional economic value by improving environmental and social performance beyond the compliance of legal standards (which manifest the internalisation of externalities by governments). As countries differ in the level of internalisation, so does the business case in these countries.

1.2   The Smart Zone

Authors such as Lankoski (2000), Salzmann *et al.* (2002), Schaltegger and Figge (2000), Schaltegger and Synnestvedt (2002) and Wagner *et al.* (2002) have discussed an inverse U-shaped curve as one of several approaches of describing the relationship between corporate economic and environmental/social performance (ESP). Figure 1 portrays the possible relationship of absolute economic performance and beyond-compliance ESP, i.e. how economic performance is affected when companies internalise external environmental and/or social effects voluntarily. The curve defines three 'intuitive' phases of the impact of ESP improvements on corporate economic performance in which all corporate sustainability initiatives are 'benchmarked' against the weighted average cost of capital (WACC) or another internal company- or project-specific (i.e. risk-adjusted WACC) 'cut-off' measure.

Section I of Figure 1 constitutes the 'smart zone' in which companies aim to invest in ESP improvements that lead to the greatest increases in economic performance. These initial 'bundles' of 'beyond-compliance' initiatives, also referred to as 'quick wins' or 'low-hanging fruits' feature the—compared to competing alternatives—greatest net present values (NPVs) (which are obviously greater than the WACC). They are followed by further investments in corporate sustainability featuring smaller NPVersus The resulting marginal increases of economic performance decrease such that improvements in corporate ESP in the smart zone eventually lead to an optimal level of economic performance. At this point, the initiatives' NPVs equal the WACC.

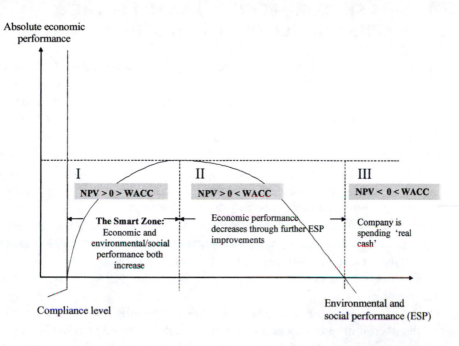

Figure 1. Relationship between economic and environmental/social performance beyond compliance

NPV = net present value. WACC = weighted average cost of capital.

Beyond this optimum (in section II), the NPV of investments that aim to achieve further ESP improvements is still positive but smaller than the WACC. Hence, ESP improvements are associated with decreases in economic performance: The company needs additional justification (e.g. strategic expenditure) to engage in such sustainability initiatives.

Section III illustrates a philanthropic level of ESP performance: Even at zero cost of capital, the NPV of sustainability initiatives is negative.

The first pre-testing of the diagnostic tool indicates that the smart zone is of considerable heuristic and motivational value for sustainability officers endeavouring to identify their company-specific business case. The concept is easily understood and engenders curiosity to figure out not only where a company is positioned on the curve but also some additional arguments for the business case.

2.   A SECTOR-SPECIFIC EXAMPLE: THE PHARMACEUTICAL INDUSTRY

The pharmaceutical industry is an interesting example because it has enjoyed high profitability and little controversy for a considerable time, in contrast to recent decades when companies such as Hoffmann-la Roche, Sandoz and Boehringer Ingelheim were in the midst of major environmental conflicts. Aging populations and increased health consciousness have driven demand, while mergers and acquisitions (M&A) contributed to rising profitability. Today, the world is a much more hostile place for pharmaceutical companies. Regulators have increased scrutiny, health management organisations are demanding huge discounts and driving the process of generic substitutions, many blockbuster patents are expiring and R&D costs are exploding. On top of this, the peace/truce with powerful non-governmental organisations (NGOs) and international organisations has vanished.

Pharmaceutical companies are currently confronted with the following sustainability issues:

- **Access to healthcare**—15% of the world's population consumes 92% of the overall drug production (the USA counts for more than half), whereas the remaining 85% of the population shares only 8%. Thus the access to affordable drugs has become a globally relevant issue and countries such as South Africa and Brazil are openly violating patent rights to produce cheaper drugs, e.g. for AIDS patients. Drug companies are being forced to reduce their prices for poorer countries (e.g. in India, the average ethical drug price is one-twelfth of that of the USA, but even this is affordable only to the better-off) and to donate drugs to foundations for especially needy patient groups. And the pressure does not stop there. In connection with this issue, the R&D priorities of the pharmaceutical companies have been heavily criticised. NGOs maintain that 90% of R&D is being devoted to only 10% of known diseases, mainly those prevalent in developed countries, and often only to remedy unhealthy lifestyles. The creation of 'lifestyle drugs' has further fuelled the criticism that killer diseases such as malaria and tuberculosis are being neglected.

- **Healthcare economics**—in developed countries also, pricing policy has come under pressure as social security systems come under stress. The USA is virtually the only country today to allow free price setting and not 'order' in one way or another the use of generics. But here also, rising costs and criticism of aggressive marketing practices with regard to doctors, and advertising tactics targeting the public, may indicate a change. The pharmaceutical companies have not been very successful in communicating that the health benefits/cost effectiveness of drug remedies are often better than other methods of treatment and that the industry is also creating positive externalities, e.g. vaccines, which also benefit those who do not use them through the containment of certain diseases and/or the positive externalities resulting from R&D.

Related to these sustainability issues are the international frameworks for enforcing patents and intellectual property rights in global trade. The industry is lobbying hard to strengthen the enforcement of this regime, but still claim that patent violations are equivalent to one third of their exports to developing countries.

Given the pressure which, in the long-run can completely undermine the current business model of pharmaceutical companies, it is no small wonder that managers in the industry see the 'licence to operate' as an important value driver for the justification of activities in corporate sustainability. Equally ranked are 'reputation' and 'brand value', since 75% of companies have experienced damage of varying degrees to their brand image in the last three years as a result either of an NGO campaign (almost 50%) or through 'conflicts with authorities' (33%). In this knowledge-intensive industry, 'intangibles' rather than physical assets determine a large part of the share price and a priority is 'to attract talent and increase employee satisfaction'.

However, these concerns are not yet leading to a clearly defined sustainability strategy in most pharmaceutical companies. The approaches differ widely and very often the 'eco-efficiency' approach is still dominant. Not that this approach does not have merit—especially in positively influencing the value driver 'cost'—but, for the pharmaceutical industry, there are limits to what can be achieved with this approach.

These findings are mirrored by evidence that there is often an absence of a sufficiently open culture to foster awareness and discussion of emerging issues. Many sustainability officers struggle to get 'buy in' from their senior management for their activities. Not surprisingly, there are only a few cases where some systematic links between overall corporate strategy and sustainability strategy are visible or that sustainability activities are integrated into functions or the organisation per se. Whereas human resources (HR) and communications are normally supportive of sustainability activities, the issues have yet to reach the R&D function and their relationship to marketing and finance can best be described as 'crowded with obstacles'.

Except for the environmental dimension, few tools exist to manage sustainability issues. Even sustainability reports are not common practice in the industry—the need for these and their content are still perceived differently by senior managers within pharmaceutical companies. Relationships with stakeholders are chequered and even moderate NGOs are generally sceptical about the transparency and credibility of pharmaceutical companies (but with differences in the industry). Relations with regulators, who at least speak the same language, are normally better—though there is a growing awareness that pharmaceutical companies had better sit up and listen to a broader variety of stakeholders. For the time being, however, the management of sustainability issues in most companies is neither proactive nor systematic.

3.   CROSS-INDUSTRY RESULTS

3.1   Influence of Social and Environmental Issues on Industries

It comes as no great surprise that an overwhelming majority of managers expect sustainability to become more important in years to come—as has occurred with its precursor, the environment, over several decades. In research, however, we have to guard against accepted 'political correctness' or 'sugar-coated answers' as the Chinese put it (Steger *et al.* 2003)—which do not reveal how decisions are made or decision-making criteria are changed in a company. More revealing is the way in which managers are influenced by sustainability issues.

Figure 2 shows the influence of social and environmental issues on different industry sectors. These answers back up statistically the results of the qualitative interviews described in the industry reports emerging from the research at IMD.

For both social and environmental issues, the average for all sectors is 3.1—slightly above the category 'fairly' (as in 'fairly influential'). Managers in the finance and technology sector perceive their business units/functions as being least influenced by sustainability issues, whereas managers in the oil and gas, food and beverage, and chemical sectors admit to being most influenced.

Interestingly, the standard derivation for answers in the environmental area, both in the sector comparison (0.58) as well as for all answers given (1.32),is higher than in the social area (0.32/1.07). This indicates that most participants selected a middle-category answer for social issues—a choice typically observed in surveys if a question is not understood or participants do not have a clear opinion.

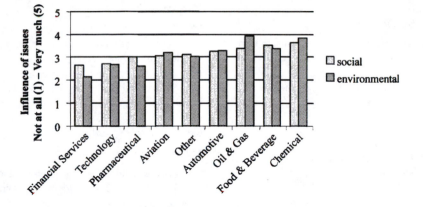

Figure 2. Influence of social and environmental issues on industries

3.2 Sector Characteristics and Main Issues

Table 1 summarises the differences between the researched sectors. The issues showing basic differences include:
- Direct impact from core business operations (aviation) versus mainly indirect implications through customer risks (finance)
- Social issues (pharmaceutical) versus environmental (oil and gas)
- Different steps of the value chain, supply (food and beverage), production (aviation) to product (automotive)
- Visible and publicly discussed issues related to the core product (e.g. oil and gas, automotive) versus side aspects of the product (e.g. pharmaceutical, food and beverage)

Table 1. Sector characteristics and main sustainability issues

Aviation	**Finance**
Characteristics	*Characteristics*
Impact mainly related directly to (core) business operation. While relative impact per passenger is decreasing, absolute impact will grow further due to strong long-term traffic growth rates (e.g. greenhouse gas emissions).	Only minor direct impact of business operations, but customers of financial products and services may have enormous impact. Hence, the big global financial companies in particular are confronted indirectly with the whole range and complexity of sustainability issues.
Main issue cluster	
- Noise and local air pollution	*Main issue cluster*
- Flight emissions	- Responsibility for whole range of indirect issues related to product portfolio and customer base (role in society)

Automotive

Characteristics

Issues around the whole value chain from suppliers to production and products. Issues are well known and broadly discussed in public, but as yet there is no customer demand for possible solutions.

Main issue cluster

- Mobility
- Energy and emissions
- Recycling
- Safety

Chemicals

Characteristics

Issues around the whole value chain from suppliers to production and products. Environmental and social issues around supply chain and production are localised, but as chemical products are integrated into every human-made product, issues related to them are widely spread.

Main issue cluster

- Environmental and safety issues around production process, (including spills and accidents)
- Impact of chemical products on health and wealth

Food and Beverage

Characteristics

Supply chain is closely connected to the ecological basis of human existence; hence the sector is confronted with all related issues, even if there is no direct responsibility. Issues around products are quite critical as they may have a direct impact on consumers' health.

Main issue cluster

- Raw material and water supply (environmental and social impact)
- Health and safety (e.g. obesity, dietary deficiencies, allergies)

Pharmaceutical

Characteristics

The industry sees its business model per se contributing to sustainability. Main sustainability issues are related to social responsibility.

Main issue cluster

- Access to healthcare
- R&D areas
- Intellectual property
- Health economics in developing countries

Energy

Characteristics

The use of the product itself is a main issue that leads, especially in the long-term, to fundamental questions on the business as a whole. In the short- and middle-term, there are a number of social and environmental issues related to search, extraction and production, refining and sales.

Main issue cluster

- Climate change
- Health and safety
- Biodiversity and nature protection

Technology

Characteristics

The industry sees its business model per se contributing to sustainability. Main sustainability issues are related to social responsibility.

Main issue cluster

- Life-cycle management
- Environmental production issues

In most sectors, managers have quite a clear perspective on environmental issues. These are often broadly discussed (e.g. emissions in the automotive industry) and are easy to classify and structure. Well-elaborated checklists exist, e.g. within established environmental management systems (EMAS,

ISO 14001). A starting point to structure the environmental impact could be the different chemical substances (carbon dioxide [CO_2], nitrogen oxides [NO_x], polychlorinated biphenyls [PCBs]), their physical conditions (liquid, gaseous or solid) or the environmental problem (air pollution, contamination, resource depletion).

All sectors in some way face the whole range of environmental issues, but with a different focus and from a different perspective. Most of the time, one sector is directly causing the impact, i.e. it has a direct impact through its core business operations and is in the 'lead' for certain issues, e.g.

- Food and beverage for issues related to agriculture
- Aviation for noise around airports
- Oil and gas sector for issues related to extraction and resource depletion.

Regarding social issues, most interviewees conceded that they lacked a clear picture and were working on a concept. In their view, social issues 'are more illusive and difficult to grasp'. One reason may be the derivation of the interviewees from the environmental area. Another may be the complexity of social issues. Whereas environmental issues are often discussed in an overall context and are quite tangible and/or visible, social issues are more likely to be discussed alone and not connected to an overall context. Interviewees often referred to just one or two main issues—generally to health and safety, (business) ethics and impact on developing countries/wealth.

Economy-dominated sustainability issues play only a minor role. Examples in the pharmaceutical sector include:

- The pricing structures for medication in the third world (malaria, HIV)
- The justification of an incredibly high profit margin while the health systems of most of the developed countries are confronted with severe and worsening financial problems.

The main economic issues are related to wealth in developing countries (e.g. oil and gas, financial sector, chemicals). And even here, it is difficult to distinguish between economic or social effects.

3.3   Stakeholders

This section gives an overview of the more proactive or reactive roles stakeholders play in terms of corporate sustainability and highlights some of the findings of our research. Figure 3 shows the level of proactiveness among general managers contacted.

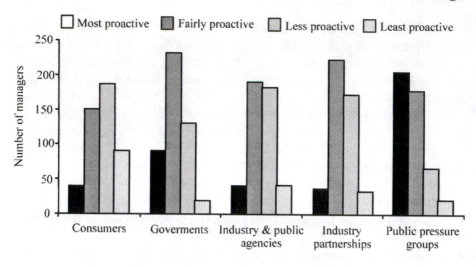

Figure 3. Level of proactiveness of stakeholders (general managers)

3.3.1   Civil Society

Local and global NGOs launch campaigns for more stringent regulations against the negative effects of corporate activities and lobby policy-makers `(Spar and La Mure 2003). Small, local public pressure groups (e.g. local residents for the aviation, chemical and utility sectors) can play a significant role in addressing specific local issues (e.g. noise, biodiversity). Their global counterparts scrutinise companies in terms of both their local and global environmental and social performance. The media play a similar part, even if they primarily take on the role of a catalyst.

Interviewees in the chemical and utility sectors do not perceive NGOs as an active threat. However, interviewees in the pharmaceutical, food and beverage, oil and gas, and technology sectors consider them—in addition to regulators—their most significant pressure group focusing on broader issues such as access to drugs, food safety and climate change rather than on local, social or environmental problems.

Public pressure depends on:

• **The visibility of the sectors' products and operations**. 'Front-line' sectors with consumer brands such as the food and beverage industry are more vulnerable. Public scrutiny of broader issues, particularly if related to developing countries, appears to be seen as a significant threat.

• **The perceived power of sectors—relative to regulators in particular**. The oil and gas and the utility sectors jointly face the issue of climate change. The utility sector is less targeted by public pressure groups because it is more closely regulated and is subject to a gradual decrease in subsidies for domestic mining activities, leading to closures and lay-offs.

3.3.2 Customers

Overall, customers (or 'consumers') appear to play the least proactive role. In particular, interviewees in the aviation, chemical, food and beverage, oil and gas, and pharmaceutical sectors indicated that their customers are mainly concerned with the lowest price or the best quality price ratios, and are basically unwilling to switch to a more expensive but more sustainable product and pay a sustainability premium. Customers in developing countries tend to focus even more strongly on the product's core functions and affordability, i.e. sustainability criteria such as low energy consumption and potential for recycling are largely ignored.

3.3.3 Regulators

Traditionally, sectors such as utilities, chemical, pharmaceutical and aviation are strongly regulated. This obvious influence, which was confirmed in our interviews, differs between developed and developing countries. The latter tend to lack regulatory standards and are mainly concerned with constant and adequate revenue flows. Hence, environmental and social issues are only gradually being taken more into consideration. The consequences are two-fold:

- NGOs take over the role of watchdog in developing countries
- In the face of this global scrutiny, companies move beyond compliance, individually or jointly (e.g. joint ventures in the oil and gas sector, Responsible Care in the chemical sector).

3.3.4 Industry

Interviewees across all sectors suggested that sustainability leaders exert significant 'pull' effects on laggards. Furthermore, they pointed to external barriers such as regulations, lack of customer demand and technological uncertainty when questioned as to why their industry does not further increase its environmental and social performance.

3.3.5 Employees

The increasingly important role of employees is indicated by the responses of sustainability officers with regard to value drivers. Although attracting

talent and increasing employee satisfaction appear to be particularly important in the very R&D-intensive pharmaceutical sector, it appears that
employees' importance is based on product development and knowledge
intensity rather than improvements in sustainability performance.

3.3.6   Shareholders

In general, shareholders (including all those labelled 'capital market' and its
related industries, e.g. investment banks) are not perceived, in other than minor or narrow aspects, as playing a part in promoting corporate sustainability. Interviewees almost unanimously pointed to the deterring role of shareholders, even if pressure on selected issues is increasing. The Carbon Disclosure Project, a group of institutional investors, is currently scrutinising the
corporate sector in terms of its CO_2 portfolio (Nicholls 2003). European
shareholders appear to exert more pressure on certain issues such as climate
change than US investors. Although mentioned in several interviews,
socially responsible investors still have only marginal influence overall.

3.3.7   Conclusions on Stakeholders

Looking at the overall results of the survey, the perceptions of sustainability
officers and general managers of stakeholders appear to be largely con-
gruent. Sustainability officers tend to have a more positive view on corporate
activities because, as the standard bearers in their company, they have to be
more optimistic. They are more aware of the proactive activities of the sector's sustainability leaders and the reactive attitudes of external stakeholders.

However, several sector-specific differences between the perception of
general managers and sustainability officers were detected in every instance.
Key differences between industries were found in terms of:
• The role of civil society and regulators, which clearly depends on
  industry-specific dynamics
• The expectation concerning shareholders' future reactions (e.g. food and
  beverage versus pharmaceutical)

Furthermore, the sectors displayed considerable similarities with regard to
consumer attitudes which, as described above, are generally seen as being a
strong barrier to sustainable development.

3.4   Value Drivers

The business case for sustainability (BCS) is built on an (economic) value-
oriented internalisation of sustainability issues. Sustainability issues emerge

due to externalities related to environmental or social effects of corporate activities on a global, regional or local level when stakeholders such as NGOs, customers and regulators increase pressure and reward improvements in companies' environmental and/or social performance.

As a strategic concept, BCS goes far beyond issue management, which is often limited to an almost ad hoc (and rarely strategic) response to an emerging issue ('fire-fighting'). It is based on certain value drivers (Rappaport 1986) that 'reconcile' improvements of corporate performance in the environmental and social dimension on the one hand and the creation of economic value on the other—through either net cost savings and/or net increases in revenues (see also Schaltegger and Figge 1997).

The economic value created by improved environmental and/or social performance is compared with value created by less sustainable, 'competing' alternatives. Hence, value drivers (Figure 4) are essentially arguments for more sustainable business practices, since they conceptualise the minimisation of opportunity costs.

The significance of value drivers depends on the underlying issues and compliance levels, which can both vary significantly, particularly between developed and developing countries. Hence, we differentiate between two main approaches to value creation:

- Risk and opportunities are operationally managed through incremental improvements in environmental, health and safety, and social performance that are primarily associated with net cost decreases, i.e. either short-term cost decreases or cost increases that are compensated for by improved reputation or the licence to operate

- Risks and opportunities are strategically managed through more radical innovation of products and services, often associated with significant changes in business models, which can have a profound impact on both operational risks and opportunities. Radical innovations are primarily associated with short-term cost increases that are compensated for by long-term revenue increases, improved reputation and a licence to operate.

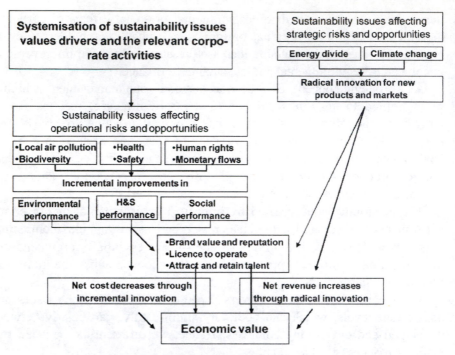

Figure 4. Value drivers

A number of interviewees mentioned social and economic development (through the provision of energy, mobility, etc.) as a significant value driver. We have not specifically elaborate further on this because:

- Social and economic development is based primarily on the rollout of conventional business models in developing countries, leading to a relative decrease in environmental impact and is, as a rule, eventually eaten up by production growth
- It is considered part of operational management of risk and opportunities

3.4.1   Empirical Evidence

As one can also see from Figure 5, managers are already beyond a mere cost perspective. The licence to operate, reputation and brand value as well as the capability to attract talent and increase employee satisfaction are considered very significant value drivers. They are even more important than risk management and cost reductions—the typical 'low hanging fruits'.

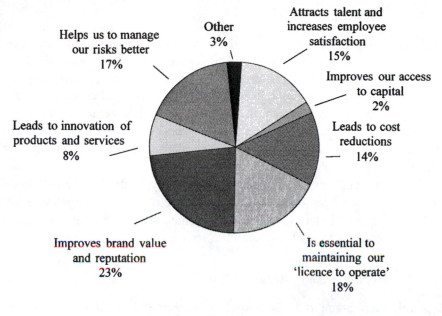

Figure 5. Importance of value drivers (sustainability officers)

Finally, the data also illustrate clearly the marginal role of improved access to capital as a value driver. In the following section, cross-industry conclusions are drawn on the importance of individual value drivers and the economic potential behind them.

3.4.2   Net Cost Decreases

Companies 'traditionally' strive for cost reductions through more (eco-) efficient (Schmidheiny 1992) and safer processes. Interviews still indicated a significant economic potential for achieving these 'easy win–wins' (particularly among the industries' laggards), which that are mainly realised by increasing operational excellence rather than ad hoc environmental, health and safety (EHS) programmes.

Data obtained from the questionnaire responses suggest that the chemical sector puts most emphasis on cost reductions and the pharmaceutical sector the least, presumably because costs are mainly associated with R&D and less with sustainability issues. The remaining industries surveyed displayed significant interest in operational risk and cost management—the oil and gas industry in risk management in particular.

3.4.3 Licence to Operate

Interviews suggest that the licence to operate plays a particularly salient role in the oil and gas, aviation, food and beverage, and pharmaceutical sectors. The aviation sector uses sophisticated models to quantify the importance of noise reduction around airports in order to maintain the licence to operate, particularly at night. In the case of the food and beverage industry, the licence to operate is the basis for today's most compelling business case. Without the introduction of sustainable fishing methods, the depletion of fish stocks will nullify a current licence to operate.

These findings from the interviews are largely confirmed by sustainability officers responding to the questionnaire; the licence to operate was most significant in the oil and gas and pharmaceutical sectors, and least significant in the financial and technology sectors.

3.4.4 Reputation and Brand Value

Reputation and brand value are closely linked to each other and also to both the licence to operate and employee satisfaction. Their importance as a value driver is substantial given today's global scrutiny of the corporate sector, as particularly indicated by sustainability officers from the food and beverage and pharmaceutical sectors, followed by the financial services and technology sectors. In contrast, reputation and brand value appear to be a less significant value driver in the oil and gas sector.

Responses from general managers on the importance of brand and reputation show a similar picture (Figure 6). Brand and reputation appear to be more important to 'front line' industries such as the food and beverage and automotive sectors, and less important to the chemical (significantly), oil and gas and technology sectors. They are affected mainly through NGO and media campaigns (particularly in the food and beverage and oil and gas sectors), whereas the pharmaceutical sector reports more conflicts with authorities. Consumer boycotts play a minor role, particularly in the oil and gas sector. NB The survey focused on incidents in the last three years, so apart from STOP ESSO, there were no significant boycotts against the oil and gas sector.

Overall, the damage from such incidents appears to be less important (bias likely) and is considered most significant by far by general managers from the automotive sector, followed by those from the chemical sector. The smallest effect is indicated by respondents from both the technology and pharmaceutical sectors.

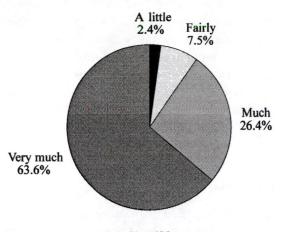

N = 492

Figure 6. Importance of brand and reputation (general managers)

3.4.5   Employee Satisfaction

As can be seen from Figure 5, attracting and retaining talent is a significant promotional factor for corporate sustainability. It appears to be most important to R&D-intensive industries (particularly in the pharmaceutical sector), and least important to the oil and gas and technology sectors.

This coincides with evidence obtained from interviewees who largely confirmed employees' underlying 'desire to be a good citizen'. They also argued that good corporate citizens have a competitive advantage over laggards in the industry due to increased employee productivity and attractiveness to recruits.

3.4.6   Net Revenue Increases

Our empirical evidence suggests that, provided distinct barriers such as lack of customer demand and/or technological uncertainty can be overcome, net revenue increases constitute a less significant value driver since they generally only materialise in the mid- or long-term.

Sustainability officers responding to the questionnaire considered the innovation of products and services to be a less important argument for promoting the concept of sustainability. (The significance of a strategic approach is presumably even smaller, since respondents are likely to primarily associate the item 'leads to innovation of products and services' with incremental rather than radical innovation.) Whereas it was considered more significant in the financial services (14%), it was perceived as less important in the pharmaceutical (0%) and oil and gas (5%) sectors.

Business opportunities were considered a significant factor in promoting sustainable business practices—slightly more important than process and product innovation. The latter were least significant in the pharmaceutical and food and beverage sectors, and most important to the oil and gas (a significant contradiction to the previous paragraph) and chemical sectors. Business opportunities, on the other hand, were perceived as most significant in the financial services sector and least significant in the pharmaceutical sector.

3.4.7   Conclusions on Value Drivers

Data obtained from both interviews and questionnaires suggest that managers tend to focus more on operational (incremental) than strategic (radical) management of risk and opportunities. The more radical innovational lever of increased sustainable business practices is largely neglected because:

- It does not work well on a business-as-usual basis due to higher internal and external barriers such as lack of expertise, mindset and even inadequate business environments
- The business case–like any strategic decision—is hard to quantify in the long-term. Overall, it appears to be weak, particularly if net revenue increases are uncertain and only materialise in the long-term. (The discounting of both positive and negative future cash flows decreases the relevance of long-term investments.)

Table 2 lists those activities that appear to have the greatest economic potential in each sector (based on our survey results and additional research).

Table 2. Corporate activities with the greatest economic potential

Sector	Corporate activities with the greatest economic potential	
	In the short-term	**In the long-term**
Automotive	Improve product-related EHS performance (also climate change)	New mobility concepts and engine technology to maintain licence to operate
Aviation	Noise reduction to maintain licence for night flights	?
Chemical	EHS-related operational excellence	New service-oriented business models ('rent a molecule')
Food and beverage	Depends on crop and product respectively: licence to operate (resource depletion, increase food safety, manage social issues in developing countries)	
Financial services	Minimise downside risk	

Sector	Corporate activities with the greatest economic potential	
	In the short-term	**In the long-term**
Oil and gas	Manage social and environmental issues in developing countries to minimise disruptions of operations	New climate-neutral products and business models
Pharmaceutical	EHS-related operational excellence	Maintain the licence to operate by providing adequate access to drugs
Technology	Improve product-related EHS performance (also climate change)	New business models (service-based dematerialisation)
Utilities	EHS-related operational excellence	New climate-neutral operations and business model (e.g. contracting)

Based on the interpretations presented above, the sectors under consideration can be categorised as follows:

- The issues for the oil and gas and chemical sectors are related both to production (short-term) and product (long-term). Both industries feature heavy assets and tend to focus on cost and risk reductions, and the licence to operate. Long life-span of product-related 'livestock' leads to incremental rather than radical innovations of products and services.

- The more front-line industries, i.e. food and beverage and pharmaceutical, are more vulnerable to reputation risk and damage to brand value. Gatekeepers influence upstream activities to some extent. Sustainable product innovations are largely neglected. The key issues are either upstream (sustainable sourcing) or downstream (access to drugs), and both are very pressing in the short-term.

- The automotive and technology sectors differ in terms of their (industrial versus private) customers and perceptions of stakeholders. However, issues are related primarily to their products' environmental and safety performance. Primary value drivers appear to be reputation and brand value.

- The aviation and financial services sectors are both service industries and feature special characteristics. Whereas financial services are essentially concerned with reputation and the minimisation of credit and under-writing risks associated with issues relevant to its customers, airlines (beyond passenger health and safety) are primarily concerned with one single issue—noise reduction and a clear business case to maintain or extend night flights. interesting

4.   CORPORATE GOALS, ORGANISATIONAL CULTURE (VISION) AND SUSTAINABILITY STRATEGY DESIGN

4.1   Corporate Goals and Strategies

Corporate strategies are driven by corporate goals and basically concern the question of what businesses the corporation should be in and how corporate headquarters should manage the array of business units. Our research showed that sustainability has no significant impact on corporate strategies in almost all the sectors studied. Across the board, interviewed company members perceived that sustainability had no impact and that main corporate goals such as profitable growth are not influenced. The chemical sector, however, represents a rare exception. While some chemical companies are trying to focus on necessary strategies to avoid negative consequences for their businesses, other companies are rethinking their entire business model and divesting themselves of business units because of risks and opportunities arising from sustainability.

4.2   Sustainability Strategy

A plethora of terminology is currently used to describe management approaches in this area:
- Corporate sustainability management (CSM)
- Corporate citizenship
- Corporate social responsibility (CSR)

This appears to depend on regional preferences (e.g. USA versus Europe). However, many of these approaches encompass similar management concepts. In addition, some entities had only an explicit environmental management (EM) approach.

Across all sectors, some companies—sometimes even when pursuing CSM or CSR approaches—had a sustainability strategy combining environmental and social issues. In some sectors, only a handful of entities interviewed had explicit sustainability goals and plans for reaching these. In some cases, such strategies are actions and measures in single business units but can also be company-wide policies geared to sustainability such as guidelines, codes of conduct, business principles, health/safety rules, etc.

Again across sectors, a few companies even pointed out that they want to change values in the long-run to better face up to risks and opportunities arising from sustainability. As corporate values represent the foundation for corporate culture, this adoption of values can also imply a change within organisational culture. An open corporate culture, in particular, is seen as important and desirable in order to improve a company's social and environmental performance while creating value for the company.

Overall, sustainability strategies are not the result of broad grass-root movements in companies, but of a top–down management approach. Therefore, it was found in all industries that the support of a board member is crucial for building and implementing effective strategies. Senior management usually assigns the responsibility to a staff function in the corporate centre, which is delegated responsibility to co-ordinate and bring forward environmental and social measures. Generally, these staff functions formulate the corporate sustainability strategy in co-operation with senior management and other departments.

5. ORGANISATIONAL STRUCTURE AND IMPORTANCE OF FUNCTIONS

5.1 Sustainability Responsibilities

The responsibility for sustainability has a different set-up in different industries. In most sectors, the concept of sustainable development emerged within Environment, Health and Safety (EHS) departments, with the HR function sometimes being involved early on in the evolution. The situation today seems to be quite diverse across—but interestingly also within—specific industries. There is not a single sector with a common approach for sustainability responsibility. In some industries, it is still the EHS department that is responsible for and is taking the lead in the process towards sustainable development. Only a few companies within the surveyed sectors have a specific department or unit called a sustainability unit; in fact, this does not appear to be a trend across sectors. Leaders such as Shell have even recently decided to dissolve their existing sustainability unit to replace it with a more integrated sustainability management system within business units. In most industries, responsibilities are split between different functions. Table 3 summarises the current situation of sustainability responsibilities within the surveyed sectors.

Table 3. Sustainability responsibility across the different sectors

	Automotive	**Aviation**	**Chemical**	**Energy**
Historical evolution:	Emerged within EHS departments	Environmental management on operational level and traditionally HR	Mainly emerged within EHS departments	Safety and Environment
Situation today;	Different companies have installed different combinations	Comparable approach between companies	Either single unit or split between environment and sustainability	Two approaches seem generally to be chosen
Unit responsible:	Head of R&D or operations in conjunction with sustainability unit	Mostly EHS function—only a few companies with sustainability unit	Often a sustainability officer or committee together with many functions	Either sustainability or external affairs function or split across EHS and HR
Hierarchical location:	Sustainability unit reporting to board level	Board member either for Public Affairs or for quality/EHS	Integrated into every function with overall responsibility at board level	Strong involvement at board level

	Financial services	**Food and beverage**	**Pharmaceutical**
Historical evolution:	Evolved within environmental management	Evolved from environmental management	EHS departments as early promoters and leaders
Situation today:	Some have sustainability unit	Different ways and options chosen	Diverse situation with different approaches chosen
Unit responsible:	Sustainability unit or part of risk management	Often a strategic co-ordination committee together with issue groups	Mostly EHS, Public Affairs, sustainability unit and/or committee
Hierarchical location:	Mostly reporting to board member	Reporting to board level with strong CEO involvement	Reporting to board member (either CEO or Public Affairs)

Interestingly, across industries, the hierarchical location of the sustainability unit/driver is very high, with most of the responsible units reporting directly to a board member and with quite an astonishing number of board members being directly involved in the progress towards sustainability.

5.2 The Involvement of Business Functions

All sustainability officers/units across the different sectors agreed that the involvement of specific functions is crucial for progress in terms of sustainable development and as a reliable indicator of 'integration'. Nevertheless, despite the strong need for functional interaction, the status quo is very varied throughout industry. Table 4 summarises the status quo of the current involvement and interaction between the unit responsible for sustainability and other business functions.

Table 4. Business functions' involvement towards sustainability

	Automotive	**Aviation**	**Chemical**	**Energy**
HR	Interacting with sustainability unit on labour-related issues	Traditionally being strongly involved	Key to setting up guiding principles for corporate. value, etc.	Are naturally concerned with social issues
EHS	Traditionally leading the path towards sustainability	Driving the evolution to-wards sustain-ability	Organisationally integrated in all companies	Core of activity
Finance/ Controlling/ Investor relations (IR)	Short-term profit orientation Providing information to capital markets	No involvement so far	Short-term thinking as barrier. Nevertheless goals set, controlled and revised	Usually most resistant, although controlling tools take soft-factor into account
Operations	Works on a daily basis on issues such as eco-efficiency	Historically this is where EHS evolved from	Involved in setting EHS standards for production	Concerned with local issues and stakeholders. Less aware of long-term strategic challenges
Marketing and Sales	Mostly seeing sustainable development as a revenue-decreasing factor	No involvement so far	Trying to offer additional services for win–win situations	Little involvement
Corporate Strategy	No direct link seen to corporate strategy	No involvement so far	Involved in risk management and issue management systems	Part integration of sustainability

	Automotive	Aviation	Chemical	Energy
R&D	Researching and developing to increase eco- and safety performance	Only on specific issues (emissions)	Key function to leverage sustainable development performance through innovations	Relative proactive attitude, since they anticipate future development
Communications /Public Affairs	Arguing in favour of a value driver perspective	Strong promoter for the concept of sustainable development	Regular dialogue between key people established	Show neutral to proactive attitude, increasingly interested in profiling renewables

	Financial Services	Food and Beverage	Pharmaceutical
HR	Promoting the drive towards sustainability	Little	Need for strong collaboration. Mostly promoting the concept of sustainable development
EHS	Department taking the lead in the organisational change process	Often separate from food safety	Key promoter and leader for sustainability
Finance/ Controlling/ Investor relations (IR)	Strong relation to risk management	Opposing the concept of sustainable development	Relationship crowded with obstacles. Mostly opposing the concept of sustainable development
Operations	Only the environmental side	Opposing the concept of sustainable development and at the same time regarded as the biggest promoter	Long history of positive interaction. Sustainable development regarded as cost-reduction factor
Marketing and Sales	Little	Opposing the concept of sustainable development	Opposing the concept because of their mindset of maximising revenue
Corporate Strategy	Traditionally strongly involved in the concept of sustainable development	Part of the strategic co-ordinating committee	Only minor involvement Neutral to the concept of sustainable development
R&D		Not sufficiently involved in sustainable development but	Sustainable development has not yet reached the function

		seen as having significant potential to promote	
Communications / Public Affairs	Concept has started out and is still to be found in corporate communication	Very significant influence in rollout	Close interaction with sustainability unit 'Mouthpiece' of the sustainability unit

Interestingly, the units opposing progress towards more sustainability and those promoting the concept of sustainable development are quite similar across industries. This is precisely what the survey revealed. Table 5 shows the results of the general manager survey for the different sectors; the top three 'opposers' and 'promoters' are given, with the respective percentages shown in brackets.

Table 5. Promoting and deterring roles of business functions

	Greatest Promoter	**Strongest Opposition**
Automotive	R&D (31.3%) Manufacturing (22.9%) HR/corporate staff (20.8%)	Finance/Controlling (44.8%) HR/corporate staff (17.2%) R&D (10.3%)
Aviation	R&D (41.7%) Manufacturing (16.7%) HR/corporate staff (8.3%)	Finance/Controlling (33,3%) Manufacturing (33.3%) Others (33.3%)
Chemical	Manufacturing (23.4%) Corporate staff (20.7%) R&D (19.6%)	Finance/Controlling (44.4%) Marketing and Sales (22.2%) Manufacturing (22.2%)
Energy	Manufacturing (23.4%) Corporate staff (20.7%) R&D (19.6%)	Finance/Controlling (28.6%) Manufacturing (27.0%) Marketing and Sales (12.7%)
Financial services	R&D (26.7%) HR/corporate staff (23.0%) Manufacturing (22.2%)	Finance/Controlling (32.7%) Marketing and Sales (32.7%) HR/corporate staff (17.3%)
Food and beverage	Manufacturing (22.6%) R&D (21.1%) Marketing and Sales (16.6%)	Finance/Controlling (29.2%) Marketing and Sales (25.0%) Manufacturing (15.3%)
Pharmaceutical	Manufacturing (28.6%) R&D (25.7%) HR/corporate staff (17.1%)	Finance/Controlling (26.3%) Manufacturing (26.3%) Marketing and Sales (21.1%)

It is interesting to note that, in some industries, manufacturing is notably seen as both the greatest promoter and the strongest opposition.

5.3   Processes

The processes, systems and tools that relate to corporate sustainability management can be categorised according to the process of building the business case for sustainability. This process includes the following steps:
- Identifying issues
- Building the business case
- Implementing the business case
- Monitoring and controlling.

Companies need to go through all these steps to comprehensively integrate corporate sustainability management.

The cross-industry comparison reveals that the overall progress that an industry has achieved in this process also determines its achievement and implementation of the respective tools. Obviously, the level of achievement differs among companies in any one sector. Therefore the results from the industry comparison always relate to the industry average. Table 6 presents the most frequently used tools across all industries.

Table 6. Corporate sustainability tools

Tools to identify the BCS	Tools to build the BCS
Stakeholder/industry dialogue Media screening Surveys/public opinion polls Benchmarking Risk management tools	Co-ordination committee discussing and pushing strategic decisions at corporate level Business teams, task forces to resolve conflicts and push CSM Strategic planning and accounting procedures that take account of environmental and/or social issues
Tools to implement the BCS	**Tools to monitor and control the implementation**
Corporate values, policies and standards that take account of environmental issues Reward and punishment systems (e.g. salary partly based on social and/or environmental performance) Management development (e.g. environmental training courses, workshops on sustainable development with senior executives) Sustainability/environmental innovation awards Product stewardship Communication tools to create awareness and understanding Internal information systems/services (e.g. Intranet, corporate TV, corporate magazines)	Measurement tools to increase transparency (e.g. measuring material and waste flows) Tools measuring resource allocation (e.g. environmental expenses) Environmental (EHS) and/or social auditing Eco-efficiency analysis Environmental accounting Due diligence environmental assessment

Tools to identify the BCS	Tools to build the BCS
Sustainability indices and ratings	
Sustainability reporting initiatives	

Interestingly, the survey revealed that no company had already developed and implemented an integrated corporate sustainability management system. Moreover, the necessity of such a system has been stressed by a majority of advanced companies.

The research shows that, so far, the overall focus of implementation processes is on environmental management. Companies report difficulty in defining social aspects and related criteria clearly. In conclusion, it turns out that companies only incrementally implement sustainability-related tools in 'tough' areas such as budgets, decision-making and remuneration. Even the most advanced companies focus their activities on soft measures such as guidelines, non-financial incentive systems, etc.

Although industries are clearly at different stages of development, they feature similar approaches in the areas of issue identification and strategy-building. The oil and gas, food and beverage and chemical industries are identified as being the most advanced in the implementation of sustainability-related systems.

6.   FINAL THOUGHTS

Putting our findings into perspective, the results supported our hypothesis that there is a business case for corporate sustainability and that it is largely sector-specific, though with variations from company to company. Regarding the country dimension, the real differences seem to be between developed and developing countries.

If there was a surprise element in our research, it was how little most companies had thought systematically about the economic logic of what they were doing in the sustainability area. Whereas the relevant issues are generally well known, the tendency is more to jump directly to issue management than to think about the relationship between issues and business value, and from there to set management priorities and to design management systems. On the one hand, this is good news with regard the need for a diagnostic tool (such as the one we have developed) to clarify this link. On the other hand, we have to admit that there is a 'fuzzy' process, not necessarily leading to clear quantitative results. However, the sustainability area is not alone in facing these uncertainties in (monetary) evaluation. The whole cluster of 'intangibles' is increasingly important as any gap between market value and book assets indicates (nobody asks the stock market for detailed reasons for the evaluation because it is a market fact).

One nagging question remains: given that customers and capital markets are reluctant to appreciate sustainability efforts, can one really claim with a clear conscience that sustainability pioneers will be rewarded? Should we perhaps admit that the anecdotal evidence tends rather to indicate that the laggards are more likely to be punished than the pioneers are to be rewarded? This might seem to be especially true given the selective pressure applied to sustainability issues (sometimes it is even surprising just how much is actually happening in companies given the low pressure related to many issues).

Finally, our research is a further reminder that what is being considered here are the externalities and not the core business of companies. A leading environmental NGO representative made the sobering contrast between the survey and his estimate: 'There is a limit of 5% plus or minus of overall company turnover that can be influenced by CSR. The rest is the daily grind of business and maximising shareholder value.' Indeed, the empirical evidence can help to take the hype out of the well-meaning propaganda put out by some governments and NGOs, and sharpen the focus on what can be done in real life.

REFERENCES

Aupperle, K.E., Carroll, A.B. and Hatfield, J.D. (1985): 'An Empirical Examination of the Relationship between Corporate Social Responsibility and Profitability', *Academy of Management Journal* Vol. 28, No. 2, 446-463.

Corbett, C.J. and Wassenhove, L.N. van (1993): 'Internalising and Operationalising Environmental Issues', *California Management Review* Fall, 116-135.

Davidson III, W.N. and Worrel, D.L. (1990): 'A Comparison and Test of the Use of Accounting and Stock Market Data in Relating Corporate Social Responsibility and Financial Performance', *Akron Business and Economic Review* Vol. 21, No. 3, 7-19.

Elkington, J. (1994): 'Towards the Sustainable Corporation: Win-Win-Win Business Strategies for Sustainable Development', *California Management Review* Winter, 90-100.

Epstein, M.J. and Wisner, P.S. (2001): 'Using a Balanced Scorecard to Implement Sustainability', *Environmental Quality Management* Winter, 1-10.

Griffin, J.J. and Mahon, J.F. (1997): 'The Corporate Social Performance and Corporate Financial Performance Debate: Twenty Five Years of Incomparable Research', *Business and Society* Vol. 365, No. 1, 5-31.

Lankoski, L. (2000): *Determinants of Environmental Profit: An Analysis of the Company-Level Relationship between Environmental Performance and Economic Performance* (Doctoral dissertation). Helsinki: Department of Industrial Engineering and Management, Helsinki University of Technology.

McGuire, J.B., Sundgren, A. and Schneeweis, T. (1988): 'Corporate Social Responsibility and Company Financial Performance', *Academy of Management Journal* Vol. 31, No. 4, 854-872.

Moore, G. (2001): 'Corporate Social and Financial Performance: An Investigation in the UK Supermarket Industry', *Journal of Business Ethics* Vol. 34, 299-315.

Nicholls, M. (2003): 'Investors Turn Up Heat on Climate Change', *Environmental Finance* March, 12-13.

Pava, M.L. and Krausz, J. (1996): 'The Association between Corporate Social-Responsibility and Financial Performance: The Paradox of Social Cost', *Journal of Business Ethics* Vol. 15, 321-357.

Rappaport, A. (1986): *Creating Shareholder Value: A New Standard for Business*. New York: The Free Press.

Rojsek, I. (2001): 'From Red to Green: Towards the Environmental Management in the Country in Transition', *Journal of Business Ethics* Vol. 22, 37-50.

Salzmann, O., Ionescu-Somers, A. and Steger, U. (2002): *The Business Case for Corporate Sustainability: Review of the Literature and Research Options* (IMD Working Paper 2002-06). Lausanne: International Institute for Management Development.

Schaltegger, S. and Figge, F. (1997): *Environmental Shareholder Value*. WWZ Studie Nr. 54, 1st edition, Basel: WWZ/Sarasin.

Schaltegger, S. and Figge, F. (2000): 'Environmental Shareholder Value. Economic Success with Corporate Environmental Management', *Eco-Management and Auditing* Vol. 7, No. 1, 29-42.

Schaltegger, S. and Synnestvedt, T. (2002): 'The Link between 'Green' and Economic Success. Environmental Management as the Crucial Trigger between Environmental and Economic Performance', *Journal of Environmental Management* Vol. 65, No. 2, 339-346.

Schmidheiny, S. (1992): 'The Business Logic of Sustainable Development', *The Columbia Journal of World Business* Fall/Winter, 18-24.

Sharma, S., Pablo, A.L. and Vredenburg, H. (1999): 'Corporate Environmental Responsiveness Strategies: The Importance of Issue Interpretation and Organisational Context', *The Journal of Applied Behavioral Science* Vol. 35, No. 1, 87-108.

Spar, D.L. and La Mure, L.T. (2003): 'The Power of Activism: Assessing the Impact of NGOs on Global Business', *California Management Review* Vol. 45, No. 3, 78-107.

Steger, U. (2002): *Corporate Diplomacy*. London: Wiley.

Steger, U., Zhaoben, F. and Wei, L. (2003): *Greening Chinese Business*. Sheffield: Greenleaf Publishing.

Wagner, M. and Schaltegger, S. (2003): 'How does sustainability performance relate to business competitiveness?, *Greener Management International*, Issue 44, Special Edition on 'Sustainability Performance and Business Competitiveness', Winter 2003, 5-16.

Wagner, M., Schaltegger, S. and Wehrmeyer, W. (2002): 'The relation between the environmental and economic performance of companies. What does theory propose and what does empirical evidence tell us?', *Greener Management International* Vol. 34, 95-108.

Zadek, S. (1999): 'Stalking sustainability', *Greener Management International* Vol. 26, Summer, 21-31.

ACKNOWLEDGEMENTS

This chapter presents preliminary and aggregated results of research carried out at the Institute for Management Development, Lausanne. The full results will be published by Macmillan in early 2006 and in a series of dissertations. The support of the whole Corporate Sustainability Management Team, especially Aileen Ionescu-Somers and Oliver Salzmann, as well as the co-operation of WWF International, is gratefully acknowledged. Furthermore, research associates Marc Brunner, Oliver Eckelmann, Achim Gebel, Claudia Schindel and Hans-Jörg Hess contributed substantially to this study.

DEVELOPING VALUE
The Business Case for Sustainability in Emerging Markets

Jodie Thorpe and Kavita Prakash-Mani
SustainAbility, UK

Abstract: While a growing body of research shows how corporate action on sustainability can improve financial performance, the focus to date has been on companies in developed markets. Based on an analysis of more than 240 case studies from over 60 countries, this study focuses on addressing the gap. It analyses the 'business case' for sustainability in emerging markets, identifying opportunities for businesses to reduce costs, increase sales, reduce risks, develop human capital, build reputation and enhance access to capital from better corporate governance, improved environmental practices, and investments in social and economic development. A business case matrix demonstrates graphically where the strongest links exist, while the discussion highlights some variations by region as well as company type. Overall, the study confirms that there are compelling commercial reasons for emerging market companies to take action on sustainability.

The late 1990s saw a rise in protests against economic globalisation and accusations that business is damaging the planet and its people, particularly in emerging markets. At the same time, policy-makers, consumers and investors have expressed concerns about sustainability and development issues, with the private sector increasingly seen as a key agent in achieving sustainable development goals. But, from the point of view of business, why should companies concern themselves with sustainability when their primary role is to provide goods and services profitably?

One answer could be that 'it is the right thing to do', that engaging in bribery or poisoning communities through industrial pollution is both illegal and ultimately immoral. However, there are many areas of corporate activity that are matters of neither legality nor morality, issues related to training, environmental innovation or community investment, for example. It is in these areas that a growing body of research has been demonstrating strong business reasons for the private sector to be concerned with sustainability. The research shows clear links between improved sustainability performance on the economic, environmental and social dimensions, and a company's financial results. (See for example, Hart and Ahuja 1996; Schaltegger and Figge 1997; Waddock and Graves 1997; Verschoor 1999; Repetto and Austin 2000; SustainAbility/ UNEP 2001; Wagner 2001; Schaltegger and Synnestvedt 2002; Waddock *et al.* 2002.)

To date, however, this research has focused almost exclusively on developed markets. The assumption is of what could be described as a 'sustainability Kuznets curve'. In other words, the relationship between sustainability performance and economic growth of a country is an inverted-U shape, with sustainability performance initially worsening but then improving with economic development. A similar relationship was originally described by Kuznets (1955) for income inequality, and later by Grossman and Krueger (1995) for environmental performance. However, without using this term, there is clearly an underlying assumption by many in the business world that the incorporation of sustainability concerns into business practice is a luxury for rich companies in developed nations, and that the primary function of the private sector in emerging markets should be as an engine of economic growth with social and environmental improvements to be considered only after a certain level of development has been achieved.

Nevertheless, like their counterparts in developed economies, businesses based in emerging markets are facing growing pressures as a result of increasing public apprehension about sustainability-related issues. Yet research into the potential business impacts for these companies has been limited. However, a new study (SustainAbility *et al.* 2002), summarised in this chapter, has begun to address this gap through a broad survey of empirical evidence from over 170 companies—small businesses to multinational corporations—in over 60 countries in Africa, Asia, Central and Eastern Europe and Latin America. It systematically analyses the strength of evidence of businesses achieving benefits such as higher sales, reduced costs and lower risks from better corporate governance, improved environmental practices, and investments in social and economic development. It aims to help business people in emerging markets who are struggling to find the right balance between financial pressures on the one hand, and growing sustainability challenges on the other. Ultimately, it makes the case that sustainability is about increasing the opportunities for businesses in emerging markets, not limiting them.

1. BUSINESS AND SUSTAINABILITY IN EMERGING MARKETS

Sustainability is moving up the business agenda globally. The growing importance of the private sector in all regions and countries at all stages of economic development has fuelled concerns about globalisation, the role of markets and global governance. Emerging market businesses are being asked to address these challenges in an uncertain political and economic environment. Companies continue to struggle against corruption, crime and lack of infrastructure, and there have been economic crises in major markets such as Argentina and Turkey. The growth of trade has slowed, while the growth of real gross domestic product (GDP) in developing countries was estimated to have increased by just 1.3% in 2001, down from 3.8% growth in 2000 (World Bank 2002).

Despite these pressing economic difficulties, the need for sustainable development is no less urgent. Poverty remains endemic: almost a quarter of the population in emerging markets lived on less than US$1 per day in purchasing power parity terms in 1999, while 28% of the world's children under five years of age are malnourished. HIV/AIDS incidence is increasing: 36 million people were affected around the world in 2000, the majority living in Southern Africa and South and East Asia. Over 1 billion people worldwide do not have access to safe water sources. It will require a contribution from all actors in society to successfully tackle these problems, and business has a key role to play.

2. THE BUSINESS CASE ANALYSIS

The need for action is compelling. But a key question is whether the enormous contribution that business could make to sustainable development can be reconciled with the private sector's need for competitiveness and profitability. As discussed by Michael Porter (1998), competitiveness derives from innovation leading either to enhanced operational effectiveness or to superior strategic positioning. Operational effectiveness—achieved, for example, through lower waste (in either materials or effort) or more highly motivated employees—results in a company saving on operational costs or creating products of greater value for which a higher price can be charged. Strategic positioning, on the other hand, is about differentiating a company from its competitors, through perhaps improved reputation, a new product design or staff training. Both aspects of competitiveness lead to superior profitability, although Porter identifies the differentiation of a company's products and services as more significant in the long term.

The business case analysis considers the impact of sustainability activities on the competitiveness of companies operating in emerging markets contexts, based on 240 case studies of corporate social, environmental and economic activities drawn from 170 companies operating in these markets. Although the term 'emerging markets' was first used by the International Finance Corporation (IFC) to refer to a fairly narrow list of middle- to higher- income economies among the developing countries, with stock markets in which foreigners could buy securities, the term's meaning has since been expanded to include more or less all developing countries. This study considered cases from over 60 countries, many of which the World Bank classifies as 'upper–middle-income', such as Botswana, Brazil, Hungary and Malaysia, but with 25% of the cases from 'low-income' countries, such as Bangladesh, Indonesia, Nicaragua and Tanzania.

Three company examples appear in this chapter, illustrating the types of case that were included in the research. The other case studies analysed are available in an online database at http://www.sustainability.com/developing-value/search.asp. These cases include all types and sizes of company from small and medium-sized enterprises to multinationals, and cover a wide range of sectors such as agriculture, manufacturing, infrastructure and information technology. The companies examined are not 'model companies', but rather ordinary businesses that have taken practical steps to address specific issues, although some of the companies have integrated sustainability more strategically in their overall processes. As one key aim of the report was to help business people in emerging markets to assess the potential impact of sustainability activities on their own business performance, the focus was on 'real-world' examples. In addition, as there is relatively little coverage in the literature on the business case for companies operating in emerging markets, the emphasis was also on gathering empirical information and providing an initial framework for analysis.

The research approach was to assess for each case whether business practices in one of seven possible sustainability areas had an impact on one or more of six possible business success measures. The sustainability factors reflect a company's 'triple bottom line' performance—social, economic and environmental (Elkington 1997)—along with the business processes that underpin this performance. They are:

1. Governance and management
2. Stakeholder engagement
3. Environmental process improvement
4. Environmental products and services
5. Local economic growth
6. Community development
7. Human resource management

The choice of these seven sustainability factors was based on Sustain-Ability's previous business case work (SustainAbility/UNEP 2001), as well as the IFC's internal framework for assessing the contribution of private-sector investments to sustainable development (IFC 2003), and aimed for overall clarity and simplicity.

The business success factors, also based on the SustainAbility/UNEP work cited above, are:

1. Revenue growth and market access
2. Cost savings and productivity
3. Access to capital
4. Risk management and licence to operate
5. Human capital
6. Brand value and reputation

These factors act as indicators of a company's competitiveness. The first two factors impact directly on the profitability of a company, and are largely a result of operational effectiveness, although innovation in product design or service provision can also influence revenues and market access. Access to capital (debt or equity) provides the funds for companies to invest in research and development or newer technologies that enhance productivity, for example, and can also directly impact a company's balance sheet through the cost of this capital. Risk management similarly has direct financial relevance by reducing costly business disruptions, but is also about building relationships with stakeholders, which can affect strategic decision-making and help a company to evolve and differentiate itself from the competition. Human capital reflects the knowledge, skills and talent of the company's workforce, and therefore has a significant impact on its ability to innovate and compete. Finally, a company's reputation, while most directly related to its strategic positioning, can also affect operational effectiveness through the ability to attract capital, quality employees and business partners, and to enter into stakeholder relationships.

The full definition of each of the seven sustainability factors and six business success factors can be found at http://www.sustainability.com/developing-value/definitions.asp.

3.   THE BUSINESS CASE MATRIX

Each case study in the database was analysed to identify links between the seven sustainability factors and six elements of business success as described above. The linkages thus identified have been summarised in a matrix (see Fig. 1), which shows the relative strength of the evidence (rather than strength of impact) linking each pair of business/sustainability factors based on the 240 case studies examined. The strength of evidence was based on both the volume of evidence relevant to each link and the nature of the evidence. Quantitative data was weighted more highly than qualitative material, while anecdotal evidence had the lowest weight. The matrix is thus a visual representation of the linkages, which answers the question: How much evidence is there that a business gains from a specific sustainability action?

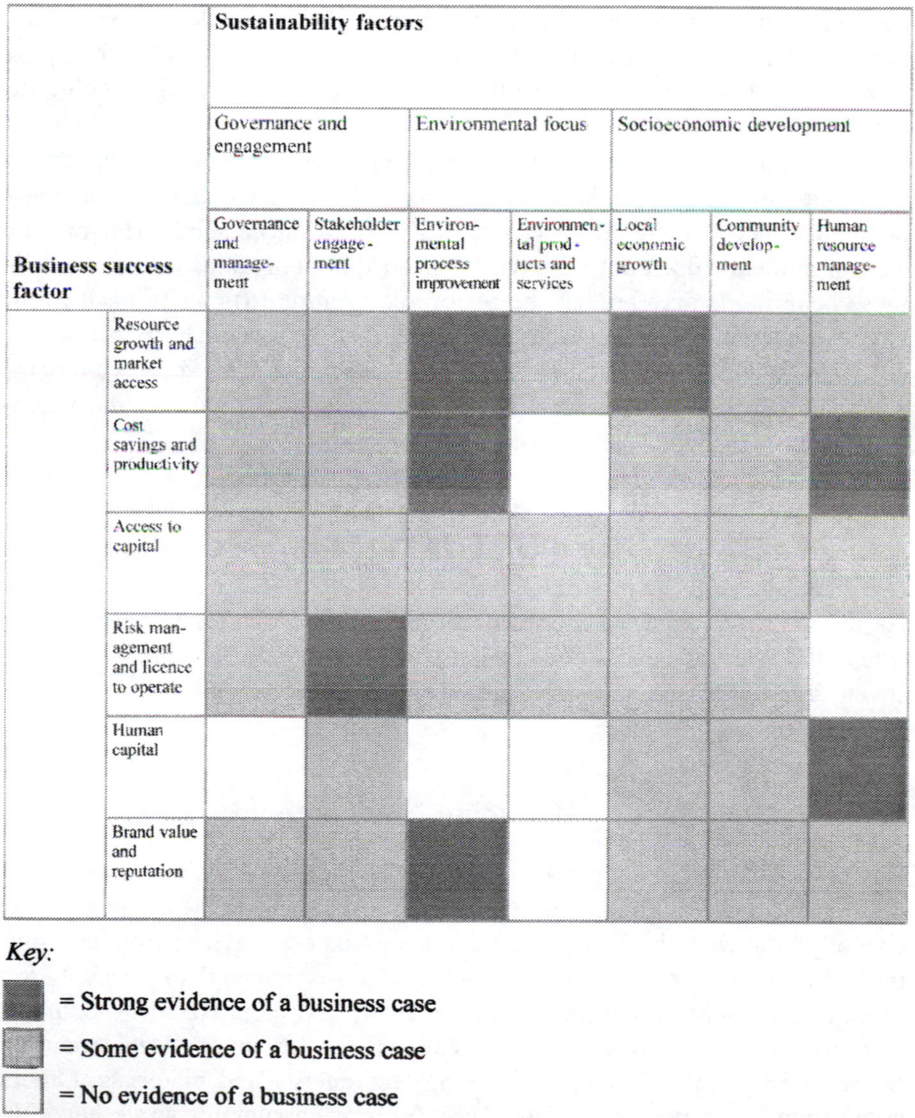

Business success factor	Sustainability factors						
	Governance and engagement		Environmental focus		Socioeconomic development		
	Governance and management	Stakeholder engagement	Environmental process improvement	Environmental products and services	Local economic growth	Community development	Human resource management
Resource growth and market access							
Cost savings and productivity							
Access to capital							
Risk management and licence to operate							
Human capital							
Brand value and reputation							

Key:

■ = Strong evidence of a business case

▨ = Some evidence of a business case

□ = No evidence of a business case

Figure 1. The business case matrix

The dark grey cells identify the strongest evidence. Companies are clearly realising the business benefit described down the left side of the matrix by taking the sustainability action identified across the top. For example, the matrix shows that a company making improvements in working conditions is very likely to achieve greater labour productivity. These key links highlight the nuggets of good practice that present the best business opportunities. The light grey cells, which fill the bulk of the matrix, represent links where there are business benefits, but the evidence is not as strong as the previous seven clear winners. These may, however, represent areas where the business case has the greatest potential to strengthen in the future. For example, there is evidence of opportunities to improve access to capital linked to all seven sustainability factors, the strongest link being to governance and management.

Six cells are uncoloured. In these areas, such as cost savings from environmental products, there are no cases showing evidence of business benefits, although there are other benefits from the sustainability factor. The lack of evidence does not necessarily mean that companies cannot achieve these benefits. It may be that the benefits are more difficult to measure or have not been measured. On the other hand, if these sustainability actions do not yield business benefits, then these might represent areas for governments and other players to assess and redesign framework conditions and incentives to strengthen the business case.

4.   THE BEST OPPORTUNITIES

As the matrix in Figure 1 shows, there are seven links for which the case study evidence of business benefits is particularly strong. The nature of these seven 'best opportunities' was explored in further detail and the findings are summarised here.

4.1   Save Costs by Reducing Environmental Impacts

Businesses can reduce costs by making environmental improvements that deliver an immediate impact on the financial bottom line. More than one in five of all the cases in the database demonstrated cost savings from environmental improvements, often described as 'eco-efficiency' (a concept first presented by Schaltegger and Sturm in 1990, and popularised by Schmidheiny [1992] and the World Business Council for Sustainable Development). Some savings flow directly from using less energy and materials. Others come from lower pollution costs in the form of charges for waste handling and disposal, fees, licences and fines for breaking environmental regulations.

Reorganising production processes, material flows and supplier relationships can also produce benefits such as higher productivity of capital and/or labour. For example, reducing waste volumes can reduce the need for labour and machines that handle waste.

4.2   Save Costs by Treating Employees Well

Effective human resource management can cut costs and boost the productivity of the workforce. Sound employment practices such as fair wages, a clean and safe working environment, training opportunities and health and education benefits for workers and families can all increase morale and productivity while reducing absenteeism and staff turnover. As well as productivity benefits, companies also save on costs for recruitment and training of new employees.

4.3   Increase Revenues through Environmental Improvements

In addition to eco-efficiency benefits, environmental process improvements can lead directly to increased revenues. Successful approaches to improving environmental impacts during production include innovating and developing new processes, viewing 'wastes' as potentially saleable by-products, and making existing products more attractive to concerned customers. Recognition as a responsible producer—informally or through formal certification: for example, ISO 14001 for environmental management systems or Forest Stewardship Council certification for sustainable forestry—can be important in opening the door to some markets in developed countries or achieving premium prices.

4.4   Increase Revenues through Enhancing Local Economic Growth

Action that helps to develop local economies, such as local recruitment, using local suppliers and providing finance and telecommunication facilities, can boost sales and may also have important public relations benefits for companies that are seen to be integrating into the community. Local small and medium-sized enterprises are involving their communities and finding innovative ways to grow sales, both locally and abroad: for example, through eco-tourism and organic farming.

4.5   Reduce Risk through Engagement with Stakeholders

Businesses can reduce financial, reputational and political risks by engaging with stakeholders and thereby obtaining a 'licence to operate', the acceptance of the company's operations by these stakeholders. Regulators grant the legal licence, but the 'local licence to operate'—sometimes the one with the greatest impact on a company's performance—is obtained through consultation and good relations with affected communities. It depends on community support for (or at a minimum a lack of opposition to) a company's activities. It can improve reputation and brand value, while lack of this licence can raise operational and production risks, and create significant costs for the company involved. The business case for risk reduction through engagement is strongest for larger companies, related both to higher societal expectations of these companies and to their often more obvious impacts.

4.6   Enhance Reputation by Increasing Environmental Efficiency

A company's reputation is an intangible asset that helps to build sales, attract capital and business partners, and recruit and retain workers. However, measurement of reputation is not as precise as for many components of business success. Most of the case evidence of improved reputation in this study was in the form of companies receiving recognition and awards from organisations, governments, rating agencies or public surveys. While awards are not always the best benchmarks for reputation and brand value, they can be seen as a reasonable proxy indicator. There is evidence of reputational gains from most of the sustainability factors, although the strongest link is from improving environmental processes. This is consistent with a recent worldwide survey (Roper 2000), which found that environmental responsibility was the third most important expectation of companies, after the basic activities of providing jobs and quality products.

4.7   Develop Human Capital through Better Human Resource Management

A quality workforce is critical for enhancing innovation and key aspects of competitiveness, such as productivity and product quality. This was found to apply in emerging markets even though in many cases there may be a large pool of available workers. Effective human resource management that sets the right polices and practices can improve the knowledge, skills, motivation, health and empowerment of workers. Aspects include providing good working conditions, paying what are seen as fair wages, providing training and development, and ensuring equal opportunities regardless of gender, race, religious persuasion or other factors. Health issues, particularly HIV/AIDS and other infectious diseases, are also pressing areas of concern for human capital. An unhealthy workforce can lead to increased absenteeism, loss of trained employees and high costs for replacement and training.

5.   THE DIVERSITY OF THE BUSINESS CASE

The business case matrix and the seven key opportunities described above illustrate the overall conclusions based on aggregate data. In addition, an initial breakdown of the cases by region and company type was undertaken, with interesting differences emerging, showing that some benefits were more marked in certain regions or for certain company types. While there is significant scope for further research to develop specific business cases by region, country, sector or company type, this initial assessment suggests that companies need to consider their own circumstances when deciding which sustainability opportunities to explore. The challenge for managers is to improve understanding of the links between sustainability performance and business success in their own particular organisations.

5.1   Results by Company Type

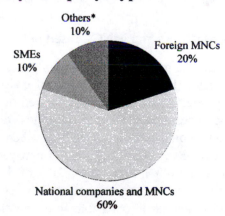

* Others include co-operatives and non-profit organisations, as well as studies that cut across types of companies.

Figure 2. Breakdown of case studies by company type

The companies were divided into the four broad categories indicated in Figure 2. National and multinational (MNC) refers to large companies based in the emerging markets, although they may have operations and customers anywhere in the world. Small and medium-sized enterprises (SMEs) are also based in the emerging markets, but are distinguished by their size. Foreign multinational (MNC) refers to companies operating in emerging markets but with their ownership based in one of the developed markets.

5.1.1 Small and Medium-sized Enterprises (SMEs)

For SMEs, many of which operate in survival mode, even small changes in revenues and costs are critical, time horizons are short and access to capital is problematic. The external sustainability drivers tend to be weaker, as these companies are likely to be under less public pressure to demonstrate high social and environmental standards compared with larger businesses. Nevertheless, a business case does exist for SMEs. It focuses overwhelmingly on cost savings (47% of the SMEs in the study benefit from cost savings, mostly based on environmental process improvements), along with revenue and market access (43% of SMEs). SMEs are leading the way in innovation and the use of 'alternative business models' in creating revenues while generating both social and economic development, through microfinance or 'digital dividend' projects, for example. Creating and supplying environmental products and services, such as eco-tourism and organic agriculture, were more important for the SMEs in the study than for other types of company. On the other hand, there were no examples of enhanced access to capital or risk management among these SMEs.

5.1.2 National Companies and MNCs Based in Emerging Markets

Over half (57%) of the examples of national companies and MNCs in the study enjoyed the greatest benefits in the form of cost savings. However, unlike the SMEs analysed, for which savings derived mostly from environmental processes, the benefits here came from almost all the sustainability factors. Several national companies and MNCs also benefited from sustainability in two ways that SMEs did not, through improved risk management (18%) and access to capital (4%). In addition, 20% of the companies in this category also enjoyed improved reputation, which resulted from a wide variety of sustainability factors: in particular, human resource management and environmental process improvements. Socioeconomic growth was a more important sustainability factor than for other categories of company.

5.1.3 Foreign MNCs

There were examples of foreign multinationals which experienced financial benefits from improved sustainability in all areas. But, compared with companies based in emerging markets, cost saving was found to be less important (30% of the foreign MNCs studied), and the focus on intangibles, including risk reduction (24%) and human and intellectual capital (11%), was found to be greater. Even more than for national companies, risk management was an important aspect of sustainability's contribution to business success for foreign MNCs. Driven by a range of stakeholder pressure both in their home country and their country of operation, MNCs based in the developed markets derive benefits from engagement and social development activities as a means of managing risk and maintaining their local licence to operate.

5.1.4   Market Focus

In addition to the type and size of company, market focus—whether the company trades domestically or internationally—also has a significant influence over how firms gain from sustainability. Export-oriented companies are more likely to concentrate on meeting international environmental and labour standards, and on adherence to recognised management systems (especially certification) in order to gain greater access to international markets and customers, and sometimes price premiums. Companies focused on the domestic market, on the other hand, respond to a wider range of local societal pressures but reap more diverse rewards. They are more likely to gain from local economic and community development, which fosters licence to operate and helps companies to further their own revenue growth. Proactive stakeholder engagement is another way in which companies producing for domestic consumption benefit, through lower risks and a reduction in costly production delays.

5.2   Results by Region

Attitudes to sustainable development vary widely from region to region, and even within regions. While broad generalisations can be dangerous, the case studies analysed show some regional differences in the opportunities being grasped by companies. This does not necessarily mean that opportunities are not available to all companies in all regions; just that local priorities and pressures play an important role in the particular benefits experienced. It may also suggest areas for cross-regional learning, both for the corporate sector and for other stakeholders that wish to help companies improve their sustainability activities.

The following analysis looks at four regions: East Asia and the Pacific, South Asia (Bangladesh, India, Nepal, Pakistan and Sri Lanka), Sub-Saharan Africa, and Latin America and the Caribbean (see Fig. 3). It is based on trends from the case studies, also highlighting some other relevant research and perspectives related to the regions. Since for all regions (except South Asia) the strongest evidence of a business case was for environmental improvements leading to cost savings, the discussion focuses on the other relevant links in each region.

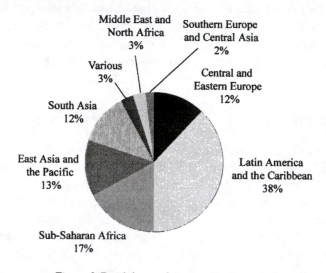

Figure 3. Breakdown of case studies by region

5.2.1 East Asia and the Pacific

Companies in East Asia and the Pacific experience strong benefits from environmental and social management systems, particularly those that are internationally recognised, such as ISO 14001 and SA8000. Production for the global market is important for many of these companies, and certification systems can help them to win international customers. Interestingly, however, cost savings are the main benefit from implementation of these management systems, even if they are developed to meet customer demands. A survey in Thailand found similar results: 76% of the respondents achieved cost savings from ISO 14001, and more than two-thirds greater efficiency (Thailand Environment Institute 1999). Another key area is corporate governance. The 1997 Asian crisis has been influential in spawning calls for greater transparency and better corporate governance in the region, and companies such as the Bank of Shanghai (see Box 1) are starting to experience benefits. It is notable that, unlike in many other regions, companies in East Asia and the Pacific did not show significant benefits from better community relations, perhaps because of relatively weaker pressure from NGOs, trade unions and consumer groups. This result is consistent with a global study by Environics International (2001), which found that only 8% of citizens in Asia had punished companies for being socially irresponsible, compared with 23% in Latin America and 42% in North America.

Box 1. The Bank of Shanghai

Location: China (East Asia and the Pacific)
Company type: national company
Sector: finance and insurance
Business case: governance and management leading to access to capital

The Bank of Shanghai (BoS) was established in 1995 through an amalgamation of 99 urban credit co-operatives. It has grown rapidly and remains the largest of about 110 'city commercial banks' in China. But it is still relatively small: 4,500 employees, 45 branches and 198 business offices. Through representation on the Board of BoS, the International Finance Corporation (IFC) has effectively assisted BoS in implementing international banking best practices and improving corporate governance. This has included, for example, annual external audits in accordance with international accounting standards and the creation of audit, compensation and risk management committees under the board of directors. As a result, BoS has become a leader and model bank in China for emulation by other city commercial banks.

The corporate governance improvements to enhance transparency and link the bank's performance to management pay scales have resulted in major improvements in the bank's asset quality and profitability, and, as a result, have made the bank more attractive to overseas investors. In December 2001, HSBC signed an agreement to acquire an 8% equity stake in the Bank of Shanghai for approximately US$62.6 million.

Source: International Finance Corporation

5.2.2 South Asia

Social issues such as harmful child labour, fair labour practices and community welfare are more prominent than environmental concerns in South Asia, the only region for which eco-efficiency benefits were not common. In some countries, such as India, large companies commonly provide comprehensive welfare benefits for employees—well beyond what would be expected in developed countries—including subsidised housing, children's education and development resources for neighbouring communities. However, indications suggest that the environment will become a more important issue in this region in future. A survey in India, for example, found that the general public perceives the primary role of companies to be providing quality products at cheap prices, but then expects them to ensure that operations are environmentally friendly and that employees are treated fairly in accordance with global standards (Kumar *et al.* 2001).

5.2.3   Sub-Saharan Africa

Despite significant commercial pressures in Africa, there was substantial evidence of a business case in the social areas, as well as a focus on human resource management. Some of the community focus may derive from governments' unwillingness or inability to provide services. Ayo Ajayi, Managing Director and CEO of UAC of Nigeria plc, says, 'In developed countries, governments provide education, health, law and order. In Africa, these are areas where companies are likely to use up their CSR budget. Good leadership is lacking in Africa' (World Economic Forum and Environics International 2002). Health is an important issue; company activities range from focusing on safe working conditions to HIV/AIDS initiatives. While it is difficult to quantify costs and benefits of HIV schemes accurately, one study found that the total cost per new HIV infection (due to sick leave, productivity loss, recruitment, training, etc.) is likely to be greater than the cost of treatment and care to keep employees in the workforce (Barks-Ruggles *et al.* 2001). Companies in Africa with a proactive approach to managing the labour force are also experiencing increased productivity and motivation, and lower staff turnover. In the area of environmental products/ services, the development of organic agriculture and eco-tourism, for example, have led to important revenue gains for African companies.

Box 2. Anglo American Corporation

Location: South Africa (Sub-Saharan Africa)
Company type: emerging market MNC
Sector: oil, gas and mining
Business case: local economic growth leading to cost savings and productivity

Anglo American Corporation is a leading mining and natural resources company, and has a long record of support for disadvantaged black communities in South Africa. One aspect of this is now known as Zimele, a Zulu/Xhosa word which means 'independence'. The unit exists specifically to build local economies, especially black communities, by helping to expand the small business sector. Originally support was aimed at micro-enterprises but now the targets are bigger, which led to the formalisation of Zimele as a self-sufficient business unit in 2000. Zimele takes a minority equity stake and may make loans to the businesses it backs. Crucially it also takes a seat on the board and continues to support the new entrepreneurs. It can call on the skills of Anglo's managers—from information technology to mining expertise—and makes sure these new businesses adopt the high standards of health and safety to which Anglo subscribes. Early in 2002 the operation had investments in 22 companies, which together provided work for 1,300 people and had revenues of 145 million rand (US$15 million). Many of Zimele's SMEs are based on linkages developed from outsourcing opportunities at the mining operations including bakeries and catering, conveyor belt maintenance, railway maintenance, engineering, fuel supplies, laundry services and garment manufacturing and transport.

Apart from the general benefits from helping to build—and being seen to build—a more vibrant economy, the Zimele operation also meshes with Anglo's policy of outsourcing many non-core operations. It means there are reliable, viable, local businesses that can become suppliers to the group with more fruitful and trusting relationships than would be the case with outsourcing based solely on price.

Source: SustainAbility Ltd

5.2.4 Latin America and the Caribbean

The most important link in Latin America (after eco-efficiency) was for cost savings and higher productivity from good human resource management. This emphasis on labour force issues may derive from the strong trade union tradition in many countries, although the role of trade unions has generally weakened in recent years. The evidence also shows that Latin American companies have improved their access to capital through actions in all seven sustainability factors, a fact that did not hold true in any other region. Governance and management systems and environmental process improvements demonstrate the strongest link to access to capital for these firms. Finally, companies in Latin America, as in Africa, are benefiting from environmental products and services, the only two regions to do so. Companies have increased revenues and accessed new export markets through organic products such as coffee in Colombia and Venezuela, and sugar and heart of palm in Brazil.

Box 3. Girsa

Location: Mexico (Latin America and the Caribbean)
Company type: national company
Sector: chemicals
Business case: environmental process improvement leading to cost savings and productivity, risk management and licence to operate, as well as brand value and reputation

Girsa invested in a comprehensive two-phase corporate modernisation programme over eight business units. From 1994 to 1998 Girsa restructured and consolidated its operations with the aim of becoming a low-cost producer and upgrading its environmental standards for more stringent regulations under the North American Free Trade Agreement (NAFTA). In the second phase, from 1999 to 2001, Girsa further modernised existing plants through quality, technology and process improvements and reduced costs, expanded capacity and established a joint venture with a leading world chemicals producer to enter niche markets. From 1991 to 1998, while production more than tripled, the plant reduced CO_2 emissions from 3.9 to 0.65 tons per ton of output, waste-water from 13.7 to 1.5 cubic metres per ton of production, and solid waste from 69.8 to 5.3 pounds. In its efforts to improve relations with the surrounding community, Girsa went beyond merely mitigating the plant's impacts. It has partnered with technical institutions and universities to offer training and conduct research and development activities, and shares its best practices with other businesses. Girsa conceives and designs all its projects considering the best cost–benefit alternatives, which in general take the new project to pollution prevention/waste minimisation options. The environmental team is an integral part of the business decision-making process of Girsa.

Girsa has invested more than US$20 million in environmental efficiency improvements, including the capture and use of energy generated in the carbon black process, which yielded US$30 million in savings and has substantially reduced emissions and waste. It also sells the CO_2 releases from one of the plants to another plant, with the net income as a percentage of sales rising from negative 40% in 1991 to 21% in 1998. The plant has gone from being a major source of controversy in the community to a model corporate citizen that locals are proud of. Formal community complaints lodged against the plant dropped from 12 in 1991 to none in 1998. It has won numerous accolades for its performance at national and international levels, including the Mexican Environment Ministry's National Quality Award in 1997 and the National Award for Ecological Merit in 1999.

Source: International Finance Corporation

6.   RECOMMENDATIONS AND CONCLUSION

Sustainability can no longer be seen as a luxury that emerging markets cannot afford. Many businesses in emerging markets have improved their competitiveness and gained valuable business benefits from initiatives that help progress towards sustainable development: good corporate governance, sound environmental practice, and social and economic development. The research outlined above highlights some of the ways in which companies that may not have previously recognised the links can find business value from sustainability, while also highlighting key differences between regions as well as between types of company. Most importantly, it confirms that there are compelling commercial reasons to take action.

This is not to say that sustainability offers a magic recipe for success. It can contribute to success, but will not offset poor business practices or compensate for bad decisions in conventional aspects of marketing, production or financial control. Companies must assess risks and analyse the costs and benefits of sustainability action as they would for other activities. For many companies, meeting minimal requirements may be all that is possible in the short term. But the successful companies in emerging markets will anticipate these growing expectations and derive value from them. The more sustainability is developed and integrated into core business management and processes, the more risks and opportunities will be better understood and managed.

The business case is evolving, reflecting changing expectations and relevance. A few years ago the environmental and social agenda was widely thought to be a fringe movement, but today companies are increasingly taking these concerns on board as their customers, investors and employees are examining their sustainability performance along the whole value chain. As this agenda continues to become more mainstream, there will be growing opportunities for companies to derive competitive advantage by incorporating sustainability into their business strategies.

REFERENCES

Barks-Ruggles, E., Fantan, T., McPherson, M. and Whiteside, A. (2001) *The Economic Impact of HIV/AIDS in Southern Africa*. Washington, DC: The Brookings Institution.

Elkington, J. (1997) *Cannibals with Forks: The Triple Bottom Line of 21st Century Business*. Oxford: Capstone Publishing.

Environics International Ltd (2001) *Corporate Social Responsibility Monitor*. Toronto: Environics International.

Grossman, G. and Krueger, A. (1995) 'Economic Growth and the Environment', *Quarterly Journal of Economics* Vol. 110 No. 2, 353-377.

Hart, S. and Ahuja, G. (1996) 'Does it Pay to be Green? An Empirical Examination of the Relationship between Emission Reduction and Firm Performance', *Business Strategy and the Environment* No. 5, 30-37.

IFC (International Finance Corporation) (2003) *Measuring Sustainability: A Framework for Private Sector Investments*. Washington, DC: IFC.

Kumar, R., Murphy, D.F. and Balsari, V. (2001) *Altered Images: The 2001 State of Corporate Responsibility in India Poll*. New Delhi: Tata Energy Research Institute.

Kuznets, S. (1955) 'Economic Growth and Income Inequality', *American Economic Review* Vol. 45 No. 1, 1-28.

Porter, M. (1998) *On Competitiveness*. Boston: Harvard Business School Publishing.

Repetto, R. and Austin, D. (2000) *Pure Profit: The Financial Implications of Environmental Performance*. Washington, DC: World Resources Institute.

Roper Reports Worldwide (2000) 'Cause Branding: Does Social Good = Market Share'. Presentation of consumer research by Roper ASW.

Schaltegger, S. and Figge, F. (1997) *Environmental Shareholder Value*. WWZ/Sarasin Basic Research Study No. 54; Basel: WWZ.

Schaltegger, S. and Sturm, A. (1990) 'Ecological Rationality: Starting Points for the Development of Environmental Management Tools', *Die Unternehmung* Vol. 4, 273-290.

Schaltegger, S. and Synnestvedt, T. (2002) 'The Link between "Green" and Economic Success: Environmental Management as the Crucial Trigger between Environmental and Economic Performance', *Journal of Environmental Management* No. 65, 339-346.

Schmidheiny, S. (1992) *Changing Course: A Global Business Perspective on Development and the Environment*. Cambridge, MA: The MIT Press.

SustainAbility, International Finance Corporation and Ethos Institute (2002) *Developing Value: The Business Case for Sustainability in Emerging Markets*. London: Sustain-Ability.

SustainAbility and UNEP (United Nations Environment Programme) (2001) *Buried Treasure: Uncovering the Business Case for Corporate Sustainability*. London: Sustain-Ability.

Thailand Environment Institute (1999) *How Can it Benefit Business? A Survey of ISO 14001 Certified Companies in Thailand*. Bangkok: Thailand Environment Institute.

Verschoor, C. (1999) 'Corporate Performance is Closely Linked to a Strong Ethical Commitment', *Business and Society Review* Vol. 104 No. 4, 407-415.

Waddock, S. and Graves, S.B. (1997) 'The Corporate Social Performance–Financial Performance Link', *Strategic Management Journal* Vol. 18 No. 4, 303-319.

Waddock, S., Bodwell, C. and Graves, S.B. (2002) 'Responsibility: The New Business Imperative', *Academy of Management Executive* Vol. 16 No. 2, 132-148.

Wagner, M. (2001) *A Review of Empirical Studies Concerning the Relationship between Environmental and Economic Performance: What Does the Evidence Tell Us?* Lüneburg: University of Lüneburg, Centre for Sustainability Management.

World Bank (2002) *Global Economic Prospects and the Developing Countries: Making Trade Work for the World's Poor*. Washington, DC: World Bank.

World Economic Forum and Environics International (2002) *The World Economic Forum Poll: Global Public Opinion on Globalization*. www.environicsinternational.com/global.

APPENDIX

Table 1 summarises the cases that made up the matrix. In each cell, the first number represents the total number of case studies corresponding to that cell. The second number in brackets represents the total score given to the cell, based on how substantial each case was judged to be. Cases with quantitative evidence of the business case were weighted more strongly than those based on qualitative evidence, which were in turn more strongly weighted than those based on anecdotal evidence: for example, a comment by the CEO, or by a major customer of the company of how a sustainability activity has affected business success.

The case studies on which this research and the 'business case matrix' were based are freely available through an online, searchable database at http://www.sustainability.com/developing-value/search.asp. The database describes companies of different sizes and from different industries, outlining the sustainability actions (environmental, social and governance) they have undertaken and the business benefits they have experienced as a result. It can be search in three ways: based on individual criteria (country, world region, sector, type of company, sustainability factor, business success factor), based on the matrix itself, or through an advanced search function that allows searching by multiple criteria or keywords. Where the information has been based on publicly available sources, the source is also provided. Please note that the information from these sources has not been independently verified by the authors of the report.

Table 1. Summary of case studies that make up the business case matrix

	Governance and engagement		Environmental focus		Socioeconomic development		
	Governance and management	Stakeholder engagement	Environmental process improvement	Environmental products and services	Local economic growth	Community development	Human resource management
Revenue growth and market access	7 (16)	1 (1)	10 (24)	7 (15)	12 (24)	12 (17)	4 (8)
Cost saving and productivity	9 (17)	4 (7)	128 (46)	0	5 (5)	4 (7)	13 (28)
Access to capital	6 (15)	1 (2)	1 (3)	3 (7)	1 (1)	1 (3)	2 (6)

	Governance and engagement		Environmental focus		Socioeconomic development		
	Governance and management	Stakeholder engagement	Environmental process improvement	Environmental products and services	Local economic growth	Community development	Human resource management
Risk management and licence to operate	4 (4)	11 (21)	7 (14)	1 (1)	4 (5)	4 (6)	0
Human capital	0	1 (1)	0	0	2 (2)	3 (5)	15 (22)
Brand value and reputation	4 (5)	2 (3)	11 (22)	0	2 (4)	10 (17)	6 (14)

ACKNOWLEDGEMENTS

This chapter summarises the report *Developing Value: The Business Case for Sustainability in Emerging Markets* prepared by the strategy consultancy SustainAbility; the International Finance Corporation (IFC), the private-sector arm of the World Bank Group; and the Ethos Institute in Brazil. See http://www.sustainability.com/developing-value.

Chapter 8

Company Cases

MANAGING SUSTAINABILITY PERFORMANCE IN THE TEXTILE CHAIN

Stefan Seuring and Maria Goldbach
Supply Chain Management Centre, Carl von Ossietzky Universität Oldenburg, Germany

Abstract: Intense global competition is a feature of the textile and apparel industry. Customer demand triggers short product life-cycles and volatile markets that react quickly to new trends. Furthermore, the textile and apparel industry is frequently held accountable for the environmental and social problems along the supply chain that occur during textile and clothing production. Leading companies have meanwhile found ways to improve the environmental and social performance of their supply chain while staying competitive in their respective markets. This chapter reports on Otto GmbH & Co. KG and Steilmann GmbH & Co. KG—two German-based companies that have introduced measures to improve the sustainability performance of their supply chain while offering environmentally improved products at competitive prices.

1. INTRODUCTION

The performance of companies is highly dependent on the performance of their suppliers and supply chain. This is the case for all three dimensions of sustainability, as environmental and social criteria have to be met while staying competitive in the market. This is especially true for the textile and apparel industry. Few other industries with the same basic conditions possess intense competition through global production as well as the environmental and social problems along all stages of the supply chain. Such problems have been addressed by various special interest groups, which demand that textile and apparel producers and retailers should obey a certain level of environmental and social standards. Meanwhile, leading companies have taken steps to not only respond to such claims, but also to manage their supply chain proactively to reduce environmental impacts during the various stages of production while taking the social needs of employees into account. This must all be done while successfully selling clothing of improved environmental performance to customers. This chapter reports on two such cases from the fashion industry and contains four sections:

First, environmental and social problems along the textile and apparel supply chain are discussed to highlight the need to improve the sustainability performance of such chains. Brief remarks on supply chain management are then made and the product–relationship matrix is introduced as a framework for systematic decisions in setting up and running a supply chain. Thirdly, the relation between sustainability and supply chain performance is addressed and two textile chain focal companies introduced—Otto GmbH & Co. KG, a leading German mail order business, and Steilmann GmbH & Co. KG, a leading European fashion producer. The product–relationship matrix is used to structure the analysis of how these companies respond to such challenges and improve their sustainability performance. Finally, some concluding remarks are made.

2.   SUSTAINABILITY IN THE TEXTILE AND APPAREL INDUSTRY

When discussing issues of sustainability within the textile and apparel industry, it is helpful to refer to the three-dimensional concept that allows environmental, social and economic issues to be taken into account. These are regularly taken up in sustainability reporting guidelines (see GRI 2002), and form a valid basis for guiding measures that need to be respected by companies. This is also in line with the United Nations Global Compact (see Internet URL: http://www.unglobalcompact.org), which was first proposed by UN Secretary General Kofi Annan during the World Economic Forum on 31 January 1999. Amid a backdrop of rising concerns about the effects of globalisation, this forum also addressed the 'triple' bottom line of sustainability. Yet companies cannot enact this by looking at their internal processes and products alone, but also must obey the supply chains of which they are a part. This is especially true for so-called focal companies that are in close contact with customers, and manage or control the supply chain (Schary and Skjoett-Larsen 2001:96).

As mentioned above, the textile and apparel industry is of particular interest because examples illustrate the pressure raised by non-governmental organisations (NGOs) on focal companies in the textile chain. Prominent examples spotlighting the textile chain are the Clean Clothes Campaign (Internet URL: http://www.cleanclothes.org), Social Accountability International (Internet URL: http://www.cepaa.org) and the Pesticide Action Network North America (Internet URL: http://www.panna.org).

These NGOs often concentrate their activities on certain issues, e.g. working conditions as a social problem or the use of pesticides in cotton farming as an environmental one. Companies placed under pressure and attacked directly include Adidas, Benetton, Disney, Levi Strauss, Nike and Rebook. Considerable public attention was generated by the activities of the Clean Clothes Campaign during the last two football World Cups in 1998 and 2002. This topic is also frequently tackled by the media such as a recent report on German TV, to name only one example of many. Problems addressed include child labour, working conditions, access to fresh water and toilets as well as the use of environmentally harmful substances used during production.

These examples illustrate the need for focal companies to obey the environmental and social dimension of their corporate activities, which call for a management of the supply chain (Myers and Stolton 1999). Traditionally, the textile industry has been highly fragmented. Products are bought from suppliers as needed and on a short-term basis (Fisher 1997:107; Forza *et al.* 2000:227). Previously, retailers were only in contact with their first-tier suppliers and did not care about environmental or social problems arising along the supply chain.

This has changed due to the pressure raised by NGOs. If focal companies want to introduce products with reduced environmental impacts, they have to manage their supply chain proactively and build relationships with, and in all stages of, the supply chain. Objectives are usually set to meet environmental and social standards while reaching competitive prices for their clothing products (Seuring 2001a, 2001b). Thus environmental and social criteria form a baseline for sustainability performance, while the competitiveness of the supply chain is achieved through successful performance in the economic arena.

3.   SUPPLY CHAIN MANAGEMENT

One of the most cited definitions of supply chain management is that of Handfield and Nichols (1999:2): 'The supply chain encompasses all activities associated with the flow and transformation of goods from raw materials stage (extraction), through to the end user, as well as the associated information flows. Material and information flow both up and down the supply chain. Supply chain management (SCM) is the integration of these activities through improved supply chain relationships, to achieve a sustainable competitive advantage.'

Therefore, the needs and abilities of all companies must be taken into account, as the competitiveness of the chain will only be as strong as its weakest link (Croom *et al.* 2000:67). Hence, the decisions framing the supply chain must be integrated into a conceptual framework for supply chain management covering both the material and information flows and their relationships. Cooper and Slagmulder (1999:10) distinguish the product and the relationship dimension, which are each subdivided into a constitutional and an operational phase.

This separation into two phases builds on life-cycle thinking. The first phase looks at the constitutional decisions taken to design the product or the supply chain. The second phase is operational, i.e. the material and information flows in the chain are performed. Therefore, within the product dimension, the two phases of product design and production are separated while the relationship dimension is split into network design and interface optimisation. Taking the two dimensions and their interrelations together, the product–relationship matrix is formed (Figure 1).

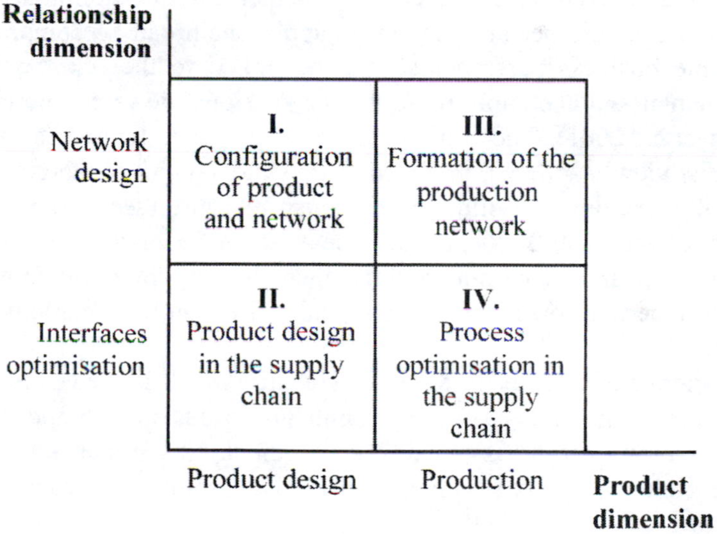

Relationship dimension

	Product design	Production
Network design	**I.** Configuration of product and network	**III.** Formation of the production network
Interfaces optimisation	**II.** Product design in the supply chain	**IV.** Process optimisation in the supply chain

Product design   Production   **Product dimension**

Figure 1. The product–relationship matrix of supply chain management (Source: Seuring 2002:18)

Within the product–relationship matrix, four fields result that can be used as a decision framework for supply chain management. These four fields constitute a decision process for managing the supply chain, which will be described below.

Competitiveness is achieved by taking a single entity view of the supply chain. Linking this to the performance debate in strategic management (Porter 1996) and operations management (Schmenner and Swink 1998), the picture of the performance frontier can be used. This implies that, when aiming to reach contrary objectives (as single companies in the supply chain might) trade-offs (Corbett and van Wassenhove 1993) are incurred only if the performance frontier is reached. Otherwise, the performance achieved concerning contrary objectives (e.g. quality and cost) can be improved towards both measures. This calls for co-operation with risk and reward sharing in the supply chain (Handfield and Nichols 1999:87), as companies within the supply chain will only invest if they believe that investments will pay off in the long run (Gunasekaran *et al.* 2001). This idea will be taken up below when discussing the relation between sustainability and business performance in the supply chain.

4.   SUSTAINABILITY AND BUSINESS PERFORMANCE IN SUPPLY CHAINS

Bringing the different issues discussed together, the question arises of how sustainable business performance in a supply chain can be comprehended. Sustainable business performance can be linked to the relation between environmental and economic performance. Various views can be identified (Wagner *et al.* 2001). The 'traditional view' assumes trade-offs, while the 'revisionist view' supposes improved environmental and economic performance of, for example, a pollution abatement measure (see also Schaltegger and Synnestvedt 2002). Integrating these views, a picture results where environmental and economic performance initially increase jointly and, following a certain level of environmental protection, the relations become negative.

In a simplified transfer to the supply chain (which is viewed as a single entity), such relations between environmental or sustainable and economic performance can also be assumed. Focal company performance is therefore dependent on that of its suppliers and is also evaluated in such terms by stakeholders.

5.   THE FOCAL COMPANIES

5.1   Steilmann and Eco-Polyester

The company, Klaus Steilmann GmbH & Co. KG, was founded in 1958 in Wattenscheid in the Ruhr region of Germany. Company headquarters are still located there today. Steilmann's core business is confectioning and clothing sales. Major customers include Marks & Spencer and C&A. In 2001, the company had a turnover of over 700 million euros and employed about 14,500 people, mainly in Rumania, where currently about 12,000 (mostly female) employees work.

Apparel made from polyester traditionally plays an important role among the product range offered to its suppliers. In the mid-1990s, Steilmann was approached by a chemical company with the suggestion that a new, environmentally improved polyester quality might be used for its products. This company had developed a new catalyst for the polymerisation process, which uses titanium dioxide instead of antimony trioxide (antimony is a heavy metal closely related to arsenic), thus eliminating the problem of heavy metal usage in the polymerisation process. During subsequent production steps, small quantities of antimony spill over into the waste water.

5.2   Otto and Organic Cotton

Otto GmbH & Co. KG is the largest mail order business in the world. Otto was founded in 1949 in Hamburg, Germany. While its headquarters remain there, the Otto Group currently consists of 90 companies in 23 countries, employing almost 76,000 people worldwide with a turnover of 23.5 billion euros in 2001. Exceeded only by Amazon.com, Otto runs the second-largest online shop in the world. The products traded by Otto cover a wide range including clothes, electronics and household appliances.

Otto started introducing environmentally improved apparel into its collections in the early 1990s. These optimisations comprised both cotton and other fibre collections and aimed at limiting harmful substances at the product level. In 1997, Otto decided to go one step further and extended the optimisations to the production process up to the 'cradle' of cotton apparel production, the cotton plant. The aim was to provide sustainable cotton clothing for a highly fashionable mass market. The challenge was realising a value-adding process in which economic, ecological and social aspects would be equally respected. These sustainable cotton clothes were not to cost considerably more than conventional ones while at the same time maintaining Otto's high quality and fashion standards. The major question arising in this context was not only how to solve the technical problems of sustainability, but how to co-ordinate the activities of the highly complex network of different partners involved (Goldbach 2002, 2003; Kogg 2003).

6.   MEASURES FOR SUSTAINABILITY PERFORMANCE IN THE TEXTILE CHAIN

In this section, the product–relationship matrix is applied to illustrate which measures Otto and Steilmann implemented to improve the sustainability performance of their supply chains. Even though these measures were triggered by the will to sell products with an improved sustainability performance, many issues are mirrored in conventional supply chain management literature and are related to general trends in supply chain management.

6.1   Configuration of Product and Network

The configuration of product and network covers the strategic decisions in which products and services are offered in co-operation with other companies. This includes the question of how the co-ordination among supply chain partners can be organised most efficiently and effectively. Within supply chain management, it is assumed that intermediate forms of co-ordination that have neither the disadvantages of hierarchies nor those of free, unlimited markets are superior to both extremes of the continuum (Schary and Skjoett-Larsen 2001).

Concerning sustainability performance, this dimension includes the definition of environmental and social criteria for supplier evaluation laid down in the supplier and purchasing guidelines of Otto (Otto 2001, 2002) and Steilmann (Steilmann 1999, 2000), and in additional 'codes of conduct' for social standards to be met by suppliers. These guidelines include social aspects taken up from wider standards that include:

- No child labour is to be used as defined by UN standards
- The right to form and join trade unions is not suppressed
- Working conditions are safe and do not impair the health of employees

The rather normative requirements are combined with the strategic goal of the focal companies and their will to sell products sourced in this fashion on competitive markets. Thus, the following three fields of the product–relationship matrix help to set this into action.

6.2   Product Design in the Supply Chain

Product design in the supply chain aims to utilise the research and development know-how of suppliers. New materials or process technologies are developed and need to be integrated into the supply chain because they might set the trend for new products; this can be observed regularly in the apparel industry (Fisher *et al.* 1994:84) This leads to strategic sourcing decisions in which a company must conclude which parts of the product development process belong to its core competencies, which parts can be outsourced in strategic partnerships, and which parts can be purchased on commodity markets.

This field specifies the product to be produced and sold. Usually, the focal companies design the clothing products they want to sell and then look for a supplier who is able to produce them at the specified price (Seuring 2001b:76). In both cases (i.e. organic cotton and eco-polyester), environmental criteria have been set that ensure that the final products meet the requirement of being free from harmful substances. In the case of eco-polyester, the necessary changes in the single production stages along the supply chain made it necessary to start joint optimisation efforts with suppliers. These made it possible to fulfil all technical and cost requirements, allowing linings from eco-polyester to be introduced as part of the first step (Seuring 2001b).

Such efforts are needed if a new, environmentally improved fibre quality is to be introduced. During the design of each piece of clothing, the production requirements of suppliers must be kept in mind. This ensures that the clothing is producible for the suppliers at a reasonable cost. This leads directly to the next field.

6.3   Formation of the Production Network

Production in the textile chain is spread around the globe. Consequently, the decisions to be made within the formation of the production network involve the choice of production partners and the definition of their specific role. The processes carried out at the single production facilities, stock holding points and (delivery) cycle times must be specified, usually with the aim of achieving the lowest total cost (Romano and Vinelli 2001).

At this point, the social and environmental criteria specified are set in motion. Otto and Steilmann conduct supplier audits during which they check whether their suppliers adhere to the code of conduct and achieve the environmental standards set. But to achieve competitiveness, they have to advance further. To acquire designed products that meet all environmental and social criteria, Otto and Steilmann need to form partnerships with their suppliers.

Steilmann formed a close partnership with a textile company and a chemical company, which produces eco-polyester. This three-stage supply chain is shorter than traditional supply chains, limiting the need for co-ordination among suppliers and Steilmann (Goffin *et al.* 1997; Seuring 2001b).

Otto formed a production network for organic cotton in Turkey, where several partners are involved in several stages of the supply chain (Seuring and Goldbach 2002:356). First, this supply network guarantees the stability needed to allow all partners to achieve the environmental and social criteria set. Secondly, joint optimisation is possible within such a network across all stages of the supply chain. This allows implementation of measures for environmental improvements and cost savings. Overall, an organisational result that is able to deliver products at competitive prices (Goldbach 2002).

6.4   Process Optimisation in the Supply Chain

Process optimisation in the supply chain as the last field covers most of the traditional supply chain literature. Using a continuous improvement perspective, existing processes are analysed to identify improvement potentials. Guiding objectives are often the reduction of cycle times and inventories along the supply chain.

Such approaches were still needed in the textile chains discussed. Otto introduced a programme to help its suppliers to improve their production processes to achieve both reduced environmental impacts and improved economic performance. By creating such 'win–win' situations, the suppliers are encouraged to accept the additional requirements Otto imposes on them. These measures are of general help to the suppliers, even though they do not exclusively sell to Otto. In other words, Otto 'invests' in the suppliers, although it is not certain that either side will continue to sell or buy from the other one in the future (Seuring 2001a; Goldbach 2003).

Direct changes at the production processes allowed Steilmann and its polyester linings supplier to introduce a new mode of joint production planning. Previously, linings were manufactured in a made-to-order mode and it required a lead time of two weeks before Steilmann received linings from a supplier. In the new make-to-stock mode, which is exclusively offered to Steilmann, the new eco-polyester is held in stock in a set of predefined colours. After an order is placed, it takes only two weeks to deliver the linings to Steilmann (Seuring 2001b). Steilmann is committed to this supplier and sources all its linings exclusively from this textile company. Furthermore, to allow for easier production, Steilmann and the supplier set up a joint improvement process which, for example, led to a major reduction in the colours ordered. This created a further improvement in operations, as fewer colours ordered by Steilmann leads to fewer set-up costs at the supplier (Seuring and Goldbach 2002).

7.   CONCLUSIONS ON SUSTAINABILITY PERFORMANCE IN THE TEXTILE CHAIN

After presenting the single measures taken, the overall issues of sustainability performance in the textile and apparel industry need to be addressed. The product–relationship matrix has been used as a framework for the discussion of two cases. Only by taking all four fields into account can a complete picture be obtained.

Close co-operation is necessary for the supply chain to operate competitively. Without the co-operation of their suppliers, Otto and Steilmann would not be able to offer products that obey social standards with an improved environmental performance at competitive prices.

Looking at the sustainability performance of the textile chains discussed, it is evident that the performance among the social dimension is mainly determined by the suppliers along the textile chain. Otto and Steilmann use social audits to ensure that no problems occur and that codes of conduct are met, thus responding to pressure raised by NGOs.

The environmental dimension covers two well-known issues. Production at the suppliers has to be carried out in a way that reduces environmental impacts and the products themselves have to be environmentally friendly (this is ensured by testing them for harmful substances).

These two dimensions form the basis that allows the companies to maintain their business in the long-run. The economic dimension is closely interlinked with this: the companies have to operate in competitive markets, which is possible only by selling such products for the price of conventional ones (Meyer and Hohmann 2000).

Even though the link between the different dimensions of sustainability should not be simplified (see the comparable discussion by Newton and Harte 1997), much of the evidence presented shows that 'win–win' situations can be identified where the performance towards the social or environmental dimensions and economic success is improved. However, the measures discussed do not come without cost and effort, so negative relations between the three dimensions are also found where contrasting objectives will have to be met by supply chain partners. In such trade-off situations, no simple solution is available and only long-term commitments can help companies push their performance frontier further over time.

The cases described provide some hints on how sustainable performance and business competitiveness are interlinked. As the supply chain is the entity on which a company's success depends, future research will need to take a broader look at supply chain issues.

REFERENCES

Cooper, R. and Slagmulder, R. (1999): *Supply Chain Development for the Lean Enterprise— Interorganisational Cost Management*. Portland: Productivity Press.

Corbett, C.J. and Wassenhove, L.N. van (1993): 'Trade-Offs? What Trade-Offs? Competence and Competitiveness in Manufacturing Strategy', *California Management Review* Vol. 35, No. 4, 107-122.

Croom, S., Romano, P. and Giannakis, M. (2000): 'Supply Chain Management: An Analytical Framework for Critical Literature Review', *European Journal of Purchasing & Supply
Management* Vol. 6, 67-83.

Fisher, M. (1997): 'What is the Right Supply Chain for Your Product', *Harvard Business
Review* Vol. 75, No. 2, 105-116.

Fisher, M., Hammond, J., Obermeyer, W. and Raman, A. (1994): 'Managing Supply Meet
Demand in an Uncertain World', *Harvard Business Review* Vol. 72, No. 5/6, 83-93.

Forza, C., Pietro, R. and Vinelli, A. (2000): 'Information Technology for Managing the Textile Apparel Chain: Current Use, Shortcomings and Development Directions', *International Journal of Logistics* Vol. 3, No. 3, 227-243.

Goffin, K., Szwejczewski, M. and New, C. (1997): 'Managing Suppliers: When Fewer can
Mean More', *International Journal of Physical Distribution & Logistics Management* Vol.
27, No. 7, 422-436.

Goldbach, M. (2002): 'Organisational Settings in Supply Chain Costing', in: Seuring, S. and
Goldbach, M. (Eds.): *Cost Management in Supply Chains.* Heidelberg: Physica, 89-108.

Goldbach, M. (2003): 'Coordinating Interaction in Supply Chains—The Example of Greening
Textile Chains', in: Seuring, S., Müller, M., Goldbach, M. and Schneidewind, U. (Eds.):
Strategy and Organisation in Supply Chains. Heidelberg: Physica.

Goldbach, M., Back, S. and Seuring, S. (2003): 'Coordinating Sustainable Cotton Chains for
the Mass Market—The Case of the German Mail Order Business Otto', in: Wolters, T.
(Ed.): *Sustainable Chain Management: Transforming International Product Chains into
Channels of Sustainable Production.* Sheffield: Greenleaf Publishing (forthcoming).

GRI (Global Reporting Initiative) (Ed.) (2002): *Sustainability Reporting Guidelines 2002,
Boston* [online] [cited 31 October 2002]. Available from Internet URL: http://www.
globalreporting.org.

Gunasekaran, A., Patel, C. and Tirtiroglu, E. (2001): 'Performance Measures and Metrics in a
Supply Chain Environment', *International Journal of Operations & Production Management* Vol. 21, No. 1/2, 71-87.

Handfield, R.B. and Nichols, E.L. (1999): *Introduction to Supply Chain Management.* New
Jersey: Prentice Hall.

Kogg, B. (2003): 'Power and Incentives in Environmental Supply Chain Management', in:
Seuring, S., Müller, M., Goldbach, M. and Schneidewind, U. (Eds.): *Strategy and Organisation in Supply Chains.* Heidelberg: Physica (forthcoming).

Meyer, A. and Hohmann, P. (2000): 'Other Thoughts; Other Results? Remei's bioRe Organic
Cotton on its Way to the Mass Market', *Greener Management International* Vol. 31, 59-
70.

Myers, D. and Stolton, S. (Ed.) (1999): *Organic Cotton—From Field to Final Product.* London: Intermediate Technology Publications.

Newton, T. and Harte, G. (1997): 'Green Business: Technicist Kitsch?', *Journal of Management Studies* Vol. 34, No. 1, 75-98.

Otto (Ed.) (2001): *Code of Conduct.* (Social Standards) Hamburg: Otto.

Otto (Ed.) (2002): *'Pure-Wear' Requirements for Garments for Cellulose Fibres with Ecological Optimised Processes.* Hamburg: Otto.

Porter, M.E. (1996): 'What is Strategy?', *Harvard Business Review* Vol. 74, No.3, 61-78.

Romano, P. and Vinelli, A. (2001): 'Quality Management in a Supply Chain Perspective -
Strategic and Operative Choices in a Textile-Apparel Network', *International Journal of
Operations & Production Management* Vol. 21, No. 4, 446-460.

Schaltegger, S. and Synnestvedt, T. (2000): 'The Link between 'Green' and Economic Success: Environmental Management as the Crucial Trigger between Environmental and Economic Performance', *Journal of Environmental Management* Vol. 65, 339-346.

Schary, P. and Skjoett-Larsen, T. (2001): *Managing the Global Supply Chain.* Copenhagen: Copenhagen Business School Press.

Schmenner, R.W. and Swink, M.L. (1998): 'On Theory in Operations Management', *Journal of Operations Management* Vol. 17, No. 1, 97-113.

Seuring, S. (2001a): 'A Framework for Green Supply Chain Costing - A Fashion Industry Example', in: Sarkis, J. (Ed.): *Greener Manufacturing and Operations - From Design to Delivery and Back.* Sheffield: Greenleaf Publishing, 150-160.

Seuring, S. (2001b): 'Green Supply Chain Costing - Joint Cost Management in the Polyester Linings Supply Chain', *Greener Management International* Vol. 33, 71-80.

Seuring, S. (2002): 'Supply Chain Costing—A Conceptual Framework', in: Seuring, S. and Goldbach, M. (Eds.): *Cost Management in Supply Chains.* Heidelberg: Physica, 15-30.

Seuring, S. and Goldbach, M. (2002): 'Managing Time and Complexity to Green the Textile Chain', *Proceedings of The 2002 Business Strategy and the Environment Conference* 16-17 September 2002, Manchester, 348-359.

Steilmann (Ed.) (1999): *Steilmann Group—Suppliers' Guideline.* Wattenscheid: Steilmann.

Steilmann (Ed.) (2000): *Steilmann's Code of Conduct—Guidelines for Global Social Responsibility.* Wattenscheid: Steilmann.

Wagner, M., Schaltegger, S. and Wehrmeyer, W. (2001): 'The Relationship between the Environmental and Economic Performance of Companies', *Greener Management International* Vol. 34, 95-108.

ACKNOWLEDGEMENTS

This chapter describes work carried out during research project EcoMTex—Ecological Mass Textiles (Project FKZ 07 OWI 14/0) conducted at the University of Oldenburg, other research institutions as well as Otto and Steilmann (see Internet URL: http://www.uni-oldenburg.de/ecomtex). We are grateful to the German Ministry of Research (BMBF) for funding.

SUSTAINABILITY AND COMPETITIVENESS IN THE RENEWABLE ENERGY SECTOR
The Case of Vestas Wind Systems

Rolf Wüstenhagen
Institute for Economy and the Environment, Switzerland

Abstract: Vestas, a Danish company whose beginnings can be traced back to a black-smith's workshop founded in 1898, has become the world market leader in wind turbine manufacturing. Between 1994 and 2001, Vestas's sales have increased more than tenfold, and the number of employees increased from 643 to 5,240. While its main contribution to sustainability may be seen as increasing the market share of wind energy, thus reducing the environmental impacts of electricity generation, the company has also become a leader in terms of internal environmental management and social sustainability. Until about a year ago, the company was also a phenomenal success story in financial terms, with a share price that would have provided investors participating in the 1998 IPO with a 778% return over a four-year period. Recent industry developments, however, are more challenging for Vestas, and it remains to be seen whether the company can take its success story to the next level. This chapter presents key milestones in the company's development from niche to mass market and analyses success factors in the relationship between Vestas's sustainability performance and business competitiveness.

1. VESTAS'S HISTORY: FROM NICHE TO MASS MARKET

1.1 1898–1978: The Early Days of Vestas

The roots of Vestas date back to the end of the 19th century, when black-smith H.S. Hansen opened his first workshop at Lem, Denmark.[1] According

---

[1] Unless indicated otherwise, data in this section is taken from *The Vestas History* (Vestas 2003b), published by the company (http://www.vestas.com/profil/historie/UK/1898_1969_

to Vestas's history, Smith Hansen had a reputation for creating many ideas and showing fearless initiative, inspiring many of his colleagues at the time to start their own businesses and thus contributing to the emergence of an important centre for the blacksmith's craft at Lem. It was not until 30 years later that H.S. Hansen and his son, Peder Hansen, founded their first industrial company, Dansk Staalvindue Industri, a manufacturer of steel window frames for industrial buildings. After the Second World War, Peder Hansen formed a new company, Vestjysk Stålteknik A/S, which subsequently changed its name to Vestas. With a start capital of DKK 75,000, the Vestas team moved into manufacturing household appliances and kitchens. Over the following 15 years (1945–1960), the company's product range evolved continuously, from appliances to agricultural trailers to intercoolers. In 1960, Vestas's offices and warehouse burned to the ground and the factory had to be rebuilt. As a consequence, the company faced several years of consolidation, until it identified, in 1968, hydraulic cranes for light lorries as a promising new product area, which proved to be a major export success. A couple of years later, as the two oil crises of the 1970s hit the transport industry and lorry crane sales declined, Vestas had to look for yet another growth area.

1.2   1979–1985: First Steps in Wind Turbine Manufacturing

Inspired by the second oil crisis in 1978/79, Vestas began to examine the potential of wind turbines as an alternative source of energy. Initially, it chose the Darrieus turbine design, but after 18 months of experiments the company decided to focus on a three-blade model, which soon became the dominant design in the wind industry. In 1979, the first wind turbines were delivered to Danish customers. Subsequently, the industry experienced its first boom, mainly driven by government incentives in Denmark and the United States. Vestas started serial production of 55 kW wind turbines in 1980. By 1985, the number of employees increased to 800. It was also in 1985 that Vestas introduced pitch-regulation, a major technological innovation that optimises the energy output of a wind turbine by constantly adjusting the angle of the blades to current wind conditions. By the end of that same year, Vestas had sold 2,500 wind turbines to the US.

UK.html), as well as a variety of other company publications, particularly annual reports and stock exchange announcements.

1.3   1986: Crisis and Turnaround

The strong exposure to the US market turned from a blessing into a curse for Vestas when, at the end of 1985, the California tax credit legislation expired. As a consequence, Vestas's US market collapsed and, after a rescue plan failed, it filed for bankruptcy in October 1986. As the reason for the collapse lay primarily in the change of the regulatory framework rather than in Vestas's products, a major restructuring finally led to the establishment of a new company called Vestas Wind Systems A/S in 1987. After large parts of the Vestas Group had been sold off, the new company emerged as a wind energy pure play, managed by the new CEO, Johannes Poulsen, with a dedicated team of 60 employees.

1.4   1987–1997: Strong Organic Growth

It soon became apparent that the new Vestas was set to become a unique success story. The years 1987 to 1997 saw a sequence of international expansion, technological innovation and ever-larger orders. The company set up subsidiaries in India (1987), Germany (1989), Sweden, the US (both in 1992), and formed the joint venture, Gamesa Eolica, in Spain (1994), where Vestas holds 40% of the shares and Gamesa, the parent company, 51%. The Spanish market became particularly important in the mid-1990s, when large utilities started placing large orders to benefit from government incentives. In terms of technology, Vestas gradually increased turbine size—as did the other industry players—with every new generation of their product. Having entered the wind turbine business with a 55 kW machine in 1980, the company introduced its V39-500 kW turbine in 1990, followed by the V44-600 kW turbine in 1994 and the V66-1.65 MW turbine in 1997. Today, the company is operating the first prototypes of its V90-3.0 MW turbine scheduled for serial production in 2004.

Most of Vestas's exceptional growth during this period was organic, accelerated only by selected acquisitions: DWT, Danish Wind Technology, in 1989 and Costas Computer Technology A/S, a long-standing supplier of software and components for Vestas's wind turbine control systems, which was taken over in 1999. When expanding into new international markets, the company often chose to form a joint venture together with a well-established partner in the target country, as was the case with Vestas RRB India Ltd, or the joint venture with Energy System Taranto S.p.a. in Italy. In countries where Vestas felt comfortable that it knew the market, however, it went in with fully owned subsidiaries, as in the US, Sweden and Germany.

This decade also saw Vestas's first turbine deliveries to a smaller off-shore project, involving ten 500 kW turbines in the Baltic Sea in 1995. Also in 1995, the company exceeded 1,000 employees for the first time and generated more than €200 million in revenues, a 66% growth rate over the previous year (for convenience, all financial figures in this chapter have been converted from Danish crowns to euros at the exchange rate of May 2003 [1 DKK = €0.13475]). It became increasingly clear that, in order to maintain the pace of growth, the company needed additional sources of capital. Two years later, in 1997, the company introduced two new turbine models and consequently posted a slight loss, despite sales growth (in MW) of 24%. Therefore, in early 1998 CEO Johannes Poulsen announced that the time had come to float the company on the Copenhagen Stock Exchange, stating that, in his opinion, 'there is no doubt that in future environmental factors will play an increasingly large role in any political and probably also any commercial decision'.[2]

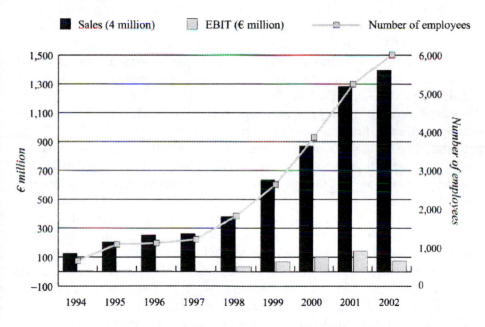

Figure 1. Growth in Vestas's sales, earnings before and after tax (EBIT) and number of employees 1994–2002 (Source: Vestas company data)

1.5   1998–2001: IPO and Hypergrowth

Vestas's initial public offering in April 1998 was a big success. The shares were eight times oversubscribed and the company raised €175 million of fresh equity capital to finance its future growth, including new international subsidiaries and new fibreglass production and turbine assembly facilities. In

---

[2]   Press release announcing initial public offering (IPO), 23 March 1998.

the year of the IPO, Vestas increased revenues by 45% and started production in its newly established Italian subsidiary in July 1998. Within its first
year, the Italian subsidiary generated revenues of €35 million with just 50
employees. 1999 saw the opening of a new blade factory in south-eastern
Denmark, an area of high unemployment that provided good recruiting
opportunities for Vestas, as well as the launch of a prototype V80-2.0 MW
turbine. 1999 became another record year for Vestas, largely because of
exceptional growth in the US market. At the end of 1999, the production tax
credit (PTC), an important financial incentive to wind energy generators in
the US, expired. Thus, a large number of project developers ordered turbines
before the end of the year to take advantage of the incentive. As a result,
Vestas increased sales by 66% and more than doubled profits compared with
the previous year. In 2000, growth continued, fuelled, among other things,
by the largest order ever for wind turbines, received by Vestas's Spanish
joint venture Gamesa from Energia Hidroeléctrica De Navarra, worth more
than €600 million. Vestas also expanded to Japan, co-operating with Toyota
and Kawasaki, and received large orders from FPL Energy LLC in the US
following extension of the PTC for two years.

2001 brought more good news for Vestas, when it was chosen as the
supplier for the first major offshore project in the North Sea (Horns Reef),
the largest offshore order to date, worth around €130 million. 2001 was also
the year with the strongest growth in the global wind energy market in
history, increasing by 51% over 2000 levels. In this year, Vestas achieved a
market share of 24.1% and was clearly the market leader. However, 2001
can also be seen as a turning point in Vestas's history in several respects.
Remarkably, on the morning of 11 September 2001, the company announced
that 59-year-old CEO, Johannes Poulsen, who had led the company since it
was formed in 1987, had decided to resign from his position at the General
Meeting in April 2002. Also, increasing strategic differences between Vestas
and Gamesa led to a sale of Vestas's 40% stake in the joint venture in
December 2001. In hindsight, Vestas had ultimately helped to grow a major
competitor that was now seeking independence. Finally, the outlook for the
US market looked uncertain following another expiration of the PTC. Owing
to altered political priorities in the aftermath of 11 September and conten-
tious issues in the proposed US energy bill, PTC extension was eventually
delayed until March 2002. The company ended 2001 with 5,240 employees,
a tripling in the three years since the IPO.

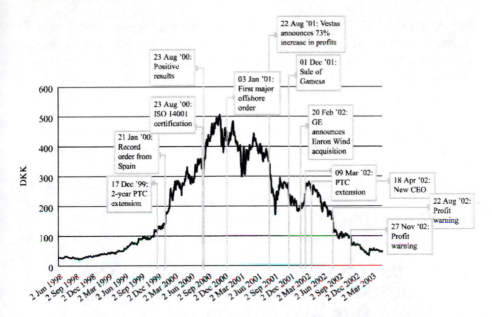

Figure 2. Major events influencing Vestas's share price over the past five years (Source: Data from Copenhagen Stock Exchange, events from company publications, industry associations)

1.6   2002 Onwards: Changing of the Guard and New Challenges

The beginning of the post-Poulsen era at Vestas was challenging in many ways. The inauguration of Svend Sigaard, the former CFO and new CEO, was accompanied by the news that a major competitor had entered the market: General Electric (GE). The large US engineering conglomerate announced in February 2002 that it had acquired the assets of Enron Wind. GE's entry was not just negative news: after all, it also provided the industry with a lot of credibility because an established player was acknowledging the growth potential in the wind market. It may also not be fully accidental that legislation extending the PTC was passed only five weeks after GE had announced its market entry. Nevertheless, given GE's expertise from the conventional power business, its strong distribution channels in North America and its financial strength, this clearly became an important new competitive threat for Vestas. After the first year of operating in the wind industry, GE is now expected to achieve 45% market share in the US, partly selling to its own projects developed by GE Wind, while Vestas's sales in the US market seem to have slowed down. The development of the euro/dollar currency exchange rate accentuates the challenge for Vestas. In addition, during 2002, Vestas struggled with technical problems on its new flagship V80-2.0 MW turbine and faced delays at the high-profile Horns Reef offshore project, which eventually resulted in cost overruns of €15–17 million. Looking positively at this, Vestas has had an opportunity to learn important lessons for the emerging growth market of offshore wind parks, and is now established as the market leader in the European offshore market with a 37% market share. Also, thanks to its size, Vestas is better positioned to cope with the larger risks in this market than most of its competitors (except GE and Gamesa).

In contrast to the previous boom years, 2002 ended with the company's announcement that, after the second profit warning in three months, it had to lay off 495 employees, the first downsizing since 1986.

2.   SUSTAINABILITY PERFORMANCE AND BUSINESS COMPETITIVENESS AT VESTAS: KEY SUCCESS FACTORS

Looking at the development of Vestas from a bankrupt company in 1987 to the world market leader in wind energy in 2001, a number of key factors can be identified that have contributed to successful growth. Five important points are discussed below: (1) Vestas's vision for both the company and the industry; (2) the management of internal growth; (3) international expansion; (4) the politics of wind energy; and (5) social responsibility and environmental management.

2.1   A Clear Vision for Vestas and the Industry

A strong point differentiating Vestas from many of its peers is that the company has always had a very clear vision and strategy that was simple to communicate and thus to be shared by its employees and stakeholders:

> With quality and care we use the wind to generate competitive, clean and renewable energy. In the future, this energy will cover a substantial part of the global energy supply and contribute to sustainable development for the benefit of future generations. Vestas is to be the international market leader in the field of wind power systems—valued by customers, shareholders, employees and other stakeholders (Vestas 2003a: 8).

Unlike, for example, many of the large utility subsidiaries looking at the renewable energy market, Vestas is clearly convinced that this sector will experience strong growth and is determined to lead the market. A number of Vestas's actions also showed that they understood that one company could not build the market alone and that there was room for others to grow as well. In addition to their vision, other elements of Vestas's mission statement were also well thought through. For example, Vestas calls its core values, which are the foundations of its corporate culture, 'integrity, care, the power to act, and development'. This shows that they are aware of the trade-off between being a reliable and trustworthy partner on the one hand, and the necessity to take initiative and be competitive on the other. In fact, this can be seen as a very conscious interpretation of the two facets inherent in sustainable development.

Finally, Vestas also had a very clear-cut strategy to achieve its goal of being an international leader with sufficient financial strength to continue internationalisation: 'Vestas' strategy is to supply customised wind power solutions based on standard wind turbines and standardised options that can generate electricity of the optimal quality at the most competitive price' (Vestas 2003a: 9).

Again, this demonstrates how the company was well aware of the trade-offs it had to cope with as a growing company. As a market leader, it had to focus on relatively standardised products, and was careful to adapt the level of customisation to the needs of appropriate target segments. This also meant that, unlike in its early days, Vestas was not the number one supplier for a small farming co-operative that wanted to buy just one turbine. Leaving this market for smaller competitors, it managed to satisfy large customers such as FPL Energy, a subsidiary of a major US utility, which buys hundreds of wind turbines at a time. Vestas was also conscious of the importance of competitive prices for the industry to grow, and was committed to delivering lower cost per kWh with every new product it launched. This was key for wind energy to become cost-competitive with conventional power generation, and consequently to develop from a green niche to the mainstream power market.

2.2 Managing Internal Growth

The next step from having a well-formulated vision and strategy is to put it into practice, including the important issue of organisational development to manage growth. Here again, Vestas did an extraordinary job. Four examples illustrate this.

1. When Vestas set up new facilities, it formed 'flying squads', consisting of staff from existing operations across the company. For example, when the new Italian subsidiary was formed in 1998, employees from the Netherlands and Germany, who had gone through the process of starting up operations in their own facilities, went to Italy for a limited period of time to train the local staff and supervise the ramp-up process. This had

two positive effects for the company: first, new capacity came online much faster and smoother and, second, the assignment to a foreign subsidiary was a motivating form of job enrichment for the members of these teams.

2. Even before managing the ramp-up process, Vestas acted wisely when it came to choosing locations for new facilities. These were usually situated in areas of high unemployment, which made it convenient for Vestas to hire skilled and unskilled labour. Setting up a blade factory in Nakskov, Denmark, in 1999/2000 was one such example, and the location of the German blade factory in Lauchhammer, in the heart of the former East German brown coal district, was no less prudent. The inauguration of the factory in the middle of the 2002 federal election campaign by German Chancellor, Gerhard Schröder, received positive media coverage, since Vestas's investment represented one of the few growth sectors in the middle of a region with 20% unemployment.

3. Another aspect of managing internal growth is to take care of employee retention and enable the staff members to take a fair share of the company's success. This was achieved through employee share programmes, which were very well received among the staff. For example, in November 2000 more than 80% of employees entitled to purchase Vestas shares made use of this option.

4. Vestas has consistently put special emphasis on training its employees. In 2002, the company went one step further by founding the Vestas School, which also works with external training providers.

These examples show how managing internal growth has become one of Vestas's core competences and illustrate how the company could possibly cope with annual growth rates of more than 30% throughout a decade.

2.3   International Expansion

As mentioned above, Vestas's vision showed that the company's frame of reference was the international market from the very beginning. In fact, the old Vestas, in the 1950s, had a tradition of exporting a substantial part of its production to other countries. This of course also reflected the relatively limited size of the Danish home market. Nevertheless, this international orientation helped the company to gain a competitive edge over many of its competitors in the wind industry that were more nationally focused. The strong presence on the North American market in particular has, of course, also been the source of painful lessons for Vestas, probably most pronounced in the mid-1980s. The company has learned its lesson, and recognised that broader international diversification is the best way to manage risk and grow continuously despite the boom-and-bust cycles in some markets. Between 1987 and 2001, the company set up ten international subsidiaries across three continents. This diversified portfolio paid off in 2002 when the large US market—where Vestas had traditionally held a leading position—declined by 75% year-on-year. Thanks to a growth of 45% in markets outside the US, Vestas could still slightly increase its 2002 sales (Vestas 2003a: 21).

Looking at the apparent success of Vestas's internationalisation, however, one should not gloss over the challenges that the company met on the way. A particular example of things not going smoothly was the experience with Gamesa in Spain. When Vestas originally entered into the joint venture, Gamesa Eolica, in 1994, it anticipated building yet another subsidiary that would help to grow the market for Vestas technology in Spain. Initially, expectations were met, as the strong sales growth in the Spanish market demonstrated. However, over time strategic differences emerged over the relative contribution of the two partners to the success. This latent conflict intensified when Gamesa decided to go public in 2000, using the growing wind energy sector as a key argument to convince investors of its attractiveness. In fact, however, Gamesa did not have any proprietary technology, but licensed the technology from Vestas. In addition, the licence was exclusively limited to the Spanish market, so Gamesa under the existing constellation could not grow into markets such as Italy and Greece. Vestas considered different options to solve the conflict, but realised that, given the ownership structure, there was no way for it to get beyond a 49% minority holding in Gamesa Eolica. So, even if it led to a substantial loss of licence fees from Spain and, longer-term, to the creation of a serious competitor, in December 2001 Vestas decided to sell its 40% stake in Gamesa Eolica for €287 million to Gamesa, the parent company. The fact that the price of the transaction was largely regarded as relatively favourable for Gamesa once again underlined Vestas's commitment to integrity and to the development of the wind industry as a whole rather than focusing on short-term gains.

2.4   The Politics of Wind Energy

The electric power sector is a heavily regulated industry and, in the case of renewables, the role of government incentives to bring these young technologies to market adds to the importance of politics. Looking at the growth of wind turbine capacity over the past decade, two conclusions can be drawn. First, among all renewable energies, wind energy is certainly the one that is closest to making the transition from niche to mass market, with more than 30,000 MW capacity installed worldwide and annual growth rates of 33% over the past five years (see Fig. 3). Second, Germany and Spain account for more than half of the world market today, and these markets have largely been driven by government regulation. Both countries, through their feed-in tariffs, pay relatively generous incentives to wind energy generators that enable cost competitive wind power production at good and medium-quality sites. Going forward, government policies aimed at mitigating climate change are expected to further support wind energy. Governments also play a role in providing start-up incentives for offshore projects in some countries. So, the importance of politics is probably here to stay, although costs continue to come down and are as low as 2–3 cents/kWh in the most attractive projects today.

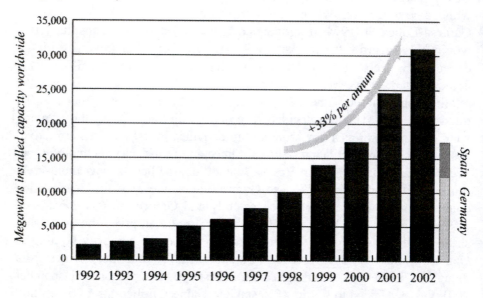

Figure 3. Growth of global wind energy capacity 1992–2002 (Data source: BTM Consult)

In addition to this long-term influence of politics, an interesting analysis from Bishop and Stettler (2003) demonstrates that there is also a measurable short-term influence of regulatory decisions on wind energy companies. They plotted the share prices of four listed wind energy pure plays in the period before and after the latest PTC extension in March 2002. In the few days following the PTC extension, share prices of those companies with a significant exposure to the US market, namely Vestas and NEG Micon, appreciated by more than 30% (see Fig. 4).

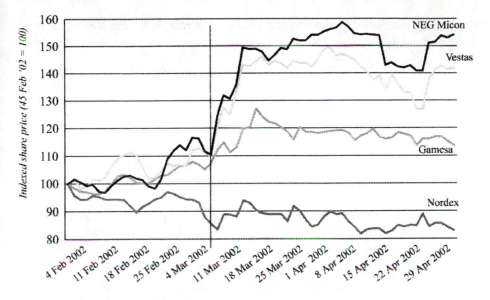

Figure 4. Share price performance of wind energy stocks following the
9 March 2002 PTC extension (Source: adapted from Bishop and Stettler 2003; Data:
Copenhagen Stock Exchange, Yahoo Finance)

Because the influence of politics on the wind energy market is clearly documented, the important question is: what can a company such as Vestas do to manage this? First of all, it appears that it can easily become a victim of unpredictable changes in the policy framework. The 1986 collapse of the US market was one example, and stop-and-go policies continue to characterise US wind energy policy today. When the PTC once again expired at the end of 2001, Vestas had anticipated a PTC extension before year-end, similar to 1999. Therefore it had kept its capacity at levels that would enable quick response to increasing demand at the beginning of 2002. However, legislation was delayed in the political process, and 1,200 Vestas employees had to work short hours for three months.

That is not to say that Vestas has not worked to actively influence the political process. In fact, the decision to situate the planned US manufacturing facility in Portland, Oregon, was directly related to political support for wind energy. As the company announced the plan for the Portland plant, CEO Johannes Poulsen stated outright:

The strong regional support of wind energy generation and considerable support for the extension of the Production Tax Credit, made by particularly Governor John A. Kitzhaber and his staff, Portland Mayor Vera Katz and staff, Port of Portland Director Mr Bill Wyatt has confirmed our belief that Portland and Oregon is a good strategic fit for Vestas (Vestas press release, 3 April 2002).

And, even after the company had to withdraw its plans following the decline in US business, the governor of Oregon continues to be a strong supporter for Vestas when it comes to making the case for wind energy in the political debate in Washington, DC.

2.5   Social Responsibility and Environmental Management

Finally, we come to those issues that are most commonly associated with sustainability in the context of large companies. It is no coincidence that this section is at the end of the factors that we identified for Vestas's success. As the company has grown from a small pioneer to a major industry leader, more formal aspects of social responsibility and environmental management have come into place. But, rather than being the origin of Vestas's sustainability management, these systems can be seen as supporting the company's core sustainability mission, which is to focus on an environmentally benign technology and to transform the electric power industry by growing the market share of wind energy.

In August 2000, Vestas achieved ISO 14001 certification for the environmental management system established at the Danish parent company. CEO Johannes Poulsen explained the relevance of this step for the company as follows:

> Vestas has always given high priority to the environment, but it is only now that we have received certification of our environmental management system that we are able to document our efforts. Wind turbines themselves are environment-friendly, so it is naturally important to us that they are also manufactured and maintained in an environmentally responsible manner (Vestas press release on ISO 14001 certification, 23 August 2000).

In May and July 2002, respectively, the Italian and three Danish subsidiaries followed. As for occupational health and safety, the parent company completed certification according to the British OHSAS 18001 standard in August 2001. Further certification processes are under way. Today, thanks to this formalisation of environmental, health and safety management in combination with the environmental advantages of its product, the company is included in all major sustainability stock indices: namely, the Dow Jones Sustainability World Index (DJSI World), the Dow Jones STOXX Sustainability Index (DJSI STOXX), the FTSE4Good Europe Index, and the FTSE-4Good Corporate Social Responsibility Index.

Nevertheless, as a pioneer that has lived through the ups and downs of the wind industry, the company is well aware that good social and environmental performance is not enough to be sustainable, as a statement from its annual report points out:

> Social responsibility is a natural part of Vestas' management philosophy and value set, and Vestas exercises its social responsibility both internally within the Group and externally with reference to the surrounding community. Vestas' desire for sustainable development for the company encompasses social responsibility, environmental responsibility and financial profitability (Vestas 2003a: 16).

3. OUTLOOK: DEFENDING A LEADING POSITION IN A CHANGING MARKET

As indicated above, simultaneously with the changing of the guard at Vestas, market conditions have significantly changed in the industry. A number of challenging factors are currently coming together: the US power market is facing overcapacities in the aftermath of the gas bubble, reducing the attractiveness of new power generation capacity; US utilities' credit ratings have deteriorated, making it more difficult for Vestas's US customers to develop projects; the US dollar exchange rate has declined, making Vestas's exports less competitive; Vestas faces strong competition from GE in North America; the German on-shore market is saturating; promising new growth markets such as France seem not to be getting off the ground, while European offshore markets are characterised by delays and demanding technological issues. Finally, the financial community criticises Vestas for its high degree of vertical integration that leverages the current market downturn. The new CEO, Svend Sigaard, can certainly not complain about a lack of challenges. The question arises whether the core competences of Vestas— growing organically and acting as the vertically integrated market leader— will be a successful model in a potential phase of industry consolidation. In terms of Vestas as an organisation, after years of hypergrowth with little time to consolidate, followed by an unfamiliar experience when almost 10% of the employees were made redundant at the end of 2002, it remains to be seen how the company makes the transition from seemingly effortless growth to what might become a new turnaround situation.

At least there is little doubt that the market potential for wind energy continues to be huge: governments around the world are struggling to achieve Kyoto targets and wind energy is practically the only renewable energy technology that is very close to being cost-competitive today. So, if the sustainability analysts are right, Vestas should be able to bear that challenge successfully and reinvent itself once more in its long history. Building on the entrepreneurial qualities that have characterised the company since the days of blacksmith H.S. Hansen and his son will certainly help.

REFERENCES

Bishop, A. and Stettler, J. (2003) *Wind Industry: Playing the Waiting Game*. London: Dresdner Kleinwort Wasserstein.
Vestas (2003a) *Annual Report 2002*. Ringkøbing, Denmark: Vestas.
Vestas (2003b) *The Vestas History*. Ringkøbing, Denmark: Vestas.

ACKNOWLEDGEMENTS

The author thanks Bill Moore, PhD candidate at the University of St Gallen, for valuable comments on a previous version of this chapter. Also, the author thanks his former employer SAM Sustainable Asset Management AG for enabling him to gain the background experience in the wind energy industry that helped in preparing this case study. All remaining errors are in the sole responsibility of the author.

PATH-DEPENDENT THINKING AND ECO-PRODUCTS
An Empirical Study of Socio-Cognitive Models and Product Propositions of Ford and Volvo Cars

Mats Williander
Fenix Centre for Research on Knowledge and Business Creation, Chalmers University of Technology, Sweden

Abstract: The debate as to whether it pays to be 'green' or under what circumstances it pays to be green may underestimate the issue of the ability of companies to create value in environmentally benign offerings captured from customers or other economic actors. This chapter address this issue by looking into why two companies in the automotive industry do not sell their environmentally benign car offers in sufficiently high volumes and briefly compares with two alternative and potentially more successful offerings. The study reveals that the industry's perceived reluctance towards becoming more environmentally friendly may not be rooted in a lack of willingness, lack of ethics or lack of belief in the strategic relevance of environmental issues. Instead, it may be caused by institutionalised perceptions and engineering practices creating a bias in the understanding of consumers' behaviour-driven expectations on environmentally benign products. Consumers follow rational choice on environmental issues in situations of high private cost, relatively independent of their attitude. The study indicates that 'high cost' may be very low, which suggests a need for innovative solutions addressing not only the monetary issue but also the symbolic, behavioural and organisational attributes of the product. Findings from the comparison suggest a potential solution in bundling common-good and private-good attributes.

1.   INTRODUCTION

There is an interesting and highly relevant debate on the greening of industry: what gains may be made in 'going green', under what circumstances, and for whom. There are general strategic views (Hart 1997), debates on how to attain them (Hart and Milstein 1999; Kemp *et al.* 1998; Newton 2002; Schnaiberg and Gould 1994) and interaction effects of regulation (Palmer *et al.* 1995; Porter and van der Linde 1995; Rugman and Verbeke 1998; Wallace 1995). When companies are studied more closely, further suggestions arise such as ethical aspects (Payne and Raiborn 2001), organisational culture (Harris and Crane 2002), insurance issues (Minoli and Bell 2003), management compensation schemes (Lothe and Myrtveit 2003) and corporate non-monetary measures (Figge *et al.* 2002), production-oriented aspects (Hart and Ahuja 1996), product-oriented aspects (Hart 1995), and, in more general economic terms for the company, whether it pays to be green or not (Elkington 1994; Hart and Ahuja 1996; Maxwell 1996; Payne and Raiborn 2001; Porter and van der Linde 1995; Reinhardt 1998, 1999; Walley and Whitehead 1994).

The debate, as such, can be criticised from several perspectives (Newton and Harte 1997), including bias in the research itself (Huesemann 2002). A potential explanation for the differences in findings that cause this debate and a possible framework for how to improve understand and guide future research was suggested by Schaltegger and Synnestvedt (2002). They indicated that there is a potential risk that the common research approach might not be sufficient when, as in this case, the issue is complex and multi-dimensional, the question may have been put wrongly, and where the context may have to be taken into consideration in a fundamentally different way. The complex reality may require an interdisciplinary approach to provide suggestions for solutions with practical and theoretical relevance. This chapter, an empirical study made as an insider/outsider research approach (Bartunek and Louis 1996), is one contribution to an interdisciplinary approach. The more detailed reason for this study and its scope is to improve our understanding of how the private attributes and environmental attributes of environmentally benign products can be conflicting or supporting, depending on product typology and the social meaning of the product.

In many businesses, the offered products can be environmentally improved without any change to their private attributes such as green electricity (Rowlands *et al.* 2003). Yet other businesses may experience a positive correlation between environmental improvements and private attributes, as potentially found in dishwashers, refrigerators and washing machines (Strannegård 1998), where improved environmental performance in general has a positive impact for instance on energy consumption, an attribute of private concern. For such businesses, going green is mainly an issue of bringing an attractive environmentally benign value proposition to an established market and obtaining customer acceptance (Reinhardt 1998). However, there are important industries, not least the automotive industry, that depend on complex networks of related businesses that have been developed over several decades to become strong, convergent and difficult to change (Hård and Jamison 1997; Hård and Knie 2001; Kemp *et al.* 1998; Newton 2002), and where symbolic and behavioural aspects of the product may be in conflict with environmental improvements.

'Greening' such industries is not only a matter of providing more environmentally benign products to the consumer, but of achieving a regime shift affecting multiple businesses and networks, and to 'change an integrated system of technologies and social practices' (Kemp *et al.* 1998:184). For the individual company, either the product must be made to fit the existing network of related businesses such as the fuelling infrastructure, or a parallel system has to be developed, potentially including change of societal discourse in what Kemp *et al.* (1998:183) call 'co-evolution and mutual adaptation'. Greening of industry and consumers becomes a reciprocal interaction between human action, technology and societal structures (Orlikowski 1992), in which history has created a path-dependent socio-cognitive model of technology evolution (Garud and Rappa 1994) affecting the decision criteria of both companies and consumers.

The understanding of this reciprocal interaction and how to design environmentally benign technology within the constraints of the institutional context can profoundly affect a company's competitiveness. This empirical study looks into this issue by comparing the launch and sales of environmentally benign alternative-fuelled cars by two different car manufacturers in three different countries. Neither of them has managed to turn environmental benignity into a competitive advantage. The case reveals a bias in understanding of how to meet customers' behaviour-driven expectations with environmental products in the existing societal context. The effect either becomes an externalisation of the cost or a market failure, or both. The chapter speculates on the bundling of product properties for the common-good and private-good as one possible solution and makes a brief comparison between Volvo's and Ford's methane-fuelled vehicles versus Toyota's hybrid vehicle and Saab's ethanol-based vehicle.

Bundling of common-good properties and private-good properties in products seems to be something of a blind spot in research. Research on attribute bundling that specifically addresses the combination of common-good and private-good product properties and how this may affect consumer behaviour is therefore proposed.

The chapter has the following structure. First, there is a brief literature review on economics, markets and consumers in the greening of industry. Secondly, the methodological issues of the case studies are addressed. Thirdly, the empirical material is explored and, finally, some findings and implications are discussed in more detail.

2.   ECONOMICS, MARKETS AND CONSUMERS

One relatively normative view on the greening of industry is that industry has substantial responsibility for the environmental impact of its products during use. Responding to this responsibility is also the right thing to do from a long-term profitability perspective (Hart 1997; Payne and Raiborn 2001; Porter and van der Linde 1995). Another view from economic theory opposes the argument that increased environmental performance and increased profits may go hand in hand. Maxwell (1996) and Walley and Whitehead (1994) argue that win–win rhetoric does not work. Maxwell rhetorically asks: 'After all, the purpose of environmental regulation is to internalise the costs of pollution, which are usually borne by the public. If regulation internalises costs, can they lead to greater profit?' (Maxwell 1996:60)

A third view, also from economic theory, brings a balance to the topic by suggesting that the question 'does it pay to be green?' is put wrongly and hence cannot be answered categorically, since it depends on the industry and the company (Reinhardt 1998). Reinhardt's view is that environment is no different than any other aspect of strategy or management. In order to succeed in deriving competitive advantage from environmental concern, companies need to create value and capture it from customers, suppliers or other economic agents. Their ability to do so depends on the structure of their industry, the government regulatory framework and executives' own creativity in defining the nature of competition in their business. These are the factors that influence corporate success more generally and, consequently, Reinhardt suggests that we can make significant progress in addressing environmental problems if we analyse them as we would other business issues (Reinhardt 1998:46). While Reinhardt's view is primarily market-oriented, a higher-level corporate view, looking at business operation in general, finds neither positive nor negative correlation between shareholder value and environmental protection (Schaltegger and Figge 2000). Inspired by these suggestions and findings, this view is applied to the cases in this chapter. The choice was made to analyse the cases from a marketing perspective using the theory of competitive rationality (Dickson 1992). This theory provides the means to evaluate the logic behind a company's creation of a product proposition (the microprocedural perspective), as well as the logic of consumers (the macrobehavioral perspective). However, as the focus in this paper is on products, market and consumers, a path-dependent socio-cognitive view of technology evolution is brought in as this may prove to have a profound effect on a company's perceptions and ability to act, and hence competitiveness. We shall therefore start by looking at the social context in which the market is embedded.

With respect to institutional changes and social embeddedness, one view can be provided from the history of technology, network theory and the theory of structuration. Environmentally benign alternatives to established technological regimes need to become socially embedded in order to be considered by consumers (Hård and Jamison 1997; Newton 2002). A technological regime is defined as a combination of 'rules and beliefs embedded in engineering practices and search heuristics with the rules of the selection environment' (Kemp *et al.* 1998:182). These rules and beliefs, embedded in engineering practices, greatly influence product design and how various product attributes are bundled into a total value proposition. They emerge from historical experiences about preferences of the selection environment, i.e. the consumers. This means the existing technological regime not only influences the macrobehavioral perspective— what will be considered by consumers— but also the designing organisation's microprocedural perspective of competitive rationality—what will be considered for experimentation.

According to Hård and Jamison (1997), alternative technological offers must have a reasonable fit to the 'defining power' of established technologies in (1) symbolic, (2) organisational and (3) behavioural structures. The perception of 'reasonable' may prove crucial, as we shall see in the following case. The referred theory does not provide any detailed suggestions as to what may be considered reasonable but, on a relatively high level, it does suggest that it is important not to challenge too many of them simultaneously: 'an alternative technology seldom succeeds if it poses an alternative at all three levels' (Hård and Jamison 1997:148). These three structural dimensions constitute the societal context of the case study.

In the theory of competitive rationality, Dickson suggests that there is a continuous disequilibrium in the market (Dickson 1992). At a certain point in time, a market segment may be crowded by suppliers. This leads to low profit and hence encourages individual companies to experiment with new product propositions to improve profit. Companies scoring high on one or more of the properties—self-improvement, unbiased understanding of their customers' needs and speed to market—have competitive advantages. This is the microprocedural rationality half of the circle, which results in heterogeneity in supply. The other half of the circle is macrobehavioral. Here, consumers may perceive the new product proposition as a better one and hence create heterogeneity in demand; this makes part of the market move to this segment with higher profits. The change and the higher profit drive other companies to follow. The circle is constantly repeating and hence markets are always in disequilibrium, driven by companies' efforts to improve or maintain profits and verified through a never-ending stream of new product propositions.

One example in the car industry that indicates the importance of the symbolic, organisational and behavioural structures from the social context in which the market is embedded is the experimentation that led to sports utility vehicles (SUVs). They have higher fuel consumption, a higher price and roll over more easily due to their higher centre of gravity, yet a large proportion of car consumers perceived this proposition as 'better' as is evident in the many years of growth of this car segment at the expense of others.

From this example, it becomes clear that a 'better' proposition is what the addressed customer segment perceives as 'better' which, according to Hård and Jamison (1997) is influenced by the defining power of the existing technology in the symbolic, organisational and behavioural structures. A bigger car with a more powerful engine and a body shape radiating freedom to go anywhere, even off road, may have a symbolic and behavioural attractiveness perceived as more valuable than fuel consumption, roll-over stability and price. This 'path dependency' of manufacturers' and consumers' perceptions may be seen as incorporated in Dickson's theory of competitive rationality, since new product propositions are from a microprocedural view proposed and from a macrobehavioral view valued in any dimensions incorporated in the organisations' and customers' perception of product 'value'.

Consumer perception of good value of environmental offers is a multi-disciplinary issue. As long ago as 1982, from a social psychology point of view, Tyler et al. (1982) verified that a person's attitude and behaviour may differ substantially when common-good issues with a high personal cost were concerned. In their study on energy conservation, Tyler et al. (1982) found supporting evidence of the Defensive Denial hypothesis that states: 'Holding prosocial norms will not increase prosocial behaviour in situations in which the prosocial behaviour in question has high personal costs, because those holding prosocial norms will redefine the situation as inappropriate for norm activation.'

By combining social psychology, sociology and economy on consumer attitude and behaviour on environmental issues, Diekmann and Preisendörfer (2003) found that one may expect rational choice to be dominant in high-cost situations: 'Indeed, most of the empirical regularities that depart in a systematic way from the predictions of rational-choice seem to belong to the low-cost sector'(Diekmann and Preisendörfer 2003). Cost here is not only the economic cost, but also the perceived cost in terms of various sacrifices in any of the symbolic, organisational and behavioural structures such as, for example, decrease in convenience.

The issue of why environmentally benign product offerings do not sell seems to boil down to their perceived value to the customer. This perceived value may be judged purely from a private perspective despite its common-good value, consumer's attitude and social importance. The perceived value can be affected in at least three different ways:

(1) Through the product design and bundling of various product attributes
(2) Through additional 'value' through governmental incentives or incentives from any other economic agent
(3) Through reduction in the perceived value of existing technological regimes, for instance through governmental taxes.

Although (2) and (3) are recognised both by Reinhardt (1997) and Diekmann and Preisendörfer (2003), they are not incorporated into Dickson's theory because this does not incorporate the market's possible interaction with the social context in which it operates. Possible interactions are, for instance, internalisation and externalisation of costs, which greatly influence the perceived value of a proposition and hence the need for it to be included. Adding a context of governments and other economic actors to Dickson's theory finally gives a tool for analysing the case.

In the following case study, the reviewed theory of competitive rationality and of consumer purchasing behaviour is used with the addition of a context of other economic actors to structure the case. Given the contextual structure defined by the established dominant technology, it is shown that a 'cost' in any of the symbolic, organisational, behavioural or monetary dimensions of an environmentally benign product alternative, although potentially perceived as low from an attitudinal perspective, tends to quickly become high from a behavioural point of view, which may be an important cause of environmentally benign product failures.

3. METHODOLOGY

A case study is suitable when research focuses on specific phenomena in a clearly defined system and where the aim is towards insight, discovery and interpretation rather than hypothesis testing (Merriam 1994). The findings, although not statistically generalisable, aim to achieve analytical generalisation on classes of phenomena of which the case is an instance (Merriam 1994:25). A 'clearly defined system' affects issues of contextual and temporal boundaries (Dubois and Araujo 2004). In case studies including networks and relations such as 'clean' cars in the automotive industry, contextual and temporal boundaries emerge and unfold during the research process and therefore require a relatively open-ended process of inquiry compared with surveys and other population/analytic approaches which 'require rigidly de-limitable cases, assign them generic properties and refuse all transformations on the nature of the cases' (Dubois and Araujo 2004:209).

To collect data, interviews were conducted with project team members in the two focal companies. Managers in functions such as product planning, market and sales, new product development and senior management were interviewed at both Volvo and Ford. An interview guide was developed and adhered to during the open-ended interviews, which lasted for about an hour and a half. All interviews were recorded and significant passages were tran-scribed. In addition to the interview material, internal documents were col-lected and examined.

Interviewing is a commonplace method for data collection in qualitative research (Fontana and Frey 1994; Kvale 1996). The data analysis of qualitative material puts certain demands on the researcher (Huberman and Miles 1994; Silverman 1993). Rather than just pigeonholing different quotes into categories as in the grounded theory model (Glaser and Strauss 1967), researchers employing a qualitative method need to engage actively in an interpretation of the empirical material.

In the present study, the empirical material was coded along different emic categories (Boje 2001), i.e. in categories that made sense to the prac-titioners and were used by the practitioner verbally. Such categories were market demands, customer expectations, policy issues, management deci-sions, company strategy, development issues, infrastructure dependence, etc. The case message is, however, structured according to the theory used for analysis, i.e. in the three main sections of microprocedural rationality, macromarket behaviour, and government and other economic actors.

In structural terms, the study reported in this chapter is on what Bartunek and Louis (1996) call an insider/outsider research methodology. One of these authors is a practising manager at Volvo Car Corporation, which has been owned by the Ford Motor Company since 1999. Working as a practising manager within the automotive industry allows detailed know-how and a broad contact network for better access to, and understanding of, the indus-try's practices and mechanisms. The other author is an academic researcher at a university of technology and served as the outsider, i.e. the role serving to maintain a critical distance to the empirical material. Being able to com-bine an insider's know-how and access to practices with an outsider's distance and critical reflection on the insider's findings is the main strength of the insider/outsider research design.

4. THE CASE STUDY

4.1 Company Background

Volvo Car Corporation is a Swedish car manufacturer and was part of vehicle manufacturer Volvo AB until 1999 when it was sold to the Ford Motor Company. The headquarters are still located in Gothenburg, Sweden, and the business is run as a subsidiary of Ford. Volvo has been in business for more than 75 years and has about 27,000 employees worldwide. It produces passenger cars and sells about 450,000 annually through independent dealers worldwide.

As a subsidiary of Ford, Volvo's revenue and profit figures are not published, but 2004 was a record year for Volvo in terms of both volume and profit. Ford has been in the car making business for 100 years and has some 313,000 employees. It sells about 6,700,000 vehicles annually and generates revenues of 125.5 billion euros from its worldwide operations.

These two companies have independently brought alternative-fuelled vehicles to the market; both have chosen to offer methane-fuelled vehicles. Methane is either obtained from fossil sources (often referred to as compressed natural gas [CNG] or from renewable sources (often called biogas). This chapter uses the abbreviation CNG in the way that practitioners use it, even though their methane-fuelled cars can run on methane from any source.

4.2 The Microprocedural Rationality to Start Experimenting

Ford's interest in methane started towards the end of 1979. At that time, there was a general interest at Ford in alternative fuels such as ethanol, methanol, liquefied petroleum gas (LPG) and methane. So when Ford's subsidiary in Brazil made a direct request in 1979 for engineering help to provide ethanol-powered cars (a concept promoted in Brazil for state financial reasons), Ford formed a small team to look into a whole range of alternative fuels, of which methane was one. At Ford's research laboratory, the team developed a range of similar vehicles that could run on the various fuels.

Two laws enacted by the US government to address growing concerns over energy dependency gave further impetus to Ford's microprocedural rationality. The Alternative Motor Fuel Act 1988 was designed to encourage car makers to produce alternative-fuelled vehicles, while the Energy Policy Act 1992 mandated fleet customers—especially governmental fleets—to buy and use alternative fuel vehicles (AFVs). The Manager of Policy and

Business Strategy at Ford stated: 'Ford read those acts as a sincere move by the government that wanted us to move into that business.'

Volvo's path to methane-powered passenger vehicles came from a strategic belief that growth potential existed through more focused exploitation of the company's core values of safety, quality and environmental care. Simultaneously, the local municipal government adopted an initiative driven by concerns about the local air quality of Gothenburg. Furthermore, post-sale vehicle conversions to methane, which were being carried out in parts of Europe, concerned Volvo for crash-safety reasons. Volvo Cars' senior managers formed a small team to look into more environmental friendly fuel alternatives and joined the network created by the Gothenburg municipal government to address local air quality issues (see Internet URL: http://www.businessregion.se/upload/pages/planet_folder.pdf).

Both Ford and Volvo found strategic relevance in starting to experiment with more environmentally benign product propositions. Both companies responded positively to governmental concerns and both have invested considerably 'up front' in these projects. An estimate by the Manager of Policy and Business Strategy at Ford indicated that: 'Ford alone has spent more than $100 million to develop these cars'. (In January 2005, $100 million was equivalent to 76.5 million euros.)

4.3   Engineers' Interpretations of How to Provide Customer Value

Since the aim was to offer a vehicle that could run on an alternative to petrol, it became quite natural both to Ford and Volvo, given their existing engineering practices, to put their efforts into modifying the powertrain to accommodate that fuel and not to develop a completely new car or to bundle the modified powertrain with other car attributes. The manager of the development project at Ford remembers: 'Ford's project goal was to keep other car attributes the same, to make a "transparent functional vehicle".'

Ford's vehicles were dedicated to CNG, taking maximum advantage of that fuel. Ford offered both underfloor tanks and an alternative with an additional tank in the luggage compartment. The combination gave a range of 250 miles, so the CNG range came close to being on a par with traditional vehicles. The additional cost of a car for methane use ranges from 3450 euros (for a car with one steel tank) up to 6120 euros.

Gas storage is inherently more expensive than petrol storage. The tank and high-pressure solenoids needed to provide enough gas for a reasonable distance drive up costs; this cost penalty will remain even at high production volumes. With many years in the business, the Manager of Policy and Business Strategy at Ford concludes: 'I personally, in 23 years of doing this, cannot think of a high pressure cylinder being produced at such low cost as petrol tanks.'

Ford did not initially invest in bifuel development because it believed that CNG had an environmental message which bifuel vehicles do not have. Ford thought that, eventually, the consumer was going to heed the environmental message. They never did, so Ford complemented its gas-fuelled car with bifuels in 1994. The bifuel vehicles have a full-size petrol tank, with gas tanks placed around it to minimise engineering cost. A research project looked specifically at tank alternatives, but eventually found that the economic benefits from more major changes were just not there. Instead, the luggage storage area was used for tanks as well in order to provide enough gas for a reasonable driving range.

So far Volvo has focused solely on bifuel vehicles because it believes that the infrastructure around the world is too limited for consumers to consider dedicated CNG cars. As at Ford, engineering efforts were directed towards making the bifuel car as similar as possible to the petrol version in terms of all attributes other than those related to fuel. The development ambition was captured in the team's consumer-oriented catch-phrase 'no sacrifices'. This led Volvo to develop a unique underfloor, lightweight tank solution with multiple gas tanks to allow for full luggage space and capacity. This solution required a smaller petrol tank, meaning that the range on petrol or CNG was about 300 km for each.

Engineers at both Ford and Volvo demonstrated the same roles and beliefs embedded in their engineering practices. They tried to make the cars as similar as possible. They believed in an environmental message and they made certain trade-offs based on these beliefs between engineering cost, range and luggage space,

4.4   Macrobehaviour: Buyers' Preferences and Wants

Consumer priorities among various product attributes are important factors in their perception of a product's value. One such attribute is fuel economy, which consists of the two elements of fuel consumption and fuel cost.

Fuel costs differ significantly between the EU and the USA, and hence create differences in US buyers' preferences and wants in comparison with EU buyers. In absolute figures, the petrol price in Europe is equivalent to about 3.62 euros/gallon compared with 1.15 euros/gallon in the USA (November 2003). The EU uses fuel tax differences to promote certain fuels over others. Diesel engines are more efficient than petrol engines and fuel energy content varies; these differences mean that a fuel economy comparison requires a recalculation from fuel price. Recalculation gives the fuel running cost, based on approximate fuel price levels in October 2003 as shown in Table 1.

Table 1. Fuel running cost, based on approximate fuel price levels

	Petrol	Diesel	CNG
Germany	100%	58%	39%
Sweden	100%	62%	67%
USA	100%	–	67%

What can be seen from Table 1 is that Germany promotes CNG significantly in both relative and absolute terms. Sweden promotes CNG versus petrol, but significantly less so. With low absolute fuel prices in the USA, the difference, although relatively as great as in Sweden, has a substantially lower economic impact for US consumers. This also became clear in a discussion with the Group Vice President of Corporate Affairs at Ford World Headquarters about US car customers in general: 'If we ask: "Do you want a big vehicle with the fuel economy of a small vehicle," they will say yes. And if we then tell them: "I can't give you that, what do you want to compromise on?" they will compromise on fuel economy. We have small vehicles for sale, but they don't buy them. We don't say "don't buy them!" They just don't.'

The fuel price differences created in Germany has resulted in relatively high consumer interest in bifuel vehicles, both from private households and fleet customers, while interest is lower in Sweden, especially from private households.

Fuelling infrastructure is another 'cost' for consumers to consider. A Ford interviewee commented on this: 'The infrastructure is a key issue. A customer of a natural gas vehicle is as much a potential customer to the vehicle as he is to natural gas. He must be able to see both of them to consider either of them.' In the USA, the number of CNG fuelling stations has grown during 23 years from about 600 to 1,600; in comparison, there are roughly 175,000 petrol stations available in the USA.

When the fuel price difference is perceived as low, convenience becomes increasingly important. It is unlikely that you will come across a fuelling station just when you need one. There is also a need to refuel more frequently when using gas fuels due to the shorter range. In Sweden and Germany, the gas companies show substantially higher ambitions, possibly driven by the EU target for 10% of road transport to use CNG by 2020 (Commission of the European Communities 2001). The German government declared early on that taxes would be pegged for CNG for vehicles until 2020, making a manager of a German gas company conclude: 'CNG is politically chosen!' The German gas companies are jointly establishing an impressive plan of infrastructure development of 200 stations annually up to 2006, with the ambition to offer one fuelling station every 25 km in rural areas and one every 5 km in cities. Sweden is steadily improving the infrastructure, but so far only in the southern half of the country.

With an average distance driven of roughly 20,000 km annually, it takes many years for a private household to obtain a payoff from the additional price even when the car may have incentives. To give a brief indication about this time, a net present value (NPV) calculation for the Volvo Bifuel in Sweden, at an interest rate of 5%, gives a positive NPV after 10 years. This may be considerably longer than the average consumer intends to own the vehicle. For company car drivers, who normally do not have to take any financial risk in terms of product quality, residual value, etc., economy still ranks high in their evaluation of product and fuel propositions. A survey of 341 Volvo bifuel company car drivers in Sweden produced the response shown in Table 2.

Table 2. Responses of a survey of 341 Volvo bifuel company car drivers in Sweden

Why did you choose Volvo Bi-Fuel as your company car?	
Private economy	74%
Environment	23%
How much do you run on gas?	
Between 81% and 100%	72%
Between 61% and 80%	19%
What are the reasons for running on petrol?	
Driving in areas lacking CNG/CBG fuelling stations	50%
Limited availability of fuelling stations requires more travel planning	27%

A substantial part of the cost of ownership of a car comes from its residual value and, for CNG vehicles, the residual value has so far been lower than for a similar petrol version. A staff technical specialist at the Ford Scientific Research Laboratory gives his view on this problem: 'I am not certain that use of gaseous fuels for vehicle use makes sense. One issue is the number of filling stations and convenience of refuelling. But you have a number of other things, not least the range. Customers, given many choices, do not choose CNG. The initial buyer may get incentives that partly may compensate for that, but the second or third buyer buys a lot of the inconvenience but gets no incentive for it. So the residual value diminishes.'

Fleet customers such as airport shuttle companies and taxi companies do not necessarily experience the same drawbacks. A fleet owner may get a payback from the fuel price difference in less than a year due to high mileage, even in the USA. Closed-loop operation such as shuttle buses can have their own filling station and still make a business case out of it. Many fleet owners drive and own the car until the end of its life, and hence do not suffer from any residual value problem.

5. THE CONTEXT OF GOVERNMENTS AND OTHER ECONOMIC ACTORS

5.1 Incentives and Taxes

Prices for diesel and petrol fuels are substantially lower in the USA than in Europe, basically due to differences in tax policy. With low taxes on vehicle fuels, government does not have any substantial opportunity to use that instrument to create consumer interest in an alternative fuel. The Manager of Vehicle Energy Planning at Ford World Headquarters said: 'The US has state tax and federal tax on fuels. But neither group will use it for social purposes. It is strictly highway funding. When they want to promote alternative fuels, they typically use incentives on the car purchase price.' The incentives never fully offset the additional costs of the alternative-fuelled vehicle, but typically cover about half the additional price.

The Swedish government has reduced carbon dioxide taxation on CNG and biogas, and has decided to give incentives in terms of reduced tax for environmentally benign company cars. A 20% tax reduction versus the same petrol car is given to ethanol- and methane-fuelled vehicles, including bifuel versions; 40% tax relief is given for hybrid vehicles and electric vehicles. The implementation of this tax relief system has significantly increased the sale of such cars. Lack of other general incentives is evident in very low sales to private households while sales to fleet customers are often possible for environmental reasons, which may rank higher in Swedish society than in the USA.

The German government's tax decision has created a substantial price benefit for CNG as a fuel for vehicles. In the German market, gas companies run incentive programmes for methane-fuelled cars from time to time, at best covering 25% of the additional car price. A substantial share of the bifuel sales, about 40% for Volvo, goes to private households while the rest is fleet sales. German company car taxes are based on car price, which becomes a disincentive for environmentally benign cars, which carry a higher price tag and, consequently, no bifuels are sold as company cars in Germany.

5.2   The Issue of Many Fuel Choices

The US law that mandated government departments and fleets to buy and use AFVs provides a whole list of fuels to choose from such as electricity, natural gas, ethanol, methanol and biodiesel. Different states promote different alternative fuels for various reasons; Minnesota promotes ethanol while Texas promotes propane, California CNG, etc. Of course, this makes it difficult for customers who use their cars across states.

With limited cost and effort, a petrol-driven car can be made to also run on ethanol. Ford calls these cars 'flexi-fuel' vehicles. They can run on any blend of petrol and ethanol up to 85% ethanol (known as E85). Although there are only around a hundred ethanol fuelling stations in USA, mainly concentrated in Minnesota, a lot of flexi-fuel vehicles are sold. The Ford AFV North American Marketing, Sales and Business Manager said: 'When we sell our Flexi-fuel vehicles, we know—the customers even tell us—that they have no intention whatsoever to fill one single drop of ethanol. But they met the mandate.' The Manager of Policy and Business Strategy at the Ford Scientific Research Laboratory continues: 'And we [the US] never build an infrastructure that will manage to fuel all ethanol vehicles. We build hundreds of thousands of flexi-fuel vehicles and none of them run on ethanol.' Although it may be difficult for governments to choose only one fuel as an alternative, promoting a broad range may be contrary to the initial objective of establishing alternative(s).

A fuel research specialist at Ford comments: 'Too many alternative fuels have been promoted, which means none of them have developed an infrastructure that is good enough for consumers to consider. In the USA, there are about 1,600 CNG fuelling stations versus 175,000 petrol stations. It's a 1:100 ratio. Regarding alternative fuels, there are a lot of advocates that don't necessarily look upon them from a rational standpoint. Working on alternative fuels for almost 20 years, we should as a collective have been able to choose one and worked on it to become seriously competitive. This has not been done, but instead every alternative fuel has had its advocate, and resources have been spread to become so diluted no alternative fuel is seriously considered.'

Germany's early promotion of CNG and considerable price differentiation seems to have brought considerable stability to the market and faith in the fuel. Private households consider the car/fuel, as do fleet customers. Disincentives in the company car tax system in Germany mean that company car drivers do not.

The Swedish company car tax system seems to be sufficient to encourage Swedish company car drivers to consider a more environmentally benign vehicle. Owners, however, including companies providing these company cars, do not find value in the proposition and hesitate to buy.

6.   A BRIEF LOOK AT TWO ALTERNATIVE
PRODUCT PROPOSITIONS

Two interesting and contrasting alternative to the Ford and Volvo engineering approaches are the Toyota Prius hybrid electric vehicle (HEV) and the Saab Bio Power ethanol vehicle. Both these alternatives can use the existing infrastructure of fuelling stations without range limitations. Both create distinct symbolic values without requiring any (or very limited) change in organisational and behavioural dimensions of consumption.

The hybrid technology in the Prius improves energy efficiency, which translates into improved fuel economy, but the car still runs on petrol. The price difference of the car is in the same range as for a methane-fuelled vehicle. They often also receive approximately the same governmental incentives. The reduction in fuel consumption roughly translates into the same fuel cost saving as when driving on methane in Sweden and the USA. Thus, from a purely economic perspective, these cars show equal attractiveness.

However, the Prius brand exists only for the hybrid, which means a Prius owner is an HEV owner, and it shows. A symbolic value for the buyer is substantiated externally through a unique body style and internally through a 'high tech' interior with, among other things, a display showing the real-time energy flow between the various components in the driveline. The car is advertised as a 'high tech' advanced hybrid with low fuel consumption and where the environmental performance is a bonus. The driver/owner is constantly reminded of and rewarded for the fact that the Prius represents leading-edge technology, fuel savings and environmental performance combined in these symbolic attributes.

The product proposition does not challenge any of the behavioural or organisational dimensions of the existing dominant technology. No alternative fuel is required, and range can be not just equalled but also potentially improved due to the car's higher energy efficiency. Toyota sold 53,293 hybrid electric vehicles in 2003 and 62,000 from January to June in 2004. The company announced plans to increase production capacity by 50% in 2005 to 15,000 hybrid electric vehicles a month. The hybrid segment is growing rapidly in the USA, although from small start numbers, and Toyota sells over ten times more hybrids than Volvo and Ford sell methane-fuelled vehicles combined.

Saab recently launched its Bio Power ethanol vehicle in Sweden. It can run on any blend of petrol and ethanol. From a design perspective, Saab's solution has similarities to Volvo's and Ford's methane propositions. The car looks the same and, in fact, is mostly identical to its petrol cousin. There is, however, a symbolic and a monetary difference that may turn this offer into a success—though it is too soon to judge.

The monetary one is the price difference. Ethanol is liquid and can be stored in the same tank as petrol and blended with petrol, while the tank system for methane is very expensive. The additional price can therefore be limited to about 880 euros compared with Volvo's about 330 euros for methane (at 1 SEK = 0.110 EUR and car prices in Sweden, January 2005). These cars are, nevertheless, subject to the same company car tax incentive in Sweden.

The other difference, a symbolic value, is the fuel-engine combination. Saab chose a turbo engine for its ethanol variant and, when run on ethanol (E85), this engine can use the characteristics of ethanol to provide 30 hp more, as well as more torque. When run on pure petrol, it performs like its petrol cousin, providing 150 hp. This symbolic value of engine power comes at a lower cost with ethanol than with petrol. The additional price for a 35 hp more powerful petrol engine is about 1,650 euros, which makes the symbolic value of the Saab Bio Power also price-competitive in relation to the existing dominant technology. The potential lack of infrastructure for ethanol fuelling pumps turns this car into an 'ordinary' 150 hp Saab, but without any other sacrifices.

The product proposition may challenge the organisational dimension to some extent since range is somewhat lower on ethanol due to its lower energy density. Although the Saab has just been launched and no sales figures are yet available, a hint as to its potential can be given by looking at Ford Focus sales figures in Sweden. Ford does not provide any power increase in their ethanol vehicles, i.e. no symbolic value. The main consumer benefit when choosing a Focus Flexi-fuel (the ethanol version of the Ford Focus) over an ordinary Focus is only the external incentives such as the 20% company car tax relief and free parking in some cities. In 2004, Ford sold about 6,500 Focus vehicles in Sweden, of which about 5,500 were the Flexi-fuel ethanol version.

7. THE UNRECOGNISED BIAS AND ITS CONSEQUENCES

This case study analyses the product value propositions provided by Volvo and Ford through their more environmentally benign methane-fuelled vehicles offered in Sweden (Volvo), Germany (Volvo) and the USA (Ford). Encouraged by Reinhardt's (1998) suggestion that we can make significant progress in addressing environmental problems if we analyse them as we would other business issues, the case was structured using the theory of competitive rationality provided by Dickson (1992) into two perspectives: the microprocedural rationality perspective of the company; and the macrobehavioral perspective of consumers. Since stimuli from other economic actors are an important element of competition, the context of government and other economic actors was included to make the analysis tool complete.

From a microprocedural rationality perspective, some product typologies such as cars become more costly with improved environmental performance, even at high volumes. This is not surprising since improved product performance of many kinds comes at a cost. Of crucial importance, though, is the fact that environmental performance is a common 'good'. The theory of competitive rationality asserts that a product offering that target consumers perceive as less attractive than existing offerings will fail on the market.

Research on consumer purchasing behaviour shows that willingness to pay, which is also realised in purchasing actions, is fairly limited for improved common-good attributes in the case of perceived high-cost product propositions. It is therefore interesting to observe that the expressed objective of both these car companies was to design cars as equal as possible to their traditional counterparts in all attributes other than environmental performance. This approach makes it extremely easy for consumers to relate price difference to improved common good, and consumer behaviour in high-cost situations follows the theory of rational choice. With their engineering practices, these companies interpret structural requirements from the dominant technology, challenges in regime shifts and consumer demands in ways that leads them to develop propositions against findings from theory of consumer behaviour and of competitive rationality. That is, they do not manage to create product propositions with perceived improvement in value as seen from a consumer behavioural perspective, though it may be perceived as an improvement from an attitudinal perspective. These two companies show bias in their understanding of what consumers perceive as high-cost.

From a macrobehavioural perspective, consumers can be found who are willing to pay the additional price for the improved common good only, though they are, as Diekmann and Preisendörfer (2003) point out, the exception. Not only is the price higher, some attributes of personal importance such as range and luggage space are also difficult to keep on a par with petrol-driven cars. The cause of this disincentive may be a matter at least partly outside the control of the car manufacturer. Not only can the design trade-off that has to be made be based on consumer preferences, it is affected adversely by structural limitations, in this case due to the inferior infrastructure of CNG filling stations. The design becomes a disincentive for most potential customers and cannot survive competition from the established technological regime without continuous and substantial incentives from other economic actors. The combination of product proposition and consumer behaviour creates a need for an externalisation of the cost, and the recipient becomes the context of governments and other economic actors such as the governments of Sweden and Germany and the gas companies in Germany.

A brief comparison of Volvo, Ford, Toyota Prius and Saab models shows that Volvo and Ford have made product propositions where the price for the environmental attributes could be easily identified by the consumer and where the symbolic, organisational and behavioural attributes have never been on a par with, or above those of, the existing dominant technology. The consumer price for Saab's environmental part of its product proposition could also be easily identified. However, the price increase is competitive when combined with a symbolic value of increased engine power. The car underperforms slightly in the behavioural attribute when run on ethanol due to the lower energy density of ethanol. The environmental attributes of the Toyota Prius cannot be identified economically, as the Prius does not exist in any other version. The Prius is 'bundled' into an offering where the price of the common good and private good cannot be separated. The car does not underperform in any of the structural dimensions. It is sold to the paying customer on the basis of its advanced technology and fuel economy, with environmental performance as a 'bonus'.

Reverting to speculations and noticing that Ford has a CEO who expresses environmental ambitions, that Volvo has had 'environment' as a core value for decades, while Saab and Toyota at least until recently have not stated publicly any specific environmental product ambitions, one may ponder if a company's environmental attitude and ambition potentially introduce a bias that overrate the threshold for when cost for common good is judged 'high' by consumers.

From the perspective of governments and other economic actors, the case indicates that product propositions that are designed for incentives may become so to some extent because of structural causes such as limitations in infrastructure for the alternative fuel. A governmental strategy to promote a range of alternative technologies and fuels may adversely affect each alternative's chances of surviving and becoming interesting enough for consumers to consider.

Drawing on the addressed theories and cases, one can argue that it may be problematic but not impossible for businesses such as the automotive industry to provide improved environmental performance that the consumer is prepared to pay for. Product typology and the product's social meaning may affect how improved environmental performance is perceived by the consumer. From a company perspective, a conscious bundling of product attributes may be a successful way of bringing environmentally benign alternatives to the market.

In this case, bundling means improved environmental performance combined with product improvements that the consumer is likely to desire. The bundling can be made to create value in any of the three structural dimensions as well as monetary value. Governmental incentives may be seen as a type of bundling, although they are normally monetary and limited in time while product attribute bundling may create more long-lasting values and hence be of substantial importance in the greening of industry and consumers. One possible problem with bundling may be the potential view that the same bundling without the environmental improvement is more likely to show higher profitability. To avoid premature speculation, however, this environmental perspective of bundling requires more research.

This chapter supports Reinhardt's suggestion (1998) that significant progress can be made in addressing environmental problems if they are analysed in the same way as other business issues. This chapter makes such an analysis and found that some companies' institutionalised perceptions may misguide their environmental ambitions while others manage to create product propositions that are both environmentally improved and considered by consumers.

When applying Hård and Jamison's suggestion (1997) that alternative technological offers must have a reasonable fit to the defining power of established technologies to environmental issues, given the findings on consumer behaviour in these cases (Diekmann and Preisendörfer 2003), reasons are found to suggest that, for private consumers, 'high cost' is rather low and most likely not related, or only weakly related, to product price or environmental seriousness. On the other hand, willingness to pay for what is perceived as private good may be considerable, given the actual price span of cars of over a factor of 20.

There may be reasons to question the general emphasis on incentives as a means of changing environmental behaviour (Diekmann and Preisendörfer 2003; Kemp et al. 1998). Although incentives may close the gap between consumer attitude and behaviour and indeed affect the consumer's perceived value of a proposition, that option may also exist in the bundling of attributes for the common and private good in products and may be more long-lasting. The substantial difference in consumer willingness to pay between common-good and private-good attributes also encourages further research on potential bundling opportunities.

The claim that actors representing the established technological regime are generally not interested in stimulating new competing technologies (Kemp et al. 1998) cannot be verified in this study. The companies showed no lack of willingness to encourage new competing technologies. Neither did they show lack of persistence in their efforts. Volvo has engaged in the methane-fuelled vehicle endeavour for more than ten years, surpassed by

Ford's 25 years. Economic theories on bundling are completely lacking when it comes to the potentially highly relevant issue of bundling of attributes for the common and private good in products such as cars. Hence, the issues addressed in this chapter seem to have significant relevance not just for managers but also for science.

8.   CONCLUSIONS

Not surprisingly, environmentally benign product propositions have to be competitive to succeed in the marketplace. Research on consumer behaviour shows us that our expectations on consumer willingness to pay for environmental improvements should be kept low. One possible way to address this problem of increased cost for improved environmental performance and low willingness to pay may be through design choices such that the perceived value increases or at least is kept on a par in the structural dimensions defined by the existing dominant technology. Such structural improvements are 'private-good' and hence increase willingness to pay substantially over willingness for 'common-good' improvements. This type of 'bundling' of private-good and common-good product attributes is probably not easy to doe—not least because of companies' path-dependent and institutionalised engineering practices and search heuristics. Hence, in an increasingly environmentally aware society, those companies that learn how may expect sustained competitive advantage.

The recommendation to managers is to look into the potential and opportunities offered by the bundling of the common and private good in products. Researchers are recommended to look at the apparent blind spot of bundling of common and private good into environmentally benign products and how that affects the perceived value.

REFERENCES

Bartunek, J.M. and Louis, M.R. (1996): *Insider/Outsider Team Research.* Thousand Oaks: Sage.

Boje, D.M. (2001): *Narrative Methods for Organisation Research & Communication Research.* London, Thousand Oaks, New Delhi: Sage.

Commission of the European Communities (2001): *Communication from the Commission to the European Parliament, the Council, the Economic and Social Committee and the Committee of the Regions* (Proposal for a Council Directive COM (2001) 547 Brussels) [online]. Available from Internet URL: http://europa.eu.int/comm/energy/res/legislation/doc/comm2001-547-en.pdf.

Dickson, P.R. (1992): 'Toward a General Theory of Competitive Rationality', *Journal of Marketing* Vol. 56, Issue 1, 69-83.

Diekmann, A. and Preisendörfer, P. (2003): 'Green and Greenback: The Behavioral Effects of Environmental Attitudes in Low-cost and High-cost Situations', *Rationality & Society* Vol. 15, 441-472.

Dubois, A. and Araujo, L. (2004): 'Research Methods in Industrial Marketing Studies', in: Håkansson, H., Harrison, D. and Waluszewski, A. (Eds.): *Rethinking Marketing - Developing a New Understanding of Markets*. Chichester: Wiley, 207-228.

Elkington, J. (1994): 'Towards the Sustainable Corporation - Win-Win-Win Business Strategies for Sustainable Development', *California Management Review* Vol. 36, 90-100.

Figge, F., Hahn, T., Schaltegger, S. and Wagner, M. (2002): 'The Sustainability Balanced Scorecard - Linking Sustainability Management to Business Strategy', *Business Strategy and the Environment* Vol. 11, No. 5, 269-284.

Fontana, A. and Frey, J.H. (1994): 'Interviewing', in: Denzin, N.K., Lincoln, Y.S. (Eds.): *Handbook of Qualitative Research*. London: Sage, 361-376.

Garud, R. and Rappa, M.A. (1994): 'A Socio-Cognitive Model of Technology Evolution: The Case of Cochlear Implants', *Organisation Science* Vol. 5, 344-362.

Glaser, B.G. and Strauss, A.L. (1967): *The Discovery of Grounded Theory*. New York: De Gruyter.

Harris, L.C. and Crane, A. (2002): 'The Greening of Organisational Culture - Management Views on the Depth, Degree and Diffusion of Change', *Journal of Organisational Change Management* Vol. 15, 214-234.

Hart, S.L. (1995): 'A Natural-Resource-Based View of the Company', *The Academy of Management Review* Vol. 20, 936-960.

Hart, S.L. (1997): 'Beyond Greening: Strategies for a Sustainable World', *Harvard Business Review* Vol. 75, No. 1, 66-77.

Hart, S.L. and Ahuja, G. (1996): 'Does it Pay to be Green? An Empirical Examination of the Relationship between Emission Reduction and Company Performance', *Business Strategy and the Environment* Vol. 5, 30-37.

Hart, S.L. and Milstein, M.B. (1999): 'Global Sustainability and the Creative Destruction of Industries', *Sloan Management Review* Vol. 41, No. 1, 23-33.

Hård, M. and Jamison, A. (1997): 'Alternative Cars: The Contrasting Stories of Steam and Diesel Automotive Engines', *Technology in Society* Vol. 19, 145-160.

Hård, M. and Knie, A. (2001): 'The Cultural Dimension of Technology Management: Lessons from the History of the Automobile', *Technology Analysis & Strategic Management* Vol. 13, 91-103.

Huberman, A.M. and Miles, M.B. (1994): 'Data Management and Analysis Methods', in: Denzin, N.K. and Lincoln, Y.S. (Eds): *Handbook of Qualitative Research*. London: Sage, 259-309.

Huesemann, M. H. (2002): 'The Inherent Biases in Environmental Research and their Effects on Public Policy', *Futures* Vol. 34, 621-633.

Kemp, R., Schot, J. and Hoogma, R. (1998): 'Regime Shifts to Sustainability through Processes of Niche Formation: The Approach of Strategic Niche Management', *Technology Analysis & Strategic Management* Vol. 10, No. 2, 175-195.

Kvale, S. (1996): *InterViewing*. London: Sage.

Lothe, S. and Myrtveit, I. (2003): 'Compensation Systems for Green Strategy Implementation: Parametric and Non-Parametric Approaches', *Business Strategy and the Environment* Vol. 12, 191-203.

Maxwell, J.W. (1996): 'What to do When Win-Win Won't Work: Environmental Strategies for Costly Regulation', *Business Horizons* Vol. 39, No. 5, 60-63.

Merriam, S.B. (1994): *Fallstudien som forskningsmetod*. Lund: Studentlitteratur.

Minoli, D.M. and Bell, J.N.B. (2003): 'Insurance as an Alternative Environmental Regulator: Findings from a Retrospective Pollution Claims Survey', *Business Strategy and the Environment* Vol. 12, 107-117.

Newton, T.J. (2002): 'Creating the New Ecological Order? Elias and Actor-Network Theory', *The Academy of Management Review* Vol. 27, 523-540.

Newton, T.J. and Harte, G. (1997): 'Green Business: Technicist Kitsch?', *The Journal of Management Studies* Vol. 34, No. 1, 75-98.

Orlikowski, W.J. (1992): 'The Duality of Technology: Rethinking the Concept of Technology in Organisations', *Organisation Science* Vol. 3, 398-427.

Palmer, K., Oates, W.E. and Portney, P.R. (1995): 'Tightening Environmental Standards - The Benefit-Cost or the No-Cost Paradigm', *Journal of Economic Perspectives* Vol. 9, 119-132.

Payne, D.M. and Raiborn, C.A. (2001): 'Sustainable Development: The Ethics Support the Economics', *Journal of Business Ethics* Vol. 32, No. 2, 157-168.

Porter, M.E. and Linde, C. van der (1995): 'Green and Competitive: Ending the Stalemate', *Harvard Business Review* Vol. 73, No. 5, 120-134.

Reinhardt, F.L. (1998): 'Environmental Product Differentiation: Implications for Corporate Strategy', *California Management Review* Vol. 40, No. 4, 43-73.

Reinhardt, F.L. (1999): 'Market Failure and the Environmental Policies of Companies: Economic Rationales for 'Beyond Compliance' Behavior', *Journal of Industrial Ecology* Vol. 3, 9-21.

Rowlands, I.H., Scott, D. and Parker, P. (2003): 'Consumers and Green Electricity: Profiling Potential Purchasers', *Business Strategy and the Environment* Vol. 12, 36-48.

Rugman, A.M. and Verbeke, A. (1998): 'Corporate Strategies and Environmental Regulations: An Organising Framework', *Strategic Management Journal* Vol. 19, 363-375.

Schaltegger, S. and Figge, F. (2000): 'Environmental Shareholder Value: Economic Success with Corporate Environmental Management', *Eco-Management and Auditing* Vol. 7, 29.

Schaltegger, S. and Synnestvedt, T. (2002): 'The Link between 'Green' and Economic Success: Environmental Management as the Crucial Trigger between Environmental and Economic Performance', *Journal of Environmental Management* Vol. 65, 339-346.

Schnaiberg, A. and Gould, K.A. (1994): *Environment and Society - The Enduring Conflict.* New York: St. Martin's Press Inc.

Silverman, D. (1993): *Interpreting Qualitative Data.* Thousand Oaks: Sage.

Strannegård, L. (1998): *Green Ideas in Business.* (Gothenburg Research Institute) Gothenburg: School of Economics and Commercial Law, Gothenburg University.

Tyler, T.R., Orwin, R. and Schurer, L. (1982): 'Defensive Denial and High Cost Prosocial Behavior', *Basic and Applied Social Psychology* Vol. 3, 267-281.

Wallace, D. (1995): *Environmental Policy and Industrial Innovation - Strategies in Europe, the US and Japan.* London: Earthscan Publications Ltd.

Walley, N. and Whitehead, B. (1994): 'It's not Easy being Green', *Harvard Business Review* Vol. 72, No. 3, 46-52.

HONDA AND TOYOTA: USING SUSTAINABILITY IN A NEW COMPETITIVE BATTLEGROUND

Peter A. Stanwick and Sarah D. Stanwick
Department of Management and School of Accountancy, College of Business, Auburn University, USA

Abstract: The role of addressing sustainability has increased in importance for companies across the globe. As various stakeholders demand that corporations consider long-term sustainability in their operations, companies must address these challenges in their day-to-day operations. One industry that has a high level of visibility as it pertains to sustainability issues is the automobile industry. Vehicles that use internal combustion engines are a visible example of how humankind can have a significant, positive impact on the environment. Two companies in the forefront of addressing environmental issues in the automobile industry are Honda and Toyota. These two companies have taken a leadership role related to sustainability issues due to the long-term vision of their corporate leaders, as well as the necessity to be environmentally proactive in their native country of Japan.

1.   INTRODUCTION

Since the 1990s, the relationship between environmental and economic performance has received an increased level of attention in the academic arena. With the recent conclusion of the World Summit on Sustainable Development in Johannesburg, the debate continues to focus on how businesses can focus on stakeholders' needs of environmental sustainability while also addressing stockholders' needs of financial performance (Walley and Whitehead 1994). It is through this increased focus on stakeholder needs that businesses realised that improved environmental performance could translate into establishing or sustaining a competitive advantage for the company. This is in contrast to the 'traditionalist' view presented by Wagner (2000) and Wagner *et al.* (2001). The traditionalist view of the relationship between environmental and economic performance is a negative relationship (Friedman 1970). The underlying assumption is that it becomes more costly to increase environmental performance and that the costs outweigh the economic benefits (Walley and Whitehead 1994). In contrast, Wagner (2000) and Wagner *et al.* (2001) presented the revisionist view which states that there is a strong positive relationship between environmental and economic performance. The revisionist view is based on the foundation that companies that are proactive environmentally are able to make significant gains in the market place and are able to yield positive financial returns for their environmental commitment. Schaltegger and Figge (2000) argue that the level of corporate environmental protection does not add or reduce shareholder value per se, but that the value of the company's environmental performance impacts shareholder value through the way in which corporate environmental management is developed and implemented.

By differentiating the company's strategy through proactive environmental involvement, a company can separate itself from its competitors (Hart 1995; Porter 1991; Porter and van der Linde 1995; Reinhardt 1999a). In addition, improved environmental performance may yield significant cost savings that will also allow the company to enhance its competitive position (Reinhardt 1999a; Schmidheiny 1992). By developing alternative manufacturing processes or incorporating advanced technology in the manufacturing process, companies are rewarded by not only increasing their compliance demands for improved environmental performance, but also may be able to generate a reduction in production costs, increased efficiencies, reduction of compliance costs and a reduction of future legal liabilities (Porter and Esty 1998, Reinhardt 1999b).

This is one of the underlying arguments presented by Porter and van der Linde (1995). They believe that pollution and waste products are inherent in an inefficient production process and that the hidden costs of pollution such as wasted resources and employee effort are not identified since they buried within the life-cycle costs of the product. Porter and van der Linde (1995) argue that the increase in the level of innovation by adopting environmental proactive strategies can more than offset the financial costs of such investments.

In addition, companies are better able to serve the needs of customers by incorporating the most advanced technology in their operations. As a result, they are able to capitalise on the benefits of being the first mover in the industry (Porter and Esty 1998). Using event studies, White (1995) and Klassen and McLaughlin (1996) found a positive relationship between positive environmental practices (via a comprehensive environmental management programme) and stock returns, and a positive relationship between corporate environmental awards and abnormal stock returns. Cohen *et al.*

(1995) also found a positive relationship between corporate environmental performance and the level of profitability of the company. Their work was extended by Hart and Ahuja (1996), who found that companies that reduce emissions and other pollution levels had higher levels of company performance based on return on sales and return on assets within one or two years of when the pollution reduction strategies were implemented.

Hart and Ahuja's (1996) work is supported by Gallarotti (1996), who stated that pollution reductions should be considered an opportunity for financial reward and not a cost of doing business. King and Lenox (2002) found that companies that implemented waste prevention strategies not only achieved lower emission levels but also high levels of profitability. These results extend the work of King (1995) and Majumdar and Marcus (2001), who claim that waste reduction benefits the company by creating a new learning opportunity for it. This opportunity gives the company an ability to establish new revenue growth through strategy and technology developments (Hart 1997).

Focusing on the environment from a sustainability perspective, Hart (1995, 1997) proposed that enlightened companies understand the importance of establishing long-term objectives in order to ensure environmental sustainability. Hart (1995) argues that companies need to view the natural environment from a natural-resource based perspective. Just as the traditional resource-based view of the company examines how capabilities and resources are used to develop a competitive advantage, the natural-resource based view of the company examines these same components from a natural environment perspective. Hart (1997) states that companies that have incorporated environmental capabilities into their strategic focus will yield excess profits compared with their competitors.

Hart (1997) proposed a four-stage process that includes pollution prevention, product stewardship, clean technology and sustainability vision. As a result, companies have the ability to be proactive environmentally and are rewarded with high levels of financial performance by integrating their competitive strategy with their commitment to the environment. By presenting a long-term perspective, Hart (1995, 1997) suggest that companies should consider environmental investments from a sustainability perspective and not from a short-term rate of return perspective.

Russo and Fouts (1997) found a positive relationship between environmental and company performance using a resource-based view of the company. They also found that the relationship was moderated by the growth level of the industry. The positive relationship became stronger as the growth rate of the industry increased. King and Lenox (2001) also found that industry was an important variable to consider in this relationship and showed that a higher environmental performance of a company relative to other companies in the industry had a positive impact of its financial performance.

Dowell *et al.* (2000) examined the relationship between multinational enterprises (MNEs) and the establishment of a global environmental standard through their corporate environmental policy. They found that MNEs that adopted a single comprehensive global environmental standard had a higher market value than those companies that used less stringent country standards. Dowell *et al.* (2000) concluded that countries that have less stringent standards attract companies that have a lower level of quality and are less globally competitive.

These studies highlight the assumed belief stated by Reinhardt (1999a) that companies should make decisions on environmental expenditures just as they would with any type of expenditure expected to result in a positive return from the investment. Reinhardt (1999b) argues that environmental investments are converted to positive financial gains based on:

- Increased efficiency
- Increased demand for the company's products
- Reduction of the threat of the negative image
- Increases in the ability of the company to attract more qualified employees.

In addition, Reinhardt (1999b) recommends that companies need to consider their economic standing, the structure of the industry in which they compete and the company's capabilities as they incorporate environmental decisions within their strategic decision-making process to maximum the return on the environmental investment. As a result, Reinhardt (1999a, 1999b) recommends that environmental investments should be based on the specific financial characteristics of each company and that a standardised 'one size fits all' approach to environmental investments is not a viable approach.

In their extensive review of previous research pertaining to the relationship between environmental and economic performance, Wagner *et al.* (2001) concluded that earlier reviews of the literature revealed a moderate positive relationship between environmental and economic performance. However, Wagner *et al.* (2001) continued by stating that more recent studies examining this relationship showed a significant relationship; however, it is not clear whether it is positive or negative.

Resent studies such as those by Wagner *et al.* (2001) and Schaltegger and Synnestvedt (2002) state that the lack of a concise conclusion could be due, in part, to the variance in the studies based on impact factors such government regulations, industry structure, country location, the measurement of environmental and economic performance, and the size of the company. For example, environmental performance has been measured using emission levels such as the Toxics Release Inventory, environmental compliance expenditures and environmental rankings (Wagner 2000). Economic performance has traditionally been measured from a market perspective (stock price) or through accounting measurements such as return on assets (ROA) and return on sales (ROS) (Wagner *et al.* 2001). Therefore, as stated by Schaltegger and Synnestvedt (2002) and as supported by the work of Hart (1995, 1997) and Reinhardt (1999a, 1999b), the relevant question may not be 'does it pay to be green?' but should be 'when does it pay to be green?'

Schaltegger and Synnestvedt (2002) address this issue by proposing that academic research examining this relationship should also incorporate eco-efficiency performance as a variable. Eco-efficiency performance is the middle ground or a combination of both environmental and economic performance. Schaltegger and Sturm (1990; cited by Schaltegger and Figge 2000) define eco-efficiency as the ratio between the value added for the company and the environmental impact added or the ratio between economic performance and environmental performance. By adding this measure to the analysis, researchers will be able identify the direction of the causation between environmental and economic performance.

The causal effect between environmental and economic performance is also critical in understanding this complex relationship (Schaltegger and Synnestvedt 2002; Wagner *et al.* 2001). The direct and indirect impact that environmental and economic performance have on each other makes it difficult and challenging to identify the impact different variables have on this relationship. It can be argued that strong environmental performance can lead to a strong economic performance through competitive advantages and cost savings, and that a strong economic performance can lead to strong environmental performance by allowing the company to allocate resources for resolving environmental issues.

This chapter examines how two companies in the same industry 'compete' for high levels of environmental, social and economic performance. We selected this approach because it gave us the opportunity to identify in specific detail how environmental issues are integrated in the day-to-day operations of the two companies. In addition, a case analysis allows us to highlight the similarities and differences in the relationship between the environmental and financial performance for these two companies. By performing a side-by-side comparison, a rich level of content is available to identify the subtle and not so subtle differences between the two companies using the natural environment as an opportunity to enhance their competitive advantage.

The same industry was selected as the unit of analysis since it allows a direct comparison between companies. In addition, it will include the same level of industry-related environmental costs such that the environmental impacts will be the same for both companies (Luken *et al.* 1996). Honda and Toyota were selected because these competitors are closely matched from both a competitive and environmental strategy perspective. However, this chapter highlights not only the similarities, but also the differences in their strategic approaches to dealing with the natural environment and financial performance.

2. THEORETICAL FOUNDATION OF THE RELATIONSHIP BETWEEN SUSTAINABILITY PERFORMANCE AND BUSINESS COMPETITIVENESS

In the past, research examining the relationship between environmental and financial performance has been limited, being based on subjective measures of environmental performance and relatively small sample sizes (Cohen *et al.* 1995; Konar and Cohen 1997). In addition, traditional studies did not examine the different strategic focuses that companies implement to increase their level of environmental performance (Wagner *et al.* 2001). These different strategic focuses could range from adjusting a number of areas:

- The raw materials used
- The manufacturing process
- The disposal of end of production waste products.

Previous studies on the relationship between sustainability performance and business competitiveness can be classified into three major categories: (1) event studies; (2) model portfolios of environmentally reactive companies; and (3) multiple regression analysis (Wagner *et al.* 2001).The focus of this chapter is to extend the model portfolio classification of companies by comparing and contracting the relationship between environmental and financial performance for two companies in the same industry.

3. BACKGROUND OF HONDA AND TOYOTA

3.1 Background of Honda

Established in 1948, Honda has evolved from engine-powered bicycle manufacturing to being a global leader in a diverse number of industries. It employs over 120,000 employees across the globe. Honda manufactures products that include engines, generators, lawn and garden products, outboard motors, personal water craft, pumps, scooters, snow blowers, financial services, motorcycles, all-terrain vehicles (ATVs) and automobiles. Although Honda competes in a number of different product categories, as shown in Tables 1 and 2, 80% of its revenue is generated from automobiles and 13% from motorcycles. Therefore, these are the two areas through which Honda's commitment to sustainability is discussed.

Table 1. Summary of Honda's financial information (Source: Honda 2002a, 2002b)

	2002	2001	2000
Net sales and other operating revenue	7,362,438	6,463,830	6,098,840
Operating income	639,296	406,960	426,230
Net income	362,707	232,241	262,415
Number of employees	120,600	114,300	112,400

Consolidated numbers in billions of Yen unless otherwise specified

Table 2. Breakdown of Honda's net sales and other operating revenues by segment and region in 2002 (Source: Honda 2002a, 2002b)

Sales by segment	
Automobiles	80%
Motorcycles	13%
Others	4%
Financial services	3%
Net sales and other operating revenue by region	
North America	56%
Japan	25%
Europe	8%
Others	11%

3.2   Background of Toyota

Established in 1937, Toyota started as a manufacturer of weaving equipment. In 2002, Toyota became the third largest automobile manufacturer in the world. In 2001, Toyota sold almost 6 million vehicles and employed over 246,000 employees. A summary of Toyota's financial results are shown in Tables 3 and 4. Toyota's automobile business, including its finance operation, accounts for over 90% of the total revenues for the company. Therefore, Toyota's automobile operations are discussed as they relate to its commitment to sustainability.

Table 3. Summary of Toyota's financial results (Source: Toyota 2002a)

	2002	2001	2000
Net revenue	14,316,874	13,137,070	12,649,777
Operating income	1,093,632	790,729	698,561
Net income	556,567	674,898	481,936

Consolidated numbers in billions of Yen unless otherwise specified

Table 4. Breakdown of Toyota's net sales and operating revenues by region in 2002 (Source: Toyota 2002a)

Net sales and other operating revenue by region	
North America	15%
Japan	76%
Europe	5%
Others	4%

3.3   Honda and Toyota's Overall Commitment to Sustainability

Both Honda and Toyota have established formalised policies and procedures to ensure a high level of commitment to sustainability. Honda's environmental statement is shown in Box 1 and Toyota's environmental statement in Box 2.

Honda's philosophy pertaining to the environment can be summarised by PDCA (Plan Do Check Action). Honda's commitment is based on planning for long-term environmental solutions, implementing those actions, verifying the results of the actions and making any follow-up adjustments when necessary. A summary of Honda's commitment to sustainability is shown in Figure 1.

Honda established a world environmental committee in 1995 to address environmental issues from a global perspective. Its world environmental committee receives direct reports from:

- Each of the four major business operations (motorcycle, automobile, power products, service parts)
- Each of the five regional operations (Japan, North America, South America, Europe, the Middle and Near East and Africa, Asia and Oceania)
- Each of the five functional operations (purchasing, administration, business management, Honda R&D Company Ltd, Honda Engineering Company Ltd)
- The Green Factory Project
- The New Recycle Project

- The Life Cycle Assessment Project

Thus, environmental issues are fully integrated into the decision-making process at Honda.

Box 1. Honda's environmental statement (Source: Honda 2002b:5)

Honda's Environmental Statement

'As a responsible member of society whose task lies in the preservation of the global environment, the company will make every effort to contribute to human health and the preservation of the global environment in each phase of its corporate activity. Only in this way will we be able to count on a successful future not only for our company, but for the entire world.'

We should pursue our daily business interest under the following principles:
1. We will make efforts to recycle materials and conserve resources and energy at every stage of our products' life cycle from research, design, production and sales, to services and disposal.
2. We will make every effort to minimise and find appropriate methods to dispose of waste and contaminants that are produced through the use of our products, and in every stage of life cycle of these products.
3. As both a member of the company and of society, each employee will focus on the importance of making efforts to preserve human health and the global environment, and will do his or her part to ensure that the company as a whole acts responsibly.
4. We will consider the influence that our corporate activities have on the regional environment and society, and endeavor to improve the social standing of the company.'

Established and announced in June 1992.

Toyota established its environment committee in 1992. Toyota has a different approach to Honda pertaining to reporting responsibilities and environmental issues. Instead of linking different operations directly with its corporate environmental committee, Toyota links the environmental committee to other environmental committees. These other environmental committees include product design, production and recycling. In addition, sub-environmental committees are linked to the various operations.

Box 2. Toyota's environmental policy (Source: Toyota 2002c:10)

Toyota Earth Charter (April 2000)

I. BASIC POLICY
Contribute towards a prosperous 21st century society
Aim for growth that is in harmony with the environment and set a challenge to achieve zero emissions throughout all areas of business activities

Pursue environmental technologies
Pursue all possible environmental technologies, developing and establishing new technologies to enable the environment and economy to co-exist

Take action voluntarily
Develop a voluntary improvement plan, based on thorough preventive measures and compliance with laws, that addresses environmental issues on global, national, and regional scales while promoting continuous implementation

Work in co-operation with society
Build close and co-operative relationships with a wide spectrum of individuals and organisations involved in environmental preservation, including governments, local municipalities, and related companies and industries

II. ACTION GUIDELINES
Always be concerned about the environment
Work toward achieving zero emissions at all stages, i.e., production, utilisation, and disposal
-Develop and provide products with top-level environmental performance
-Pursue production activities that do not generate waste
-Implement thorough preventive measures
-Promote businesses that contribute towards environmental improvement

Business partners are partners in creating a better environment
Co-operate with associated companies

As a member of society
Actively participate in social actions
-Participate in creation of a recycling-based society
-Support environmental government policies
-Contribute to non-profit activities

Toward better understanding
Actively disclose information and promote environmental awareness

---

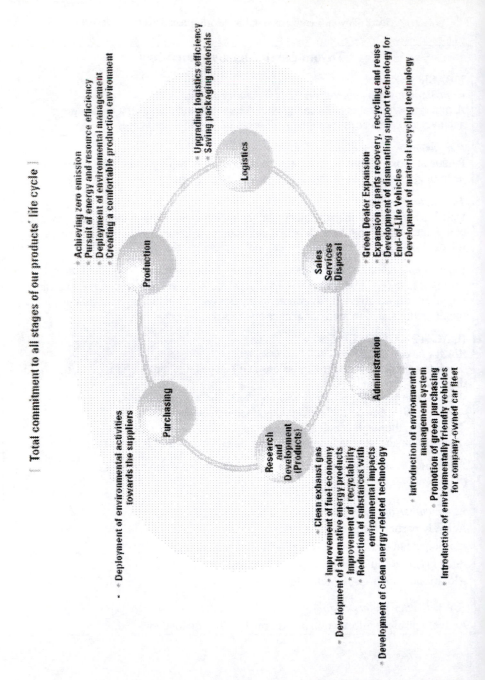

*Figure 1.*Honda's integrated commitment to sustainability (Source: Honda Ecology 1999:15)

The sustainability challenges facing both companies include the various areas in which environmental concerns may be created. As presented in Honda's *Ecology* report (Internet URL: http://www.environment.honda-eu. com) and shown in Box 3, there are a number of diverse environmental issues that must be addressed by both companies. Both Honda and Toyota are meeting these challenges by examining how their actions can be environmentally proactive while also allowing each company to differentiate their products. These issues can be addressed by examining solutions such as:

- Making the exhaust gas cleaner
- Improving the fuel efficiency of the vehicles
- Reducing the noise level of the engines
- Developing alternative energy products
- Improving the recyclability of the vehicles
- Reducing the use of substances with high negative environmental impacts

Box 3. Environmental challenges facing vehicle manufacturers in the use and disposal of products (Source: Honda Ecology 1999:19, Honda 2002b:6)

Environmental challenges:

Global warming
Depletion of natural resources
Air pollution
Waste
Destruction of the ozone layer
Water pollution
Soil pollution
Noise

Major commitments of Honda Corporation's domains used to face these challenges:

Products:
Clean exhaust gasses
Improvements in fuel economy
Noise reduction
Improvements in recyclability

Purchasing and Production:
Promotion of green purchasing
Promotion of green factories

Logistics:
Promotion of green logistics

Sales and Services:

Promotion of green dealers

Disposal and Recycling:
Increasing the recovery, recycling and re-use of parts
Technical support for the proper disposal and recycling of end-of-life products

Administration:
Promotion of green offices

4.   HONDA AND TOYOTA'S SUSTAINABILITY STRATEGY PERTAINING TO POLLUTION EMISSIONS

Both Honda and Toyota use low emissions as a means to develop and sustain a competitive advantage. This is due, in part, to the increasingly stringent standards that have been established in two keys markets for these companies—Japan and California. Through the Ministry of Land, Infrastructure and Transport, the Japanese government has established emission standards that are used to classify emission levels. If emission levels are 25% below the 2000 exhaust emission standards, the vehicle is classified as 'good'. If the emission levels are 50% below the 2000 standards, the vehicle is classified as 'excellent', and if the emission levels are classified as 75% below the 2000 level, the vehicle is classified as 'ultra'.

4.1   Honda's Response to Low Emissions

In fiscal year 2000, Honda sold 576,587 cars in Japan that were classified as 'excellent', representing 73% of total sales in Japan for that year. By 2001, 855,892 or almost 96% of the cars sold in Japan were classified as low emission vehicles.

In 2000, Honda had a number of low emission vehicles that were top in their class for fuel efficiency. They included the Civic iE (19.4 km/l), the CIVIC FERIO (1.5 litre lean burn engine 20.0 km/l) and the Stream (2.0 litre DOHC i-VTEC topped its class in fuel economy of 14.2 km/l lean burn NO_x adsorbing catalyser). The DOHC i-engine is a high-fuel economy engine with clean exhaust emissions. This type of engine uses Honda's own variable valve timing and lift electronic control system (VTEC), which also enhances the fuel efficiency of the vehicle.

Based on the low emissions classifications, in 2002 Honda had four types of vehicles classified as 'ultra': (Civic [Types B and G], Civic Ferio [Type C], Civic Hybrid) and 12 types of vehicles classified as 'excellent' (CR-V,

HR-V, That's, INSPIRE, INTEGRA, CIVIC Type r, Step Wagon, Saber, Vamos, Fit, MOBILIO, Life).

4.2   Toyota's Response to Low Emissions

Toyota uses a number of different avenues to increase the level of fuel efficiency of its products. These include:

- Reducing of the weight of vehicles
- Improving the level of combustion efficiency
- Implementing more efficient engines, including direct-injection lean burn engines.

Toyota uses a Variable Valve Timing-Intelligent (VVT-i) system that results in higher fuel efficiency and lower exhaust emissions. The VVT-i system is used for all of Toyota's new models and any existing models that are redesigned. Toyota also reduces emissions by reducing the level of air resistance through implementing more aerodynamically viable designs. In addition, it is are beginning to implement the Toyota Stop and Go System ,which reduces fuel consumption and the level of exhaust emissions when the vehicle is at a complete stop. The Stop and Go system is a manual system in the Vitz and an automatic system in the Crown Comfort.

In 2002, Toyota had seven types of vehicles classified as 'ultra' for low emissions. They include the Premio (1.5 litres, 16.4 km/l), Platz (1.0 litres, 19.6 km/l), Allion (1.5 litres, 16.4 km/l), Vitz (1.0 litres, 19.6 km/l) Estima Hybrid, Camry and Soarer. As part of its environmental management programme, Toyota has carried out life-cycle assessment (LCA) on the Premio and Allion. The results showed that these two types of vehicles generate less environmental impact compared with conventional vehicles. In addition, the Toyota Crown with a mild hybrid system has been classified as 'excellent' for emission levels. Toyota also has 14 types of vehicles that have been classified as 'good' in relation to emission levels. They are the: bB OPEN DECK, Will Vs, Altezza Gita, Ipsum, Windom, Corolla Spacio, Gaia, Crown (including Crown Sedan, Estate, Comfort, patrol car) Nadia, Noah/ Voxy, Vista/Vistra Ardeo, Brevis/Progres, Premio/Allion and Mark ii Blit.

5.   USING ALTERNATIVE ENERGIES AS A FUEL SOURCE

5.1   Honda's Strategy Pertaining to Alternative Energies

5.1.1   Hybrid Cars

In 1999, Honda introduced its first hybrid car. The Honda Insight uses Honda's Integrated Motor Assist (IMA) system. IMA uses the engine as its primary source of power and the motor as an auxiliary power source. The Insight also has a light weight aluminium body to enhance fuel efficiency. The Insight is able to travel 35 km on one litre of gasoline and has the highest fuel efficiency in the world for its class. The Insight has a 1-litre lean burn VTEC engine, which is the lightest engine in the world. The lean burn engine is based on the combustion of lean fuel. The lean fuel engine is designed to use more air in the air-fuel ratio than a conventional engine, creating a more fuel-efficient burning process.

When the Insight accelerates, the motor that is linked directly to the crankshaft is activated. When the car is decelerating and/or braking, the motor works as a generator to reclaim the energy. The Insight also has an auto idle stop system, which automatically stops the engine when the car comes to a complete stop.

In December 2001, Honda introduced its second hybrid. Instead of developing a new model, Honda developed the Civic Hybrid. As with the Insight, the Civic Hybrid can make the claim that it has the world's best fuel economy (46 miles per gallon [mpg] in the city and 51 mpg on the highway) for its class which is a five passenger gasoline-powered mass production vehicle.

5.1.2   Natural Gas Vehicle

In 1997, Honda introduced its first mass-produced natural gas vehicle (NGV). It began selling it in Japan and the USA in 1998, and in Europe in 1999. The CIVIC GX has a near zero level of emissions released. This vehicle meets the zero emission standards in Japan and the USA and is estimated to be able to travel 376 km with one tank of natural gas fuel. Natural gas is a logical alternative to gasoline since it has a much cleaner exhaust gas and natural gas reserves are more plentiful compared with oil. The CIVIC GX is classified as an ultra low emission vehicle in Japan. In addition, in the USA, the CIVIC GX meets the Super Ultra Low Emission Vehicle Standards (SULEV) for California and is certified by the California Air Resource Board (CARB) as having zero evaporative emissions and 15-year durability certification for exhaust emissions.

5.1.3   Fuel Cell Vehicle

In 1999, Honda introduced the FCX-V1 and FCX-V2—the next generation of fuel cell vehicles. The fuel cells generate electricity via a chemical reaction. This reaction occurs at a relatively low temperature, thus generating energy conversion efficiencies. The only by-product of the reaction is water.

Two types of fuels are used in this fuel cell technology. Both hydrogen and methanol have been used as the raw fuel needed to make the chemical reaction. Before this technology can be introduced commercially, a number of issues need to be addressed:

- The supply and storage of hydrogen
- The additional weight of the vehicle
- The high cost of the vehicle.

Honda hopes to have a commercially available vehicle available by 2008.

5.1.4   Electric Vehicles

Honda has developed an electric vehicle (EV) called the Honda EV Plus. Introduced in 1996, it went on sale in the USA in 1997. The EV has a highly efficient water-cooled motor and long-lasting nickel metal hydride batteries. The EV is able to travel 200 km on a single charge.

Honda has extended its commitment to electricity-based vehicles by establishing an insulated community that uses only electric or hybrid vehicles for transportation. The Intelligent Community Vehicle System (ICVS) in Singapore shares the use of environmentally friendly vehicles. People who live in the community are given membership and they are allowed to pick up and drop off any of the vehicles at three designated ports. Members are able to check the availability of vehicles via cell phone or the Internet. Honda has also developed a similar system in California called CarLinkII. In this programme, members share the use of CIVIC ULEVs, which are ultra low emission vehicles.

5.1.5   Other Vehicles: Motorcycles

In 1999, Honda introduced the Hyper VTEC motorcycle engine. The Hyper VTEC uses Revolution-Modulated Value Control (REV) technology to achieve the maximum balance between power and environmental performance. This engine is used in Honda's CB400 Super Four Motorcycle. In 2001, Honda introduced its environmentally friendly Silver Wing motorcycle. The Silver Wing was able to achieve a clean emission level that was half of the acceptable rate in Japan for carbon monoxide, hydrocarbons and nitrogen oxides.

5.1.6   Other Vehicles: Electric Scooters

Honda developed an electric scooter in 1994. The CUV ES is designed for consumers who make short trips in congested urban areas. It was originally designed for Japanese consumers. The scooter can be recharged using a household 100-volt outlet. From a single charge, the scooter can travel up to 60 km. The battery will retain the charge for up to 8 hours. Honda has also introduced an electric motor assisted bicycle called the RACOON COMPO. The RACOON COMPO is a lightweight bicycle that can be folded into small areas and, like the CUV ES, is also designed for short trips in congested urban areas.

5.2   Toyota's Strategy Pertaining to Alternative Energies

5.2.1   Hybrid Vehicles

Toyota has three hybrid models—the Prius, Estima Hybrid and Crown (with mild hybrid system). In March 2002, the total sales of the three models surpassed 100,000 vehicles. Of these, approximately 12,000 Estima Hybrids and 2,000 Crowns have been sold. Box 4 shows the greenest vehicles of 2002 as rated by the American Council for an Energy Efficiency Economy.

Box 4. Greenest vehicles of 2002 (Source: Internet URL: http://www.hondacars.com)

---

1. Honda Insight (gasoline electric hybrid)
2. Honda Civic GX (natural gas)
3. Toyota RAV4 EV (electric)
4. Toyota Prius (gasoline electric hybrid)
5. Honda Civic HX (gasoline)
6. Toyota Echo (gasoline)
7. Nissan Sentra (California-only edition, gasoline)
8. Honda Civic (All models nationwide, gasoline)
9. Mitsubishi Mirage (gasoline)
10. Toyota Corolla (gasoline)
11. Chevrolet Prizm (gasoline)
12. Saturn SL (gasoline)

The hybrid models are based on the Toyota Hybrid System-Mild (THS-M), which consists of a small motor that also serves the function of a generator and which is connected directly to the engine by an auxiliary system drive belt. When the vehicle is started, the motor is used to start the vehicle and the engine is also started. When the vehicle is driven during normal conditions, the engine moves the vehicle. During deceleration and/or braking, the vehicle captures electricity that is stored in the battery via energy regeneration. When the vehicle comes to a complete stop, the engine stops and the motor provides energy to the vehicle.

The Prius has a US Environmental Protection Agency (EPA) fuel economy rating of 52 mpg in the city, 45 mpg on the highway and 48 mpg combined. Toyota began selling the Prius in North America in July 2000 and it is currently the best selling hybrid sold there. Furthermore, Toyota has formed a partnership with ExxonMobil to develop cleaner burning fuels. Toyota has also formed a partnership with General Motors to develop advanced technology related to hybrid and other types of alternative energy vehicles.

5.2.2   Fuel Cell Hybrid Cars

Introduced in 2001, Toyota's Fuel Cell Hybrid Vehicle (FCHV) uses hydrogen as the base fuel.

Figure 2 shows how Toyota's fuel cell system works. Toyota's current version of the FCHV is called the FCHV-4 and is being developed for eventual full-scale commercial release. Toyota has introduced FCHV cars in 2004 in Japan, the USA and Europe. One of the major benefits of FCHV is the energy efficiency. Using high-pressure hydrogen, the FCHV can be three times more efficient than gasoline vehicles and 1.5 times more efficient than gasoline hybrid vehicles. As with the Honda fuel cell vehicle, the only by-product from this process is water.

Toyota has also embraced the shared community concept as it relates to sustainability. Toyota has developed the Crayon EV Commuter System, which has served various communities since 1999. This system is based on the shared use of compact electric vehicles. This system has been used in California with Toyota's eco-commuter (e-com). E-com is a two-seat vehicle that is electric and battery operated. In addition, Toyota has developed the Intelligent Multi-mode Transit System (IMTS), which is part of Toyota's commitment to future means of transportation. This is a system where specially designed buses move automatically in a single line on specific roads developed for this system. The buses can also be used manually on any road when they are not linked to the automated system.

■ Structure of a Fuel Cell

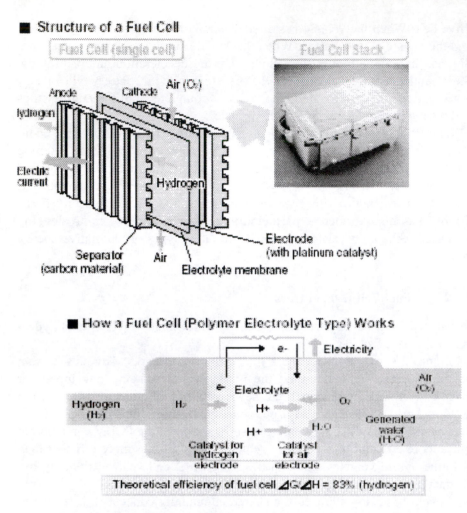

Figure 2. Toyota's cell fuel system (Source: Toyota 2002b:54)

6.   OUTREACH TO VARIOUS STAKEHOLDERS

6.1   Honda's Strategies to Address Stakeholder Concerns

Honda ensures that its commitment to sustainability is followed through during the selling process. Honda sends each dealer a comprehensive list of materials, including policies and procedures to follow as well as guides for increasing consumer awareness of how Honda is implementing environmentally friendly strategies in its vehicles. Each dealer must implement an environmental management system (EMS) that includes the handling and disposal of end-of-life products. In Japan, the EMS includes Honda's Good Green Dealer Certification system, which evaluates the dealer's environmental performance. Dealers certified as 'green dealers' receive various promotional materials, including posters and brochures, to increase customer awareness.

Honda releases information for its stakeholders pertaining to the environment through various media. Some of the communication channels used include brochures, environmental and corporate annual reports, and Honda's website.

In addition, Honda sponsors environmentally friendly vehicle fairs and exhibitions, and holds special events to introduce new products and/or the development of new types of technologies.

Honda also participates in its Eco Wagon programme, which is used to expose children to environmental issues. In addition, Honda has developed the 'Joyful Forest' project. This project involves the reforestation of Mongolia in the People's Republic of China. In addition, Honda is involved in reforestation activities in Japan.

6.2   Toyota's Strategies to Address Stakeholder Concerns

At Toyota, dealers are responsible for establishing environmental response plans and actions, and are required to incorporate them into their policies and procedures. Toyota publishes the Toyota Eco Communication News, which is sent to each dealer to highlight information pertaining to actions that are needed based on a particular environmental issue.

Dealers have the option of allowing the lease or rental of hybrid vehicles; the Prius has been available since 1998 and the Estima Hybrid since 2001. This allows consumers to 'test drive' these vehicles over an extended period of time before they make the commitment to buy a hybrid vehicle.

Toyota has comprehensive environmental training programmes for all of its employees. In addition, specialised environmental training has been developed for department general managers and employee positions considered critical to business operations.

Toyota established a formalised stakeholder dialog over a two-day event in 2001. The theme of the meeting was the role of corporations in sustainable development. Stakeholders included non-profit organisations (NPOs), academic researchers and consumers. In addition, Toyota holds an annual environmental forum which consists of lectures, panel discussions and displays of the latest products that incorporate environmental awareness.

7.   SUSTAINABILITY IN NON-VEHICLE INDUSTRIES

Toyota became involved in the biotechnology business in Indonesia in 2001 with Mitsui and Company. By using sweet potatoes as the raw material, the joint venture is able to produce animal feed and biodegradable plastics (polylactic acid). Biodegradable plastics are derived from plants that capture carbon dioxide. Production from the feed processing plant is expected to top 100,000 tonnes annually in the near future. The production of the biodegradable plastics started in 2004. The development of the biodegradable plastics will aid the drive towards long-term sustainability for vehicle parts. Toyota is testing the durability and level of heat resistance in hopes of eventually using these plastics in the vehicle manufacturing process.

Toyota is also involved in the afforestation business. Toyota has established the Toyota Roofgarden Corporation, which uses peat mined in China to construct roof gardens. Roof gardens have the ability to reduce the 'heat island' effect of large urban cities.

Toyota is developing eucalyptus trees that yield a 40% higher volume of wood. The Australian Afforestation Pty. Ltd was founded in 1998 and is responsible for promoting sustainability in forest products. The tree project is located in Western and Southern Australia and covers approximately 861 hectares of land. Toyota is also involved in the reforestation in China with the goal of reforesting 1,500 hectares in three years.

Toyota is also involved in the home building industry. Toyota's Housing Group has developed environmentally friendly housing designs that include improving levels of insulation, lighting, management of chemicals, reduction of waste during the manufacturing process and water conservation.

8.   CONCLUSIONS

8.1   Inward versus Outward Environmental Approach

This examination of how two companies in the same industry address the relationship between economic and environmental performance has yielded a number of interesting results. To paraphrase Charles Dickens, it is definitely a tale of two strategies. We view Honda and Toyota as developing fundamentally different strategic approaches to deal with sustainability issues. We classify Honda as having an inward environmental strategy and Toyota as having an outward environmental strategy. An inward environmental strategy looks at incremental avenues in order to expand a company's relationship with sustainability issues. An outward environmental strategy is based on expanding product lines in order to address sustainability issues.

Honda's corporate strategy is based on related diversification, which allows Honda to develop synergistic relationships with its various business units. Honda has a number of different product categories including automobiles, motorcycles, lawn mowers, boat engines and other engine-based product lines. Therefore, Honda has the luxury of receiving the shared benefits of centralised research and product development. As a result, Honda can have a significant impact on sustainability issues by focusing on improvements in its existing core products through advanced technology. Furthermore, Honda focuses on 'retrofitting' some of its existing product models to be more sustainable. The actions of Honda are consistent with the use of a sustainability balanced scorecard approach to business strategy (Figge *et al.* 2002). Figge *et al.* (2002) argue that economic, environmental and social performance should be integrated in the strategic decision-making process. Honda views the environment as another type of decision that needs to be incorporated into each business unit within the corporation. As a result, topics such as emission levels, energy intensity, waste and material inputs are not considered from a sustainability perspective, but are incorporated in the means of production. Through the synergistic benefits of a related diversified strategic focus, Honda is able to use this integrative tool to improve its environmental and economic performance. Thus, Honda is an excellent example of how a company can use eco-efficiency strategies (Schaltegger and Figge 2000; Schaltegger and Synnestvedt 2002) to develop and maintain a competitive advantage and to address the concerns raised with sustainability issues.

Toyota has an opposite combination of corporate and environmental strategic focus. Toyota can be more closely defined as using a single business corporate level strategy. The dominant focus is on automobiles and the financing of automobiles. Therefore, Toyota's strategic focus is based on its single core product category. As a result, it does not have the same strategic opportunities that Honda has when addressing sustainability issues. Due to its limited corporate strategy, Toyota has taken an outward approach to sustainability issues. An outward environmental approach introduces new products within Toyota's single product category to help capture the strategic benefits of sustainability. Thus, Toyota's perspective on competitive advantage and sustainability is to develop a more comprehensive product line to address various customer needs with respect to sustainability issues.

An example of the differences in the product line strategy is shown in Box 4; in this list of the Greenest Vehicles of 2002, both Honda and Toyota have four entries in the top 12. However, three of the four entries for Honda are various versions of the Honda Civic but all four entries for Toyota are different models.

8.2   Differences in their Description of their Environmental Commitment

Boxes 1 and 2 highlight the environmental policies of the two companies. Although similar in some aspects, there are subtle differences in these disclosures. The Honda environmental statement is very general in description and addresses the interests of stakeholders other than employees only in very general terms. The Toyota policy not only identifies the specific sustainability issues that Toyota is committed to address but also presents actionable goals which Toyota is trying to accomplish. In addition, Toyota gives more detail about how it will address the issues of various stakeholders.

This difference in the presentation of their environmental commitment may be based on their different environmental strategies. By using an integrative eco-efficiency approach to sustainability, Honda does not identify much specific detail on sustainability issues since the environment is already integrated within the strategic decision-making process. An example of the integrative approach to decision making is presented in Figure 1. As was mentioned previously, sustainability is just another factor incorporated into the decision-making process.

On the other hand, Toyota does not have the luxury of using the synergistic benefits of related diversion to enhance its commitment to sustainability. Thus, it is more likely to consider sustainability as a separate and not as an integrative decision-making process for strategic development. As a result, Toyota is deliberate in identifying specifically how its commitment to sustainability can help various stakeholders and is more specific about the type of goals that it is attempting to achieve.

8.3   Economic Performance and Market Location

One question that may arise from this analysis is whether one environmental strategic focus yields a higher level of economic performance than another. The results show mixed results, which Wagner et al. (2001) highlighted as a common occurrence (see Tables 1 and 3). If net income is calculated as a percentage of sales, Honda had a higher financial performance in 2000 (4.30% versus 3.80%) and 2002 (4.92% versus 3.88%), but a lower financial performance than Toyota in 2001 (3.59% versus 5.13%). This supports Wagner et al.'s argument (2001) that the relationship between environmental and economic performance is hard to identify and difficult to measure accurately.

Another interesting factor is the primary market focus of Honda and Toyota. Again, the two companies have a very different philosophy concerning which markets to penetrate (see Tables 2 and 4). Honda is heavily dependent on the US market (56% of sales), with Japan a distant second (25% of sales). Alternatively, Toyota has over three-quarters (76%) of its sales in Japan. Again, this supports the argument that the relationship between environmental and economic performance is country-specific (Wagner *et al.* 2001). The different governmental regulations and customer needs in Japan and the USA allow both Toyota and Honda to have different environmental strategies while both being equally effective from an economic performance standpoint. This also supports Toyota's outward environmental philosophy on sustainability. Due to limited oil resources and land area, Japanese consumers are more willing to accept new automobile models that address sustainability issues. In contrast, Honda's dependence on the USA for profitability supports its inward approach to sustainability. American consumers are more willing to try new technology in the form of alternative energy sources as long as the product is consistent. Since Honda has established a strong positive brand image with the American consumer, Honda can effectively add sustainability 'new' models that are actually current versions of their existing models, which have been retrofitted for the new type of technology.

In conclusion, this analysis has highlighted how two companies that are headquartered in the same country and that compete in the same industry can have very different approaches to sustainability. A significant result of this analysis is that the type of corporate strategy a company implements has a direct result on the approach it takes when addressing sustainability issues. The level of diversification impacts the type of opportunities that are available to the company as it tries to incorporate the environment in its strategic decision-making process. Companies with different corporate strategies place different emphasis on the value drivers of shareholder value (Schaltegger and Figge 2000). Through high levels of diversification, Honda makes different decisions on level of capital investment and value and sales growth than Toyota. As a result, both Honda and Toyota develop environmental shareholder value, but their process to achieve it varies based on their corporate level strategy.

REFERENCES

Cohen, M.A., Fenn, S.A. and Naimon, J. (1995): *Environmental and Financial Performance: Are They Related?* Nashville: Owen Graduate School of Management, Vanderbilt University.

Dowell, G., Hart, S. and Yeung, B. (2000): 'Do Corporate Global Environmental Standards Create or Destroy Market Value', *Management Science* Vol. 46, 1059-1074.

Figge, F., Hahn, T., Schaltegger, S. and Wagner, M. (2002): 'The Sustainability Balanced Scorecard-Linking Sustainability Management to Business Strategy', *Business Strategy and the Environment* Vol. 11, 269-284.

Friedman, M. (1970): 'The Social Responsibility of Business is to Increase its Profits', *New York Times Magazine* 13th September, Vol. 33, 122-126.

Gallarotti, G. (1996): 'It Pays to be Green: The Managerial Incentive Structure and Environmentally Sound Strategies' *Columbia Journal of World Business* Vol. 30, 38-57.

Hart, S. (1995): 'A Natural-Resource-Based View of the Company', *Academy of Management Review* Vol. 20, 986-1014.

Hart, S. (1997): 'Beyond Greening: Strategies for a Sustainable World', *Harvard Business Review* Vol. 75, 66-76.

Hart, S. and Ahuja, G. (1996): 'Does it Pay to be Green? An Empirical Examination of the Relationship between Emission Reduction and Company Performance', *Business Strategy and the Environment* Vol. 5, 30-37.

Honda (2002a): *Annual Report.* Tokyo: Honda.

Honda (2002b): *Environmental Annual Report.* Tokyo: Honda.

Honda (2005) *Ecology*, http://www.environment.honda-eu.com/reports/Honda%20Ecology %20Full.pdf.

Honda Ecology (1999): *Honda Environmental Conservation Activities 1999.* Tokyo: Honda.

King, A. (1995): 'Innovation from Differentiation: Pollution Control Departments and Innovation in the Printed Circuit Industry', *IEEE Transportation Engineering Management* Vol. 2, 270-278.

King, A. and Lenox, M. (2001): 'Lean and Green: Exploring the Spillovers from Lean Production to Environmental Performance', *Production Operations Management* Vol. 10, 244-256.

King, A. and Lenox, M. (2002): 'Exploring the Locus of Profitable Pollution Reduction', *Management Science* Vol. 48, 289-299.

Klassen, R. and McLaughlin, C. (1996): 'The Impact of Environmental Management on Company Performance', *Management Science* Vol. 42, 1199-1214.

Konar, S. and Cohen, M.A. (1997): *Does the Market Value Environmental Performance?* Nashville: Owen Graduate School of Management, Vanderbilt University.

Luken, R., Kumar, R. and Artacho-Garces, J. (1996): *The Effect of Environmental Regulations on Industrial Competitiveness of Selected Industries in Developing Countries.* (Paper presented at the 5th Greening of Industry International Conference, Heidelberg, 24-27 November 1996) Heidelberg: Greening of Industry.

Majumdar, S. and Marcus, A. (2001): 'Rules versus Discretion: The Productivity Consequences of Flexible Regulation', *Academy of Management Journal* Vol. 44, 170-189.

Porter, M. (1991): 'America's Green Strategy', *Scientific American* Vol. 264, No. 4, 168.

Porter, M. and Esty, D. (1998): 'Industrial Ecology and Competitiveness: Strategic Implications for the Company', *Journal of Industrial Ecology* Vol. 2, No. 1, 35-43.

Porter, M. and Linde, C. van der (1995): 'Green and Competitive: Ending the Stalemate', *Harvard Business Review* September/October 1995, 120-134.

Reinhardt, F. (1999a): 'Bringing the Environment Down to Earth', *Harvard Business Review* Vol. 77, 149-157.

Reinhardt, F. (1999b): 'Market Failure and the Environmental Policies of Companies', *Journal of Industrial Ecology* Vol. 3, 9-21.

Russo, M. and Fouts, P. (1997): 'A Resource-Based Perspective on Corporate Environmental Performance and Profitability', *Academy of Management Journal* Vol. 40, 534-559.

Schaltegger, S. and Figge, F. (2000): 'Environmental Shareholder Value: Economic Success with Corporate Environmental Management', *Eco-Management and Auditing* Vol. 7, 29-42.

Schaltegger, S. and Sturm, A. (1990): 'Ökologische Rationalität'. In: *Die Unternehmung*, Nr. 4, 1990, 273-290.

Schaltegger, S. and Synnestvedt, T. (2002): 'The Link between 'Green' and Economic Success: Environmental Management as the Crucial Trigger between Environmental and Economic Performance', *Journal of Environmental Management* Vol. 65, 339-346.

Schmidheiny, S. (1992): *Changing Course: A Global Perspective on Development and the Environment.* Cambridge: The MIT Press.

Toyota (2002a): *Annual Report.* Tokyo: Toyota.

Toyota (2002b): *Environmental Report.* Tokyo: Toyota.

Toyota (2002c): *North American Environmental Report.* Tokyo: Toyota.

Wagner, M. (2000): *The Relationship between the Environmental and Economic Performance of Companies: What Does Theory Propose and What Does Empirical Evidence Tell Us?* (Paper presented at the ESST Annual Conference, Strasbourg, May 2000) Strasbourg: ESST.

Wagner, M., Schaltegger, S. and Wehrmeyer, W. (2001): 'The Relationship between the Environmental and Economic Performance of Companies: What Does Theory Propose and What Does Empirical Evidence Tell Us?', *Greener Management International* Summer 2001, 95-108.

Walley, N. and Whitehead, B. (1994): 'It's not Easy being Green', *Harvard Business Review* May/June 1994, 46-52.

White, M. (1995): 'The Performance of Environmental Mutual Funds in the United States and Germany: Is there Economic Hope for 'Green' Investors?', *Research in Corporate Social Performance and Policy Supplement* Vol. 1, 325-346.

INCREMENTAL CHANGE TOWARDS SUSTAINANBILITY

Integrating Human and Ecological Factors for Efficiency

Suzanne Benn[1] and E. Jane Probert[2]

[1]*School of Management, University of Technology, Sydney, Australia;*
[2]*European Business Management School, University of Wales Swansea, Swansea, UK*

Abstract: This chapter presents case studies of two companies, one based in South Wales, UK, and the other in New South Wales, Australia. Both companies have successfully carried out incremental changes that have integrated economic aims with environmental improvements and local social sensitivity. We argue that the competitiveness of these companies is facilitated by their proactive and co-operative environmental management philosophy. A key capability underpinning the environmental success of both organisations is networking with regulators and with local community. Another is the systematic approach to human resource functions. The chapter thus raises suggestions concerning the integration of the human and ecological sustainability of corporations.

1. INTRODUCTION

This chapter examines the relationship between human and ecological forms of corporate sustainability. We define corporate human sustainability as the contribution that the corporation makes to sustaining and developing a just and equitable workplace and society. Corporate ecological sustainability is the contribution the corporation makes to the support and renewal of the biosphere. We examine the sustainability of the management practices of two companies that are linked in that they share two key characteristics: their capacity to network with stakeholders and a system based approach to human resource management. In each company, these characteristics underpin eco-efficiency measures and are a common factor in maintaining their competitiveness.

INCO Europe Ltd is situated in South Wales, UK, and its core product is based on old technology—the manufacture of nickel. However, it is adapting its products and processes to meet new demands and to fulfil the requirements for economic success. The Panasonic TV Factory is a branch of Matsushita Electric Co. (Aust) Pty Ltd situated in New South Wales, Australia; it is part of the electronics sector and, as such, represents successful new technology.

These two organisations are both on the path towards sustainability and their progress towards ecological and human sustainability can be assessed according to the phase model developed by Dunphy *et al.* (2003). Using an integrated approach to human and ecological sustainability, this model, which is summarised in Table 1, defines key steps along the way to the sustainable organisation. It can be used as a tool to enable comparison between organisations in terms of their progress to sustainability. Unlike other eco-ordering models such as those proposed by Freeman *et al.* (2000), Hunt and Auster (1990) and Roome (1992), this model draws together the two forms of sustainability. It does not assume a linear progression nor does it intend to 'lump' companies together (Newton 2002:529), but to present a series of ideal types for comparison reasons only.

The following sections describe the companies, the management practices that have facilitated the shift to their current positions and the reasons why they have not progressed further in either human or ecological terms. In both cases, the link between their human and environmental sustainability practices and their competitiveness is emphasised.

Table 1. Phases in the development of corporate sustainability

	Human Sustainability	Ecological Sustainability
Level 1 **Rejection**	Employees and subcontractors exploited. Community concerns are rejected outright.	The environment is regarded as a free good to be exploited.
Level 2 **Non-Responsiveness**	Industrial Relations (IR) a major issue with the emphasis on cost of labour. Financial and technological factors exclude broader social concerns. Training agenda focuses on technical and supervisory training.	Environmental risks, costs, opportunities and imperatives are seen as irrelevant.
Level 3 **Compliance**	Human Resource (HR) functions such as IR, training, Total Quality Management (TQM) are instituted but with little integration between them.	Ecological issues likely to attract strong litigation or strong community action are addressed.

	Human Sustainability	Ecological Sustainability
Level 4 **Efficiency**	Technical and supervisory training augmented with interpersonal skills training. Teamwork encouraged for value-adding as well as cost-saving purposes. External stakeholder relations developed for business benefits.	ISO 14000 integrated with TQM and Occupational Health and Safety (OH&S) systems or other systematic approaches with the aim of achieving eco-efficiencies. Sales of by-products are encouraged.
Level 5 **Strategic** **Pro-activity**	Intellectual and social capitals are used to develop strategic advantage through innovation in products/processes/services.	Environmentally sustainable innovations such as product redesign are seen as a source of competitive advantage.
Level 6 **The Sustaining Corporation**	Key goals both inside and outside the company are the pursuit of equity and human welfare and potential.	The company works with society towards ecological renewal.

2.   THE PANASONIC TV FACTORY: MELCOA PTY LTD

The Panasonic TV Factory is a branch of Matsushita Electric Co. (Aust) Pty Ltd Matsushita was rated in 1997 by *Fortune* magazine as one of 13th largest manufacturers in the world and one of the top three in the electrical appliances industry. It commenced operations in western Sydney in 1968 and now has 160 employees and produces 1,000 televisions per day. The company operates in a high labour cost environment—of the 13 companies manufacturing televisions from bare board to final product 20 years ago in Australia, only Panasonic remains. This area of Sydney is the third largest business area in Australia, with as many as 75,000 operating businesses.

2.1   Ecological Sustainability

The ecological sustainability initiatives at Panasonic have been driven by two employees—the personnel manager and the purchasing supervisor. They were prompted into action in 1992 by the high costs of landfilling waste. At first, they met informally to organise the sale of by-products, the purchasing manager using his informal purchasing networks to get recycling initiatives under way. Initial savings (such as 25% reduction of landfill costs in the first year) convinced management that being environmentally responsible could increase competitiveness. The bottom line in Panasonic's competitive business is economic survival and savings were obviously being made through reducing energy use, as well as reducing waste. By 1997, the informal meetings had evolved into a planned and structured approach to pollution prevention through recycling, energy efficiency and supplier choice. An environmental management system (EMS) was implemented to assess, manage and minimise the impact of business operations on the environment. In 1998, the EMS was formalised by certification under ISO 14001 and, in 1999, targets for waste reduction were initiated.

Panasonic has also capitalised on the diverse networks of local business interests to decrease its waste outputs and avoid costs. Instead of paying for landfill, it now has ingenious arrangements with a range of local companies for either the sale or free removal of by-products. Pallets are sold to a fencing company and plastics of all types, dross from solder machines and scrap metal are recycled. Cabinets are removed by a local company and used as bases for worm farms. Cardboard cartons are resold; selling the cartons pays for waste disposal costs. Foam is a major waste, but 100% now goes to a building company to be incorporated into concrete slabs for road building.

All major suppliers have been contacted and informed of the importance of environmental considerations in purchasing decisions. For instance, a number of supply materials have been phased out due to their toxicity, detergents are selected according to environmental criteria and safety data sheets are kept on chemicals. Energy efficiency is also encouraged. Renovations have been selected that will have the spin-off of better insulation. A process of zoned lighting has commenced and notices above switches encourage employees to turn off lights. The credibility gained from these small wins for the concept of eco-efficiency has persuaded senior management to include major energy saving initiatives in new warehouse and building sites.

In 2000, the company gained 1st place in the Western Sydney Industry Awards category 'Integrating Environmental Systems, Products and Technology into Business Practices'. The company is now committed to contributing funds to support kerbside collection of household wastes and to support a pilot television collection and recycling initiative.

Panasonic has a proactive and collaborative relationship with regulators, reflected in the fact that it was the first electronics company in Australia to sign up for the National Packaging Covenant—a voluntary code for packaging initiated by the Australian Government.

2.2   Human Sustainability

The human resource policy is strongly paternalistic, couched in a business perspective largely driven by cost. For instance, the personnel officer's role has now expanded to include official environmental responsibilities on top of his original duties. However, while the setting of targets and planning is still done by the personnel manager and the purchasing supervisor, there is now top–down support for the EMS. Expert consultants and external auditors are employed by the organisation to maintain and update the EMS and all staff are put through environmental training programmes. A pamphlet, *Employees Guide to the Environmental Management System*, has been printed and the staff canteen has an environmental notice-board.

According to the personnel manager, such management practices have given staff a sense of ownership of the company's environmental achievements. This is demonstrated by the fact the EMS is now on the agenda of every third monthly communication meeting. Staff have also become engaged as a result of the setting of realistic and quantitative targets and implementing practical everyday pollution prevention and energy saving measures. Annual and cumulative savings from reducing waste and energy use have been documented graphically and are available to staff. The meeting is led by the managing director and addressed by various speakers on issues such as attendance, internal sales and profitability.

Television manufacture requires the compiling of many different components and is dependent on a skilled assembly line. The company has a policy of continually upgrading skills through attendance at accredited courses, setting competency standards and awarding medals. Many employees have visited Matsushita training centres in Malaysia, Japan, and taken study tours to similar centres in Europe. Almost all employees see the company as a long-term employer and there is a low level of staff turnover.

Even though the parent company is a multinational, Panasonic tries to concentrate on the Penrith community. For instance, there is a community welfare committee that makes shopfloor decisions about product gifts. Staff assist during paid time in the local 'meals-on-wheels' programme for the elderly and infirm. In 1998, Panasonic was one of only three companies in Australia identified by Volunteering Australia as being genuinely involved in projects that promote community well-being. According to the personnel manager, the community welfare programme at Panasonic is only a 'tiny initiative' involving less than 1% of total work time per week. He points out that, although the impact is small in terms of cost and the company donates only as much as it can afford, there is a big impact in terms of reputation.

The workplace culture at Panasonic has been inspired by the management philosophy of its founder, Konosuke Matsushita. While Matsushita saw management objectives as grounded in values that abide by the 'laws of nature and society', he was also committed to 'throwing himself into maximising the useful life of every available resource' (Sato 2000:40). According to this philosophy, human resources are to be used as productively as possible. The current preparations for the Matsushita 35th anniversary celebrations at Penrith reflect the paternalistic aspect of this culture. They include personal gifts and improvement of amenities for employees, gifts to the community and employee involvement in a local species tree planting program in the nearby area.

3. INCO EUROPE LTD

The second study focuses on the INCO nickel refinery at Clydach near Swansea, in South Wales, UK. The refinery has been operating at the site since 1902 and uses the unique carbonyl process to produce nickel in a range of physical forms. The plant produces over 41,000 tonnes of nickel products per year. The main product is nickel pellet used in the stainless steel and high nickel alloy industries. Also produced are special forms of pellet for electroplating applications. The nickel powders produced at Clydach are used for powder metallurgy and in nickel battery applications. Newer higher value/lower volume products such as nickel foam and nickel fibre have specialist applications in the automotive, electronics and leisure industries (INCO 2002.) INCO's corporate policy, expressed in its values and principles, is to go beyond compliance to give long-term risk avoidance and stability.

The INCO Group is a global company. The turnover of the whole of the INCO Group is US$ 2.2 billon. Approximately 10,000 people are employed by the company worldwide. At Clydach, 260 people are employed. The annual growth rate in the nickel industry is approximately 4%.

3.1 Environmental Initiatives

In 2000, the plant won the Wales Environment Award for companies with more than 250 employees. INCO also gained ISO 14001 certification in the same year. This certification proved very helpful when writing the site's application for an Integrated Pollution Prevention and Control (IPCC) permit. The Pollution Prevention and Control Regulations have been introduced as a result of the EU's IPPC Directive, which is designed to prevent, reduce and eliminate pollution at source through the prudent use of natural resources. These Regulations are a major driving force for environmental improvement and the Environment Agency is responsible for ensuring compliance with them in England and Wales.

The nickel industry is associated with major occupational health and safety (OH&S) issues. At Clydach, nickel carbonyl and carbon monoxide used in the production of nickel from a nickel oxide concentrate are highly toxic. INCO's integrated systems are designed with the aim of fully integrating quality, environment, health and safety management. INCO managers consider that these system give its products a competitive advantage over cheaper products from other producers. The company is currently making its way towards an OH&S standard (ISO 18001).

The company also has a proactive and collaborative approach to regulators and is actively involved through the Nickel Development Institute with EU and US legislators on the development of health and safety regulations relating to nickel. INCO is currently looking at improving its stack emissions. Although these emissions are well within legal limits, work is now concentrating on this area and INCO is currently looking at new abatement measures. The company feels that it is better to be ahead of any possible changes in legislative limits and, perhaps, even influence the direction. The emphasis is on a transparent, working relationship with the regulator.

In moving towards better environmental performance, INCO follows the procedure of identifying significant aspects of the plant in terms of environmental management impact such as severity, quantity and legislation. Each is given a rating and high scores are emphasised in efficiency measures. The Business Unit then sets targets for the delivery of improvement schemes that focus on eco-efficiency measures such as reducing energy usage, recycling and improving operations. Participation in the voluntary 'waste busters' programme has resulted in the generation of a number of good ideas for energy savings.

Recycling of timber used in packaging is an example of one of these eco-efficiency measures. Before the scheme started, timber used for packaging was nailed to the floor of the containers, which made it useless afterwards. Now the timber is cut to longer lengths and wedged into the containers, allowing for subsequent re-use. The company has also introduced a recycling process that enables the full recovery of the nickel oxide from the delivery packaging. This has eliminated the need for disposal of the delivery packaging as special waste and also saves the company £100,000 per year.

INCO collects all waste and segregates it at source. Fluorescent tubes, wood, pallets, scrap metal, metal drums, cardboard and general waste are all separated out so that very specific figures for each type of waste are available. When opportunities arise the waste is sold or taken off-site for recycling. Scrap metal (steel), cardboard, pallets and office paper are sold.

The environmental benefits of INCO's environmental management programme are numerous. All surface and process water streams at the refinery are collected in the effluent treatment plant where over 99% of the nickel present is recovered before the water is discharged to a local river. As a result of continually trying to measure and improve environmental performance, the plant has achieved 65% reduction in effluent discharges since 1995. The discharge of soluble nickel is well below the Environment Agency's specified limit. According to the environmental superintendent, the plant's performance is now as good as they can get it with available technology. INCO is looking at the installation of a magnetic water treatment system to reduce lime deposition in the effluent plant. The next improvements will be water reduction and water recycling.

The benefits also include a 70% reduction in waste sent to landfill and a recovered material value of over £100,000 from shredding and segregating waste materials. The company always seeks to segregate its waste, but has to make sure there is a market for the materials. Over the past three years, it has reduced its emissions to air by over 40%. INCO participates in its sector's Climate Change Agreement (CCA) and has meet the target set for the past two years. The company is now in a position to 'bank' (after verification by external auditors) the 10,000 tonnes of carbon dioxide it has saved. Nuisance to the general public in the form of noise from INCO activities has also been alleviated.

3.2   Human Sustainability

The change agent at INCO was a new production director who arrived from Canada and decided to introduce a number of initiatives including the aim to achieve ISO 14001 in line with corporate policy. Staff describe the director as being very decisive and giving strong leadership.

Employees are trained according to ISO 14001 requirements and some are trained as auditors for ISO 14001. Each business unit has an employee evaluation each year, when training needs are agreed for the following year. Business unit teams meet for half an hour each morning and there is good communication through managers to team leaders and process technicians.

A major influencing factor is that many of the employees live locally. The plant is one of the biggest employers in the area and many employees stay 30 years with the company. The Environmental Superintendent takes a proactive attitude to the community and has a loose network of community members that assists in identifying any areas of complaint. The operation at Swansea has a Community Liaison Committee, which consists of council members, community members, school governors, teachers and other community representatives. It meets every two months to discuss community issues in relation to INCO. INCO supports the local community development plan and the community development officer is based at the plant. In ten local schools, INCO supports an industry information programme that is integrated into the curriculum. Retired employees often bring parties of schoolchildren from local schools to visit the plant. The company organises open days when the public are encouraged to visit the site.

According to INCO managers, the social or community programme costs the company approximately £12,000 a year. They are not sure how much it benefits the company as they cannot quantify it.

4.   OPERATIONAL CHANGES FOR SUSTAINABILITY

Incremental organisational change is ongoing, systematic and gradual. Unlike radical transformational change it is not spectacular, but yet can offer real benefits to organisations (Stace and Dunphy 2001). In the instance of the two corporations studied here, the enabling influence for sustainability is not a transformational 'green' culture or a crusading 'green' morality (Newton 2002), but incremental change in the day-to-day activities of the company.

The change agents in each case are middle managers with good net-working skills with regulators, the community and other organisations. In these companies, these change agents develop adaptive relationships with regulators and reduce business risks associated with future legislative change. They network with other businesses to reduce waste or proactively search out community opinion in order to forestall complaints. Put simply, each company is prepared to invest in the development of social capital. While the motivation for this may be instrumental, this shared norm of 'I'll do this for you now if you do something for me later', allows communities to bind (Adler and Kwon 2002), as well as giving the company the 'right to grow' in the future (Elkington 1999).

These findings support those made by Crane (2000), and Green *et al.* (2000) which suggest that it is not necessary to create radical cultural 'green-ing' or to espouse the tenets of deep ecology in order to develop environ-mental improvements. Our case study findings also support the work of Newton (2002), who argues for the importance of interdependency networks in organisational greening.

The research presented here indicates that it is not a 'green' culture that is needed for more radical change for sustainability, but a culture that fosters innovation. Both the organisations in our study are supported in their ability to move to the efficiency phase of sustainability by the paternalistic head office or parent company, but yet are denied the flexibility needed to innovate beyond to the strategic phase of sustainability (see Table 1). Both have loyal workforces (long-term employees) drawn from the local commu-nity. As a result of these factors, the two companies fall short of adopting the strategy of making a more comprehensive use of employee human potential, achieved through broader and interpersonal development schemes. INCO, furthermore, illustrates the pragmatic difficulties in moving to a fully strate-gic position in a competitive industry sector. The company has developed new products, which have reduced material throughput, but its main efforts remain focussed on the larger and more stable market for nickel pellet.

Despite these issues, considerable progress to sustainability has been made by both companies. Through a series of incremental changes, both organisations have moved to the efficiency phase of human sustainability, enabling eco-efficiency measures to be successfully implemented. People in both organisations are seen as a source of increased productivity and their skills increased accordingly. Both organisations emphasise training and have good communication procedures in place. Workplace systems are installed to ensure high work efficiency. Better environmental performance is enabled through these TQM-based systems and is seen as a way of reducing operational costs. Systematic reviews have enabled ongoing reduction in resource use. Internal benchmarking and the implementation of management systems such as ISO 14001 built on the TQM base are key factors in reaching and remaining at this stage. As Dunphy *et al.* (2003:140) point out: 'the efficiency approach represents a natural move to sustainability because it builds on existing operational and technical capabilities and is a natural extension of installing compliance systems. But as Gratton (2000) observes, such an approach may be only give limited competitive advantage as it may be readily imitated by competitors. It does not offer the long-term strategic competitive advantage that a more innovative approach to change can provide.

5.   CONCLUSION

These case studies demonstrate that human and ecological sustainability are integrated processes. In these organisations, the ecological capability has been built upon and developed through the building of human resource and stakeholder relationship-building capacities—what we term human sustainability.

REFERENCES

Adler, P. and Kwon, S. (2002): 'Social Capital: Prospects for a New Concept', *Academy of Management Review* Vol. 27, No 1, 17-40.

Crane, A. (2000): 'Corporate Greening as Amoralisation', *Organisation Studies* Vol. 21, 673-696.

Dunphy, D., Griffiths, A. and Benn, S. (2003): *Organisational Change for Corporate Sustainability.* London: Routledge.

Elkington, J. (1999): *Cannibals with Forks.* Oxford: Capstone Publishing.

Freeman, R., Pierce, J. and Dodd, R. (2000): *Environment and the New Logic of Business.* Oxford: Oxford University Press.

Green, K., Morton, B. and New, S. (2000): 'Greening Organisations: Purchasing, Consumption and Innovation', *Organisation and Environment* Vol. 13, 206-225.

Hunt, C. and Auster, E. (1990): 'Proactive Environmental Management: Avoiding the Toxic Trap', *Sloan Management Review* Winter, 7-18.

INCO (2002): *INCO Homepage* [online]. Available from Internet URL: http://www.incoltd.com.

Newton, T. (2002): 'Creating the New Ecological Order? Elias and Actor-Network Theory', *Academy f Management Review* Vol. 27, No. 4, 523-540.

Roome, N. (1992): 'Developing Environmental Management Strategies', *Business Strategy and the Environment* Vol. 1, No. 1, 11-24.

Sato, T. (2000): 'Konosuke Matsushita: His Life and Legacy' (Industrialists of the 20th Century), *Asia 21* January 2000.

Stace, D. and Dunphy, D. (2001): *Beyond the Boundaries*. Sydney: McGraw Hill.

Chapter 9

Environmental Management Systems and Competitiveness

ISO 14001

Profitable? Yes! But is it eco-effective?

Jost Hamschmidt and Thomas Dyllick
University of St Gallen, Switzerland

Abstract: Do environmental management systems (EMSs) effectively support the eco-logical performance of companies and are they sufficient to meet the challenge of continuous environmental improvements? These questions were targeted by a research project of the Institute for Economy and the Environment at the University St Gallen. In this chapter we reflect on the results of a written survey covering more than 150 ISO 14001-certified companies in Switzerland. The survey's focus is on the ecological and economic effectiveness of EMSs. It is deepened by the analysis of several case studies with a focus on EMS impact on environmental learning processes within companies. Our results show that the companies are largely satisfied with the ecological and economic effects of their EMSs. However, the potential benefits of EMSs are often not systematically explored by companies. We could identify several key areas for potential improvements: integration, audit culture, strategic objectives and authority relationships. The findings suggest that additional measures need to be considered in order to support the eco-effectiveness of ISO 14001-certified companies.

There is a growing body of literature on the international diffusion of en-vironmental management systems (EMSs) and the economic ratio behind this phenomenon (see e.g. Delmas 2001; Enroth *et al.* 2000; Steger 2000). However, little emphasis has yet been put on the role of EMS with regard to its potential for driving companies towards eco-effectiveness. 'Effective-ness' here means 'doing the right things' in order to reach absolute environ-mental performance improvements. This goes beyond the common under-standing of eco-efficiency ('doing the things right'), which generally aims at reducing negative environmental impacts per unit of output. This chapter aims to evaluate the potential of ISO 14001 to generate processes of change in companies, based on empirical results from Switzerland.

In 1999 the Institute for Economy and the Environment at the University of St Gallen carried out the first representative survey of all ISO 14001-

certified companies in Switzerland (Dyllick and Hamschmidt 2000). The focus of the study was to evaluate the effectiveness of EMSs in Swiss companies:

- What kind of organisations are certified to the ISO 14001 standard?
- What are the companies' expectations?
- What measures do they actually take based on their EMS?
- How do they perceive the economic and environmental effects of their EMS?

In this chapter, we first concentrate on some key findings of the study. We then give some additional information based on the results of four case studies done subsequent to the questionnaire study, and pinpoint the potential for improving EMS effectiveness. Finally, we explore the incentives of the ISO 14001 standard (ISO 1996) for guiding developments in the direction of environmental sustainability.

1. DESIGN OF THE SURVEY

Starting from the results of existing empirical studies about EMSs in Germany (e.g. Prehn *et al.* 1998; UNI–ASU 1997), we designed our study to look at EMS effectiveness and at development processes initiated and supported by EMS. The structure of the questionnaire is reflected in the model shown in Figure 1.

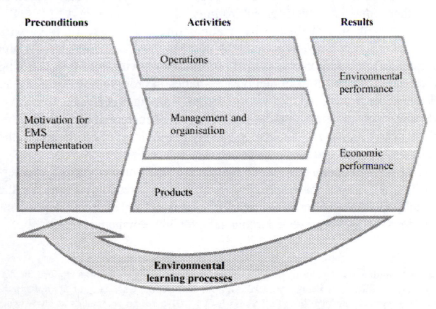

Figure 1. Structure and content of the survey

The model distinguishes between three different categories: preconditions, activities and results of EMS. With regard to preconditions, the perceptions of company environmental exposure (e.g. importance of environmental problems and stakeholders) were collected and the motivations for implementing an EMS. With regard to activities undertaken, the measures taken in three different areas were surveyed—the area of operations, management and organisation, and products. With regard to the results, the environmental and economic performance related to the EMS was asked for. Furthermore, we wanted to learn more about environmental learning processes occurring over time and resulting from the experiences drawn from using the EMS.

The questionnaire was sent to the EMS management representatives of all ISO 14001-certified companies in Switzerland as of 31 March 1999. A total of 348 certified organisations received the questionnaire; 158 questionnaires (45%) were returned. Looking at the total number of companies certified in Switzerland at the time, this figure represents 54% of all companies, as a number of big companies got more than one certificate.[1] It has to be assumed that the questionnaires returned are biased towards the environmentally more active companies, as these tend to respond more willingly to surveys such as ours. Thus, as often in cases like this, the results may be a bit too optimistic, although more pessimistic results would even strengthen our own interpretation. Apart from this non-response bias, it has to be noted that our findings reflect subjective perceptions from the viewpoint of environmental managers. Quite naturally, the findings would be different, too, if we had collected more objective evidence concerning activities taken and results from EMSs or if we had asked more people with different responsibilities inside their companies than for environmental management and EMSs. We have dealt with this challenge by triangulating our survey findings with additional information (environmental policies, environmental targets and programmes). In addition, we carried out interviews with different certifying bodies and conducted four in-depth case studies in order to develop a deeper understanding of EMS-induced environmental learning processes.

Some observations are in order concerning the structure of our sample:
- The distribution across industries closely resembles the distribution in the population of all certified organisations.
- Some 62% of companies in our sample are small or medium-sized enterprises, with fewer than 250 employees; the corresponding figure for the total population of certified organisations is 74%. Therefore, big organisations are over-represented in our sample: 38% compared with 26%.

---

[1] In the meantime the number of ISO 14001 certifications in Switzerland has topped the 800 mark. The Institute for Economy and the Environment at the University of St Gallen publishes a regularly updated list of all Swiss ISO 14001-certified companies at www.iwoe. unisg.ch/iso14001.htm.

- Some 73% of the companies in our sample had no previous experience with systematic environmental management. This finding was surprising: ISO 14001 obviously contributes significantly to the diffusion of environmental management in Swiss companies, who otherwise would not introduce systematic environmental activities. In other words: EMSs are not primarily a tool for green companies and environmental pioneers. On the contrary, close to three-quarters of the certified companies entered new territory with the decision to implement an EMS.
- A total of 50.3% of the companies in our sample were certified in 1996 or 1997 ('old' EMSs); 49.7% were certified in 1998 or 1999 ('new' EMSs). The distribution of previous experience with systematic environmental management across old and new EMSs is almost exactly the same. This means that it has not been the case in Switzerland that environmentally progressive companies were the first to be attracted to EMS certification. The mix of three-quarter inexperienced and one-quarter experienced companies remained very stable instead over the years 1996– 99.

2. RESULTS

2.1 Expectations from Implementing Environmental Management Systems

Why did the companies surveyed implement an EMS? What were their expectations? Figure 2 shows the results. At the top of the list of expectations is the improvement of public image and achievement of ISO 14001 certification. This means companies primarily expect external recognition for their EMS activities. Internal aspects such as the systemisation of existing environmental activities and risk minimisation follow in positions 3 and 4. In contrast, identification of cost reduction potential is only at position 6. The large number of very different but highly valued reasons for EMS implementation suggests that EMSs are not perceived as instruments serving only a very specific, narrowly defined purpose, but much rather as broad, general instruments serving a wide array of purposes. In addition, economic purposes dominate over environmental purposes, and external demands are clearly considered to be more important reasons for EMS implementation than are internal goals.

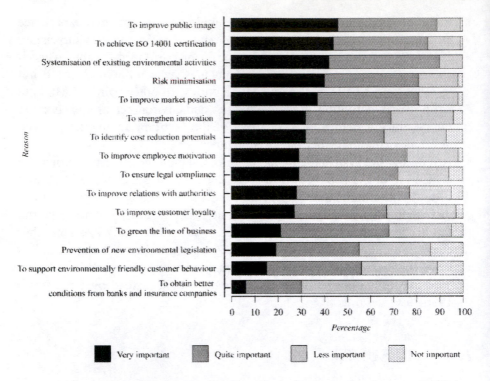

Figure 2. Expectations from implementing an environmental management system (EMS) in the surveyed Swiss companies (*n* = 158)

2.2   Environmental Management System Activities

Very different expectations for implementing EMSs such as improving public image, efficiency improvements, risk minimisation and market-oriented positioning strategies make it probable that EMS-induced activities are also as manifold. We therefore asked for information on the resources spent on the three areas of operations, management and organisation, and products. The results show that by far the most resources are spent on operations (e.g. on technical optimisation of production and operating processes). Significantly fewer resources go into the areas of management and organisation and products. However, when asked for their future plans, a compensatory effect appears from the answers given. They plan not only to increase the level of total spending but also to invest a significantly higher proportion of their resources into the areas of management and organisation as well as products. This leads us to hypothesise that there will be a shift in focus with regard to resource deployment towards products as well as towards management and organisation as the companies have taken care of the main problems in their operations and as EMS-related learning effects begin to show.

2.2.1 Operations

Environmental activities related to operations focus on the company's processes. In the field of operations the introduction of systematic waste management (implemented 'to a large extent' by 55% of the companies surveyed) and the systematic measuring of material and energy flows (43%) are at the top of the activities that have been undertaken so far. Concerning the use of environmental protection technologies, end-of-pipe measures (39%) are still more common than the application of integrated technologies (35%). Further measures such as optimisation of logistics, supplier ratings or office and building ecology were implemented by less than 20% of the enterprises. As a rule it can be perceived that the activities are performed to a higher degree where economic benefits and environmental improvements run parallel. Measures that do not suggest direct economic benefits are less frequently taken. For the future, a much higher level of activities in general is expected by the companies. Major increases are planned to occur in the area of integrated environmental protection technologies and in the areas of logistics and of supplier relations. From this, a trend towards a greening of the supply chain can be derived.

2.2.2 Management and Organisation

In the area of management and organisation, making environmental protection a line responsibility is the measure taken by most companies (38% say they have done this 'to a large extent'), followed by training of employees (32%). Less than a third of the companies integrate environmental targets into their business planning (29%) or use systematically environmental performance indicators (25%). Additional activities, such as systematic use of suggestion schemes (19%), benchmarking with other enterprises (4%) or the evaluation of employees based on ecological criteria (3%), are rarely used. Altogether, the level of activity is substantially lower than in the area of operations. It is worth mentioning that almost a third of the companies surveyed (32%) indicated that they are engaged in external environmental reporting, and a further 25% plan to do so, although this is not formally required by ISO 14001.

2.2.3 Products

Activities in the area of product ecology are focused on environmental improvements with regard to products and services throughout their total life-cycle. The level of activity in this area is considerably lower than in the area of operations but is also slightly lower than in the area of management and organisation. Some 35% of the companies surveyed undertook measures 'to a large extent' concerning the elimination of environmentally hazardous products or particular elements thereof. In a distant second are improvements in packaging (23%). Additional measures, such as the inclusion of environmental arguments into commercial advertisements (19%), systematic specifications as part of product development (19%), customer information (18%) or the application of life-cycle assessments (5%), are used by only a small number of companies. These low numbers show that product-related activities are considered by only a small minority of certified companies. Obviously, they are not considered as being strategically relevant. However, and again, product-related activities are planned to be increased considerably in the future. Even though it is difficult to judge how realistic these plans are, they demonstrate clearly a strong feeling of deficiency in this area on the part of the companies surveyed.

2.2.4 Evaluation

Altogether, our findings show that EMSs are strongly focused on processes and structures inside the companies surveyed. Environmental measures in the area of operations dominate clearly relative to measures in the areas of management and organisation or products. This result is surprising and is inconsistent, because the dominant objective associated with EMS implementation is to improve the company's public image. How is this objective to be reached if the measures taken are focused on internal processes? The figures are precariously low concerning the areas of training (only 32% have taken measures 'to a large extent') and inclusion of systematic environmental specifications in product development (19%). In these areas, ISO 14001 contains clear specifications for companies that should be realised before they get certification. Deficiencies in certification practices become clear, even though the companies give high ratings in general to their certification organisations. Further results of the survey show that companies indicate a higher level of activity:
- When they had had experience with systematic environmental management before certification
- When they obtained ISO 14001 certification earlier than did others (1998 or before; having 'old EMSs')

- When they are members of ÖBU (Schweizerische Vereinigung für Ökologisch bewußte Unternehmungsführung), the Swiss association for environmentally responsible management

3. ENVIRONMENTAL PERFORMANCE OF ENVIRONMENTAL MANAGEMENT SYSTEMS

3.1 Focusing Attention on Environmental Issues

A general effect of EMS implementation is a clear strengthening of the idea of environmental management and its economic potential as a business topic in Swiss companies. No less than 92% of the surveyed environmental managers acknowledged that EMS introduction led to an increase in importance of environmental topics in their companies (46% agree; 46% strongly agree). EMSs not only focus attention on environmental issues but also strengthen the sense of obligation in management. This reinforces the position of environmental managers in the company. Furthermore, EMSs focus attention on the economic potential of environmental management and supply the systems and procedures to exploit that potential. Beyond these general observations, however, what does the more specific environmental performance of EMSs look like?

3.2 Modest Eco-efficiency Improvements

Some 60% of the companies experienced at least 'some decrease' in their material and energy flows in relation to turnover (concerning use of materials, use of energy, waste production and use of hazardous materials). Only 10%, however, reported a 'strong decrease', and 30% either did not measure the changes or even experienced a worsening in situation. These results have to be evaluated as rather modest improvements in eco-efficiency, since the areas covered typically represent easy win–win situations, where economic advantages run in parallel with ecological improvements.

The results are even more modest when we look at absolute decreases in material and energy flows. Some 50% of the companies experienced at least 'some decrease', but only 10% reported a 'strong decrease'; 40% did not know or even experienced an increase. From this, it becomes clear that relative improvements in eco-efficiency are often offset by expansions in production. In addition, a clear majority of companies (about 60%) assign to EMSs only a supportive influence with regard to the effects on environmental performance. Only some 15% of the companies perceive a decisive influence for EMSs. A further 15% of the companies did not perceive any influence regarding EMSs. How can these results be interpreted? For a large majority of the companies EMSs obviously are not integrated into regular planning and controlling activities. Such systems take on more of an instrumental character for implementing independently developed environmental objectives and targets.

Looking at products, the companies reported that only small decreases with regard to environmental impacts had occurred since EMS implementation. A total of 48% of the companies surveyed reported 'some decreases', but only 6% reported 'strong decreases'; 35% were unable to report any EMS-induced changes. Fully 17% did not know. Not knowing at all has to be considered as being the poorest answer of all, since EMSs above all should create knowledge and sensitivity, even before improvements in performance occur. It has to be concluded that EMSs play only a supporting role and lack real influence on product improvements. In view of the fact that no fewer than 32% of the same environmental managers surveyed viewed product-specific environmental impacts as important, there is a large gap between problem perception and activities undertaken.

4.   ECONOMIC PERFORMANCE OF ENVIRONMENTAL MANAGEMENT SYSTEMS

How can the costs and benefits of EMS be assessed? The implementation of an EMS is costly. But systematic environmental management explores benefits with regard to profitability and competitiveness as well. So what is the net economic effect of EMS investments?

4.1   Costs

Costs were differentiated in set-up costs (internal costs and advisory costs), certification costs and annual operating costs. The average total costs for the set-up and operation of an EMS amount to 287,000 Swiss francs (CHF287,000). There are big cost differences, however, depending on size. For small businesses (1–49 employees) the average costs are CHF93,000, for medium-sized businesses (50–249 employees) CHF154,000 and for large companies (250 or more employees) they amount to CHF535.000. Looking at relative costs, however, the total costs per employee range from CHF5,400 per full-time employee in small businesses to CHF500 per full-time employee for large companies. The average cost amounts to CHF2,000 per employee. It should be added, however, that the factual basis for these figures is very weak. Only 19% of the companies surveyed measured their internal costs, and only 11% measured their operational costs. The figures reported by the companies therefore are based on rough estimates. How good they are cannot be judged from the data collected.

4.2   Quantifiable Monetary Benefits

What are the monetary benefits of EMSs? The empirically determined mean value of the annual benefits reported is CHF167,000. Large differences exist with regard to business size: in small businesses the average benefits are CHF22,000, in medium-sized companies the average benefits are CHF110,000 and in large companies the average benefits amount to CHF343,000. This results in an average payback period of only 2.2 years. EMSs obviously represent economically very interesting investments, also when compared with other investments. These results differ, depending on size. While the payback period is 2 years and less for large and medium-sized companies, it is close to 11 years for small companies. A word of caution is in order here as well: these figures are based mostly on bold estimates. Only 6% of the companies surveyed do measure the benefits, 47% make an estimate and fully 47% do not answer the question at all, because they cannot or do not want to quantify the economic benefits of their EMS. The question remains: why are the economic benefits of EMSs—and also its costs—measured so rarely?

4.3   Non-monetary Benefits

The economic benefits of EMSs go far beyond the quantifiable economic benefits and cover very diverse aspects. In a differentiated evaluation of 11 different categories of non-monetary benefits, the most important is system-atisation of existing environmental activities. Some 76% of all companies judged this to be of 'high value' for them. In second and third place are assurance of legal compliance (59%) and risk minimisation (58%). A total of 50% of the companies (fifth place) perceived high value in the exploitation of cost reductions, and 41% saw value in employee motivation (seventh place). Compared with these internal benefits, the external benefits are esti-mated to be somewhat smaller. Some 52% of the companies assume there is a large benefit for the corporate image (fourth place) and 47% (sixth place) see high value with regard to their relationship with public authorities. Only 32% see high value in EMS-induced improvements in innovation (ninth place) and in market position (28%). These small market effects of EMSs should not come as a surprise to the observer in view of the low level of activity in the areas of product and market communications. Fewer than 20% of the enterprises use environmental arguments in their advertisements or inform the public on environmental aspects of their products and services. In addition, since only 3% of the companies do market research concerning the environmental behaviour of customers and competitors, it is not surprising that environmental marketing and differentiation strategies have not been seriously pursued so far. Still weaker are the effects regarding improved conditions from banks and insurance companies. Only 13% of the companies could see a substantial benefit in this area.

Even if the external effects of EMSs seem to be small, the overall economic satisfaction with EMSs from companies' point of view is significantly higher than expected. These findings were clearly acknowledged in four case studies (Hamschmidt 2001). It can be concluded that the process-oriented management system approach of ISO 14001 often generates unexpected operative benefits regarding organisation, communication and transparency within companies.

5.   EFFECTIVENESS OF ENVIRONMENTAL MANAGEMENT SYSTEMS: POTENTIAL FOR IMPROVEMENT

The incentive of certification ensures the set-up of the EMS and the required infrastructure. This is essential but not sufficient for effective improvements over time. If the system is to lead to continuous improvements in the EMS and environmental performance as required by ISO 14001, it needs different and stronger incentives. These can come from different sources: from the company itself, from customers, financial markets or authorities. If these incentives are missing or if they remain weak, as the empirical observations indicate, the firm's interest in EMSs may recede over time.

We observed different internal and external potential for improvements. Apart from improvements to external incentives, modifications inside the companies are needed in order to increase the ecological effectiveness of EMSs. Four areas are judged to be particularly important:
- Integration of the EMS with other management systems, particularly with the general management system
- The development of an audit culture oriented towards learning
- The strategic orientation of the EMS
- Use of the EMS as a basis for a different relationship with public authorities

5.1   Integration

A major incentive for the integration of different management systems is the elimination of multiple efforts for documentation, operation and certification of the management systems. Often, integration of management systems is restricted to areas such as quality, health and safety, and environmental management. This partial integration has to be considered a necessary but not sufficient step, however. Integration of management systems and activities must mean integration into the general management system, where business planning, control and reporting takes place. As long as environmental planning and control is separated from business planning and control, no real integration or efficiency of activities will be achieved.

5.2 Audit Culture

Audit culture is a crucial point for achieving ecological improvements. In our case studies, internal audits were indeed perceived as important drivers for the process of continual improvement. In contrast, we observed quite critical perceptions of external certification audits. Two quotes from different case studies might illustrate the point:

> I expected a more detailed examination. Instead, the auditors were fixed on procedures and documented processes. Nobody was interested in what was going on outside (Environment Manager, Landis Bau AG, Zug).

and

> We just did not accept certain auditors anymore. 'Hello, how are you'— that's not enough for our company development (CEO, Frigemo AG, Neuchâtel).

The quotes show that external compliance audits in the tradition of the 'old' ISO 9001 audit culture often lack incentives for continual improvements. Audits can be a powerful tool for achieving effective improvements. However, in practice, an over-emphasis on compliance and conformance to standard requirements often does not support the intended improvement process. In future, the function of certification audits as enablers for continual improvements should be developed.

5.3 Strategic Objectives

Normative, strategic and operational issues are given very different weights in the ISO 14001 standard. The demand for an environmental policy addresses the normative level. Most elements of the standard, however, address operational issues, whereas strategic issues are not addressed at all. For instance, nowhere in the standard can the manager find help in identifying environmental market potentials and in identifying changes in the business environment as a starting point for a reduction of environmental risks.

However, there is an abundance of detailed specifications that concern the operational level. As a consequence, the companies are preoccupied with fulfilling the operational demands of the standard instead of being directed to strategically interesting perspectives. However, the development of strategies is of fundamental importance for improving the effectiveness of EMSs over time.

5.4   Relationships with Public Authorities

Apart from the company's own management, public authorities are considered to be the most important stakeholders by the companies surveyed. Their demands and expectations strongly influence the implementation and further development of EMSs. The attitude of the authorities in relation to ISO 14001 as a new instrument for the private sector is thus of high importance for the further development of EMSs. EMSs can facilitate co-operation between public agencies and enterprises. If state authorities develop an approach to EMSs that rewards high-performance EMSs, the diffusion and effectiveness of EMSs could be improved.

EMSs are flexible management systems. Beyond the 'hard' demand for adherence to legal compliance and the establishment of the formal system structures, it is the company's decision to set its own emphasis and priorities. The differences in quality between existing EMSs are large. Until now, EMSs have lacked transparency since there are no requirements for active external reporting activities. It is recommended that transparency between the certified companies be enhanced so that top environmental performers who go far beyond compliance with regulatory requirements be recognised and encouraged.[2] The ISO 14001 standard itself gives few incentives for initiating processes of fundamental change towards environmental sustainability.[3] However, it is a well-tried starting point for the development of a continual improvement philosophy and the establishment of environmentally oriented control systems. The approach can serve as a first step towards eco-effective value creation. Implementing an EMS therefore needs to be viewed as the beginning of a transition process towards corporate ecological sustainability rather than the end of the process (Dyllick and Hockerts 2002).

---

[2]   An interesting approach is that of the US Environmental Protection Agency's National Environmental Performance Track Programme (EPA 2000), which might be a blueprint for a similar European initiative.

[3]   These incentives might be provided by different existing and future management system standards that are currently being developed in different initiatives, such as the The Natural Step (Nattrass and Altomare 1999), the Sigma Project (2001) of the British Standards Institution and diverse sustainability balanced scorecard (SBSC) projects (e.g. Bieker *et al.* 2001).

6.   CONCLUSIONS

EMSs fulfil the expectations of the companies regarding the systematisation and controlling of environmental relevant processes and economic performance. The achievement of innovations and improvements in market success, however, are to be regarded as an unfulfilled challenge for EMS application. Moreover, regarding the expectations that companies have when implementing an EMS, we have to conclude that companies look for external improvements in public image, but they find internal assurance with regard to their systems and processes.

From the environmental policy perspective, EMSs seem to be useful but not sufficient for effective ecological improvements in companies. The 'eco-efficiency revolution' has not yet taken place in most companies with an EMS. Since ISO 14001 does not explicitly refer to environmental sustainability it is not surprising that the ecological results remain modest. In addition, the market signals for product-oriented environmental innovations are still too weak to drive the necessary strategic adjustments of certified enterprises towards profitable environmental innovations.

Potential for improvements could be identified in the better integration of EMSs into the core processes in companies, a more strategic application of EMSs and the introduction of further measures to create greater transparency concerning the environmental performance of EMSs. Furthermore, stronger incentives from different stakeholders, such as market participants or state authorities, are needed in order to drive companies more effectively in the direction of environmental sustainability.

REFERENCES

Bieker, T., Dyllick, T., Gminder, C.-U. and Hockerts, K. (2001) 'Towards a Sustainability Balanced Scorecard: Translating Strategies into Multi-objective Sustainability Management', *Proceedings of the 10th Business Strategy and the Environment Conference, Leeds 2001*. Shipley: ERP Environment, 22-31.

Delmas, M. (2001) 'Stakeholders and Competitive Advantage: The Case of ISO 14001', *Production and Operations Management* Vol. 10 No. 3: 343-358.

DeSimone, L. and Popoff, F. (1997) *Eco-efficiency: The Business Link to Sustainable Development*. Cambridge, MA: The MIT Press.

Dyllick, T., and J. Hamschmidt (2000) *Wirksamkeit und Leistung von Umweltmanagementsystemen*. Zurich: VDF-Verlag.

Dyllick, T. and K. Hockerts (2002) 'Beyond the Business Case for Corporate Sustainability', *Business Strategy and the Environment* Vol. 11 No. 2: 130-141.

Enroth, M., Zackrisson, M. and Widing, A. (2000) *Environmental Management Systems: Paper Tiger or Powerful Tool?* Working paper; IVF Research Publication 00828; Stockholm: Industrial Research Institute.

EPA (US Environmental Protection Agency) (2000) *National Environmental Performance Track Programme*, www.epa.gov/performancetrack.

Hamschmidt, J. (2001) *Wirksamkeit von Umweltmanagementsystemen*. Dissertation; Bamberg, Germany: Difo-Druck.

IEE–USG (Institute for Economy and the Environment, University of St Gallen) (ed.) (monthly) Swiss Companies with an ISO 14001 Certificate, monthly updated list, www. iwoe.unisg.ch.

ISO (International Organisation for Standardisation) (1996) *ISO 14001: Environmental Management Systems. Specifications with Guidance for Use*. Geneva: ISO.

Nattrass, B. and M. Altomare (1999) *The Natural Step for Business: Wealth, Ecology and the Evolutionary Corporation*. Gabriola Island: New Society Publishers.

Pearce, D. (1993) *Blueprint 3: Measuring Sustainable Development*. London: Earthscan Publications.

Prehn, M., Richter, G., Schwedt, B. and Tiebler, P. (1998) *Auswertung der Ergebnisse von Modellprojekten zur Umsetzung der EG-Umwelt-Audit-Verordnung*. Ed. Umweltbundesamt (UBA); text 20/1998; Berlin: UBA.

Sigma Project (2001) 'The Sigma Project: Sustainability in Practice', Sections 1–3, 4–6, Appendices A–F (July 2001 version), downloadable at www.projectsigma.com.

Steger, U. (2000) 'Environmental Management Systems: Empirical Evidence and Further Perspectives', *European Management Journal* Vol. 18 No. 1: 23-37.

UNI–ASU (Unternehmerinstitut–Arbeitsgemeinschaft selbständiger Unternehmer) (1997) *Öko-Audit in der mittelständischen Praxi*. Bonn: UNI–ASU.

THE PROMISES AND PITFALLS OF ISO 14001 FOR COMPETITIVENESS AND SUSTAINABILITY

A Comparison of Japan and the United States

Eric W. Welch[1], Ashish Rana[2] and Yasuhumi Mori[2]

[1] *University of Illinois at Chicago, USA;* [2] *National Institute for Environmental Studies, Japan*

Abstract: This chapter investigates the theoretical and empirical reasons why Japan leads the world in adoption of ISO 14001, while the US lags, and the comparative effect of ISO 14001 on environmental performance of adopters in both countries. Findings suggest that institutional barriers to adoption are much higher in the adversarial policy climate of the US than in the more reciprocal policy climate of Japan. Expected benefits of adoption are lower than the reported realisation, and this finding is significant for some categories such as competitive market advantage and relationships with regulators. Findings regarding the effect of ISO on environmental performance are mixed, but generally point to a relatively limited effect. We conclude that, even if ISO 14001 has a moderate effect on firm environmental action, the structural barriers in the US generally limit the viability of these types of voluntary policy.

Adoption of the international organisation for standardisation (ISO) 14001 environmental management system standard is an organisation-level decision undertaken primarily by private-sector facilities. While it is generally hoped, and often assumed, that adoption of ISO 14001 leads to improvements in both environmental management and economic competitiveness of the facility, the nature of the relationship between economic and environmental performance has been shown to be complex and variable (Wagner *et al.* 2001; Schaltegger and Synnestvedt 2002). Around the world, adoption rates differ significantly among nations with Japan as a world leader and the United States as a world laggard (Welch *et al.* 2002). And, while recent literature on voluntarism indicates that national institutional frameworks within which facilities operate create nuanced incentive structures that can favour or disfavour, accelerate or decelerate adoption by facilities (Prakash

1999; Delmas 2002; Kollman and Prakash 2002), little research has been undertaken to compare the ISO 14001 experiences of Japan and the US.

This chapter represents findings from the first survey designed to simultaneously compare ISO 14001 perspectives and resulting behaviour of US and Japanese manufacturing facilities. The primary research questions are: why are adoption rates so much higher in Japan than in the US and what are the different effects of adoption in the US and Japan? To investigate potential answers to these questions, the rest of this chapter is presented in five parts: a comparison of the status of ISO adoption in Japan and the US; a discussion of the literature on voluntarism and ISO 14001 adoption; a description of the survey design and data; the analysis; and a final conclusion section.

1.   ISO 14001 IN JAPAN AND THE UNITED STATES

ISO 14000 comprises a set of environmental management standards and guidelines for such activities as environmental performance, auditing, labelling and life-cycle assessment that was initially established in 1996 by the International Organisation for Standardisation.[1] Organisations seeking ISO 14001 certification must undertake four broad steps: define an environmental policy, develop an environmental plan, implement the plan and continually monitor the implementation process. The detail behind these broad categories is generally extensive, complex and costly for the organisation to accomplish (Zharen 1995; Cascio 1996; Delmas 2002).

Japan is by far the world leader while the US comes in sixth with comparatively low adoption rates. As of June 2002, Japan had twice as many new adoptions as the next nation, Germany, and more than four times the number of US adopters (see Fig. 1). New adoption rates over time indicate that the gap between US and Japan appears to be increasing rather than decreasing (see Fig. 2). These gaps provided the initial motivation for this study.

---

[1]   http://www.iso.ch, November 2002

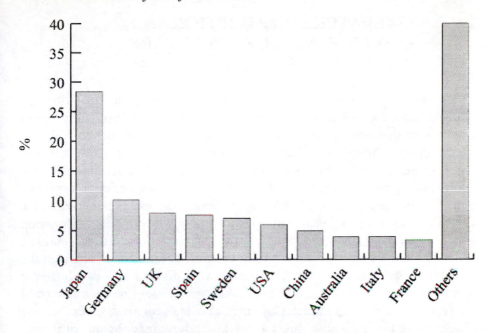

Figure 1. Top ISO adoptions by country, June 2002 (Source: ISO,
http://www.ecology.or.jp/isoworld/english/analy14.htm)

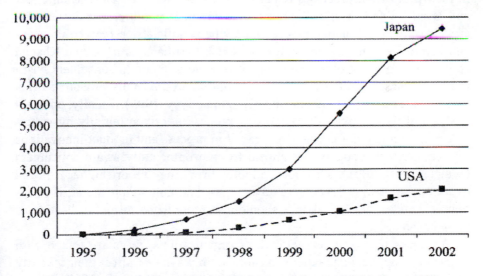

Figure 2. Comparison of new ISO 14001 adoptions in Japan and USA (Source: ISO,
http://www.iso.ch/iso/en/prods-services/otherpubs/pdf/survey11thcycle.htm)

2.   LITERATURE ON ADOPTION AND EFFECTIVENESS OF VOLUNTARY INSTRUMENTS

In general, the literature that analyses voluntary environmental activities by polluters wrestles with two questions: what drives firms to volunteer and to what extent does voluntarism result in measurable environmental and economic change (Arora and Cason 1996; Khanna and Damon 1999; Alberini and Segersen 2002; Melnyk *et al.* 2002)? To take the first question first, the certification process is time-consuming and costly to the polluting organisation. Not only are there certification and information search and costs, there is also the potential for legal challenges resulting from required information disclosures (Quazi 1999; Russo 2001; Delmas 2002). As rational entities, adopting facilities must perceive that the returns of certification outweigh the investment and risk. In general, returns can be divided into two different types: direct economic advantage and indirect advantages through improved network relations, both of which may enhance overall competitiveness.

Opportunities to realise direct economic advantages for the firm may occur as they prepare for certification; facilities may realise a variety of technological and managerial opportunities to cut material and energy waste in their production processes (Gray *et al.* 1996; Fielding 1998; Schaltegger and Burritt 2000). Moreover, firms that voluntarily address environmental aspects of their production processes may be beneficially perceived in financial markets as carrying lower levels of risk (Williams *et al.* 1993; Khanna and Damon 1999). Voluntarism may also serve as a cue to consumers wishing to purchase products and services from environmentally proactive firms (Williams *et al.* 1993; Arora and Gangopadhyay 1995). Finally, internal analysis of waste streams and decision processes, driven initially by voluntary programme requirements, may result in process and product innovations that create new products that appeal to environmentally aware consumers (Wagner *et al.* 2001). Therefore, adopter firms may report higher *a priori* expectations of direct economic advantages than non-adopters and, if adoption delivers as anticipated, they should also report *a posteriori* realisation of these advantages.

As nodes in a complex network of organisations, firms are linked with regulators, suppliers and other stakeholders in ways that affect their viability in the market (Finneman and Clarke 1996; Clarke and Roome 1999; Roome 2001). Adoption of an environmental management system such as ISO 14001 is often thought to provide advantages within these networks. For example, regulatory agencies may increasingly reward firm voluntary environmental efforts with reduced oversight, reporting requirements or less adversarial relationships (Lyon and Maxwell 2002; Alberini and Segersen

2002). Smoother interaction with regulators probably also reflects good relationships with other stakeholders such as environmental groups (Bucholz 1993; Dillon and Fischer 1992; Berry and Rondinelli 1998). Additionally, as the global environmental management system becomes increasingly diffused, certified facilities may be preferred business partners (Kollman and Prakash 2001; Delmas 2002). If such advantages help to drive adoption of ISO 14001, adopters should report higher *a priori* expectations and *a posteriori* incidences of network facilitation than non-adopters.

Despite the fact that ISO 14001 is a global standard, adoption takes place in a national institutional context. The literature indicates that expectations and realisations of the costs and benefits, as well as the effects of adoption on environmental performance, depend on the institutional setting within which facilities operate. Generally, scholars have found that business–government relations in the US are more adversarial than in Japan, where they are found to be more co-operative and mutually supportive (Okimoto 1989). Similarly, environmental policy in the US has been characterised as highly antagonistic, in which strong environmental groups demand strict, legally enforceable command-and-control regulation (Kollman and Prakash 2002). The Japanese regulatory climate, by contrast, is often perceived to be more reciprocal such that government and business share authority in both the economic and environmental domains (Samuels 1987; Welch and Hibiki 2002). With respect to environmental policy, an adversarial climate often creates a tradition of mistrust which generally leads government and environmental groups to discount a firm's voluntary action as motivationally suspect, while the firm is less likely to trust government with disclosure of environmental information that might be used against it at some future point (Kollman and Prakash 2001). Russo (2001: 27) also suggests that the adoption of ISO 14001 represents a signal to the external institutional environment; in contexts where adoption is not necessarily considered to be an important signal of commitment, there will be lower levels of adoption. While these arguments may help explain the gap between ISO 14001 adoption rates in Japan and the US, they have not been tested directly.

As noted by Kollman and Prakash (2001), the institutional perspective should also help to predict national differences in outcomes of adoption of voluntary programmes such as ISO 14001. For example, disclosure of environmental information may be lower in an adversarial than in a consensual national context. In addition, firms in a stricter command-and-control environment may have already implemented more targets and be more environmentally efficient than firms in less adversarial environments. However, in many areas, prediction of facility expectations and realisations about the benefits to voluntarism is difficult. For example, voluntarism may lead to a comparatively greater perceived improvement in relations with regulators in adversarial contexts simply because the expectations are much larger, or because there is a stronger tradition of self-regulation in a non-adversarial environment. On the other hand, volunteers in an adversarial environment may, for historical reasons, severely discount their ability to bridge this gap.

3.   DATA AND DESCRIPTIVE STATISTICS

This chapter utilises cross-national survey data of private-sector ISO 14001 adopters and non-adopters that were collected simultaneously in Japan and the United States between March and May 2001. Samples in both countries were taken from two primary populations of facilities: ISO adopters and non-adopters. For the Japan survey, each of the two primary strata were subdivided into four industry substrata (electronics, electrical power, electric machinery and chemical manufacturing), while the US sample was further divided into nine different industry substrata (electronic equipment, electric power, industrial and commercial machinery, chemicals and allied products, rubber and plastics, primary metal industries, fabricated metal products, paper and allied products, transportation equipment). The US sample contained more industries because too few facilities had adopted ISO 14001 in any four industry classifications (by two-digit SIC code).

In the US case, a random sample of 726 ISO adopters was combined with a random sample of 1,675 US facilities. The survey was administered according to a modified Dillman method (2000). Of the 698 valid ISO adopter and 1,489 non-adopter surveys sent out, we received 143 (20.5%) and 97 (6.5%) usable responses, respectively. The total response rate for the survey was 11.0%. This low response rate creates potential for bias; however, it is not an unusual rate for environmental surveys of private-sector firms (Melnyk *et al.* 2002). Our analysis indicates that, in general, responses by industry and by size do not differ significantly from proportions in the random sample. Nevertheless, generalisation from the US portion of this study to US facility environmental behaviour more broadly is problematic and should be done with care.

The Japanese survey was administered at approximately the same time using the same survey design. A total of 3,227 facilities were randomly selected. Of 1,515 ISO adopters and 1,712 non-adopters surveyed, facilities provided 1,237 (82%) and 481 (28%) usable responses, respectively. This translates into an overall response rate of 56%. Table 1 provides descriptive statistics for the survey. Employees, capital and operating budget are all measured as categorised ranges where a lower categorical value represents a lower range of actual values. (For example, number of employees is measured on the following scale: 1 < 50 employees, 50 ≤ 2 < 300, 300 ≤ 3 < 1,000, 1,000 ≤ 4 < 5,000, 5,000 ≤ 5.) Revenues are reported as percentages.

Table 1. Descriptive statistics of ISO and non-ISO adopters in the US and Japan

	ISO-certified		Non-certified	
	Japan	**US**	**Japan**	**US**
Employees	2.78 (0.82)	2.87 (0.96)	2.17 (0.93)	1.60 (0.94)
Capital	1.85 (0.35)	3.62 (0.64)	1.90 (0.31)	2.28 (1.15)
Operating budget	1.54 (0.50)	3.98 (1.23)	1.71 (0.45)	3.07 (1.35)
Revenue from Japan sales	81.20 (34.39)	4.94 (10.29)	91.52 (17.55)	0.97 (2.52)
Revenue from US sales	7.69 (13.46)	81.81 (19.63)	2.86 (7.43)	95.01 (10.01)
Revenue from European sales	5.67 (10.04)	11.07 (14.02)	2.31 (6.86)	3.33 (8.06)
Proportion local voluntary agreement	0.48	0.37	0.24	0.18
Proportion environmental division	0.93	0.75	0.54	0.27
Proportion environmental manager	0.96	0.87	0.63	0.36
Manager involved in top meetings	5.66 (2.07)	5.07 (1.77)	5.13 (2.42)	5.19 (1.71)
Environment FTEs	5.36 (8.59)	3.71 (11.00)	2.32 (4.96)	3.23 (13.43)
Sub-sample size	1237	143	398*	75*

* Facilities certified in other EMSs were removed from the sample.

Comparison of the size of firms in the two samples shows that US adopter firms have larger capital and operating budgets and more employees than their Japanese counterparts, while US non-adopters have fewer employees but larger budgets. Within Japan, ISO facilities have more employees but smaller capital and operating budgets than non-ISO facilities. Within the US, ISO firms are much larger on all three counts. The proportion of facilities having an environmental division or an environmental manager in Japan is higher than in the US (adopter and non-adopter alike), and Japanese adopters report the highest average number of full-time environmental employees.

Nearly 50% of the Japanese and less than 40% of US ISO adopters reported having entered into a voluntary environmental agreement with a local government agency. Non-adopters in both nations report much lower levels of such agreements. Finally, Japanese and US adopters are more involved in international trade than non-adopters. In sum, ISO adopters in both countries are generally larger, more involved in trade and have more substantial environmental management structures than non-adopters.

4.   ANALYSIS

This section is divided into three parts, each of which compares adopters and non-adopters in the US and Japan from different perspectives. The first section compares US and Japanese expectations of the benefits of certification with their realisation of those expectations. The second section examines the effect of ISO 14001 adoption on environmental and economic values of the facility. The final section analyses the effect of adoption in both countries on environmental practices of facilities.

4.1   Expectations versus Realisations

ISO 14001 adopters were first asked about the extent to which they believed that certification would benefit them along multiple dimensions (listed in Tables 2 and 3). Each was then asked to indicate the extent to which their expectations were realised along the same dimensions. Expectation was measured from low (1) to high (7) and realisation from none (1) to full (7).

Table 2. Expectation of ISO 14001 benefits

	Japan		US	
	Recently certified	**Early certified**	**Recently certified**	**Early certified**
Market advantage from green consumers	4.41 (1.67)	4.55 (1.69)	4.46 (2.08)	4.50 (1.81)
Ability to attract high-quality employees	3.62 (1.58)	3.42 (1.52)	2.77 (1.61)	3.12 (1.72)
Government reimbursement of certification costs	1.95 (1.55)	1.69 (1.82)	1.31 (1.01)	1.29 (0.73)
Competitive advantage in production	4.87 (1.41)	4.96 (1.45)	3.96 (1.82)	4.55 (1.67)
Better relations with regulators	4.09	4.17	4.54	4.89

	Japan		US	
	Recently certified	**Early certified**	**Recently certified**	**Early certified**
	(1.69)	(1.79)	(1.88)	(1.57)
Reduced regulatory requirements	n.a.	n.a.	2.50 (1.82)	2.58 (1.11)
Reduced pressure from external groups	2.79 (1.58)	2.65 (1.61)	2.73 (1.80)	2.93 (1.71)
Economic advantage with ISO suppliers	4.15 (1.82)	4.00 (1.77)	3.38 (2.02)	3.75 (1.86)
Tax relief from government	2.63 (1.67)	2.59 (1.60)	1.58 (1.27)	1.28 (0.62)
Sub-sample size	319	915	26	94

n.a. = not applicable

Table 3. Realisation of expected ISO 14001 benefits

	Japan		US	
	Recently certified	**Early certified**	**Recently certified**	**Early certified**
Market advantage from green consumers	3.73 (1.44)	3.99 (1.48)	2.84 (2.30)	3.54 (2.08)
Ability to attract high-quality employees	3.31 (1.36)	3.37 (1.41)	1.92 (1.53)	3.21 (1.96)
Government reimbursement of certification costs	1.94 (1.41)	1.63 (1.27)	1.36 (1.32)	2.05 (2.18)
Competitive advantage in production	4.24 (1.30)	4.55 (1.42)	3.24 (1.98)	4.26 (1.92)
Better relations with regulators	3.40 (1.64)	3.72 (1.73)	3.12 (1.92)	4.41 (1.89)
Reduced regulatory requirements	n.a.	n.a.	1.80 (1.58)	2.46 (2.06)
Reduced pressure from external groups	2.89 (1.44)	3.00 (1.55)	2.20 (1.83)	3.20 (2.08)
Economic advantage with ISO suppliers	3.62 (1.56)	3.68 (1.61)	2.04 (1.57)	3.22 (2.09)
Tax relief from government	2.09 (1.33)	1.99 (1.38)	1.40 (1.32)	2.01 (2.12)

n.a. = not applicable

Results shown in Table 2 indicate that facilities held comparatively higher expectations in four areas: market advantage from green consumers, competitive advantage in production, better relations with regulators, and economic advantage from ISO suppliers. Firms had relatively moderate expectations of attracting higher-quality employees and reducing pressure from external groups. It is interesting to observe that they had low expectations of tax relief from government, reimbursement of certification costs by government and reduced regulatory requirements, even though they had expected to improve relations with regulators. This may indicate that firms were relatively realistic in formulating their expectations. Note that because this was an *ex post* survey, some of the responses to these questions may be biased due to hindsight and other factors.

Two other observations can be made from Table 2. First, in the Japanese case, recently certified firms scored higher than early adopters across five of the eight dimensions. This trend is reversed for the US sample: seven of the nine dimensions had lower scores for recent adopters than for early adopters. Hence, recent adopters may be more optimistic than early adopters in Japan, while recent adopters are more pessimistic than early adopters in the US. Second, in all but two cases—reduced pressure for external groups and better relations with regulators—overall expectations are higher for Japanese than for the US firms. These findings may indicate limited support for institutional theory: firms in less adversarial environments may be generally more responsive to co-operative policy regimes and, because relations between government and business are already strong in less adversarial countries, expectations for improvements in ties with regulators are lower than for firms in more adversarial environments.

The results in Table 3 indicate that there may be some time delay in the realisation of expected benefits from ISO adoption: in general, early adopters perceive higher levels of realisation than recent adopters. This observation is in keeping with findings from other research (Bansal 2002). Comparing Tables 2 and 3, facilities report that their expectations have not been realised. There are a few exceptions to this. One is the perceived realisation of reduced pressure from external groups by both groups of Japanese facilities and by early adopters in the US. Second, low expectations of government reimbursement of certification costs have generally been realised by all four groups of facilities.

To further analyse this data, differences in ratings for realisations and expectations were computed for each category (Japan/US–recent/early adopters). Early adopters are defined as those facilities that adopted ISO 14001 before December 1999. When the realisation rating matches the expectation rating, a difference score of zero is recorded. If the realisation score is higher (lower) than the expectation score, the result is a positive (negative) difference. The magnitude of difference indicates how well the realisation fulfils the expectation. Figure 3 shows the analysis of difference in realisations over expectations for each of the eight dimensions. In these charts, the rating differences were plotted on the x-axis and the proportion of firms on the y-axis. Thus, each point on the chart represents the proportion of firms having a particular ratings difference. The graphs show that in all categories a majority of facilities report no difference between realisation and expectation scores. Another interesting observation is that large differences, whether positive or negative, are observed only for a small proportion of firms. This implies that most facilities felt either only marginally better off or marginally worse off with respect to their expectations about the benefits from adopting the ISO system. When we compare the proportion of facilities on the positive difference side with the proportion on the negative difference side, we notice that, except for Japanese firm and US early adopters' responses to 'reduced pressure from external groups' and US firm responses to 'government reimbursement of certification cost', the balance tilts towards the negative side for all the counts. This contrast is sharp for 'market advantage from green consumers', 'ability to attract high-quality employees', 'improved relations with regulators' and 'advantage from ISO-certified suppliers'. It appears that expectations of the two commonly touted indirect benefits of ISO adoption, improved regulator relationships and supply chain effects, are unrealistically high and not easily fulfilled. In addition, expectations of direct competitive and market advantages are unrealistically high.

To determine statistically whether adopting ISO fulfilled expectations, a nonparametric equivalent of the t-test—the Wilcoxon Signed-Rank test—was performed on the pairs of expectation and realisation responses. The null hypothesis is that differences between ratings of realisations and expectations are centred on 0 and the alternative hypothesis is that ratings are different (accept null at $p > 0.05$). The z and p statistics are given in Figure 3.

Except in a few cases, the test is significant at the 5% significant level. Exceptions where there is no statistical difference between realisations and expectations are: 'market advantage from green consumers' and 'tax relief from the government' in the case of late adopters in Japan; 'advantage from ISO-certified suppliers' and 'tax relief from government' in the case of late adopters in the US; and 'advantage from green consumers' and 'better relations with regulators' in the case of early adopters in the US. In all other cases the ratings are statistically different, hence we can be confident about the basic conclusions drawn in the analysis of Tables 2 and 3, and in Figure 3. Direct consumer benefits and indirect supplier and regulatory benefits are

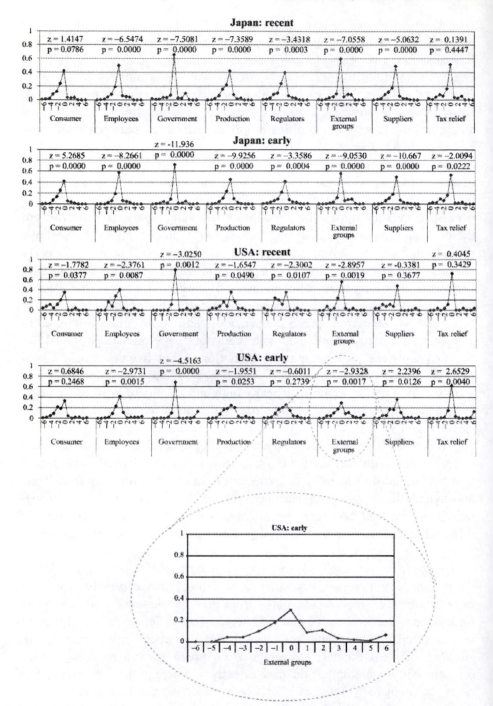

Figure 3. Proportion of respondents by magnitude of difference in realisations of expected
benefits over expectations (see text for explanation)

Notes for Figure 3:
1. z and p values refer to the Wilcoxon Signed-Rank statistic and associated probability, respectively.
2. Please refer to Tables 2 and 3 for description of categories (e.g. 'Consumer' means 'market advantage from green consumers')
3. 'Reduced regulatory requirement' was dropped from this analysis since no data for Japan exists.

poorly perceived by firms; two of those, consumer advantages in Japan and the US and regulatory advantages in the US, have relatively high expected benefits, but low realisation.

4.2   Environmental Values

To explore differences in values between ISO and non-ISO firms, respondents were asked to indicate the extent to which their efforts on each of the eight actions listed in Table 4 were driven primarily by a concern for environmental quality or by a concern for economic competitiveness. They were to rate each of the factors on a response scale of primarily environmental quality (1) to primarily economic competitiveness (7). Table 4 presents the averages of responses for each category of firms for Japan and the US.

Table 4. Effect of ISO 14001 on firm values (environment versus competitiveness)

	Japan		US	
	ISO-certified	Non-certified	ISO-certified	Non-certified
Reducing raw materials	4.44 (1.45)	4.43 (1.46)	4.94 (1.43)	5.20 (1.55)
Increasing recycled inputs	3.33 (1.53)	3.66 (1.55)	3.81 (1.66)	4.25 (1.72)
Energy efficiency	3.62 (1.60)	4.12 (1.51)	4.88 (1.54)	5.27 (1.65)
Reducing water use	3.39 (1.55)	3.89 (1.50)	3.81 (1.52)	3.97 (1.91)
Reducing CO_2	2.82 (1.43)	3.24 (1.51)	2.91 (1.48)	3.35 (1.78)
Reducing waste	2.55 (1.44)	3.08 (1.55)	4.26 (1.60)	4.20 (1.94)
Increasing product life	4.05 (1.48)	4.38 (1.48)	4.92 (1.64)	5.06 (1.73)
Developing environmentally benign products	3.15 (1.57)	3.45 (1.56)	3.84 (1.55)	3.74 (1.70)

On the whole, Japanese facilities score higher environmentally than US firms. This is true even when non-certified Japanese firms are compared with certified US firms. Moreover, ISO-certified firms in both nations perceive themselves to be, almost across the board, more environmentalist than non-certified firms. Researchers have surmised that ISO 14001 does not 'convert' firms towards greater environmentalism, rather that more environmental firms are more likely to adopt voluntary programmes in the first place. To test this, we compared responses of early and late adopters, expecting that if some kind of conversion process takes place, early adopters would score lower on the scale. Results showed no significant differences between the two groups in either country. Therefore, it appears that a self-selection bias does dominate with respect to values.

Detailed analysis of Table 4 shows that Japanese firms believe waste and CO_2 reduction to be primarily matters of environmental quality, while reducing raw materials and increasing product lifetime are driven more by economic competitiveness concerns. Other actions fall somewhere in between the two cases. CO_2 reduction by US firms is associated primarily with environmental values, while economic considerations drive efforts to reduce raw material use and increase product lifetime in both countries. In addition, US firms consider energy efficiency improvement to be primarily economically driven. Interestingly, reducing waste also appears to be more strongly influenced by economic considerations in the US than in Japan. This may reflect higher ultimate costs of waste management in the US (Aoki and Cioffi 1999).

4.3   Environmental Practices

This section examines five categories of environmental practices—general environmental action, disclosure, targets, supplier action and policy change—to determine the effect of ISO 14001 adoption on the environmental practices of firms. Borrowing from a similar question used by Ramus and Steger (2000), firms were asked to indicate, yes or no, whether they engaged in 11 different environmental activities including: publish an environmental policy, publish an annual environmental report, use eco-labelling, apply environmental considerations to purchasing decisions, use life-cycle analysis, systematically reduce fossil fuel use, systematically reduce toxic chemical use, undergo environmental audit using a third-party organisation, use eco-efficiency principles, publicly report toxic chemical use and keep track of environmental expenses. The first row in Table 5 shows the average number of these practices reported. ISO-certified firms in Japan and the US have higher average scores than non-certified firms in their respective countries. Moreover, Japanese certified firms report higher scores than US-certified firms, while the Japanese non-certified firms indicate lower scores than US non-certified firms.

Table 5. Changes in firm environmental practice

	Japan				US			
	ISO-certi-fied	Non-certi-fied	Re-cently certi-fied	Early certi-fied	ISO-certi-fied	Non-certi-fied	Re-cently certifi-ed	Early certi-fied
Environ-mental action	7.46 (1.74)	4.56* (2.17)	6.71 (1.80)	7.98* (1.65)	7.33 (1.50)	4.80* (2.07)	7.40 (1.62)	7.20 (1.28)
Disclosure	2.76 (1.16)	1.47* (1.56)	2.44 (1.16)	2.96* (1.17)	2.32 (1.09)	0.87* (1.07)	2.27 (1.20)	2.54 (0.93)
Supplier action	2.80 (0.98)	1.85* (0.87)	2.51 (0.93)	3.04* (0.99)	2.44 (0.99)	1.68* (0.81)	2.17 (0.96)	2.64* (1.07)
Targets	4.36 (1.79)	2.07* (2.11)	3.79 (1.73)	4.77* (1.82)	4.57 (1.61)	3.24* (1.64)	4.18 (1.57)	4.98* (1.60)

* Significant difference of means ($p < 0.05$)

Regarding disclosure practices, firms were asked to indicate whether they make available each of ten different types of environmental information (energy use, raw material use, water use, CO_2 production, air pollution, waste, recycling, environmental expenses, objectives and audit results) to different levels of internal stakeholders (top decision-makers, general management, all employees) and external stakeholders (publicly on request or all public and stakeholders). Firm disclosure was scaled from 1, for disclosure to top managers only, to 5, for full disclosure to the public. Thus an average of scores represents the degree of disclosure openness of the firm. Row two in Table 5 shows that certified firms in both countries have more open disclosure policies than the non-certified firms in their respective countries. In addition, although overall disclosure levels are low, those in Japan are higher than in the US. This is in keeping with expectations attributed to institutional theory in which polluters in more adversarial policy contexts are less likely to divulge information that could be used against them at some future point in time.

Another important aspect of private-sector environmental practice concerns how firms influence the environmental behaviour of their suppliers. Respondents were asked how often (1 = never; 5 = always) they carried out each of four types of actions: review supplier's past environmental records, confirm supplier ISO certification, review evidence showing supplier's environmental commitments, and review supplier's environmental audit. Resulting average scores, provided in row 3 of Table 5, show that ISO-certified firms tend to take these actions more often than non-certified ones. Findings also show that on average certified and non-certified US firms do less to evaluate the environmental practices of suppliers than their Japanese counterparts.

These trends are partially reflected in the numbers of targets that firms set for their environmental performance. Firms were asked whether they had established specific environmental targets in eight areas: reduction of raw material use, increased use of recycled inputs, energy efficiency, reduction of water use, reduction of CO_2, reduction of waste production, increased product lifetime and developing more environmentally benign products. The last row of Table 5 shows that on average ISO-certified firms have established a higher number of targets than non-certified firms. However, as might be expected from institutional theory, basic target levels are higher in the adversarial policy environments.

In general, it appears that Japanese adopter firms are somewhat more environmental than US adopter firms. In addition, difference-of-means tests indicate that ISO adopters score significantly higher than non-adopters in all cases for both countries. To test whether self-selection applies here, we again separated ISO adopters into two categories: early and recent adopters. Findings showed that early adopters in Japan reported significantly higher average levels of all four types of environmental action, while the same was true for supplier action and target development in the US. At face value, this finding seems to run counter to predictions, indicating some real effects of adoption over time. However, it is also possible to interpret this finding to mean that the most environmentalist facilities adopted ISO first and the more recent, second wave, simply runs fewer programmes, discloses less, has a smaller number of targets and checks suppliers less frequently.

5.   DISCUSSION

This chapter had two objectives: to explore the reasons for the difference in adoption rates of ISO 14001 between US and Japan, and to analyse the extent to which ISO 14001 makes a difference in environmental outcomes. Institutional theory and findings from other literature were used to guide the analysis. We utilised data from a cross-national survey of ISO adopters and non-adopters.

Findings generally support expectations of institutional theory that voluntary policies are better suited for non-adversarial contexts, such as Japan, than for adversarial contexts, such as the US. Expectations were generally higher in Japan than in the US, and, while recent US adopters are generally more pessimistic than early adopters, the opposite is true in Japan. Clearly, Japanese firms tend to believe that adoption will result in a broader scope of benefits, direct and indirect, than do US firms. The primary exception concerned US adopters' expectations that regulatory relationships would improve. This finding can be explained as a manifestation of the adversarial climate of the US (Kollman and Prakash 2001). It can also be interpreted as evidence that voluntarism is used consciously and proactively by US firms to influence future regulation (Lyon and Maxwell 2002).

Nevertheless, on average, expectations were not realised. Respondents do not perceive that the expected benefits of certification were fulfilled. This finding was especially sharp (significant) with respect to expectations about green purchasing for recent adopters in the US and Japan, and for expectations about improved relationships with regulators for early adopters in the US. It appears either that the highly publicised benefits of adoption are not being fulfilled, or that firms are being unrealistic in their *a priori* assessments of the benefits. Regardless, this finding may have particularly important implications for the future diffusion of ISO 14001. For example, broader understanding of the perceived gap between expectation and realisation of improved relationships with regulators may actually raise a barrier to adoption in the US. This finding also shows the inherent structural barriers to voluntary policies in adversarial policy environments more generally.

Analysis of the comparative effect of ISO adoption on environmental values is at once suggestive and inconclusive. Compared with non-adopters, ISO adopters in both countries reported environmental considerations to weigh more heavily as determinants of facility actions. However, follow-up analysis found no evidence indicating that early adopters were more environmentalist than recent adopters. These findings support the idea that more environmentalist firms are more likely to adopt, and that adoption has little effect on their outlook. Hence, based on this analysis, ISO does not appear to affect the fundamental balance of values of the firm.

Other analysis showed that ISO adopters in Japan and the US significantly outperformed non-adopters in all four areas. Japanese ISO firms also reported slightly more environmental activity in three areas—breadth of activities, disclosure and evaluation of suppliers—than US firms. Areas predicted by institutional theory to favour US non-certified firms—targets and breadth of action—were indeed found to have higher reported values than those of Japanese non-adopters. We tested whether self-selection was at work here, and found that early Japanese adopters reported significantly higher averages for all four categories than did non-adopters, and US early adopters reported significantly higher averages for two of the four categories. On the one hand, this indicates that ISO may be associated with some enhancement of environmental action over time. On the other, early and late adopters may simply represent two categories of firms: very environmentalist and moderately environmentalist.

The seemingly contradictory findings, that adoption leads to no change in environmental values, but may lead to change in environmental action, could point to the flexibility and longer-term effects of the standard. Once adopted, the continuous evaluation and improvement elements of the standard may rationalise a continuous improvement cycle, something that proponents often hope occurs. This hypothesis is developed by Dixit and Olson (2000). However, firms are able to make these improvements in ways that do not betray their fundamental values. Ultimately, these findings may indicate that ISO 14001 is living up to its label as a 'flexible standard' and, as others note, allows some firms the ability to 'catch up' to environmental best practices of their respective industries (Russo 2001: 26; Russo and Corbett 2001: 27).

While this conclusion may be optimistic, it is important to return to the first observation of this chapter, that diffusion rates of ISO 14001 in the US are far below those of Japan. The US, as the world's largest economy and, in many cases, largest polluter, appears to have an institutional context that inhibits its ability to diffuse voluntary programmes and policies. Adoption of a voluntary instrument appears to have a higher threshold for viability in adversarial policy environments such as the US. If so, then the speed of diffusion in adversarial nations will depend on either the market or regulatory benefits of adoption. Firms in adversarial environments may need a stronger push or pull to adopt, but once adoption takes place the standard may work as designed, encouraging continuous improvement of environmental performance. To further the chances of success in the US (and other adversarial nations), regulators and other stakeholders will need to develop stronger incentives or disincentives for adoption (as did Germany in the case of EMAS; Kollman and Prakash 2001). Unfortunately for the US, the fractured nature of the political system makes a co-ordinated effort on this front all the more difficult.

BIBLIOGRAPHY

Alberini, A. and Segersen, K. (2002) 'Assessing Voluntary Programs to Improve Environmental Quality', *Environmental and Resource Economics* No. 22: 157-184.

Aoki, K. and Cioffi, J.W. (1999) 'Poles Apart: Industrial Waste Management Regulation and Enforcement in the United States and Japan', *Law and Policy* Vol. 21 No. 3: 213-245.

Arora, S. and Cason, T. (1996) 'Why Do Firms Volunteer to Exceed Environmental Regulations? Understanding Participation in the EPA's 33/50 Program', *Land Economics* No. 72: 413-432.

Arora, S. and Gangopadhyay, S. (1995) 'Toward a Theoretical Model of Emissions Control', *Journal of Economic Behavior and Organization* No. 28: 289-309.

Bansal, P. (2002) 'The Corporate Challenges of Sustainable Development', *Academy of Management Executive* Vol. 16 No. 2: 122-131.

Berry, M.A. and Rondinelli, D.A. (1998) 'Proactive Corporate Environmental Management: A New Industrial Revolution', *Academy of Management Executive* Vol. 12 No. 2: 1-13.

Bucholz, R.A. (1993) 'Corporate Responsibility and the Good Society: From Economics to Ecology: Factors which Influence Corporate Policy Decisions', *Business Horizons* Vol. 34 No. 4: 1-19.

Cascio, J. (1996) *The ISO 14000 Handbook*. Milwaukee: ASQ Quality Press.

Clarke, S. and Roome, N. (1999) 'Sustainable Business: Learning-Action Networks as Organizational Assets', *Business Strategy and the Environment* Vol. 8 No. 5: 296-310.

Delmas, M. (2002) 'The Diffusion of Environmental Management Standards in Europe and in the United States: An Institutional Perspective', *Policy Sciences* No. 35: 91-119.

Dillman, D.A. (2000) *Mail and Internet Surveys: The Tailored Design Method*. New York: John Wiley, 2nd edn.

Dillon, P.W. and Fischer, K. (1992) *Environmental Management in Corporations*. Medford, MA: Tufts University Center for Environmental Management.

Dixit, A. and Olson, M. (2000) 'Does Voluntary Participation Undermine the Coase Theorem?', *Journal of Public Economics* No. 76: 309-335.

Fielding, S. (1998) 'ISO 14001 Delivers Effective Environmental Management and Profits', *Professional Safety* Vol. 43 No. 7: 27.

Finneman, S. and Clarke, K. (1996) *Strategic Management: A Stakeholder Approach*. Boston: Pitman.

Gray, R., Owen, D. and Adams, C. (1996) *Accounting and Accountability*. London: Prentice Hall.

Khanna, M. and Damon, L.A. (1999) 'EPA's Voluntary 33/50 Program: Impact on Toxic Releases and Economic Performance of Firms', *Journal of Environmental Economics and Management* No. 37: 1-25.

Kollman, K. and Prakash, A. (2001) 'Green by Choice? Cross National Variations in Firms' Responses to EMS-based Environmental Regimes', *World Politics* Vol. 53 No. 3: 399-430.

Kollman, K. and Prakash, A. (2002) 'EMS-based Environmental Regimes as Club Goods: Examining Variations in Firm-level Adoption of ISO 14001 and EMAS in UK, US and Germany', *Policy Sciences* No. 35: 43-67.

Lyon, T. and Maxwell, J. (2002) 'Voluntary Approaches to Environmental Regulation: A Survey', in: Frazini, M. and Nicita, A. (Eds.): *Economic Institutions and Environmental Policy*. Aldershot: Ashgate Publishing.

Melnyk, S.A., Sroufe, R.P., Calantone, F.L. and Montabon, F.L. (2002) 'Assessing the Effectiveness of US Voluntary Environmental Programmes: An Empirical Study', *International Journal of Production Research* Vol. 40 No. 8: 1,853-1,878.

Okimoto, D. (1989) *Between MITI and the Market: Japanese Industrial Policy for High Technology*. Stanford: Stanford University Press.

Prakash, A. (1999) 'A New-institutionalist Perspective on ISO 14001 and Responsible Care', *Business Strategy and the Environment* No. 8: 322-35.

Quazi, H.A. (1999) 'Implementation of an Environmental Management System: The Experience of Companies Operating in Singapore', *Industrial Management and Data Systems* No. 7: 302-311.

Ramus, C.A. and Steger, U. (2000) 'The Roles of Supervisory Support Behaviors and Environmental Policy in Employee "Ecoinitiatives" at Leading-edge European Companies', *Academy of Management Journal* Vol. 43 No. 4: 605-626.

Roome, N. (2001) 'Conceptualizing and Studying the Contribution of Networks in Environmental Management and Sustainable Development', *Business Strategy and the Environment* No. 10: 69-76.

Russo, M.V. (2001) 'Institutional Change and Theories of Organizational Strategy: ISO 14001 and Toxic Emissions in the Electronics Industry', lcb1.uoregon.edu/mrusso/ISO_Study.htm, 10 March 2002.

Russo, M.V. and Corbett, C.J. (2001) 'ISO 14001: Irrelevant or Invaluable?', *ISO Management Systems* December 2001: 23-27.

Samuels, R.J. (1987) *The Business of the Japanese State: Energy Markets in Comparative and Historical Perspective*. Ithaca: Cornell University Press.

Schaltegger, S. and Burritt, R. (2000) *Contemporary Environmental Accounting: Issues, Concepts and Practice*. Sheffield: Greenleaf Publishing.

Schaltegger, S. and Synnestvedt, T. (2002) 'The Link Between "Green" and Economic Success: Environmental Management as the Crucial Trigger between Environmental and Economic Performance', *Journal of Environmental Management* No. 65: 339-346.

Wagner, M., Schaltegger, S. and Wehrmeyer, W. (2001) 'The Relationship between the Environmental and Economic Performance of Firms', *Greener Management International* Issue 34 (Summer 2001): 95-108.

Welch, E.W. and Hibiki, A. (2002) 'Japanese Voluntary Environmental Agreements: Bargaining Power and Reciprocity as Contributors to Effectiveness', *Policy Sciences* Vol. 35 No. 4: 401-424.

Welch, E.W., Mori, Y. and Aoyagi-Usui, M. (2002) 'Voluntary Adoption of ISO 14001 in Japan: Mechanisms, Stages, and Effects', *Business Strategy and the Environment* Vol. 10 No. 1: 43-62.

Williams, H., Medhurst, J. and Drew, K. (1993) 'Corporate Strategies for a Sustainable Future', in: Fischer, K. and Schot, J. (Eds.): *Environmental Strategies for Industry: International Perspectives on Research Needs and Policy Implications*. Washington, DC: Island Press, 117-146.

Zharen, W.M. (1995) *ISO 14000: Understanding the Environmental Standards*. Rockville, MD: Government Institutes, Inc., 39-49.

ACKNOWLEDGEMENTS

We acknowledge the generous funding for this project from the Japan Ministry of Environment Global Environment Research Fund. The Global Environment Research Program aims to promote multidisciplinary and international research through sponsoring projects that facilitate interaction among researchers and the accumulation of scientific knowledge for the protection of the global environment. We also thank the anonymous referees for their helpful comments and suggestions.

WHAT MAKES ENVIRONMENTAL MANAGEMENT SYSTEMS SUCCESSFUL?

An Empirical Study in the German Manufacturing Sector

Boris Braun

Department of Geography, Otto-Friedrich-University, Bamberg, Germany

Abstract: Environmental management is becoming an increasingly important issue for manufacturing companies. This chapter determines the factors that are responsible for the successful implementation of standardised environmental management systems on the company level. The multivariate empirical analysis draws on a large-scale survey regarding the implementation of the EMAS system by German manufacturing establishments. The findings reveal that, irrespective of general characteristics such as size and industry, there is considerable company-specific scope for achieving improvements in environmental protection. The success of environmental management systems is positively correlated with profitability. Other important success factors are the environmental commitment of management and employees, and the integration of companies in information networks and in favourable, innovative regional milieus. The findings allow some specific conclusions to be drawn for the management of companies as well as for regional and local policy-makers.

1.   INTRODUCTION

In the future, environmental sustainability will be an increasingly important factor in determining the competitive success of manufacturing industries. Theoretical work as well as empirical studies show that economic and ecological goals do not necessarily contradict each other (see, for example: Porter and van der Linde 1995; Wagner *et al.* 2001). However, the environmental challenge requires considerable changes in the organisation and the management of companies, as they have to respond to ever-tightening environmental legislation and to the needs of more environmentally aware consumers, investors and employees. This chapter explores an important facet of these profound changes, namely, the implementation and organisation of an environmental management system (EMS) as way to combine sustainability and competitiveness. It concentrates on the question: which factors make environmental management systems successful on the company level?

While end-of-pipe measures against negative environmental impacts of production processes dominated in the 1970s and 1980s, environmental management initiatives and management-based instruments became the trends of the 1990s. The early 1990s saw a growing interest in the concept of corporate environmental auditing around the globe. The progress made over the years resulted in the publication of the Eco-Management and Audit Scheme (EMAS) (Council Regulation 1836/93) by the European Communities in 1993. With EMAS, the European Communities supplied a voluntary, market-oriented instrument for European manufacturing companies to help them improve their environmental performance and to prove this to external interested parties by publishing a validated environmental statement. A global environmental management standard, ISO 14001, was launched by the International Organisation for Standardisation in 1996. Both standards are comparable in their major objectives. They can be used as guidelines for the implementation of an EMS and can lead to either registration (EMAS) or certification (ISO 14001). Both standards aim at the continuous improvement of a company's environmental performance and help to systematise the company's environmental strategies, policies, programmes and actions. Many European companies perceive the two systems as complementary rather than as exclusive. The experiences of companies with environmental management systems do not differ significantly with respect to the formal standard. The reformulation of EMAS (EMAS II), which became effective in April 2001, further strengthened the links between the two systems.

From a political as well as from a business perspective, a critical issue is how far environmental management systems can support efficient solutions to environmental problems (Coglianese and Nash 2001). The answer to this question will undoubtedly influence the future acceptance of environmental management standards. In particular, EMAS will only be successful as an instrument of environmental policy if it leads to ecological, economic and technological gains.

2. ENVIRONMENTAL PERFORMANCE, COMPETITIVENESS AND MANAGEMENT SYSTEMS: THEORY AND EMPIRICAL EVIDENCE

Discussions about the relationship between environmental and economic success reveal basically two lines of argument. Sceptical commentators argue that there is a fundamental conflict between the environmental performance of companies and their competitiveness because environmental gains are only possible with additional costs, thus causing competitive disadvantage (e.g. Walley and Whitehead 1996). In the 'traditionalist' view of standard microeconomic theory pollution-abatement measures are predicted to increase production costs (Wagner *et al.* 2001). More recently, proponents of a positive causal link between environmental and economic performance argue that decreasing resource inputs and pollution reduction provide cost savings by increasing efficiency or reducing future compliance costs. These cost saving effects are widely discussed in the environmental accounting literature (e.g. Schaltegger and Burritt 2000). Porter and van der Linde (1995) suggest that environmental regulation does not only result in environmental gains but also helps to make companies more competitive and innovative (see also: Pickman 1998; Porter 1991). They theorise that opportunities for profitable pollution reduction exist because managers often lack the experience and skill to understand the full cost of pollution. Similar ideas have been proposed by Panayotou and Zinnes (1994) based on principal agent theory and network externalities (see also Braun 2003). The 'green' marketing literature concentrates on communication strategies, product innovations, new market opportunities and first-mover advantages in order to explain the competitive advantage of good environmental performance (Belz 2001; Meffert and Kirchgeorg 1998; Ottman 1992; Spiller 1996).

Empirical studies have also lent support to the 'win–win' hypothesis. Apart from case studies reflecting the experiences of individual companies or small numbers of companies, a growing empirical literature has applied econometric techniques to test the win–win hypothesis (see Wagner *et al.* 2001 for a more detailed overview and typology). However, the results of these studies are contradictory. While some studies indicate a positive relationship between economic and ecological performance (e.g. Fritz 1995; Hart and Ahuja 1996; King and Lenox 2001; Klassen and McLaughlin 1996; Klassen and Whybark 1999; Russo and Fouts 1997; White 1996), others seem to prove almost exactly the opposite (e.g. Christmann 2000; Jaggi and Freedman 1992).

One reason for these contradicting results is differing methodologies and performance measures. There is obviously a wide variance in the relationship between different types of economic and environmental performance, such that a general relationship is difficult to identify. Moreover, the relationship might be rather dynamic and changing over time (Schaltegger and Synnestvedt 2002). Another important reason for the contradictory results of the empirical studies might simply be the fact that not every environmental management is good environmental management and that not every progress in environmental performance is also necessarily favourable in economic terms. Thus, success depends not so much on the implementation of environmental management in general, but on the exact characteristics of the environmental management system in place. Possibly it pays to reduce pollution by certain means and not by others—or only companies with certain attributes can reduce their pollution in a profitable way.

Recently, larger surveys of companies that have implemented standardised environmental management systems (EMAS or ISO 14001) have been conducted (e.g. Dyllick and Hamschmidt 2000; Freimann and Schwedes 2000; Günther 1998; Heinelt and Malek 1999; Hillary 2000; Hillary *et al.* 1998; Seidel and Weber 1998; Umweltbundesamt 1999; UNI/ASU 1997). Their results tend to support the assumption that the implementation of environmental management systems pays off in the long-run, basically due to savings in energy, raw material and waste disposal costs. Positive market effects normally remain small. The average payback periods have been estimated to be between 1.5 and 2.5 years, irrespective of the standard applied (see, for example: Hamschmidt and Dyllick 2002; UNI/ASU 1997). However, a closer look at the results reveals considerable variance between individual companies. For small companies, for example, the payback period tends to be much longer than for bigger ones.

However, the factors responsible for ecologically and economically successful implementation of environmental management have not been systematically covered by the existing studies. It is this question that this chapter will explore by applying a multivariate statistical model.

The following sections approach the theme of successful industrial environmental management in two steps. The first step investigates how far central goals of industrial environmental management have been achieved by German enterprises. The second step is a statistical analysis of the factors that are significant for successful environmental management. On the basis of the empirical findings and their discussion, recommendations to improve environmental and economic performance are offered.

2.1   Data and Methodology of the Empirical Study

The analysis is based on data from a representative sample of German manufacturing establishments validated according to EMAS I. It covers 385 establishments—more than 40% of all validated manufactures in Germany by the beginning of 1998. Thus, the sample is large enough to guarantee representative results for EMAS-validated manufacturing sites in Germany.

A comparison between the responding manufacturing establishments and the parent population on a number of control variables indicated that the structure of the respondents does not differ significantly from the parent population. The manufacturing enterprises in the sample represent very different ownership characteristics, size groups, industries and location types. In order to avoid problems of serial correlation when dealing with multi-site companies, only one site per company has been included in the survey.

In addition to the quantitative information provided by this sample, qualitative experience was gained from more than 70 company interviews in Germany and the UK (see Braun 2003; Braun and Grotz 2002). These interviews provided background information for the interpretation and assessment of the results of the statistical analyses.

2.2   Success Dimensions of Environmental Management

Identification of the success dimensions of environmental management evokes the same problems as the evaluation of economic success in general. Difficulties arise especially because of the subjectivity of the term 'success' and the different indicators to measure it (see Rudolph 1996). In broad terms, however, it is possible to identify four general success dimensions of environmental management from which measurable success indicators can be derived. The four dimensions are:

* The economic dimension (cost-effectiveness)
* The ecological dimension (decreasing energy and raw material input)
* The technological dimension (innovation activities)
* The communication dimension (enhancing the dialogue with stakeholders)

2.2.1   The Economic Dimension: Costs and Benefits

Environmental management standards are generally accepted in the private sector only if they lead to substantial cost savings or to new market opportunities. Yet, interviews with companies reveal that the chances of developing new markets or increasing market shares as a consequence of environmental management are still low. A process in which the fulfilment of environmental management standards becomes a necessity within supply chains is developing only slowly. At least until now, the cost side of environmental management is more important for the companies.

Cost savings, however, depend on the specific situation in each company. While some companies show net losses from having implemented an EMS, others show considerable gains. Thus, 58% of the surveyed manufacturing establishments claimed that they were able to achieve cost reductions within the first year after the system came into operation (Table 1). In most cases, cost-effectiveness had been achieved by optimising the production process— mainly resulting in a considerable reduction of energy inputs and in harmful by-products. For a majority of manufacturing establishments (61%), total expenses for establishing and running the system still exceed cost reductions. This partly contrasts with other studies that indicate rather short payback periods (e.g. Dyllick and Hamschmidt 2000; UNI/ASU 1997) and supports more sceptical views (e.g. Umweltbundesamt 1999:39). However, it has to be kept in mind that the data reliability of all surveys is limited because 'costs' and 'savings' are very often not covered adequately by the costing systems within the companies.

Table 1. Selected indicators for successful implementation of EMS (Source: own survey of German manufacturing companies 1997/98)

	Number of establishments sampled		
	Yes (as %)	No (as %)	N
Cost-effectiveness of EMS (after the first year of operation):			
Running expenses reduced by EMS	57.5	42.5	334
Cost savings higher than costs for running the EMS	38.6	61.4	202
Changes in resource consumption (during and after implementation):			
Total decrease of energy and raw material consumption (a)(b)	31.6	68.4	313
Total decrease of water consumption (b)	34.7	65.3	303
Total decrease of fuel oil consumption (b)	30.5	69.5	203
Total decrease of electricity consumption (b)	24.3	75.7	309
Total decrease of natural gas consumption (b)	20.0	80.0	235
Total decrease of petrol consumption (b)	15.2	84.8	191
Relative decrease of energy and raw material consumption (a)(b)(c)	62.9	37.1	270
Relative decrease of water consumption (b)(c)	63.8	36.2	264
Relative decrease of fuel oil consumption (b)(c)	62.5	37.5	177
Relative decrease of electricity consumption (b)(c)	57.2	44.6	269
Relative decrease of natural gas consumption (b)(c)	53.8	46.2	204
Relative decrease of petrol consumption (b)(c)	52.0	48.0	171

	Number of establishments sampled		
	Yes (as %)	No (as %)	N
Environmental innovations (as a result of EMS):			
Product innovations	17.2	82.8	378
Process innovations	52.1	47.9	378
Environmental communication with relevant stakeholders:			
Successful environmental communication (d)	30.4	69.6	368
'Very strong' or 'strong interest' in company's EMS (ten most important stakeholders)(e):			
Employees	73.5	26.5	362
Owners, shareholders	60.6	39.4	350
Government, authorities	55.4	44.6	368
Customers	51.4	48.6	358
Other companies and competitors,	36.7	63.3	346
Insurance companies	35.3	64.7	360
Non-governmental environmental organisations	34.3	65.7	362
Trade, industry associations	31.4	68.6	359

(a) For selected inputs (water, electricity, gas, fuel oil, petrol), mean of input figures available
(b) Decrease of more than 5 % between 1995 and 1997
(c) Estimates based on input and output figures available
(d) Profiles of environmental stakeholder demands and stakeholder interest in EMAS coincide
(e) Self-assessment of companies on a scale from 1 (very little) to 5 (very strong)

2.2.2 The Ecological Dimension: Decreasing Resource Consumption

Cost reductions are often closely related to a more efficient use of natural resources. The issue of resource consumption is a decisive criterion to assess the quality of EMAS as an instrument of environmental policy. Such evaluations are difficult to accomplish, however, because in many cases there is a lack of reliable data on resource and energy consumption—even more so on emissions of specific pollutants. For this reason, the data presented here can provide only a rough indication of the environmental effects of EMAS.

Overall, about one-third of the surveyed adopters of EMAS in Germany were able to reduce their total resource consumption between 1995 and 1998. This result applies to the reduced consumption of water (35%), fuel oil (31%), electricity (24%), natural gas (20%), and petrol (15%). Reductions in relation to output are even more important than such absolute reductions. The percentage of manufacturing establishments that achieve economies in relative terms is considerably higher because most plants increased their output in monetary as well as in physical terms (Table 1). However, it is almost impossible to determine or quantify the exact impact of EMS on the overall resource consumption because the relevance of other organisational and technological changes is often substantial.

2.2.3   The Technological Dimension: Environmental Innovations

Technological innovation is another important dimension of successful environmental management. The complex relationship between environmental protection and technological innovations is still not fully understood despite substantial research activities in this field in recent years (e.g. Hemmelskamp *et al.* 2000). According to recent research findings environmental innovations tend to create first-mover advantages predominantly for those companies active in growth markets. In declining markets, traditional cost-oriented process innovations are often a better way to sustain competitiveness.

Due to the process-oriented nature of EMS, innovations are mainly process innovations (Table 1). In some cases, the adoption of environmental management actually resulted in a substantial change of manufacturing processes. In contrast, product innovations have been relatively minor and mostly related to changes in the manufacturing process. It has to be stressed, however, that environmental innovations are not necessarily 'high tech' innovations. Rather, they are frequently an intelligent and consistent application of well-known techniques, machines and materials.

2.2.4   The Communication Dimension: Environmental Dialogue with Stakeholders

From the beginning, hope for improvements in the communication between enterprises and the public has been one of the central elements of EMAS. The critical role of environmental communication was also stressed by those who have based their work on the stakeholder approach (Donaldson and Preston 1995; Freeman 1984; Grafé-Buckens and Hinton 1998).

A stakeholder is defined as any person or organisation who is affected or affects the way in which a company manages its business, e.g. shareholders, employees, customers, banks, environmental organisations and the state. In order to be successful in the long-term, enterprises have to find a sustainable balance of these different stakeholder demands. Regulation has been an important instrument in pushing private companies towards improved environmental performance. More recently, there is also increasing pressure from a growing number of other stakeholders including customers, neighbours, non-governmental organisations (NGOs) and the media. In order to improve corporate relationships with various stakeholders, companies need to be able to identify these stakeholders and to assess their influence (Madsen and Ulhøi 2001; Figge and Schaltegger 2000).

Table 1 lists the groups of stakeholders that were the most interested in the environmental management of the surveyed enterprises. The empirical results suggest that EMAS and the environmental statement have so far not contributed significantly to a functioning communication on environmental issues between companies and their external stakeholders. In particular, communication with so-called diffuse stakeholders (local communities, non-governmental environmental organisations, the media, etc.) is still difficult for many companies (see also Braun *et al.* 2001). Even according to comparatively low standards, not more than 30% of the surveyed enterprises could be classified as successful with respect to their environmental communication.

2.3 Determinants of Successful Environmental Management

If environmental management has the potential to combine ecological and economic gains, not all companies are able to profit from these 'win–win opportunities' or 'double dividends'. This potential remains untapped in many companies. Only a fraction of the EMAS-validated manufacturing enterprises in Germany could be labelled 'ecological pioneers'. This leads to an important question: what are the internal and external determinants that are responsible for an ecologically and economically successful implementation of EMS within manufacturing establishments?

2.3.1 Basic Assumptions and Hypotheses

Relatively little systematic research has been carried out on the success factors of environmental management. Moreover, this work is concerned only marginally with spatial factors and relies mostly on rather anecdotal evidence or small company samples (see Freimann and Schwedes 2000; Hillary 2000; Sutton 1997). Consequently, there is no comprehensive or generally accepted theory from which hypotheses could be derived. However, promising lines of theoretical explanation are provided by several approaches:

- Economic research that tries to identify critical success factors of private businesses (Steinle 1996; Steinle *et al.* 1998)
- The resource-based view of the company (Hart 1995; Russo and Fouts 1997)

- The stakeholder approach (Freeman 1984; Donaldson and Preston 1995; Grafé-Buckens and Hinton 1998)
- Network/milieu theories in economic geography and regional science (Braczyk *et al.* 1997; Camagni 1991; Cooke and Morgan 1993; Maillat 1998; see Störmer 2001 on the role of networks in environmental management and sustainable development).

Based on the assumptions of these theoretical approaches and experiences from company interviews, it is assumed that successful implementation of environmental management is positively connected to both (favourable) company-internal and external (regional) factors. The first set of (internal) factors is further differentiated as: (a) environment-related and (b) general internal factors. The second set is further differentiated as: (c) regional and (d) non-regional factors. A fifth intermediate category is defined as: (e) network factors. Network factors, by their nature, hold a position between purely internal and external factors. Network relations have to be actively pursued by the company itself, but they also rely on external conditions, which cannot be influenced significantly by a single enterprise (e.g. the existence of network partners within the region). Figure 1 represents this complex of different success dimensions and different success factors graphically.

The following six specific hypotheses can be deduced from these relationships:

1. Environmental management opens up considerable scope for individual implementation strategies. This hypothesis suggests that company-specific efforts in environmental protection are more important for successful environmental management than general characteristics or the regional setting of an enterprise.
2. Economic and ecological benefits are closely related. According to this hypothesis, profitable enterprises are more successful in implementing EMS than less profitable ones.
3. Limited internal resources impede an adequate implementation of environmental protection measures on the company level. Companies that have been assisted by external environmental consultants and supported by public funds are more successful in implementing an EMS.
4. Manufacturing establishments rely on their local and regional environment. Positive externalities (localisation and urbanisation economies) increase the chances of successfully implementing an EMS. This is an advantage for manufacturing establishments located in urban agglomerations and/or technologically dynamic regional settings.
5. Integration within environment-related inter-company information networks supports the successful implementation of an EMS. Apart from

regional networks, extra-regional exchange of information is also important.

6. Environmental protection and environmental management at the company level are basically reflections of increasing pressures from the outside world. This hypothesis suggests that manufacturers who see themselves confronted with intensive stakeholder demands are more successful in implementing EMS than manufacturers who do not yet feel the full effects.

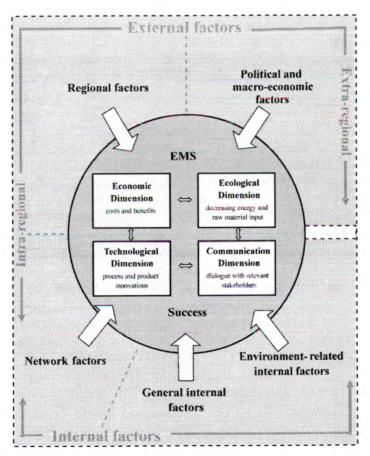

Figure 1. Determinants and dimensions of successful environmental management in the manufacturing industry

2.3.2 Logistic Regression and Model Variables

Logistic regression is used to estimate the impact of internal and external parameters on the successful implementation of EMS. The logistic regression model is basically a non-linear transformation of an ordinary linear regression. While the dependent variable must have a binary format, variables of all scales are accepted as independent variables.

In the following logistic regression models, successful implementation of environmental management is described by five dependent variables. First, COSTRED (Model 1) measures the economic effects (reduction of running expenses for raw materials, energy, waste treatment, etc.). Secondly, RESOURCE (Model 2) measures the environmental effects (decrease of energy and raw material consumption) of environmental management. A third dependent variable, INNOVATE (Model 3), serves as an indicator for innovation processes initiated by environmental management. The fourth dependent variable, ENVCOMM (Model 4), indicates achievements in communicating with relevant stakeholders of the enterprise. The last variable, SUCCESS (Model 5), represents a more comprehensive overview. It is derived from the first four dependent variables and comprises different dimensions of EMS success.

In a second step, 30 independent variables were selected for which explanatory potential can be assumed. Almost all variables were derived from the representative survey of EMAS-validated manufacturing establishments. There are only three exceptions. PATINT, a measure for the innovative character of the regional milieu, comes from the German Patent Atlas (Greif 1998). ENVREG, an indicator for the state of the environment within the region, was taken from Korczak (1995). The classification of the variable AGGLO is based on the spatial typology of settlement patterns from the Bundesamt für Bauwesen und Raumordnung (1999).

The full set of selected indicators and variables is presented in Table 2. In most cases, clear causal effects (and signs) from the set of hypotheses can be expected. The effects of some general company-internal factors such as industry (INDUSTRY), size (SIZECOM, SIZESITE), age (AGECOM, AGESITE), and market orientation (EXPORT) are more difficult to assess. Depending on the success criterion in question, different signs could be expected. For this reason, neutral effects were assumed for this set of variables.

Table 2. Variables of logistic regression models

Dependent variables (success indicators)	
COSTRED	Running expenses reduced by EMS (yes=1, no=0)
RESOURCE(a)	Relative decrease of energy and raw material consumption (yes=1, no=0)
INNOVATE	Product or process innovations as a result of EMS (yes=1, no=0)
ENVCOMM	Environmental communication successful (yes=1, no=0)
SUCCESS	Comprehensive indicator for EMS success (three or four success indicators=1, less than three success indicators=0)

Independent variables—internal factors related to environmental protection

INNOPROD(b)	(+)	Environmental product innovations (yes=1, no=0)
INNOPROC(b)	(+)	Environmental process innovations (yes=1, no=0)
EARLY	(+)	Adoption of EMAS before July 1996 (yes=1, no=0)
ISO9000	(+)	Additional ISO 9000 certification (yes=1, no=0)
INTEGRAT	(+)	Quality and environmental management systems integrated (yes=1, no=0)
ISO14001	(+)	Additional ISO 14001 certification (yes=1, no=0)

Independent variables—internal factors related to environmental protection

COMMIT	(+)	EMS initiated and supported by top management (yes=1, no=0)
EMPLOY	(+)	Interest of employees in environmental issues, scale from 1 (min.) to 5 (max.)
ENERGY	(+)	On-site usage of renewable energy (yes=1, no=0)
ECOPROD	(+)	Eco-aspects considered in product development (yes=1, no=0)
ADVERT	(+)	Environmental characteristics of products emphasised in advertising campaigns (yes=1, no=0)

Independent variables—general internal factors

INDUSTRY	(o)	Dummies for different industries (yes=1, no=0)
GROUP	(o)	Subsidiary or branch plant (yes=1, no=0)
SIZECOM	(o)	Total number of employees (ln)
SIZESITE	(o)	Number of employees on the validated site (ln)
AGECOM	(o)	Age of company (in years) (ln)
AGESITE	(o)	Age of establishment (in years) (ln)
PROFIT	(+)	Profit situation, scale from 1 (very poor) to 5 (excellent)
EXPORT	(o)	Exports as % of total production output (by tonnage)
RESEARCH	(+)	R&D expenditure as percentage of total turnover

Independent variables—network factors

NETREG	(+)	Regular exchange of information with other companies on environmental issues, local and regional levels (yes=1, no=0)
NETNAT	(+)	Regular exchange of information with other companies on environmental issues, national and international levels (yes=1, no=0)
CONSULT	(+)	Assistance by external environmental consultant(s) (yes=1, no=0)
STAKE	(+)	Median strength of stakeholder demands, scale from 1 (min.) to 5 (max.)

Independent variables—external factors (regional and extra-regional variables)

WESTEAST	(+)	Location of establishment in Old or New Länder (West=1, East=0)
AGGLO	(+)	Location of establishment (urban agglomeration=1, rural area=0)

PATINT	(+)	Regional patent intensity (patent applications per 100,000 employees, annual average 1992–1994) (Source: Greif 1998)
ENVREG	(+)	Regional situation of natural environment, scale from 0 (very un-favourable) to 1.000 (very favourable) (Source: Korczak 1995)
SUPPORT	(+)	EMAS process supported by public funds (yes=1, no=0)

In brackets: expected sign of regression coefficient
(a) Also independent variable in model 1
(b) Not tested in models 3 and 5

In an analysis of direct effects between 'success indicators' and 'success factors', the majority of relations reveal the expected signs. On the other hand, only a relatively small number of potential success determinants indicate significant positive effects on all dependent variables. This indicates that success factors can have quite selective impacts on different aspects of environmental management. Thus, it is useful to calculate separate regression models for different dimensions of successful EMS implementation. The small number of significant relations also makes it necessary to limit the number of independent variables in the statistical models. Due to a stepwise backward exclusion of variables, with $P > 0.2$, only statistically relevant parameters are included in the logistic regressions.

2.3.3   Results of the Logistic Regression Models.

The logistic regression results are presented in Table 3. This table includes regression coefficient estimates (B) and their significance as well as partial correlation coefficients (R) to indicate the contribution of the respective co-variate to the overall model. Positive B-coefficients indicate an increasing probability, while negative B-coefficients indicate a decreasing probability of positive values of the dependent variable. All models are significant at the 1% level according to model χ^2 statistic. The percentages of correct predictions are also acceptable (71–75%).

The results of the logistic regression models can be summarised as follows:

- **Model 1 (COSTRED).** The probability of actually achieving cost reductions is significantly increased if business establishments reduce their overall resource consumption (RESOURCE) and if they generate environmental product and process innovations (INNOPROD, INNOPROC). The environmental commitment of the employees is also important (EMPLOY). Experience already gained with environmental management (EARLY) is another, although less significant, component that is positively related to the ability to cut costs. General internal factors are less influential. Neither industry and profits nor size seem to have a significant effect. The more complex impact of 'size' deserves a closer look. Additional χ^2 tests show that small manufacturing establishments, especially those with less than 50 employees, have difficulties achieving cost-effectiveness. The most successful establishments are medium-sized with 50 to 500 employees. The role of regional and network variables is also contradictory. On one hand, the regression results reveal that companies do not depend too much on their external environment. On the other hand, the innovation dynamics of the regional environment (PATINT), as well as the integration in regional information networks (NETREG), seem to increase the ability of manufacturing establishments to realise cost savings.

- **Model 2 (RESOURCE).** Environmental gains (RESOURCE) are more difficult to predict from the given set of independent variables than cost savings. According to Model 2, only two variables influence the probability of achieving reductions in the overall resource consumption in a significant way. Decreasing resource consumption depends on specific and very individual parameters (experience, market-opportunities, technology, etc.). These parameters are difficult to measure due to their diverse and often problem-oriented character. Nevertheless, the positive sign for PROFIT tends to confirm the assumption that there is a close correlation between economic success and environmental progress. Again, the impact of 'size' proves to be more complex than the regression model suggests. As is clear from cross-tabulations and χ^2 tests, reductions in the consumption of energy and resources significantly increase above a threshold of about 750 employees. Large manufacturing establishments still have an advantage in resource and energy efficiency. The roles of process and product innovations (INNOPROD, INNOPROC) and of progressive environmental technologies (ENERGY, ECOPROD) are surprisingly limited. The same is true for almost all of the external and network variables. The influence of external consultants (CONSULT) is inverse to the expected effect. An explanation for this could be that consultants are commissioned primarily by companies that have difficulties in establishing a working EMS. Experienced companies, on the other hand, are mostly able to implement an EMS without the help of external consultants.

Table 3. Logistic regression results (Source: own survey of German manufacturing companies 1997/98

Independent Variable	Model 1 COSTRED B	Sig.	R	Model 2 RESOURCE B	Sig.	R	Model 3 INNOVATE B	Sig.	R	Model 4 ENVCOMM B	Sig.	R	Model 5 SUCCESS B	Sig.	R
RESOURCE (+)	0.411	**	0.114		not tested			not tested			not tested			not tested	
INNOPROD (+)	0.819	***	0.164		-			not tested			not tested			not tested	
INNOPROC (+)	0.381	**	0.112		-			not tested			not tested			not tested	
EARLY (-)	0.421	*	0.070	0.261	n.s.	0.012		-		-0.410	**	-0.074		-	
ISO9000 (-)		-			-			-							
ISO14001 (+)		-			-		0.274	*	0.058						
COMMIT (+)	0.428	**	0.118		-		0.557	*	0.106						
EMPLOY (-)		-			-		0.460	***	0.138	0.402	**	0.075	0.486	**	0.119
ENERGY (-)								-		0.735	*	0.058			
ECOPROD (+)															
ADVERT (+)											-		0.254	*	0.051
GROUP (o)							-0.310	**	-0.077						
PROFIT (+)	0.327	**	0.086	0.433	**	0.093	0.486	**	0.106		-		0.467	**	0.098
NETREG (+)		-		0.220	n.s.	0.011	0.319	**	0.082		-		0.368	**	0.106
NETNAT (-)				-0.457	**	-0.104		-					0.252	**	0.048
CONSULT (+)					-			-			-				
STAKE (-)	0.007	**	0.091		-		0.005	*	0.059	0.887	***	0.215	0.459	***	0.049
PATINT (+)													0.006	**	0.082
Constant	-1.116	n.s.		-0.677	n.s.		-3.801	***		-3.850	***		-6.211	***	
Number of cases	223			194			241			281			254		
Model Chi² [df]	55.1 [7]	***		15.3 [4]	***		44.8 [7]	***		30.4 [4]	***		48.1 [7]	***	
Correct predictions (as %)	74.4			71.0			70.5			75.5			72.8		

In brackets: expected sign of regression coefficient
B: Regression coefficient, R: Partial correlation coefficient
Level of significance: *10 %, **5 %, ***1 %, n.s. not significant

- **Model 3 (INNOVATE)**. The ability to generate technological innovations seems to be primarily influenced by the degree of commitment to environmental protection (COMMIT, EMPLOY, ISO 14000), economic success (PROFIT) and the integration in national or international information networks (NETNAT). Moreover, the process is supported to a minor degree by an innovative regional environment (PATINT). Subsidiaries or branch plants are less successful when it comes to technological innovations (GROUP). The statistically irrelevant effect of R&D expenditure (RESEARCH) on environmental innovations is surprising at first sight, but can be explained by the dominating process character of most environmental innovations. Process innovations (as confirmed by other research work) are less dependent on expensive R&D activities compared with product innovations.

- **Model 4 (ENVCOMM)**. The relatively high percentage of correct predictions can be attributed to a small number of independent variables. Successful environmental communication is basically influenced by environment-related internal factors (ENERGY, ECOPROD) and—most importantly—by the intensity of stakeholder demands (STAKE). The more demanding the stakeholders, the harder will enterprises try to fulfil these demands. This can be interpreted as a particular form of a demand-pull situation. The negative sign of EARLY may imply the existence of learning-processes between 1995 and 1998. More surprisingly, some plausible potential determinants do not prove statistically relevant, e.g. size or industry.

- **Model 5 (SUCCESS)**. The independent variable SUCCESS serves as a comprehensive indicator for successful environmental management, which summarises the findings of Models 1 to 4. About 30% of all surveyed manufacturing establishments were classified as successful implementers of environmental management. With the exception of the variable ADVERT, indicating environment-related product advertising, no new factor was added to the model equation. Some success factors, however, confirm their importance. According to Model 5, the environmental commitment of employees (EMPLOY), the profit situation (PROFIT), the dynamics of innovations in the regional environment (PATINT) and the integration into information networks (NETREG, NETNAT) are the most important factors responsible for the overall success of EMS.

It has to be stressed that the logistic regression models are exploratory in character and that not all possible determinants can be depicted empirically. The models, for example, do not reveal any significant impact of the variable INDUSTRY. However, some specific industries differ from this general picture. Manufacturers of medical instruments, for example, stand out positively in most of the success dimensions tested. Other industries, notably textile, clothing and furniture manufacturers, attract attention because of below-average results. The first two of these industries show considerable deficits in terms of either energy and resource savings, or environmental innovations. The chemical industry reveals further differences. Chemical plants normally generate an above-average rate of product and process innovations. Yet, their achievements in cost cutting and the reduction of direct environmental effects by production are rather limited. These limitations probably do not reflect 'backwardness'. It is more likely that the chemical industry, which is very sensitive and politically controlled in its environmental effects, no longer enjoys easily an accessible reduction potential compared with other industries.

2.3.4   Interpretation of the Empirical Results

If the findings of the empirical analysis with the basic hypotheses are confronted, a rather diverse picture emerges. While hypotheses 2 and 5 are basically confirmed by the empirical results, hypotheses 1, 4 and 6 are only partially confirmed and, despite its general plausibility, hypothesis 3 cannot be confirmed. Neither support by public funds nor external environmental consultants have a significant impact on the critical success dimensions of environmental management.

In general, the empirical findings reveal that there is a considerable company-specific scope for achieving improvements in environmental protection (hypothesis 1). General company characteristics such as size, industry or product range have only a limited impact on successful environmental management. This is not to say that size does not matter at all, but its influence on environmental performance is neither continuous nor linear and often eclipsed by other factors.

Irrespective of long-term structural characteristics such as size and industry, companies have enough room to find individual windows of environmental opportunity. Experience with management systems may help to find these windows but it does not guarantee that all possibilities of optimisation become apparent. As Hamschmidt and Dyllick (2002) point out, environmental management systems themselves give only little incentives for initiating processes of fundamental change towards environmental sustainability. Rather they are starting points for the development of a continual improvement philosophy. Environment-related internal factors in general tend to play an important role for costs, innovations and communication issues.

Within the group of these environment-related factors, the commitment of employees to environmental protection proves to be an especially influential factor. This shows quite clearly that the implementation of formal management structures is not sufficient. Environmental protection depends very much on the quality of managerial decisions as well as on the motivation and participation of every member of the company. The company actually has 'to live' environmental care (Freimann and Schwedes 2000:104). The formal implementation of an EMS may only serve as a reinforcing mechanism (Nash and Ehrenfeld 2001:79).

Economic success and environmental performance show the expected close correlation (hypothesis 2). The reduction of costs and environmental gains are closely related and profitable enterprises are significantly more successful in environmental management than less profitable ones. These findings tend to confirm older empirical results at the company level (e.g. Fritz 1995; Hart and Ahuja 1996; Russo and Fouts 1997) and more generally the optimistic win–win expectations of Porter and van der Linde (1995) or Panayotou and Zinnes (1994).

Interestingly, the ability to reduce running expenses through the EMS is not related statistically to the profit situation of a company. This can be interpreted as an indication of the causal relationship behind the link between environmental and economic success (see Schaltegger and Synnestvedt 2002). It not simply the positive cost effect of environmental management that makes companies more profitable. It seems to be more likely that profitable companies are well-managed companies that are successful in many fields of business, including environmental management. Furthermore, environmental management can hardly be seen as a general or even dominant success factor (see also Steinle *et al.* 1998). It is only one out of several management options that may increase a company's competitiveness. Economic success does not 'automatically' result from any environmental activity. Competitiveness very much depends on the managerial ability to improve environmental performance in an economical way.

Hypothesis 4 has only been partly confirmed by the empirical results. 'Environmental pioneers' are not at all tied to a specific regional or local setting. Urban agglomerations are not necessarily a better breeding ground for environmental innovations than rural areas. Manufacturing establishments in the periphery are not at a disadvantage, at least not with respect to the environmental performance. The same seems to be true for manufacturing establishments in East Germany. The regional innovation climate is obviously more important than general location factors.

Positive externalities and spill-overs within innovative milieus have a significant positive impact on cost savings and innovations. Regular exchange of information in environment-related networks has also proved to be a rather important success factor for environmental management (hypothesis 5). This result can be interpreted as an empirical confirmation of the 'network paradigm', which emphasises the role of co-operative linkages and the exchange of implicit or tacit knowledge (see Cooke and Morgan 1993; Feldman 2000; Schamp 2000; Störmer 2001).

Even though environmental management standards as such can be seen as a classic example of almost ubiquitous codified knowledge, at least some tacit knowledge appears to be necessary in order to implement these systems successfully at the company level. Inter-company co-operation seems to be even more important for environmental issues than for other areas of business. A closer look reveals that local and regional networks are particularly relevant for cost-related questions. For technological innovations, however, national or even international networking seems to be more important. These results are more or less in line with recent work on innovation-oriented inter-company co-operation (e.g. Grotz and Braun 1997; Koschatzky 1998). Although these authors tend to be more sceptical with respect to the overall relevance of networks, they also stress the dominating role of extra-regional linkages for technological innovations.

Despite a highly significant impact of stakeholder demands on the effectiveness of environmental communication, it is too early to speak of stakeholder demands as a general success factor. External stakeholders are having only a marginal influence on the economic, ecological, and technological dimensions of environmental management. Therefore, hypothesis 6 is only partly confirmed. This result is not completely consistent with the theory that regards stakeholder pressure as a major driver behind environmental improvement (see Braun 2003), but it is more or less in line with other empirical studies that also found a relatively weak influence of stakeholders other than state authorities, owners or employees (e.g. Braun *et al.* 2001; Madsen and Ulhøi 2001; Wagner and Schaltegger 2001). However, this situation might have improved since 1998 when the survey was conducted. Moreover, it should be considered that internal stakeholders—most prominently the employees of a company—are among the most important success factors for environmental management.

3.   CONCLUSIONS FOR REGIONAL POLITICS AND PRIVATE ENTERPRISES

This analysis provides a number of specific conclusions for regional policy as well as for individual manufacturing companies. From the perspective of regional policy, it is important to note that the environmental performance of enterprises is neither limited by the industrial structure nor by the settlement pattern of a region. For these reasons, regional economic policy that aims for environmental protection and economic growth is appropriate for peripheral areas with small-scale industries. In general, three points of reference for regional political initiatives are particularly promising.

The first group of initiatives relate to the promotion of environment-related networks that enhance a quick and co-operative exchange of experiences. These regional networks should remain open to the outside world to avert the danger of lock-ins. They should also be connected at a trans-regional level to similar networks in other regions. In particular, the UK experience with so-called 'green business clubs' could be helpful in this context (Braun and Grotz 2002). A second group of initiatives relate to the creation of open communications between enterprises and their external stakeholders (public authorities, politicians, neighbours, environmental organisations, regional customers and suppliers). Provided the immediate effects of this kind of regional communication are not overestimated, the long-term potentials are high. A third group of initiatives relate to the promotion of environmental innovations in the public sector as well as in the private sector. These initiatives will not be instigated primarily by environmental politics. Yet they may serve environmental protection as well as economic interests.

With regard to manufacturing enterprises, favourable preconditions for environmental strategies depend upon the particular strategic goals desired by the company (Figure 2). These goals relate to cost-effectiveness, reduction of resource and energy consumption, implementation of environmental process and product innovations, and improvement of environmental communication. In exploring the relationships between success indicators, strategies and management goals two aspects need to be underlined. First, success factors tend to have a selective effect on different dimensions of environmental management. This means that the question of which factors should be particularly promoted depends on an enterprise's main strategic goals. Secondly, the success factors, which can be identified from this study, do not necessarily imply progress in environmental protection. They only make progress more probable.

Within the list of success factors for environmental management, two groups can be distinguished. The factors of the first group can be influenced directly by management. These are classical environmental strategies. The factors of the second group either cannot be influenced effectively by the company's management (especially regional aspects) or they rely on the general, non-environmental characteristics of an enterprise (e.g. profit situation, size). Thus, this second group of success factors describes the framework conditions for decisions aimed at environmental protection. Recommendations for company-related management strategies need to bear in mind the importance of these conditions. In practice, many of the success factors are in some way concentrated on communication aspects—both within the company and between the company and the outside world.

Goals of environmental Management	Success factors identified	
	Strategies	**Favourable preconditions**
	• Reduction of resource and energy consumption	• Medium-sized manufacturing establishment
Cost-effectiveness ⇐	• Promotion of process and product innovations	• Innovative regional environment
	• Fostering regular information exchange with other firms	• Existence of partners for co-operation within a region
	• Building-up understanding and environmental commitment of all employees	
Reduction of resource and energy consumption ⇐	• Commitment of management to environmental protection	• Good profit situation
	• Fostering environmental competence in the company	• Large manufacturing establishment
	• Commitment of management to environmental protection	• Good profit situation
	• Additional ISO-certification	• Independent company or establishment
Implementation of environmental process and product innovations ⇐	• Fostering regular information exchange with other firms	• Innovative regional environment
	• Building-up understanding and environmental commitment of all employees	
Improvement of environmental communication ⇐	• Implementing publicly visible environmental protection measures (renewable energies, environmentally friendly products, etc.)	• Good profit situation
		• Strong interest of internal and external stakeholders in environmental issues
	• Implementing environment-related advertising strategies	

Figure 2. Company-related strategies for the achievement of the central goals of environmental management

In many respects the findings of this study are in line with the results of other recent surveys conducted within and outside Germany in the field of environmental management (e.g. Umweltbundesamt 1999; Dyllick and Hamschmidt 2000) Even though the data are now almost five years old and some aspects might well change over time, the basic findings still appear valid. Thus, there are clear indications that the implementation of environmental management differs significantly from country to country, even within the European Union (Braun and Grotz 2002; Hillary *et al.* 1998).

Therefore, initiatives such as the European Business Environment Barometer that aim at the collection of comparable international data (Baumast 2000; Baumast and Dyllick 2001) are important as they potentially provide a chance to analyse the success factors of environmental management systems in a broader European context.

REFERENCES

Baumast, A. (2000): *Environmental Management in Europe. Results of the European Business Environmental Barometer (E.B.E.B.) 1997/98* (IWÖ Discussion Paper No. 79). St. Gallen: Institute for Economy and the Environment, University St. Gallen.

Baumast, A. and Dyllick, T. (Eds.) (2001): *Umweltmanagement-Barometer 2001* (IWÖ Diskussionsbeitrag Nr. 93). St. Gallen: Institute for Economy and the Environment, University St. Gallen.

Belz, F.-M. (2001): *Integratives Öko-Marketing. Erfolgreiche Vermarktung von ökologischen Produkten und Leistungen.* Wiesbaden: Gabler.

Braczyk, H.-J., Cooke, P., and Heidenreich, M. (1997): *Regional Innovation Systems: The Role of Governance in a Globalised World.* London: ULC Press.

Braun, B. (2003): *Unternehmen zwischen ökologischen und ökonomischen Zielen. Konzepte, Akteure und Erfolgschancen des industriellen Umweltmanagements aus wirtschaftsgeographischer Sicht.* Münster: Lit Verlag.

Braun, B., Geibel, J. and Glasze, G. (2001): 'Umweltkommunikation im Öko-Audit System— von der Umwelterklärung zum Umweltforum', *Zeitschrift für Umweltpolitik und Umweltrecht* Vol. 24, 299-318.

Braun, B. and Grotz, R. (2002): 'Environmental Management in Manufacturing Industries: A Comparison between British and German Companies', in: Schätzl, L. and Revilla Diez, J. (Eds.): *Technological Change and Regional Development in Europe.* Heidelberg: Physica, 273-292.

Bundesamt für Bauwesen und Raumordnung (1999): *Aktuelle Daten zur Entwicklung der Städte, Kreise und Gemeinden.* Bonn: BBR.

Camagni, R. (Ed.) (1991): *Innovation Networks: Spatial Perspectives.* London: Belhaven Pinter.

Christmann, P. (2000): 'Effects of 'Best Practices' of Environmental Management on Cost Advantage: The Role of Complementary Assets', *Academy of Management Journal* Vol. 43, 663-680.

Coglianese, C. and Nash, J. (Eds.) (2001): *Regulating from the Inside: Can Environmental Management Systems Achieve Policy Goals?* Washington D.C.: Resources for the Future Press.

Cooke, P. and Morgan, K. (1993): 'The Network Paradigm: New Departures in Corporate and Regional Development', *Environment and Planning D* Vol. 11, 543-564.

Donaldson, T. and Preston, L.E. (1995): 'The Stakeholder Theory of the Corporation: Concepts, Evidence, and Implications', *Academy of Management Review* Vol. 20, 65-91.

Dyllick, T. and Hamschmidt, J. (2000): *Wirksamkeit und Leistung von Umweltmanagementsystemen: Eine Untersuchung von ISO-14001-zertifizierten Unternehmen in der Schweiz.* Zürich: vdf Hochschulverlag.

Feldman, M.P. (2000): 'Location and Innovation: The New Economy Geography of Innovation, Spillovers, and Agglomerations', in: Clark, G.L., Feldman, M. and Gertler, M. (Eds.): *The Oxford Handbook of Economic Geography.* Oxford: University Press, 373-394.

Figge, F. and Schaltegger, S. (2000): *Was ist 'Stakeholder Value'? Vom Schlagwort zur Messung.* Lüneburg: University of Lüneburg, Chair of Environmental Management.

Freeman, R.E. (1984): *Strategic Management. A Stakeholder Approach.* Boston: Pitman.

Freimann, J. and Schwedes, R. (2000): 'EMAS-Experiences in German Companies: A Survey on Recent Empirical Studies', *Eco-Management and Auditing* Vol. 7, 99-105.

Fritz, W. (1995): 'Umweltschutz und Unternehmenserfolg. Eine empirische Analyse', *Die Betriebswirtschaft* Vol. 55, 347-357.

Grafé-Buckens, A. and Hinton, A.-F. (1998): 'Engaging the Stakeholders: Corporate Views and Current Trends', *Business Strategy and the Environment* Vol. 7, 124-133.

Greif, S. (1998): *Patentatlas Deutschland.* München: Deutsches Patentamt.

Grotz, R. and Braun, B. (1997): 'Territorial or Trans-Territorial Networking: Spatial Aspects of Technology-Oriented Co-operation within the German Mechanical Engineering Industry', *Regional Studies* Vol. 31, 545-557.

Günther, K. (1998): 'Betriebliches Umweltmanagement setzt sich in der Praxis durch. Ergebnisse der UNI/ASU-Umweltmanagement 1997' *UmweltWirtschaftsForum* Vol. 6, No. 1, 16-20.

Hamschmidt, J. and Dyllick, T. (2002): 'ISO 14001: Profitable—Yes! But is it Eco-effective?', *Greener Management International* Vol. 34, 43-54.

Hart, S.L. (1995): 'A Natural Resource-Based View of the Company', *Academy of Management Review* Vol. 20, 986-1014.

Hart, S.L. and Ahuja, G. (1996): 'Does it Pay to be Green? An Empirical Examination of the Relationship between Emission Reduction and Company Performance', *Business Strategy and the Environment* Vol. 5, 30-37.

Heinelt, H. and Malek, T. (1998): 'Öko-Audits in deutschen Betrieben. Zum Ausmaß und den Hintergründen einer Erfolgsstory—auf Basis einer schriftlichen Befragung', *Zeitschrift für Umweltpolitik und Umweltrecht* Vol. 22, 541-566.

Hemmelskamp, J., Rennings, K. and Leone, F. (Eds.) (2000): *Innovation-Oriented Environmental Regulation. Theoretical Approaches and Empirical Analysis.* Heidelberg: Physica.

Hillary, R. (Ed.) (2000): *ISO 14001: Case Studies and Practical Experiences.* Sheffield: Greenleaf Publishing.

Hillary, R., Gelber, M. and Biondi, V. (1998): *An Assessment of the Implementation Status of Council Regulation (No 1836/93) Eco-management and Audit Scheme in the Member States* (Final Report). London: Centre for Environmental Technology, Imperial College of Science, Technology and Medicine.

Jaggi, B. and Freedman, M. (1992): 'An Examination of the Impact of Pollution Performance on Economic and Market Performance: Pulp and Paper Companies', *Journal of Business Finance and Accounting* Vol. 19, 697-713.

King, A. and Lenox, M. (2001): 'Does it Really Pay to be Green? An Empirical Study of Company Environmental and Financial Performance', *Journal of Industrial Ecology* Vol. 5, 105-116.

Klassen, R.D. and McLaughlin, C.P. (1996): 'The Impact of Environmental Management on Company Performance', *Management Science* Vol. 42, 1199-1214.

Klassen, R.D. and Whybark, D.C. (1999): 'The Impact of Environmental Technologies on Manufacturing Performance', *Academy of Management Journal* Vol. 42, 599-615.

Korczak, D. (1995): *Lebensqualität-Atlas.* Opladen: Westdeutscher Verlag.

Koschatzky, K. (1998): 'Company Innovation and Region: The Role of Space in Innovation Processes', *International Journal of Innovation Management* Vol. 2, 383-408.

Madsen, H. and Ulhøi, J.P. (2001): 'Integrating Environmental and Stakeholder Management', *Business Strategy and the Environment* Vol. 10, 77-88.

Maillat, D. (1998): 'Vom 'Industrial District' zum Kreativen Milieu: Ein Beitrag zur Analyse der gebietsgebundenen Produktionsorganisationen', *Geographische Zeitschrift* Vol. 86, 1-15.

Meffert, H. and Kirchgeorg, M. (1983): *Marktorientiertes Umweltmanagement. Konzeption—Strategie—Implementierung.* Stuttgart: Schäffer-Poeschel.

Nash, J. and Ehrenfeld, J.R. (2001): 'Factors That Shape EMS Outcomes in Companies', in: Coglianese, C. and Nash, J. (Eds.): *Regulating from the Inside: Can Environmental Management Systems Achieve Policy Goals?* Washington D.C.: Resources for the Future Press, 61-81.

Ottman, J.A. (1992): *Green Marketing. Opportunity for Innovation.* Lincolnwood: NTC Publishing.

Panayotou, T. and Zinnes, C. (1994): 'Free-Lunch Economics for Industrial Ecologists', in: Socolow, R., Andrews, C., Berkhout, F. and Thomas, V. (Eds.): *Industrial Ecology and Global Change.* Cambridge: University Press, 383-397.

Pickman, H.A. (1998): 'The Effect of Environmental Regulation on Environmental Innovation', *Business Strategy and the Environment* Vol. 7, 223-233.

Porter, M.E. (1991): 'America's Green Strategy', *Scientific American* April 1998, 168.

Porter, M.E. and Linde, C. van der (1995): 'Green and Competitive: Ending the Stalemate', *Harvard Business Review* Vol. 73, No. 5, 120-133.

Rudolph, H. (1996): 'Erfolg von Unternehmen. Plädoyer für einen kritischen Umgang mit dem Erfolgsbegriff', *Aus Politik und Zeitgeschichte* Vol. 23, 32-39.

Russo, M.V. and Fouts, P.A. (1997): 'A Resource-Based Perspective on Corporate Environmental Performance and Profitability', *Academy of Management Journal* Vol. 40, 534-559.

Schaltegger, S. and Burritt, R. (2000): *Contemporary Environmental Accounting: Issues, Concepts and Practice.* Sheffield: Greenleaf Publishing.

Schaltegger, S. and Synnestvedt, T. (2002): 'The Link between 'Green' and Economic Success: Environmental Management as the Crucial Trigger between Environmental and Economic Performance', *Journal of Environmental Management* Vol. 65, 339-346.

Schamp, E.W. (2000): *Vernetzte Produktion. Industriegeographie aus institutioneller Perspektive.* Darmstadt: Wissenschaftliche Buchgesellschaft.

Seidel, E. and Weber, F.M. (1998): 'Die EMAS-Praxis in Deutschland. Ergebnisse einer kritischen Bestandsaufnahme', *UmweltWirtschaftsForum* Vol. 6, No. 1, 22-27.

Spiller, A. (1996): *Ökologieorientierte Produktpolitik—Forschung, Medienberichte und Marktsignale.* Marburg: Metropolis.

Steinle, C. (1996): 'Erfolgsfaktoren und ihre Gestaltung in der betrieblichen Praxis. Empirische Ergebnisse und Handlungsempfehlungen', *Aus Politik und Zeitgeschichte* Vol. 23, 14-23.

Steinle, C., Thiem, H. and Böttcher, K. (1998): 'Umweltschutz als Erfolgsfaktor—Mythos oder Realität?', *Zeitschrift für Umweltpolitik und Umweltrecht* Vol. 21, 61-78.

Störmer, E. (2001): *Ökologieorientierte Unternehmensnetzwerke. Regionale umweltorientierte Unternehmensnetzwerke als Ansatz für eine ökologisch nachhaltige Wirtschaftsentwicklung.* München: VVF Verlag.

Sutton, P. (1997): 'Targeting Sustainability: The Positive Application of ISO 14001', in: Sheldon, C. (Ed.): *ISO 14001 and Beyond. Environmental Management Systems in the Real World.* Sheffield: Greenleaf Publishing, 211-242.

Umweltbundesamt (1999): *Betrieblicher Umweltschutz mit System. EG-Umweltaudit in Deutschland* (Erfahrungsbericht 1995 bis 1998). Berlin: Umweltbundesamt.

UNI/ASU (Unternehmerinstitut/Arbeitsgemeinschaft Selbständiger Unternehmer) (1997): *Öko-Audit in der mittelständischen Praxis—Evaluierung und Ansätze für eine Effizienz-steigerung von Umweltmanagementsystemen in der Praxis*. Bonn: UNI e.V.

Wagner, M. and Schaltegger, S. (2001): 'Umweltmanagement in deutschen Unternehmen—der aktuelle Stand der Praxis', in: Baumast, A. and Dyllick, T. (Eds.): *Umweltmanagement-Barometer 2001* (IWÖ Diskussionsbeitrag Nr. 93). St. Gallen: Institute for Economy and the Environment, University St. Gallen, 5-15.

Wagner, M., Schaltegger, S. and Wehrmeyer, W. (2001): 'The Relationship between the Environmental and Economic Performance of Companies. What does Theory Propose and What does Empirical Evidence Tell Us?', *Greener Management International* Issue 34, 95-108.

Walley, N. and Whitehead, B. (1996): 'It's Not Easy being Green', in: Welford, R. and Starkey, R. (Eds.): *Business and the Environment*. London: Earthscan Publications, 36-44.

White, M.A. (1996): *Corporate Environmental Performance and Shareholder Value*. Charlottesville: McIntire School of Commerce.

EDITORS

Schaltegger, Stefan, Prof. Dr rer. pol., Chair of Environmental Management, University of Lüneburg, Centre for Sustainability Management, University of Lüneburg, Scharnhorststr. 1, D-21335 Lüneburg, Germany, Email: schaltegger@uni-Lüneburg.de

Professor Schaltegger is full professor for Management and Business Economics at the University of Lüneburg, Germany and director of the Centre for Sustainability Management (CSM). He is head of the MBA sustainability management programme 'Sustainament' (Internet URL: http://www.sustainament.de) and chairman of the Environmental Management Accounting Network (EMAN) Europe (Internet URL: http://www.eman-eu.net). His research deals with sustainability management including sustainability accounting, information management, sustainable finance, sustainable entrepreneurship and strategic environmental management. He is on the board of a number of international scientific associations and journals (including *Business Strategy and the Environment, Corporate Social Responsibility and Environmental Management, Greener Management International, Progress in Industrial Ecology* and *International Journal of Business Environment*).

Wagner, Marcus, Dr. rer. pol., MBA, Dr Theo Schöller Chair in Technology and Innovation Management, Technische Universität München, Arcisstr. 21, 80333 Munich (Germany), Email: wagner@wi.tum.de

Dr Wagner is assistant professor at the Business School of the Technical University of Munich. He is an associate research fellow at the Centre for Sustainability Management, University of Lüneburg, where he also teaches on the MBA programme 'Sustainament'. His research is concerned with innovation and technology management as well as sustainability management in areas such as co-operation in innovation and sustainable and environmental innovation. Dr Wagner was also a lecturer/author at Hagen University (microeconomics; growth, distribution, business cycles; environmental accounting and performance indicators; environmental economics). From 2002 to 2005, he worked as a senior manager/manager in the semiconductor and chemicals industries. In 2001, he was scientific advisor to the Global Reporting Initiative.

AUTHORS

Ball, Robert, Prof. Dr, Dean of the Faculty of Management, University of Stirling, Stirling, Scotland (UK), email: rob.ball@stir.ac.uk

Batenburg, Ronald, Dr, Department of Information and Computing Sciences, Utrecht University, PO Box 80089, NL 3508 TB The Netherlands, email: r.s.batenburg@cs.uu.nl

Benn, Suzanne, School of Management, University of Technology, Sydney (Australia), email: suzanne.benn@uts.edu.au

Bönning, Matthias, Oekom Research AG, Goethestr. 28, 80336 Munich (Germany), email: boenning@oekom-research.com

Braun, Boris, Prof. Dr, Department of Geography, Otto-Friedrich-University Bamberg, Am Kranen 12, 96045 Bamberg (Germany), email: boris.braun@ggeo.uni-bamberg.de

Clausen, Jens, Dr, Borderstep Institut für Innovation und Nachhaltigkeit gGmbH, Hausmannstr. 9-10, 30159 Hannover (Germany), email: clausen@borderstep.de

Cheng, Deborah, Global Footprint Network, 1050 Warfield Ave, Oakland, CA 94610 (USA), Phone: +1 510 839-8879, email: info@footprintnetwork.org, homepage: http://www.footprintnetwork.org

Dyllick, Thomas, Professor of Environmental Management, Managing Director, Institute for Economy and the Environment (IWOE–HSG), University of St Gallen, St Gallen (Switzerland), email: Thomas.Dyllick@unisg.ch

Farrell, Frank, Environment Agency, Rivers House, Bridgwater, Somerset TA6 4YS (UK), email: frank.farrell@environment-agency.gov.uk

Figge, Frank, Dr rer. pol., Lecturer, School of the Environment, University of Leeds, Leeds LS2 9JT (UK), email: frank@env.leeds.ac.uk

Goddard, Trevor, Lecturer, School of Occupational Therapy, Curtin University of Technology, GPO Box U1987, Perth WA 6845 (Australia) and Deakin University, Corporate Citizenship Research Unit (Australia), email: t.goddard@curtin.edu.au

Goldbach, Maria, Dr, Research Co-ordinator EcoMTex, Supply Chain Management Centre, Institute for Business Administration, Faculty of Business, Economics and Law, Carl von Ossietzky Universität Oldenburg, 26111 Oldenburg (Germany).

Goldfinger, Steve, Global Footprint Network, 1050 Warfield Ave, Oakland, CA 94610 (USA), email: info@footprintnetwork.org, homepage: http://footprintnetwork.org

Hahn, Tobias, Dr rer. pol., Institute for Futures Studies and Technology Assessment (IZT), Schopenhauerstr. 26, 14129 Berlin (Germany), email: t.hahn@izt.de

Hamschmidt, Jost, research associate, Institute for Economy and the Environment (IWOE–HSG), University of St Gallen, St Gallen (Switzerland), email: Jost.Hamschmidt@unisg.ch

Hitchens, David, Professor of Applied Economics, School of Management and Economics, 25 University Square, Queen's University Belfast, Belfast BT7 1NN (UK), email: d.hitchens@qub.ac.uk

Keil, Michael, IÖW (Institute for Ecological Economy Research), Hausmannstr. 9-10, 30159 Hannover (Germany), email: michael.keil@hannover.ioew.de

Kitzes, Justin, National Accounts Program, Global Footprint Network, 1050 Warfield Ave, Oakland, CA 94610 (USA), phone: +1 510 839-8879, email: justin@footprintnetwork.org, homepage: http://www.footprintnetwork.org

Koehler, Dinah A., Sc.D., Economics and Decision Sciences Research National Center for Environmental Research 8722F, 1200 Pennsylvania Avenue, NW, Washington, DC 20460 (USA), email: Koehler.Dinah@epamail.epa.gov

Knörzer, Andreas, Bank Sarasin & Co. Ltd, Elisabethenstraße 62, 4002 Basel (Switzerland), email: andreas.knoerzer@sarasin.ch

Lankoski, Leena, Visiting Researcher, INSEAD Business in Society (IBiS) Research Centre, INSEAD, Boulevard de Constance, 77305 Fontainebleau (France), email: leena.lankoski@insead.edu

Lee, Ki-Hoon, Prof. Dr, Environmental Management Centre, POSCO Research Institute (POSRI), PORSI Bldg.147, Samsung-dong, Kangnam-gu, Seoul 135-090 (Korea), email: euroben@dreamwiz.com

Lindblom, Josefina, Dr, Institute for Prospective Technological Studies (IPTS), World Trade Centre, Isla de la Cartuja, 41092 Sevilla (Spain), email: josefina.lindblom@jrc.es

Madsen, Henning, Associate Professor, PhD, Department of Information Science, The Aarhus School of Business, Fuglesangs Allé 4, 8210 Aarhus V (Denmark), email: hem@asb.dk

Martiniak, Chris, Global Footprint Network, 1050 Warfield Ave, Oakland, CA 94610 (USA), phone: +1 510 839-8879, email: info@footprintnetwork. org, homepage: http://www.footprintnetwork.org; and University of Michigan Business School (USA), email: martinic@umich.edu

Monfreda, Chad, Sustainability and Global Environment Program, University of Wisconsin, Madison (USA), email: clmonfreda@wisc.edu

Mori, Yasuhumi, Dr, Senior Research Associate, National Institute for Environmental Studies, 16-2 Onogawa, Tsukuba, Ibaraki (Japan), email: mori-y@nies.go.jp

Odom, Sonja Lynn, PhD, Department of Mechanical Engineering, Laboratory for Sustainable Solutions, University of South Carolina, 300 Main St, Columbia, South Carolina, 29112 (USA), email: odoms@engr.sc.edu

Petersen, Holger, Dr rer. pol., Umweltbank AG Nürnberg, Flössaustraße 92, 90763 Fürth, and Centre for Sustainability Management (CSM), University of Lüneburg (Germany), email: holpetersen@yahoo.de

Piñeiro Chousa, Juan, Professor with Tenure at the Department of Finance and Accounting, University of Santiago de Compostela, Avda. Alfonso X O Sabio, Facultade de Administración e Dirección de Empresas, 27002 Lugo (Spain).

Plinke, Eckhard, Bank Sarasin & Co. Ltd, Elisabethenstraße 62, 4002 Basel (Switzerland), email: eckhard.plinke@sarasin.ch

Prakash-Mani, Kavita, SustainAbility Ltd, 11–13 Knightsbridge, London SW1X 7LY (UK), email: prakash-mani@sustainability.com

Probert, Jane, European Business Management School, University of Wales Swansea, Singleton Park, Swansea, SA2 8PP (UK), email: j.probert@ swansea.ac.uk

Rana, Ashish, Dr, Research Fellow, National Institute for Environmental Studies, 16-2 Onogawa, Tsukuba, Ibaraki (Japan), email: ashish.rana@nies.go.jp

Rennings, Klaus, Dr, Centre for European Economic Research (ZEW), PO Box 103443, 68034 Mannheim (Germany), email: rennings@zew.de

Romero Castro, Noelia, Associate Professor at the Department of Finance and Accounting, University of Santiago de Compostela, Avda. Alfonso X O Sabio, Facultade de Administración e Dirección de Empresas, 27002 Lugo (Spain), email: noeliarc@lugo.usc.es

Rosinski, Nikolaus, Generation Investment Management LLP, 4 Cork Street, London, W1S 3LG (UK), email: niki.rosinski@generationim.com

Schröder, Michael, Dr, Centre for European Economic Research (ZEW), PO Box 103443, 68034 Mannheim (Germany), email: schroeder@zew.de

Seuring, Stefan, PD Dr, Senior Lecturer, Supply Chain Management Centre, Institute for Business Administration, Faculty of Business, Economics and Law, Carl von Ossietzky Universität Oldenburg, 26111 Oldenburg (Germany), email: stefan.seuring@uni-oldenburg.de

Spirig, Kuno, lic. oec. HSG, lic. phil. I, Managing Director, Valde Value Development GmbH, Fuhrstraße 31, CH-8820 Wädenswil-Zürich (Switzerland), email: spirig@uudial.ch

Stanwick, Peter A., PhD, Associate Professor, Department of Management, College of Business, Auburn University, 440 Lowder Business Building, Auburn, AL 36849-5241 (USA), email: pstanwik@business.auburn.edu

Stanwick, Sarah D., PhD, Associate Professor, School of Accountancy, College of Business, Auburn University, 345 Lowder Business Building, Auburn, AL 36849-5247 (USA), email: stanwsd@auburn.edu

Steger, Ulrich, Prof. Dr, Professor for Environmental Management, Alcan Chair, International Institute for Management Development (IMD), Ch. de Bellerrive 23, PO Box 915, CH-1001 Lausanne (Switzerland), email: steger@imd.ch

Thankappan, Samarthia, School of Management and Economics, 25 University Square, Queen's University Belfast, Belfast BT7 1NN (UK), email: s.thankappan@qub.ac.uk

Thorpe, Jodie, SustainAbility Ltd, 11–13 Knightsbridge, London SW1X 7LY (UK), email: thorpe@sustainability.com

Trainor, Mary, School of Management and Economics, 25 University Square, Queen's University Belfast, Belfast BT7 1NN (UK), email: m.trainor@qub.ac.uk

Triebswetter, Ursula, Dr, IFO Institute for Ecological Research, Poschingerstr. 5, 81679 Munich, Postfach 860460 (Germany), email: utriebswetter @aol.com

Ulhøi, John P., Professor, PhD, Department of Organisation and Management, The Aarhus School of Business, Haslegaardsvej 10, 8210 Aarhus V (Denmark), email: jpu@asb.dk

Wackernagel, Mathis, Dr, Global Footprint Network, 1050 Warfield Ave, Oakland, CA 94610 (USA), Phone: +1 510 839-8879, email: mathis@ footprintnetwork.org, homepage: http://www.footprintnetwork.org

Welch, Eric W., Assistant Professor, Graduate Program in Public Affairs, University of Illinois at Chicago, 412 S. Peoria St., Room 138, Chicago, Illinois 60607 (USA), email: ewwelch@uic.edu

Wellington, Fred, Sustainable Enterprise Program, World Resources Institute, and formerly Environmental Management Program, University of San Francisco (USA), email: fwellington@wri.org

Williander, Mats, PhD Student and Business Strategy Manager, Fenix Centre for Research on Knowledge and Business Creation, Chalmers University of Technology, Vera Sandbergs allé 8, SE 412 96 Göteborg (Sweden), phone: +46 31 325 0418, email: williander@fenix.chalmers.se

Wüstenhagen, Rolf, Dr, Vice Director, Institute for Economy and the Environment, University of St. Gallen (IWOe-HSG), Tigerbergstraße 2, 9000 St Gallen (Switzerland), email: rolf.wuestenhagen@unisg.ch

Ytterhus, Bjarne, Associate Professor, Department of Economics, Norwegian School of Management, Nydalsveien 37, 0484 Oslo (Norway), email: bjarne.ytterhus@bi.no

Ziegler, Andreas, Centre for European Economic Research (ZEW), PO Box 103443, 68034 Mannheim (Germany), email: ziegler@zew.de

INDEX